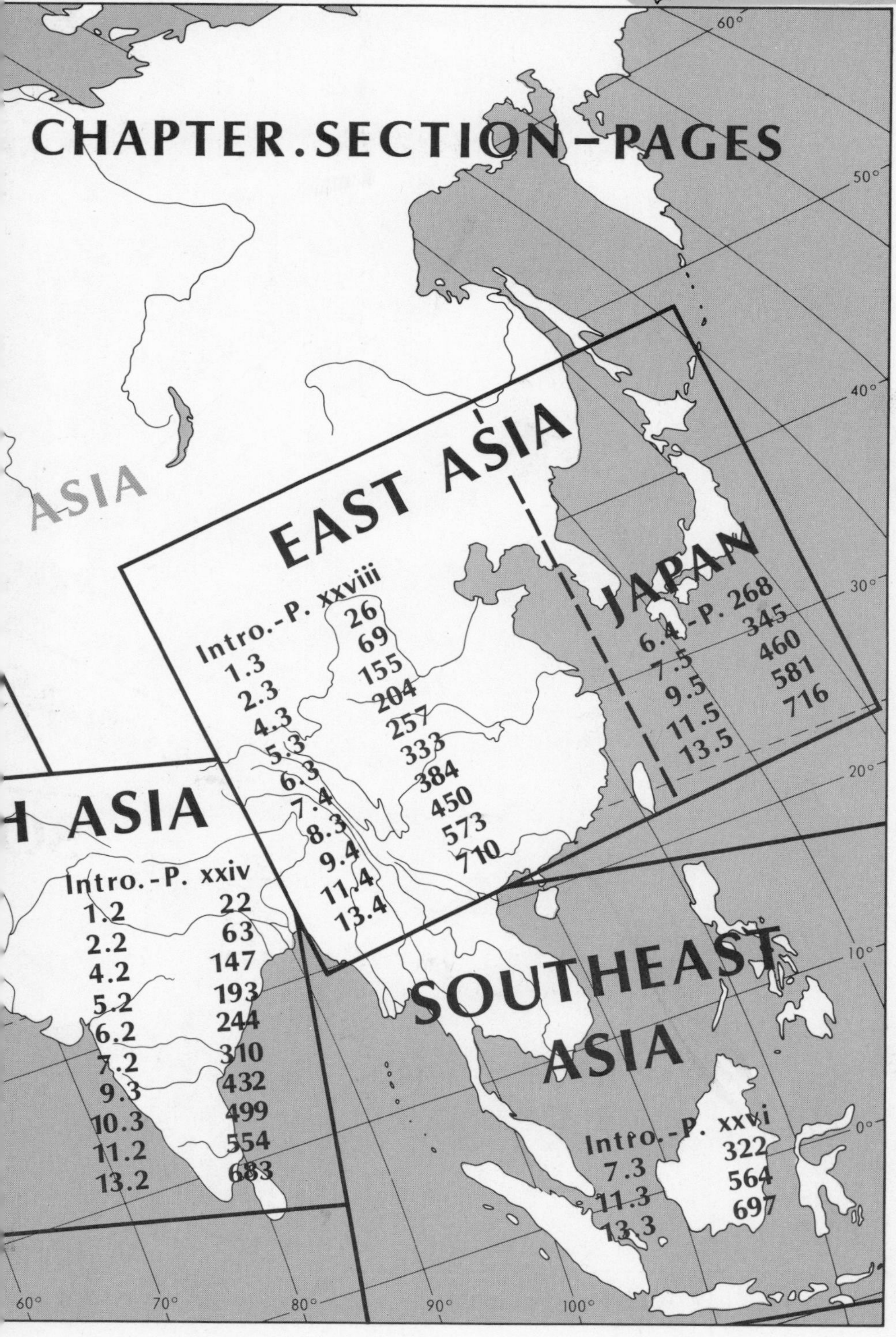
CHAPTER.SECTION–PAGES
ASIA
EAST ASIA
Intro.-P. xxviii
1.3 26
2.3 69
4.3 155
5.3 204
6.3 257
7.4 333
8.3 384
9.4 450
11.4 573
13.4 710
JAPAN
6.4-P. 268
7.5 345
9.5 460
11.5 581
13.5 716
H ASIA
Intro.-P. xxiv
1.2 22
2.2 63
4.2 147
5.2 193
6.2 244
7.2 310
9.3 432
10.3 499
11.2 554
13.2 683
SOUTHEAST ASIA
Intro.-P. xxvi
7.3 322
11.3 564
13.3 697
60°
50°
40°
30°
20°
10°
0°
60°
70°
80°
90°
100°

Comparative History of Civilizations in Asia

Comparative History

Edward L. Farmer
UNIVERSITY OF MINNESOTA

Gavin R. G. Hambly
UNIVERSITY OF TEXAS AT DALLAS

Volume I: 10,000 B.C. to 1850

# of Civilizations in Asia

David Kopf
UNIVERSITY OF MINNESOTA

Byron K. Marshall
UNIVERSITY OF MINNESOTA

Romeyn Taylor
UNIVERSITY OF MINNESOTA

ADDISON-WESLEY PUBLISHING COMPANY

Reading, Massachusetts
Menlo Park, California
London • Amsterdam
Don Mills, Ontario • Sydney

Title page photo: Ruins of Chinese military storehouse, Tun-Huang, ca. 52 B.C. From M. Aurel Stein, *Ruins of Ancient Cathay,* London: Macmillan and Co., Ltd., 1912.

 Printed in the United States of America. Published simultaneously in Canada. Library of Congress Catalog Card No. 75–12095.

ISBN 0-201-01998-1
ABCDEFGHIJ-HA-79876

This book is dedicated to our children:

Amy	Jessica	Maximilian
Byron	Jim	Michelle
Charles	Joy	Sally
Dan	Judy	Sarah
Edward	Lara	Walter

Contents

List of Maps

Preface

The day has long since passed when one could seriously question the desirability of including at least an introductory treatment of Asian history in the content of a liberal education. Yet the general reader, the student, or the teacher attempting to come to grips with the history of Asia is faced simultaneously with two formidable problems. The first is the need to assimilate a vast amount of unfamiliar information. The second is the need to order that information into meaningful units, to relate it to the rest of one's knowledge and to decide what is essential and what is less important. The purpose of this book is to help solve these problems by providing a broad framework and flexible method for thinking about the history of the peoples of Asia. The approach adopted, which involves the comparative study of civilizations, is described in detail in the Introduction. Here we will address the questions of why we have written such a book and how we think it can be used in teaching.

The Problem of Perspective

It is an understandable, if lamentable, fact that the curriculums and teaching resources of colleges and universities in the English-speaking world are heavily weighted toward the values and institutions of the European and American past. This condition is a natural result of the fact that the study of history, and to a lesser extent the other humanities and social sciences, has been motivated by a desire for self-understanding, by the search for a cultural self-image. Interest in other peoples and other traditions has been relegated to a secondary position. This has been particularly true of Asian studies, as a function of both physical and cultural remoteness from Western life. In recent decades, however, interest in the world outside the West has increased markedly and efforts have been made to include the history of most areas of the globe within the scope of a liberal education. In part at least this is due to the recognition that self-understanding is achieved through an understanding of the "other." Once one accepts the desirability of including Asian history in the undergraduate curriculum one is faced with formidable practical problems. Prominent among these problems is the question of scale. More than half of the people in the world are Asians. The size and diversity of Asia as a cultural unit is suggested by the fact that thirteen of the twenty principal spoken languages are Asian, while only six are of European origin.

The challenge for an introductory course in Asian history is how to give a meaningful account of this vast sector of the world, with less resources and less class time than is normally devoted to the cultures of the West. Two considerations, one theoretical and one practical, enter at this point. The first consideration is that Asia is too large, too complex,

Principal World Languages	Millions of Speakers	European	Asian
1. Mandarin	639		x
2. English	352	x	
3. Russian	226		x
4. Spanish	208	x	
5. Hindi	205		x
6. Arabic	121		x
7. Bengali	120		x
8. German	120	x	
9. Portuguese	120	x	
10. Japanese	109		x
11. Malay-Indonesian	93		x
12. French	87	x	
13. Italian	60	x	
14. Urdu	57		x
15. Punjabi	53		x
16. Telugu	53		x
17. Tamil	52		x
18. Korean	51		x
19. Marathi	49		x
20. Cantonese	47		x

Source: The World Almanac & Book of Facts 1975 (New York, 1974), p. 295.

and too diverse to be treated as a single unit in the way Europe or Latin America can be. It is necessary, therefore, for the purpose of analysis to divide Asia into smaller, more cohesive subdivisions. A reasonable division of the world into regions would separate Asia into five parts: West Asia, South Asia, East Asia, Southeast Asia, and Central Asia.

	North	South					Asia		
Region	America	America	Africa	Europe	**West**	**South**	**Southeast**	**East**	**Central**
Area (Mil. Sq. Mi.)	9.4	6.8	11.5	3.7	2.5	1.6	1.7	3.9	7.7
Population (Millions)	335	206	374	659	130	724	297	956	158

Once Asia is broken into manageable and meaningful units the question arises as to how to treat several units at once. The approach offered in this series is to view the subdivisions of Asia from a comparative perspective.

The practical consideration that faces the instructor trying to teach a course covering the whole of Asia is the fact that no single individual scholar can hope to acquire a detailed familiarity with all areas of Asia. All too often the solution is to teach about China or India and let the rest go. The virtue of a comparative approach is to create flexibility by allowing one to extend inquiry from the relatively familiar to the relatively unfamiliar while retaining a balanced perspective.

How to Use This Book

This book is designed for use by an instructor who is more familiar with one subdivision of Asia than with the others. The organization of each chapter is intended to facilitate the extension of inquiry comparatively from known subject matter to the relatively unknown. Structurally, each chapter is composed of a "process" section (abbreviated P) and "pattern" sections (organized from west to east) describing historical events in the various subdivisions of Asia. For example, in Chapter 4 the process section (4.P) analyzes the formation of universal empires, while the patterns describe specific empires: the Achaemenids (4.1), the Mauryans (4.2) and the Ch'in-Han (4.3). This combination of process and patterns gives the reader a great freedom of choice in selecting a strategy for using the book.

The instructor need not follow the book section by section as it is printed. Instead his or her lecturing and reading assignments can be varied to use some or all of the chapters, some or all of the patterns within the chapters. The patterns within each chapter are in reality separable subchapters, which can be read in any order desired since they are numbered arbitrarily according to geographical position. The instructor should break up chapter assignments to meet the needs of a given course. We suggest a number of course formats in which the book could be used:

1. As it stands the book is an overview of all of Asian history from the eastern borders of Europe to the Pacific and from the birth of civilization to the present. The stress in this overview is placed on the identification of a number of significant stages of historical development in the life of civilizations and on clarification of the social and cultural subdivisions within Eurasia. On this scale there is no possibility of surveying in detail the history of each civilization. This overview has utility both for the beginning student who wants a sort of world map for future study and the advanced student who knows about one area and wants to extend his or her knowledge to others.

2. Less inclusively, one could survey just two civilizations using the processes as a basis for discussion and assigning only the two relevant patterns in each chapter. The instructor, of course, has the flexibility of choosing to lecture primarily on the area with which he or she is most familiar and perhaps assigning additional reading to supplement the text on the other area. Many variations are possible along these lines.

3. For a topical survey of one time period a course could be built around a single theme such as the universal religions discussed in Chapter 6. In this treatment the process portion of Chapter 6 would supply questions to be pursued in depth for a whole term. Chapter 3 on ethical protest and reform ideologies could be read for background, and the patterns in Chapter 6 could be supplemented by additional readings such as those suggested in the bibliography section appended to the chapter.

4. In the survey of a single area of Asia this book could be treated as a supplementary reading in which the process sections, particularly, might be used to formulate questions.

5. At a more advanced level, the process portions of the book could be used to provide a structural format for a seminar or discussion course. The patterns would supply minimum background for the discussion of unfamiliar areas, while the bibliographies would supply a starting point for those reading in depth on a given area and for those preparing papers.

6. The reader will note from the maps and the process format that the scope of this comparison could be extended beyond Asia to include all of Eurasia. That the patterns are confined to Asia alone is primarily a matter of practical considerations such as the amount of space required. Certainly lectures or readings on Western "patterns" (Rome, Christianity, etc.) would comfortably fit the structure of the comparison. Some instructors may wish to attempt such inclusions, which are often most stimulating. The authors have on numerous occasions benefitted in their own course from guest lectures by colleagues in ancient and medieval history. The last four chapters can likewise be expanded to a global range (Africa, Latin America, North America) since the processes associated with European maritime domination, nationalism, and modern change were not constricted by the confines of the Eurasian landmass.

The point of these remarks is to urge readers to use this book with flexibility according to their needs and circumstances. It is not intended to be a definitive account of all aspects of Asian history. Rather, it is intended as an introduction and as a tool to facilitate open-ended and comparative inquiry. Certain questions are raised in each chapter, and the descriptive material is necessarily oriented toward those questions. The reader should be prepared to challenge both the questions and the interpretations at any point. The value of the comparative format is not in the precision of the answers as much as it is in the way it formulates questions and clarifies basic assumptions in preparation for further study.

Bibliography

The scope of Asian history and the volume of scholarship on Asia defy any effort at definitive condensation. What we have tried to do in each chapter is suggest further readings that will provide practical beginning points to the reader who wishes to know more. In our selections we have usually included standard textbooks and reference works, and where possible we have indicated works available in paperback. For more detailed bibliographical guidance, however, more specialized works should be consulted. Among the most useful are:

Howard, Harry N., *et al.*, eds., *Middle East and North Africa: A Bibliography for Undergraduate Libraries* (Williamsport: Bro-Dart Publishing Co., 1971), 80 pp.

Hucker, Charles O., *China: A Critical Bibliography* (Tucson: University of Arizona Press, 1962), 125 pp.

Mahar, J. Michael, *India: A Critical Bibliography* (Tucson: University of Arizona Press, 1964), 119 pp.

Silberman, Bernard S., *Japan and Korea: A Critical Bilbiography* (Tucson: University of Arizona Press, 1962), 120 pp.

Tregonning, Kennedy G., *Southeast Asia: A Critical Bibliography* (Tucson: University of Arizona Press, 1969), 103 pp.

Bibliography of Asian Studies, annual volumes published by the Association for Asian studies since 1971 (September 1970 issue). Prior to 1970 this work appeared as the fifth issue of the *Journal of Asian Studies.* This is the best source for recent Western-language works on Asia except for West Asia. However, one must look through each volume to get the publications of each year, and the citations do not contain annotations as do the critical bibliographies listed above.

Authorship

This book grew out of an undergraduate survey course taught for many years at the University of Minnesota. It was David Kopf's inspiration in 1967 to integrate the course by treating all Asia in a common format instead of assigning a given number of weeks to East Asia and a like number to South Asia. From that beginning four historians, specialists in modern India, premodern China, modern China, and modern Japan, became engaged in a collaborative teaching enterprise, which required each of us to expand the horizons of our teaching, to view our own areas of specialization from a comparative perspective, and often to engage in an extended, even heated, debate. Because no two history texts, particularly those dealing with different areas of Asia, treated history from a comparable perspective or in comparable units, we decided to develop our own teaching materials. In the most fundamental sense this book is a joint effort, the product of many continuing dialogues, and the writing itself has been a stimulating and rewarding experience. We were joined in the undertaking by Gavin Hambly of Yale University, who brought to the project a welcome familiarity with Iran, Central Asia, and Muslim South Asia. Writing and revision, which took five years and consumed a great deal of paper, was often interrupted by periods of research abroad and the normal strains of personal and professional life. Inevitably many changes were made in the design of the book and in the choice and definition of processes. While comments, suggestions, and criticisms were freely exchanged through several drafts, the primary responsibility for writing the individual sections was distributed as follows:

Edward L. Farmer: Introduction; 1.2 Harappan Civilization; 2.2 Aryan Civilization; 4.P Processes in the Rise of Universal Empires; 6.2 Hinduism; 9.P Processes of Early Modern Empires; 9.4 Ming and Ch'ing; 10.P Processes of Decline; 10.4 Decline of Ch'ing; 11.3 Western European domination in Southeast Asia; 11.4 Maritime Integration in China; 12.3 Disintegration in China; 13.3 Nationalism in Southeast Asia; 13.4 Nationalism in China; 14.3 Change in Southeast Asia; 14.4 Change in China.

Gavin Hambly: 4.1 Achaemenid Empire; 4.2 Mauryan Empire; 5.1 Parthians and Sasanids; 5.2 Kushanas and Guptas; 6.1 Islam; 7.1 Fragmentation in West Asia; 7.2 Fragmentation in South Asia; 8.2 Mongol Empire in West Asia; 8.4 Timur; 9.1 Ottomans; 9.2 Safavids; 9.3 Mughuls; 10.1 Decline of Ottomans; 10.2 Decline of Safavids; 10.3 Decline of Mughuls; 11.1 European Domination in West Asia; 12.1 Disintegration in West Asia; 13.1 Nationalism in West Asia; 13.2B Nationalism in South Asia among Muslims; 14.1 Change in West Asia.

David Kopf: 11.2 Western European domination in South Asia; 12.2 Disintegration in South Asia; 13.2A Nationalism in South Asia among Hindus; 14.2 Change in India.

Byron K. Marshall: 6.3 Buddhism (Japan portion); 7.5 Cultural Synthesis in Japan; 9.5 Tokugawa; 10.5 Decline of Tokugawa; 11.5 Maritime Integration in Japan; 12.P Processes of Disintegration; 12.4 Disintegration in Japan; 13.5 Nationalism in Japan; 14.P Processes of Change; 14.5 Change in Japan.

Romeyn Taylor: 1.1 Mesopotamian Civilization; 1.3 Shang Civilization; 2.1 Political Organization of Mesopotamian Civilization; 2.3 Shang and Chou China; 3.1 Hebrew Prophets and Zoroaster; 3.2 Mahavira and Buddha; 3.3 Reform Ideology in Chou China; 4.3 Ch'in-Han Empire; 5.3 Late Han and Three Kingdoms; 6.3 Mahayana Buddhism; 7.3 Fragmentation in Southeast Asia; 7.4 Fragmentation in China; 8.P Processes of Central Asian Domination; 8.1 Formation of Mongols; 8.3 Mongol Domination in East Asia.

Joint Authorship: *Farmer* and *Kopf*: 11.P Processes of Maritime Integration; 13.P Processes of Cultural Renaissance and Nationalism; *Kopf* and *Marshall*: 3.P Processes of Crisis and Ethical Protest; 6.P Processes of Universal Religions; 7.P Processes of Regional Fragmentation; *Kopf* and *Taylor*: 1.P Processes of Birth of Civilization; 2.P Processes of the Political Organization of Civilized Societies; 5.9 Processes of the Persistence of Empire.

Acknowledgments

Inevitably, in a project which has gone on as long as this one has, many people make contributions which the authors wish to acknowledge as best they can. The heroine of our entire effort has been Sue Cave, who, with occasional help from Kathy Cooper and Carley Albrecht, typed the entire manuscript at least three times, often at dazzling speed. The staff at Addison-Wesley understood what we were trying to do at the outset, brought the five authors together and set us to writing, and saw us through the long years of revision. Over the years our colleagues at the University of Minnesota have been tolerant of our struggles with a joint lecture course and an integrated manuscript. Among those who have lectured in the survey or made other contributions are Bernard Bachrach, Robert Berkhofer, Stephen Blake, Jerry Clinton, Stephen Dale, Tom B. Jones, Lothar Knauth, David Lelyveld, Richard Mather, Angus McDonald, Larry Moses, John Perry, Tom Noonan, Robert Poor, Stuart Schwartz, and Ira Spar. Our sternest and most constructive critics have been the teaching assistants who joined us in the classroom: Thomas Allsen, George Chang, Amalendu Chakraborty, Robert Dillard, Richard Heitler, Roland Higgins, Yun-yi Ho, Tai-yung Lin, Bonnie McKellar, Bruce Robinson, Patrick Roche, Kristina Kade Troost, Wallace Witham, and Dante Yip. Special thanks are due to Dorothy Larson and Lorraine Mix of Central Duplicating and Pat Burwell and Sandy Haas of the Cartography Lab of the University of Minnesota for expert help in many crucial points of production. The staff of the History Department at the University of Minnesota, particularly Gretchen Asmussen, Dennis Clayton, and Doreen Haven, gave institutional support and personal encouragement for which we are most grateful.

September 1976

E.L.F.
G.R.G.H.
D.K.
B.K.M.
R.T.

Introduction

The *Asian* in the title of this book indicates in a general way what part of the world is to be considered. Its use, however, may lead to certain misunderstandings unless its implications are examined. The conventional practice of dividing the Eurasian landmass arbitrarily into two "continents," Europe and Asia, along a line through the Ural Mountains reinforces the mistaken idea that Europe and Asia are equivalent historical entities. In fact, however, the Asian part is very much larger than the European and is the home of at least three civilizations. This means that while to study the history of Europe is to study one civilization, to study the history of Asia is to study several civilizations at once.

Because there is no single Asian civilization, it follows that there can be no uniform history of Asia. The familiar history of "Western civilization," which traces the evolution of a common cultural tradition from Greek and Roman origins through the Middle Ages to modern Europe and the United States, has no parallel in Asia. The history of Chinese civilization in East Asia or of Indian civilization in South Asia, to cite the two most obvious examples, would each be comparable to the history of Western civilization in Europe. Thus it becomes necessary to dispense with the notion of an Asian civilization and to distinguish several distinct cultural traditions, which shared the single common characteristic of being non-European. The problem is to decide which units to deal with and how to approach them. In this book Asia will be divided into five culture zones, three of which are clearly identified with civilizations, and their history will be treated comparatively.

Three cultural areas of Asia are historically comparable to Europe in the sense that major civilizations have evolved in them. Unfortunately, in the English language there are no common names for these areas as there is for Europe, a fact that makes it difficult to perceive their cultural unity. Consequently, we are forced to the expediency of labelling these civilizations by the geographical terms for the regions in which they developed: *West Asia, South Asia,* and *East Asia*. These terms, while graceless, at least avoid the parochialism of Europocentric terms (Near East, Middle East, Far East). They also avoid the imprecision and confusion of usages that derive from a single nation (Indian civilization, Chinese civilization) or religion (Islamic civilization). West Asia designates a polycentric culture zone that includes the Arabian peninsula, the Fertile Crescent, Turkey, Iran, and the southern flanks of the Soviet Union; by South Asia we mean the Indian subcontinent; while East Asia includes China and the adjacent territory of Korea, Japan, and Vietnam. Two other subdivisions of Asia, which have historically interacted with these areas, are *Southeast Asia* and *Central Asia*. Southeast Asia, while it was a meeting place and zone of interaction with the four major civilizations of Eurasia, displayed a high degree of cultural diversity and did not itself develop a unified civilization. Central Asia was generally inhospitable to the development of civilization, although in some parts of this region oasis cities flourished as local variants or blends of the major civilizations.

What do we mean by civilization? The term is used here not as a value judgment but to designate the largest distinct culture-bearing units—the evolving configuration of social norms, traditions, and institutions that came to be widely shared by the population of the major subdivisions of Eurasia. The reason civilizations are defined in this book in terms of the common and enduring culture of great regions is not to denigrate local cultures, much less national histories, which are the proper concerns of anthropologists and historians. The reason is to underscore the scale of the subject matter to be dealt with. We are looking only at the broadest outlines of historical development and generalizing about changes taking place through the entire span of human history and across the expanse of the world's most extensive landmass. It is simply not possible to pay detailed or consistent attention to local affairs.

The search for that which was widely accepted and enduring in Asian culture tends to lead one to elite culture, to the values and ideas that found expression and hence preservation in the written record of the literate classes. In this sense civilization is equated in large part with the "great tradition," or the high culture, of a region in contradistinction to local customs. This is not to say that ordinary people are of no interest or that what is noteworthy in human culture has been the product of the rich and powerful alone, for all classes of society have participated in the human experience and all have contributed to the cultural heritage. Nevertheless, it is the educated few who have tended to share common perceptions and practices over large areas. Just as Latin was known to educated individuals all over Europe, so classical Chinese served as a *lingua franca* among the speakers of many dialects in China as well as among the educated in Korea, Japan, and Vietnam. Moreover, our present state of knowledge regarding the history of the common people in Asian societies is very limited, and what information there is has often been filtered through the eyes of the literate class.

The formation of the great cultural traditions of Eurasia was a cumulative development that took place in historical time. While each civilization was unique, reflecting the particular circumstances of its situation, certain broad parallels are apparent which allow comparative generalization. In many cases these parallels may be the products of fundamental changes in economic organization, technology, social organization, or the accumulation and interpretation of traditional beliefs. For example, the development of agriculture played an important role in the origin of civilization; likewise, religions in each case helped shape basic social values; and in modern times, the complex of factors we call industrialization upset the traditional social order. The overview of Asian civilizations that follows assumes comparability and often seeks parallels on this very abstract level. However, several warnings are in order. First, no claim is made that all civilizations developed in the same stages and by reason of the same causes; in some cases the reader may be struck by similarities, while in other instances it is the differences that stand out. Second, we are not asserting that we have found the motivating forces that made civilizations the way they were, or even that the causal factors were the same in each case. Third, the reader is reminded that the comparisons ventured here are undertaken on the broadest scale and that an analysis that helps our understanding at the most general level may obscure it at a more detailed level. In this connection the reader should bear in mind the very loose and broad meaning we are giving to the word *civilization*. For example, while we may treat East Asia as a culture zone with a common civilization, generalizations about the whole area will not always hold true for all societies within it. Japan, for instance, shares many traits with China but differs from the latter sufficiently for it to be viewed as a distinct culture within the broader civilization. The problem is one of scale; the generalizations this comparative approach allows should not be endowed in the reader's mind with the sanctity of historical law.

To put the scale of this comparison into perspective, think of the entire history of Western civilization, and then consider how to organize a study of three other civilizations of a comparable magnitude. In such an undertaking, two approaches common to introductory history texts are precluded. The first is the consideration of national history. There are too many nations and peoples in Asia to attempt a coherent account of their histories within two volumes. The second approach, which might be useful if one were dealing with a single civilization, is the chronological survey. That survey format would not fit the history of Asia easily because of the diversity of the area. In place of these familiar forms of organization, a somewhat different framework will be employed here—selective comparison in chronological sequence. The structure and the terminology of this comparison need to be explained.

Process, Pattern, and Period

The comparative perspective is useful in studying Asian civilizations for two principal reasons. First of all, by treating the history of the civilizations comparatively, one underscores the differences among them and hence their separateness in a way that dispels the notion of an Asian unity. Second, comparison stimulates awareness of contrasts, raising questions about differences as well as similarities, questions that often would not occur if one were dealing with a single civilization. Thus, for example, if one studied only European history one might accept as "normal" and not question the fragmentation of the Roman empire into many states. But if one also considers the fact that the Chinese empire was reunited during the medieval period, one is prompted to try to account for the differences. The point here is not that a comparative method automatically yields answers to such questions, or that it can prove any particular theory of history, but merely that it helps to challenge assumptions and suggest fruitful questions. Another way to put it is to say that comparative history forces one to make basic concepts explicit. In this book the analytical concepts used to guide comparisons are called *processes* and the historical examples that are compared are referred to as *patterns*.

A *process* is a developmental phenomenon that can occur in different times and regions. It is described in broadly generalized terms so that the definition will fit various societies and cultures. An example of a process might be urbanization. One would find urban communities forming in all parts of the world at various times, although they would differ in appearance and the motive for forming them could vary widely. Thus one city might form as a castle town, another as a trading center, and a third as a place of worship. At the beginning of each chapter a process section will discuss a number of historical developments in the abstract to provide a guide or framework for the comparative sections to follow. For example, the birth of civilization will be discussed in terms of such processes as the development of agriculture, urbanization, and the invention of writing. We emphasize that the processes selected for discussion in each chapter are not fixed and rigid categories setting the limits on historical reality, or Platonic ideals representing the essence of the truth. Rather, they are commonsense formulations for the purpose of facilitating discussion. In this sense the processes are arbitrary; they are chosen on heuristic grounds. A different list of processes could have been used for most chapters, and each process could have been defined differently. In the case of urbanization, for example, the process can be conceived in a number of ways. Cities can be defined in terms primarily of trade, or the density of population, or their status in a political hierarchy. Each such alternative will produce a different process, which in turn will alter the comparison of cities in Japan, Iran, and elsewhere. The function of the processes, then, is to structure the comparison of civilizations in Asia and not to make a definitive statement about their history—still less to explain Asian history in causal terms.

Patterns, in the usage of this text, are the events in the particular subdivisions of Asia which are being compared. The beginnings of civilization, which will be discussed at the outset of Chapter 1 as processes, will then be viewed in three historical patterns: Sumerian civilization in West Asia, Harappan civilization in South Asia, and the Shang civilization in

East Asia. Whereas the processes are stated abstractly, the pattern sections are concrete and descriptive. It is the task of the reader to test the processes against the patterns in each case to see where there is similarity and where difference.

A third element in this scheme is *period*. Obviously, the comparable events in the history of various civilizations are not always going to be found in the same span of time. For this reason comparison must take into account the notion of period. In each chapter the reader will find a statement about the time period covered by each of the patterns. Sometimes the patterns will not even overlap in time. Evidence of the beginnings of civilization in Mesopotamia is much older than that of comparable developments in the Indus valley and northern China, so the patterns discussed in the first chapter will diverge chronologically. Generally speaking, the time periods diverge most widely in chapters covering the remote past and correspond most closely in those covering more recent periods, with the chapters covering the modern period overlapping broadly.

Chapter Topics

The comparison of civilizations in Eurasia entails certain assumptions about the classification of civilizations as cultural entities with uniform or similar attributes. A historical comparison entails assumptions about the relationships among the civilizations. The selection, arrangement, and interpretation of subject matter is influenced by assumptions about these questions. The perspective adopted here can be clarified by stating what it does not assume. First of all, we are not primarily concerned with seeking the origins of civilized values or institutions; we are not trying to trace civilization or its constituent elements back to some primal source. While the diffusion of cultural elements from one area to another is fully recognized, and even becomes a major theme of some chapters, the ancestry of a civilization is not a central concern of this work. Second, interaction among civilizations is not the focus. Contact between one part of Eurasia and another, the influence of one culture on another, is a constant and substantial portion of our picture, but it is not the interaction itself that is of primary interest, but the effects of interaction on the civilizations involved. Third, and by the same token, the uniqueness of each cultural tradition is not to be stressed. Most historians write about some aspect of their own historical tradition and thus are involved in developing a cultural self-image, a perception from the inside. While the comparative format recognizes both relatedness and distinctness, it is concerned less with grasping the peculiar essence of a particular civilized tradition than with generalizing about the common characteristics of a number of traditions.

The problem is to accommodate a comparative format to historical subject matter. A sociologist or a political scientist might be content to compare family structure or governmental institutions in various societies without regard to the historical epoch. This study, however, is historical in that the topics are arranged in a chronological order and the sequence of patterns contributes to the continuity of the whole. Since cultural traditions grow by accretion, it is important to see how they evolved over time. In this sense the earlier chapters are background to the later chapters. Thus, the ethical protest ideologies—which included, for example, that of the historical Buddha—are discussed in Chapter 3. These ideologies were later important in giving form to the universal religions—for example, Buddhism—dealt with in Chapter 6. Nevertheless, the reader is reminded that more attention has been given to the comparison across civilizations within each chapter than to the continuity within each civilization from one chapter to the next. In fact, the chapters are intended to cut across the flow of history at points of interest without promising to connect the spaces between in a uniformly detailed manner.

Another point to be clarified is that the chapters are not concerned with a uniform set of questions or perspectives. The scale of comparison differs—one chapter may deal with a thousand years, another with a half century; in some chapters an extended empire is the subject, while others might deal only with a small number of seminal thinkers. A further variation is introduced by the level of abstraction. Where the chapter on universal religions generalizes about the evolving faith of hundreds of millions of worshippers, the earlier account of ethical protest ideologies deals with the doctrines of a few individuals. Most important is the fact that the topics of various chapters pose different questions. A rough characterization of these differences in perspective can be presented in tabular form:

EVOLUTIONARY DEVELOPMENT	INSTITUTIONS	SOCIAL BREAKDOWN	ELITE VALUES IN CRISIS	REGIONAL INTERACTION
1. Birth of Civilization	4. Universal Empires	7. Regional Fragmentation	3. Ethical Protest	8. Central Asian Domination
2. Political Organization	6. Universal Religions	10. Decline of Empires	5. Persistence of Empire	11. Maritime Integration
14. Modern Change	9. Modern Empires	12. Cultural Disintegration	13. Renaissance and Nationalism	

The first two and the last chapter attempt to analyze the way that changing economic and social conditions affected culture. Three chapters deal with periods of unity, either political or religious, while three others consider periods of social breakdown and cultural disintegration. The perception of social crisis is the main topic of another three chapters, while regional interaction—including attempts to unify Eurasia—is the main theme of the remaining two.

Viewed sequentially, the chapters trace the evolution of human society in Asia by attempting to identify major points of change. Chapter 1 examines the processes by which civilization came into being, while Chapter 2 discusses the emergence of the state and kingship as a response to the problems caused by the growth of civilized society. In Chapter 3 we consider the protests and ethical prescriptions that were elicited in the first millennium B.C. by the incessant and escalating conflict among the newly evolved states. One solution to the dilemma, political unification on a basis as wide as the whole civilized world, or culture zone, was accomplished by universal empires, the subject of Chapter 4. The decline and collapse of universal empires were followed by attempts to resurrect them and to preserve their heritage (Chapter 5), but the more significant development was the rise of universal religions (Chapter 6), which promised mankind a new security independent of the structure of the state. A period of regional fragmentation (Chapter 7), rich in local cultural development, was followed by the heroic effort of the Central Asian peoples under Mongol leadership to unify the Eurasian world by military conquest (Chapter 8). Following the Mongol irruption, new empires (Chapter 9) were formed in the heartlands of the old civilizations. Their survival into modern times in a progressively weakened condition is the subject of Chapter 10. The extension of European activities by land and sea increased the intercourse between Europe and the civilizations of Asia, leading by the nineteenth century to the consummation of European domination over much of Asia (Chapter 11). This development, which hastened the introduction of forces of change, accelerated the cultural disintegration of Asian societies (Chapter 12). The response of Asian people to the ascendancy of Westerners assumed the form of cultural renaissance and nationalist movements (Chapter 13). In Chapter 14 the processes of modernization are examined in the context of their impact on the cultural traditions of Asian societies.

This brief summary should make clear that the chapter topics have been chosen to touch on a few periods of significant innovation and of crisis. The intent of this scheme is to give the reader an introductory grasp of some of the most interesting developments in the history of human societies in Asia and a framework with which to seek and sort out the vast store of information that further reading can provide.

The Geographical Setting

Now that the scheme of the book has been introduced, something about the setting in which these historical developments transpired remains to be said. The practice throughout the book will be to present the patterns in a geographical order moving from west to east. Here, some basic features of each culture zone of Asia will be reviewed and considered in order to orient the reader for the text that follows. The five subdivisions will be conventionally designated by the terms West Asia, South Asia, Southeast Asia, East Asia, and Central Asia.

West Asia is the name we use to designate the area commonly referred to in everyday English as the Middle East or the Near East—terms we abjure because they define the region from a European standpoint. (From the perspective of California or Hawaii, China is the "Near West" and Arabia the "Far West.") As a culture zone and a center of civilization, West Asia is less cohesive and more polycentric than either South Asia or East Asia. It is helpful to think of the area in terms of the three dominant regions that mark its poles—Iran (formerly Persia) to the east, the Arabian peninsula to the south, and Turkey, or Anatolia (the ancient Asia Minor), to the northwest. The physical dispersal of these subcenters of West Asia is an important feature of an area that has served to link Europe and Africa with Central Asia, South Asia, and East Asia by means of age-old caravan trails. In the northwest, Anatolia projects outward toward Europe in the shape of a rectangular peninsula bounded on the north by the Black Sea, on the south by the Mediterranean, and on the west by the Aegean Sea. The Sea of Marmara, with narrow straits—the Dardanelles to the south, the Bosporus to the north—links the Aegean to the Black Sea and physically separates Anatolia from Thrace, with Istanbul (originally Byzantium, later Constantinople) on the European side. Northeast of Anatolia, the Caucasus region lying between the Black Sea and the Caspian Sea connects West Asia with the Volga-Don steppes in what is now the Soviet Union. This region includes the Soviet republics of Georgia, Armenia, and Azarbayjan, which adjoin Turkey and Iran. Along the southern shore of the Caspian Sea run the Elburz Mountains, demarcating the northern extremity of the Iranian plateau, while to the east of the Caspian the arid region comprising the present-day Turkmen, Uzbek, and Tadzhik republics of the Soviet Union, bordering Iran and Afghanistan, acts as a glacis linking West Asia with the true steppelands of Central Asia beyond the Syr Darya. Iran, consisting of a vast plateau broken by ranges of mountains (of which the Zagros to the west and southwest have tended to insulate Iran to some extent from the course of events in Mesopotamia) is the prime link area of West Asia, with its eastern extension in what is now Afghanistan acting as a major funnel for intercourse with South Asia. Mesopotamia (now Iraq), the great agricultural basin between the Euphrates and Tigris rivers, lies at the center of West Asia, where the first Asian civilization was born. The Tigris and Euphrates empty their waters into the Persian Gulf, a body of water that is constricted at its mouth by the Strait of Ormuz and opens onto the Gulf of Oman and the Arabian Sea. These bodies of water, which have long provided avenues of commerce with the East, frame the eastern and southern coastline of the Arabian peninsula, a vast tract of desert and semiarid regions which lies between Mesopotamia and the northeastern coast of Africa. Separating the two continents is the Red Sea, on the eastern side of which is the region of the Hijaz with the important Muslim religious centers of Medina and Mecca. At the northern end of the Red Sea, Egypt is separated from Palestine by the Sinai peninsula, a heart-shaped body of land defined on the east by the Gulf of Aqaba and on the west by the Gulf of Suez, where canals have at various times provided a link with the Mediterranean. The Levant is the name given by Europeans

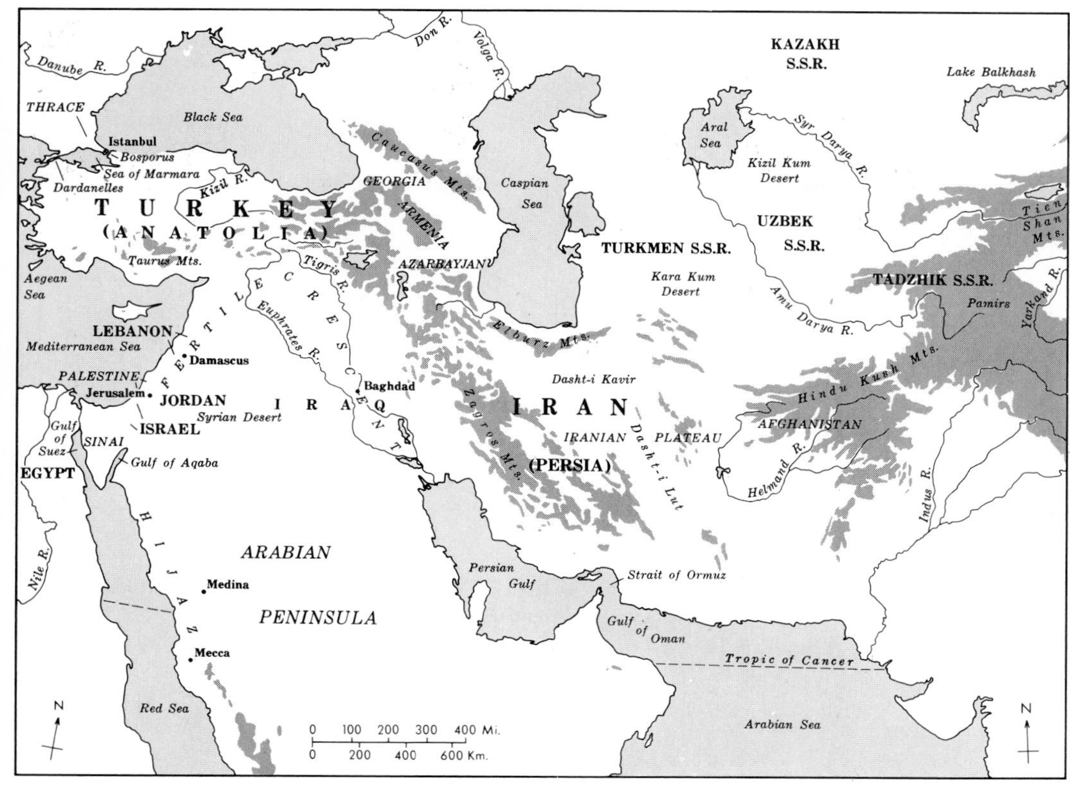

Map 1 West Asia

to the eastern coast of the Mediterranean, consisting of Syria and Palestine—the western arc of the curving belt of arable lands extending westward out of Mesopotamia known as the Fertile Crescent—and including the region long known to Christians as the Holy Land. The modern states of Jordan, Israel, Lebanon, Syria, and Iraq contain such historic centers as Jerusalem, Damascus, and Baghdad.

South Asia, the Indian subcontinent, has throughout its history interacted with West Asia and Central Asia along overland communication routes. India has also played a role as an intermediary in maritime trade between Southeast Asia and areas to the west, and South Asian values and institutions have made a profound impact on the culture of both peninsular and insular Southeast Asia. Natural barriers, the mountains of Tibet and western China and the nearly impenetrable jungles of Burma, have contributed to preventing direct commercial or military contact between India and China, but cultural contacts have been profoundly important, particularly the spread of Buddhism from South Asia to East Asia. For the purposes of this text, our focus in South Asia lies in the northern part of India, in particular the watersheds of the Indus and the Ganges rivers. This was the locus of the earliest civilized communities in South Asia and later of the greatest states. The Indus flows in a southwesterly direction from its headwaters in the Himalayan Mountains. The Indus plain is bordered on the west by the foothills that rise up to the mountainous massif of central Afghanistan and extend westward into the region known as Baluchistan, where they descend toward the Makran coast of the Arabian Sea some two degrees north of the Tropic of Cancer. Land routes lead westward from the Indus basin to Iran through Kandahar and, farther north, through Ghazni and Kabul. From the Kabul valley, passes lead northward

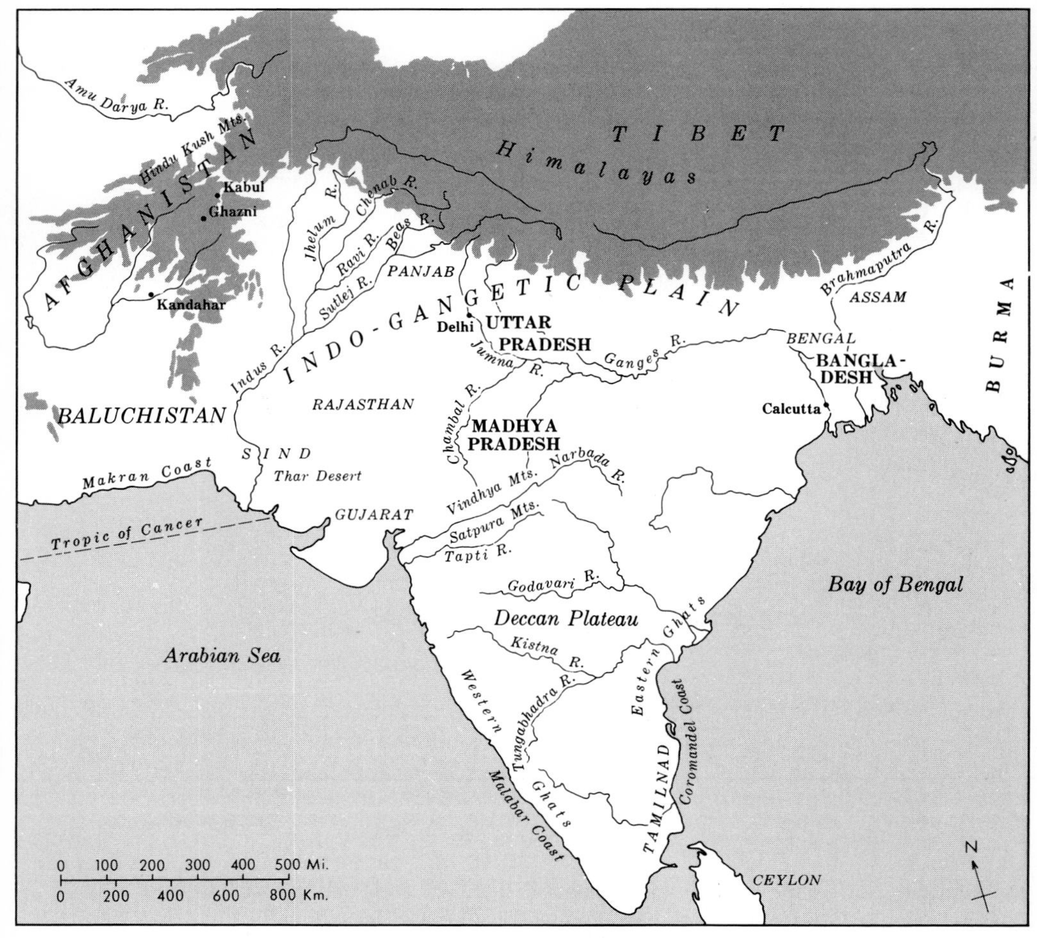

Map 2 South Asia

across the Hindu Kush Mountains into Central Asia. The major tributaries of the Indus flow across the Panjab, or "Land of the Five Rivers"—the Jhelum, the Chenab, the Ravi, the Beas, and the Sutlej. To the south the Indus region is cut off from the rest of the subcontinent by the Thar, or Great Indian Desert, and the arid portions of Rajasthan. From the Jumna, on which Delhi stands, and the upper reaches of the Ganges, the eastern arm of the Indo-Gangetic plain stretches some nine hundred miles to the sea near the modern city of Calcutta. The other major river of the north, the Brahmaputra, after leaving Tibet flows westward across Assam and turns south to form, with the Ganges, the vast deltaic region of Bengal, an important cultural subdivision of South Asia, currently divided between India and Bangladesh. The Narbada River, which flows west into the Arabian Sea, and the Vindhya and other low ranges running from west to east across the subcontinent have served to isolate the Deccan plateau and the far south of the peninsula from the north. The hilly terrain of much of central and southern India has tended to inhibit communication by land, prompting coastal peoples to turn to the sea. The Western Ghats, a range of mountains running close to the Arabian Sea, define the narrow coastal plain known in the far south as the Malabar coast. On the other side of the peninsula a wider coastal plain known as the Carnatic separates the Eastern Ghats from the Coromandel coast, facing the Bay of Bengal. The island of Ceylon, now the nation-state of Sri Lanka, which lies off the southern tip of the peninsula, is properly part of South Asia, but will play no part in our story.

Geographical factors have affected the history of civilization in South Asia in a number of important ways. The relative isolation of the southern coastal regions from the northern plains has meant that the former, which have had the most intensive contact with other cultures by sea, have had a relatively slight impact on the heartland of South Asia. In the north, exposure to invasion from West Asia and Central Asia has made possible repeated incursions into the Indian subcontinent by peoples who brought with them alien cultural influences, which constitute important elements in the pattern of South Asian civilization. In the Ganges region and in certain other areas, the rhythm of seasonal rainfall, the monsoon, caused by heavy rains drawn inland from the Indian Ocean by rising hot air in the warm season, followed by a dry period in the winter when cool air flows south from the Central Asian landmass, made possible an intensive rice agriculture and a dense population.

Southeast Asia includes both the arc of mainland Eurasia west of India and south of China and the thousands of islands of the Indonesian and Philippine archipelagos. Between China and Indochina, however, there is no sharp line of demarcation either in the form of a physical boundary or an historically stable political and cultural division. In the island world, common usage excludes Sri Lanka (Ceylon) on the west and Taiwan to the north from inclusion in Southeast Asia. From an analytical perspective, in terms of social and cultural history, a strong argument could be made for including those islands with their neighbors in Southeast Asia.

The dominant characteristic of the physical geography of Southeast Asia, and a fact that goes far towards explaining why a culturally uniform and politically organized society never developed in the area, is the fragmentation and dispersal of the habitable land over great distances separated by mountains and water. The land area of Southeast Asia totals some 1.5 million square miles, slightly less than South Asia, and yet this land extends over an area that is some two thousand miles from west to east and a similar distance from north to south. Most of the major rivers of mainland Southeast Asia originate in the eastern end of the Tibetan plateau, where they are flanked by the headwaters of the Brahmaputra and the Yangtze. The Irrawaddy and the Salween are the principal rivers that flow southward through Burma, reaching the Andaman Sea on the western side of the Malay peninsula. In Thailand the Chao Phraya (Menam), a relatively short waterway, enters the Gulf of Thailand near the modern capital of Bangkok. The principal river of Indochina, the Mekong, flows for half its length through China before it enters Laos, defining for a distance the border between that country and Thailand before it enters Cambodia and crosses South Vietnam in the area known in French colonial times as Cochin China, where it debouches into the South China Sea. Along its course the Mekong passes the present capitals of Luang Prabang and Vientiane in Laos and Phnom Penh in Cambodia. The Red River, which originates in southwest China, flows to the sea across North Vietnam, the area once termed Tonkin by the French, and then passes through the city of Hanoi before it reaches the Gulf of Tonkin, a body of water that is defined by the southern projection of the Chinese Luichow peninsula and Hainan Island.

In general, the mountains of the mainland run north to south between the rivers just described, a fact that, together with the prevalence of heavy jungle cover, contributes to the isolation of the valleys. Another isolating feature is the extremely extended coastline. The coastline of Burma runs south from Bangladesh in the Arakan Mountain region until it reaches the Irrawaddy River delta, where it runs briefly eastward to the south of the Pegu Range before turning south along the Tenasserim coast on the Malay peninsula. The Malay

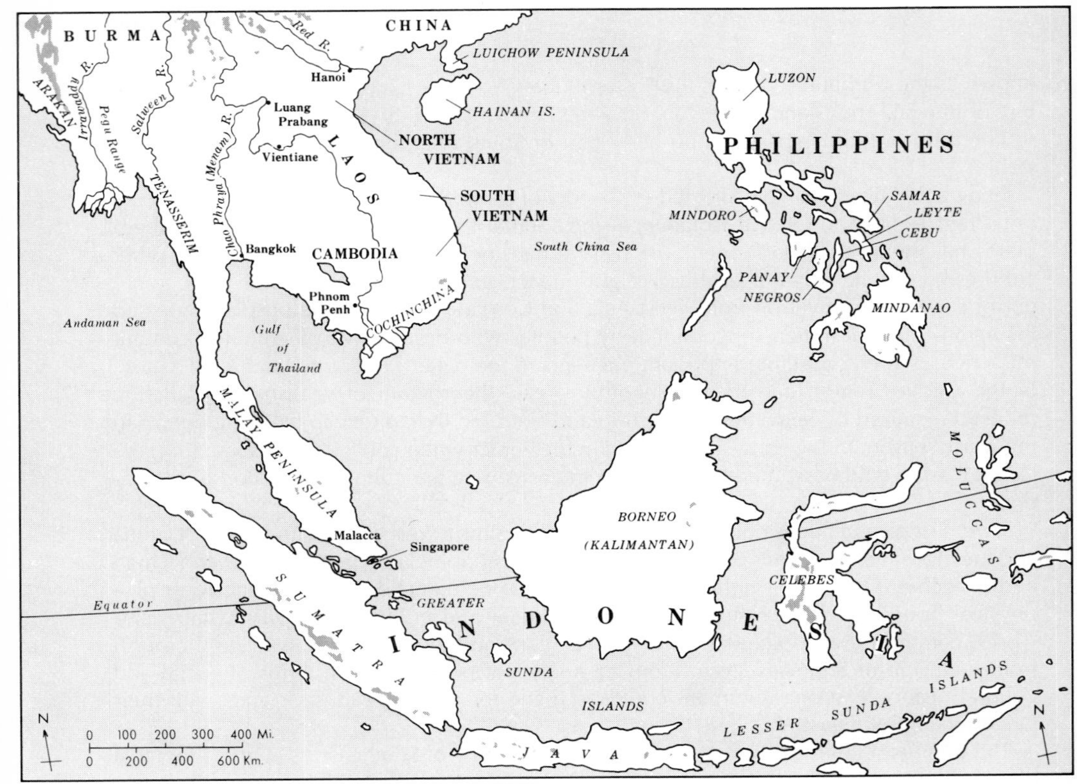

Map 3 Southeast Asia

peninsula is a long narrow arm of land that effectively lengthens the distance by sea between the western and eastern coasts of the mainland. As a consequence of this fact, such locations as Malacca and Singapore, at the tip of the peninsula, became strategic points for the control of sea-lanes and commerce. On the eastern side of the peninsula the Gulf of Thailand forms a southward-facing arc of coastline, while the elongated coast of Vietnam faces eastward toward the South China Sea. Since the political boundaries of Southeast Asia are of recent historical origin, the reader is advised that contemporary national terms are employed here for convenience purposes only.

The islands of the Indonesian archipelago are conventionally grouped into the Greater Sunda Islands, the Lesser Sunda Islands, Celebes, the Moluccas, and New Guinea (Irian). The Greater Sundas include the major islands of Sumatra, Borneo (Kalimantan), and Java. The Lesser Sundas and the Moluccas were important in the spice trade but have played a minor role in the history of Southeast Asian civilization. The principal islands of the Philippines are Luzon, Mindoro, Panay, Negros, Cebu, Samar, Leyte, and Mindanao. Southeast Asia lies on both sides of the equator, but only a tip of Burma extends north of the Tropic of Cancer. This fact, together with the abundance of rainfall, made wet-rice agriculture possible on the limited floodplains and deltas of the great rivers, but in mountainous areas the leaching effects of heavy rains often dictated a migrant slash-and-burn pattern of agriculture. Most important for cultural history, the accessibility of this fragmented landmass from the sea made Southeast Asia uniquely susceptible to the penetration of cultural influences from other parts of Eurasia. India certainly had the greatest impact, but Chinese institutions and values played a strong part in shaping Vietnamese culture, and Chinese commerce and immigration is an important feature throughout Southeast Asian history. Arab trade has long been important, and much of the population professes the Islamic faith. In modern times European and Japanese occupation and administration have introduced a further heritage of influences from those areas.

East Asia, by virtue of its physical location, was the most remote of the culture zones of Eurasia, but not isolated from the others. Its boundaries are indistinct. China, Vietnam, Korea, and Japan are the most important societies that have shared in a common East Asian civilization. The minority groups of southern and western China and the Tibetans, Mongols, and Manchus have periodically been drawn into the Chinese state and thus qualify as at least participants in the creation of the common cultural traditions of East Asia. Contact between East Asia and the other centers of civilization was limited by the great distance around Southeast Asia by sea, the mountains of western China, and the deserts of Central Asia. China proper is defined on the west by the Tibetan massif and on the north by the break between the steppe and sown, roughly along the line of the Great Wall. River valleys and their floodplains have provided the best locations for agriculture. In the south the Hsi (West) River meets the sea near Canton and Hong Kong. The Yangtze crosses the middle of China from the great Szechwan Basin in the west, through the lake country and the complex network of inland waterways, and past Nanking and Shanghai in the east. To the north, silt from the Yellow River (Huang Ho), which has altered its course north and south of the Shantung peninsula, has accumulated to form the north China plain, which stretches seven hundred miles from Nanking to Peking. Between the Yangtze and Yellow rivers is the transitional zone that marks off the warm south, where crops may be grown the year round, from the north, where cold air from Siberia makes winters frigid. In Manchuria the Liao River courses the wide valley east of the Greater Khingan Mountains and south of the Lesser Khingan Range. The Liaotung peninsula projects toward the Shantung peninsula to form the Po Hai, a northern annex to the Yellow Sea.

The Korean peninsula is demarcated by the Yalu River on the west and the Tumen on the east. The four main islands of the Japanese archipelago are, from north to south, Hokkaido (the last to be fully settled by Japanese), Honshu (the locus for most of the developments treated here), and the smaller islands of Shikoku and Kyushu. Formed originally by volcanic action, these islands are predominantly mountainous terrain. Both settled agriculture and urban life have occurred primarily on the coastal plains or in narrow valleys created by rivers debouching into the sea. The largest and most fertile of the plains are located on the island of Honshu, around the modern city of Tokyo and in the region of the neighboring cities of Osaka and Kyoto. These, and many smaller fertile plains, face the Pacific Ocean or the Inland Sea passage between Honshu and Shikoku and now, as in previous periods, have the highest concentration of population. Unlike China and other continental regions, there are no great rivers or, with the exception of Hokkaido, extensive grasslands for herding. Again with the exception of Hokkaido, the climate is made moderate by the warm ocean currents. One other geographical fact that has had important ramifications for Japanese history is its relative isolation. Over one hundred miles separate Japan from the tip of the Korean peninsula, the closest contact with mainland Asia. China lies several hundred miles southwest over rough waters. This has meant that the Japanese could interact with other East Asians, but it was difficult for outsiders to force that interaction or to incorporate Japan into a larger political unit.

Central Asia, or Inner Asia, is the expanse of steppes, deserts, and mountains that extend across Eurasia from the Caspian Sea and the Ural Mountains to Manchuria. Low rainfall and severe annual temperature variation made most of this area unsuitable for agriculture and therefore generally inhospitable to dense urban habitation. The peoples who lived in this region developed an economy and social organization based on a highly specialized form of animal husbandry. This style of life, which depended on seasonal migrations in quest of

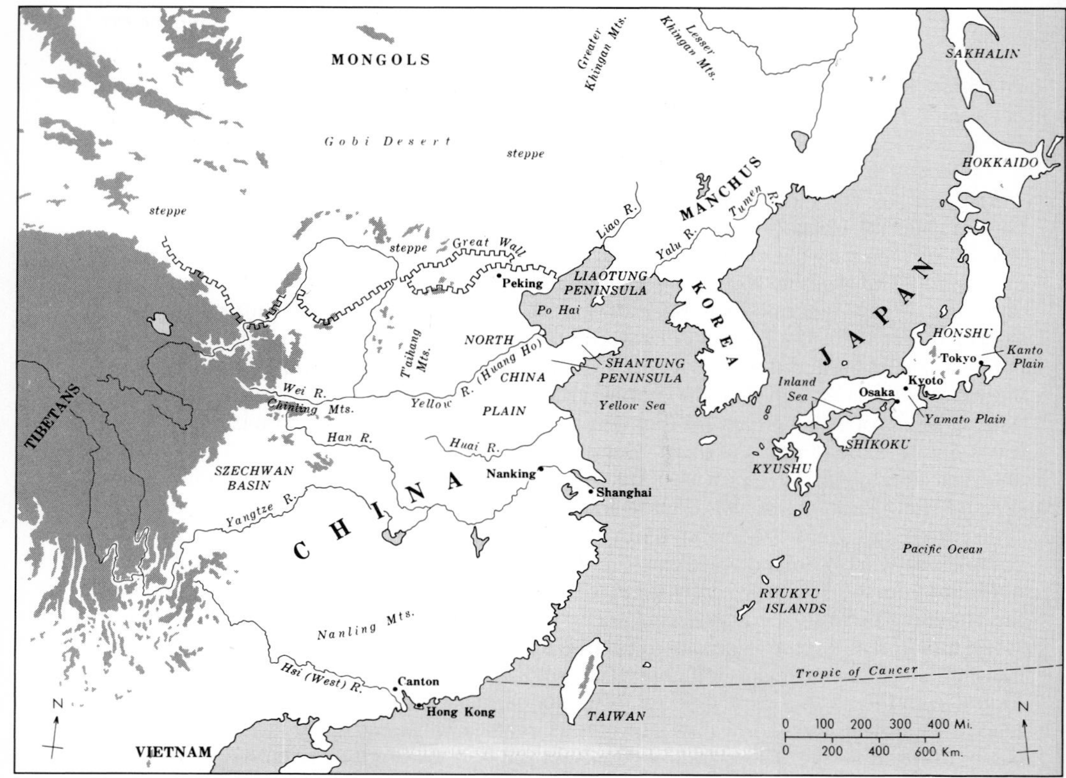

Map 4 East Asia

new grazing grounds, has been termed nomadic pastoralism. Where cities did occur in Central Asia, in the oases, on the river banks, and on the caravan routes, they were primarily extensions or outposts of the great sedentary civilizations (mainly Iranian and Chinese) on the fringes of Central Asia. The Volga River flows southward into the Caspian Sea. East of the Volga, in a north-south direction, lie the Ural Mountains, the conventional demarcation line between Europe and Asia. To the southeast lies the Aral Sea, fed by the Syr Darya (Jaxartes), which rises in the foothills of the Tien Shan Mountains, and the Amu Darya (Oxus), with its headwaters in the Pamirs. Across this region lay the land routes that connected West, South, and East Asia and passed through such ancient centers as Bokhara, Samarqand, Kashgar, and Khotan. East-west travel had to go north of the Tibetan plateau and either north or south of the Takla Makan desert, which lay between the Kunlun and Tien Shan mountain ranges. North of the Tien Shan Mountains lies the area to which the Russians have given the name of Semirechie, grasslands extending from the vicinity of Lake Balkhash in the west in the direction of the Altai Mountains to the northeast. Eastwards, beyond the pass known as the Dzungarian Gates, lie Dzungaria and Mongolia. Mongolia is bordered on the north by Lake Baikal and several mountain ranges, on the east by the Greater Khingan Mountains, and on the south by China, with the Gobi desert acting as a barrier separating them. Central Asia was important to the Eurasian civilizations in two respects. First of all, its caravan routes and oases facilitated the exchange of goods, peoples, and ideas between the centers of sedentary civilization. Second, it acted as a great reservoir from whence nomadic pastoralists, when mobilized for war, could strike at those same centers of sedentary civilization with devastating effect.

BIBLIOGRAPHY

Bagby, Philip, *Culture and History: Prolegomena to the Comparative Study of Civilization* (University of California Press paperback, 1963), 244 pp. An effort to apply anthropological insights to the creation of definitions and guidelines for the comparison of civilizations.

Kroeber, Alfred L., *Anthropology* (New York, 1923; revised 1948), pp. 311-85. Chapters 8 and 9 of this work provide an influential early discussion of pattern and process which differs in some respects from the definitions employed here.

————, *An Anthropologist Looks at History* (University of California Press paperback, 1963), 213 pp. Posthumous essays of a great anthropologist, including seven papers dealing with the comparison of civilizations.

McNeill, William H., *The Rise of the West: A History of the Human Community* (University of Chicago paperback, 1963), 828 pp. A brilliant and readable overview of Eurasian history with a tendency to stress interaction and influence among civilizations.

Redfield, Robert, *The Little Community and Peasant Society and Culture* (Chicago University Press, 1960), 182 pp. and 92 pp. The second of these combined essays contains some of the reflections of a noted anthropologist on the relationship between the local community and the civilization.

GLOSSARY

Civilization. The largest distinct cultural unit in human organization consisting of shared social norms, traditions and institutions persisting through historical time from one generation to the next. Usually this involves a "great tradition" fostered by a literate elite that consciously promotes the core values.

Culture zone. A subdivision of Asia characterized by common cultural traits, in some cases a common civilization.

East Asia. The western Pacific coast and islands including China, Japan, Korea, and sometimes Vietnam and extending inland to Tibet, Chinese Turkistan, and Mongolia.

Great tradition. The values and conventions of a dominant elite consciously propagated over a span of generations as the core of a civilized tradition. The great tradition is normally embodied in literature that is widely disseminated throughout a culture area, in contrast to a little tradition, which is embodied in the local community and tends to be orally transmitted.

Pattern. A particular instance of a generalized process of social change characterized by the influence of the physical location, historical antecedents, and social condition.

Period. The historical era or division of time in which a particular topic is discussed in this text.

Process. A characterization of social change in general terms without reference to a particular time and place, used for purposes of analysis and comparison of specific instances.

South Asia. The Indian subcontinent including the present-day territory of Pakistan, India, Bangladesh, and Sri Lanka (Ceylon).

Southeast Asia. The region south of East Asia and east of South Asia, including the arc of the Eurasian mainland from Burma to Vietnam and the islands of the Indonesian and Philippine archipelagos.

Steppe. Treeless, often arid plains of the Eurasian heartland.

West Asia. Known also as the Middle East or Near East, this area includes Turkey, Iran, and Arabia and the Fertile Crescent. For the purpose of this text, it also includes Afghanistan and the Soviet Central Asian Republics.

The Birth of Civilization in Asia

10,000 B.C. to 1000 B.C.

This book is a history ot civilization in three great culture areas: West, South, and East Asia. It begins therefore with the attempt to answer the questions when and how the societies inhabiting these regions first became civilized. The answer that one arrives at depends partly on the way in which civilization is defined. Here, a civilized society is one that is organized around permanent seats of religious or political authority. Such seats of authority are defined as cities, so societies became civilized as they generated urban centers. Such a minimal definition allows for the fact that the transition from precivilized to civilized society was gradual, taking place over thousands of years. It also allows for the fact that many features of precivilized society, such as the organization of agriculture in village communities, continued to exist in the civilized societies. Similarly, some of the characteristics commonly associated with civilizations, such as the building of fortifications and the use of conventional signs for record keeping, may have occurred in noncivilized contexts.

Before societies became civilized, they had long settled down in agricultural villages. The transition from hunting and gathering to village agriculture then merged gradually into the transition to civilization. The processes that provide the terms of comparison in this chapter thus fall into two categories: those antecedent to civilization, and those of the birth of civilization. Search for the origins of civilization leads back into the fateful venture of deliberately altering the natural ecological system by cultivating the soil, selecting seeds, selecting and breeding animals. Closely associated with this battery of technological innovations in food production were certain changes in patterns of settlement, social organization, and religion. Institutionalized religion with temples and ceremonial specialists offered a means of integrating and harmonizing the increasingly complex and competitive societies, and this in turn stimulated the development of new techniques of production and distribution and the growth and enrichment of cities.

Three great floodplains rimmed by uplands provided the settings of early civilization in Asia: Mesopotamia (modern Iraq); the Indus valley (northwest India); and the Yellow River valley (north China). The civilizations of all three regions revealed in their origins the distinctive styles and symbols that made them recognizably the ancestors of their modern descendants despite the transformations that all of them have since undergone.

PROCESSES

Antecedents to Civilization

a. Agricultural revolution
b. Sedentarization
c. Social stratification

The Birth of Civilization

d. Religious sanction of stratified society
e. Urbanization
f. Occupational differentiation and technological innovation
g. Writing

PATTERNS

1. **The Birth of Mesopotamian Civilization in West Asia**

2. **The Birth of Harappan Civilization in South Asia**

3. **The Birth of Shang Civilization in East Asia**

1. BIRTH OF CIVILIZATION

		1	2	3
	EGYPT	MESOPOTAMIA	INDUS VALLEY	CHINA
9000 B.C.				
		Broad spectrum gathering in the uplands, shifting settlement		
8000				Broad spectrum gathering in the uplands, shifting settlement
				Microlithic culture (north China)
		Jericho		
7000		Grain agriculture in uplands Settled villages Jarmo		
				Cord-marked ceramics (south China)
		Ali Kush		
6000		Ceramics Irrigated agriculture, beginning of settlement of lower Mesopotamia Eridu		
				Yangshao Grain agriculture in uplands, settled villages
5000				

		Northwestward spread of irrigated agriculture on the floodplain Ubaid		
4000			Emergence of villages and towns supported by agriculture	
		Uruk Urbanization, temple building, copper casting, writing		
3000	Protodynastic, Dynasties 1-2 Old Kingdom 3000-2300, Dynasties 3-4 Great pyramids 2800-2400	Early Dynastic City walls, bronze casting	Flourishing of Harappan culture in and around the Indus valley and beyond	Lungshan Spread of agriculture to north China plain; rice cultivation in south China
2000	Middle Kingdom 2050-1800, Dynasties 11-12 Hyksos invasions 1750-1550 New Kingdom 1565, Dynasties 18-20 Hyksos driven out		Approximated date of the disappearance of Harappan civilization	Shang Urbanization, temples, palaces, bronze casting, writing
1000				Chou

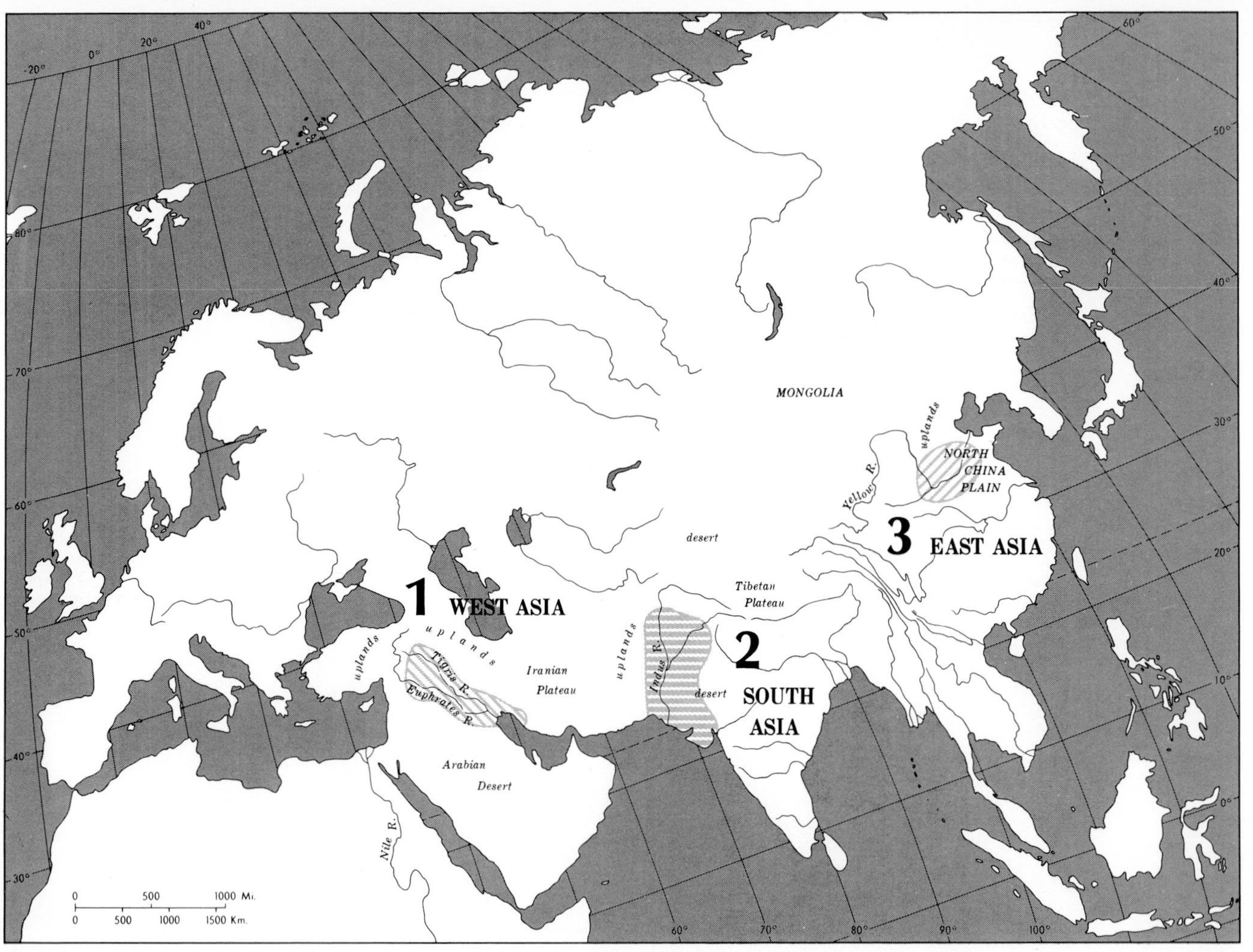

Map 5 The birth of civilization in Asia

PROCESSES

The generations of people in different parts of the world who made the long passage from hunting and gathering to village agriculture and from village agriculture to the highly differentiated and fast-changing condition we call civilization knew not what they were doing. They could not know the cumulative long-term consequences of their own intelligent, ad hoc responses to immediate problems. One cannot be certain that people would have willingly marched into the civilized condition if they had known what they would find on their arrival there.

The most promising approach to the problems of prehistory and early history is the formulation of hypotheses regarding the processes of social change and of interaction between human communities and their environments. The resources of many disciplines, including archaeology, anthropology, botany, history, geography, and ecology, among others, are being brought to bear on this task. In this chapter and those that follow, a comparative approach is adopted. Processes will be offered as reasonable hypotheses to explain change in an effort to get beyond the compartmentalization of human history in abstractions such as "Western civilization" or national or racial "genius." The question of whether agriculture, for instance, or writing, was invented only once in Eurasia and then diffused to recipient societies will appear to be very largely beside the point. Both of these technical systems are important because they were adopted and locally developed as useful solutions to similar needs.

THE PERIOD

The subject of this chapter falls entirely within the long period from 10,000 B.C. to 1000 B.C., a much longer period than that covered by all the remaining fourteen chapters. The discipline of history depends heavily on written materials for its data, and writing did not appear until about 3500 B.C. Surviving written documents are still scarce or otherwise relatively unsatisfactory at the beginning of the first millennium B.C. For the earliest stages in the emergence of civilized societies, therefore, it is necessary to rely on the work of archaeologists for all, or at least much, of our data. Moreover, the dating of preliterate stages rests on inferences from the stratigraphy (soil layers) in excavated sites and on analysis of samples of radioactive carbon, both of which methods require wide margins of error. The transition to agriculture, on present evidence, began around 8000 B.C. in West Asia; around 5000 B.C. in north China; and not later than 3500 B.C.—and probably much before—in northwest India. Two other areas may be added for comparison: south China, about 7000 B.C.; and central Mexico, about 3000 B.C. Also roughly and somewhat arbitrarily, the emergence of civilization can be dated by the formation of urban complexes in West Asia about 3500 B.C.; in northwest India about 3000 B.C.; and in north China about 1700 B.C. If this marks the onset of civilization, where do we place the end of the beginning? All three of our primary civilizations (and others that lie outside Asia) soon underwent a fateful change in their social organization: they came under the political and military domination of hereditary dynasties. Kings experimented with novel means of extending and maintaining their dominion, mobilizing the resources of the lands and peoples subject to them, and engaging their domestic and foreign rivals in war. With this turn of events, civilization entered the stage of state organization, which will be treated in the following chapter. On this basis, the period of the present chapter will end with the beginning of the dynasty of Akkad in West Asia in 2334 B.C.; the Aryan settlement and the end of the Indus civilization in India about 1750 B.C.; and the Chou conquest in north China in 1028 B.C.

ANTECEDENTS TO CIVILIZATION

a. Agricultural Revolution

The domestication of plants and animals increased the production of food in a given area of land, and this effect was magnified over centuries of technological change, leading to more effective systems of cultivation. It was not necessarily the case that the irrigation farmer, for example, could produce more food than a hunter and gatherer of wild foods in a favorable setting, but it was the case that many more people could now occupy a given area, and their maximum production was over and above what they needed for subsistence, that is to say, their potential agricultural surplus *in the aggregate* was far in excess of the potential surplus in the same area in a hunting-gathering economy. This increase in the aggregate surplus meant that greater quantities of food and off-season manpower were within the reach of urban centers as these developed at a later time. The material and energy were now at hand with which to construct ever more imposing temples, palaces, and walls and to support a growing number of religious and administrative specialists and craftsmen. But this is only to say that the agricultural revolution was a necessary precondition of the city and of civilization. It is equally important to understand that the shift to agriculture and husbandry may have set in motion processes of social change that drove the original societies of village farmers toward the formation of stratified (class-structured) societies, the dominance of cities, and eventually the formation of kingdoms. These processes will be considered in their turn.

Hunting and gathering societies normally maintain themselves in a state of balance, or equilibrium, with the resources of their environment. Enough game is available to permit them to meet their needs with a few days' effort in a week's time. Why, then, did the inhabitants of certain areas undertake the domestication of plants and animals? One theory that is both inherently reasonable and consistent with the evidence runs as follows: The late Paleolithic population subsisted on a relatively narrow diet of easily obtained species. A transition to broad-spectrum gathering occurred when areas that were ecologically highly favorable to human occupation underwent sufficient population growth for pressure on the food supply to be noticeable. This resulted in an outward migration of some groups into surrounding marginal areas that were somewhat less desirable. This in turn resulted in an excess of population in the marginal area and made it necessary for the inhabitants to experiment in the use of a much wider range of plant and animal foods. The resulting broad-spectrum pattern resulted in a rich and varied diet, and the practice became general even in the original optimal areas. Among the new foods were cereal grains, which were collected in the wild state, and new tools and utensils were devised for their preparation and storage. Such plants were most abundant in mountainous areas of low rainfall and light forest cover. In some places, perhaps encouraged by periodic set fires, meadows were formed that contained almost pure growths of wild wheat, barley, or other cereal. Such areas now became the optimal zones and sustained growing populations. Again, outward migrations into marginal zones became necessary. The migrants, now habituated to grains as an important part of their diet, attempted to grow them in their new environments. The simplest form of grain cultivation in wooded areas was slash-and-burn agriculture, in which trees were killed by girdling and burned to make clearings. The soil was loosened with digging sticks and the seeds sown broadcast. Moisture was sufficient on the upper slopes to permit maturation of the crops for a few years before desiccation, erosion, or the growth of weeds made it necessary to burn a new clearing. Further population growth led to new migrations downward into areas where cultivation was more difficult. Where rainfall was inadequate, for example, sites often had to be selected on the borders of marshes or beneath cliffs where the runoff was sufficient to maintain soil moisture. A high water table made it possible for water to be drawn from wells or water holes for application to the growing grain. In a still later stage in the development of grain agriculture, farmers moved out onto the great alluvial plains, like those of Mesopotamia, the Indus, and north China. Here the agricultural potential was enormous, but before it could be fully realized generations of small-scale efforts and, eventually, large-scale projects were required to solve the problems of drainage and irrigation.

The tendency to concentrate on grain did not end the need or the taste for other foods. Husbandry developed in close association with agriculture. In different regions, sheep, goats, pigs, cattle, dogs, or poultry might be kept to supply meat. A modest number of livestock could be maintained at very little cost, pasturing in fallowed land, cropping stubble after harvest, or even turning excess grain into meat in a year of bumper harvests. Since agriculture eventually came to be concentrated near surface water, fish, shellfish, and waterfowl were also major sources of protein. On the uncultivated margins of the agricultural communities, other groups came to specialize in herding and traded their stock for grain from the villagers, thus giving rise to a classic social and cultural contrast: that between farmer and pastoralist. Arboriculture came, in time, to enrich the diet with a local supply of nuts and fruits from groves and orchards. Wild game was still favored too, but increasingly this would have to be obtained in trade from people still inhabiting the mountains, or killed by hunting parties.

b. Sedentarization

Even before the agricultural revolution, groups of people, presumably extended families, were able to settle for relatively long periods of time if the supply of natural food was abundant and reliable. Typical economic bases for such villages might be lake fishing or wild-grain harvesting. Archaeologists have found in different parts of the world pre-agricultural villages with clay-walled houses, basketry, lined grain-storage pits, and refined equipment for fishing, hunting, and the collection, grinding, and cooking of grain. In some areas there were substantial pottery industries. In retrospect all of this may be regarded as preparation for agricultural village life and, eventually, the formation of cities. The domestication of plants and animals made it possible for vastly greater numbers of people to settle down in villages and to systematically explore and learn to exploit the resources of their landscape. Moreover, as the population densities grew in village farming societies, kin-related communities remained in regular contact with one another and through social and economic interaction began to form larger, transcendent communities.

c. Social Stratification

Without exception, civilized societies have been characterized by division of the population into classes and status groups. Where division into classes has occurred, certain groups of families or individuals within the society control a disproportionate share of the productive resources, while others have only limited or conditional access to these resources. More specifically, in a stratified society based mainly on grain agriculture, most of the working population can gain access to suitable land only by sharecropping, paying rent, working for pay, or doing forced labor on lands controlled by others. The class structure of the society may be described in terms of the exact form of such relationships. Status, on the other hand, involves the rank ordering of groups in the society according to formal criteria of prestige, such as titles, forms of address, and ceremonial rules, and the specification of appropriate life-styles, including kinds of clothing, accessories, and houses permitted to persons of each rank. Ordinarily, class and status tend to be harmonized by according higher status to those having greater control over resources, but social change, such as the formation of an important merchant class (which occurred later than the period covered by this chapter), may disrupt the mutual adjustment of class and status. In this case, an old landowning aristocracy may have enough political and coercive power to deny high formal status to merchants, even though some of the latter may be wealthy.

Hypothetically, at least, the simplest form of society is the egalitarian, in which responsibility and respect flow to the strongest and most resourceful members of a band of hunters and gatherers. But rank ordering by status, probably always present in some degree, gains in importance. For example, in a settled village where several individual small households belonging to an extended family (that is, all claim descent from a common ancestor) form an economically integrated community, sharing work and goods, community direction and management is generally invested in persons rank ordered by some principle of family relationship—for example, the eldest son of the eldest son of the common ancestor. This is probably the kind of social system represented by the archaeologically found villages of the agricultural revolution. Many villages, all very much alike, may be found scattered over a tract of cultivable land. Within each village there may appear indications of differences in rank or status—for example, a larger house foundation standing in the center of a circle of smaller houses. Although there may be specific formal, symbolic recognition of differences in status, there is still no stratification, no class. The leaders of the community have the responsibility of assuring an equitable distribution of tasks and goods to all and cannot extract a disproportionate share for themselves. All share about equally in abundance or scarcity.

The transition from rank society to stratified society was inseparable from the emergence of civilization. Involved in the concept of stratified society were, first, concentrations of resources and wealth, which stimulated and subsidized an elaboration of all forms of technology; and second, the creation of social tensions between those with full and those with more or less restricted access to resources, which gave rise to conflict and the formation of effective systems of religious, military, and political control and mediation. The central sites of such systems were the nuclei around which the first cities arose, with their proliferating skills and broadening intellectual life.

But how may we account for the shift to stratified society? A number of ecological, demographic, and sociological processes in various combinations were probably involved. First, the development and improvement of agricultural techniques had the effect of concentrating a progressively larger proportion of productive capacity on a diminishing proportion of the land. It has been estimated, for instance, that about 35 percent of the land area of Iran could have sustained a hunting-gathering economy, while only about 10 percent was suitable for agriculture of any kind, and a mere 1 percent could be irrigated. At the same time, however, the amount of food yielded by an acre of land under irrigated agriculture may be ten times greater than the amount that would be obtained by hunting and gathering. Second, sedentarization of agricultural communities probably gave rise to strong proprietary feelings of communal attachment to particular parcels of land. This sense of ownership may have been intensified in a shift from slash-and-burn agriculture to permanent-field agriculture with fallowing and irrigation. Third, owners of the most productive and drought-proof land were able to survive bad years better than people of more vulnerable villages. Fourth, the possessors of stores of food in a temporarily distressed economy could turn this to advantage in their economic relationships with less fortunate neighbors, perhaps by requiring them to provide labor in building or irrigation work in return for grain, and this in turn would increase still further the disparity in control of resources. When such unequal relationships were regularized and formalized over a period of time, the result was a stratified society.

THE BIRTH OF CIVILIZATION

d. Religious Sanction of Stratified Society

Wherever civilizations developed out of precivilized societies, their first cities were formed around ceremonial centers. As archaeologists dig down through progressively earlier occupation layers in primary urban sites, they can sometimes trace the city's origins back to a simple shrine, the "ancestor" of increasingly elaborate temple complexes. Moreover, the temple complex is so consistent and so striking an accompaniment of primary urban origins that one is led to the conclusion that institutionalized religious beliefs played a key role in the formation of civilized society and the first cities. Indeed, as societies came to be stratified, their inequities could have been regularized and explained only in religious terms; secular ideologies had not yet come into existence. This was an age dominated by mythopoeic thought, when people had not conceptually detached themselves from their setting and still experienced a sense of intimacy with the forces of nature. Plants, animals, rivers, the sky, sun, and planets were experienced as living presences and tended in the course of time to be personified as anthropomorphic divinities. With the elaboration of myth in early civilized times, cosmic phenomena such as the birth of the universe, the progression of the seasons, and the flooding of the rivers, and human dramas such as triumphs and defeats on the fields of battle could all be explained in terms of divine drama, or mythology. In this developing mythopoeic context, agricultural village communities joined technical means of ensuring good crops and herds, such as seed selection and irrigation, to religious means, such as the maintenance of cults for the propitiation of life-giving powers, although the technical-religious distinction was not made at that time. There were many possible kinds of cult. Some had reference to universal phenomena, such as the powers of the sun, while others were local or otherwise particular, such as the spirit of a particular hill, stream, or sacred grove. Another kind of cult that was widespread, but of variable importance, was that of ancestor worship. An extended family might reinforce the solidarity of the group by elaborating the cult of a mythical, or divine, ultimate ancestor. The rise of a specific group to a position of local or regional dominance was necessarily reflected in the growing eminence and power of its cult. When tribute or labor service was demanded of subordinate groups, this was expressed as a contribution to the cult, and the imputation of selfishness on the part of the dominant group was thereby avoided. Service of the cult was held to be in the interests of all. It may have been by some such process that favored local shrines became great ceremonial centers commanding the labor and treasure of broad regions.

e. Urbanization

The distinguishing feature of civilization is the city. There is much disagreement as to what constitutes a city, however, and this requires a definition that will serve the purposes of our argument. A minimal definition is: the geographically fixed cultural focus and organizing center of all the communities in its region. Several implications of this definition should be noted. One is that it implies a hierarchy of communities—for example, a city standing in some functional relationship to all the villages subject to its control. Another implication is that if the main organizing principle of the society in question is religious, the heart of the city will be a temple complex; if political, a palace; if commercial, a market place; if military, a fortress; or some combination of these functions and institutions. A third implication is that the civilized society must not be equated simply with its most dramatic manifestation, the city itself, but must be seen as a whole, comprising city and village, townsman and farmer. If the city is defined in this way, it becomes unimportant to determine exactly when a temple complex has gathered around it a sufficiently large and concentrated population to count as really urban. A common form among early cities was settlement-group urbanism, in which a central core of temples and palaces was occupied by ruling families and their household staff, while farmers and artisans of various kinds lived in their own villages nearby, so that the whole group of settlements constituted a dispersed city. A compacted city with a dense population living within confining walls usually represented a later stage of development.

1.1a

1.1b

1.2

Samples of early writing all show signs of having evolved from pictographic and symbolic characters. The soft clay tablets marked with a seal or stylus, common to both West and South Asia, were not used in China.

1.1 Photograph and transcription of an early Sumerian tablet. This inscription, a list of proper names, was written around 3000 B.C. Courtesy: Publications of the Joint Expedition of the British Museum and the University Museum, Philadelphia, to Mesopotamia.

1.2 Impression of a typical Harappan seal depicting an ox with a saddlecloth facing a cult object or stand. The script at the top has not been deciphered. Courtesy: American Oriental Society, Item No. 28, Plate 52, from E. J. H. Mackay, *Report on the Chanhu-daro Excavations, 1935-36* (AOS Vol. 20).

1.3 Undershell of a tortoise inscribed by diviners of the Shang court. The shells were cracked by heating and the cracks interpreted as answers from the spirits. Dark area shows rubbings of the original; diagram gives modern equivalents of the ancient script. Courtesy: Institute of History and Philology, Academia Sinica, Taipei. First published by the Institute.

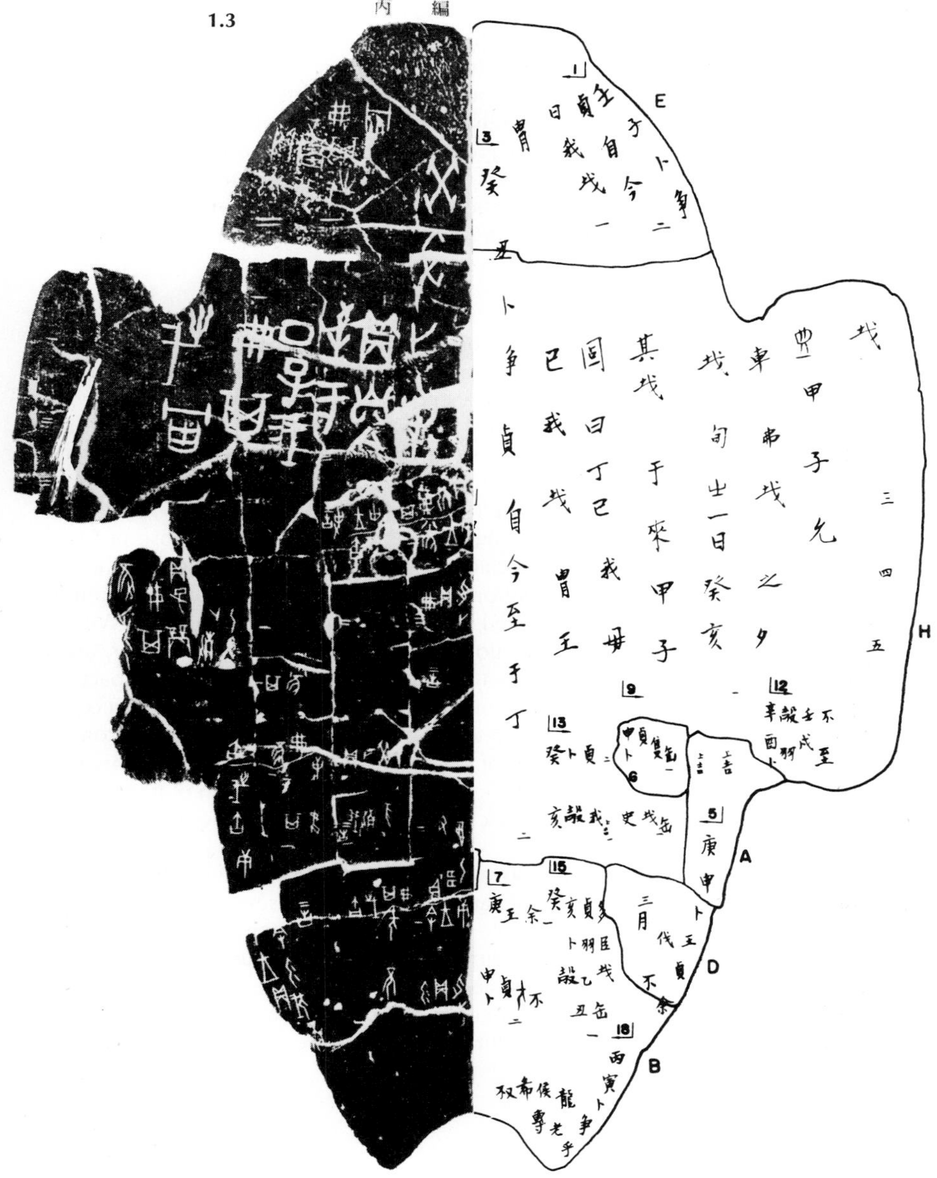
1
3
E
H
9
12
13
6
5
A
7
15
D
18
B

f. Occupational Differentiation and Technological Innovation

The development of a wide range of new techniques occurred simultaneously with the economic differentiation of the stratified and urbanizing society into specialized occupational groups. As the dominant class drew on the material and human resources of the region to construct and maintain ever more monumental temples and palaces, it created a demand for new skills. Despite the old saw, "necessity is the mother of invention," however, the relation between need and innovation remains obscure. But if the problems are important and the proposed solutions effective, a new technique should result. Urbanization required improved means of transporting food and other goods in very large quantities. Common solutions of the problem included the combination of the wheel (probably first used in pottery making) and animal power in the first wagons, and the combination of boat and wind power in sailing craft. The building of large structures demanded stronger materials than mud and wattle. The need was variously met by the arts of masonry, beam-and-pillar construction, and brick baking. The aesthetic side of life was also developed beyond its precivilized levels with the application of greater skill to old and new materials to make sculptures, jewelry, textiles, and vessels and to make buildings more ornamental and impressive. The organization of food production on large estates of temples and leading families encouraged specializations in fishing and husbandry, with a resulting gain in efficiency.

g. Writing

The most characteristic and, in the long run, possibly the most important of all the innovations associated with the development of civilization was the invention of systems of record keeping and communication which did not depend on the spoken word. This invention was eventually associated with the occupational specialization of the scribe, or clerk. Some systems were very simple, such as the knotted strings by which the Incas of Peru kept track of inventories, the conventional symbolic arrangements of cowrie shells among the Yoruba in West Africa, the original pictographic scripts of Sumer, Egypt, and China. Some of these were followed by such developed scripts (logographic or alphabetic) as those of China, Sumer, and the Mediterranean. Within the category of communications systems, the decisive transformation occurred with the invention of phonetic or mixed semantic and phonetic scripts, using signs that could be combined to represent the spoken language. With this invention, the range of written communication could be made as wide, as clear, and as flexible as speech itself. The effect was, to a significant degree, to overcome space and time. Lengthy and complicated statements could be transmitted over great distances, and one generation could bequeath verbatim to another cosmologies, mythologies, chronicles, epics, stories, and love poems. This fact was of inestimable help in the large-scale organization and administration of society and in the maintenance and adaptation of tradition. The complex and dynamic culture of civilized society had found a vehicle for its transmission and growth.

The learned class, the literati, was also associated with protosciences that involved the systematic observation and recording of natural phenomena. Astronomical observation, carried out over long periods, made it possible for the several early civilizations to work out accurate and useful calendars and to predict many regularly recurring events such as conjunctions of planets and constellations, and lunar eclipses. The development of such skills increased the authority of those who could command them and were of practical value in scheduling and organizing agricultural tasks that were tied to the seasons of the solar year.

PATTERNS

1. THE BIRTH OF MESOPOTAMIAN CIVILIZATION IN WEST ASIA

The first part of this chapter suggested a model, or general explanation, for the origin of civilizations. The early civilizations of Sumer in West Asia, of the Indus valley in South Asia, and of north China in East Asia can now be compared in terms of the model. The earliest civilization was that of Sumer. Observance of chronological order is useful in this case in order to do justice to the arguments that certain elements of one civilization may have diffused to the other civilizations. The reader should bear in mind, however, that when Indians or Chinese think of "ancient history," they think of their own early civilizations rather than of West Asian civilization as Americans and Europeans tend to do.

Antecedents to Civilization

Long before the first civilization with its cities and towns appeared in Sumer, the necessary preliminary stages had been reached in the surrounding uplands. The transition from hunting and gathering to sedentary village agriculture had already been completed in such areas as Palestine, Syria, and Anatolia, when Mesopotamia (the valleys of the Tigris and Euphrates rivers in modern Iraq), relatively backward until then, suddenly forged into the

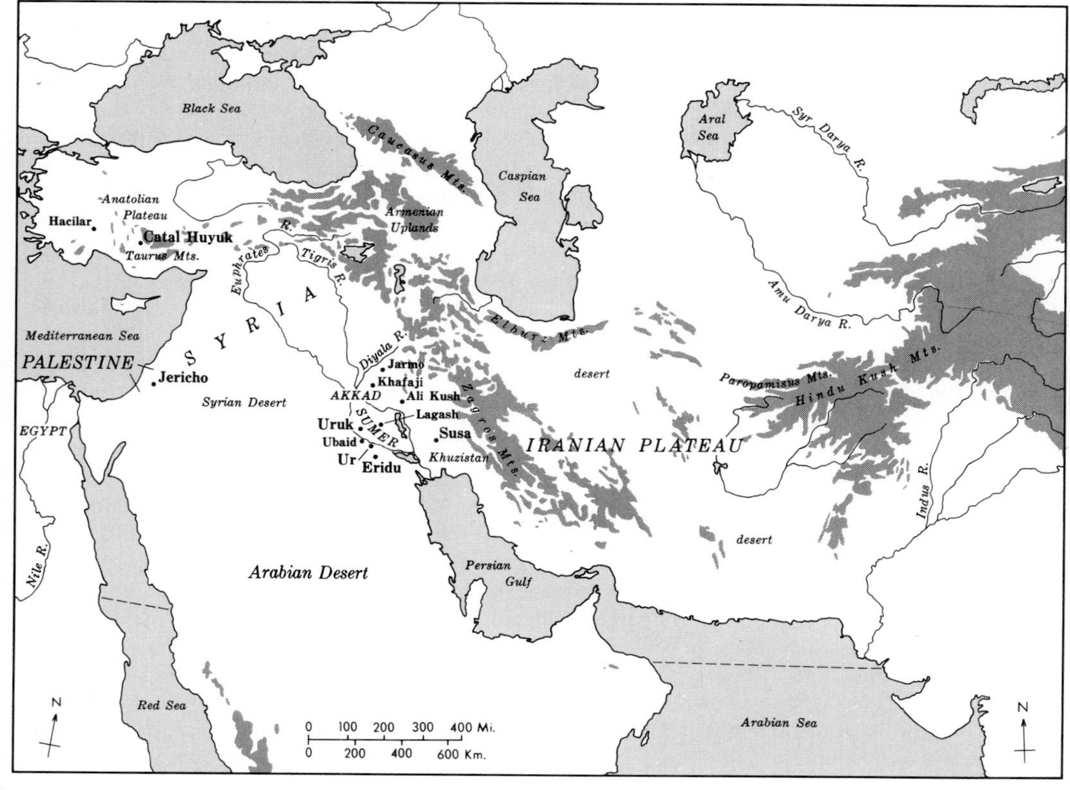

Map 6 The birth of Mesopotamian civilization, to 2334 B.C.

lead. The geographical setting of the antecedents to West Asian civilization is therefore found in areas around Mesopotamia, and it is only later that the scene shifts to Sumer itself.

The dominating feature of West Asian geography is the broad zone of high and often rugged country comprising the Anatolian plateau (modern Turkey) in the west and the Iranian plateau in the east, connected by ranges that meet in the area where the frontiers of modern Turkey, Iran, and Iraq converge. To the north are the Caucasus and the Elburz mountains, the latter extending eastward in an almost unbroken chain of low ranges to meet the Paropamisus and, eventually, the massive Hindu Kush in central Afghanistan. To the south, facing Syria and Mesopotamia, lie the Taurus and Zagros ranges. In the early postglacial period, when the transition to agriculture began, the climate was probably much the same as it is today. North of the upland zone, the Russian and Central Asian steppes had a temperate climate with harsh winters, while to the south of it, the climate was dry with hot summers and mild winters. In the Zagros and Taurus mountains, the higher altitudes were temperate and the rainfall was moderate. Here were located the headwaters of the Tigris and Euphrates, with their tributaries. Here also grew the wild ancestral forms of the wheat and barley that became the basic grains of West Asian agriculture. Wheat grew wild in Palestine, Anatolia, northern Syria, and the Zagros. Barley was found in the same regions and extended farther eastward through the Elburz and into what is now Russian Turkistan. The genetic stock of West Asian animal husbandry was also native to these regions, where the habitats of the ancestors of domesticated sheep, goats, and cattle all overlapped with the basic wild grains.

In the ninth millennium B.C. the uplands were populated with very small communities that moved about, occupying temporary sites usually for no longer than a single season and then moving on in search of food. Their diet included nuts, legumes, fish, and fresh-water mollusks, as well as game, and their increasing reliance on grain is attested to by the sickles and stone grinding tools found in their habitation sites. Until actual specimens of the food grain are found dating from this period, there is no reason to suppose that agriculture had yet begun. It is more likely that the inhabitants simply harvested in season the fields of wild grain that grew on the relatively dry, lower southern slopes of the mountains.

On present evidence, there were at least three main early centers of agriculture in West Asia. Two of these, southern Anatolia and the Syro-Palestine area, were near the Mediterranean. The third was in the Zagros Mountains on the eastern flanks of Mesopotamia. The discovery of domesticated grains in cultural contexts dating back to 7000 B.C. in all three areas proves that agriculture had begun by that time. Some of the early farming villages, favored by their local environment, grew large and prosperous. In the Syro-Palestine area, the site of Jericho has furnished a long and virtually unbroken cultural record from the preagricultural Natufian culture, before 9000 B.C., down to the abandonment of the site around 6000 B.C. Until about 8000 B.C. the site was visited seasonally by hunters, who were attracted to a nearby spring and worshipped at a shrine that underlay the later town. There followed a permanent settlement that grew to a population of about two thousand. Houses, storage rooms, and a wall and tower testify to the energy and organization of this large community. Grinding implements suggest a reliance on grain, but whether this was wild or cultivated remains uncertain. Dry farming (unirrigated agriculture) was likely, however, given the size and permanence of the village. The diet was supplemented by hunting and by domesticated goats. A new population moved in around 7000 B.C., remained for a millennium, and then abandoned the town. In southern Anatolia, the sites of Hacilar and Catal Huyuk furnish a comparable record of development, beginning with the cultivation of barley, wheat, and lentils and the domestication of the dog by 7000 B.C. The growth of Catal Huyuk (occupied 6700-5700 B.C.) outstripped even that of Jericho and reached an estimated ten thousand population. Here, the archaeological record testifies to a highly elaborated religious life, expressed in a great number of shrines rich in religious iconography. Whether Jericho and Catal Huyuk should be classed as cities is a debated question. By our definition they may well have been cities, but more would have to be known about their relationship with other communities before they could be said to have achieved regional domination.

For all their early brilliance, however, Jericho and Catal Huyuk faded from the scene before they could become the centers of sustained cultural development. This may have been because they soon outstripped the agricultural resources within their reach. The early agriculture of the Zagros was more important for the development of West Asian civilization, because village farmers of that region descended to the floodplain of lower Mesopotamia and began to lay the economic and social foundations of the later urban communities of Sumer. Zagros agriculture probably began in the north, around the headwaters of the Tigris. Domesticated seeds were then used in spreading grain agriculture southeastward to the central and southern Zagros, which lay beyond the natural habitat of the wild wheat and barley. The reason that the Mesopotamian plain, apart from its northern fringes, was settled first by farmers from the southern, rather than the northern, Zagros may have been that conditions on the southern portions of the plain were peculiarly suited to cultivation by small, family-sized groups with simple tools. Village farming subsequently advanced upstream, where problems of floodcontrol and irrigation were more difficult and required improvements in technology and social organization for their solution.

A preagricultural phase of intensified food gathering in the northern Zagros is associated with the Zarzian microlithic culture, characterized by fine stone points and blades. Seasonal sites of a slightly later culture, around 9000 B.C., yield evidence of a shift toward plant foods, perhaps including wild grains. The earliest domestication of sheep may have occurred in this context. No continuous cultural sequence has been found here like that at Jericho, however. An important early agricultural site at Jarmo was occupied around 6750 B.C. Here a community of about 150 people cultivated wheat, barley, and lentils and collected wild foods for four hundred years or more. In the central Zagros, permanent village agriculture is represented by a settlement of about 6300 B.C., where barley was grown. The further diffusion of agriculture to the southern Zagros is reflected in the site at Ali Kush. Originally a winter encampment of goat herders, a permanent farming village was established here by 6500 B.C., with cultivated barley and wheat supplemented by game, fish, and mollusks. This venture into agriculture did not prove successful in the long run, however, with grain production reaching a peak later in the seventh millennium, then by about 5700 B.C. giving way to pastoralism again. Elsewhere in the region agriculture continued, and around 5500 B.C. the first irrigated agriculture had begun on the southeastern margins of the Mesopotamian lowlands near Susa in the Khuzistan region of Iran. Here beneath the Zagros foothills, rainfall was low enough to make dry farming hazardous, yet sufficient to provide some support for early experiments with irrigation.

A few more generalizations are in order regarding the early agriculture in the West Asian uplands. The first is that the size of the villages, with rare exceptions, was limited. Here there were only small interior basins, enclosed plains, or narrow valley bottoms separated by more difficult terrain. The village agricultural thrust toward civilization began in this setting, but it could continue only in the potentially richer environment of the alluvial lowlands. Second, permanent settlement involved the development of new building techniques as caves were abandoned for temporary tent or reed-hut camps in the open, and these, in turn, were replaced by houses with walls of clay slabs, mud-plastered frames, or sun-dried bricks. Increasingly one may also find evidence of an interest in comfort and convenience, such as baking ovens and flues to clear smoke from the rooms. Plastered walls, sometimes with painted decoration, and quantities of ornamental objects indicate an aesthetic awareness. More significant in this regard is the proliferation of ceramic styles—plain, painted, and with impressed designs and in an immense variety of forms. Some styles were local and evanescent, while others were widespread and more enduring, providing useful indications of the sequential and contemporary relationships of different cultures or phases of cultural change. The making of pottery appears to have begun in the mid-seventh millennium, at least five hundred years later than agriculture, and in the same regions: Anatolia, northern Syria, and the Zagros. Third, the presence of shrines, religious figures, and paintings prove, if they do not explain, the religious concern of the village farmers. The religious or magic handling of the problem of death is indicated by burial practices including the use of red ochre and the placing of burial objects in the graves. The contrary concern with life and fertility is thought to be indicated by female figurines and occasional phallic objects. Finally, and of great importance for the prehistory of West Asia, is the existence of long-distance trade in valuable and easily transported materials. With sedentary communities occupying the same villages for hundreds of years, patterns of exchange developed on such a scale that the size and prosperity of several communities, including those of Jericho and Catal Huyuk, have been attributed at least in part to their having had a strategic role in interregional trade involving Anatolia, the Red Sea, the Mediterranean coast, and the Jordan valley.

The oldest known settlement in lower Mesopotamia, the land of Sumer, is represented by the lowest culture stratum at Eridu. Between Eridu and the Zagros lay a zone of dunes and marshes along the lower course of the united streams of the Tigris and Euphrates and, beyond them, the undulating plain of Susa, or the land of Elam. At Eridu's back was the eastern margin of the Arabian desert. Downstream was the delta bounded by the northern shore of the Persian Gulf, and upstream was the central floodplain lying between the two rivers where their courses diverged. Geography and the evidence of archaeology suggest that the region of Eridu was settled by people who had already engaged in irrigated agriculture in the vicinity of Susa on the plain beneath the southern Zagros. Farmers may have settled for a time on the delta before moving to the lower end of the central floodplain. The early settlement at Eridu was connected with the Persian Gulf by lakes and waterways that have long since vanished. Here an abundance of fish balanced the diet of irrigated grain, and the farmers may well have been preceded by fishermen inhabiting reed huts like those in the earliest levels of Eridu. From such beginnings, around 5000 B.C., village agriculture spread into the central floodplains where the cities and civilization of Sumer were later to emerge.

The Birth of Civilization

In the setting of lower Mesopotamia, or Sumer, the development of urban civilization went forward from the middle of the fourth millennium on the foundations laid by the village agriculturalists of the floodplain. Nearly all the early cities were in the region of the central floodplain, which measured about three hundred miles from the confluence of the Tigris and Euphrates upstream to the region of Akkad, where the two rivers closely approach each other. At its widest point, this plain is about one hundred and fifty miles across. Here, as in the lower floodplain below the confluence, the plain was dissected by distributaries of the great rivers, breaking through their banks and making their own channels. The early settlements clung to the low banks of the smaller streams and basins. The first irrigation channels were short and easily dug by small groups. Larger systems based on the Euphrates and one of its main branches (the Tigris was swifter and its channel too deep for easy irrigation) required the large scale of social organization associated with urbanization. Flooding in the plain was generally shallow because of the level terrain. Flood water trapped in natural basins was used for irrigation, and the deposit of silt helped maintain the fertility of the soil. The slow-moving Euphrates was also serviceable in water communications and so contributed to the economic, cultural, and eventually, political unity of the region. The central floodplain also presented the inhabitants with certain difficulties, however. One was that the flooding sometimes occurred too late in the spring and damaged the growing grain. Another was that the intense summer heat and low humidity resulted in a high rate of

Main Periods of Mesopotamian Archaeology
Eridu 5500-4300 B.C.
Ubaid 4300-3500 B.C.
Early Uruk 3500-3100 B.C.
Uruk IV and III 3100-2900 B.C.
Early Dynastic 2900-2334 B.C.

evaporation. This, in turn, resulted in a gradual accumulation of salts in the irrigated fields. In time, barley replaced wheat because of its higher tolerance for salt, and eventually even barley grew poorly, causing parts of the plain to be abandoned by the farmers.

The history of settlement in lower Mesopotamia may be conventionally divided into the following periods: Eridu, 5500-4300 B.C.; Ubaid, 4300-3500 B.C.; Uruk, 3500-3100 B.C.; Uruk IV and III, 3100-2900 B.C.; and Early Dynastic, 2900-2334 B.C. These terms, excepting the last, are archaeological references to sites and occupation levels with their associated cultural forms. The course of change was slow at first. Eridu was joined by other fishing and farming communities that had formed clusters in favored locations across the plain by 3500 B.C. Eridu itself, after as much as two millennia of occupation, had a population of only about four thousand. In the Uruk period, Eridu and some of the other villages of the lower end of the central floodplain increased in size and regional importance, becoming cities in the sense of our definition of the word: their shrines became large temples that served as cult centers for the surrounding villages. In Uruk IV and III, urban society developed farther north as some of the villages in the middle and upper portions of the plain became cities. Uruk IV and III and the Early Dynastic period also saw the development of writing and the beginnings of warfare and political organization, which will be treated in the following chapter. As implied in the term Early Dynastic, the inhabitants of Mesopotamia then entered, however uncertainly, the historic period, for which archaeologically found documents and written myth, epic, and history in combination begin to provide information on persons, events, laws, and institutions. Only with the appearance of written documents, moreover, can the dominant inhabitants be identified as Sumerians, as speakers of the Sumerian language. There is linguistic evidence that unidentified other peoples had occupied the region earlier, and on archaeological evidence it has been suggested that the Sumerians arrived as late as the Uruk IV period, when certain innovations occurred in temple architecture. Since connections with the Susa region and, perhaps to a lesser extent, with the north and west were reflected in cultural styles, it seems probable in any case that a continued drift of peoples into Mesopotamia provided an ethnically various population, which at least from Uruk IV was to remain under Sumerian domination until the rise of Akkad.

The transition from village agriculture to urban civilization in Mesopotamia occurred within the single millennium, from 3500 to 2334 B.C., with the Early Dynastic period also representing a transitional period from temple-centered communities to politically organized kingdoms. This transformation may be grasped in terms of several different orders of social and cultural change interacting with one another to generate further change. On this assumption any given change may have been both cause and effect.

Graves containing burial objects of great or of little value and indications of elaborate or simple ceremonial have been noted in sites of precivilized village agriculture. These point to a rank-ordered society, in which a family head, for example, may have been especially honored in death so that his or her spirit would continue to guide and give good fortune to the survivors. The settlements in lower Mesopotamia were probably of this type until the Uruk period. The mature urban society of the Early Dynastic period, however, was stratified, with distinct classes. There were wealthy, aristocratic families who owned most of the agricultural land and who played an oligarchic role in managing the religious, civil, and military affairs of the communities. Written records document the recognition of different categories of dependency, including slaves, hereditary corvée workers and soldiers, and tenants. Associated with stratification was the development of property rights in land and of customary law regulating its sale and use. Ownership does not seem to have pertained to individuals, however, but to corporate groups such as families or temples. The change from rank-ordered to stratified society appears to have come about gradually, with some stratification in the Uruk period, more in Uruk IV and III, when slavery appeared, and still more in the early stages of Early Dynastic. The explanation therefore is probably not to be found in a simple, dramatic fact of conquest, although ethnic conflicts cannot be altogether ruled out as a cause of stratified society, as seen in the enslavement of war captives. The more important cause appears to have been the mounting pressure of population on easily irrigated land. Families and temples that controlled the best land had a double advantage; the others had either to cultivate marginal land, raise sheep or goats on the semidesert between the settled areas, or gain access to land as tenants or laborers. The owners of good land could add to their wealth by using the labor of others, and they could use their wealth to buy land and to undertake the extension of irrigation and drainage systems, thereby further enlarging their holdings. The tendency toward concentrations of wealth may have been reinforced by lineage stratification within the village and urban communities. The sorting out of lineages within an extended family accords higher status to those closer to the principal line of descent. This higher status may be used to justify retention of a disproportionate share of the common property, to the disadvantage of the junior lines. Finally, given some drifting of families—either people who in-migrated or people made homeless by drought or flood—there were "outsiders" around the cities, who could easily have been reduced to dependent status.

The role of temples in the formation of urban communities in Mesopotamia was undeniably important. At a time when men universally confronted their natural environment as a living presence and not, in our detached way, simply as a set of inanimate things to be analyzed and used, certain places were felt to have exceptional spiritual significance. The local spirit of a spring, a lake, or a sheltered hillside might be served with offerings and provided with a shrine by those who lived there. Flourishing farming villages invested a part of their growing resources in the services of the local cults that were thought necessary to ensure good harvests and good health. Moreover, wealthy landowning families left their fields in the hands of managers and built town houses near the cult centers. Here as absentee landlords they shared in the variety and excitement of life in the developing cities. Excavation of urban sites in Sumer have revealed the building, rebuilding, enlargment, and elaboration of shrines and temples. No less than eighteen building levels have been identified at Eridu, with a tiny shrine on the eighteenth level, probably used by fishermen, and on the sixth level, corresponding to about 3500 B.C., a large temple with nave and rows of adjoining rooms, which measured overall about 75 by 40 feet. In the Uruk IV period, temples became both larger and more elaborate. Although mud-brick construction continued, rows of columns now appeared, perhaps in imitation of wooden buildings in the Zagros region. Columns and exterior walls were ornamented with colorful mosaics of clay nails with painted heads. The sudden advance in scale is suggested by an Uruk temple of Uruk IV that measured overall about 180 by 70 feet. These structures were made even more imposing by the fact that the successive building levels had raised their foundations until they stood at the top of artificial mountains, or ziggurats. Even after the late Early Dynastic and Akkadian periods, when the temples began to be rivaled in some cities by the palaces of kings, they continued to hold a prominent place in Mesopotamian society.

Nothing is known specifically about the cults and ceremonials of the first shrines, but in the literate period the gods of the principal cities can be identified. The attributes of the gods and goddesses are preserved in the mythology and there is documentary evidence of the way in which some of them were served by their worshippers. The gods and goddesses were not merely symbolized by their likenesses in the temples, but were thought to be quite literally embodied in them. The temple therefore was the god's or goddess' house, and the temple staff was his or her household. The gods and goddesses were served meals twice each day in the ceremony of offering. Dishes prepared in the temple were presented to the god or goddess and he or she, it was believed, consumed the nourishing essence of the food by looking at it. Thus nourished, the god or goddess maintained his or her vitality and the power to protect and bestow blessings upon the community. The temple household included a "wife" or "husband" for the god or goddess, priests who waited on the divinities, and a great number of administrators, clerks, craftsmen, and menials.

Written documents throw some light on the temples' social and economic roles. During a time when the urban society was becoming stratified into classes and differentiated into occupational groups, the temples and their cults expressed and fostered the subjective solidarity of the community. Where a whole community might once have worshipped together at a village or domestic shrine, priests and priestesses chosen from leading families now assumed the task of communication with the divine powers on behalf of all. Common people were not allowed inside the temples but were permitted a glimpse of the god or goddess as the statue was carried through the streets in the new-year festival. Documents also show that the temples were great landowning corporations, or more precisely, functioned as stewards in the management of estates that were said to be owned by the gods they served. For all their wealth and eminence, however the temple officials did not constitute a theocracy. Effective authority in historical times, and probably earlier as well, was held by the great families. Landed estates and the very idea of property in land must have arisen first among the families, because the temples, as the guarantors of community solidarity, could have had no need for properties of their own, and they could have had no rivals against whom to assert any proprietary rights of their own until private estates had begun to form. The temples therefore may best be understood as having been joint undertakings of the great families, maintained in the interest of communal order and prosperity. The temple estates may have been organized on the model of private estates to provide continuing support for the myth of divine ownership, a device to cover the case of a communal property surviving in the context of a social system increasingly given to private proprietary rights.

Unfortunately for our knowledge of patterns of urbanization in Mesopotamia, archaeologists have usually concentrated their efforts on the ceremonial centers, with their temples and their works of art. What evidence there is, however, is consistent with the assumption that until the Early Dynastic period the ceremonial centers, with their associated communities of craftsmen, clerks, and priests, were sustained by tribute received from surrounding villages, the temple and its hinterland together representing a city of the settlement-group type—a cluster of small, specialized communities around the controlling center, rather than a compact, continuous urban mass. During the Early Dynastic period and after, cities became more compact and were sometimes more confined within defensive walls. The increasing incidence of warfare accounts for the change, and improvements in land and water communications made it easier for supplies to be delivered to the consuming centers and for laborers to go out to their fields. In some cases, farm workers occupied temporary quarters during seasons of agricultural work and returned to the cities at other times. Some notion of the scale of urbanization before the time of Akkadian rule may be obtained from estimates made for the city of Lagash around 2400 B.C. The area subject to the city's control was some three thousand square kilometers, or the equivalent of an area around the city with a radius of about twenty miles. Another clue is the estimate of a population of twelve thousand for the Early Dynastic city of Khafaji in the lower Diyala in Akkad. Urban houses there were of mud brick and were closely built on narrow alleys.

The division of ordinary houses into five to ten rooms at this time suggests that they were occupied by extended families.

The differentiation of urban populations into occupational specialties and the development of new or improved techniques were encouraged by the investment of communal and private wealth in buildings and artifacts. In architecture, limestone masonry made its appearance in a few buildings of the Uruk period. Domes, corbelled barrel vaulting, and the keystone arch were used in underground tombs or in buildings above ground in the Early Dynastic period. Metallurgy and carpentry were mutually supportive with the manufacture of a variety of cast copper tools for woodworking, including axes, adzes, and saws. In the Uruk period, copper was cast by the *cire-perdue* process, in which a ceramic mold was baked around a wax model and the molten wax drained off through holes in the mold. In late Early Dynastic times, copper was alloyed with tin to make bronze. From Uruk IV, pottery was made on the wheel, itself an innovation of great long-term significance, and was being mass-produced by professionals. The growing popularity of metal goods, however, contributed to a decline in the quality of ceramic wares. Also from Uruk IV, four-wheeled carts with solid wheels and drawn by domesticated onagers (a variety of wild donkey) were added to the older boats and sledges. Two-wheeled carts and chariots are found in Early Dynastic strata, the latter used for military purposes. A taste for luxury and elegance among the wealthy was expressed in the production of finely wrought jewelry using semiprecious stones, gold, and silver. Representational art of a high order appears in the cylinder seals of Uruk date, and musical instruments, including the harp and lyre, have been found in Early Dynastic sites. The combination of quality with quantity in material production points to the formation of groups of specialist artisans in the service of the estates or producing for sale.

The first language to be given written form was Sumerian. The earliest found Sumerian documents, which were produced around 3100 B.C., early in Uruk IV, represent writing in the most primitive sense. Ownership of a quantity of goods might be indicated by a tag bearing a seal impression to identify the owner and a set of marks equal to the number of objects. The growing need for record keeping demanded something better, however. The kind of object in question was indicated by a representational sign, a recognizable but highly conventionalized sketch of the head of a cow, for example. The use of unique seals to identify persons was impracticable where a large number of names had to be recorded, as in a temple storehouse, but most names were difficult or impossible to symbolize by representational signs. Scribes were compelled to find some way to suggest the sound of the name by means of conventional signs. This was done initially by taking representational signs and letting them stand for sounds and combining them to approximate the name. Thus *Matson* might now be written with signs for *mat* and *sun*. Once the possibility of phonetic representation was discovered, its use spread rapidly. The adoption of a standard syllabary (syllabic signs) and standard ways of writing them required a high degree of organization, however, which was provided by scribal schools, where the conventions were thoroughly learned. The use of clay as the main writing material and a squared stick or stylus to impress characters on the surface led to the evolution of the cuneiform (angular-form) style of writing. Cuneiform characters became so conventionalized and so simplified that they were no longer recognizable in their original representational forms. Once the writing system had been refined for effective communication in the Sumerian language, it was adapted to other languages as well, such as Akkadian, Babylonian, Assyrian, Elamite, Hurrian, Hittite, and Urartian. The invention and development of writing in Mesopotamia had important consequences for society and culture. It was crucial to the process of concentrating and regulating community resources for religious and urban development. It was also associated with the emergence of the literati, or scholars, as an occupational group. The literati gained in importance not only by their key role in administration but also in their role as shapers and transmitters of the cultural tradition.

2. THE BIRTH OF HARAPPAN CIVILIZATION IN SOUTH ASIA

The breakthrough of human social and economic organization from a hunting and gathering existence to village and then city life supported by agriculture was completed in South Asia in the third millennium B.C. This first civilization in the Indian subcontinent, referred to as the Indus Valley civilization, or, after one of its major urban centers, as the Harappan culture, flourished during the period 2350 to 1750 B.C. Unlike the early civilized cultures of Mesopotamia and northern China, which held a prominent place in the later historical traditions of those areas, the very existence of an early Indus Valley civilization was unsuspected until the advent of modern archaeology. Scientific excavations were begun under the British in the twentieth century, and the advent of radiocarbon dating techniques in recent years has considerably clarified the chronology of Harappan culture. The picture that emerges from the archaeological record is that of a civilization that predated the earliest historical events recalled in the oral tradition of Vedic legend. The Vedas are associated with the Aryans, speakers of an Indo-European language who entered India from the northwest, almost certainly as conquerors, at about the time the Indus Valley civilization came to an end. Thus, the first civilization in South Asia did not become an acknowledged part of Indian historical consciousness until modern times. Although it developed later in time than the first civilization in Mesopotamia and may have benefitted from precedents established in West Asia, Harappan culture was sufficiently distinct to dispel any notion that it might be a mere offshoot of another civilization.

The Setting

The Indian subcontinent is a distinct region of the Eurasian landmass, bounded by the broad expanse of the Himalaya Mountains in the north and by the sea on the eastern and western sides of the peninsula. While South Asia is defined by geographic boundaries, it is also linked to other regions. On the eastern coast and the southern tip of the peninsula the sea provided access to Ceylon, the islands and coastline of Southeast Asia and, at some periods, East Asia. In the west the sea has provided routes of trade and contact with the Arabian peninsula, the east coast of Africa and, more recently, Europe. At its northwestern corner the Indian subcontinent is connected to West Asia and Central Asia by land routes that carried many peoples back and forth in historical times. To the north and east the barrier of the Himalayas and the dense jungles of Burma restricted contact with Tibet and southwestern China to the occasional passage of the hardiest travelers. The dominant area in the cultural history of South Asia is the great Indo-Gangetic plain, stretching from west to east across the northern edge of the peninsula and encompassing the watersheds of the major river systems. South of the Narbada River lies the Deccan plateau, consisting of hills and valleys poorly connected to the northern plain, often facing as much toward the sea as toward the north.

The locus of the Harappan culture was northwestern India and Pakistan: the valley of the Indus River; the Makran coast and the hill country of Baluchistan to the west; the Panjab ("Land of the Five Rivers") and the Rajasthan desert to the east; and the regions of Kutch, Kathiawar, and Gujarat to the southeast.

A variety of Stone Age sites have been discovered throughout the Indian subcontinent and Ceylon indicating human habitation for many millennia. The Neolithic settlements that gave rise to civilized culture were located in the hill country of Baluchistan and date from about 3500 B.C., several thousand years later than similar sites in Mesopotamia. In these sites there is evidence of domestication of sheep, goats, and oxen. Houses were constructed of pressed earth and later of mud brick. Wheel-thrown painted pottery was manufactured in local styles, and some copper appears among a variety of stone and bone tools. The existence of bread ovens and stone grinding tools offers evidence that cereals were part of

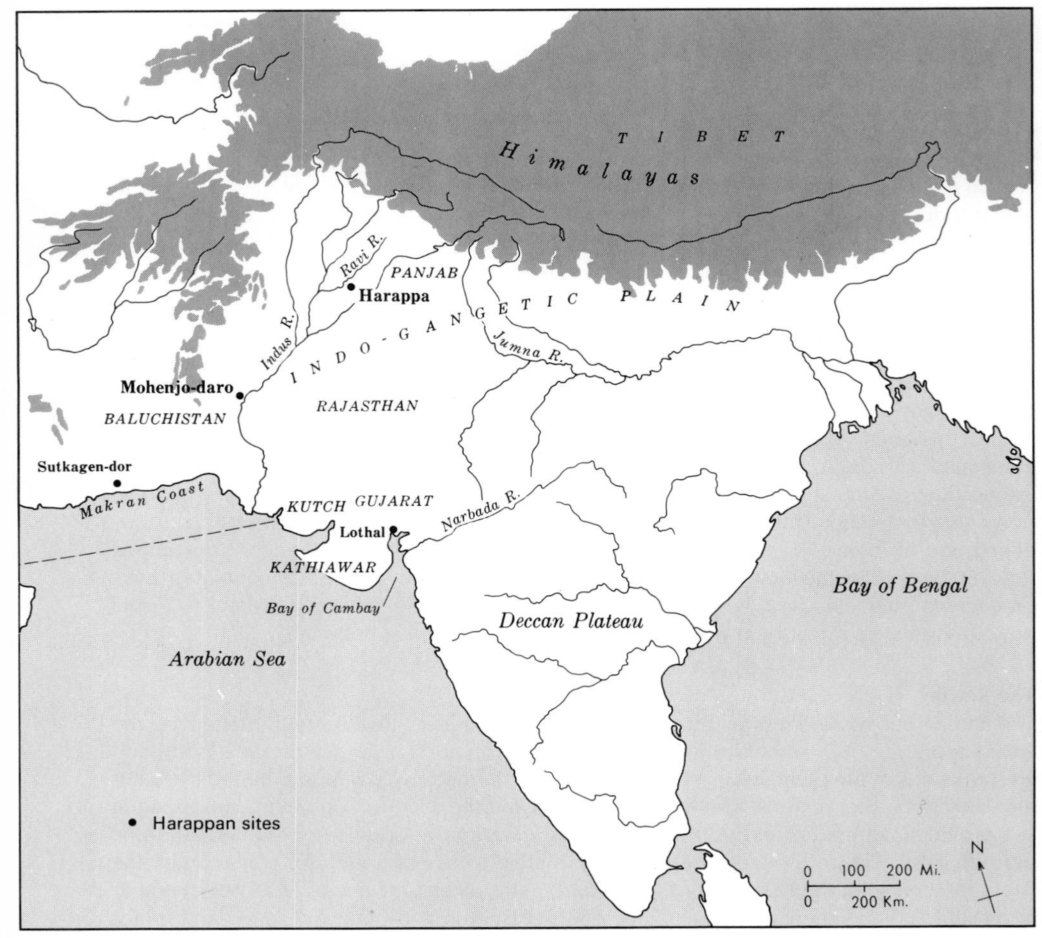

Map 7 The birth of Harappan civilization, to 1750 B.C.

the diet. Proliferation of settlements and the extension of sedentary life to the Indus plain took place around 3000 B.C. Many sites in the Indus region show signs of occupation for as much as five centuries before the emergence of a Harappan civilization. In many cases characteristics of this early culture still appear in the Harappan phase, indicating that there was considerable continuity at the local level.

Harappan Civilization in the Indus Valley

The Indus valley, with its broad floodplain, offered a rich environment for the expansion of agriculture. Silt deposited by the seasonal flooding of the river provided a vast expanse of easily worked soil that needed neither plowing nor fertilizer. The survival of a permanent settlement on the floodplain depended upon, in addition to agricultural techniques, the capability to take effective measures against the inundations of the river. The existence of towns and cities thus required the technology for mass production of fired bricks and a social organization capable of mobilizing the populace to construct sturdy walls, dikes, and levees. The cities were built on great platforms of earth raised above the plain and were surrounded by high walls, both of which were periodically rebuilt and added to as time went by. The two main centers of Indus Valley civilization were Harappa, on the Ravi in the Panjab region, and Mohenjo-daro, on the Indus some 150 miles from its mouth. Both cities were divided into two portions—the city proper and to the east a smaller but higher unit usually referred to as a citadel, an arrangement still found in some South Asian cities. One possible explanation for these separate units is that the lower town represents the older settlement and that the citadel, with its higher walls, is the product of intruders who imposed themselves on the earlier inhabitants. In both of these cases the citadels were about 1400 feet in length from north to south and half as wide. The platforms of the lower towns were at least three miles in circumference with evidence of building extending farther out. Existing remnants of the citadels rise 40 feet above the plain, and excavations have shown that culture-bearing strata at Mohenjo-daro extend 40 feet below the surface of the plain. The wall of the citadel at Harappa, composed of mud brick with a baked-brick facing, was 50 feet thick. The population of Harappa and Mohenjo-daro was probably in the vicinity of forty thousand persons each. In addition to these principal centers, separated by four hundred miles, some seventy other known sites are scattered over an area of about half a million square miles.

The regularity of design that the Harappan sites reveal must have been the result of a highly organized society, but no details of such an order are known. The uniformity of Harappan culture was introduced rather suddenly over a wide area, suggesting a rapid social change. For example, the grid network of streets with a fixed width and right-angle intersections was the same at various locations, often being imposed over earlier irregular streets. Even the size and shape of bricks were standardized, as were weights and measures. Copper tools and bronze and copper vessels changed little over several centuries. The pottery, which could not have come from a common source, also displayed a marked uniformity.

Large buildings, lavatories, cesspools, sewers, drains, and gutters still evident in the surviving brick-remains attest to the high standards of urban life. The large populations of Harappa and Mohenjo-daro depended for their support on the surplus of an extended agricultural hinterland. How this surplus was collected and the nature of the social ties that bound the countryside to the city are obscure, but the evidence of food collection is undeniable. Enormous granaries with loading platforms and air vents were constructed for the storage of a food supply. Wheat and barley were the principal grains in a diet that included legumes, dates, and meat from sheep, goats, cattle, and domestic fowl. Cotton was woven for cloth. Large workshops and barrackslike structures, which may have housed laborers, suggest that some kinds of manufacturing and processing were organized on a large scale. The labor force in these great cities must have included—in addition to those who tilled the field and tended the animals—potters, metal workers, construction workers, managers who supervised the collection, storage, and distribution of grains, and people who processed and distributed a variety of food and household items. Many routine tasks, such as the weaving of cloth, the transport of grain, or the construction of brick walls, could conceivably have been accomplished as secondary occupations by nonspecialists or as part of a service obligation imposed on the populace at large. The same may be said of military service, although direction, organization, and command must have been provided by specialists with defined social roles. In the absence of adequate written records little can be deduced concerning the government and social stratification of Harappan society.

The existence of a large brick pool, or "great bath," at Mohenjo-daro has prompted speculation that ritual bathing might have been practiced under the direction of a priestly class. The bath itself was 39 feet long, 23 feet wide, and 8 feet deep, with brick stairways leading into the water at each end. The bath was constructed of watertight layers of mortared brick and had a large drain that led out to the side of the citadel mound. Adjoining the bath were rows of small private chambers with drains, which might have been used for washing purposes. Religious information from pottery decorations, seals, and figurines reveals certain continuities between Harappan values and later Indian religious practice. The pipal leaf, the swastika, the bull, and the figure of a mother goddess are themes that were to persist in later time. There are also hints of a cult of tree spirits and of a god who was the lord of all beasts. An interest in fertility is evidenced by the lingam, or phallic symbol, yet another element that persisted in Hinduism.

Harappan writing is preserved on small stone and clay seals that have survived in large numbers. Some seals combine pictures of animals and humans along with written script, while others are abstract and symmetrical in design. The brevity of the seal inscriptions has inhibited definitive interpretation, so that the use of these documents to reveal the workings of Harappan civilization has remained limited. The distribution of the seals, however, tells something of the trade and cultural contacts of the Indus Valley civilization. Seals of the Harappan type have been found in deposits in Mesopotamia, indicating trading contacts during the period 2350-1770 B.C. Harappan towns at Lothal on the Bay of Cambay and at Sutkagen-dor on the Makran coast were centers of sea trade. At Lothal a brick-edged enclosure 730 by 120 feet appears to have been a port facility, improved with a sluice gate at one end so as to keep ships afloat in the harbor during the low tide.

The present-day location of Sutkagen-dor, thirty miles from the shoreline, is indicative of the environmental changes that have occurred in the last four millennia. Evidence of repeated and serious flooding has been cited as a possible explanation for the decline of the Indus Valley civilization. Mohenjo-daro shows signs of constant rebuilding, as the walls and platforms were raised to keep the city above the rising floodplain. Greater uniformity and crudity in the upper levels—a shift to undecorated pottery, for example—may be indicative of an environmental challenge that severely taxed the society's capacity to respond. One prominent theory is that geological changes in the lower Indus valley caused the river to back up into a giant lake, which submerged the low-lying cities and deprived the peripheral areas of the heartland of their civilization. Another line of explanation, not necessarily in conflict with the first, stresses invasion by Aryan peoples as a factor in ending the Harappan phase of occupation. Clusters of skeletons in disorderly positions at the uppermost stratum of Mohenjo-daro are possible evidence of a massacre of the city's inhabitants. Relative dating among sites indicates that the Harappan phase persisted longer at the peripheral locations, in the south along the coast and in the east toward the Ganges. For whatever reason, the first civilization of the Indian subcontinent disappeared around 1750 B.C.

3. THE BIRTH OF SHANG CIVILIZATION IN EAST ASIA

Chinese civilization is the oldest in East Asia, but it is younger than those of West and South Asia. The inhabitants of north China made the transition from hunting and gathering to village agriculture around 5000 B.C. This, in turn, generated the social, economic, and cultural forces that led to the emergence of the Shang dynasty urban civilization around 1600 B.C. Memories and myths of the origins of Chinese civilization have been preserved down to modern times in the early literary works, but archaeological research began only in the 1920s, and then under difficult conditions of war and revolution. As a result, much of what is known about prehistoric and early historic China has been discovered only during the past twenty-five years by the archaeologists of the People's Republic. The archaeological record provides a rapidly growing body of information, including excavated written documents, which can be combined with the traditional written materials to illuminate the history of the earliest farmers and townsmen in China.

The Beginnings of Agriculture in China

As far back as the evidence goes, Chinese grain agriculture has been divided roughly into two realms: a northern region of millet and later of wheat, and a southern region of rice cultivation. The line of division between north and south runs west to east along the Ch'inling mountain range of southern Shensi, and the Huai River. North of this line, the summer rainfall provided by the monsoon winds from the southeast coast is lighter and more variable than it is in the south. This, combined with the lower average temperatures and shorter growing season in the north, accounts for the persistent contrast in natural vegetation and in cultivated plants. The study of the origins of Chinese civilization is focused mainly on the north because it was along the western margins of the north China plain that cities first appeared. Some attention has to be paid to the south as well, however, because the transition to agriculture occurred there about as early as in the north, and evidence of southern influence is found in the record of the emerging civilization in the north.

North China may be divided into two contrasting kinds of natural setting: the northern uplands and the north China plain. In its natural state, the plain was probably dissected by many shifting distributaries of the Yellow River and was subject to annual flooding over wide areas every fall. The plain was built up over many millennia by the accumulation of silt deposited by the river. A denser growth of trees, shrubs, grasses, and reeds than existed in the loess upland probably made this a more inhospitable area for farmers, despite its great potential agricultural wealth. Like the great floodplains of Mesopotamia and the Indus, this was long to remain a relatively undeveloped area, while the surrounding uplands provided the setting for the early development of agriculture. West of the north China plain lie the northwest uplands. This region corresponds roughly to the modern provinces of Kansu, Shensi, Shansi, and western Honan. The north-south range of the T'aihang Mountains make an abrupt transition from the western margin of the plain to the eastern portion of the upland in much the same way as the Zagros divide the lowland of Mesopotamia from the Iranian plateau. Most of the upland is covered by a deep mantle of windblown soil (loess) deposited there by winter winds from inner Asia. The crest of the Ch'inling Mountains marks the southern margin of the loess region; the Fen River valley marks the eastern margin; and the Ordos desert forms the northeastern margin. Elevations are mostly between 3,000 and 5,000 feet above sea level.

It was the loess-covered portions of the upland that provided the setting for the first agriculture in north China. Over much of this region, annual precipitation is sufficient for a rainfall agriculture based on drought-resistant grains, but the margin of safety is small, and in a dry year crops may fail. In contrast with the climatic system of West Asia, which is marked by winter rains and spring flooding, the loess upland has most of its rain in July and August, with autumn flooding downstream on the north China plain. Upland farmers have always faced the problem of conserving enough soil moisture from light winter snows and rains to get their seedlings well started before the heavier rains of summer. At least by early historical times, and probably earlier, they developed effective means of doing this. The climate is cooler, on the average, than in West and South Asia, with strong seasonal variations. Monthly averages in northern Shansi, for example, vary from about twenty degrees in December and January to about eighty degrees in July. Although present conditions are probably somewhat drier than those of seven thousand years ago, pollen studies show that even then the natural vegetation of the loess upland was dominated by grasses and woody plants of kinds typical of arid regions. Woodlands were sparse and were predominantly evergreen.

Before the first appearance of grain agriculture there was a period during which the inhabitants found new means of collecting food and probably broadened their diet. In the

Map 8 The birth of Shang civilization, to 1028 B.C.

early postglacial period, from about 12,000-8000 B.C., the region of Inner Mongolia and the Ordos still had many lakes and rivers that have since dried up. The remains of campsites by these vanished bodies of water show a transition to a microlithic culture—so called from its production of fine small stone points and blades. These and the presence of fishing gear point to the importance of fish and small game in the diet. Shell heaps show that freshwater mollusks and ostrich eggs were also eaten in large quantities. The preagricultural peoples of south China and Southeast Asia, meanwhile, developed their skills in hunting, collecting, fishing, and boat building. Before entering upon grain agriculture, they probably began to domesticate other kinds of edible plants in village gardens. Their distinctive ceramic ware, which antedated the domestication of grain, was the cord-marked pottery, made by impressing cords or basketry against the unfired surface of the vessels. The making of this kind of pottery spread northward over the Ch'inling divide and even across Mongolia to the region of Lake Baikal. From the Ch'inling region and beyond, the cord-marked wares were associated with the beginnings of agriculture and constituted the mainstream of Chinese ceramic tradition through the Neolithic and into the Bronze Age.

The farmers of north China were probably descended from the makers of the microliths and cord-marked pots who lived in that region. First on the southern portion of the loess upland, then spreading westward up the valley of the Wei River and its tributaries and eastward toward the north China plain, agricultural villages came to be established on natural terraces lying out of reach of floods in the valleys. This early village farming culture is called Yangshao, from one of the first sites to be found, or the Painted Pottery culture, from its most distinctive artifacts. The most important grains were domesticated varieties of the wild millets native to the region. These formed part of a diet that still included various wild grains and vegetables, fish, and game, including birds. When the cultivation of millet began is still unknown, but it was well established by 5000 B.C. The loess soils were easily worked, well drained and, because of the dry climate, not thickly bound by roots. Fields were burned over and then cultivated with digging sticks. With little or no irrigation, the open fields dried out rapidly and had to be abandoned in favor of new ones. The principal domesticated animals were the dog and the pig, with rare occurrences of cattle.

The Yangshao lived in villages of semisubterranean houses. Walls of mud-plastered branches, and thatched roofs were raised over pits frequently circular in plan which were dug down a few feet into the earth. Grain was stored in deep underground granaries, which sometimes had staircases cut into their lime-plastered walls. In some villages, houses were arranged in a circle, their doors facing inward towards a long house that was divided into a number of apartments. A village commonly had three or four sites: one or two dwelling sites, an area of pottery kilns, and a graveyard. The form of the village and the practice of differentiating burials by age and sex suggest that the communities may have been extended families. Settlement at this stage, however, was not fully sedentary. The form of agriculture made it necessary for the population to move from time to time in search of new land to clear. Where many layers of Yangshao remains are found on top of one another, this was the result of repetitive, rather than continuous, occupation of the site. This successive settlement and abandonment is reflected by pollen counts that show the predominance of domestic and wild plants in alternating layers.

The Yangshao villagers were skilled and versatile craftsmen. In pottery making their ordinary wares continued the cord-marked tradition, but their finest pieces, including ceremonial wares, were painted with red and black pigments in bold stylized and geometric designs. They were also skilled in making bone tools and implements such as awls, needles, and fishhooks. Tools of polished stone included axes, chisels, knives, hoes, sickles, grinders, and fishnet sinkers. Arrowheads and spearheads were made of bone or stone. Pottery impressions reveal a wide variety of basketry weaves; hemp and silk fibers were woven into cloth.

A second Neolithic village farming culture of north China, the Lungshan, also called the Black Pottery culture, overlapped in time with the Yangshao, but was generally later and was at least partly derived from it. The most significant changes that occurred in the transition from Yangshao to Lungshan were developmental and geographic. In a developmental sense, Lungshan marked the transition from the early village agriculture of Yangshao to the urban civilization of Shang. The geographic change was the much larger and climatically more diverse area occupied by the Lungshan. Beginning a little before 3000 B.C. and continuing for about a millennium, sites of transitional, or early Lungshan, type spread eastward from western Honan to the mountain margins of the north China plain in central Shantung and thence to the sea; southward into the Huai and Yangtze valleys, down the south China coasts and across to the island of Taiwan. The processes involved in this expansion are still very much in doubt and may have included some combination of migration, cultural diffusion, and indigenous development. Subsequently, distinctive regional variants of Lungshan culture emerged in different regions. One of the principal regional differences was that millet continued to be the dominant cultivated grain in the north, while Lungshan communities in the Huai and Yangtze valleys cultivated rice. Rice cultivation in south China began around 3000 B.C., probably near the confluence of the Han and Yangtze rivers (the region of modern Wuhan). The early form of rice culture did not depend on irrigation, as it usually does at the present time. The first grain farmers in south China domesticated native varieties of wild rice by sowing the seeds in natural swamps and shallow lakes. The expansion of millet agriculture onto the north China plain, crucially important though it was in the long run for the subsequent development of Chinese civilization, involved only modest improvements in agricultural techniques. Notably, the Lungshan farmers probably did not yet employ irrigation. In the uplands, the fields on the terraces were too far above the rivers and the water table for convenient irrigation with river water or water drawn from wells. Where ditches were dug on the north China plain, they were more likely to have been used to drain off floodwaters than to irrigate.

Lungshan communities were, in general, larger and more permanent than those of the Yangshao culture. Those in the south or on the north China plain were built on mountain foothills or on the low mounds formed on the floodplain by the old riverbanks of abandoned watercourses. The eponymous site in Shantung, which represents a late phase (perhaps even contemporaneous with Shang), was surrounded with a wall. This need not have been for purposes of military defense, however, but may have served as protection against flooding. Although one cannot now be certain that individuals or families were exclusively or mainly engaged in different occupations in the Neolithic villages, the growing mastery of a wide range of techniques suggests a tendency in that direction. As early as the Yangshao stage, the ceramic industry produced some well-made and magnificently decorated wares. Local traditions in form and decoration may reflect hereditary family crafts. Some of the painted pieces bear designs that may have had a religious function, and one of these may even represent a shaman, or spirit medium. The Lungshan sites show greater technical mastery with wheel-made pottery in many new shapes, including some elegant thin-walled black ware that may have been produced in sets for an elaborate ceremonial of a kind that is much better known in Shang and later contexts. The inventory of stone tools was now larger and appears connected with an interest in skilled carpentry. The appearance of a class of religious specialists in Shang is anticipated in Lungshan sites where uninscribed bones used in spirit communication have been found. There is even some evidence for the beginning of social stratification in the differentiation of burials on a basis other than age or sex and in the concentration of jade artifacts—a possible store of value—in a certain quarter of a village.

The Emergence of Civilization in China

Some aspects of the development of civilization in China anticipate processes, to be discussed in the next chapter, relating to the formation of the state. Whereas the political organization of society in West Asia under hereditary monarchies was preceded by a long period of growth of urban civilization, in the case of China, kingship and urban civilization occur almost simultaneously about the time of the establishment of the Shang dynasty (traditional dates 1766-1122 B.C., but 1600 B.C. is more realistic for the year of the founding). This difference between the Chinese and West Asian cases implies not that different processes were at work, but that the same processes overlapped instead of being separated in time. In this section, discussion of Shang China will be focused on social and cultural aspects of urban civilization generally, leaving the origins of Chinese political institutions for more intensive treatment in the following chapter. Briefly, the reason for the difference appears to be that by the time that urban civilization emerged in China, peoples occupying the uplands around the urbanized plains area were well advanced in pastoral economy, including horse raising, and had mastered the making of bronze weapons about as early as had the urban plainsmen. This meant that even as certain Neolithic communities were developing into urban centers of trade and religious activity, they were drawn into conflict with well-armed, aggressive pastoral neighbors, and they had to arm and organize themselves for war. As in West Asia (in the period to be discussed in the following chapter), this had the effect of generating a military aristocracy and the institutions of kingship.

The oldest surviving Chinese literary works containing information on ancient Chinese history were composed in approximately their present form only in the second half of the first millennium B.C. or later. These works contain what appear to be edicts, regulations, descriptions, songs and poems, and other matter pertaining not only to the Shang and the succeeding Chou dynasty, but to a Hsia dynasty that was supposed to have preceded the Shang and to several obviously mythical rulers who were believed to have ruled even earlier than Hsia. If there really was a Hsia dynasty, it would have corresponded to the late Lungshan period in north China, but no archaeological evidence of it has been found. Until and unless this happens, it must be assumed that the Hsia state was at best a small rival state or tribe defeated by the Shang. The Shang dynasty, however, is known archaeologically from a large and rapidly growing number of excavated sites.

The main area delineated by the known Shang cultural sites is a crescent starting west of the modern Loyang then running east along the south bank of the Yellow River, turning north near modern Chengchow and continuing in that direction for some 250 miles. Outside this area, sites have been found near the western foothills of the mountain area of central Shantung, and one site south of the Ch'inling Range in the Han River valley near Nanyang. From the distribution of the sites and the relative ages of their earliest Shang strata, it appears that Chinese urban civilization may have begun on the floodplain near Loyang bounded by the Yellow River on the north and the Ch'inling Range on the south. It then spread eastward to the lower end of the T'aihang Mountains and northward along the western margin of the plain, never venturing very far from the T'aihang foothills, except for a few outposts similarly situated on floodplains with mountains at their backs. In other words, Shang civilization began and developed in a zone of contact between the Lungshan agricultural communities of the floodplain and the diverging pastoralism of the adjacent uplands. Here some agricultural communities, perhaps favored over others by their location, may have prospered and grown not only as centers of agricultural production but also as places of exchange between the agricultural products of the plain and the stone, ores, timber, fuel, and livestock of the uplands. And as these centers grew, their cults and great families grew with them in wealth and prestige.

Literary sources hold that the Shang realm was ruled successively from seven different capitals. The first two have been tentatively identified with recently excavated sites near Loyang and Chengchow, respectively. By far the most productive site, however, was one of the first to be discovered: the royal tomb and cult complex near Anyang. This site was occupied near the end of the Shang period and may have been its last capital. The small size of the site in comparison with the much larger Shang city at Chengchow and the fact that it does not appear to have been walled have led some scholars to suspect that there is a large habitation site nearby still awaiting discovery. In any case, archaeologists working at the Anyang site from 1928 to the present, despite interruptions by war and revolution, have unearthed a rich mass of cultural material including building foundations, bronze weapons and ritual vessels, ceramic wares, and perhaps most important, tens of thousands of written documents in the form of inscribed bones and tortoise shells used by diviners to communicate with the spirits.

The many excavated Shang sites together provide a picture of a long developmental sequence running through the Yangshao, Lungshan, and Shang periods. The onset of urban civilization is indicated in the earliest Shang strata by the appearance of impressive cult centers. These are marked by pounded-earth building platforms of large or extremely large size (one of these at the presumed first capital near Loyang is more than one hundred yards long and wide) and by evidence of large-scale sacrifice of animal and human victims. Heavy concentrations of divination bones also testify to the elaboration of religious cults and the formation of a priestly class of specialists in spiritual communication. The archaeological evidence also confirms intense social stratification and occupational differentiation throughout the Shang period. Both habitation and burial sites reveal a sharp differentiation between an aristocracy and the lower classes. The former seems to have enjoyed a virtual monopoly on the use of bronze in the form of ritual vessels and weapons and armor. The aristocrats' palatial dwellings were built near the temples and altars and at least in some cases were marked off by a surrounding wall. The aristocratic tombs, especially but not merely those of the kings, were richly furnished with goods and sacrificial vicitms. By contrast, the common agricultural workers lived in much the same style as their Neolithic predecessors, in small, semisubterranean houses, and used stone hoes, knives, axes, and sickles in their work. The cities of Shang resembled one another in their overall pattern. The aristocratic and cult complex stood at the center, and distributed through a large surrounding area were small settlements of specialized economic function. There were, for example, settlements complete with workshops for bronze casters, potters, and bone workers. A larger number of settlements housed ordinary peasants. On this evidence, it is probable that the major occupations had come to be monopolized by specific lineages, which preserved and improved their craft techniques and were hereditarily bound as groups to the service of the aristocratic households.

Although all Shang sites have much in common, there is evidence of cultural development during the dynasty's six centuries. The earliest evidence of bronze casting in China coincides with the beginning of the period. The Loyang site contains a few simple forms: knives, fishhooks, awls, and a bell. At Chengchow, cast-bronze ceremonial vessels appear. Although these are small and often poorly made, they mark the advance of bronze technique. The Anyang ceremonial bronzes represent the highest technical stage. The ornamentation of the most successful vessels is flawlessly executed and their size is sometimes astonishing; the largest known Anyang vessel is a single casting of more than one ton in weight. Another and more abrupt change was the Shang adoption of the two-horse chariot during the Anyang phase. Although there is no evidence of horse chariots in the Loyang and Chengchow sites, they are prominent in the vicinity of the last capital. The chariot came to be regarded with such awe as a symbol of aristocratic power that the late Shang rulers performed ritual sacrifice of chariots complete with horses and drivers. The Shang system of writing undoubtedly developed during the dynastic period, and archaic and relatively "modern" styles appear in the Anyang inscriptions. The origins of the system remain obscure, however. In early Shang strata near Loyang, markings on some pottery vessels may represent early written forms, but there is still no satisfactory evidence. The reason for this is probably that Shang scribes ordinarily wrote on strips of wood or bamboo, which were then tied together with string to constitute books. Among the characters written on the oracle bones is a pictograph of such a book. Although a few wooden books have survived from the later Chou dynasty, none of Shang date has yet been found, and it is possible that all of them have disintegrated.

Shang religion is known mainly from the oracle-bone inscriptions and from the great tombs. Although there were cults of very different kinds, the most important of all was that of ancestor worship. The domination of society by an aristocracy was sanctified and regularized by the invention of a celestial court presided over by an awesome principal god, Shang Ti, who was attended by the spirits of generations of deceased kings, queens, and noblemen. At least some, if not all, of the nature spirits were integrated into this divine order, with the spirit of the wind, for example, serving as Shang Ti's messenger. The ancestral spirits were thought to play an active and determining role in the affairs of the living. Good and bad fortune were understood as expressions of favor or disapproval on the part of the ancestors. Therefore, it was of the utmost importance that the ancestors be served meticulously and without limit. Although some form of ancestral cult became a permanent feature of Chinese society, it had its most extravagant expression in the Shang. Not only were the kings in almost constant communication with their ancestors through the taking of oracles, but the number of human victims sacrificed for burial in their tombs and in their temple foundations sometimes ran into the hundreds. In West Asia, only the human sacrifices of the royal tombs of the Third Dynasty of Ur bear comparison with those of Shang. When the royal lineage and perhaps other nobles had monopolized the religious function on behalf of the whole society, securing the blessings of timely rains, good harvests, and victory in war, then the gulf between aristocrat and commoner had become almost total.

Technological innovation and development were associated with the beginnings of urban culture in China, as they were in the other areas of early civilization. It should first be noted, however, that there seems to have been little advance in the techniques of agriculture at this time. Despite some recent readings of certain oracle-bone characters, there is little reason to believe that ox plowing appeared in Shang or even in early Chou. Cultivation was still by hand, and the hoe blades were of stone and the sickles of stone or wood set with teeth or shell. Bronze agricultural tools were so rare that there is little doubt that the use of this metal was denied to the common people. Even for irrigation the evidence is inconclusive, and large-scale water control may not have been undertaken until late in Chou. The absence of major advances in agricultural technique may have been offset by efficient organization of manpower under aristocratic control and by the abundance of potentially fertile land awaiting cultivation by fire, digging stick, and hoe. By contrast, striking advances were made in other fields. Bronze was one of the most important. The making of a ceremonial vessel began with the creation of a ceramic model in full scale and with every decorative detail or written character incised on its surface. Wet clay was then applied to the surface of the model, removed in several sections, and fired. The sections of the mold were then locked together and fitted with internal core molds. Molten bronze was then poured to fill the space between inner and outer molds. The technique was obviously the end of a long development that took full advantage of the technical skills of the pottery makers.

Religion had to share with war the honor of benefitting most from Shang technological advance. The aristocratic metal was also used in the production of weapons, notably daggers and the characteristically Chinese *ko* halberd, a sturdy bronze blade hafted at right angles to a pole. At least one fine helmet of bronze has also been recovered from the Yin site. The two-horse chariot also represented a technological advance. These vehicles, mounted on large-spoked wheels and adorned with finely wrought bronze fittings, allowed the aristocrats to ride while others had to walk. Use of the chariot required not only the skills necessary for the construction of the vehicle with yoke and harness but also the ability to raise and train horses. From Shang times on, the horse in one way or another was a necessary part of military culture and a mark of the aristocratic style. In architecture the Shang began the construction of pounded-earth building foundations, although the same method may have been used in Lungshan for building walls. By this method, wooden forms, like our concrete forms, were constructed. Loess soil (which compacts readily) was thrown into the forms and tamped down hard with a tool pointed with stone or bronze. The resulting material was so hard that parts of some Shang dynasty walls have retained almost their original dimensions and hardness. Shang potters for the first time began making fine wares with white kaolin clay, the same material later used in the manufacture of translucent porcelain. They also began experimentation, though not very successfully, with glazes. The inventory of textiles and jade, ivory and bone products continued to grow, further reflecting the demand for luxury goods generated by the ruling class.

The greatest of Shang intellectual innovations undoubtedly was the writing system. By the time the Yin site was occupied by the Shang king P'an-keng, Chinese writing was already well developed. The earlier development is suggested by a few signs on Yangshao pots. Some three thousand different characters were employed, of which about one thousand have been identified with later forms. The Shang writing embodied all the major principles of character formation that were used in later times. Some were obviously pictographs—drawings of objects denoted by the word for which the character was intended to stand. Others were symbols, such as a single line to represent the word meaning "one" or "unity." Semantic compounds were made by combining two symbolic or pictographic elements to form a character suggestive of the word's meaning, and phonetic compounds were made by combining a phonetic element (a character standing for a word that sounded about the same as the word that was to be written) with a semantic element (a pictograph or symbol suggestive of the meaning of the word to be written). Sometimes a character was simply borrowed to represent a homophone, a method that was workable when the borrowed character was one not often used.

Writing in Shang must have had many uses. There is evidence, for instance, that laws were set down in wooden books, and Shang bronze vessels occasionally have short inscriptions. However, since bone is relatively imperishable, the inscribed oracle bones account for most of the documents that have survived. In the taking of an oracle, the surface of a piece of bone, often the shoulder blade of an ox, sometimes a human bone, or the undershell of a tortoise, was cut to form notches. A heated point of bronze was applied near a notch, causing the bone to crack. The directions of the cracks were then interpreted by the diviners, sometimes with the king himself expressing his opinion, as indicating a favorable or unfavorable response to whatever question was addressed to the spirit. In a minority of cases some inscription was made on the bone to record the spirit to whom the question was addressed, the question itself, the interpreted answer and, in rare cases, the actual outcome confirming the truth of the answer. The tens of thousands of such inscriptions have become the subject of a new field of scholarship. Although this represents only a small and highly specialized fraction of all the Shang written material, it has made possible the reconstruction of some important aspects of Shang high culture in addition to religion and society. Shang arithmetic established the decimal system in China. Numbers were expressed by compounding forms of characters standing for numbers one to ten with other characters meaning "ten," "hundred," "thousand," "ten thousand." The Shang calendars were of two kinds, solar and lunar. The solar year was calculated to be 365.25 days and was divided into twenty-four periods, which were paired to make twelve months. There was also a lunar calendar based on a calculation of 29.531 days per lunation. Intercalary months were added from time to time to the lunar cycle in order to bring it into correspondence with the solar seasons. The calendar was important for the ritually correct timing of court ceremonial and the agricultural cycle.

CONCLUDING REMARKS

When the births of civilization in these three areas of Asia are compared, a number of parallels and contrasts stand out. Most striking, perhaps, is the chronological disparity between the three patterns. The fact that civilization emerged first in Mesopotamia, later in the Indus valley, and last in China could be cited in support of the notion that civilization evolved first in one location and was later diffused to other places. The point was made in the Introduction that the main focus here is on understanding each of the civilizations in Asia by comparing them in terms of common processes rather than by tracing possible borrowing between them. For example, it should be noted that even though the first civilized settlements developed at different periods of time, there were marked similarities in the environments in which they evolved. In each case there appears to have been an interaction between highlands and river valleys, with the earliest sedentary communities forming in hill country where the breakthrough to agricultural production occurred. Expansion onto the plains of the great river system took place later, when the population was larger and more extensive agriculture became possible. What prompted these transformations, and how they occurred, is far from clear. From the relatively rich archaeological evidence in West Asia it is known that the movement toward civilization took place at many locations, with numerous repetitions and false starts. Knowledge of a similarly complex pattern in East Asia is beginning to emerge. In South Asia the links between the early agriculture of Baluchistan and the later civilization of the Indus valley are less clearly delineated, owing to the present scarcity of evidence.

Social stratification is revealed in each area by differentiated burials and distinctions in the size and location of residences. In Sumer and Shang China it is possible to discern the role of great families and extended kinship groupings, but in Harappan sites there is not the kind of evidence that permits such conclusions about the social structure. The towering citadels may have been the fortress residences of a dominant group, but this is mere speculation. Similarly, in the cases of West Asia and East Asia there is ample evidence, from well-developed temple complexes in Sumer and elaborate burial sacrifices in Shang, of the activities of priests and shamans. In the Indus valley, however, it is far from certain what structures were used for religious purposes and what kinds of activities were involved.

It is in terms of material culture that archaeological evidence is most adequate and that the best comparisons can be made. The physical appearance of early towns and cities—characterized by more densely grouped buildings, monumental architecture, and provisions for grain storage—is strong testimony to the nature of the relationship between the urban center and surrounding agricultural area. While styles and techniques of production were distinct to each pattern area, the comparability of pottery or bronze artifacts or vehicles in various areas points to the fact that people faced much the same problems in each culture. That the similarity of function is not evidence of common ancestry or diffusion is best illustrated by the case of writing. The phonetic symbols of cuneiform could not have been more different from the logographic script used in China; nor is it likely that the clay tablets of West Asia were the inspiration for the bundles of wooden strips that comprised a book in East Asia. Aside from some seals, it is not known whether there was extensive writing among the Harappans, because there is no evidence.

Having noted the shared or comparable processes in each civilization, one can ask what made each culture unique. What were the special traits of each area that were to remain characteristic of that part of Asia? How did the natural environment influence the development of civilization in each area? What features were most subject to change and which elements might have easily been diffused from one area to another?

BIBLIOGRAPHY

1.P The Birth of Civilization in Asia: Processes

Adams, Robert M., *The Evolution of Urban Society* (Chicago, 1966), 191 pp. Chapters 1-3 offer a comparative study of the development of civilization up to the stage of political organization.

Braidwood, Robert J., and Gordon R. Willey, eds., *Courses Toward Urban Life* (Chicago, 1962), 371 pp. Articles collected in this volume furnish material for comparative study of the origins of civilization in different parts of the world.

Childe, V. Gordon, *What Happened in History* (Pelican Book, 1942), 286 pp. A classic interpretive account of the origins of civilization in West Asia. Chapters 1-7 are pertinent to this section.

Flannery, Kent V., "Origins and Ecological Effects of Early Domestication in Iran and the Near East," in Peter J. Ucko and G. W. Dimbleby, eds., *Domestication and Exploitation of Plants and Animals* (Chicago, 1969), 1126 pp. This article includes a concisely stated model of the transition from hunting and gathering to agriculture.

Fried, Morton H., "On the Evolution of Social Stratification and the State," in S. Diamond, ed., *Culture in History* (New York, 1960), pp. 713-31. Available in Bobbs-Merrill reprint.

Wheatley, Paul, *The Pivot of the Four Quarters* (Chicago, 1971), 602 pp. Chapter 3 compares the place of ceremonial centers in the formation of cities.

1.1 The Birth of Mesopotamian Civilization in West Asia

Frankfort, Henri, *The Birth of Civilization in the Near East* (Anchor paperback, 1956), 142 pp. Chapters 1-3 are a readable introduction to early Mesopotamia.

Hallo, William W., and William Kelly Simpson, *The Ancient Near East* (New York, 1971), 319 pp. Chapters 1 and 2 present up-to-date scholarship on early Mesopotamia.

Jones, Tom B., *Ancient Civilization* (Chicago, 1960), 476 pp. Chapters 1-3 survey the origins of civilizations in West Asia and in Mesopotamia in particular.

——————, ed., *The Sumerian Problem* (Wiley paperback, 1969), 142 pp. Focused on the problems of the origins of the Sumerians, this collection of readings provides a survey of changing modes of scholarship.

Kramer, S. N., *The Sumerians* (Phoenix, 1963), 355 pp. Broadly informative monograph on the culture and society of early Mesopotamia.

Malaart, James, *Earliest Civilizations of the Near East* (McGraw-Hill paperback, 1965), 143 pp. A copiously illustrated introduction to Neolithic archaeology. Especially informative on Anatolian sites.

1.2 The Birth of Harappan Civilization in South Asia

Allchin, Bridget, and Raymond Allchin, *The Birth of Indian Civilization—India and Pakistan before 500 B.C.* (Penguin paperback, 1968), 365 pp., illustrations. This is a comprehensive and authoritative synthesis of the archaeological knowledge of prehistoric South Asia.

Basham, A. L., *The Wonder That Was India* (Evergreen paperback, 1959), pp. 1-26. A colorful account of the beginnings of Indian civilization in a lively, illustrated introduction to pre-Muslim culture in South Asia.

Dales, George F., "The Decline of the Harappans," *Scientific American* 214.5: 92-100 (May, 1966). Presents the thesis that flooding destroyed Mohenjo-daro.

Majumdar, Ramesh C., H. C. Raychaudhuri, and Kalikinkar Datta, *An Advanced History of India,* third edition (New York, 1960), pp. 9-23. A scant outline of Indian prehistory in a standard textbook.

Thapar, Romila, *A History of India,* Vol. 1 (Penguin paperback, 1966), pp. 15-49. Summary of the earliest period of Indian history in a readable standard source.

Wheeler, Sir Mortimer, *The Indus Civilization,* third edition (Cambridge University Press paperback, 1968), 144 pp. Brief but authoritative description of Harappan culture with photographs, diagrams, and maps.

1.3 The Birth of Shang Civilization in East Asia

Chang Kwang-chih, *The Archaeology of Ancient China,* second edition (Yale paperback, 1968), 483 pp. Chapters 1-6 survey the archaeology of China from Paleolithic cultures through Shang.

Creel, H. G., *The Birth of China* (Ungar paperback, 1937), 402 pp. Chapters 4-14 provide a readable introduction to Shang civilization. Watson, below, should be used to bring the archaeology up to date.

Ho Ping-ti, "The Loess and the Origins of Chinese Agriculture," *American Historical Review* 75.1: 1-35 (1969). Richly informative study of the beginnings of agriculture in north and south China.

Li Chi, *The Beginnings of Chinese Civilization* (University of Washington paperback, 1957), 123 pp. A classic account of the study of Neolithic and Shang cultural remains in the Anyang region.

Watson, William, *Early Civilization in China* (McGraw-Hill paperback, 1966), 143 pp. Illustrated survey of ancient archaeology of China.

Wheatley, Paul, *The Pivot of the Four Quarters* (Chicago, 1971), 602 pp. Chapter 1 provides a synthesis of scholarship on Shang civilization.

GLOSSARY

Aryans. Speakers of an Indo-European language who invaded India from the northwest in the second millennium B.C.

Deccan plateau. The great tableland of Central India south of the Narbada River.

Domestication. The domestication of plants and animals involves the long-term modification of wild species under human control which results in new varieties. Thus, for example, there are heavy-yielding, drought-resistant varieties of grains that owe their existence to centuries of cultivation and seed selection by farmers.

Harappan culture. The earliest civilization of South Asia, so named from the type site, the ruins of the city of Harappa in the Panjab.

Lineage. A common-descent group, more specifically the descendants of a single ancestor usually reckoned through the male line of descent as in a patrilineage.

Loess upland. The region of high elevation and mostly rugged terrain in north China west of Fen River in central Shansi. Loess is a deposit of windblown soil found in great depth in parts of the upland.

Logograph. A written sign, often representing an object, which stands for a spoken word.

Lungshan. The place-name of a neolithic archaeological site in Shantung and, by extension, the designation of the Black Pottery culture, or culture phase.

Myths. Myths were dramatic retellings or reenactments of such great events as the creation of the world or the return of spring. Natural events were experienced as the acts of personified forces, and the human community participated in them through the myths and their associated ceremonial. Myths were also extended to human affairs such as the origin of communities, institutions, or customs.

Neolithic. Literally, the "new stone" age. This name was first given to cultures characterized by flaked or chipped stone tools that were then improved by grinding or polishing. Neolithic in later usage, however, has come to denote the period when food was first obtained by agriculture and husbandry, and metal tools and utensils were not yet in use.

Nomadism. Groups of people that move about at seasonal intervals and have no fixed habitation are nomadic. Nomads are ordinarily hunting or pastoral people, but they may also practice some agriculture.

Panjab. The land of the five rivers, the headwaters of the Indus, historically important as a transit zone between the Gangetic plain and Central Asia.

Pastoralism. The economy and way of life of societies that depend mainly on raising animals for subsistence. Pastoral peoples graze their livestock ordinarily on land not well suited to agriculture, but obtain agricultural products by trade or raiding.

Priest or priestess. In the most general terms a specialist in the performance of religious ceremonial or divination. Such a person is ordinarily recognized as being qualified by ordination, inheritance, or some outward sign of unusual spiritual powers.

Vedas. Religious hymns and texts dealing with both ritual and philosophical speculation transmitted for generations among the Aryans through memorization and recitation; the oldest sacred texts of Hinduism.

Yangshao. The place-name of a Neolithic archeological site in western Honan, and by extension the designation of the Painted Pottery culture, or culture phase, of the loess upland.

2

The Political Organization of Civilized Societies

The Political Organization of Civilized Societies

2334 B.C. to 400 B.C.

Early civilized societies were most often organized around religious institutions, and the social order was harmonized, sanctified, and expressed by religious ceremonial. Still at an early stage in their development, however, the civilized societies came to be politically organized in states. The nuclei around which they were now to be organized were kings, courts, and royal palaces instead of priests and temples. The transition from religious to political organization was, however, gradual and incomplete, with priest and temple continuing in some kind of cooperative relationship with the new rulers. The essential function of early kingship was military leadership, and accordingly the origins of kingship were associated with an increase in the incidence and scale of warfare and a growing emphasis on the fortification of cities and the construction of fortified frontiers. The early kings assumed other functions as well, such as the promotion of accepted social values by means of codified law and the judicial process, and provision for the general welfare by organizing such projects as the construction of flood control, irrigation, and transport systems. The most striking contrast between the state and the older religious form of organization, however, was that the state, by its origin and its essential nature, represented the society under its military aspect and mobilized for struggle. Politically organized societies therefore tended to expand by military and political means.

The first states made their appearance early in the literate, or historical, period, which means that the surviving documentation is scarce and difficult to interpret. Several processes may be suggested, however, as having been involved in the origins of political organization. As civilized societies developed in area, population, and wealth, they became increasingly differentiated among occupational and status groups and this increasing complexity undermined the religious sanctions of social order. At the same time, the expansion of the early civilized communities with their agricultural hinterlands brought them into conflict over the diminishing free resources of land and water. Moreover, a pastoral-nomadic "counterculture" emerged along the outer frontiers of the civilized world, and this gave rise to endemic conflict between farmers and herdsmen. For all these reasons, it became necessary for the civilized communities to establish military leaders, first temporarily and eventually hereditarily, to organize them for war.

In the three main Asian culture areas of Mesopotamia, northern India, and north China, state building proceeded rapidly, and warfare was more common and destructive. The consolidation of political power by successful states in each case led to the formation of great kingdoms such as those of Assyria, Magadha, and Ch'in, which laid the foundations for the first universal empires, the subject of a subsequent chapter.

2

PROCESSES

Internal and External Conflict

a. Social conflict
b. Cultural and stimulus diffusion
c. Conflict between steppe and sown
d. Warfare and the origins of militarism

The Formation of Monarchies

e. Political differentiation
f. Hereditary monarchy
g. Legal codification

PATTERNS

1. **The Political Organization of Mesopotamian Civilization in West Asia**

2. **The Political Organization of Aryan Civilization in South Asia**

3. **The Political Organization of Shang and Chou China**

2. POLITICAL ORGANIZATION

		1	2	3
	EGYPT	MESOPOTAMIA	SOUTH ASIA	CHINA
		Beginning of kingship, *lugal*		
	Old Kingdom 3000-2300, Dynasties 3-4			
2600 B.C.		Akkadian military domination, kings of Kish		
		Iron in Anatolia		
2400				
	First Intermediate Period, Dynasties 7-10	Sargon of Akkad, r. to 2279		
2200		Gutian invasions		
	Middle Kingdom 2050-1800, Dynasties 11-12	Ur III, 2117-2004, Neo-Sumerian Isin and Larsa, 2025-1763		
2000				
		Law codes, chariotry		
1800	Second Intermediate Period, Dynasties 13-17			
		Hammurabi, r. 1792-1750	Destruction of Harappan civilization; waves of Aryans enter India from the northwest	
1600		Kassite domination		

	New Kingdom 1565, Dynasties 18-20	Steel or iron in Anatolia? "Dark Age," no records		Shang Dynasty ca. 1600-1122
1400		Assyrian kingdom		Capital at Anyang 1401
			Era of events alluded to in the Vedas (chronology uncertain)	Chariotry
1200				
				Western Chou 1122-771
1000			Aryans move eastward into the Ganges basin	Feudal rule
		Aramaic script	Development of agriculture, clearing of forests, use of iron	
800		Kingdom of Urartu Cavalry widely used Assyrian expansion		Eastern Chou 771-256
			Spread of literacy	League of states 681
600		Assurbanipal, r. 668-627 Nebuchadnezzar II, r. 604-562 Chaldean domination		Irrigation, iron, law codes
400			Emergence of kingdoms and republics in northern India	Warring States 453-222
200				Ch'in unification of China 221

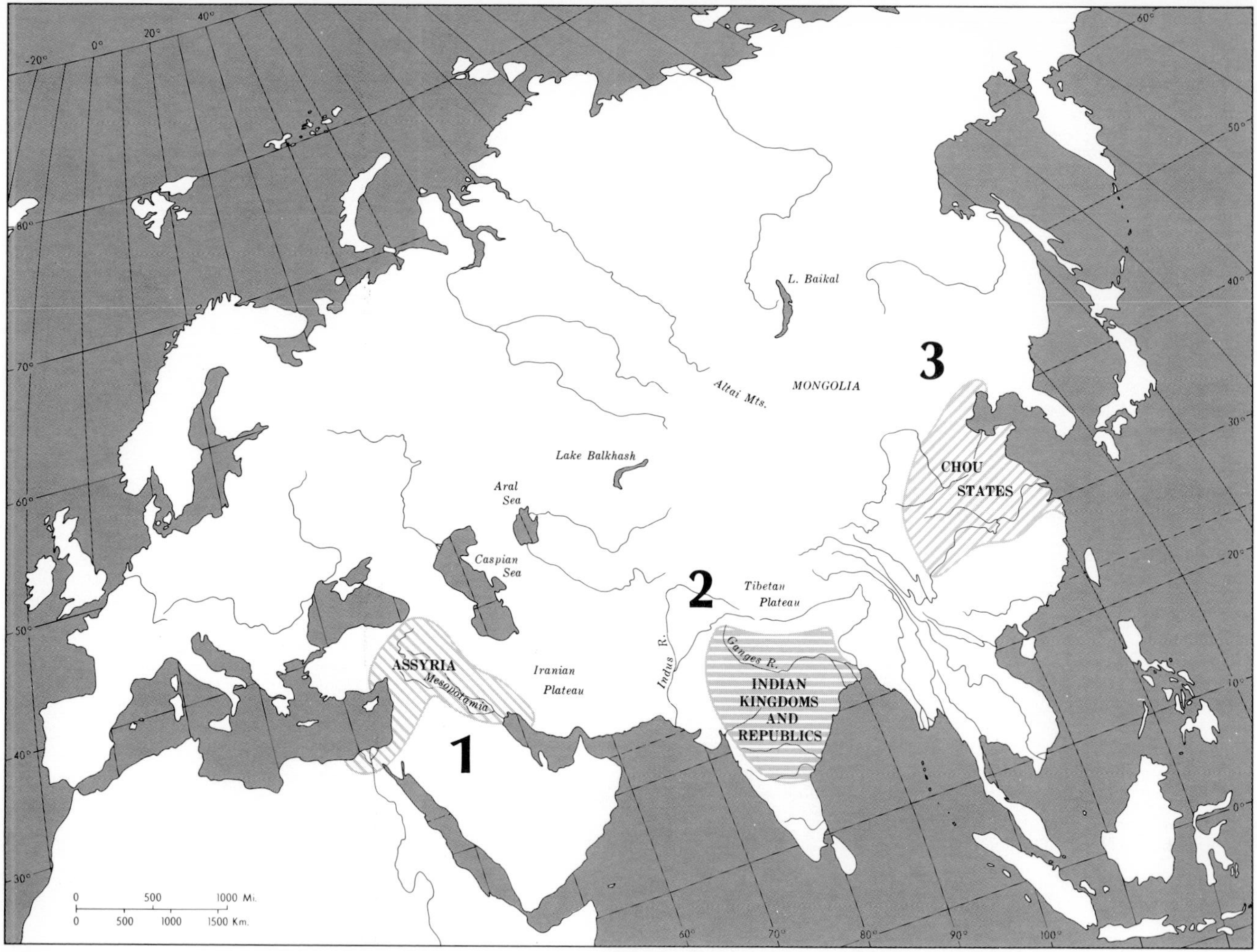

Map 9 The political organization of civilized societies

PROCESSES

The political organization of large societies under the authority of sovereigns occurred at an early stage in the development of civilization. Kingship became a permanent and hereditary institution, and sovereigns elaborated civil and military offices to give practical effect to their royal will. Material and human resources were mobilized for wars of conquest or defense, the power of the state was magnified by large-scale undertakings in transportation, irrigation, and flood control, and great kingdoms were raised on these foundations. From ancient times the state has undergone changes in form, ideology, scale, and intensity of application, but it has been in continuous existence, and is with us still.

THE PERIOD

This examination of the political organization of civilized peoples will fall within the period from 2334 to about 400 B.C. Specifically, it will begin in West Asia with the reign of Sargon I (2334-2279 B.C.), founder of the Akkadian dominion over all of Mesopotamia, and end with the fall of Assur, capital of the Assyrian state, to the Medes in 614 B.C. As outlying peoples transformed themselves culturally under Mesopotamian influences, new regimes were organized in the region by intruding militarists. The Assyrians were merely the last and most powerful in a series that spanned more than one and a half millennia. While many of the regimes were ephemeral and weakly organized, there were discernible tendencies over the long run toward more powerful organization and greater scale in area and population. Turning to South Asia, the Indian subcontinent, we are presented with a somewhat different course of development. About 1700 B.C. a shift of certain chariot-driving Indo-European peoples from Inner Asia, perhaps northern Iran, brought one of them, the Mitanni, into West Asia, where for a time in the middle of the second millennium they dominated northern Mesopotamia, and brought the other, the Aryans, into the Zagros region of southwestern Iran, the eastern extremity of the Iranian plateau, and southeastward into the Indus valley. Whereas the Mitanni marked a disruptive interlude in West Asian history, the Aryans supplanted the Indus Valley civilization and developed one of their own. The culture of Harappa and Mohenjo-daro can be said to have survived only underground, to some degree modifying the culture and religion of the intruders. The history of the period after the Aryan conquests until the fifth century B.C. must be reconstructed largely from oral literature preserved by rote memorization across successive generations. Even this material, however, offers evidence of the growth of kingdoms and the gradual reemergence of a new agricultural economy and new urban centers. This consideration of South Asia ends with the rise of the great kingdom of Magadha about 600 B.C. In East Asia, large-scale political organization was achieved by the Shang dynasty and extended by the Chou following its conquest of the Shang in 1122 B.C. The end of this period in the Chinese context will fall in the Warring States period, around 400 B.C. As in West and South Asia, the expansion of the Chinese culture area and the growth of increasingly powerful forms of political organization will be found to have occurred.

INTERNAL AND EXTERNAL CONFLICT

The formation of great political systems in antiquity may best be understood as arising from the growth of conflicts within and among societies. Societies became increasingly differentiated in economic classes and in status and occupational groups, and concentrations of wealth appeared both in the hands of private groups and in the temples and palaces. Social and economic conflicts became too intense and too complex to be reliably mediated and resolved by the old collective community organizations. Kings were able to strengthen their political authority by assuming the tasks of law and order: the powers of police, lawmaking, and justice. At the same time, the institution of kingship was strengthened by the increasing scale and destructiveness of wars among societies or states. Rulers engaged in wars of aggression either to enlarge their domains or to reduce their rivals to tributary status. The scale and intensity of political and military activity was enormously expanded by the diffusion of elements of civilized culture from the older urbanized regions to larger and larger areas. New kingdoms were formed on the widening frontiers of civilization and with this, new possibilities for aggrandizement were opened up. Finally, as the spread of civilized culture, with its agricultural and urban economic basis, approached its permanent ecological limits, where lack of water or the steep pitch of mountains made agriculture unrewarding, a new kind of frontier emerged, that between farmers and herders. Where farmers encroached on lands more suitable for the raising of sheep, horses, and cattle, others evolved the pastoral-nomadic way of life, specializing in stock raising and obtaining grain and other goods from the farmers and townsmen. The relationship between farmer and herder tended to be an antagonistic one, despite the trade that developed between their complementary economies. They struggled over the land and mounted raids on one another's territory. The pastoral peoples pioneered the development of chariot and cavalry warfare, were well supplied with horses, and used these advantages with devastating effect against the civilized societies. The rulers of the latter found in this another role to enhance their authority and prestige, that of defenders of civilization against the "barbarism" of the grasslands and forests.

a. Social Conflict

In the first chapter it was suggested that religious cults were generally helpful in resolving the tensions inherent in stratified society. But religious sanction of social order can be effective only insofar as there is a consensus on the sacred basis of the society. Civilized societies became increasingly complex. Village communities in the urban hinterlands might elaborate their own tenacious local cults; hereditary occupational groups, such as weavers or bronze casters, reinforced their community solidarity by developing their own protective religious beliefs and practices. The interaction of several large, urban-centered communities with one another brought different urban cults into conflict, requiring an accommodation of their different specific beliefs. While the ability of religious institutions to provide for social harmony was being weakened, social conflicts became more difficult to reconcile or to contain. Leading families, strong by reason of prestige and wealth, engaged in mutual rivalry, thereby precluding the possibility of stable oligarchic control. Moreover, population in older urban centers sometimes outgrew the land available to support and employ it, which resulted in the formation of a class of alienated and troublesome people on the margins of the society. These might be increased in number by the arrival of destitute pastoralists or other nonagricultural people driven from their old habitats. This, added to the entrenchment of rival occupational or ruling elements in the urban communities, undermined community solidarity and led to internal strife.

b. Cultural and Stimulus Diffusion

The areas in which civilizations began were necessarily small, but in this period they expanded rapidly. The growing population of farmers and townsmen gradually brought new lands under cultivation, which accounts for a part of this phenomenon. Equally or more significant were the processes by which elements of civilized culture influenced the development of widening circles of surrounding societies. While pockets of civilized society were appearing in a few narrow areas, they engaged the peoples around them in various forms of economic and cultural exchange. Where geographic settings permitted, the full range of agricultural and urban life was attained. Elsewhere, the scope of cultural influence was more restricted. Cultural diffusion takes place when a cultural trait, such as the ox-drawn plough or the potter's wheel, is adopted by one people from another. Certain conditions have to be met before it can occur, and it may spread rapidly or very slowly in the recipient culture, depending in part on the resistance it encounters. In order for a nonagricultural people to become farmers, for example, changes eventually have to appear in virtually the whole pattern of culture—in the social organization, religion, proprietary rights, housing construction, diet, etc. For such a transformation to occur at all, the society affected must already be disposed by its indigenous processes of change to move in that direction; or it must be strongly motivated, as by fear of famine. Stimulus diffusion, which is also a form of invention, is harder to prove historically because it involves the spread of an idea or principle. The most obvious examples include phonetic systems of writing, in which knowledge of one writing system inspired the invention of another one for use with a different language.

c. Conflict between Steppe and Sown

Pastoral nomadism was a way of life as highly developed and specialized in its way as was civilized society, and yet it presented the most striking contrasts to it. Where civilized society tended toward concentration of populations, the pastoralists were dispersed. The grasslands most often inhabited by the latter had a relatively low carrying capacity; a large area was necessary to support each animal. The herds had to be small enough to allow each animal to find sufficient grass in the occupied area, and the herds had to be far apart to prevent overgrazing. The effect of this was to make it necessary for the herdsmen to live in small, dispersed groups, usually families. Where the farmers and townsmen were virtually rooted in their habitations, the nomadic pastoralists were mobile. The scarcity of good grazing and seasonal changes in temperature and rainfall required the herdsmen to adopt cyclical patterns of migration, whether from valley to distant valley or from lower to higher slopes on a mountainside. These extreme traits of pure nomadic pastoralism were modified where there occurred, in various combinations, mixed economies of agriculture and husbandry and such other occupations as mining, iron working, and trapping. In terms of social organization, the extended family or clan was stronger and more persistent than it usually was among civilized peoples, and in place of territorial monarchies one finds tribes (associations of clans) or federations of tribes. Pastoral-nomadic societies were generally poor in material possessions and were physically hardened by the harsh conditions under which most of them lived.

Their way of life conferred certain military advantages on them vis-à-vis the sedentary peoples. The armies of the latter were helpless in the grasslands if they remained for any length of time, owing to the difficulty of maintaining lines of supply, so the pastoralists had little to fear if they could retreat deep into their own territory. On the other hand, the mobility of the pastoralists allowed them to concentrate large forces quickly for raids or occasionally even wars of conquest against sedentary enemies. Pastoral nomadism in its specialized form developed later than agriculture and in relation to it, combining its own supplies of meat and milk with the grain purchased or extorted from the farmers.

d. Warfare and the Origins of Militarism

Apart from small-scale and occasional raiding, warfare was primarily an activity of the civilized societies and their pastoral-nomadic neighbors. It implied more than simply large-scale violence. It also presupposed the institutional means for the mobilization of the resources of a society on a large scale, and this further presupposed the existence of specific cultural values and ideological justifications that supported the war-making enterprise, with all its costs and hazards. There had to be a government capable of identifying, recruiting or conscripting, training, and equipping soldiers. Even in the absence of a specific military class, which occurred later, armies had to be assembled, organized, and led. Defensive

2.1

2.2

The development of chariot warfare was characteristic of both the chronic armed conflict that accompanied the evolution of political organization and the social tension associated with the emergence of kingship and ruling classes. Hunting and fighting from chariots were favorite occupations of the nobility. As these illustrations make clear, a comparable military technology was shared across Eurasia.

2.1 Egyptian chariot drawn from a bas-relief in the tomb on Thut-mose IV. Source: Howard Carter and Percy E. Newberry, from *Tomb of Thoutmosis IV,* Westminster, Archibald Constable and Co., 1904.

2.2 Assyrian bas-relief, one of a series depicting the heroic deeds of Assurnasirpal II (883-859). Horse-drawn chariots are prominent in these scenes of war and hunting. The king is shown here hunting lions from his chariot. Courtesy: Trustees of the British Museum.

2.3 Drawing of Aryan chariot based upon literary evidence from the *Rigveda.* No remains or contemporary representations of an actual Aryan chariot are known to have survived. Courtesy: Penguin Books Ltd., from Stuart Piggott, *Prehistoric India.*

2.3

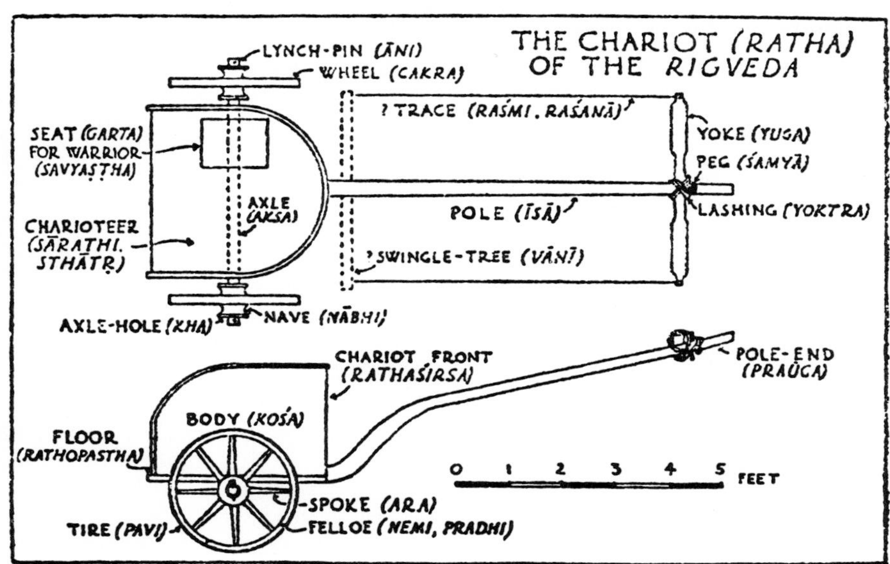

2.4 Shang dynasty chariot sacrifice with two horses and driver (partially visible behind). This well-preserved specimen was excavated in 1972 near Anyang. The chariot is an improved verşion of a type that first appeared in West Asia around 1600 B.C. The practice of chariot sacrifice exemplifies the combination of war and religion in early Chinese political organization. Source: *K'ao Ku,* July 1972, Plate 2, No. 2.

preparations had to be made, such as the construction of forts and city walls and the accumulation of reserve supplies of food. On the side of ideology, the cult of the military hero and the creation and preservation of epic literature appeared in association with the institutionalization of warfare. The development of war and kingship were mutually reinforcing. As military emergencies became more frequent and more acute, there was greater need for kings as the persons permanently responsible, directly or by delegation, for the provision of defense. On the other hand, the king could increase his own authority and prestige by victorious leadership in wars that he himself provoked, which contributed to the frequency of wars. In extreme cases, as near the end of our period, one may find instances of militarism, the domination of a society by rulers and officials with a military orientation.

THE FORMATION OF MONARCHIES

e. Political Differentiation

Government is common to all human communities, whether of clan, village, tribe, or city organization, but the state involves something more than mere government, and it appeared later in the historical record. In the first chapter, for example, evidence was cited for various forms of government in early civilized communities, but they were without the clear differentiation of a specific political role and function. The state may be said to have existed when two conditions were satisfied: when authority over war and justice was vested in a permanent institution, usually a monarchy, and when the ruler had at his disposal enough coercive force, military or police, to compel obedience to his authority if it should be challenged. Permanence was indicated by hereditary rulership within a dynasty, as well as by continuity (subject to modification) of the symbols, ceremonial forms, and ideological sanctions of the ruler's authority. The war-making authority was indicated by the reliability of the means by which the ruler was able to assemble an army and by his freedom to make decisions relative to war and peace. Authority to uphold justice in the relations among his subjects was commonly reflected in attempts by the ruler to draw up general principles and procedures for the resolution of disputes and the punishment of crimes.

Several implications of this definition should be noted. Since political authority had now become specific and demonstrable, it was essential that the ruler be able to distinguish precisely between those who were subject to his authority and those who were not. This was often done on a territorial basis, so that all persons within certain boundaries were subjects. From this arose the idea that when an army of one state crossed the territory of another, the "sovereignty" of the latter had been violated. But the distinction could be made on nonterritorial grounds as well. Where boundaries were difficult to establish, as among the pastoral nomads, the ruler-subject relationship depended on a formal acknowledgement of personal authority on the part of the nobility, as in a feudal system. The state also implied an increase in scale over that of earlier forms of government, such that the ruler could not deal with all his subjects directly and face to face even if he chose to. Although the state implied the differentiation of a specific political function within the social order, it was not necessarily *secular* in the sense of nonreligious. Indeed, in the period we deal with in this chapter, political ideology had a strongly religious orientation.

f. Hereditary Monarchy

The monarch in the setting of his court and his capital symbolized the political community over which he ruled. As leader vis-à-vis other states, he held the fate of the whole society in his hands, and he represented the last court of justice for his subjects. His authority, his ability to impose his own will upon the society, was subject to practical limitations, however. These included his dependence on officials for information, advice, and the execution of his policies and the restraints imposed by ideology. If the monarchy was traditionally justified by its commitment to justice and the security of the whole society, then the ruler's failure to provide these, or his pursuit of contradictory aims, might be taken as legitimate grounds for his overthrow. The sovereign, therefore, had to refrain from playing the tyrant if he wished to be secure on his throne. One way in which monarchical power was made more secure was by making it hereditary. By this means, the number of legitimate rivals was reduced to those near relatives who qualified under the rules of succession. Another buttress of monarchy was the elaboration of a splendid court and capital city. If the city was unrivaled by any other in wealth and population, and if the ruler's palace was unrivaled within the city by any other household, it was easier for him to command the followers and the resources needed for his defense.

g. Legal Codification

Closely associated with the formation of kingdoms was the royal practice of compiling systematic catalogs of basic laws or principles. This did not constitute legal codification in the modern sense of the organization and standardization of existing legal practice, but aimed at stating permanently and authoritatively the goals of the monarchy as guardian of justice in the society.

The subject of Chapter 3 will be the ideological reactions against the increasingly harsh and burdensome domination of civilized societies by great royal regimes, which were usually more committed to their own aggrandizement than to the welfare of their subjects. The systematic search for new ethics and new intellectual orientations was represented by a remarkable cluster of thinkers who were nearly contemporaneous around 500 B.C. The present chapter will depict the social, political, and cultural changes that culminated in the unsettling and creative age in which they lived.

PATTERNS

1. THE POLITICAL ORGANIZATION OF MESOPOTAMIAN CIVILIZATION IN WEST ASIA

Urban society had developed in Sumer by the middle of the fourth millennium B.C. and by the early third millennium had spread across the central floodplain from the confluence of the Tigris and Euphrates upstream to the vicinity of Akkad. The original pattern of settlement was one of strings of cities, with their associated fields and villages, following the major river channels across the plain. Between these urban clusters were areas of grasslands and desert. The cities were oligarchic communities of landowning families. Their massive temples symbolized their aspiration to communal order and regulated relations between the cities and the gods that watched over them. Public affairs of a secular sort were managed by citizen assemblies, which were convened as circumstances required. Although there was extensive trade among the cities, there was little political interaction, and wars were uncommon and relatively insignificant. Then, between the beginning of the Early Dynastic period, around 2900 B.C., and the reign of Sargon of Akkad some five hundred years later, a major transformation occurred: the organization of Mesopotamian society in territorial kingdoms and the commitment of resources in men and goods to the pursuit of politics and war. From Sargon's time to the conquest of Babylon in 539 B.C. by the rising Achaemenid universal state of Iran, the scale of political organization was vastly expanded and new techniques of domination and control were instituted.

These changes in scale and in form of organization were very largely the consequences of growth in several senses of the word. In Mesopotamia itself, population continued to grow while the best land was brought under irrigation and the further expansion of intensive agriculture became increasingly costly. The greater scarcity of land reinforced patterns of social stratification, limiting the freedom and economic opportunity of many. The control over land and water tended to develop into political authority, and contributed to the growth of states. In another sense of growth, the field of political and military interaction in West Asia expanded enormously, as the peoples of the surrounding grasslands and mountains were drawn into cultural and trading relationships with the cities of the plain. The ambitions of would-be conquerors among both the civilized peoples and their neighbors on the frontiers expanded accordingly, and insofar as they were successful their kingdoms grew ever larger.

THE PERIOD

The long period from 2900 to 539 B.C. may conveniently be divided into three parts: from 2900 B.C. to the career of Sargon (2334-2279 B.C.); from Sargon to the Dark Age (ca. 1600–ca. 1400 B.C.); and from the Dark Age to the Achaemenid domination in the sixth century B.C. During the first of these three periods, hereditary kingship made its initial appearance. During the second, the functions of kingship were enlarged and the organization of government greatly elaborated. At the beginning of the third period, the expansion of civilized society and the spread of its influence brought new actors, peoples from the remote northern and eastern frontiers, onto the Mesopotamian stage. Under their domination there may have been a temporary abandonment of the durable clay tablets in favor of more perishable materials, because there is an almost total gap of about two hundred years in the documentary record. It is in this sense that the period may be called a "dark age." After Mesopotamia reemerged into the light of history in the fourteenth century B.C., Babylonia, the old land of Sumer and Akkad, was politically overshadowed in the north by the Assyrian kingdom. Assyria, in its largest expansion, set a new standard for scale of political organization in the seventh century by bringing under its rule not only Mesopotamia and Syria, but for a time, at least, even Palestine, the Sinai peninsula, and Egypt as well.

Periods of Political Organization in West Asia
Early Dynastic 2900-2334 B.C.
Kings of Kish 2700-2600
First Dynasty of Ur 2600
Sargon to the Dark Age 2334-1600 B.C.
Dynasty of Akkad 2334-2154
Third Dynasty of Ur 2112-2004
Isin and Larsa 2017-1763
First Dynasty of Babylon 1894-1595
Dark Age to fall of Assur 1600-614 B.C.
Dark Age 1600-1400
Kassite Dynasty ?-1157
Assyrian expansion 883-627

The Beginnings of Sumerian Kingship before Sargon

In Sumerian society, land was the most important form of property and the principal source of income. In the Early Dynastic period, ownership of land had become highly concentrated in large estates. The largest of these were the great manorial establishments of the temples, but there were wealthy private estates as well, which were the property of the leading citizens. Ordinary free citizens, or commoners, might also own private plots. Lands belonging to the estates were cultivated by peasants in various states of dependency, either as rent-paying tenants or as serfs. The larger estates, especially those of the temples, had their own administrative staff and supplemented their agricultural income by operating workshops with dependent artisans and laborers. Landless individuals or families within the city were normally absorbed as dependents of the estates, whether as peasants in the fields or as artisans or laborers living in the city. Domestic slavery also existed, but does not seem to have been economically important. People who could not find a place in the private or temple economy of the city might subsist for a time on charity, but would soon have to move away. This pattern proved extremely stable because it prevented the formation of a large, uncontrolled proletariat within the city and also averted the formation of an open market economy and a merchant class. Produce entered the city mainly as rent or manorial deliveries from the fields owned by estates and was distributed by the owners among their dependents. Similarly, the absorption of artisans in temple and domestic workshops reduced the need for trading in handicrafts. When goods were exchanged within the city, the transactions were subject to regulation and control by public authority.

There was, however, an extensive trade among cities and between the cities collectively and the surrounding peoples of grassland and mountain. Stone, metallic ores, and timber had to be obtained in exchange for grain, textiles, or other finished goods. But even this trade was powerless to break down the urban social order, because it was carried on by professionals who served as agents for the temples and private establishments. They, in turn, dealt with counterparts who were similarly controlled. Prices, quantities, and standards were established by contract or custom, and the traders subsisted on wages or commissions rather than on price variations in a market. Moreover, when outsiders came to do business, they were required to live in the harbor quarter, outside the city proper. Successful traders appear to have moved up into the city to join the older gentry. Thus it was that although the cities of Mesopotamia were tied into a vast network of long-distance trade, the land-based manorial establishments remained intact and kept control of the city.

While the heads of temple and private establishments were ordinarily competent to govern their dependents, some kind of city government was required to manage common activities and to keep the peace among the citizens. For these purposes, the citizens gathered from time to time in a civic assembly. The probable exclusion of women and of unfree persons such as serfs and slaves reduced membership in the assembly, and representatives of gentry families played a leading role in its deliberations and decisions. Some assemblies were bicameral, indicating a formal subdivision of the citizens into gentry and commoners. In the course of time, final authority of the community tended to pass from the general assembly to the higher chamber. The assembly's powers were important and pervasive within the community. Serious crimes were judged by it, the death penalty was inflicted, and disputes over property were arbitrated. Ordinary administrative functions were performed both by the temple staff, which had the authority to establish norms and standards, and by certain officers, such as the *ensi,* who had charge of the city's collective agricultural tasks, irrigation, and public works. The importance of the citizen assembly as a focus of civic identity is revealed by the fact that one of its functions was to elect the *en,* or "consort"—wife or husband—of the principal god or goddess. The responsibility of the divine spouse was to ensure, by his or her charismatic powers, the fertility of the fields and the abundance of the harvests.

The temple was certainly an institution as old as the city, and the assembly may have been just as old, growing out of the governance of the preurban agricultural clan village. The institution of kingship in Sumer was of much later origin, first appearing in a rudimentary form around 3000 B.C. Kings of the Early Dynastic period were sometimes called *en* and sometimes *lugal*. The origins of kingship are therefore to be sought in these two municipal offices. The *ens* as male consorts of city goddesses sometimes assumed administrative functions in addition to the basic cultic role. Originally elected for a limited term, the *ens* of some cities assumed responsibilities of such importance that they were able to make the position permanent and hereditary. In cities protected by male deities, however, the chief living consort was a priestess and was not qualified for military leadership. This role was given to the *lugal,* who was elected by the assembly as a war leader to defend the city in a time of emergency. He had no connection with the temple, no ritual function, and was selected for his military ability and for his membership in a powerful patrician family rich enough to provide men and equipment.

The transformation of the temporary offices of *en* and *lugal* into the institution of kingship is at the heart of the evolution of the political organization of Sumerian society. First, the kings made their office hereditary and claimed to have received their authority from their tutelary gods. Divine sanction was affirmed by annual consecration of the king by priests in the main temple, and divine attributes of the royal person were believed to be displayed in the radiance, or "halo," that surrounded him. Victory in battle and the prosperity of the people were seen as additional proofs of the king's enjoyment of the favor of the gods. The kings thereby wrested sovereign rule of the city from the hands of the assembly, which had sanctioned the offices of *en* and *lugal* in the first place. Second, their assumption of sovereign independence allowed them to pursue goals of their own choosing, subject to little or no effective control by their citizen-subjects. This in turn encouraged the kings to extend their effective power far beyond the limits of the city-state by means of war and conquest.

Several factors contributed to this development. In the beginning the most important was the fact that the private and temple estates had a limited capacity to absorb unattached individuals and families. Consequently there developed in the grasslands and desert areas around and between the irrigated lands a shifting population of herdsmen, poor farmers, and marauders. They included people who had drifted in from the Syrian and Arabian deserts, as well as others who had abandoned the cities. Not only did they not belong to any city, but they were positively hostile to urban life and its values. They represented, in effect, an antiurban counterculture, attached to their freedom and proud of their skill in warfare. The presence of this threat in the countryside made it necessary for the cities to look to their defenses. But the Sumerian cities were so strongly oriented toward agriculture and trade that they were not at all eager to take up the challenge. The presence of a growing number of Semitic names along the *lugals* suggests that the city leaders were inclined to turn to the same alien element to protect them. Thus, although the cities seem to have been little troubled by internal social strife such as might give rise to a strong political system, significant conflicts did develop within the larger context of Sumerian society as a whole.

A second factor in the transition from urban community to territorial state was the expansion of the Mesopotamian cultural area, principally into the north. The northern limits of the central plain, where the Tigris and Euphrates approach each other, were a Sumerian cultural frontier region around 3000 B.C., and the new cities located there such as Kish and Babylon were growing in wealth and commercial importance. But this region was especially vulnerable to the infiltration of desert peoples from the west and north. By the middle of the third millennium it was becoming as much Akkadian as Sumerian in language. Although the newcomers were heavily influenced by Sumerian culture, adopted intensive agriculture, and organized their communities on much the same political and religious principles, they appear to have retained something of a regional identity in opposition to the older cities of the south. Thus it was that this mid-Mesopotamian region came to be known as Akkad, in contrast to the land of Sumer, downstream. Likewise, on the southeastern frontier of Sumer, the land of Elam, where there was an urban society almost as old as that of Sumer itself, developed its own regional cultural traditions under Sumerian influence. Gradually and sporadically at first, these regional frontiers became zones of political and military conflict, with Kish becoming a political center in Akkad and Susa in Elam. Under these circumstances the scale of political action grew to include all of

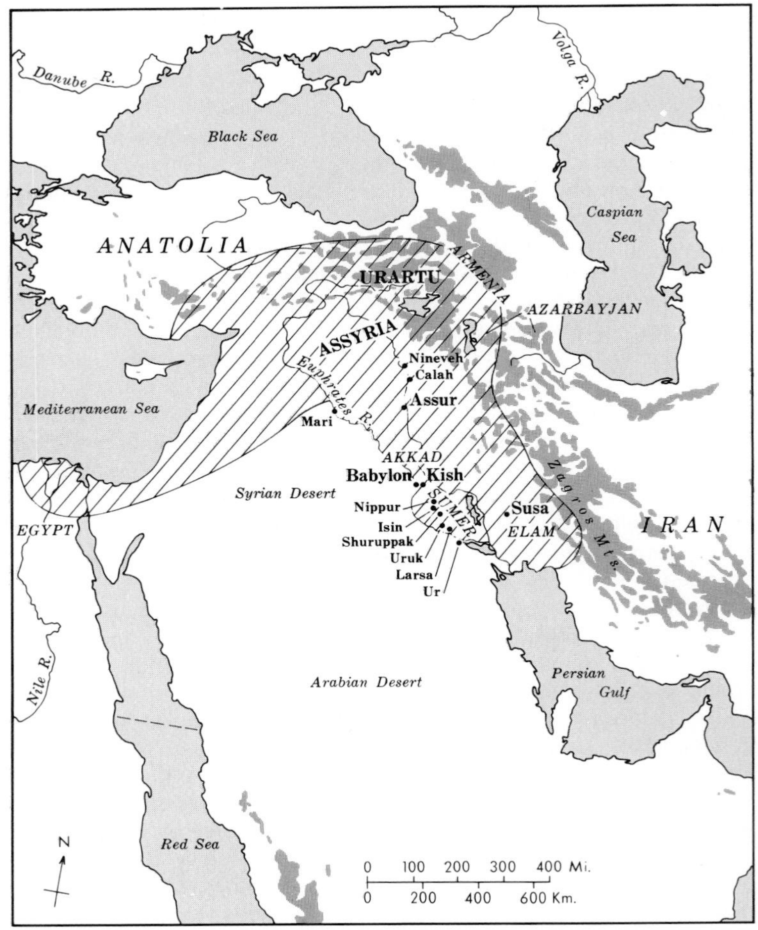

Map 10 Assyria, seventh century B.C.

Mesopotamia and western Iran. The dyed-in-the-wool provincialism of the Sumerian cities made it difficult for them to cooperate on a regional scale, but the attempt was occasionally made. The first indication of Sumerian solidarity appears faintly in the tradition, current in the Early Dynastic period, that accorded a uniquely sacred status to the city of Nippur and its cult of the mighty and warlike god Enlil. The temple of Enlil may have served as a place of assembly for representatives of the cities to discuss problems of regional scope and even to elect a common king to organize for collective defense. Kings and conquerors faithful to Sumerian tradition were careful to legitimize their authority by honoring Enlil. Perhaps a more important, and certainly a better documented, factor in the development of kingship was the attempt by the Akkadian kings of Kish around 2600 B.C. to establish their control over all Mesopotamia. Time and again they sent their fleets down the rivers to pillage and subjugate the great cities. Although they may have attempted to make their control permanent by establishing garrisons, their organization was ineffectual and the cities soon reasserted their independence. From this time on, however, warfare was frequent, if not continuous, and the kings, as the organizers of defense or attack, were able to assert more easily their military dominance throughout the region. This also was the period in which it became usual for cities to surround themselves with fortifications and for all who could do so to crowd within the walls.

The governments of the early kings were patrimonial in the sense of being an extension of the royal household. In many instances, at least, they were also in some sense foreign to the cities they ruled. Both these facts help to account for the instability of Sumerian kingship. With regard to the first point, the meaning of *lugal*, "great householder," is suggestive. Royal officials were identified as "slaves" on their seals of office, which indicated at least ideally a relationship of total dependence vis-à-vis the ruler. Moreover, officials were often given such domestic titles as cupbearer or musician, whatever their real functions may have been. This patrimonial form of rule accounts for the otherwise inexplicably large numbers of individuals listed in domestic-service categories in palace records at Shuruppak, for example. Also, as the institution of kingship developed, the kings themselves were often not deeply rooted even in their capital cities. They might have come as outsiders in the first place, with their personal followings, and they commonly claimed that authority had been granted them by a divine authority superior to that of their capital city, such as Nippur's Enlil, or Inanna of Kish. They recruited new followers wherever they could, bringing them in from other cities. Much of their military manpower was also recruited at large, and their great personal estates made it unnecessary for them to depend on local taxes. Another and very important source of the king's financial independence was the accumulation of war booty resulting from successful campaigns. Under these circumstances the old assemblies lost ground to the growing royal power, and they retained only a limited authority, mainly judicial, although they had to share even this function with the king and his officers. Many more cities were not the seats of royal palaces but were ruled by officials sent out from the capital city. For them the king's authority was even more obviously alien, and therefore resented. Thus it was that the governments of the early kings had shallow political roots in urban society and were easily destroyed by military defeat or overthrow by palace coups.

Kingship and the State from Sargon to the Dark Age: 2334-1600 B.C.

Sargon, founder of the dynasty of Akkad, is more a legendary than a historical figure. Although one might wish that his rule were better documented, his prominent place in West Asian cultural tradition is sufficient measure of his importance. His glorious image, as shaped by the makers of his legend, became a standard and a model in northern Mesopotamia for more than a thousand years after his time. Like the kings of Kish before them, Sargon and his heirs maintained a military domination over Sumer and Akkad from their Akkadian capital, but their conquests reached farther and made a more enduring impression.

Before the time of Sargon, the upper marches of Mesopotamia (later called Assyria) were already settled by large numbers of Akkadians, who were assimilating the older culture of the farthest outposts of Mesopotamian civilization, such as those at Mari, Assur, and Nineveh. Thus the Moses-like legend of Sargon's Akkadian origins was apocryphal but poetically just, in having him abandoned by his mother to float down the Euphrates to Kish, where he was saved and brought up by a poor gardener. Under the protection of the goddess Ishtar (Sumerian Inanna), guardian of Kish, he became a cupbearer in the service of the king. Owing to a ritual fault on the part of the king, Sargon broke with him and founded a new city at Akkad. Sargon's founding a new city was probably a historical fact and set a precedent that was successfully emulated by Amorite and Assyrian rulers in later times. The new city was occupied by Akkadian followers under his control, and, unlike the Sumerian and Akkadian kings before him, Sargon did not have to live as the guest of a city with an ancient and parochial tradition. With an immense palace entourage of more than five thousand, he began the transition from patrimonial to bureaucratic administration and financed his government by taxation. In an expedition to the south he captured the mayor of Uruk, who had claimed with some exaggeration to be the ruler of the entire world. Sargon then brought his captive to Nippur, where he accepted appointment by the god Enlil to supreme rulership and brought the mayor before the god as a trophy. Sargon then completed the conquest of Sumer and established his control over Assyria and Elam as well.

Invasions by Amorites from the north and Gutians from the Zagros broke up the Akkadian kingdom around 2200 B.C., hardly a century after its founding. The Gutian invasion was a new and shattering experience for the cities of Sumer, because never before had they been conquered by a people so different in culture. The Gutians were representative of the large-scale pastoral-nomadic societies that were then forming beyond the frontiers of civilized society, and their conquest of southern Mesopotamia was a prelude to the Dark Age that was soon to follow. Roused to a new sense of their collective identity, the Sumerian cities under the leadership of a king of Uruk drove out the Gutians and thereby made possible the reunification of Sumer and Akkad under the Third Dynasty of Ur (2112-2004 B.C.). To the grandeur of the royal tradition of Sargon, the Third Dynasty joined a characteristically Sumerian bureaucratic administration and brought the art of government to a new level of effectiveness. The rule of Ur ended spectacularly in the destruction of that city by an Elamite invasion, and until the reign of Hammurabi (1792-1750 B.C.), Mesopotamia was once again divided among a number of states, the most important of which were the kingdoms of Isin and Larsa, ruled by Sumerian and Amorite kings, respectively. The Amorite Hammurabi and his heirs in their capital in Babylon revived the Sargonid tradition of northern domination and maintained it until Mesopotamia passed under the control of Hurrian and Kassite newcomers around 1600 B.C..

Pious Sumerians blamed the eventual destruction of the Akkadian kingdom on the sacrilegious conduct of Naram-Sin, Sargon's third heir. According to the traditional account, Naram-Sin caused himself to be addressed as God of Akkad in violation of sanctified practice, and in a war with Nippur he destroyed Enlil's temple. The offended god then avenged this transgression by sending the Gutian invaders into Mesopotamia. Apart from the explanation offered by the legend, the Akkadian kings appear to have failed in at least two important respects. Succession to the throne was badly managed, with several reigns terminated by palace coups. In the absence of an orderly transition of authority, the state was vulnerable to attack at the beginning of each reign. The other obvious difficulty lay in the control over the cities of the south. Akkadian rule was resented by the Sumerian cities, and they had to be conquered again by each of the Akkadian kings. This may have been due in part to the fact that the Akkadians were perceived as aliens. They had long been present in Sumerian society and had had a share in its formation, but the dynasty of Sargon and his heirs changed the terms of the cultural issue by fostering the development and official use of an Akkadian written language, using an adapted cuneiform system. This, and the translation of parts of the Sumerian literary heritage into Akkadian and later into Babylonian and Assyrian, meant that even while appropriating much of the Sumerian cultural tradition, the Akkadians and the others were turning the tables on their hosts and requiring them eventually to master the new languages. The Akkadian rulers also acquired landed property in the conquered cities and distributed it among their followers, thereby establishing a pattern of colonialism. No less provocative was the practice of transporting people from their native places to other sites, where they might be settled as soldiers or workers. It may be significant that while the cities of the south revolted with great regularity, those of Sargon's homeland in the Akkadian north appear to have accepted readily the authority of the court in Akkad.

For all the bitterness with which they were remembered in Mesopotamian literature, the Gutians left little enduring cultural impact on the region. Indeed, by breaking the Akkadian control, they may have facilitated the strong revival of Sumerian art and literature that culminated during the succeeding period. Of all the cities of Sumer, Uruk, ancient home of the sky god, An, was especially suited to the role of leader in the expulsion of the Gutians. But seven years after Utukhegal, king of Uruk, had made that city the capital of a unified Sumer and Akkad, he was displaced by one of his governors, who then proceeded to found the Third Dynasty of Ur. The second king of the dynasty, Shulgi, appears from the documents of his reign to have been a creative administrator and bureaucrat. To strengthen his political control he personally appointed a great number of officials not only as governors of regions or as mayors (ensi) of subject cities, but even as managers of temple workshops. Records were kept in minute detail, and the weights and measures Shulgi adopted for his state remained standard throughout Mesopotamia until the Achaemenid period. The impulse toward clarification and standardization was also reflected in one of the early attempts at codification of law. In one respect, however, the Ur kings did violence to Sumerian tradition: they claimed divine status. They may have done so in order to justify their practice of appointing the *ensi* of other cities. The *ensi,* originally the communal managers of agricultural work, were regarded as divinely appointed city officials. Had they been appointed instead by mere mortal rulers, their authority might well have been questioned, so the kings claimed divinity in order to avoid this difficulty. But for all their skill, the Ur rulers were generally on the defensive on their eastern and northern frontiers. The Amorites, now following on the heels of the Akkadians, were settling in the middle region of Mesopotamia. The fourth king of the Ur dynasty was driven to the desperate and unsuccessful expedient of constructing a great wall 170 miles in length across the valley not far above Babylon, terminating in a fort on high ground at each end. The wall was easily flanked, however, and soon the Amorites were moving downstream again. In the last reign, Hurrians, newcomers to the Zagros, and Elamites entered the plain from the east and Ur was destroyed by the latter.

The transition in political organization to territorial kingdoms and from Sumerian to Semitic formulations of Mesopotamian culture culminated in the Hammurabi dynasty, or First Dynasty of Babylon. The two centuries of the Isin-Larsa period, from the end of the Third Dynasty of Ur to the conquests of Hammurabi, were marked by the last literary expressions of Sumerian tradition, including the law code of Lipit-Ishtar, and by the last supplement, with the dynasty of Isin, to the Sumerian king list. At the same time, the establishment of Amorite kingdoms in several cities, including Larsa and Babylon, reflected the acculturation of the western Semitic Amorites to urban Mesopotamia and their assumption of the role of perpetuators of the indigenous civilization. Thereafter, literary Sumerian rapidly became a dead language, used by scribes for the copying and transmission of ancient texts.

Hammurabi was the sixth in a line of obscure Amorite rulers of Babylon. His father began the expansion of their kingdom by conquests in the south. The decline of Assyrian power in the north provided Hammurabi with the opportunity to extend his power in that direction. At its greatest extent, his First Dynasty of Babylon dominated Syria and approached the Mediterranean, as well as controlling most of Mesopotamia, although the far south and the region of Elam retained their independence. The rule of Babylon was widely resisted, however, both north and south, and even Hammurabi late in his reign emulated the practice of Ur by constructing a long wall for the protection of the capital region. Thus the frontier between Mesopotamia and the Syrian steppe and desert reasserted itself, with Amorites first being walled out by the Sumerians, then themselves walling out their newly arrived relations from the West. In the later political tradition of the Assyrian north, Hammurabi shared honors with Sargon, whose work of conquest and organization he had revived and carried forward. But he is most commonly remembered in recent times for his legal code, an almost complete copy of which was found in the Elamite city of Susa, far from his capital. Comparison with surviving fragments of older codes does not suggest that this one was innovative.

Hammurabi's code was reproduced in many copies for distribution to his officials, who were to be guided by them in their administration of justice. The 282 articles reflect major preoccupations and current attitudes towards justice in Babylon. Agriculture is strongly emphasized in defining mutual rights and obligations between landowner and tenant and between landowner and hired laborer. Common interest in production is acknowledged in penalties for failing to cultivate the land in one's charge and for causing damage to the fields of others by not maintaining dykes and ditches in good order. Commercial relations, credit, and marital relations are also covered. In crimes of violence, it is made clear that the relative status—gentry, commoner, or slave—of the individuals involved is to be taken into consideration. Crimes committed against persons of lower rank are less severely punished. The readiness to resort to the death penalty for many forms of theft suggests the intense interest in security of property that must have prevailed among the upper classes. The role of the king and his officers in maintaining peace and order within a stratified society is thus implicit in the code. The king did not, however, claim his own person to be the source of law and justice. The rules of law were held to be contained in the totality of cosmic principles, called *kittum,* and guaranteed by the sun god, Shamash (Sumerian An), who was especially concerned with justice. The king was understood simply to receive the law from Shamash and make it known to his officers and subjects.

As written Sumerian became a dead language, Akkadian began to give way to the closely related Old Babylonian, which was eventually to be the classical language of Mesopotamia. Over the long period from the time of Sargon to the Dark Age, the major mythological, epic, and historical texts assumed their definitive form. They represent a late and probably self-conscious reshaping of earlier tradition, which was genuinely attested to only in a fragmentary way by early Sumerian tablets. The mythological literature contains elements of the oldest strata of Mesopotamian culture, and by projecting the ancient social order into the "history" of the gods, it provides information about the institution of the civic assembly and the origins of kingship. The epics, of which the *Gilgamesh* is now the best known, were the product of a somewhat later time and represent conditions of the Early Dynastic period and later. Here, the cult of the warrior hero became a major theme for the first time. *Gilgamesh,* to be sure, gains in interest by introducing with power and sensitivity the universal existential dilemma of human mortality. Historical literature was uninspired, consisting of terse and generally uninformative chronologies. The Sumerian king list, however, which was completed near the beginning of the Third Dynasty of Ur, is interesting in that it assumed that Mesopotamia had always been governed by a single monarch, and accordingly it assembled the king lists of all states, including the many that had existed simultaneously, and arranged them in a single series stretching back into the remote past. This error not only reveals the Sumerians' distorted view of their own history, but also shows how firmly they were now committed to the principle of a single monarchy over the old city-states. This whole literary corpus, by the end of the First Dynasty of Babylon, had assumed the status of a classical heritage and would be carefully preserved under royal patronage until the coming of the Achaemenids.

From the Dark Age to the Achaemenid Empire

From about 1600 B.C., Mesopotamia was affected by a further expansion of the West Asian cultural area, which took the form of the development of new regional civilizations on the Mesopotamian frontiers and under Mesopotamian influence. This in turn may be explained in part by an unprecedented large-scale movement of peoples of mixed pastoral-nomadic and agricultural economies out of the grasslands of Central Asia in all directions. Anatolia was settled by the Hittites and the Luvians. The Hittites, in eastern Anatolia, developed a distinctive urban civilization using a cuneiform script for one of its writing systems and until the thirteenth century B.C. maintained a powerful kingdom bordering on northern Syria. The Iranians moved southward, gradually settling among the villagers of the Iranian plateau and the Zagros Mountains. As early as the Third Dynasty of Ur, Hurrian groups entered Syria and Mesopotamia from the east, where they assimilated readily to the indigenous culture and added their own language to the growing list of those written in cuneiform script. Around 1600 B.C., Mitannians entered Syria from the east and established a kingdom around the headwaters of the Tigris. At the same time, Kassites descended from the Zagros and founded the dynasty that reigned at least nominally over Mesopotamia until the twelfth century B.C.. From about 900 to 600 B.C. a kingdom was formed in Urartu (Kingdom of Van) on the northern frontier of Assyria. The Urartians also adopted a cuneiform script in place of an earlier one of their own invention. These movements of peoples associated with the outward drift from the Central Asian steppes brought into West Asia new techniques of horse chariotry and, from about the ninth century B.C., cavalry warfare. In self-defense, the indigenous peoples of the area adopted the new methods. There were other migrations as well, including the one that brought the Hyksos along the eastern Mediterranean coast and into Egypt, where they established a new kingdom. From about 1300 B.C., the Arameans began settling in Syria and subsequently moved down into Mesopotamia. The Arameans, around 1000 B.C., adopted an alphabetic script derived from the Phoenician script. This writing was so much more efficient than the cuneiform that even in Mesopotamia it began to displace the indigenous system, at least for everyday business and administrative uses. These displacements and fusions of peoples and cultures should not be perceived as catastrophic collisions, however; they seem, rather, to have occurred piecemeal and over sufficiently long periods of time to permit cultural and political adjustments to take place. Their principal effect was to create a much wider civilized world, extending from the Mediterranean across Syria and Iran to northwest India.

It was within this great cosmopolitan world that the Assyrian kingdom emerged in the fourteenth century B.C. and carried forward the political and cultural traditions of Mesopotamia. The sacred city of the Assyrians, Assur, was named for their principal god. Assur was situated on the banks of the Tigris and controlled one of the main trade routes between the Persian Gulf and Anatolia. The city was ruled from Babylonia by Sargonic governors from about 2300 to 2000 B.C. Then, during a brief first period of independence, Assur prospered as a commercial center, spawning Assyrian merchant colonies as far afield an Anatolia. Their trade curtailed by the formation of the Hittite state, the Assyrians came under Babylonian control for two centuries, from about 1850 B.C., and then were subject to the northern power of Mittani for three centuries more. In the middle of the fourteenth century B.C., defeat of the Mittanians by the Hittites made it possible for Assur to recover its independence and to become a major power for the first time.

For some seven hundred years, an Assyrian kingdom with its capital at Assur (then at Calah in the eighth century B.C. and Nineveh in the seventh) maintained itself and at times achieved an almost imperial scale and intensity of domination. Throughout this period, the northern frontier was held by strong states such as those of the Hittites, Neo-Hittites, Urartians, and Cimmerians. Assyrian expansion, therefore, was usually westward into Syria and Palestine or southward into Babylonia. By 1200 B.C. Assyrian rule had been consolidated in a core area along the Tigris from Akkad to Nineveh. In this upper region of Mesopotamia most of the population formed a looser and more scattered pattern than in the urbanized south. Except for the irrigated valley bottoms, this was a land of agricultural villages subsisting on rainfall agriculture and of upland slopes that supported pastoral communities. Under these conditions, a military aristocracy was formed, which developed an unstable pattern of feudal relationships through war and political competition and subsisted on the tribute its members could exact from the villages. The economic resources of Assyria were modest at best, which made it expedient for the Assyrian kings to send plundering expeditions into regions of greater wealth. Consistently unable to exercise permanent control over the larger cities, the Assyrians relied heavily on a tactic adopted long before, but on a smaller scale, by the First Dynasty of Babylon: the forced resettlement of conquered populations in new cities that could then be centrally controlled and taxed.

The height of Assyrian power was reached during the period of the ninth through the seventh centuries B.C. The boundaries were extended until they enclosed the entire Fertile Crescent from Elam to the Nile and its outer frontiers in the Zagros, Azarbayjan, and Armenia. The resources of this state were immense, with the agriculture of Mesopotamia and Egypt, the timber and minerals of the mountains, and the trade of the eastern Mediterranean. Several factors, including iron metallurgy and improvements in administration, contributed to this elevation of political organization to a new level of efficiency. The smelting of iron ores may have begun between 3000 and 2500 B.C. in Anatolia, but the transformation of the soft-iron bloom into wrought iron by heating and hammering was a costly procedure. Moreover, wrought iron was too soft to hold an edge, and tools or weapons made of this material had to be reheated and sharpened so frequently as to make them impracticable. Bronze continued to be preferred until the discovery of steel around 1500 B.C. Iron was converted into steel by the introduction of carbon either at the time of smelting or afterward by reheating it in a bed of burning charcoal. Initially a closely held Hittite monopoly, the making of steel spread after 1200 B.C., and it subsequently contributed to advances in other fields such as agricultural and military technology. Command of this improved metal significantly added to the wealth and power of the state. Another factor was the growth and refinement of the civil and military administration of the empire. Different forms of control were used in different regions. In the central region and in a few strategically important areas farther away, provinces were formed and placed under the local control of royal governors. The provinces in turn were subdivided into smaller units, each with its own complement of officials. The officials at all levels were held responsible for observance of policies and regulations laid down by the central government and were subject to investigation upon the filing of complaints by other officials or even by ordinary subjects. Both civil and military officials were granted grain fields to support them and their households. Taxation in these directly administered areas was standardized and included a levy of 25 percent on grain and 10 percent on straw. There were also taxes on livestock and on trade and communications, and subjects were conscripted for labor and military service. Remoter parts of the empire were controlled indirectly through vassal kings. These were bound by oath-sanctioned treaties to furnish regular tribute and to provide military aid when it was demanded. Communications were provided by royal roads with post stations and great numbers of official messengers. Surviving documents prove the amplitude of official correspondence from outlying provinces, including reports on local conditions and requests for guidance. An important limitation on the power of royal authority, however, was the survival of countervailing special rights and privileges of the ancient and venerated cities of Mesopotamia. Even the city of Assur itself, through its temple corporations, sometimes frustrated the royal will.

The ideology of the Assyrian state developed under strong Babylonian influence, and the Assyrian rulers generally acknowledged their debt to the more ancient civilization to the south. A thirteenth century B.C. ruler was the exception that proved the rule. He destroyed the walls of Babylon and carried off its divine Marduk, and was subsequently killed for this and other impieties by outraged Assyrian conservatives. The greatest monument to Assyrian respect for Babylonian culture was the great library of King Assurbanipal (r. 668-627 B.C.), who collected important documents from all parts of his realm. The library he assembled contained the core of the Sumerian-Babylonian cultural tradition. There were some differences, however, between Assyrian and Babylonian politics. Whereas the Babylonian kings were not priests, despite their claim to divine sanction, the Assyrian rulers were the high priests of the cult of Assur. Moreover, against the feudal and aristocratic background of Assyrian society, the kings were first among equals with respect to other aristocratic families and consequently had to show due regard for their pride.

The Assyrian state was split by a civil war between Assurbanipal and his brother in the middle of the seventh century B.C.. This provided the restive and obstinately independent Babylonian cities with the opportunity to revolt under the leadership of the Chaldean tribesmen of the lower Mesopotamian swamplands. An independent Chaldean dynasty was established in 625 B.C.. As Assyria and the Chaldeans fought over control of Mesopotamia, a new and greater power was forming in the east. Under Cyaxares (r. 625-593 B.C.) the Median descendants of the Iranian settlers on the plateau organized a kingdom based on the region east of the central Zagros. In 612 B.C., Cyaxares' armies destroyed Nineveh and ended the Assyrian kingdom in 609 B.C.. Another Iranian group, the Persians, had occupied the lower Zagros region and Elam. Allied with the Chaldeans in their war with Assyria, they attacked from the south while the Medes were advancing from the east. The Chaldeans became the heirs of the Assyrian empire and briefly controlled the entire Fertile Crescent from the Persian Gulf to the Mediterranean, but they fell in their turn to their former Persian allies, losing Babylon, their capital, in 539 B.C..

2. THE POLITICAL ORGANIZATION OF ARYAN CIVILIZATION IN SOUTH ASIA

With the breakup of the Indus Valley communities around 1750 B.C., the first phase of Indian civilization came to an end. Urban life disappeared and a millennium passed before South Asia produced another urbanized and literate society. This Gangetic, or Aryan, civilization, which became literate in the middle of the first millennium B.C., was the accomplishment of a people known as Aryans, whose culture was distinct from that of the Harappans. The Aryans were pastoral people who entered India from the northwest and may well have been responsible for the destruction of the existing civilization in the Indus region. The story of their migrations, their conquests, their gradual conversion to agriculture, and the development of kingdoms is completely undocumented and can only be pieced together from fragmentary bits of evidence. It is assumed here that it took more than ten centuries for the Aryans to achieve literacy around 700 B.C., although no documents survive that predate the rock inscriptions of Ashoka from the third century B.C.

Most of the evidence for the early Aryan presence in India must be gleaned from the Vedas—the oldest surviving oral literature in South Asia, which was passed on from generation to generation through memorization and recitation. *Veda,* which means "knowledge," or "spiritual knowledge," is a general term covering a vast body of hymns, prayers, charms, and sacrificial formulas as well as prose passages of explication and philosophical speculation. The oldest of these works, the *Rigveda,* consists of 1,028 hymns to various Aryan gods and is believed to date from the time when the Aryans were still located in the Panjab region. Later epics, the *Ramayana* and the *Mahabharata,* refer to political events of the period 1000-700 B.C. in the Ganges basin to the east.

The Aryans were seminomadic herdsmen who originated in the steppe lands of Central Asia and were related to the other pastoral peoples who pressed southward into West Asia in the second millennium B.C. The term Aryan refers properly to the type of language these intruders spoke. Sanskrit, the language of the Vedas, is classified as an Indo-European language and shares many roots with all the Slavic, Germanic, Romance, and Iranian languages. Common English words such as father and mother can be shown to be closely related to their equivalents in Sanskrit. The penetration by the Aryan tribes of the agricultural plains of the Harappans was a classic example of the conflict between pastoral nomads and sedentary agriculturalists which was to be repeated again and again throughout Eurasian history. The Aryans had domesticated the horse, which they used to devastating effect in warfare, usually in conjunction with a light, two-man chariot with spoked wheels. They were mobile, they were adept at warfare, and they had better weapons than did the Harappans. Judging from the Vedic hymns to their sky gods, the Aryans gloried in war. The god Indra was described as the breaker of cities, and there exist lines about driving out the dark inhabitants and burning their cities. Their enemies, presumably the Harappans, were depicted as dark, snub-nosed people who lived in fortified strongholds and had many cattle. They were despised for their worship of a mother goddess, animal deities, and the phallus.

Following their intrusion into the Panjab, which is reflected in the Vedas, the Aryans pushed eastward into the then heavily forested watershed of the Ganges and gradually underwent a transformation from nomadic pastoralism to agriculture. The passage from the Indus watershed to that of the Ganges was accomplished across a corridor bounded by the Indian desert on the south and the foothills of the Himalayas on the north where the distance from the Sutlej River in the west to the Jumna River on the east was only eighty miles. This area, where the Jumna runs parallel to the Ganges before joining it, served as a strategic link between the two halves of northern India. Its importance is attested to by the later location there of Delhi and, slightly to the north, Panipat and Karnal, the scenes of famous battles. Vedic testimony to the movement eastward is provided by references to the fire god, Agni, burning the earth, which suggest the process of clearing the jungle. Archaeological excavation of sites in the upper Gangetic region has revealed a characteristic painted gray ware thought to be associated with the Aryans, deposited above earlier remains, particularly those of fragments of an ochre ware produced by pre-Aryan occupants of the region. The introduction of iron took place in the period 1000 to 500 B.C. The appearance throughout the Ganges region and the Panjab of a northern black polished ware is evidence of the emergence of a uniform culture that might be referred to as a Gangetic civilization. City life developed in the Jumna-Ganges region during the same period in which the use of iron first appeared there and in the locale in which the *Mahabharata* recounts the rivalry of wealthy, civilized states.

The economy of the Aryan intruders was initially based on cattle, which were used as a measure of value and receive prominent mention in connection with disputes, warfare, and prayers for prosperity. The horse was also accorded special reverence and was the cult object of the most spectacular sacrifice of the Aryans. The principal Aryan gods were the agencies of nature deified: heaven, earth, the sun, the dawn, fire (Agni), and even the plant soma, which gave an intoxicating beverage used in religious ritual. Considerable equality of the sexes is indicated by the fact that both men and women took part in religious ceremonies and in composing commentaries on the hymns. Poetry was particularly highly developed, but music also received considerable attention, with the flute, lute, harp, cymbals, and drums being among the principal instruments. Gambling with dice was very popular and its folly is vividly described in the Vedas. During the move into the forested Gangetic region, iron probably played an important role in clearing new lands for raising crops. A mixed agriculture with both animal husbandry and the cultivation of grains, now including rice, and some use of techniques of manuring and irrigational techniques came into existence by the late Vedic period. The shift to agriculture brought with it a greater differentiation of occupations, with the appearance of carpenters, weavers, potters, tanners, and copper, bronze, and iron workers. Trade developed again with Mesopotamia, and by the second half of the first millennium B.C., money circulated in the form of punch-marked silver and cast coins of copper in round and rectangular shapes.

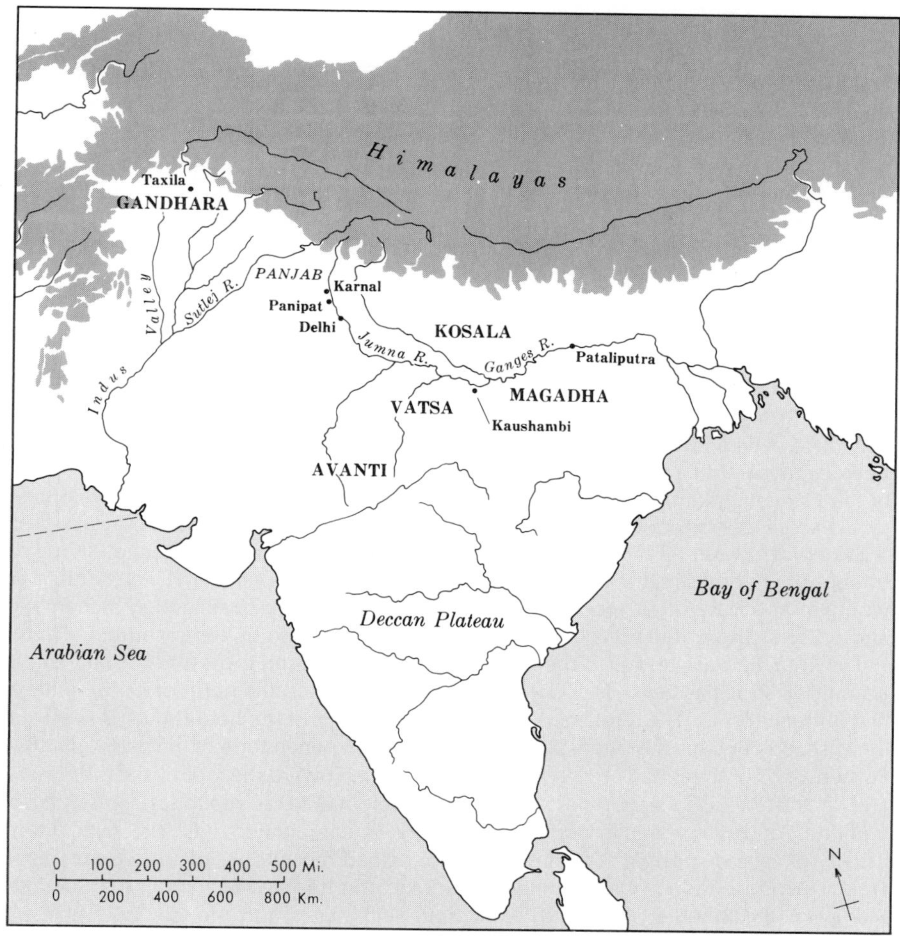

Map 11 Aryan civilization, seventh century B.C.

The process of social stratification can be seen in the *Rigveda* to have already differentiated the population into four distinct groups by about 1000 B.C. The Aryans initially recognized three divisions: warriors, who were more or less an aristocracy; priests; and common people. Once the Aryans had subjugated the Harappan territories, a new category was created for the indigenous people, called Dasas, who were darker skinned than the Aryans and who were treated as inferiors. From this four-part division evolved the system of caste, which eventually became a characteristic feature of South Asian civilization. The Sanskrit word for caste, *varna,* means "color," and so perhaps derived its usage in part from this original distinction between the Aryans and the Dasas. The basic four segments were: (1) warriors, or aristocracy *(kshatriyas);* (2) priests *(brahmans);* (3) cultivators *(vaishyas),* many of whom later became landlords, traders, and artisans; and (4) ritually unclean groups *(shudras),* many of whom later became cultivators. The first three of these groups were defined primarily by occupation, but the fourth seems to have been perceived in some special ethnic sense, a fact that helps explain why the *shudras* were barred from Vedic ritual and continued to worship their own gods. By the time of the Buddha (ca. 500 B.C.) Sanskrit had become a classical language with a written script, restricted in its usage mainly to the brahmans, while popular variants, Prakrits, served the needs of everyday speech. As we shall see in the next chapter, the message of the Buddha was popularized in this common tongue rather than in the language of the priests. Caste distinctions became hereditary and were later reinforced by conventional forms of address and rules, such as those against members of different castes eating together. It should be noted that the evolution of caste was a gradual process and, furthermore, that in later times there developed subcastes, which in fact became more important in everyday life than the four original divisions outlined in this rather simplified sketch.

The early Vedic tribes were patriarchal groupings composed of groups of related families. The word for these family groups later came to be used to mean "village" as nomadic units were converted to sedentary residence. The early tribal leader or chief, called *raja,* was elected by the tribe for leadership in war. He was not divine, had no religious functions, and no revenue system, but he did receive gifts in kind. Two assemblies, the *sabha,* which may have been a council of elders, and the *samiti,* which may have been a meeting of all freemen, dealt with affairs of the tribe. In the course of warfare among the tribes for control of the Gangetic plain, the tribal chief evolved into a hereditary king. The development of royal sacrifices forged a link between the king and the priesthood, and kingship came to be regarded as divine. As kingship evolved, the process of political differentiation led to the establishment of distinct officers of the state. Among the new elements were a chief priest, who was at once a ritual specialist and an adviser, a military commander, a chamberlain, and officers whose functions may have been those of treasurer and revenue collector.

The *Mahabharata,* which is the longest poem in the world, gives an epic and legendary account of struggles between tribal kingdoms over lands to the north of Delhi in the early first millennium B.C. The *Ramayana,* which tells the story of the hero Rama, is set farther to the east and contains passages suggestive of the Aryan penetration of the peninsula. By 600 B.C. two kinds of states had emerged in northern India. Toward the foothills of the Himalayas and in the Panjab, smaller states, sometimes referred to as republics, preserved older traditions of government through an assembly in conjunction with the *raja,* who was usually of *kshatriya* origin. These republics remained repositories of early traditions resistant to the imposition of brahmanical orthodoxy, and it is significant that the Buddha and Mahavira, the founder of Jainism, were from such states. On the Gangetic plain, large kingdoms emerged, the most important of which were Kosala, Magadha, Vatsa, and in central India, Avanti. To the west the Panjab state of Gandhara, with its capital at Taxila, was tributary to the Iranian Achaemenids. Gandhara served as a link with West Asia and as a conduit of religious influences in both directions. The political centers of these rival kingdoms developed into major cities. For example, Kaushambi, the capital of Vatsa, located on the Jumna, was four miles in circumference and had ramparts thirty feet high, faced with brick and topped with rectangular towers.

Of the four largest kingdoms, it was Magadha that eventually triumphed. The policy of expansion was initiated by a ruler named Bimbisara, who probably reigned sometime during the middle decades of the sixth century B.C. He strengthened his capital with stone walls, employed war elephants in battle, and formed marriage alliances with other states. Bimbisara's successor, who came to the throne by parricide, continued this expansion. It was he who built a fortification near the Ganges which was to grow into the great city of Pataliputra, future capital of the Mauryan empire. The precise dates and details of successive rulers of Magadha are unclear, but the state remained the most powerful on the Gangetic plain. In the fourth century B.C. it could field an army rated by Greek authors at 200,000 foot soldiers, with cavalry, chariots, and elephants numbered in the thousands. This force was never tested against the Greeks, however, since Alexander's campaign into India in 326 B.C. penetrated no farther than the Panjab, and the Macedonian conqueror died in 323 B.C. without consolidating his hold on that region. In the east, the usurpation of the throne of Pataliputra by Chandragupta Maurya in 321 B.C. marked the establishment of the first great empire in Indian history, a development that will be described in Chapter 4.

3. THE POLITICAL ORGANIZATION OF SHANG AND CHOU CHINA

The early political organization of Chinese society was largely the work of two successive dynasties: Shang and Chou. The five hundred years of the Shang corresponded to the period of the emergence of Chinese civilization, and it also saw the establishment of hereditary kingship. The Shang kingdom was conquered in 1122 B.C. by the rival state of Chou, which had earlier established itself in the Wei valley. Chou culture and society differed in some respects from those of Shang, and the conquest of Shang resulted in a new cultural synthesis, so that each dynasty made its contribution to the later political tradition.

During the period of the Chou dynasty (1122-256 B.C.) the Chinese world from the Inner Mongolian frontiers to the Yangtze valley and from the sea to the Tibetan plateau enjoyed a period of rapid growth in population (from perhaps two million to around fifty million) and in economic wealth. The spread of grain agriculture across the north China plain, which had begun in late Neolithic times, continued at an accelerating rate through the Chou. The long, steady rise of the rice economy of the south continued at the same time, but still on a smaller scale. This development of the agrarian economy was associated with an expansion of trade and of regional economic specialization, chiefly in luxury goods. These increased resources in population and wealth were not destined to serve the interests of the Chou monarchy, however. On the contrary, they provided the economic basis for the development of many strong and aggressive states both within the old Chou kingdom and on its frontiers.

The Chou realm gradually broke apart into a large number of practically sovereign states, which then engaged one another for several centuries in political and military struggles that did not come to an end until all the losers were absorbed by the victors and the state of Ch'in finally defeated and swallowed the last of its rivals in 221 B.C.. The breakdown of the old order was inseparably linked to the birth of a new one. In the course of the deadly competition of rival states, the Chou aristocracy and its manorial estates were swept away. The peasants and artisans became the direct subjects of powerfully organized bureaucratic states geared for war. The new institutions and methods of government created during this period of severe trial provided the political foundations upon which the Chinese universal state of Ch'in and Han was soon to be raised.

Chinese historians have divided the Chou dynasty into several periods, which are helpful in keeping the processes of political organization in proper chronological perspective. The period from 1122-771 B.C. is called Western Chou, because the kings maintained their court and royal government at the city called Hao near Sian in the Wei valley. In 771 B.C. there was a dispute over the rejection of a royal heir and the nomination of a new one. The defeated court faction joined with a vassal state and with the Jung barbarians of Shensi and invaded the capital, killed the king, and drove the original heir apparent eastward to the secondary capital near Loyang. The location of the new capital gave its name to the later period, Eastern Chou. Already in decline by 771 B.C., the Chou kings were now seldom more than nominal and symbolic rulers and often found themselves the pawns of their former vassals. The state was finally extinguished in 256 B.C.

2.3 Political Organization: Shang

Periods of Political Organization in China
Shang Dynasty 1600-1122 B.C.
Chou Dynasty 1122-256 B.C.
Western Chou 1122-771 B.C.
Eastern Chou 771-256 B.C.

The Shang State

According to the literary sources, the Shang king P'an-keng assumed the throne in 1401 B.C. and crossed the Yellow River to reestablish his court in a new capital near modern Anyang. The kings remained there until the Chou conquest in 1122 B.C.. All the archaeologically found Shang documents were written during this period. For the two centuries of Shang rule prior to the move to Anyang there is no contemporary written documentation. Consequently, most of what can be said about the Shang state pertains to the second half of its long history. Since many of the inscriptions are addressed to or refer to the pre-Anyang rulers, however, they do provide some information on the earlier period and particularly on the royal succession.

The fact that the Shang dynasty survived for some five hundred years is surprising if one assumes that it was the first Chinese monarchy and, as traditional Chinese sources would have us believe, that it ruled the whole Chinese world of its day. It is much more likely, however, that Chinese kingship first developed during the seventeenth and sixteenth centuries B.C. in several emerging cities of the western Honan–Lungshan region and that the Shang hegemony over a large area was established only gradually, and mainly by military superiority. Rival states subsequently formed on the Shang frontiers. The high level of Chou culture at the time of the Chou conquest of Shang suggests that it may have become at least equal to Shang in wealth and power by that time. Shang documents could be expected to present a view of Anyang as the single Chinese seat of sovereign authority, but from the frequency of military operations undertaken by the Shang kings it would be reasonable to infer that their domination was widely opposed.

The Shang monarchy developed in the context of an aristocratic society. Chariot-driving militarists armed with bow and arrow and with bronze weapons and armor were organized in lineages that were sanctified and sustained by ancestral cults. The wealth invested in the service of ancestors appears in the bronze ritual vessels and in the remains of animal and human sacrificial victims. Oracle-bone inscriptions place the Shang kings at the center of this class of titled nobles and territorial lords. It is reasonable to suppose, therefore, that Shang kingship originated in the role of war leader within a stratified society. The state, then, served both to mobilize the aristocrats for war and maintain and regulate their high status, and to support their control over the subject class of artisans and peasants. Ancestral and local cults, which had probably existed in Neolithic times, were retained by the new military aristocracy as important additional means to assert and maintain its social prestige and political authority. The most potent and the most lavishly served of all these cults were those of the Shang kings at Anyang, which was in keeping with their pretensions to rulership over the other great houses.

The core of the Shang state was the royal house. By the late reigns of Shang the common-descent group to which the kings belonged had grown to a great size. The way in which it was organized is much disputed, however. One current theory holds that the royal branch of the ruling clan was subdivided into five lineages, which intermarried according to a regular pattern. Two of these lineages, however, were closer than the others to the main patrilineal line of descent within the royal branch, and so provided most of the kings. However the ruling clan and its royal branch may have been organized, the oracle bones and the royal tombs provide evidence enough of the power and effectiveness of the ancestral cult. The king's patriarchal authority over a numerous and usually obedient kinship group provided him with a large pool of potential officials to serve him. The addition of slaves, who were probably war captives, to serve as officials according to their ability, and the commissioning of royal consorts (the status of women was relatively high at this time) rounded out the patrimonial foundation of Shang government.

The Shang capital was regarded by its inhabitants as the center of the universe. Palaces, altars, and tombs were carefully oriented toward the four cardinal directions, and the Chinese world was correspondingly divided into the four quarters. The king himself asserted his unique sovereignty by using the royal first person pronoun *yü-i-jen,* "I, The One Man." In practice, however, the Shang kingdom was neither universal nor confined within clear territorial boundaries. The immediate vicinity of the capital appears to have been closely controlled by royal administration. The discovery of a large storehouse of agricultural tools near Anyang suggests that the fields around the capital may have been cultivated by gangs of peasant conscripts working under the direction of royal overseers. Beyond this, the central portion of the kingdom, as defined by the successive capitals and the royal tombs associated with them—that is, the narrow crescent running from Loyang to Anyang—may have constituted the Shang patrimony. Beyond, and possibly within, this area lay territory occupied by semiindependent titled aristocrats who acknowledged Shang suzerainty by sending tribute or performing military service. These nobles were sometimes, but not necessarily, members of the royal house. At a greater distance were more or less definite frontiers dividing people of Shang culture from "foreigners." Shang authority over these outer regions was relatively weak and easily challenged.

The royal government was provided with a large administrative staff. The bone inscriptions are rich in official terminology, and many of the titles appear later in the Chou documents. Unfortunately, however, the documents yield few clues as to the actual functions of the officials and how they were recruited and managed. Many among the most important of them were of a priestly or clerical character, having to do with divination, performance of ceremonial, and the compilation and preservation of records. Terms for military officers imply that some specialization of functions had taken place. Horse-drawn chariots were accompanied by large numbers of foot soldiers, who were probably peasant conscripts. The principal weapons were the compound bow, knife, and dagger-axe. The scale of civil and military mobilization achieved by Shang government is suggested by archaeological and documentary evidence. The Shang capital near Chengchow was surrounded by a pounded-earth wall with a total length of about four miles and a height of more than thirty feet. It has been estimated that its construction would have required the labor of ten thousand workmen over a period of about ten years. The number of workers actually employed is unknown, but this was obviously a large and long-term undertaking. As for military operations, Shang documents refer to expeditions of from one thousand to at least ten thousand men, and a campaign into the Huai valley under the last Shang king lasted 260 days or more.

The Chou State

The Chou people began their transition from village agriculture to civilization before they conquered the Shang, and they did so in a setting already familiar to us from our study of the north China Neolithic. For several hundred years the Chou or their ancestors had moved about in the loess upland of Shansi and Shensi, where they were in close proximity with the developing pastoral societies of Tibet and Mongolia. Indeed, they may themselves have combined pastoralism with the agriculture they had seen so long practiced in the Neolithic nuclear area. They developed under Shang cultural influence among the upland barbarian tribes known to the Chinese as the Jung. From the oracle bones we know that they came within the political sphere of Shang and were attacked by an army sent from

Anyang around 1300 B.C. Subsequently they were regarded by the Shang as their subjects. At the time of their conquest of the north China plain, the Chou were already living in towns, casting bronze weapons and ritual vessels, fighting from horse-drawn chariots, and using the Shang script for inscriptions that attest to their intense interest in political organization. Their traditions, as recorded in the classical literature, tell us more. Although they worshipped a miraculously born agricultural deity, Hou Chi, "Lord Millet," as their clan founder, they accounted for their barbarian and pastoral antecedents with a legendary tale that tells of Lord Millet's son going to live among the barbarians. This device, identification of a civilized ancestor who made himself at home in a barbarian tribe, is a common theme in Chou literature and obviously served to reconcile civilized ex-barbarian peoples to their uncivilized origins. Chou legend goes on to tell of a much later leader, whom they called Duke Tan-fu, who taught his people two of the arts of civilization: permanent agriculture and the building of walled and fortified cities. The duke's successor married a Shang noblewoman, and their son, posthumously named Wen Wang (the "Civilized King"), laid the political and military foundations of the Chou kingdom. According to Chou tradition, Wen Wang survived capture and imprisonment by the Shang and, by war and diplomacy, forged a powerful federation of upland tribes and strengthened his political control over them by building a new capital city just west of modern Sian. All this he bequeathed to his son Wu Wang (the "Martial King"), conqueror of Shang.

In 1122 B.C., Wu Wang led his clansmen and his tribal allies out of the passes and marched north along the edge of the plain to the Shang capital. The city was taken and burned. Although the site continued to be occupied by villagers, it never recovered as a place of any importance and has been locally known to this day as Yin Hsu, "Ruins of Yin." Chou court poetry presents this as a victory of epic proportions and as the fulfillment of a divine mission to rule the world. The tradition grandly proclaims that the Chou supreme deity, Heaven, gave them their victory although their army was outnumbered by 700,000 to 50,000. Actually, it seems that most of the Shang army at that time was away from the capital campaigning against the eastern barbarians, but the absurdity of the claimed ratio testifies to the sense of heroic pride among the victors. So far there is no evidence to show that the Chou enjoyed any notable technological advantage in their war against Shang, but the fact that they had long experience of warfare with other peoples of the uplands suggests that they may have had better horses and been more skillful in chariot fighting than the urbanized Shang aristocrats on the plain. Because of the rather loose character of the Shang realm with its many dependencies, however, the work of the conquest was far from done. After the death of Wu Wang and the accession of his young son as Ch'eng Wang, the new king, aided by his uncle, the Duke of Chou, had to suppress a coalition of Shang and Chou aristocrats that resisted his authority. The Chou conquest thus furnished the new dynasty with a heroic origin and with three charismatic heroes whose names have retained their majestic aura throughout three millennia of Chinese history: Wen Wang, Wu Wang, and the Duke of Chou.

The final subjugation of the Shang by the Chou during the reigns of Wu Wang and Ch'eng Wang involved the destruction of the old political order of north China. After putting down the unsuccessful revolt against their conquest, the Chou systematically removed whole Shang communities—aristocrats and dependents—from their original domains and transported them great distances. Some were settled near modern Loyang, where a secondary royal capital was built. (According to a later tradition, the Duke of Chou wanted the king to reside there but was overruled.) Others were moved far to the east, where they provided labor and all necessary skills for the support of new Chou outposts in barbarian territory. Although Shang aristocratic lineages survived this displacement and their royal clan was allowed to continue its ancestral cult, political power above the local level had been struck from their hands and it became the task of the Chou to build a new

Map 12 Chou China, 1000-1400 B.C.

state. In this undertaking, they started with the original federation of clans and tribes that they had led to victory, but they could not count on the cooperation of Shang aristocracy in the conquered regions. The alien conquerors had to improvise a government by sharing their sovereignty among their ablest and most trusted military leaders. The relationships between king and vassal were personal and based on mutual interest. Family ties were also important, with most, though by no means all, of the new fiefs being given to members of the royal clan. The Chou practice of polygamy resulted in a rapid proliferation of collateral lineages capable of governing new territories. The remaining fiefs went to military leaders who headed other clans. Many titles of nobility and names of administrative offices were taken over from Shang (some of them even before the conquest), but noble and official titles were bestowed rather indiscriminately with little sense of an orderly hierarchy of ranks or of a consistent relationship between title and function. Also, as in early feudalism in the West, the mutual obligations of ruler and principal vassal were not clearly expressed in the acts of investiture.

What held this rough feudal structure together generation after generation through Western Chou? One factor was the presence of external enemies. Rivalries among the feudal lords were controlled by the need for an effective defense against the barbarians on all sides, who did not passively accept the emergence of the aggressive new regime. The kings continued, at least into the early decades of the Eastern Chou period, to play an important part in the organization of the collective defense of the kingdom. Moreover, many of the strongest and potentially most dangerous of the vassal states were on the marchlands of the kingdom and were fully occupied with their own defense. Another factor was the solidarity of the royal clan, but this was a diminishing asset because the junior lineages grew ever further apart from the senior line and increasingly were preoccupied with their own interests.

Shang-Chou cultural synthesis began before and continued after the conquest. We have already noted that Chou inscriptions used the Shang writing. Also, although there were some modifications in the forms and motifs of the bronze ritual vessels as between late Shang and early Chou, these clearly fall within the same civilization. In the first few reigns after the conquest there occurred a remarkable synthesis of the two state ideologies. The Shang royal court had attached great importance to the cult of the supreme Shang deity. Shang Ti was the recipient of animal and probably human sacrifices, and the court diviners communicated with him by means of the bone and tortoise oracles. Meanwhile, the Chou had evolved a state cult of their own. Their supreme deity, T'ien, or "Heaven," probably originated as the collective conception of the risen spirits of all the deceased chiefs and kings of the Chou people. T'ien came by extension also to denote the dwelling place of these spirits. The Chous sacrificed to T'ien as the Shang had sacrificed to Shang Ti, and they developed their own means of communication with the world of spirits. Where Shang royal diviners used bone and tortoise shell, the Chou diviners used stalks of the milfoil plant gathered in sacred places. The *I-Ching,* or *Classic of Changes,* originated as a manual for this procedure. After the conquest, the first Chou rulers implied in their public pronouncements that Shang Ti was simply T'ien worshipped under a different name. T'ien was now presented as a universal deity having the power to affect the fortunes of all men and to confer universal earthly rule upon living mortals, who thus reigned as Heaven's stewards. By means of this claim of universal authority and by using the terms T'ien and Shang Ti interchangeably, the victors made it difficult for the leaders of the defeated regime to appeal to Shang Ti to restore their royal patrimony. Even the methods of divination were turned against them with both the bone and milfoil methods now regularly used in Chou practice.

As with the state cults, so too in the matter of law. The first Chou kings studied the written laws of Shang, retained what they found good, and made additions from their own traditions. Cultural synthesis also occurred on the level of social institutions as a result of the absorption of the leading Shang clans into the developing Chou aristocracy. Gradually, the Chou *tsung-fa,* or "law of kindred," system came to be generally accepted throughout the aristocracy. The *tsung-fa* system was based on primogeniture (in status, not in property, which was corporately held by the whole lineage) and ranked collateral lineages according to the number of generations they were removed from the senior lineage and the seniority of the founding younger brother. Although the practice of cross-cousin marriage continued for a time in Western Chou (and survived into modern times in some parts of China), the Chou practice of royal succession from father to son (usually the eldest son of the principal wife) continued in place of the probable alternation of lineages as in Shang.

The outward diffusion of Chou culture contributed to external conflict, as powerful new states arose on the margins of the Chou realm as it was originally constituted in the early reigns. The effect was to increase the area of Chinese civilization to about a million square miles (i.e., to between a third and a fourth of the land area of China today). In the west, the state of Ch'in began in the Wei valley as a beleaguered outpost among the Jung barbarians after the flight of the Chou court in 771 B.C., and some four centuries later it emerged as a major power. In the north, the state of Chin tenuously integrated the great military power of the semibarbarous tribes of the Shansi uplands, while Ch'i, once a remote marchland of early Chou, subdued and organized the peoples of modern Shantung. Far to the northeast the state of Yen became a great power but remained barbarous in Chinese eyes because the influence of the Chou tradition was attenuated by the great distance from the center. To the south, the peoples of the middle Yangtze region passed under the control of the immense state of Ch'u, admired for its spectacular architecture, its brilliant tradition in the arts, and its poetry rich in natural and spiritual symbolism, but also feared for its power and its proud disdain for the claims of Chou sovereignty. Downstream, among the Yueh people (ancestors of the modern Yueh, or Viet, people of Vietnam), the states of Wu and Yueh dominated the lower Yangtze and Huai valleys. Upstream from Ch'u, the state of Pa appeared in the Chia-ling valley of central Ssu-ch'uan, and the state of Shu was founded in the Min valley of western Ssu-ch'uan. All of these states were erected on the foundations of regional subcultures that resulted from the stimulus and diffusion of Chou culture outward among the neighboring peoples. These new states were perceived from the center as culturally different and barbarous to such a degree as to present a real threat to the survival of orthodox Chou traditions, and yet, on archaeological evidence, it would seem that they represented regionally differentiated syntheses of Chou and non-Chinese local cultures and fell definitely within the mainstream of Chinese civilization. Their presence within the expanding Chinese world imparted to it a cosmopolitan character, whose interest and excitement can be felt in the literature of Eastern Chou.

Still farther away, in the region of modern Yunnan province and northern Vietnam, another Bronze Age culture emerged. Archaeological sites near Tali and Kunming in southwest China and the Red River valley in Vietnam reveal the emergence in Eastern Chou times of the Tien, or Dongson, culture on an unmistakably Southeast Asian cultural foundation. The northern frontiers of Chinese culture, including the Ordos, interacted not only with Chou but also, by way of western Szechwan, with the very early bronze culture of the upper Mekong in northern Thailand. This culture of the far south was long to remain outside Chinese political control, although it was linked by trade. (Vietnam was conquered by the Chinese in the second century B.C., and Yunnan only in the thirteenth century A.D.!) In the opposite direction, a Bronze Age culture on the northern slopes of the Altai Mountains reflects Shang and Chou cultural influences. Although this region was eventually incorporated within the Chinese empire (Ch'ing dynasty, 1644-1911 A.D.), it continued to be a key area in the steppe homeland of the Inner Asian nomads, the cultural and political antithesis of the urban and agricultural Chinese.

The imperialism of the warring states within the expanding Chou realm became the principal fact of Chinese political life during the latter half of the Chou. There are three main reasons why this occurred. The first is that the diffusion of Chinese culture outward among barbarian neighbors and the formation of very large and powerful border states in these areas created problems of control quite beyond the political capabilities of the Chou monarchy. The second is that the Chou house itself went into a rapid decline after 771 B.C., when the old base area in the west was surrendered to the Jung, and eventually the Chou were unable to control even the old fiefs of the inner region, to say nothing of the outer states. Still a third factor was that junior lineages of the ruling houses of the vassal states established their own clans, and in many cases they became so powerful that they were able to wrest control of the governments from their noble masters by making the office of minister hereditary. The entrenched ministerial families had scant respect for the legitimacy of the Chou feudal order, and during their heyday, which was roughly from 600-500 B.C., they served their clans' private interests by pursuing ambitious policies of interstate warfare and diplomacy. Some effort was made by heads of state to fill the vacuum left by the collapse of royal authority. One case in point was the league of states that held a dozen conferences between 681 and 643 B.C. for the ostensible purpose of settling disputes and cooperating in matters of common concern. Again, in 546 B.C. the major powers were persuaded to sign a treaty by which they renounced war as an instrument of policy. Such measures, however, were unavailing, because the rival states were so committed to political and military struggle that what appeared to be moves toward the organization of peace were merely cynical political expedients. As the wars continued, they gained in scale and ferocity. Victors routinely butchered defeated armies, destroyed or scattered the former ruling houses, and extinguished their local and ancestral cults.

Political Consolidation in Eastern Chou

The expansionism of the great states of the latter half of the Chou period gave a strong impetus to political consolidation. Rulers and ministers made use of the almost continuous military emergencies to justify the more rational and effective mobilization of their subjects for production and for fighting. As feudal obstacles to trade crumbled and communications improved, private merchants and entrepreneurs flourished and cities grew in number and in size. The steady growth of the population, sustained by a more efficient agriculture, provided more manpower to serve the ambitions of the states. By the end of the Chou, the rulers and ministers of the last surviving great states exercised real political and military power far in excess of that enjoyed by the Chou kings even when their feudal regime was at its height.

The most important means of control in the hands of rulers was administrative rationalization. The origins of Chinese bureaucracy may be found within the essentially feudal regimes of Shang and early Chou. Nearly a hundred different titles of administrators and functionaries appear in Western Chou inscriptions. By the end of that period extensive records were kept in the royal archives, including control copies of official commissions, land titles, and private contracts, and there may have been a standard money of account (originally a certain weight of silk cloth) for the control of royal finance. The value of commodities received or paid out was often expressed in terms of this unit. The greater part of royal revenue was obtained by taxation levied directly on the royal lands and indirectly on the lands of vassals. Despite all this, however, a fully developed bureaucracy was still in the future. In Western Chou the use of official titles was inconsistent, the relationship between ruler and minister was highly personal, and officials, who were generally titled nobles as well, were not salaried but were granted office lands from which they had the right to collect revenue for their support. The method of taxation was still rather primitive and inefficient. In return for the privilege of occupying and cultivating the lord's land, the peasants gave their labor to the lord, cultivating his fields, gathering wild fruits and herbs for him, and assisting him in hunting and war. Moreover, the royal officials who were employed to oversee the governments of the feudal lords had to respect their partial sovereignty, and, as noblemen themselves, they had an interest in not undermining the feudal privileges of others.

During the last centuries of the Chou, from about 500 B.C., the transition from feudal to bureaucratic rule was sharply accelerated. The aristocratic class fought a losing battle against the encroachment of state power, now in the hands of the petty aristocrats *(shih,* "knights") and even commoners, who had supplanted the great ministerial families. One way they tried to defend their position was to crystallize and standardize their ceremonial code of conduct (called *li*) and to clarify their hierarchy of noble ranks on the basis of genealogy and the *tsung-fa* system. By so doing, they were, in effect, trying to place their conduct and their privileges beyond the reach of royal authority and the new laws that were being promulgated in an antitraditional spirit of *realpolitik*. The effort, however, was doomed. On the one hand, the incessant warfare resulted in the destruction of nearly all the states and their manorial subfiefs, and this encompassed the extermination of the nobles or their degradation to the status of commoners. On the other hand, the ramification of aristocratic lineages during the middle centuries of Chou had generated the growing class of marginal, untitled, and landless aristocrats of the *shih* class. These men, proud, ambitious, and sometimes poor, provided an ample pool of available talent from which the growing state bureaucracies might be recruited.

The essential element in the new bureaucratic order was the downward extension of central administrative control by means of local government units, each headed by officials appointed and regulated by the central government. The state of Ch'u was probably the pioneer in this innovation. Ch'u society appears to have been peculiar among the states of Chou China in the relative weakness of its lineage organizations and was, therefore, less resistant to rational administrative organization. From around the middle of the fifth century B.C., Ch'u was a bureaucratic polity, with officials appointed and dismissed freely by its rulers and locally administered through centrally directed offices called *hsien* (the identical term that has denoted the county or basic administrative unit throughout the history of imperial China). The state of Chin in Shansi adopted the *hsien* unit in the interest of centralization but failed because the new offices soon were made the hereditary property of entrenched lineage groups. Farther to the west, however, the state of Ch'in succeeded in instituting the *hsien* system. As Ch'in expanded rapidly by conquest of neighboring states from the mid-fourth century B.C., the conquered territories were placed under *hsien* administration. Ch'in also adopted an intermediate administrative level called the *chün,* which stood between central and local government. This three-level hierarchy of central, regional, and local governments was finally extended to the whole of China with the Ch'in imperial conquest in 221 B.C.

While the bureaucracies were being formed, codes of law were also employed as a means of institutional change and political centralization. At the beginning of the Chou dynasty the new regime retained much of the written law *(tien,* used down to modern time to denote basic law of the state) of the Shang. How systematically these laws may have been set forth cannot be known, since the documents are lost and are known only from references in the surviving literature. Such laws were intended by the Chou to restrain the new nobility in the interests of keeping the peace among them and between them and the conquered population. As the Chou ruling house declined, the aristocratic ceremonial code, *li,* functioned as a fairly systematic customary law governing inter- and intra-familial relations. During the climactic period of internal growth and change in late Chou, the rulers and ministers of the rival states began drafting codes of law based not on tradition but on their own rational interests in enhancing their political power. The new codes, beginning in the sixth century B.C., required behavior on the part of officials and commoners which would have the effect of maximizing production of strategic commodities, state revenues, and the size and number of the armed forces, while restricting activities not conducive to state power. Naturally, such codes were attacked by the aristocrats, who found their vested interests threatened, and the controversy over them forms a part of the philosophical dialogues we will be examining in a later section.

While the political aspect of Chou society was undergoing the transformation from feudalism to bureaucracy, the economic aspect was being transformed from a decentralized manorial economy into a mixed economy of agrarian villages and aristocratic estates. The agrarian villages held their fields in common and allotted them to families of the community. The lands of the aristocratic estates were cultivated by tenants or hired laborers. As aristocratic families were destroyed in the wars, their peasant dependents were liberated from manorial control and, constituting independent peasant villages, might assume the management of the former manor lands under a system of communal ownership. Moreover, lands that had been abandoned in the flight of the cultivators from invading armies, as well as lands reclaimed by state-sponsored projects, were now subject to disposition by the state as grants to favored officers. The communal lands probably could not legally be sold, but the existence of privately held fields gave rise to a limited but socially significant market in land. Wealthy families could now gain control over agricultural production by purchasing or developing land. These changes in the land system were accompanied by an increase in trade. The redistributive function originally served by the manorial organizations, such as collecting and doling out tools, utensils, and clothing, were now taken up by small local markets, where exchanges among peasant households could take place. Integration on a larger scale is reflected in the literary and archaeological evidence of a number of large urban trading centers.

These economic changes made it easier for the states to mobilize the economic and manpower resources they required to achieve their political and military goals. The customary labor service of the former manorial dependents now gave way to the payment of taxes in the form of grain and other agricultural products, and peasants were now conscripted directly by the states for military service. Since the owners of private estates usually had some official status or political influence to protect them, it was the ordinary peasants of the independent communal villages who bore the main burden of taxation and service.

In order to benefit from the crumbling of feudal obstacles to economic integration, the states required good communications. In the north, highways had to be built, maintained, guarded against bandits, and provided with hostels for travelers on private and official business. Not only were great armies moved efficiently over the new routes, but so also were cart loads of tax grain destined for the public granaries. The state that had full granaries in its cities had a strategic advantage over a rival state because it was then prepared to withstand a long siege. In the south, as well, the states improved their communications, but there the chief means of transportation was by water. River channels were deepened and the broad plains of the Han, middle and lower Yangtze, and Huai rivers were crisscrossed by canals that doubled as irrigation channels and as transport arteries.

In view of all that has been said about warfare among the states of the late Chou period, the militarization of the society should come as no surprise. First, in the matter of scale, the facts that there were fewer but larger states, that the Chinese population was growing, and that the states were gaining greater control over their subjects all resulted in a massive increase in the size of armies. In the seventh century B.C. a large army might have thirty thousand men, but some battles of the fourth and third centuries B.C. saw hundreds of thousands engaged on each side. The larger states were able to maintain more than a million men under arms, at least for short periods of time. These immense numbers were mostly peasants conscripted by the new bureaucracies. Local administrative units were assigned military manpower quotas. Men subject to military service were equipped and trained by the state. The hazards of military duty were offset by the fact that success in war was handsomely rewarded by military-minded governments. Good soldiers rose through the ranks to become officers or even generals, and if they killed great numbers of the enemy, they might be given material rewards such as rich farm lands. The ethical and ceremonial restraints of mid-Chou aristocratic chivalry vanished with the coming of this new militarism, and where it once was the custom to give quarter to a beaten enemy, the aim of battle now all too often was the achievement of the highest possible body count. Late Chou literature, doubtless with some exaggeration, tells of the slaughter of as many as 450,000 in a single engagement. In any case, the aristocrat's war chariot had become a quaint anachronism. In the flourishing southern regions, muddy terrain and the network of waterways rendered the chariots useless. They were vulnerable in the narrow upland valleys of the northwest, and throughout the north, the art of cavalry warfare, learned from the steppe peoples by the state of Chao in northern Shensi, was being adopted as a supplement to the basic infantry force.

The Chou dynasty, especially its latter half, was a period of major civilizational growth and technological innovation, contributing to the wealth of the states and their ruling classes. In the fifth century B.C., the aristocratic bronze was joined in Chinese material culture by the democratic iron. Evidently as an outgrowth of bronze technology, the Chinese began casting iron tools, such as blades for hoes, spades, and plows, and weapons, such as swords. For the first time, the great mass of the population began to have access to the convenience and efficiency of metal. This undoubtedly contributed to the great advances in agriculture that occurred about the same time. The last centuries of Chou saw the introduction of ox plowing and of large-scale irrigation, drainage, and flood-control projects, which led to a powerful economic expansion. In bronze technology, advances were made in the direction of mass production. The external piece-molds used in casting had the decorative pattern impressed in them by means of stamps, and parts of vessels, such as legs and handles, were cast separately and then welded to the bodies. Also, many late Chou bronzes were adorned with gold and silver inlay. In building construction, tile began to replace thatch in the Western Chou, and for some purposes, such as tomb chambers, late Chou builders substituted fired bricks for pounded earth.

Political organization into large, efficiently governed states, the improvement of land and water communications, advances in technology, and the growth of population all gave a mighty impetus to economic growth. The latter half of Chou was also *par excellence* a period of metropolitan development. Highways and waterways were crowded with wagons and boats bearing goods to town and city markets. Great fortunes were made in trade, and rich merchants became the friends and creditors of rulers. Commercial growth is reflected in the appearance of cast-bronze coinage of several types with wide regional circulation, and in the enormous size and complexity of late Chou cities. One that has been excavated had an area of ten square miles. Cities now had several walled sections. Typically there was an inner wall enclosing official and aristocratic quarters, then a surrounding larger area of shops, workshops, warehouses, and houses, which was surrounded by another wall. Beyond this outer wall lay fields and peasant villages closely linked by trade to the households within the walls. Goods for interregional trade included salt, lacquer, textiles, sea foods, timber, metals, tropical fruits, ceramics, basketry, and many other wares. Most significant, however, is the fact that staple food grains were also traded on a large scale—so large a scale, in fact, that the big grain brokers' habit of buying up great quantities in times of plenty and then driving up the price and selling at maximum profit in times of scarcity led to direct government intervention. In several states, public agencies were set up to monopolize the grain brokerage business both in order to prevent hoarding and alleviate famine and in order to make a modest profit for the treasury.

The growth of the economy was not an unmixed blessing. Ordinary peasants, liberated from the manorial duties and protection of the vanishing aristocratic society, were now forced to compete for their very survival in the developing market economy. One of the new economic classes now flourishing was that of the usurer. Peasant farmers, unable to accumulate savings to any significant extent, were forced in years of famine to borrow money or, more likely, grain at whatever interest was demanded. Thus, there began in late Chou times a problem that was to be the bane of Chinese society from that time until the founding of the People's Republic. The impoverished borrower put up his land, or the right to cultivate it, as collateral. When the loan could not be repaid, the creditor foreclosed and added the land to his property. The effect was a tendency for land ownership to be concentrated and for large numbers of peasants to be forced into tenancy or day labor or even, at times, slavery or unemployment. Under such conditions there appeared a rural proletariat, insecure, disaffected and, when well led, dangerous to the state.

In other cultural contexts, we have seen the transition from temple-oriented urban community to kingship. In the Chinese case, the Shang, which is the earliest civilization yet found in China, united these characteristics. The forms of worship associated with nature and agricultural success, as well as those having to do with the clan cults, were conducted with the assistance of priestly specialists by the aristocratic clan heads themselves. The subsequent evolution of Chou kingship through a developed feudalism to sovereign dominion over a bureaucratically structured state has been sketched in the foregoing pages.

Consonant with this development was the early adoption of an ideology, based on the Mandate of Heaven and its ethical implication of just and benevolent rule, and the later elaboration of a rationalistic cosmology, a systematic description of the operations of the cosmos in terms of natural forces.

The Chou dynasty played a major part in the formation of the Chinese great tradition. In shaping their great tradition the Chinese organized their mythology and their history into a cyclical process, beginning with a series of mythical cultural heroes who invented writing, divination, and agriculture, tamed floods, built cities, and so forth. The last in this series, the tamer of floods, was made the founder of the legendary Hsia dynasty, which was allegedly overthrown by T'ang, king of the Shang state. Shang and Chou were now seen as guardians of a Chinese (or "Middle Kingdom") great tradition transcending all temporal and cultural differences, and the idea of the Chinese dynastic cycle had now been born. Each dynasty was given Heaven's mandate to rule, in recognition of the great virtue manifested by the founders. But in the course of centuries that initial virtue was dissipated, and at last the mandate was transferred to the virtuous founders of the next dynasty. Thus, by a process of simplification, the different traditions and royal cults of Shang and Chou were incorporated into a single tradition sanctified or made authoritative by its necessary relationship to a unified cosmic order.

Although the extensive economic, social, and political changes that occurred during the late Chou period provided the foundation of the Chinese universal empire of Ch'in and Han, these changes were achieved at a high cost in destructive warfare, social instability, and psychological insecurity. These uncomfortable consequences of change, and the intellectual responses to them, will be the subject of the next section on China.

CONCLUDING REMARKS

The growth of civilized communities led eventually to the emergence of kingship and the establishment of powerful states. It is clear from the patterns considered here that the same processes were at work in Mesopotamia, the Gangetic plain, and the basin of the Yellow River. In each case cities were founded over an extended area, with the result that competing political entities arose and engaged in jurisdictional disputes, rivalry, and warfare. Interaction with peoples outside the circle of civilization was another common theme, but one might ask why there was considerable variation. In Mesopotamia, for example, there is at least the hint that the Sumerians accepted alien peoples of pastoral origin in military roles to the benefit of both groups. In South Asia the evidence is extremely limited, but it would appear that the invading Aryans overcame Harappan civilization in the Indus valley before pushing eastward to the Ganges and building cities of their own. To what extent they absorbed Harappan culture cannot be determined, but they accommodated themselves to the indigenous population by means of an ethnic stratification that was later to evolve into the caste system. In China the diffusion of Shang civilization may have been largely responsible for the cultural development of the outlying Chou people, who eventually conquered Shang and successfully merged the two cultures.

As civilizations grew in extent, new cities were formed, each with its own ceremonial center and variant regional culture. In Mesopotamia and China, kinship groupings were important in the organization of wealth and power. In China the principal religious cults tended to be structured along the lines of the lineages, while in West Asia the major cults were those of the city gods. Does this difference help explain why political organization in China evolved as a loose feudal system dominated by a hereditary military aristocracy, while in Mesopotamia leadership positions evolved from what were essentially city offices? The early councils of the West Asian cities resemble in some respects the assemblies of the

Aryans in South Asia. In the case of Gangetic civilization, however, it seems probable that the assemblies evolved from the tribal organization of an earlier pastoral period.

Kingship in both Mesopotamia and the Gangetic plain developed when the functions of temporary military leaders were expanded and hereditary rule was established. In West Asia this shift was at the expense of the priesthood, which had previously been the most influential element in the cities. A question of particular interest is how accommodations between military leaders and ritual specialists were worked out and the manner in which this led to the emergence of divine kingships. Among the Aryans a different pattern of events unfolded. There, it was the warriors who enjoyed the highest stature in the tribal hierarchy and it was only after kingdoms were well established that the brahman ritual specialists managed to characterize themselves as the highest social stratum. In all cases kingship was accompanied by the elaboration of state organization, the competition for territory, and the intensification of warfare with bronze and iron weapons, horses, and chariots. The subjugation and uprooting of peoples, the carnage, and the political instability that accompanied the development of the military state led to a crisis for civilization, which will be considered in the next chapter.

BIBLIOGRAPHY

2.P THE POLITICAL ORGANIZATION OF CIVILIZED SOCIETIES: PROCESSES

Adams, Robert M., *The Evolution of Urban Society* (Chicago, 1966), 191 pp. See Chapter 4 for a comparative study of state formation.

Fried, Morton H., "On the Evolution of Social Stratification and the State," in S. Diamond, ed., *Culture in History* (New York, 1960), pp. 713-31. Concise theoretical statement; available in Bobbs-Merrill reprint.

Krader, Lawrence, *Formation of the State* (Prentice-Hall paperback, 1968), 118 pp. Discusses theories of state formation and provides examples for comparison.

Polanyi, K., ed., *Trade and Market in the Early Empires* (Glencoe, 1957), 382 pp. Collection of articles useful for the study of the economies of ancient civilizations in comparative perspective.

Woolley, Sir Leonard, *The Beginnings of Civilization* (Mentor paperback, 1965), 636 pp. Not theoretical but contains an immense amount of information on early civilizations arranged conveniently for comparative purposes.

2.1 THE POLITICAL ORGANIZATION OF MESOPOTAMIAN CIVILIZATION IN WEST ASIA

Frankfort, Henri, *The Art and Architecture of the Ancient Orient* (Pelican History of Art, 1954), 456 pp. Extensive text rich in cultural information.

Hallo, William W., and William Kelly Simpson, *The Ancient Near East* (Harcourt Brace paperback, 1971), 319 pp. The period from the first Mesopotamian kings until the formation of the Achaemenid empire is surveyed in Chapters 2-6.

Jones, Tom B., *Ancient Civilization* (Chicago, 1960), 476 pp. Chapters 7-10 survey West Asian history from about 2000 B.C. until the Achaemenid empire.

Oppenheim, A. Leo, *Ancient Mesopotamia* (Phoenix Book, 1964), 433 pp. A good complement to Kramer's *Sumerians*, an incisive study of Mesopotamian history from the early kings to the Achaemenids.

Pritchard, James B., *The Ancient Near East*, Vol. 1, *An Anthology of Texts and Pictures* (Princeton paperback, 1958), 380 pp. Especially valuable for its annotated translations of ancient texts.

Saggs, H.W.F., *The Greatness That Was Babylon* (Mentor paperback, 1962), 535 pp. Especially useful for emphasis on Assyria.

2.2 THE POLITICAL ORGANIZATION OF ARYAN CIVILIZATION IN SOUTH ASIA

Basham, A. L., *The Wonder That Was India* (Evergreen paperback, 1959), pp. 26-45, 232-56. A brilliant topical survey of pre-Muslim Indian culture by a leading authority.

deBary, W. T., ed., *Sources of the Indian Tradition* (Columbia University Press paperback, 1964), Vol. 1, pp. 1-18. Translations from the *Rigveda.*

Majumdar, Ramesh C., H. C. Raychaudhuri, and Kalikinkar Datta, *An Advanced History of India,* third edition (New York, 1967), pp. 24-66. A basic textbook account.

Piggott, Stuart, *Prehistoric India* (Penguin paperback, 1950), pp. 244-89. A scholarly account of the early Aryans with special attention to the *Rigveda* and Aryan military technology.

Thapar, Romila, *A History of India,* Vol. 1 (Penguin paperback, 1966), pp. 28-69. A lucid and concise account in a readily available source.

Wheeler, Sir Mortimer, *Early India and Pakistan to Ashoka* (London, 1959), pp. 118-33. A chapter on the Ganges civilization in a well-illustrated general work that stresses archaeological evidence.

2.3 THE POLITICAL ORGANIZATION OF SHANG AND CHOU CHINA

Bodde, Derk, "Feudalism in China," in Rushton Coulborn, ed., *Feudalism in History* (Princeton, 1956), 438 pp. A stimulating essay on Chou political institutions in comparative perspective.

Creel, H. G., *Origins of Statecraft in China,* Vol. 1, *Western Chou* (Chicago, 1970), 559 pp. A scholarly but readable study of early Chou political institutions based largely on bronze inscriptions.

Gernet, Jacques, *Ancient China* (Berkeley, 1968), 157 pp. This concise history of the ancient period is especially helpful in its account of social and political change.

Hsu Cho-yun, *Ancient China in Transition* (Stanford paperback, 1965), 240 pp. A penetrating scholarly analysis of social and political change during the late Chou period. This is the principal monograph on the subject in English.

Waley, Arthur, trans., *The Book of Songs* (Evergreen paperback, 1937), 358 pp. Waley's translation of this early Chou classic is the most informative single source book for the culture and everyday life of people in early Chou times.

Walker, Richard L., *The Multi-State System of Ancient China* (Hamden, Ct., 1953), 135 pp. This account of the disintegration of the polity of early Chou is a particularly good introduction to war and diplomacy of late Chou.

GLOSSARY

Agni. The Vedic god of fire.

Aryans. Speakers of an Indo-European language who invaded India from the northwest in the second millennium B.C.

Bimbisara. Sixth century B.C. ruler of Magadha, initiator of a major expansion of state power.

Brahmans. The priestly caste in Aryan society; originally ritual specialists, they also occupied ministerial posts and gradually rose to become the highest stratum of the caste system.

Bureaucracy. In contrast with feudalism, implies a state in which political authority is exercised through a hierarchy of public offices. Bureaucracy is characterized by impersonality, standardized procedures, and the centralization of authority. The officeholder has no personal or proprietary right to his office and is largely controlled by detailed written regulations.

Chandragupta Maurya. Late fourth century B.C. ruler who established the first great empire in India.

Dasas. The "dark ones," an Aryan name for the indigenous people of South Asia, perhaps referring to the remnants of the Harappan civilization.

Epic. Not used here in the strict sense of a poetic narrative, but as generally denoting literature, whether written or oral, which preserves the traditions concerning the heroic past achievements of a people or its leaders.

Feudalism. Used in this text in its political sense. Political authority in a feudal state is shared by a ruler with other military leaders in return for their personal support. These in their turn may have the support of still other military men, which leads to the formation of a hierarchy of lords and vassals and of states within states. Over time, members of a feudal ruling class tend to become a hereditary aristocracy and set limits to their obligations to their lords.

Hammurabi. Ruler of the First Dynasty of Babylon (r. ca. 1792-1750 B.C.), expanded his state by conquest but was most famous for the law code that was prepared in his reign and has survived largely intact.

Ideology. In this text, generally denotes ideas, beliefs, and symbols as these are used to justify the social order or the authority of the state or a political movement.

Kshatriyas. The warrior or aristocratic class in Aryan society, later to be surpassed in social stature by the brahmans.

Li. The Chinese word commonly translated "ceremonial." *Li* in the course of the Chou dynasty came to mean the highly elaborated code of conduct that governed human relations at least among the upper classes.

Lugal. A Sumerian designation of rulers having approximately the sense of "king."

Mahabharata. An epic poem recounting power struggles in north India in the first millennium B.C.; an important religous allegory in the Hindu tradition.

Manor. Denotes a landed estate managed and directed either by the owner or his steward. Farmers, artisans, and servants of a manorial estate are the personal dependents of the lord, and in return for their services to him they are entitled by custom to his protection. They are usually forbidden to move away.

Market. Refers to a competitive economic system in which goods and services are sold or exchanged for profit. This implies among other things the existence of a class of merchants. A market economy stands in contrast to a marketless economy, in which trade is conducted on the basis of negotiated or customary terms and is carried out either directly by producers and consumers as within a village, or by personal agents acting for state or temple authorities.

Prakrits. The common spoken variants of the Sanskritic mother tongue, one of which was selected by the Buddha as a popular medium of communication.

Raja. The tribal chief, originally elected to lead in war, later developed into the title for a king in India.

Ramayana. The epic tale of Prince Rama which reflects the Aryan advance into the Ganges basin early in the first millennium B.C.; subsequently a popular morality tale in the Hindu tradition.

Rigveda. The oldest collection of Vedic hymns; it may reflect the experience of the Aryans at the time they were still in the Panjab before moving eastward to the Ganges.

Sabha. A tribal council or meeting of elders in an Aryan society.

Samiti. A tribal meeting of all freemen in an Aryan tribe, as opposed to the *sabha,* or council of elders.

Sanskrit. The language of the Vedas, it is one of the oldest Indo-European tongues sharing common roots with many modern languages; it served as the classical language of the brahman elite in South Asia.

Sargon of Akkad (r. ca. 2334-2279 B.C.). He was not the first warrior king and state builder in Mesopotamia, but he was one of the most successful. His dynasty survived for nearly two centuries. The literary tradition that formed around this heroic figure was an important element in the political traditions of West Asia.

Shudras. The lowest stratum in the Aryan caste hierarchy, ritually unclean and therefore excluded from Vedic religious practice; probably these were indigenous people conquered by the Aryans. Later they became farmers.

Steppe. A general term denoting large areas of natural grasslands. More specifically, the immense tract of grasslands extending westward from the Khingan Mountains of Chinese Inner Mongolia across the Eurasian continent into eastern Europe.

Soma. A juicy plant and the intoxicating beverage made from it, celebrated in the Vedas as a deity.

Taxila. Capital of Gandhara and an important city in the Panjab for communication and trade between India and West and Central Asia.

T'ien. The name of the principal deity of the Chou people and the divine source of their rulers' authority. After the Chou conquest of the Shang, T'ien came to denote a universal and rather abstract divine power and may be translated "Heaven."

Vaishyas. Originally the cultivator class in the Aryan caste hierarchy. Later many became landlords, traders, and artisans while others remained farmers.

Varna. The Sanskrit word for caste, meaning originally color, perhaps deriving from the distinction between conquering Aryans and the darker indigenous Dasas.

Vedas. Religious hymns and texts dealing with both ritual and philosophical speculation transmitted orally among the Aryans for generations; subsequently the oldest sacred texts of Hinduism.

Wen Wang and Wu Wang. Kings Wen and Wu of the Chou dynasty. Wen Wang in Chou tradition was a paragon of justice and wisdom and laid the moral foundations for the reign of his heroic son, Wu Wang, conqueror of the Shang in 1122 B.C. The history and legends of these monarchs occupied an important place in Chinese political ideology.

3

The Crisis and Ethical Protest in the Mid-First Millennium B.C.

The Crisis and Ethical Protest in the Mid-First Millennium B.C.

600 B.C. to 450 B.C.

During the first millennium B.C. the civilizations of Asia faced a remarkably similar set of crises. The simultaneous acceleration of economic development and the occurrence of devastating wars broke down old social patterns and generated new ones. The populations of civilized societies grew rapidly on the basis of an expanding agriculture. Trade developed far beyond the levels attained in the early civilized period, and a distinct merchant class emerged. A general advance in technology was initiated by the coming of the Iron Age and the availability of metal in large quantities for tools and weapons. Within each major cultural area warfare among states was conducted on a greatly enlarged scale and with savage intensity. Whole societies feared destruction or large-scale forced migrations. Old ruling aristocracies were destroyed along with the institutions through which they had once ruled. New and more rational systems of government were created, and administrations came to be operated by career bureaucrats with a resulting increase in the despotic authority of rulers. This destruction and displacement of older social and political orders was accompanied by the dissolution of the old religious beliefs and ceremonials that had justified and sustained them.

It was in this period of crisis that some of the best known of Asia's ethical teachers emerged on the scene to denounce the conditions of their times in protests that had much in common. Confucius, Buddha, Zoroaster, the Hebrew prophets, and the other ancient Chinese, Indian, and West Asian moralists differed among themselves in the proposals they expounded, for each was the product of a particular time and a particular cultural tradition. But all shared in common a deep concern with the breakdown of the ethical standards and moral values of the time. Each in his own way protested vigorously against senseless bloodshed, greedy ambition, ruthless exploitation, and general immorality. It was this condemnation of their societies that won for them a sympathetic audience, while the way in which they drew upon and reworked the traditions of their own cultures in proposing solutions gained them a permanent place in the history of their civilizations.

Despite the separate and distinct messages of these ethical reformers, it is possible to make comparisons under a number of broad headings, including their views of the origins of evil, their interpretation of human history, their appeal for individual transformation, and their vision of a better society.

3

PROCESSES

Crisis in the Mid-First Millennium B.C.

a. Militarism and materialism
b. Elitism and political cynicism
c. Traditionalism and ritualistic formalism
d. Proletarianization and cultural alienation

The Formulation of Ethical Protest

e. Moral sensitivity and ethical dualism
f. Existential humanism and internal transformation
g. Nemesis and the reinterpretation of history
h. Universalism and social amelioration

PATTERNS

1. **Zoroaster and the Hebrew Prophets in West Asia**
2. **Mahavira and Buddha in South Asia**
3. **Ethical Protest and Reform Ideology in Chou China**

3. ETHICAL PROTEST

		1	2	3
	GREECE	HEBREWS/ZOROASTER	MAHAVIRA/BUDDHA	CONFUCIUS/LEGALISTS
		First Isaiah, ca. 740-701		
700 B.C.		Hezekiah, ca. 725-697		
		Josiah, ca. 640-609		
		Cyaxares 625-593		
600		Zoroaster, fl. ca. 588		
		Babylonian captivity, ca. 586-539		
		Second Isaiah, fl. ca. 550-540		
		Cyrus, r. ca. 550-530 Cyrus' Edict of Liberation 539, permitting return of Hebrews to Jerusalem	Bimbisara, fl. ca. 545	Confucius 551-479
			The Buddha Sakyamuni, ca. 560-480 Mahavira, ca. 540-468	
500				

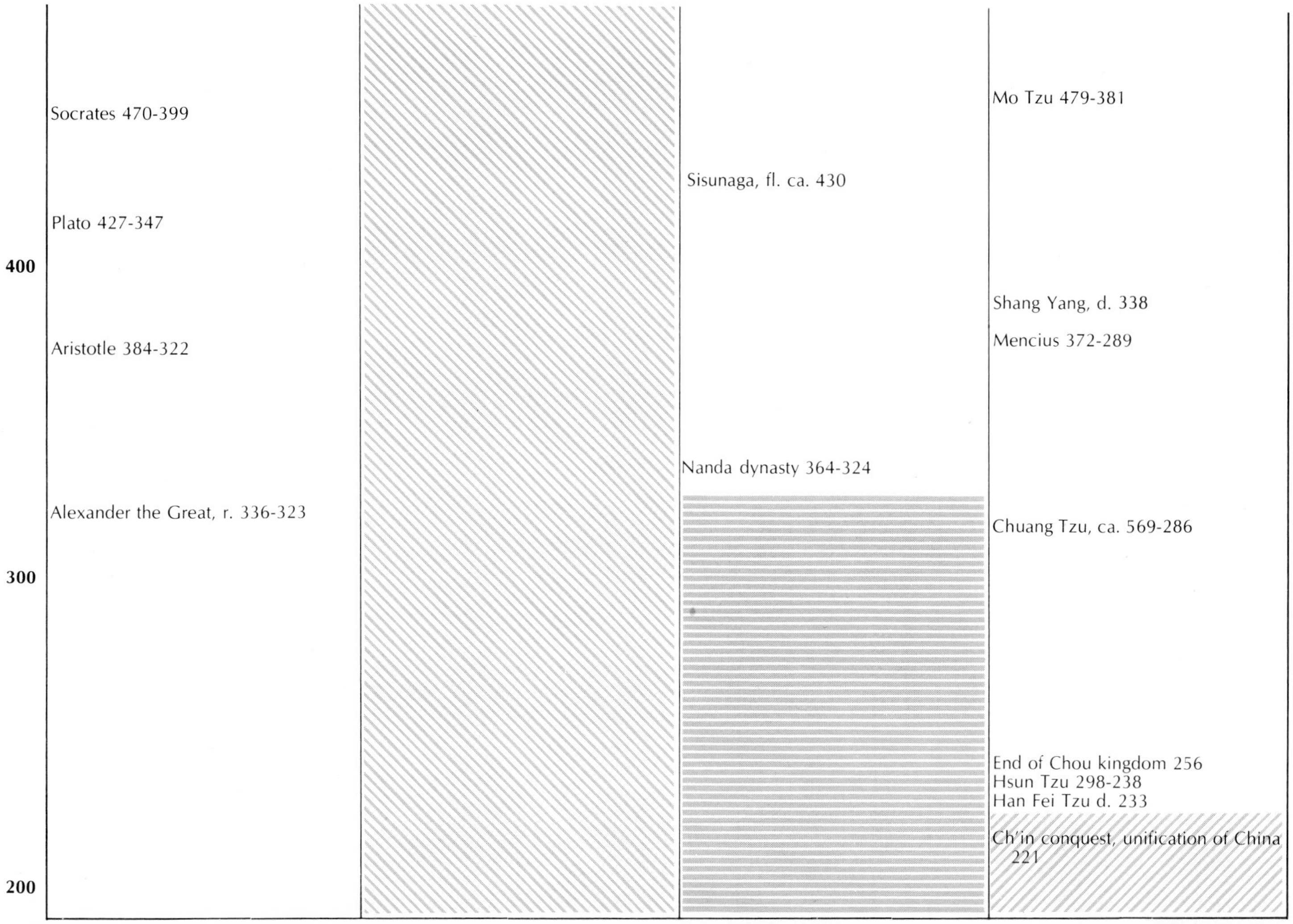

Date				
	Socrates 470-399			Mo Tzu 479-381
			Sisunaga, fl. ca. 430	
	Plato 427-347			
400				
				Shang Yang, d. 338
	Aristotle 384-322			Mencius 372-289
			Nanda dynasty 364-324	
	Alexander the Great, r. 336-323			Chuang Tzu, ca. 569-286
300				
				End of Chou kingdom 256 Hsun Tzu 298-238 Han Fei Tzu d. 233
				Ch'in conquest, unification of China 221
200				

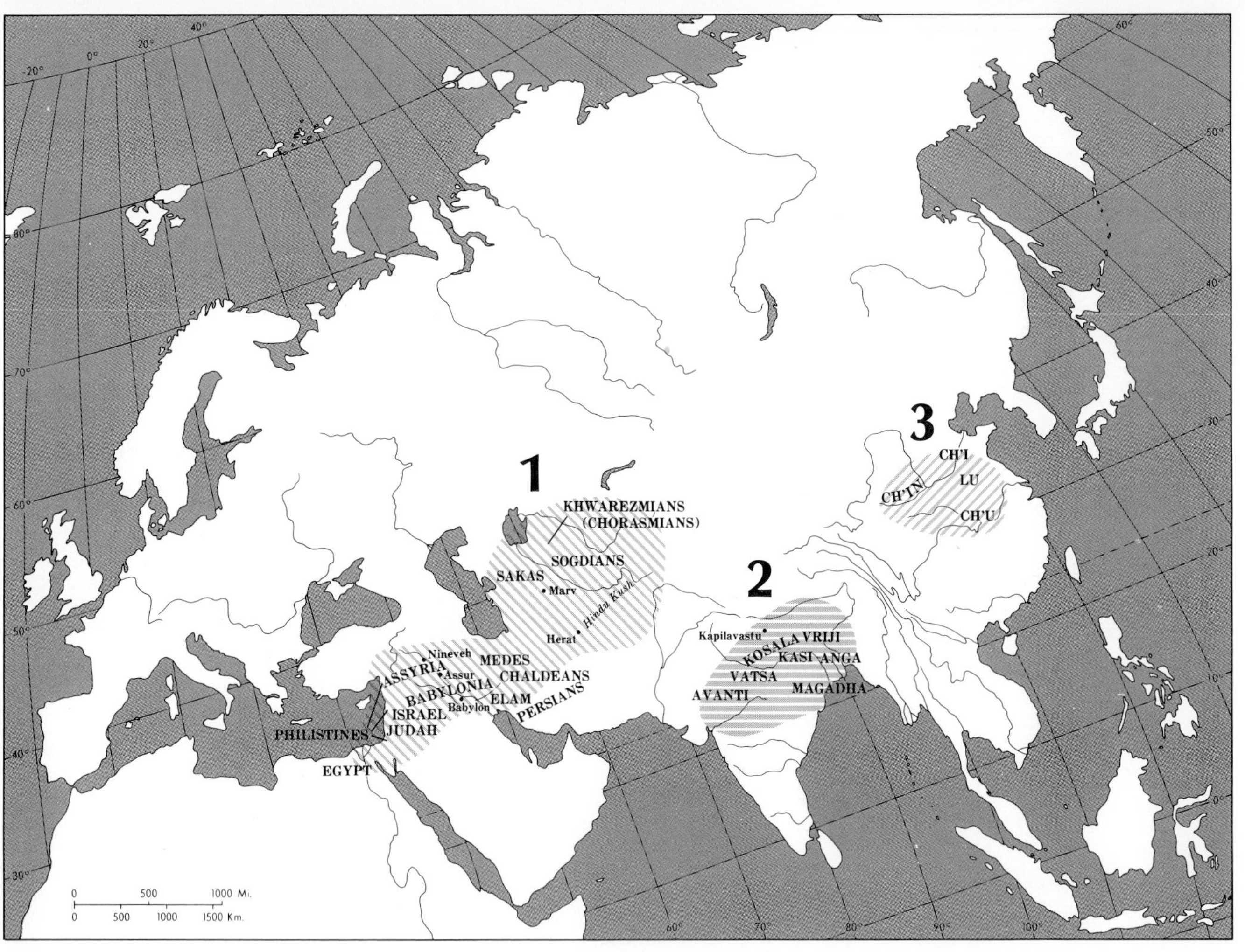

Map 13 The crisis and ethical protest in the mid-first millennium B.C.

PROCESSES

Reaction against perceived injustices or immorality is a pervasive phenomenon in the history of human societies, but in Eurasian history the two centuries between 600 and 400 B.C. stand out as a truly remarkable era of ethical protest. In this relatively brief span lived not only the Greek thinkers Socrates and Plato and the Hebrew prophets Ezekiel and Isaiah, but also the Iranian religious leader Zoroaster, the Indian moralists Mahavira and Buddha, the Chinese philosophers Mo Tzu and Confucius. These were ethical reformers whose basic ideals, although often much modified, were to form the foundations of later ideologies that continue to influence human lives even in the present day.

Here we shall attempt to compare these ethical reformers by focusing on two separate but not unrelated aspects of their lives and thought. First, there is need to explore the historical circumstances they faced in their individual civilizations. Whereas too little is known definitely about the personal lives of these men to hazard firm statements about the internal psychological experiences that led them to their beliefs, enough is known about the social conditions of their times to suggest why their ideals fell on receptive ears, spread, and became influential. Moreover, it would seem apparent that each of these thinkers was attempting to provide meaningful solutions to very real human problems—answers to questions raised by concrete situations. Thus, in order to understand the ideas they articulated, it is important to grasp the nature of the issues they confronted. Once the historical processes at work during this period have been made clearer, we can then turn to the ethical principles espoused by these moral reformers. At that point we shall stress the similarities in their basic ideals. These similarities have sometimes been said to have been due to cultural exchange, the borrowing of inspiration by one civilization from another. It can be argued that it is just as probable that conditions of crisis occurred in the separate civilizations at roughly the same time span and thus led to parallel responses.

THE PERIOD

The age of the great Asian reformers overlaps the preceding period in the growth of civilization in West, South, and East Asia, and indeed it was in many respects the processes of political organization and territorial expansion themselves that stimulated the reaction. The Hebrew prophet Ezekiel lived during the Babylonian captivity (i.e., 586-539 B.C.), shortly after the Chaldeans (or Neo-Babylonians) replaced the Assyrians in West Asia. Farther to the east, in Iran, Zoroaster (belived to have lived in the early sixth century B.C.) would have witnessed a time of political conflict preceding the establishment of the Achaemenid empire. In South Asia, by the time of Buddha (ca. 563–ca. 483 B.C.), there were over a dozen powerful states competing for dominance in northern India, including Magadha, which is sometimes compared to Assyria. In East Asia during the lifetime of Confucius (ca. 551–ca. 479 B.C.), Chinese civilization was facing its first great crisis as the Chou dynasty (1122-221 B.C.) continued its long-term disintegration.

CRISIS IN THE MID-FIRST MILLENNIUM B.C.

The processes at work in this period were in no sense unique to it. We shall note them often in discussions of political tension, social stress, and moral turmoil in other eras. We need to examine them at some length here because it was at this time that they combined to produce a period of major crisis in the ancient history of Asia. Unfortunately, in many instances specific details are not fully available to the historian, and our information is partially derived from the biased, if not necessarily distorted, views of the ethical protestors themselves, thus blurring the line between historical objectivity and subjective reaction.

Nevertheless, the broad outlines are clear enough to permit the attempt to summarize the major causes of the crises that affected all of these civilizations during the first millennium B.C.

a. Militarism and Materialism

As ancient civilizations developed and became more highly organized politically, they tended to become increasingly militaristic. Weapons and tactics became more and more brutal, often causing unparalleled hardship on the masses of the people as the violence grew in scale and intensity. Under the Assyrians, the elite of Mesopotamian society embraced a definite militaristic ethos, while in India there raged a long regional conflict of competing states eventually won by the kingdom of Magadha. In China the latter part of this period is referred to simply as the period of the Warring States. Accompanying this militarism was a pervasive atmosphere of materialism. Economic growth and technological development afforded many, especially the military and commercial elites, a new level of affluence as reward for success in materialistic competition. The crass pursuit of material wealth and hedonistic comfort often seemed the dominant motive as self-interest took precedence over ethical considerations.

b. Elitism and Political Cynicism

Parallel and closely related to military expansion and material acquisitiveness was the trend toward the cynical abuse of political power and social status. Monarchies grew more powerful as they extended control domestically through more centralized administrative structures, and at the same time they expanded their domains abroad through military conquest. Dominant commercial classes increased their profits through blatantly exploitive practices. Conservative priesthoods and other ceremonial experts took advantage of their roles to entrench themselves more firmly in an elite position. Whereas kingship was once associated with an ideal of kingly responsibility for the welfare of the common people, and indeed monarchs had sometimes formed political alliances with the commoners against exploitive elites who challenged the authority of royal government, in this period monarchs were more often allied with the various elites and exercised their royal power cynically.

c. Traditionalism and Ritualistic Formalism

A further factor in the gathering crisis within these ancient civilizations was the failure of the religious and intellectual leadership in the older centers to create new ideas or articulate moral doctrines that would have been meaningful in the conditions of the times. Instead, the priests and literati tended to look to tradition, and the dominant trend was toward the elaboration of conceptual systems built up from accumulated myths, legends, rites, and rituals. Truth and morality were sought in the rearrangement of old concepts and the greater systematization of the corpus of sanctified tradition. Traditionalism or the blind imitation of tradition had set in, often with disastrous effects on these societies. The lack of creativity on the part of priests and literati, explained in part by their desire to maintain a privileged position in society and government and in part as a response to social norms, led to an extreme conservatism in the defense of the established religions.

At the same time, ritualistic sacrifice in the name of the sacred apparently increased. The extension of royal power itself intensified the use of sacrifice, since new rituals were called for in order to guarantee the success of political programs and military campaigns. Ceremonial specialists thus actually innovated new rites and procedures for their political patrons. Ritualistic sacrifice, of course, was also in accord with the common belief in the efficacy of such acts in granting mundane success. Such sacrifice, however, had debilitating economic as well as demoralizing effects on some segments of the populace.

d. Proletarianization and Cultural Alienation

In the absence of an ethical order to moderate the abuses of materialism and self-interest, the wealthy and the powerful formed an elite that dominated society through force and collusion. The result was a widening of the social and economic distance between the privileged few and the masses. Social stratification as such had always been a characteristic of civilizations, and the peasant cultivator had always borne the burden of producing sufficient agricultural surplus to support the urban centers. But in better times the lower classes and the peasantry as a whole had been recognized as participants in the larger society. Now there was widespread economic exploitation of the peasantry, often the result of an increased commercialization of agriculture, with its concomitant tendencies toward indebtedness by cultivator to landlord or merchant. Impoverished as tenants or driven off the land to become wage laborers, these strata swelled the ranks of the proletariat, people who lost not only their former economic status but also their legal and social standing as participants in society, thereby becoming alienated from the civilized community.

Yet another cause of alienation was the expansion of civilizations to include new ethnic groups and subcultures. On the one hand, growth meant the proliferation of new and alien ideas in an often bewildering complexity. On the other hand, the conservatism of the dominant elites intensified the cultural parochialism of the dominant center, which failed to make an appropriate accommodation or to accept the new plurality of subcultures. The effect for many, especially those in the newer peripheral areas, must have been akin to the crisis of cultural identity frequently noted in our own day: assimilation into a civilized community demanded the acceptance of an orthodoxy that itself would not tolerate diversity in cultural identities. Cultural alienation, while less tangible than economic impoverishment, was nevertheless a very real factor contributing to the crisis within these civilizations.

THE FORMULATION OF ETHICAL PROTEST

The radical changes that accompanied the growth of civilizations in this age required equally radical alterations in their world views. The failure of the older centers of these civilizations to meet this challenge alienated large segments of the populace, who turned away from the orthodox moral and religious order in search of new ideas that were more relevant and meaningful to their actual experience. It was at this juncture that ethical protests were formulated by such men as Ezekiel, Zoroaster, Buddha, and Confucius. As a consequence of their lasting influence, much of the writing on these seminal thinkers has been produced by partisan advocates. Each was the founder of a religious or intellectual tradition within which later disciples were to produce complex commentaries and build sanctified systems of interpretation. Thus it is no easy task to penetrate the layers of accumulated exegesis. Moreover, these commentators have jealously guarded the claim to uniqueness made on behalf of the inspiration of their respective teachers, most often resisting attempts by historians to draw parallels or explore the striking similarities in the moral philosophies these men espoused. Nevertheless, it is both possible and fruitful to generalize on the common themes in their ethical protest.

e. Moral Sensitivity and Ethical Dualism

The first and most obvious point of similarity lies in their common rejection of the violent and selfish pursuit of materialistic goals. Although not all were pacifists in the sense that Buddha was, each was clearly reacting against the cruelty of his age, whether in the form of ritualistic killing or of warfare waged for militaristic expansion. Life in their view was more than the hedonistic quest for personal gratification or the aggrandizement of the state at the expense of others. Human conduct had to be guided by moral principles, and in order for civilization to be saved moral good had to triumph over evil. All the reformers, in their own ways and in the idioms of the cultures within which they lived, stressed the necessity of choice between good and evil. Thus, to a greater or lesser degree each developed some form of ethical dualism and each was concerned with specifying precisely what kind of behavior was evil and what kind was good. Thus, one legacy of Hebraism was its stern legalistic ethics, while the moral guidelines of Confucius were to remain meaningful in everyday conduct in China for millennia.

f. Existential Humanism and Internal Transformation

The repudiation of materialism was not, for these men, the same as a negation of all social life. On the contrary, extreme asceticism and withdrawal from the world was rejected both in their own actions and in the precepts they taught. They addressed themselves to kings as well as personal disciples and taught that even the man of commerce might achieve morality if only he first overcame evil in his daily conduct. All of these reformers were primarily concerned with human existence within society, although not all were as articulate about social relations as Confucius and none perhaps wrestled with the specific problems of governmental institutions as extensively as did Plato in Greece. Moreover, all rejected the preoccupation of established religious and intellectual ideologies with metaphysical systems. These were irrelevant to man's quest for fulfillment. In many ways the position adopted is close to that of modern existentialists in our own day, who have insisted that reality lies in human existence per se and not in the substance of ideas about that existence. It followed that blind adherence to esoteric rituals or similar attempts to manipulate fate merely obscured the truth and deflected man from the path of morality. Man was quite alone in shaping his world and must do so without providential intervention by the gods (although here the Hebrew prophets would dissent from the others). Nor was man's fate predetermined by his internal nature. Man had free will to do both good and evil.

Closely associated with existential humanism was a stress on self-knowledge and internal transformation as essential to moral goodness. Since the reformers tended to view man as the measure of all things, it followed that man had to look within himself for the altar of truth. Only through self-realization could he become a moral being and thus end individual and social suffering. The method to achieve this internal transformation was therefore crucial, and reformers gave considerable attention to it. Recommended practices ranged from rigorous self-discipline verging on asceticism to the observance of detailed rules for responsible interaction in human relations.

g. Nemesis and the Reinterpretation of History

This existential orientation and stress on internal transformation placed a great burden of responsibility on the individual. He alone was responsible for his acts; he was to choose between good and evil; and he was to give up rituals meant to coerce the spirits or manipulate fate. There was, therefore, the need for assurance that ultimately justice would prevail, that evil would be punished and virtue rewarded. Moreover, the repudiation of established ideologies required a reinterpretation of man's past, a reevaluation of the myths and historical beliefs that had been embodied in the traditional world views of these civilizations. For some reformers both needs were met by projecting the golden age into the future—an age that older views had placed in the mythical past. Thus the Hebrew prophets preached the coming of a messiah, and Zoroaster taught that there would be a day of judgment, on which retribution to the wicked and the victory of good over evil would be accomplished. The doctrine of karmic retribution offered a similar assurance of nemesis in South Asia. In the case of Confucius, however, the reward was to be found in the dispensations of a truly just society, the recapturing of the golden age in the present.

Although the break with the past is often quite apparent to later historians, it must be emphasized that the reformers themselves did not claim the role of innovators. Their attack on tradition was an attack on the misuse of the past by traditionalists. Some, like Confucius, took pains to insist that they were merely reaffirming the teachings of the sages of antiquity, the true tradition that had become distorted.

h. Universalism and Social Amelioration

The ethical protest of the first millennium B.C. was typically a call for moral reform rather than social change in the sense of the egalitarianism of the modern era. Just as the protest against the violence of militarism was not necessarily an argument for pacificism, the objection to elitism was not necessarily a demand for social equality. For these reformers the just society need not be democratic either politically or economically. Nevertheless, they were calling for the amelioration of social wrongs as well as spiritual evils, and their message often had radical implications in the context of their own times. For example, the sharp criticism of materialism was a condemnation of economic exploitation of the lower classes, and the emphasis on internal virtue demanded that the exploitive elite and the malevolent king justify their authority and position.

Moreover, these reformers appear to have intended their message to hold true for all of humankind. This meant, on the one hand, that all men (and for some, at least, even women) had the status of participants in human society, since all individuals, if not necessarily fully equal, had the capacity for self-transformation and moral goodness. As such the individual was not to be treated as a mere means to another's ends. On the other hand, universalism also implied a rejection of the cultural parochialism that underlay the oppression of peripheral peoples by the elite of a dominant center. Psychologically, these universalistic themes must have had great appeal for people no longer certain of their place in society or of their own cultural identity as minority groups within a larger civilization.

The ideas of these ethical reformers, especially their attack on externalities and their faith in the individual's capacity to find salvation for himself, were radically new in the history of Eurasia. In sum they called for a virtual revolution in morality. It is therefore not surprising that they had more appeal among the less powerful than among the more influential groups within their own societies. Despite some instances in which rulers were moved to moderate the political cynicism of the times, the immediate success of the reformers in their own day was at best limited. Although they did not all suffer the martyrdom of Socrates, condemned for corrupting Athenian youth, and were not without honor in their own land, nevertheless it was not until long after their deaths that any was to receive his place in the history of his respective civilization. As we shall see in the next chapter, this would typically follow the co-option or appropriation of their basic ideas by elites within new universal states, immense empires that unified civilizations in part by utilizing these ideas as the foundation for universalistic political ideologies.

PATTERNS

1. ZOROASTER AND THE HEBREW PROPHETS IN WEST ASIA

On the eastern and western margins of West Asian civilization, religion with a strong ethical orientation developed in contexts of social insecurity engendered by war, cultural interaction, and social change. Eastern Iran in the seventh and sixth centuries B.C. was a zone of interaction between sedentary communities based on cattle raising, agriculture, and trade and the very different society of the fully nomadic people of the Central Asian steppes. It was also a region of mingling cultural influences stemming from distant centers of civilization in Mesopotamia and perhaps from India. It was here that Zoroaster probably began his teaching some time around 588 B.C., calling on his hearers to abandon the gods and cults of ancient Iranian tradition and instead to devote themselves to the service of Ahura Mazda, divine champion of truth and justice, against the lies and wrongs of the unbelievers. In the west, the Palestinian kingdoms of Israel and Judah occupied an embattled zone between Egypt and the expanding empires of Assyria and Babylon during the eighth through sixth centuries B.C. Elements of a major cultural crisis existed in the experience of conquest and exile and in the continuing tensions between the ancient religious values of the Israelites' nomadic phase during the Exodus and the agricultural and urban cults and values indigenous to the national home in the land of Canaan. The prophets summoned their people to purge themselves of the corruptions of urbanism and the worship of false gods, and warned that failure to do so would be punished by invasion and conquest at the hands of the great powers acting as the instruments of divine wrath.

In contrast to these frontier regions, the Mesopotamian center of West Asian civilization responded to the crises of war and politics by renewed commitment to ancient religious values. The social structure of the cities proved its toughness and durability and the cities held fast to their protecting gods. Moreover, the rulers of Assyria, very much in the same religious tradition, generally respected the urban cults and allowed them to continue. Thus, basic changes in ideological orientation would come this time from the margins and not from the center of the civilization.

Zoroastrianism and the ethical monotheism of the Hebrew prophets dramatically challenged men to assure their own, and the world's, reformation by knowing and doing the right, and both exerted a strong influence on subsequent history. Zoroastrianism was later incorporated into the ideology of the empires of Iran and gave rise to the religions of Manichaeanism and Mazdakism. Zoroastrianism itself survives in the present time as a minor religion in Iran and among the Parsees of India. The religion of the Hebrew laws and the prophets has enabled its followers to maintain a collective identity in the face of millennia of exile and dispersal, and it gave rise to the religions of Christianity and Islam.

Zoroastrianism

Most of the population of the Iranian plateau lived near its outer margins, where streams descending from the mountains watered pastures for livestock and made irrigated agriculture possible. The interior was dry and sparsely inhabited. In the centuries before Zoroaster, the Persians occupied the southern portion of the Zagros, with the Medes to the north of them. In eastern Iran were Chorasmians, Bactrians, and Sogdians, who occupied the valleys of rivers flowing northwest and west from the Hindu Kush and the riverine tracts skirting the Amu Darya and its mouths. Despite the distances that separated them and their regional variations in culture and dialect, these peoples shared a relatively homogeneous Iranian heritage. One effect of this pattern was that the richest and most populous parts of Iran were exposed to attack by the civilized states of the west or by the nomads of the steppes.

The homeland of Zoroaster and his teaching was in eastern Iran. Archaeological evidence has shown that the first half of the first millennium B.C. in this region was a time of profound change. A flourishing urban civilization based on cattle raising, irrigation, and trade had begun to develop, especially in the vicinities of Marv and Herat. Large, permanent settlements were built by the peasants and pastoralists, and the presence of iron implements testifies to the fact that their material culture was fairly advanced. The extent of the ancient irrigation systems proves that there must have been an efficient and correspondingly large-scale social organization. The archaeological evidence lends support to epic traditions that there were territorial kingdoms there by the time of Zoroaster, although this cannot be proved, and such states as may have existed were soon to be absorbed in the Achaemenid empire. At the very least, the changes taking place in eastern Iran were such as to alter the forms of association in both kin and political groups and to require corresponding changes in the religion. Compounding the unsettling effects of social and cultural change was the difficulty of defending the oases against attack. The remains of horse equipment found in these sites indicate the presence of nomads, presumably Sakas (Scythians), in the area. How much contact there may have been between these eastern outposts of West Asian civilization and the populated regions of western Iran and Mesopotamia is difficult to determine, but the importance of trade would make it appear that some contact must have existed.

On the western frontiers of Iran, war and politics were building to the climactic formation of the Achaemenid empire. Assyria's "Second Empire" extended its domination over Mesopotamia and, provoked by Elamite support of local resistance, sent its armies against Elam in 636 B.C. and devastated it so thoroughly that it ceased to be a major independent power thereafter. Despite this success, Assyria was soon challenged by the Chaldean state in lower Mesopotamia and then finally destroyed by the Medes invading upper Mesopotamia from the east.

The source for early Zoroastrianism is the *Avesta,* comprising the *Gathas,* or *Hymns,* as well as additional scriptures dating from a later period. Only the *Gathas* are thought to be the words of Zoroaster. The language of the *Gathas* is archaic and difficult to understand, and the text lends itself to radically different interpretations by modern scholars. There are some probabilities most scholars can agree on, however. Zoroaster was a priest of the religion indigenous to the eastern regions of Iran and enjoyed the patronage of a tribal leader or king, Vishtaspa, whom he is said to have converted to his doctrines around 588 B.C. The *Gathas* themselves reflect a deep hostility toward the nomads, whom Zoroaster regarded as positively evil, and conversely, they express general approval of the vocations of farming and husbandry. This suggests that Zoroaster's social milieu was that of the oasis rather than of the open steppe.

The religion of eastern Iran at this time shared a common origin with that of northern India in the ancient Aryan beliefs, but it was undergoing important changes. The nature gods, who were divine representations of natural forces, were giving way to new ones who personified elements of the social order, such as contract and hospitality. The gods were now more approachable than they had been before, because Zoroaster addressed Ahura Mazda directly and familiarly in the *Gathas*. Consistent with this narrowing gap between the worlds of gods and men, the age of myth was now yielding to that of the epic. In this context of cultural change, Zoroaster formed his vision of the supreme divinity, Ahura Mazda, who epitomized the ethical good. Against him were arrayed the demonic forces of "the lie." The ethical dualism of good and evil had become for him the cosmic issue and his message was therefore universal, for all mankind. Other spirits were seen as evil powers, and in his commitment to his vision of ethical responsibility he denounced the worship of false gods and the ancient cult practices of sacrificial feasting and the use of *haoma* (the Aryan *soma*) to induce states of ecstasy. Perhaps in his own time and certainly soon after, the forces of evil were personified in the diabolical Anrya Mainyu. In compensation, Ahura Mazda was provided with a divine helper, Spenta Mainyu.

The vividness and durability of Zoroaster's image as the prophetic founder of a new religion suggests that he must have been an extraordinarily inspiring person with a message that was in some degree new and radical, but it is a matter of dispute exactly what his innovations were. It is possible that a tendency toward monotheism had already appeared in some form and even that the god Ahura Mazda had become the object of a cult. This is suggested by the fact that the early Achaemenid emperors claimed to have received Ahura

Mazda's sanction for their rule, but without explicitly acknowledging Zoroaster or his doctrines. What was most original in Zoroaster's doctrine may have been what may strike us as most significant even now: the responsibility of the people of the world for the final outcome of the cosmic struggle between good and evil. The challenge to choose and act rightly appears to be dramatic and almost overwhelming; not even Ahura Mazda could assure the final triumph of the Good unless mankind chose to tip the scales in its favor. The ethical duty of man was inescapable, and everything depended on it.

Indeed, the burden of responsibility placed on mere mortals by the teachings of Zoroaster proved to be too heavy, and in the further development of the religion, means were found to provide comfort and reassurance to the lay followers. Some of the old deities such as Mithra and Anahita were accorded a place in cult practices, fire worship became an intrinsic part of Zoroastrian religious life, fire altars and fire temples were erected over a vast area of country, and a powerful Zoroastrian priesthood came into being. Concurrently, the emphasis on duty shifted from the stark ethical challenge implicit in the *Gathas* to the correct performance of elaborate rituals.

Hebrew Prophets

The setting in which the tradition of the Hebrew prophets was formed was a marginal one in several senses of the word. Palestine, roughly equivalent to modern Israel plus western Jordan, was pressed between the Syrian desert and the Mediterranean coast. Politically, it was marginal to the powers of Egypt at one end of the Fertile Crescent and Mesopotamia at the other, and subject to invasion by the armies of both. In terms of the natural resources necessary for the development of urban civilization it was, again, marginal. There were resources enough to sustain urban settlement, but only on a modest scale and in intimate interpenetration with the economy of pastoralism. Irrigation was difficult because most of the country was hilly and lacking in surface water, but rainfall agriculture (wheat and barley) and tree crops were possible in some areas. Upland pastures were heavily used for sheep and goats. Under these conditions, there developed in Palestine a mixed economy of trade, agriculture, and herding and a mixed society of city dwellers, peasants, herders and, on the eastern and southern desert margins, full nomads, or bedouins.

The ethical monotheism of the prophets was shaped and deepened in Palestine during the frightening years of Assyrian and Babylonian invasions and conquests from the eighth through the sixth centuries B.C. To discover its roots, however, it is necessary to look back at least to the Exodus and the formation of the Israelite "nation" in the time of Moses. When the Hyksos established their domination over Egypt in the seventeenth century B.C., they were either accompanied or joined later by numbers of other migrants from Syria and Palestine, including some groups of Apiru, or Hebrews. The Egyptians soon overthrew the alien regime, however, and many of the people associated with it were now reduced to slavery or corvée labor. According to tradition, it was under Moses that many—perhaps hundreds of thousands—of these oppressed people revolted and escaped to the east. In the course of a half century or so of wandering, the refugees achieved a measure of solidarity, which was expressed in the form of a sacred contract that not only bound together the tribes and clans in a religious association, but bound all the members collectively, in a contractual relationship with the god Yahweh, or Jehovah. Yahweh, a majestic god of storm, fire, and battle, took charge of the destiny of Israel in return for the Israelites' commitment to keep his laws and commands as revealed by his prophets. Owing perhaps to the hardships and perils of the exodus, Yahwism, the cult of Yahweh, was singularly intense and approached monotheism. (It was acknowledged that other peoples had gods of their own, but the Israelities were permitted to worship only Yahweh.) This monotheistic tendency was probably reinforced by the relative lack of stratification and occupational differentiation of

Israelite society under the conditions of the exodus, and a consequent lack of motive for the formation of special cults.

The wanderers eventually settled in Palestine (the land of Canaan) early in the thirteenth century B.C. This region, which they identified as the promised land of milk and honey, was at that time inhabited by various peoples mostly speaking Semitic dialects, including Canaanite, Hebrew, and Phoenician. The northern and coastal areas especially had a long-established agricultural, town, and commercial society, and some of the Israelites at first assumed the role of pastoralists in the more arid areas that were left unoccupied. The settlement was not achieved peacefully, however, but required about a century of minor wars with the Canaanites. Israelite unity was now difficult to maintain. The community dispersed through Canaan, taking up different occupations as peasants (probably the greatest number), herdsmen, merchants, artisans, and priests. Thus scattered and differentiated, they were subject to strong Canaanite influence, especially with regard to the indigenous fertility cults. These involved the worship of various *baals* (generic Canaanite term for "gods" and "goddesses"). Propitiation of the *baals* required lavish sacrifices, including human sacrifice, and ecstatic and sexual rites that were offensive to strict followers of the Mosaic law. Yahwism was sustained in the face of widespread involvement in *baal* worship by the maintenance of several Yahweh cult centers, including a major one at Shiloh, where the Ark of the Covenant, a sort of portable temple, was installed. The centers and their priests provided a religious core around which the Israelite confederation maintained a precarious existence. Another factor working for unity was the threat of invasion by the Philistine "Sea People" during the twelfth and eleventh centuries B.C. Defense of the Palestine settlements demanded and brought about a measure of military cooperation.

The struggle with the Philistines was climaxed in 1050 B.C. by their destruction of Shiloh and temporary capture of the Ark. This catastrophe may have contributed to the Israelite transition from confederation to monarchy, but changes in the culture and society had paved the way for it. Concentration of wealth had resulted in the formation of urban oligarchies, which dominated not only the cities but their hinterlands as well. At the same time, military technology had been transformed by widespread adoption of the horse chariot. Such equipment could be afforded only by the wealthy, and only the wealthy had the leisure to make a profession of war. The effect of this was to reduce the confederacy's reliance on armies of peasant soldiers bearing simple arms. The military function had now begun to pass into the hands of the landowning families, and the social status of the peasantry declined accordingly. The first warrior-kings, Saul and David, were of peasant and pastoral background, respectively, but David and his heir, Solomon, moved rapidly to organize Israel politically as a conventional city-centered, bureaucratically managed monarchy supported mainly by agricultural taxes. Saul was elected king by the leading clans and annointed by the priest Samuel in about 1030 B.C. Before his death he had been surpassed in popular favor by David, who became king in about 1010 B.C. David defeated the Philistines and took advantage of the temporary weakness of Assyria and Egypt to expand his kingdom south to the Gulf of Aqaba and north through modern Lebanon and beyond. He established a central administration based at least partly on the Egyptian model and conducted a population census for tax purposes. Solomon continued the centralist and imperialist policies of David. His kingdom was divided into twelve administrative provinces, and the wealth and labor of the population were mobilized in the form of tax and tribute to defray the cost of military equipment (horses and chariots imported from Egypt), fortifications, palaces, and the great Jerusalem temple in which he intended to concentrate the religious authority of the state. Additional revenues came from copper mining and smelting in the south and from state trading. The regimentation and the material costs of his enterprises turned many against him, including not only the tax-paying peasants but the urban great families, who were unable to check his extravagances. So great was the resentment that when Solomon died in 925 B.C., his heir's demands on the north for taxes resulted in the formation there of the independent kingdom of Israel. During the period of the divided monarchy which followed, the south was subject to the kingdom of Judah.

The period of the confederacy and the monarchy corresponds roughly to the beginning of the continuous development and historical importance of the Hebrew practice of prophecy. By prophecy is meant the belief that Yahweh made certain individuals his worldly spokesmen. The prophet heard the word of God and then announced it to others as he had been commanded. The early prophets often formed large bands (groups of as many as four hundred are mentioned in the Bible), and in imparting the word of God they might be seized together by a kind of ecstatic frenzy. In the crises of the Canaanite and Philistine wars, these spectacles served the useful function of inspiring the warriors to heroic efforts in battle, and gave their campaigns the character of holy wars. The establishment of the monarchy also had the purpose of strengthening the nation of Israel against its enemies, but it was not entirely welcome to all of the prophets. The establishment of a king was acceptable as an emergency measure, but when the role became permanent and institutionalized, it stood in contradiction to the idea of the Mosaic covenant, which bound the people together and bound them collectively to Yahweh. The monarchy could be seen from the perspective of the conservative prophets as intruding between the people and their god. A further and persistent source of conflict was the practice of politics by the kings. Solomon especially, but others as well, found it expedient to make alliances with other states in pursuit of policy objectives. This usually resulted in necessary compromises with the alien cults, as when Solomon sealed his alliances by marrying foreign princesses and then granted them the right to maintain their own temples and priests in the vicinity of Jerusalem. This was easily represented as a source of corruption and an offense against Yahweh. Some prophets became court functionaries, providing divine counsel and legitimation as the occasion required, while others remained among the people. When popular disaffection with the kings grew strong, the free prophets, as individuals and with passionate intensity, began to speak the word of God in the streets of the cities. Their message, however, was directed not only against the wrongs and oppressions of royal government, but also against the sins and heresies of the common people. As a result, their sincerity was well established, but they were often so unpopular as to be in danger of their lives.

During the period of the divided kingdoms of Israel and Judah (926-722 B.C.), the Syro-Palestine area was divided among a great number of minor states, which formed unstable systems of alliances in which Judah and Israel often found themselves on opposing sides. The danger from the great powers added to the sense of insecurity. Judah was devastated by raids from Egypt late in the tenth century B.C., and Israel was, for a time, reduced to tributary status under Assyrian domination in the mid-ninth century. Israel was the more exposed to Assyrian aggression and prospered and declined in inverse proportion to the power and aggressiveness of the latter. A period of Assyrian decline permitted a great expansion of Israel under Jeroboam II (r.783-749 B.C.), but this was sharply reversed by renewed Assyrian aggression under Tiglath Pileser III, which culminated in the fall of Samaria, capital of Israel, in 721 B.C. Assyrian conquest ended the monarchy in Israel and reduced it to the status of a province. Tens of thousands of people were deported and replaced by alien settlers from Syria, Babylonia, and Elam. With this the buffer in the north was gone, and Judah was exposed directly to the Assyrian power. Under King Hezekiah, Judah came within the orbit of an anti-Assyrian coalition under Egyptian leadership, but this only provoked countermeasures that resulted in defeat for the allies and reduced Judah to the status of a tributary state. It was not until the Assyrian empire entered its final decline under the pressures of civil war and the attacks by the Medes and Chaldeans that Judah's King

Josiah (r. 640-609 B.C.) was able to resume the anti-Assyrian policies of Hezekiah. Between 629, the year of Assurbanipal's death, and 627, he not only achieved the independence of Judah but liberated the provinces of Israel as well and reunited the monarchy. The political policy of Josiah was matched by his program of religious reform (the Deuteronomic Reforms), by which he attempted to revive and purify the Yahwist tradition and centralize the cult after the centuries of syncretism with Assyrian, Egyptian, and other religious influences.

This longed-for liberation from Assyrian rule proved, however, to be no more than the prelude to unimaginable disasters. First, an Egyptian army of Pharaoh Neko marched north through Judah in a campaign to establish a new hegemony in the wake of the retreating Assyrians. The Judean army opposing the Egyptians was defeated at Megiddo in 609, and Josiah was killed in the battle. Judah was then subject to Egyptian political control until the army of Neko was defeated by the Chaldeans at Carchemish in 605 and forced to withdraw. From that time until 581 the Chaldeans conquered and consolidated their rule over Judah. This necessitated three major campaigns against stubborn resistance and repeated revolts. On each occasion the victorious Chaldeans, in the manner of the Assyrians before them, deported more of the great families and artisans to Mesopotamia and in the end destroyed all the cities and fortifications of Judah and reduced it to a province. This conquest and the deportations marked the beginning of the Babylonian captivity, which was to last until the foundation of the Achaemenid empire and Cyrus II's Edict of Liberation in 539, by which the exiles were allowed to return to their homeland.

The elements of crisis in Palestine may be seen both in the larger context of the Assyrian and Babylonian empires and in the more immediate context of Palestine itself. Militarism on the grand scale was not merely an instrument of state policy but was glorified as a manifestation of the charismatic legitimacy of the ruler. The Assyrians left behind them a terrible reputation for cruelty and destructiveness, but this was a consequence as much of their boasting as of their actions. The kings were in the habit of inscribing accounts of their victories in which they enumerated their booty and their captives and, with evident exaggeration, dwelt proudly on the rivers of blood and mountains of corpses that marked the battle sites. It is also certain that they were at least as brutal as other people of their day in the infliction of torture and mutilation upon important enemies, such as the leaders of revolts. Both the word and the reality of their deeds, however, made the Assyrian state feared throughout West Asia, and the Chaldeans in their turn were hardly less so. Moreover, even within so small a state as the kingdom of David and Solomon, and its twin successor states, the rulers seized the opportunity, when it was offered, to plunge into the international struggle for wealth and power. Biblical sources provide evidence enough of court debates between partisans of policies of positive military and diplomatic action and those of policies of accommodation or submission. The former represented, among others, the knightly *gibborim,* the soldiers by vocation.

One object of the militaristic and aggressive policies of the powers was the acquisition of wealth, first by looting and then by tribute or taxation. The deportation of wealthy families and artisans not only served the political purpose of weakening the conquered territories, but added to the wealth of the home cities of the empires. Sennacherib (r. 704-681 B.C.) rebuilt the Assyrian capital at Nineveh with new palaces and aqueducts. To symbolize the universality of his authority, he had a vast park constructed as a microcosm of the kingdom, with artificial mountains and with all the species of wild plants and animals that could be collected from far and near. Another and more spectacular instance was the new city of Babylon constructed by the Chaldeans and especially by King Nebuchadnezzar. This metropolis, with its temples, palaces, and famous hanging gardens, was so vast and so opulent as to inspire awe in foreign visitors and set a new standard for the West Asian city. The cost of its construction, however, strained the resources of the state and contributed to its ignominious collapse in 539 B.C. In relation to the more limited resources of Palestine, the building of capital cities under Solomon at Jerusalem and under Jeroboam II at Samaria had a comparable social impact.

In religious and cultural policy, the Assyrian state was highly conservative. The great cult center at Assur retained its importance to the end as the principal source of dynastic legitimacy, and not only in conquered provinces but even in the tributary kingdoms, official observance of the Assyrian cults was required. The old Mesopotamian cities, meanwhile, held fast to their local cults as a means to the preservation of their civic identity and its privileges. In Palestine, a conservative element in the worship of Yahweh grew with the monarchy, as an artistocratic priesthood entrenched itself in the capital under royal protection and performed ceremonial and ideological services for the kings. Under the Chaldeans' Neo-Babylonian dynasty, the ancient cults and their priesthoods demonstrated their astonishing power and vitality as crucial factors in the political organization of the state. When Nabonidus, last of the Chaldean kings, sought a more universal state ideology in the cult of the moon god, Sin, which in various forms was widely popular throughout West Asia, the priests of Marduk, patron deity of Babylon, deserted their king and delivered his capital city to Cyrus in 539 B.C. Moreover, Assurbanipal's generous patronage of the palace library and the work of restoring and copying ancient texts was matched later by the antiquarianism of Nebuchadnezzar and Nabonidus, who built a museum in Babylon to store historically important documents and artifacts that had been gathered from throughout the realm. Kings and established priesthoods were wedded to the traditions, laws, forms of worship, and cults that had served their predecessors so well in the past.

Continuing urbanization and the Assyrian and Chaldean practice of mass deportations combined to disorganize family and community structure and to undermine the stabilizing factor of traditional social and religious values. Urbanization, combined with monarchical institutions, fostered increasingly high concentrations of wealth in the hands of patrician families and widened the gulf between rich and poor. The calculated shifting about of large populations brought about the intimate mixing of populations that differed in language, religion, and social custom, which led to uncertainty, confusion, conflict, and syncretism. The socially divisive effects of urbanization and of migration were experienced to an extreme degree by the Israelites, who always had to try to come to terms with the indigenous *baal* cults of Canaan and, in addition, whose leading families repeatedly and in great numbers were transported into exile in Syria and Babylonia. Against this background the complacent ceremonialism of the professional priesthoods did not hold the needed answers for the great majority of the population, which was generally excluded from the material benefits and spiritual consolations of the royal courts and the great temples.

The Biblical prophets of the period from the division of the monarchy through the Babylonian captivity took positions consistently in opposition to the behavior and policies of the social and political leaders of their times, but the standpoint from which they looked at the world was a profoundly conservative one. They would reform the world not by revolutionary change in the social order, or by pitting class against class, but rather by improving the ethical standards of behavior at all levels of society, from the *baal*-worshipping peasant to the avaricious landlord and the vainglorious king. The core of their message, which was held consistently, was that the duty of all the "children of Israel" was to honor their side of the covenant with Yahweh. The ethical duty of man was summed up in the Decalogue, or Ten Commandments, attributed to the divine inspiration of Moses. Only so long as these were kept could the worshippers of Yahweh expect to enjoy his protection. If they were not kept, then no amount of ceremonial observance and making of offerings, whether in the temple or in the home, would appease his wrath. While they did not advocate the abolition of traditional forms of worship, they perceived the danger that ceremonialism might be abused as a substitute for the harder and more essential duty to act rightly according to the laws. For this reason, the priests who served in the courts and the great temples were often the targets of the wrath of the prophets.

The ethical regeneration of society was the personal responsibility of every Israelite and not a matter to be dealt with merely on the level of the ruling class of royal and patrician families. The Mosaic covenant was not merely between Yahweh and a representative (for example, a king) of the people, but collectively and directly involved all as parties to it. Thus, Yahweh might punish all for the sins of one. Furthermore, a mere show of compliance with the law was not enough; the concept of righteousness came to be a matter of whole-hearted, positive assertion of principle in action, a conviction expressed by the prophet Micah when he said, "He hath shown thee, O man, what is good; and what doth the Lord require of thee but to do justly, and to love mercy, and to walk humbly with thy God?" Given this understanding of the covenant, the prophets undertook to make right action a matter of conscience in all men. Laws and their enforcement were necessary in an imperfect world, but this was irrelevant to the main issue, which was to create a society of morally autonomous individuals acting freely in accordance with their consciences and not under compulsion.

The simple appeal to conscience, however eloquent it may have been, was not enough. According to the prophets, threatened punishment and promised reward were and remained the divine instruments by which men would ultimately be made over and the Kingdom of God realized. The troubled course of the history of Palestine provided an abundance of exemplary material for the prophets to use in expounding this thesis. The history of the nation of Israel was reinterpreted as the record of divine intervention, and it gave to the Bible a markedly political character. Because the kingdoms in Palestine were small and relatively powerless in the face of the imperialism of Assyria, Babylon, and Egypt, these great states came to be regarded as instruments of Divine Providence. The destruction of Samaria in 721 B.C., for example, was used by the prophet Isaiah as a warning to the kingdom of Judah that it could expect a similar fate if it did not repent of its evil ways. On the issues of royal foreign policy, the line generally held by the prophets was that the conventional political wisdom of kings and statesmen in relying on armed force and the formation of alliances was offensive to Yahweh, because it implied a lack of trust in him and an unwillingness to accept the moral imperatives demanded by the covenant. Not at all surprisingly, their advice to the kings that they trust in Yahweh fell on deaf ears. The armies were still maintained at great cost and alliances continued to be made with idolatrous foreign rulers. In the face of this perversity, the prophets continued to hurl their warnings of divine retribution. The prophert Jeremiah, in the last days of the kingdom of Judah, incurred the wrath of the priests by asserting not only that the kingdom would be conquered but that the great Jerusalem temple, claimed by the priests to be the very home of Yahweh, would be demolished. Although their prophesies of future events were frequently wrong, this did not destroy the credibility of the prophets' teaching. The interpretation and reinterpretation of catastrophes new and old provided them with sufficient vehicle for their message.

While it is true that the prophets were not social revolutionaries and that they demanded repentance of everyone, they leveled their heaviest charges against the great. Their words therefore reflect actual social conditions as these were seen from an antielitist point of view. The prophets themselves were of varied social backgrounds. Many were descended from the patrician families of the cities, but, owing to their disaffection with the ethical standards of their class, they took up the role of champions of the oppressed and identified themselves with the idealized tradition of a simpler and less corrupt condition in the time of the Exodus. One of the first and most memorable of the prophets' protests against the selfish abuse of power was that of Elijah against King Ahab of Israel. Ahab's wife, Jezebel, obtained a vinyard for him by bribing men to make false charges of blasphemy and treason against the owner, Naboth. Naboth was convicted on the perjured testimony and stoned to death, after which Ahab expropriated the property. Elijah then took to the streets to denounce the king as a murderer and prophesied his doom. Similarly, the Judean prophet Isaiah in the late eighth century B.C. foretold the punishment of the great families that by one means or another had built up great estates and reduced the peasants to the condition of serfs or tenants: "Woe unto them that join house to house, that lay field to field, till there is no place [for others] that they may be alone in the midst of the earth! In mine ears said the lord of hosts, of a truth many houses shall be desolate, even great and fair, [and] without inhabitant."

In the religion of the prophets there developed a deep and ineradicable tension between the particularism of the specific convenant between Yahweh and his people, the nation of Israel, and the universalism implicit in the notion that the destinies of all peoples were controlled by the same god. At least in the early form of the covenant it was taken for granted that other peoples also had their gods, but the seemingly endless train of disasters following the division of the kingdom required the worshippers of Yahweh to believe either that their god was too feeble to protect them or that the disasters were intended by him as punishment for their sins. In the latter case, Assyria and Babylonia, for example, were as much controlled by Yahweh as was Israel itself, and in this sense he was a universal god. Furthermore, as the frequency and extent of the disasters became quite unbearable, as in the destruction of the temple and the Babylonian exile, more emphasis was placed by the second Isaiah upon the expectation of the day of Yahweh, when he declared to his people that it would come about that the kings of the world would "bow down to you and lick the dust of your feet." In a somewhat similar vein earlier, Micah had looked toward the day when the many nations would "beat their swords into plowshares and their spears into pruning-hooks." Herein a contradiction was established between the real present, when the particularism of the covenant was still effective and Yahweh's control of other nations was for the single purpose of holding his people to the covenant's terms, and, on the other hand, the ever unrealized future Kingdom of God, when all nations would join with Israel in the universal worship of Yahweh.

2. MAHAVIRA AND BUDDHA IN SOUTH ASIA

During the seventh and sixth centuries B.C., the Indian subcontinent underwent accelerating changes in society, politics, and religion. During this period, local and long-distance trade by land and sea developed rapidly, which in turn generated new mercantile and artisan groups. Great cities appeared again for the first time since the collapse of Harappa and Mohenjo-daro. The expanding Aryan society in the north incorporated non-Aryan populations, with their various social and religious differences. The growing agricultural base was a field for profitable investment by wealthy families, and peasant families and villages were reduced to tenantry. At the same time the territorial monarchies of the Indus and Gangetic plains gained at the expense of the old tribal associations and competed with one another for regional dominance. With increasingly elaborate administrative systems, they tapped the wealth of the developing economy in order to build up their armed forces and create more splendid courts and capitals. During the sixth century B.C., as weaker states were annexed by the stronger, the victors became greater in size and fewer in number until most of northern India was subject to the authority of the single great kingdom of Magadha.

The kingdoms were primarily the creation of the *kshatriya* and brahman aristocrats in a marriage of military and religious authority. The kings and priests shared an interest in the careful and minute regulation of society and in the formulation and imposition of religious and ideological orthodoxy, so as to enhance their control over the states. The concentration on statecraft and the acquisition of political power created a climate of ruthlessness in the royal courts to such an extent that monarchs often died at the hands of their sons who were impatient to inherit the throne. When new directions in thought appeared in northern India, however, it was not primarily in the region of the great kingdoms, where the weight of brahmanical orthodoxy and royal power discouraged innovation, but among the tribal republics north of the great plains areas and in the foothills of the Himalayas. It was in this setting that Mahavira, founder of Jainism, and the Buddha were born and educated.

In India in the sixth century B.C. there were philosophical and religious speculations across a wide range of positions, from atheism and materialism to devotional theism. The two schools of that time that achieved the most lasting success were those of Jainism and Buddhism. Jainism became widely popular in north India and has survived to the present with about two million followers. Buddhism, in contrast, spread rapidly within India only to disappear there almost completely owing to the success of later forms of Hinduism. But because Buddhism in its Mahayana and Theravada forms spread widely throughout East and Southeast Asia, it survives outside India as a major religion.

South Asian Civilization in Crisis

Around 600 B.C. northern India was ruled by scores of states, including monarchies and republics, and these were linked in rival systems of alliances or hierarchies of dominant and subject states. The ambitions of sixth century rulers went far beyond the creation of such diffuse arrangements of political power, however, and it became the main object of statecraft and war to annex and absorb weaker states into ever greater and more firmly centralized kingdoms. As this concentration of power progressed, warfare grew accordingly in scale and intensity. Moreover, the fact that the price of defeat was likely to be the destruction of the state and the displacement of its ruling clans embittered the international conflicts. Not only victory, but mere survival, depended on the maintenance of standing armies and the fortification of important cities. Since the quality of armed forces was as important as their size, military technology advanced and became more costly. War fleets were built for fighting on the rivers, catapults to hurl boulders became necessary in siege warfare, and mobility was increased by the lavish use of horse chariots and war elephants.

The political map of northern India was transformed by the unification of the entire Gangetic basin by the state of Magadha. This required the labors of two dynasties, that founded by Bimbisara about 545 B.C. and that founded by Sisunaga about 430 B.C. A third dynasty, the Nanda (364-324 B.C.), consolidated the earlier Magadhan conquests and laid the foundation of the great Mauryan empire, which will be discussed in the following chapter. The westward expansion of Magadha involved the ultimate destruction and disappearance of the major kingdoms of Kasi, Kosala, Vatsa, and Avanti. The northern border was extended by the annexation of the tribal oligarchy of Vriji, and command of the trade route down the Ganges to the sea was attained by the conquest of the wealthy commercial state of Anga. A large number of smaller states were also absorbed.

This political process was accompanied by extensive social and economic change. The navigable waterways of the Ganges region lent themselves to a great expansion of trade. Because goods could be moved inexpensively by boat, local markets developed, and although most villages continued to be largely self-sufficient in crafts as well as in food, some craft villages appeared, occupied largely by specialists in a single trade. Commerce on a larger scale was concentrated in cities that grew up along the principal rivers, especially at points where rivers flowed together. Even sea trade had begun to develop from the lower Ganges to other parts of India and to Southeast Asia. The relative intensity of trade is suggested by the appearance at this time of a monetary system of coined copper and silver, supplementing the more primitive barter and gold bullion of earlier times. Goods involved in trade were probably of high value in proportion to weight, such as textiles (cotton, silk, muslin, embroidery), iron, jewelry, ivory, and gold. This expansion of trade was reflected in the formation of a merchant class, which constituted an important part of the urban population.

In the context of a somewhat commercialized economy, the peasant villages began to be invaded by outside interests. Although villages in the northwest may still have been based on common landownership by extended-family communities, those in the Magadhan region were characterized by the division of land into small family holdings, with village control over purchase and sale probable and with common village regulation of irrigation. In some villages of the Magadhan region, at least, wealthy urban or aristocratic families began building large private estates, thereby disrupting traditional patterns of village solidarity and cooperation. These estates were worked by hired laborers, who came to be regarded as being very near the bottom of the social scale.

Other changes were taking place in the upper strata of the society. The intensity of the political competition among the states and the drive for rationalization of administration had disastrous consequences for many families of the *kshatriya* class. In many of the states absorbed by Magadha, *kshatriyas* along with the brahmans had formed the core of the ruling class. Some of them may well have found places in the service of their conquerors, but many certainly did not. The Nanda dynasty was founded by a *shudra,* the son of a barber, and he and his early successors are held by somewhat later accounts to have been so hostile towards the aristocratic strata as to have deliberately undertaken to destroy the *kshatriyas* as a class. If this was their intention, they were obviously unsuccessful, but the claims of birth in the hierarchies of professional civil and military officials did not count for as much as before. It has been suggested that many of the *kshatriyas* left the uncongenial setting of the great monarchies for the more conventional Aryan world of the republican states in the north.

With the administrations of the great kingdoms growing beneath them, the perch of kings and their brahman priests and ministers became ever higher. The king was once, in theory, a temporary chieftain of a tribe or federation, but by the sixth century B.C. monarchy had become hereditary and absolute, and by the magic mediation of the brahmans between the gods and the earth it had become divine as well. For an entire year after his coronation, a new king underwent ritual purification and consecration so that at the end of this procedure he might be reborn as a divinity. Periodically thereafter his powers were renewed by sacrificial rites. Sacrifices in the royal cult were carried out on a vast scale, as though by their very extravagance they could magnify the divine might of the king. All of this made the kings somewhat dependent on the brahmans, and the position of the latter was strengthened within the royal courts. The courts and capital cities became increasingly luxurious as taxes and tribute flowed into them from the royally appointed or confirmed village headmen and the regional and capital administrations. The immense riches of the Nanda treasury were notorious, and that dynasty was long remembered for its rapacity. The ruling elite of the great kingdoms were thus increasingly remote from their hard-pressed subjects.

In the face of all these social, economic, and political changes, the brahmans, in order to protect their eminent position, continued to elaborate their ceremonial functions, make extravagant claims regarding their magical powers, and prescribe increasingly detailed rules and regulations for the social order. In the *Brahmanas,* commentaries on the Vedic sacrificial rites, the brahmans developed the procedure whereby they periodically reenacted the primal sacrifice of the cosmogonic god, Prajapati. Not only did the king, the state, and the social order require their ritual mediation, but without their performance of this rite, the entire universe would cease to exist. They appear also to have taken a positive interest in attempting to perfect the social order by fixing the status of the hereditary occupational groups, or subcastes within the castes *(varna),* so that their relative status might be clarified and the ritually correct customary behavior enjoined on all of them.

Under these conditions of change, uncertainty, danger, and opportunity, there was in the sixth century B.C. a general surge of intellectual and religious skepticism and innovation. Social and political realities had outgrown the ancient rules and patterns and new visions of order were required to restore a sense of purpose and direction to the lives of people of all classes. The great monarchies were too well administered and policed to make it at all likely that there would be successful challenges to the brahmanical establishment, even though the kings themselves might indulge a personal interest in some of the novel doctrines and practices that came to their attention. A more favorable environment was that of the old republics on the northern frontiers of Magadha and Kosala.

Jainism and Buddhism

Even as the brahmans elaborated their legal and ceremonial order in the kingdoms, their doctrines and their pretensions to cosmic power were greeted with increasing skepticism by intellectuals of the day, especially in the northern republics. Leadership in the development of new directions in philosophy and religion was taken up largely by wandering hermits and ascetics, who were often of *kshatriya* origin and quite independent of the brahmans and their tradition. The rise of eremetism and asceticism in the sixth century B.C. may have reflected the fact that many *kshatriya* families were being pushed out to the margins of social and political power by the expanding and centralizing monarchies. Their pursuit of new forms of truth and their assumption of the role of teachers were consistent with their felt need for responsibility and dignity. Because they were freed from the constraints of brahmanical orthodoxy, they were able to doubt every generally accepted proposition and, also, to draw on the nonbrahmanical and even non-Aryan religious and cosmological beliefs and practices of the peasant villages. The practice of asceticism was originally regarded as a means to the acquisition of magical power, even as the brahmans used elaborate ritual procedures for the same end. The willing acceptance of indigence and suffering also came to be valued as a path to spiritual salvation. In this sense it implied the conquest of selfish and materialistic desires and, in some cases, constituted a penance for such faults in the past. Elements of the rural religion that were now gaining in respectability included belief in transmigration of souls, the maintenance of local cults around sacred places *(caityas)*, such as sacred groves or mounds inhabited by spirits, and the hope for an afterlife in paradise as a reward for loving devotion to a beneficent god. Within the Aryan tradition itself, as expressed in the later Vedas, the roles and relative importance of the gods were changing, and daring questions about the origins of the universe reflected growing uncertainty even among the brahmans themselves.

Given the wide range of speculation and the diversity of religious beliefs in the late Vedic period, Jainism and Buddhism appear as just two among many emergent systems of thought, and although both obviously drew on ideas that were already becoming popular, it is impossible to discover precisely their original doctrines or where they came from. Jainism is associated with the person of Mahavira, an aristocratic member of a leading clan in the Vrijian republic. He was born in approximately 540 B.C, and died in 468, which, according to Jain tradition, was the year in which Vriji was annexed by Magadha. The Buddha's dates are more uncertain, but 563-483 B.C. is a commonly accepted approximation. The Buddha was the heir of the chief of the Sakya tribe, which had its capital at Kapilavastu in the foothills of the Himalayas. Both schools competed with each other and with other rivals as well for lay support and patronage. Although their doctrines were significantly different, the traditional accounts of the careers of these two founding figures show significant parallels. Both rejected the status, wealth, and power that were properly theirs by inheritance, cut themselves off from the world in which they had been reared, and took up the life of the wandering ascetics. Both attained enlightenment, gathered disciples about them, and in doing so created the core around which their two religions developed.

Jainism was an atheistic doctrine that held that the universe was eternal and therefore uncreated and self-sustaining. The basic constituents of the universe were souls *(jivas),* of which there were an infinite number, and nonliving entities *(ajiva).* All things, whether living or nonliving in our sense of these terms, were produced by their interaction, and all things had souls as well as material embodiment. Souls were forever subject to *samsara,* or transmigration from one material form to another, and in the course of their successive existences they tended to acquire an ever heavier burden of subtle, finely divided matter. The soul was imagined as brilliant and the matter was cloudy or turbid, and as it accumulated it obscured the pure brightness of the soul. This heavy burden of matter was identified by the Jains with *karma,* the principle of "causation." The accumulation of *karmic* matter was a consequence of one's actions, and the *karma* as it accumulated disposed one to further actions that would in turn result in new accumulations of *karma.*

Given this view of the nature of existence, the Jains understood salvation to mean the escape of the soul from its adhering *karma* and its upward flight to live on forever in a realm of pure bliss. This goal was believed to be almost impossible to attain, and the rare free souls were revered as *tirthankaras,* or "makers of the river crossing." Such beings were so completely removed from the world as to be inaccessible to prayer and so might be contemplated as inspiring models for emulation but not worshipped as gods. Without possibility of any supernatural assistance, each was responsible for the working out of his own salvation. As the Jain religion developed, it enumerated the rules that must be followed if salvation were to be achieved. The rules, however, amounted to a severely regulated life that could be managed only by monks. The monk was forbidden to kill, steal, lie, have any sexual activity, or own property. So strict was the prohibition against killing that the monks not only were held to a vegetarian diet, but their food had to be cut and harvested by laymen. The layman, obviously, was denied hope of salvation because he accumulated *karma* in the course of serving the monk. The Jain rules imply an ethical pattern aimed at overcoming all the appetites and impulses that led to *karma*-building actions. They thereby struck at the family by devaluating procreation and at the state and its ruling classes by identifying killing and the ownership of property as obstacles to salvation. The point of view from which Jain ethics were developed was essentially individual and pragmatic, however, and not social and contractual as in the case of the Hebrews. The standard of right and wrong was the consideration of the favorable or unfavorable effect of any action on the shedding of *karma* and on progress towards one's own salvation.

The doctrines of the Buddha were also directed toward the definition of the way to escape from *samsara,* but they were defined from a perspective different from that adopted by the Jains. Early Buddhist teaching, insofar as it can be reconstructed, denied the existence of any permanent entity, the soul included. All things are unstable combinations of some or all of the five elements: matter and form, sensations, perceptions, psychic constructions, and conscious thought. In human experience the five refer to tangible material; impressions of material things through the five senses and the intellect; awareness of the sensory experiences; states of mind, attitudes, inclinations, emotions; and finally, conscious thought, the exercise of reason. What is described here is a psychological process and not an object. Nowhere in this is there a self or a soul. Paradoxically, however, Buddhism also accepted the principles of *samsara* and *karma,* despite there being no discrete and abiding soul that could be subject to them. An existence began with the association of the five elements, continued through a lifetime of continuous flux and transformation, and ended in death with the separation of the elements. However, the nonmaterial elements were then recombined with new matter and form and a new existence began. Moreover, the form and condition of the new existence were determined by the accumulated effects, or *karma* (here a nonmaterial principle, in contrast to Jainism), of good and bad deeds associated with the nonmaterial elements of the old existence.

Given the difficulty of understanding the operation of *samsara* and *karma* in the absence of souls, naturally most Buddhists assumed the existence of the soul despite the early teachings to the contrary. But the notion of not-soul *(an-atta)* is important, because it is precisely the illusion of soul or self that stands in the way of salvation. If one could but understand the truth that there is no soul or any other permanent thing, there would be an end to the frustrations and sufferings that are experienced by all who are prisoners of the illusion of self. This is because when the illusion of self is gone there are no dispositions to act, and where there is no action, there is no *karma,* or "causation," and the chain of existences, or *samsara,* is finally broken. To state this more concretely, where there is no self-illusion there is, for example, no sexual craving, and where there is no sexual craving there is no procreation, no commencement of new existences.

All this is summed up in the Four Noble Truths: that life entails suffering; that suffering arises from craving; that suffering is ended with the overcoming of craving; and that the overcoming of craving is achieved by following the Eightfold Path. The Eightfold Path was the prescribed pattern of life, learning, and meditation, at the end of which one might attain enlightenment in a burst of intuitive understanding. The path was that of the monk dedicated to salvation. The enlightened one was an *arhat,* whose death would not lead into another existence but would be followed by the transcendent and indescribable condition of *nirvana.* Although salvation was probably not absolutely denied to the layman, the most he could reasonably hope for would be to perform so many good deeds in his lifetime that his next existence would be raised by his accumulated good *karma* to a more nearly perfect form and a step closer to eventual salvation. Although most early Buddhist scripture was prepared by and for monks, some instruction was given to laymen to help them in their quest.

Buddhist ethics differed in important respects from that of the Jains. Although both systems shared the belief that self-regarding desires give rise to suffering and lead away from salvation, Buddhist demands were more reasonable and had a positive aspect to balance the negative. Where for the Jains it was believed that the more terrible the self-denial, the better for one's spiritual progress, the Buddhist laws were less severe. Mahavira was believed by his followers to have starved himself to death and thereby provided them with a good example. The Buddha, by contrast, did not attain enlightenment until he had abandoned asceticism in favor of meditation, and he died at an old age of an illness he contracted after eating a good meal. Although the Buddhist monks were required to abstain from the same attachments as were the Jains, they did not go to such extreme lengths to do so. Moreover, since the Buddhists valued the good *karma* obtained by good deeds, they developed a positive side in their ethics which emphasized unselfish attention to the needs of others. This sometimes took the form of providing nursing and medical care for the sick, for example.

Both Buddhism and Jainism were asocial in the sense that they regarded disengagement from the entanglements of life in society as prerequisite to salvation. In order to achieve this they soon created the monastery as a place of retreat from the temptations of the world. Wandering Buddhist monks settled near the *caityas* to receive alms from pilgrims and built *stupas,* or reliquary shrines, and monasteries for themselves. The monastic communities *(sangha)* were in principle free of caste distinctions, places where all were brothers in the law and judged according to their own spiritual merits. They were self-governing on the principles already established in the tribal oligarchies (also called *sangha*), with the election of leaders and the collective determination of policy by discussion and voting in assemblies.

Jains and Buddhists were not social and political activists demanding reform and putting pressure on the ruling groups. However, their doctrines and their way of life, although directed away from the world, may be regarded as an implied protest against the violence and greed of the larger society around them. In their monasteries they attempted to create an alternative model and give effect to their principles. Large numbers of people were moved by their examples. Several of the rulers of Magadha and the other monarchies patronized Buddhist or Jain teachers, perhaps because they found their doctrines more attractive and more persuasive than those of the brahmans. The *sangha* expanded to such an extent that by the fourth or third century B.C., Buddhism had become the strongest of Indian religions, at least as measured by the building of monastery temples. This implied not only the ordination of great numbers of monks but also the generous patronage of wealthy lay supporters. Funds for the construction and-maintenance of the temples came mostly from the urban commercial class, chiefly *vaishyas* by caste, who benefitted from the caste-free principles of the non-Vedic religions. The Buddhist patrons, at least, also were assured that their generous donations to the *sangha* would earn them good *karma* and bring them a little closer to their own salvation in a later existence. Just how much effect Jainism and Buddhism may have had on Indian society as a whole is difficult to say, but they did provide an alternative life for all those who took the monastic vows and offered guidance and encouragement to the even larger numbers of lay patrons who sought new meanings amid the hazards and uncertainties of life in a time of rapid political and social change.

3. ETHICAL PROTEST AND REFORM IDEOLOGY IN CHOU CHINA

Perhaps nowhere more than in China was it the case that the processes of external and internal growth brought breakdown and disintegration in their train. Even as the sober and soldierly rule of early Chou feudalism gave way to an overgrown, refined, and status-conscious aristocracy and as the literati, the men of learning, organized and clarified a Chinese great tradition, the political order of the kingdom was being torn apart by interstate warfare. New families from the lower aristocratic orders and even commoners were fighting and scheming their way into positions of power. In due course, most of the aristocratic families and their manorial establishments were swept away in wars of extermination and a new order of bureaucratic sovereign states was constructed on the ruins of the old. The political and social crisis was matched by an intellectual and religious crisis. The rules, values, and religious beliefs of the dying order were irrelevant to the new. Men simply did not know any longer how they ought to behave in the new roles of statesman, bureaucrat, merchant, or free peasant. Even more fundamentally, the very meaning of existence was called in question and became the subject of heated debate. Yet Chinese civilization survived this, its first great crisis. That it did so was partly because the crisis brought forth a great burst of creative effort on the part of a number of men of genius, character, and insight.

Political Change and Social Crisis in Late Chou

Long before the late Chou age of militarism and imperialism, people had formed the habit of comparing the present unfavorably with the past. Most basically, surviving fragments of Chinese mythology reveal that in China, as in many other cultures, it was believed that when the world was young, men and gods happily consorted together until some ritual fault was punished by man's fall from grace. Ever afterwards, a great abyss was set between men and gods, which made necessary the complicated patterns of divination, sacrifice, prayer, and shamanism by which communications were maintained between the worlds of gods and men. Such myths may have formed the traditional root of late Chou speculation on the primal, or natural, state of man. Nearest to the archaic vision was that of a world in which men lived in perfect freedom—freedom from constraining ties of family, community, or state—so that all old people were one's parents, all children were one's own, all men were brothers, and there was no material property, no "mine" and "thine." Even the days of the first Chou kings, idealized as a time of peace, plenty, order, and justice, were inferior to this, because a virus of selfishness and violence had called for a just state, with its kings, officers, and laws to furnish models of good behavior and to punish the incorrigible. By Confucius' day, around 500 B.C., the actual state of the world presented a dismal contrast with even the historical age of the good Chou kings, to say nothing of the mythical utopia. The royal authority was despised, and statesmen were preoccupied with wars, preparation for wars, and cynical diplomatic maneuvers.

The insecurity and dangers of the times contributed to a flourishing sacrificialism. Because a minister's or a nobleman's word was seldom worth anything now, the innumerable treaties among powers seem invariably to have been reinforced by mighty oaths sealed by sacrificial rites. At the same time, rulers of states, in constant fear for the survival of their houses, redoubled their efforts to please the spirits of place and clan with sacrificial offerings of fine animals. Yet this lavish use of sacrifice was the very undermining of the practice. The most solemn oaths were broken with impunity, sometimes even to the great advantage of the guilty party, and heads of state registered their pathetic complaints that despite their care and generosity in the performance of sacrifice, they had been deserted by their protecting spirits. As a consequence, a mounting skepticism about the usefulness of sacrifice and even about the very existence of spirits mocked the efforts of those who clung to the old beliefs and practices.

Certainly, one of the main intellectual trends of the late Chou era was the general assault on traditional values. Conservatives of the day were seen by their opponents as the reactionary survivors of a vanishing order, whose pedantic preaching upon religious orthodoxy and the authority of the past had become a cause of unrest among the masses. Some of the leading political thinkers of the day, those of the Legalist school, were striving to perfect a "rational" order of maximum state power and efficiency and resented the invocation of a hallowed past against their programs of reform and development. Others, of the Taoist persuasion, sought the spiritual liberation of mankind from both the conventional ceremonialism of the conservatives and the regimentation of the radicals. Legalists and Taoists alike, but for different reasons, poked fun at the notion that the sage rulers of antiquity who devoted lives of unremitting toil to the service of their subjects ought to be held up as models for emulation. Blind traditionalism was no longer a tenable position for any who aspired to political or intellectual leadership. Only such schools as those of Confucius and Mo Tzu would be able to salvage something from the past by reinterpreting it and modifying its prescriptions.

Chinese cultural parochialism appeared early and became increasingly visible during the Eastern Chou period. Already in texts of the Western Chou, one finds the occasional use of words that had the sense of "Chinese" in contradistinction to "foreign" or "barbarian." Chinese sometimes identified themselves as the "Hsia people," by which they meant that they were the bearers of the great tradition of the legendary Hsia dynasty, running through Shang to their own Chou. In other texts they called themselves the "Hua people." This "Hua," which usually has the sense of "flower," is the same word that occurs with the meaning of "Chinese" in the modern name *Chung-hua jen-min kung-ho-kuo* ("Chinese People's Republic"). How it came to mean "Chinese" is a matter of conjecture, but it has been identified as, among other meanings, the ancient name of a holy mountain near the confluence of the Wei and Yellow rivers. The term *Chung-kuo* becomes more common in Eastern Chou, having the sense of "The Central States," or that part of the Chou realm that had been occupied earlier by Hsia and Shang. *Chung-kuo* in later contexts is currently translated "Middle Kingdom."

The cultural standard by which Chinese distinguished themselves from non-Chinese in mid- and late Chou was essentially the meticulous adherence to the aristocratic code, *li*, or "ceremonial," which governed the forms of social intercourse and genteel life-style. This standard could be put to political use, as in 632 B.C., when the central state of Lu attacked the state of Ch'i on the pretext that the Ch'i ruler had lapsed into barbarian custom instead of following *li* on the occasion of a visit to the Lu court. The frontier states could be parochial, too, when they chose. An envoy of the southern state of Ch'u protested an invasion by the state of Ch'i by pointing out that their countries had so little in common that even their horses and cattle could not breed with each other. Although Chou literature reveals an occasional yearning for foreign culture or romanticizes barbarian virtues, a much more common attitude is one of complacent superiority. Mencius, the fourth century B.C. follower of Confucius, resented the success of a scholar from the state of Ch'u in propagating his unorthodox (i.e., non-Chou) doctrine among the central states and attacked him as a "shrike-tongued barbarian from the south whose doctrines are not those of the ancient kings." ("Shrike-tongued" is a northerner's perjorative description of the southern speech.) Mencius had no doubt that foreigners should learn from the true Chinese and not the other way around: "I have heard of men using the doctrines of our great land to change barbarians, but I have never yet heard of any being changed by barbarians."

The breakdown of the Chou feudal order and the destruction of the aristocratic class engendered a widespread crisis of identity throughout Chinese society. It became increasingly difficult for people to know what roles to play in society and how to play the roles they had chosen. The old standards of loyalty to the king and his commands and to the gradually formed and elaborated *li* code no longer held meaningful answers. The Chou kings were ineffectual and *li* was ignored by generations of rulers and statesmen who ran their governments on "rational" principles of expediency. At the highest level, rulers commonly became the instruments of the great families entrenched in high office. How ought the role of minister be defined under these circumstances? If he could no longer be judged by his obedience to the ruler, by what standard should he be judged? Whose interest ought he serve, and what kinds of interest are legitimate? How does the minister now conduct himself in relation to his ruler? Mencius once became involved in a seemingly absurd and insoluble contest over "face" with a ruler seeking his advice. Although Mencius wanted to counsel him and the ruler wanted to be counselled, each had a different view of the relationship. Mencius sought the upper hand as teacher to pupil, and the ruler, as ruler to subordinate. When artistocratic families were suffering destruction and degradation and positions of civil and military command were being distributed to men of marginal or common family background, how was the déclassé aristocrat to understand his place in society? Was he still obliged to find some way to continue in a leading role? And how was he to live by *li* in a world increasingly dominated by people who had little knowledge or understanding of the aristocratic code? Even among the common people, great changes had set in. The destruction of the manorial communities in which they had once found their places compelled them to establish new relationships with the world beyond the house and village. One sign of the readjustment was the universalization of surnames, once an aristocratic prerogative, among the people. The term "old hundred names," which had once referred to the aristocracy, now became a synonym for "everybody." Even the practice of ancestral worship and the maintenance of the local cults became private family and village functions, because the manorial families were no longer there to perform these socially necessary rites as a function of the political order. In a deeper sense, the very ground of human behavior, the way in which people thought about themselves and their choices, had shifted beneath their feet. The old order had been guaranteed by all the ancestral and local cults, and yet that order was collapsing. Could anyone any longer believe that ceremonially correct behavior and conscientious performance of sacrifice were the certain path to success and safety? But how then was one to distinguish the right path from the wrong one? Such were some of the deep uncertainties that drove men of late Chou to urgent reflection upon the basic principles of man, nature, and the cosmos.

The deliberate pursuit of material wealth by rulers and subjects became a live issue in late Chou times. Already in mid-Chou, the elaboration of the aristocratic ceremonial code imposed on the leading clans the necessity of matching their wealth to their status. Dress, architecture, furnishings, ritual vessels, chariots and horses, all had to meet the standard of elegance required for each noble rank. But the proliferation of lineages strained the economic resources of the clans' fiefs and office lands. The resulting struggle for wealth was exacerbated by the ceremonialism of the period. The subsequent decline and destruction of aristocratic houses in the wars of late Chou times changed the terms of the struggle without alleviating it. Ambitious families of marginal or common origin needed wealth in order to emulate the material standards of the declining aristocratic order and thereby establish their social prestige. Officials, generals, and merchants competed for wealth, and everyone resisted the mounting demands of the government tax collectors. The rulers and ministers strove to enlarge the state revenues at the expense of their subjects by more effective means of tax collection, public commodity monopolies, and price controls. The opening up of the economy that resulted from the breakdown of the manorial system created new opportunities for trade, usury, and the accumulation of private estates. The life-style of the wealthy in late Chou times is reflected archaeologically in the abundance of material remains. The art of bronze casting enjoyed a brilliant renaissance in works of the so-called Huai style. Here the awesome symbolic presence of the Shang and early Chou vessels yielded to subtlety and elegance. Animal-form motifs dissolved into a delicate tracery of patterns and textures that appear to be of purely aesthetic intent. Conspicuous consumption, with no ceremonial excuse, appears in the lavish use of gold and silver inlay in some bronze vessels. Late Chou homes and tombs were furnished with brilliant-colored lacquer ware, an art form perhaps of southern origin that was now coming into its own. Silk cloth, known from Shang and possibly Neolithic sites, now was produced in greater variety and elegance of woven patterns. The materialism of late Chou, as manifested in the work of its artisans, underscored the fact of the widening gap between very rich and very poor and, as we shall see, the luxurious life of the rich was roundly condemned by the reformers.

In mid-Chou times, aristocrats and commoners were firmly distinguished in their roles and in their different life-styles, but they were still, for the most part, bound together within their manorial communities. They prospered or suffered together (albeit not in the same degree) in good times and bad, and they participated together in the service of the local cults. With the destruction of fiefs and manors in late Chou and the emergence of the state, the old sense of community disintegrated. The new elite now stood over the masses full of political cynicism and the pride of power and with little sense of a common humanity. The *Book of Lord Shang,* a Legalist text, for example, argues that the more ignorant the people are, the better it is for the state:

> If dignities are not conferred nor office given according to standards of education, then the people will not prize learning nor, besides, will they disparage agriculture. If they do not prize learning, they will be stupid and, being stupid, they will have no interest in outside things.[1]

[1] J. J. L. Duyvendak, ed. and trans., *The Book of Lord Shang* (University of Chicago Press, 1963), pp. 176-77.

From an altogether different perspective, Mencius, who did believe in learning as a qualification for office, made what is probably the classic statement of the elitism of the scholarly officials when he said:

"Some labor with their minds and some labor with their strength. Those who labor with their minds govern others. Those who labor with their strength are governed by others. Those who are governed by others support them; those who govern others are supported by them." This is a principle universally recognized.[2]

Mencius himself was very comfortably supported by others, even when he was not employed in any official capacity. When he was taken to task for this by one of his disciples, his answer provided a justification for the inclusion of literati in the socially supported elite, whether they were in office or not:

P'eng Keng asked Mencius, saying "Is it not an extravagance to go from one prince to another and live upon them, followed by several tens of carriages, and attended by several hundred men?" Mencius replied, "If there be not a proper ground for taking it, a single bamboo cup of rice may not be received from a man. But if there be such a proper ground, then Shun's receiving the empire from Yao is not to be considered excessive. Do you think it was excessive?" Keng said, "No, but for a scholar performing no service to receive his support notwithstanding is improper." Mencius answered, ". . . Here now is a man who, at home, is filial, and abroad, respectful to his elders; who watches over the principles of the ancient kings, auditing the rise of future learners (i.e., of rulers who are disposed to listen to his advice) and yet you would refuse to support him. How is it that you give honor to the carpenter and carriage-wright, and slight him who practices benevolence and righteousness? . . . He deserves to be supported and should be supported."[3]

Much has already been said about political cynicism in late Chou—the casual breaking of treaties, the ruthless extermination of defeated enemies. But a quotation from the Legalist book *Han Fei Tzu* may serve to show how deep and how refined that cynicism had become. The master, Han Fei, was discussing the proper technique for a minister in steering his master while remaining in his good graces:

Suppose, for example, the monarch you are addressing is bent on maintaining a high reputation and you appeal to him only on grounds of material gain, he will regard you as a person of low principles, treat you with no consideration or respect and henceforward exclude you from his confidence. If, on the other hand, he is bent on material gain and you appeal to him on grounds of reputation, he will regard you as lacking in common sense and out of contact with realities, and will not make use of you. Again, if he is secretly bent on material gain, but professes outwardly to care only for maintaining a high reputation, he will pretend to be pleased with you, but in reality will keep you at a distance; should you appeal to him on grounds of material gain, he will secretly follow your advice, but will outwardly disown you. All this must be taken into consideration.[4]

Han Fei Tzu, it might be added, for all his cleverness, was put to death on the advice of a rival minister, who in his turn was also put to death. A cruder statement than Han Fei Tzu's, which appears in the *Book of Lord Shang,* achieves what must have been the very last word in cynicism:

If virtuous officials are employed, the people will love their own relatives, but if wicked officials are employed, the people will love the statutes. To agree with and respond to

[2] James Legge, trans., *The Works of Mencius* (Clarendon Press, 1895), Bk. III, Pt. I, Ch. 4.
[3] Legge, *Mencius*, Bk. III, Pt. II, Ch. 4.
[4] A. Waley, *Three Ways of Thought in Ancient China* (George Allen & Unwin, 1939), p. 185. By permission of George Allen & Unwin.

others is what the virtuous do; to differ from and to spy upon others is what the wicked do. If the virtuous are in possession of evidence, transgressions will remain hidden; but if the wicked are employed, crimes will be punished. In the former case, the people will be stronger than the law, there is lawlessness in the state, but if the law is stronger than the people, the army will be strong. Therefore it is said: "Governing through good people leads to lawlessness and dismemberment; governing through wicked people leads to order and strength."[5]

Given the harsh and dehumanizing spirit of the age, it is to be expected that the condition of the peasantry should be poor or worse. A text that has come down to us from about 400 B.C. describes what should be the optimum budget for an ordinary household of that time. The farmer is assumed to have the use of a hundred Chinese acres of land (which he owns or which is allotted to him by his village) and to pay only the required tax of one-tenth of his harvest. Deducting the tax and that part of his harvest needed to feed himself and his family, the farmer converts the rest of his harvest to copper cash by selling it in the market. Then, after making his customary contributions to the local earth god and other shrines and purchasing clothes, he has already exceeded his income. If there had been a death in the family, he would also have had to pay funeral costs and he could have been responsible for special government levies above the regular tax. At best, then, the peasants were sinking slowly into debt, and in a bad year, their circumstances were hopeless.

Ideology of Ethical Reform

At least by Shang times there were learned men who had a command of reading and writing and who were formulators and custodians of tradition. But the profession of the scholar, the literatus who made a living as a private teacher supported by a band of disciples or who traveled about from state to state preaching his doctrines and seeking employment by the rulers, had its great flourishing in the late Chou period. Confucius (551-479 B.C.) was the first such teacher we know of. In Taiwan, Confucius' birthday is still celebrated as "First Teacher Day." In the fourth century B.C., not only were there thousands of teachers, but they and their disciples had sorted themselves out into followings according to their doctrines, the so-called hundred schools. The most important of Confucius' followers were Mencius (372-289 B.C.) and Hsun Tzu (298-238 B.C.). The Mohists, followers of Mo Tzu (479-381 B.C.), were an early rival school. The Confucians probably originated among the scribes, astronomers, archivists, and historians, whose tradition of service was as old as Chinese civilization itself, a tradition already a thousand years old. Although these functionaries had been members of the aristocracy, in the tough, masculine feudal world of early and mid-Chou times, they had come to be known as *ju,* "the weaklings." Confucius and his followers accepted the epithet and proudly flung it in the faces of their detractors. The Mohists were recruited from among the knights-for-hire, a class of petty aristocrats. Both Confucians and Mohists were deeply committed to the great tradition of past dynasties (Confucius "followed Chou," whereas Mo Tzu claimed to be following Hsia), but they sought to reinterpret it in order to bring about social and political reform. Two other important schools were the Legalists and the Taoists. Major Legalists were Shang Yang (d. 238 B.C.), Shen Pu-hai (d. 337 B.C.), and Han Fei (d. 233 B.C.). The Legalists, in a single-minded pursuit of public order, brilliantly articulated the political science of the day, carefully separating statecraft from ethics and tradition. Classical Taoism is represented by two texts of composite authorship: one, the *Tao-te Ching,* associated with the shadowy and perhaps mythical figure of Lao Tzu (d.ca.400 B.C.?) and the other, the *Chuang Tzu,* associated with Chang Chou (ca. 369-ca. 286 B.C.). The Taoists rejected the traditionalism

[5] Duyvendak, *Lord Shang,* p. 207.

and the ethical principles of the Confucians and Mohists and opposed the power-seeking and cynical manipulations of the Legalists. Instead, they sought social and personal tranquility through quiet contemplation leading to an intuitive grasp of an underlying metaphysical reality. Their methods enabled one to overcome obsessive and anxiety-ridden involvement in worldly affairs without necessarily withdrawing from the world.

With all their differences, the major late Chou schools of thought were alike in their preoccupation with the problem of violence and sought an end to the incessant warfare of their time. Each pointed the way to a society living peacefully under the authority of a supreme ruler. The Confucians believed that a new Chou might arise if only a ruler would come forward wise and benevolent enough to move mankind to goodness by his example and his teaching. In their new order, human society would harmonize and be made beautiful by universal acceptance and understanding of *li,* the traditional ceremonial. Every man would then know his duty and, of his own free will and according to his own understanding, would do his duty though it might cost him his life. The society in all its personal relationships would be governed by the principle of shared humanity *(jen)* and each would take his place in the society at the level appropriate to his achieved moral character. The Confucians were not pacifists inasmuch as they were prepared to fight and die in a just cause, but they were absolutely certain that the good society could not be founded on violence. As Confucius put it:

Govern the people by regulations, keep order among them by chastisements, and they will flee from you, and lose all self-respect. Govern them by moral force, keep order among them by ceremonial *(Li)* and they will keep their self-respect and come to you of their own accord.[6]

Mencius went further and dogmatically promised the rulers of the world that the path to victory over all rivals and the attainment of universal rulership lay through nonviolence:

Mencius went to see the King Hsiang of Liang. On coming away from the audience, he said to some persons, "When I looked at him from a distance, he did not appear like a sovereign; when I drew near to him, I saw nothing venerable about him. Abruptly he asked me, 'How can the empire be settled?' I replied, 'It will be settled by being united under one sway.' 'Who can so unite it?' I replied, 'He who has no pleasure in killing men can so unite it.' 'Who can give it to him?' I replied, 'All the people of the world will unanimously give it to him. Does your majesty understand the way of the growing grain? During the seventh and eighth months when drought prevails, the plants become dry. Then the clouds collect densely in the heavens, they send down torrents of rain, and the grain grows and flourishes. When it does so, who can keep it back? Now among the shepherds of man throughout the empire, there is not one who does not find pleasure in killing men. If there were one who did not find pleasure in killing men, all the people in the empire would look towards him with outstretched necks. Such being indeed the case, the people would flock to him as water flows downward with a rush which no one can repress.' "[7]

Even in the matter of sacrifice, which was valued by the Confucians at least partly on social and ethical grounds, the violence of ancient practice was tempered. Animals still had to be offered to the spirits, as they were enjoyed by the living, but the almost-vanished practice of human sacrifice was utterly abhorred. By late Chou times, clay figurines of men and women were placed in the graves replacing sacrificial victims, but Confucius was so disturbed by the implications of this practice that he bitterly denounced even this.

At the opposite extreme, the Legalists sought to end violence by means of violence. If one

[6] A. Waley, trans., *The Analects of Confucius* (Macmillan, 1958), Bk. II, Ch. 5. Reprinted with permission of Macmillan Publishing Co., Inc. © 1958 by George Allen & Unwin, Ltd.
[7] Legge, *Mencius*, Bk. I, Pt. I, Ch. 6.

state were so effectively organized for war that it could crush all its rivals, wars would cease. Once unity was reestablished and laws were codified and rewards and punishments were meted out with implacable regularity, then internal order would have been assured. The Mohists, in the spirit of their soldierly calling, tried to stop war by hiring themselves out as invincible specialists in defensive warfare. Wars would cease when the states made aggression unprofitable by their impregnable defenses. They also argued for an omnipotent state based on a social contract in which every man would surrender his will to his superior and the ruler would surrender his own to Heaven. The operative principle of this utopian order was to be what Mo Tzu called universal love. In contrast to the Confucians, who respected the greater love one bears to those nearest, the Mohists argued for the greater social usefulness of the principle that everyone must regard every other person's interest exactly as he would regard his own. Universal acceptance of this principle would lead to the required merging of wills and would guarantee the beneficient character of the perfected society.

The Taoist position with regard to violence is more difficult to state. In most of the literature of the school, opposition to war is implied, but is not explicit. The Taoists argued against the benevolence of the Confucians and the universal love of the Mohists as leading to a disposition to meddle in the affairs of others and to limit one's own and other people's spiritual freedom, thereby doing great harm. They argued instead for the recovery, through quietism, of naturalness and of spontaneity of feeling and action, and for shedding the bonds of conventional morality and social controls. In their perfected state, men would live in small communities simply and in enjoyment of nature. Paradoxically, however, they left room for an all-powerful, sage emperor, one who, having fully merged into the underlying metaphysical principle of the creating and transforming Tao, would thereby likewise become indestructible and omnipotent. But such a sage emperor, unified with Tao, would do no violence to naturalness and spontaneity in the world itself created by Tao.

For Confucius, the existential challenge to choose the good was the dominant theme of his life and his teaching. Life was a succession of choices and, because the will was free and because by study and the exercise of reason right and wrong could be known, there was no possible excuse for making wrong turns. Of free will, he said, "The gentleman does not permit himself to be used" (literally, "The gentleman is not a tool"). And, "The commander of an army may be captured, but you cannot capture the will even of the humblest of men." But it was not given to men to know the right by divine revelation or by literal application of sacred law. Heaven, standing for a moral universe, "willed" the right, but Heaven's will was hard to know. A disciple said, "Our master's views concerning culture and the outward manifestations of goodness we are permitted to hear; but about the original nature of man and the ways of Heaven, he will not tell us anything at all." A man may know the right only when he has prepared himself by a lifetime of effort of mind and will: "The master said, 'I am not one of those having innate knowledge. I am simply one who loves the past and who is diligent in investigating it.' " Also: "The Master said, 'Give me a few more years so that I may have spent a whole fifty in study, and I believe that after all I should be fairly free from error.' " As to the method of study, Confucius urged his students to avoid the twin perils of mindless pedantry and undisciplined speculation: "If you study but do not think, you toil in vain. If you think but do not study, you are in grave danger!" But study cannot be an end in itself; it is the means to the end of self-realization, and the self is realized in right action: "Tzu-kung asked about the true gentleman. The master said, 'He does not preach what he practices until he has practiced what he preaches.' And, 'To see what is right and not do it is cowardice.' " Indeed, the good life is demanding. In the words of one of the disciples, "The true knight of the way must perforce be both broad-shouldered and stout of heart; his burden is heavy and he has far to go. For shared humanity is the burden he has taken upon himself; and must we not grant that it is a heavy one to bear? Only with death does his journey end; then must we not grant that he has far to go?"

Such a life is an act of faith. Confucius had occasion to be quite explicit on this point, because in his lifetime he had little influence beyond the circle of his loving disciples. Specifically, he placed his faith in Heaven, which he saw guaranteeing the eventual triumph of the right and, as the cause of inexplicable events, of fate. For example, when one of his favorite disciples died, Confucius asserted that Heaven had taken him from him. But:

> When the master's life was endangered in the state of K'uang, he said, "When King Wen died, did not civilization [here a play on words; *wen* meaning 'civilization' is the Wen of King Wen] survive down to our time? If Heaven had intended civilization to perish, later generations would not have had the honor of continuing it. Since Heaven does not intend civilization to perish, what can the men of K'uang do to me that would affect its survival?"[8]

None of the other schools poses an ethical existentialist challenge like that posed by Confucius. The Mohists, for example, believed that the individual in the good society would be relieved of the burden of choice: "What the superior thinks to be right, all shall think to be right. What the superior thinks to be wrong, all shall think to be wrong." Moreover, since the operative principle of universal love was argued on utilitarian grounds and since historical examples were adduced to show that wrong behavior was always punished by Heaven and the spirits, even the initial commitment of the individual to the social contract was not presented as an act of faith, but as an advantageous bargain. Likewise, the Legalists submerged the issue of the meaning of individual existence in the collective good of the state, an abstraction personified by a ruler. The Taoists were not ethical existentialists, in that they intended to transcend conventional ethics through quietism and the attainment of naturalness and spontaneity and through their doctrine of *wu-wei,* or "nonaction" (meaning the renunciation of action directed toward conscious ends). However, the very renunciation of ends and the pursuit of spontaneity involved a leap of faith in Tao, or "natural process," and in its transforming and creative power. In this sense, therefore, Taoism might be described as a form of religious existentialism, taking religious in a nontheistic, nonanthropomorphic sense of the word.

The process of internal transformation in Chinese culture was already well begun by Confucius' time. Once it was believed that when people died, they *became* spirits (*shen,* a word also denoting gods generally). When sacrifices were offered to an ancestral spirit, one of the ancestor's living descendants purified himself by a period of abstinence and assumed the role of personator, (*shih,* literally "the one laid out," i.e., "corpse") inviting the spirit to take possession of his body and in this way participating in the ceremony. From this came the idea that the bodies of the living were ordinarily inhabited by spirits and that these spirits left their bodies at the moment of death. Thus the quality of spirituality was internalized quite literally and became a property of humans generally. Similarly, correct conduct, *i,* was internalized as conscience, the faculty by which one knows or feels what is the right thing to do. Unlike his later disciples, Mencius and Hsun Tzu, Confucius did not attempt to plumb the mysteries of the human spirit, or human nature, but he ardently believed in the reality of a shared humanity and in the capacity of all men to grow in wisdom, righteousness, and altruism. Confucius undertook to show his disciples the path of self-cultivation. Self-cultivation involved, for example, the development of a sense of propriety by internalizing *li,* or "ceremonial," by study and practice of the forms and by sensitivity to their meanings. Similarly, one developed *i,* or "conscience," by careful discrimination of right and wrong, by bravely doing what was right, and by merciless self-

[8] Waley, *Analects*, Bk. IX, Ch. 5.

criticism. Thereby the principles of right and wrong come to be internalized as an integral part of one's character.

The Legalists went to quite the opposite extreme and, instead of proposing the internalization of propriety, righteousness, or other principles, insisted on the externalization of all values in the form of the laws and edicts of the state. The Legalists analyzed human motivation simply into two traits, fear (of pain, death, deprivation, etc.) and desire (for comfort, status, wealth, etc.). So long as no values were internalized by the people the people could be completely controlled by the sovereign, who made the laws and saw that they were enforced with rewards and punishments. This was consistent with the Legalist approach to reform; they wanted to reform the institutions, the manner of organization, of society, whereas Confucius wanted to create the good society by reforming men. The Taoists found all value in nature and therefore held men to be good insofar as they acted naturally. They internalized the goodness of nature by finding it in the nature of man, human nature. They saw the propriety and conscience of the Confucians as having been contrived outside nature and imposed on human nature, crippling and distorting it. Thus, they were led to call for the liberation of men from conventional morality and life-styles. Confucius' disciple Mencius would seem to have combined both the Confucian and Taoist senses of internalization by insisting that human nature was naturally good, in a conventional sense of good. Man's lesser nature, comprising his appetites for food and sex, he shared with other animals, but he was also endowed, uniquely, with a greater nature, which comprised the beginnings of, or innate dispositions toward, the four virtues: shared humanity *(jen),* righteousness *(i),* propriety *(li),* and wisdom *(chih),* Thus, he found no contradiction between the introspective search going back to one's original child nature, on the one hand, and cultivating the conventional virtues by study and practice, on the other hand. Hsun Tzu, coming about three generations after Mencius, when the crisis of civilization was at its most agonizing stage, was pessimistic about human nature, which he believed to be naturally bad, in the sense of being innately selfish (not in the Judeo-Christian sense of original sin). He argued, therefore, that introspection was useless and that the only road to self-realization lay through internalization of the values and ceremonial bequeathed from the sages of antiquity.

The golden age of antiquity became a frame into which most of the schools could project their visions of the good society. The Legalists were the main exception; they believed the past to be irrelevant and that the habit of seeking guidance from the sages of antiquity was utter folly. Han Fei Tzu ridiculed traditionalism with a parable of the stupid farmer. One day when the farmer was at work in his fields, a rabbit dashed away and ran headlong into a tree. The farmer picked up the stunned animal and took it home for dinner. Afterwards, he posted himself by the tree and waited for another rabbit to come along. The farmer who expected "history to repeat" was no more foolish than the traditionalists who approached a current problem of government by trying to discover what Yao or Shun had done in an analogous case. The Confucians, on the contrary, treasured the literature that had come down to them from an earlier time and studied it with the utmost seriousness. Although they were aware of contradictory precedents, as in the ceremonial practices of Hsia, Shang, and Chou, they still believed in their value and, in general, leaned on Chou tradition because it was the most adequately documented. Yet for all their scholarly seriousness, their readings of ancient texts were apt to be forced and moralistic. For example, in the *Analects* of Confucius:

Tzu-kung said, " 'Poor without cadging, rich without swagger.' What about that for a motto?" The Master said, "Not bad. But better still, 'Poor, yet delightin in the Way; rich yet a student of ritual.' " Tzu-kung said, "The saying of the *Songs (Shih-Ching),*

As thing cut, as thing filed,
As thing chiselled, as thing polished,

refers, I suppose, to what you have just said?" The Master said, "Now Ssu, I can really begin to talk with you about the *Songs,* for when I allude to sayings of the past, you see what bearing they have on what was to come after."[9]

However, the couplet quoted by Tzu-kung was taken from a love song and had nothing to do with a gentleman's cultivation of a good character; the lines were spoken by a woman in love, praising her lover's elegance. Confucius was so committed to the notion that the Chou tradition was the repository of value that he made King Wen the vessel of *wen* ("civilization") in the passage cited earlier, and adopted the Duke of Chou as his personal hero and model in all things. It was perhaps for this reason that followers of Confucius for the next twenty-four centuries venerated the Chou and all the institutions and doctrines that they attributed to its great founders.

Among early Confucians, Hsun Tzu was undoubtedly the archtraditionalist. Because his pessimistic estimate of human nature left him with the problem of accounting for the creation of the good institutions of Chou, which he held to be the *sine qua non* of human society, he created his own history of the golden age:

If men are of equal power and station and have the same likes and dislikes, then there will not be enough goods to supply their wants and they will inevitably quarrel. . . . The former kings regulated the principles of ritual in order to set up ranks. They established distinctions between rich and poor, eminent and humble, making it possible for those above to join together and watch over those below. This is the basis upon which the people of the world are nourished. This is what the *Documents (Shu Ching)* means when it says, "Equality is based upon inequality."[10]

But,

Someone may ask whether ritual principles and concerted activity are not themselves a part of man's nature, so that for that reason the sage is capable of producing them. But I would answer that this is not so. A potter may mold clay and produce an earthen pot, but surely molding pots of clay is not part of the potter's human nature. . . . The sage stands in the same relation to ritual principles as the potter to the things he molds and produces.[11]

With Hsun Tzu's essays, the traditional account of the origins of civilization had achieved its most rational form. Originally, the elements of civilization were perceived as the invention of the gods. Then the gods were reduced to human dimensions and, like Yao, Shun Yü, and Hou Chi, were made into kings or ministers and worked into "history" as inspired mortals. Now for Hsun Tzu the rites and regulations of the sages were not inspired, or works of genius, but the products of prosaic mental toil, of the laborious exercise of reason.

For the Taoists, the golden age did not begin with the sages of Chou tradition; it ended with them. When the rulers of Hsia, Shang, and Chou invented ceremonial and the conventional virtues and taught them to their subjects, men no longer knew who they really were or how to behave naturally. The Taoists' golden age was an age of innocence, since ruined by civilization and now recoverable only by emptying oneself of all the mental baggage of the conventional society.

The ethical sensitivity of Confucians and Mohists was expressed in rather different ways. Confucius returned again and again to the cultivation of the quality of shared humanity as

[9] Waley, *Analects*, Bk. I, Ch. 15.
[10] Burton Watson, trans., *Hsun Tzu: Basic Writings* (Columbia University Press, 1963), p. 36. By permission of Columbia University Press.
[11] Watson, *Hsun Tzu*, p. 164.

the core of his ethical teaching. This quality was manifested in action as the altruistic support of others:

As for shared humanity—you yourself desire rank and standing. You want to turn your own merits to account; then help others to turn theirs to account—in fact, the ability to take one's own feelings as a guide—that is the sort of thing that lies in the direction of shared humanity.[12]

The injunction to behave altruistically implied its negative form, the duty not to behave selfishly or to take advantage of others. Because he was often in poverty and without employment, Confucius knew well the temptation to accept office expediently on improper terms, but he insisted that he would suffer any hardship rather than do so. But seeming virtue is all too easily achieved and Confucius gave much thought to the issue of sincerity in all conduct. In ceremonial, for example, one's feelings must accord with the symbolic meaning of the act:

High office filled by men of narrow views, ritual performed without reverence, the forms of mourning observed without grief—these are things I cannot bear to see![13]

Or, in one's relations with the living, to pretend to a virtue one does not possess is behavior unworthy of a gentleman:

How can we call even Wei-sheng Kao upright? When someone asked him for vinegar he went and begged it from the people next door, and then gave it as though it were his own gift.[14]

Underlying these propositions there would appear to be an aristocratic sense of honor, which linked Confucius to the passing Chou order. A sense of honor no doubt may also be found in the Mohists' insistence on severe discipline and obedience within their own knightly society, but they chose to stress logical demonstration and the principle of utility in their ethics. For instance, consider the following argument against the graded affection of the Confucians and for the Mohist principle of universal love:

Suppose . . . a man is buckling in his armor and donning his helmet to set out for the field of battle. . . . Now let us ask to whom would he entrust the support of his parents and the care of his wife and children? Would it be to the universal-minded man or to the partial man? It seems to me that, on occasions like these, there are no fools in the world.[15]

The parting soldier would, of course, leave his family in the care of the Mohist on the ground that he would care for his friend's children as if they were his own rather than trust the Confucian, who, the Mohist believed, would give first consideration to his own relatives. Mencius was unimpressed with the Mohists' utilitarian ethics but lapsed into utilitarian logic in attacking their views. The king of Liang asked him for advice that would "profit" his kingdom. Mencius indignantly pointed out to him that this way of thinking about rulership would bring about results exactly opposite to his intention. Ministers would consider how to "profit" their families, and lower members of society would seek to "profit" themselves, thereby endangering the kingdom.

The idea of nemesis, or retributive justice, is extremely important in Chinese thought. We have seen that the Chou royal tradition established the belief that the founders of Hsia and

[12] Waley, *Analects*, Bk. VI, Ch. 28.
[13] Waley, *Analects*, Bk. III, Ch. 26.
[14] Waley, *Analects*, Bk. V, Ch. 23.
[15] Burton Watson, trans., *Mo Tzu: Basic Writings* (Columbia University Press, 1963), p. 42. By permission of Columbia University Press.

Shang and, of course, of their own Chou had all been great and good men and that the last rulers of Hsia and Shang had been evil men who merited their fate when Heaven took the rule from them. In Confucius, however, the belief in a just world is certainly attenuated. There is nothing mechanical or certain about the prospering of a good man or the destruction of a bad one, but in his references to his own sense of mission and to the power of Heaven, Confucius acknowledges that in some inscrutable way and over the very long term, justice is done and the right way prospers. Mencius, as we have seen, is more dogmatic in his assertions about the rewards and punishments that shall be visited upon good and evil rulers. The Mohists, also, insisted on the principle of retribution, but for them the rewards and punishments were meted out in a most literal fashion by supernatural agency: "If someone kills an innocent person, then Heaven will send down misfortune upon him. Who is it that kills the innocent person? A man. And who is it that sends down the misfortune? Heaven." Also, in explaining the disordered and violent condition of society in his time, Mo Tzu said, "It all comes about because people are in doubt as to whether ghosts and spirits exist or not, and do not realize that ghosts and spirits have the power to reward the worthy and punish the wicked." Such notions did not generally find a place in official ideology in later times, but continued to be a vivid element in popular religion.

In one sense or another, all the schools we have considered were characterized by *universalism*. For the Confucians, perhaps the classic formulation is Confucius' own assertion that "by nature, men are nearly alike; by practice, they grow far apart." Thus, it was possible for him to recognize that there were important cultural differences among the peoples of the Chinese world and still assert that these were *merely* cultural and subject to change through education. Legalist theories of statecraft were grounded in a universal human psychology, the Mohists admitted of no qualifications in the universality of their general-will community, and the Taoists' were opposed to all the cultural forms and values that altered the natural state of man.

Although Confucius asserted that he "followed Chou" and that he was a "transmitter" and not an innovator, if his teachings are seen in their late Chou context, he appears to us as a social reformer. At a time when ascriptive status, the determination of status on the basis of birth and artistocratic family law, was yielding to the forces of political competition, he accepted the end of hereditary aristocracy. He made it a point to accept anyone eager for learning as his student and he insisted on the right of those who were commoners to hold whatever public office they were qualified for by training and achievement. So far, one might say as much about the Legalists, who also were interested in the recruitment of the ablest candidates for positions of office. But we have also noted that the Confucians and the Legalists had very different notions of what consitituted a qualified official. The Confucians insisted on character, which included moral standards, refinement, and candor, in addition to intellectual capacity. The Legalists, as we have seen, did not necessarily attach any positive value to moral characteristics but were interested in a combination of cleverness and technical competence. Consistent with these conflicting positions, the Confucians envisioned a harmonious, hierarchical society orchestrated by the *li,* which would have been internalized in all through education, a society in which there would be no contradiction between the ends of individual self-realization and the needs of society because it was precisely in the service of the just society that the essentially social nature of man was fully realized. The Legalists, on the other hand, would use codified law, with its scale of rigorously enforced rewards and punishments, as a means of imposing order externally and would employ "rational" techniques of bureaucratic management in the government. The Mohists would have achieved social reform both by institutional change—the creation of a totalitarian state—and by reforming men in the matters of frugality, simplicity, and awe of the spirits. The Taoists would not have wished to be characterized as reformers at all in any conventional sense, because this would run counter to their principle of *wu-wei,* avoidance of action directed to conscious ends. Yet, despite their protests, they must be counted as reformers too because of their devastating critiques of conventional morality and the confinements of social custom.

Among the Confucians, Mencius was the most explicit in his proposals for the reform of society. In the sections on growth and crisis of civilization, we have observed the proletarianization and pauperization of the peasantry that followed the breakdown of the feudal government and the manorial economy. Mencius tackled this problem directly by proposing land reform and educational programs for the common people. With regard to the first, he reinterpreted the manorial land tenure system of the past and adapted it to current circumstances. Agricultural land was to be marked off in one-*li* (Chinese mile) squares. Each square was to be subdivided into nine smaller squares. The eight outer squares were to be occupied separately by eight peasant families, leaving an unoccupied center square to be cultivated by all eight families in common. Each family was to support itself on its own allotment by growing grain and producing silk, and the product of the central plot was to be delivered to the state as taxes. (The central plot in this system thus represents the "lord's land" of the early manorial system.) This system implied the abolishment of private investment in land and would also have the effect of at least partially reversing the commercialization of the economy that had been underway during the late Chou. Schemes such as that proposed by Mencius, as we will see later on, were typical of the perennial efforts through twenty-five centuries to solve the problem of social instability in the countryside. In addition to these economic measues, Mencius also proposed the establishment of a hierarchy of official schools for public instruction. Adoption of these measures, he believed, would give rise to a society in which all men would find their rightful places, would be appropriately rewarded and, perhaps most important, would understand and cheerfully accept their obligations.

CONCLUDING REMARKS

Each of the three Asian civilizations treated here clearly can be said to have been undergoing crises during the middle of the first millenium B.C., and the literature of that time shows that the crisis was perceived as serious. Evidence of the crisis and contemporary statements about it all point to basic similarities in its underlying causes: the violent struggles for political power as epitomized by the Assyrian military campaigns; the cynical manipulation of acquired power as seen in the justifications put forth by the Chinese Legalists; the ineffectual reliance on magic, ritual, and sacrifice by an orthodox priesthood such as the brahmans in India; and widespread suffering among the lower classes in all three civilizations.

Despite the great differences in the cultural traditions that shaped the way in which individuals perceived the reality of their times and expressed their reactions to these crises, these moralists shared a set of common concerns: How was man to define, and then live up to, the demands of morality and live in harmony with himself and his fellow men? The answers given to these fundamental questions ranged along a broad continuum. In the Taoist and Buddhist texts the primary emphasis was placed most often on the individual achieving a personal spiritual tranquility, from which harmony among men would naturally result. Confucians, while also insisting on the necessity of internalizing ethical truth through self-cultivation, concerned themselves to a greater extent with social life. The Hebrew prophets and Zoroaster devoted more attention than did their South and East Asian counterparts to man's relationship with the cosmos, although the Hebrews definitely denied that a mere legalistic conformity with God's will without internalization was sufficient for the truly moral man.

Such differences in views would no doubt have produced lively debates if these men or their disciples had ever met in face-to-face discussion. What should not be lost sight of, however, is the fact that they would have agreed on many questions as being meaningful and worthy of debate despite the different stands they would have taken. For example, just as Confucians and Mohists in China debated the relative importance of family, one could have asked of Mahavira, Buddha, or the Hebrew prophets, What was the place of marriage and parenthood in the good society? What of equality and inequality between the sexes or classes of people? Were political rulers essential to social life and on what basis was their authority justified? How was the meaning of the historical experience of man to be understood? What was the fate of those who pursued hedonistic pleasure and material comfort at the expense of others? The historian must also ask, What types of people proved most receptive to these ethical teachings? What is the significance of the fact that geographically these teachers often appear first on the periphery of older centers of civilization? How did rulers and other elites respond to these calls for moral reform? What was the role of such ideology in the economic and political behavior of social groups? Information on some of these and other questions can be found in the bibliographical items that follow here.

BIBLIOGRAPHY

3.P THE CRISIS AND ETHICAL PROTEST IN THE MID-FIRST MILLENNIUM B.C.: PROCESSES

Dawson, Christopher, *Dynamics of World History* (Mentor paperback, 1962), pp. 115-24, 168-88. Sections on "Religion and Life of Civilizations," "The Coming of World Religions," and "Stages in Mankind's Religious Experience" offer another perspective.

Jaspers, Karl, *Socrates, Buddha, Confucius, Jesus* (Harcourt Brace & World paperback, 1962), 104 pp. A prominent philosopher's attempt at comparative analysis of what he calls "the paradigmatic individuals."

Toynbee, Arnold, *Study of History*, Vol. 4, *The Breakdown of Civilizations* (New York: Oxford University Press, Galaxy paperback, 1963), 656 pp. At times ponderous but nevertheless a provocative scheme for the comparative study of crises in ancient civilizations.

3.1 ZOROASTER AND THE HEBREW PROPHETS IN WEST ASIA

Bendix, Reinhard, *Max Weber* (Anchor Book paperback, 1962), 522 pp. Chapter 7 presents Weber's sociological analysis of ancient Israel.

Duchesne-Guillemin, Jacques, *Zoroastrianism* (Harper Torchbook paperback, 1966), 175 pp. Surveys the history of Zoroastrian beliefs and symbols.

Frye, Richard N., *The Heritage of Persia* (New York, 1966), 349 pp. This general history includes a concise account of Zoroaster and his times.

Hallo, William W., and William Kelly Simpson, *The Ancient Near East* (Harcourt Brace paperback, 1971), 319 pp. Chapter 5 presents the outlines of the West Asian political setting of the development of the prophetic traditions.

Henning, W. B., *Zoroaster, Politician or Witch Doctor?* (London, 1951), 51 pp. This short but scholarly study examines a variety of interpretations of the prophet's life and teachings.

Orlinsky, Harry, *Ancient Israel* (Ithaca, 1965), 195 pp. A concise history of the people of Israel and the development of their religion.

3.2 MAHAVIRA AND BUDDHA IN SOUTH ASIA

Basham, A. L., *The Wonder That Was India* (Evergreen paperback, 1959), 568 pp. Buddhism and Jainism and their antecedents are treated in pp. 232-97.

Bendix, R., *Max Weber* (Anchor Book paperback, 1962), 522 pp. Chapter 6 presents Weber's sociological insights into religion in India.

Conze, E., *Buddhism: Its Essence and Development* (Harper Torchbook paperback, 1951), 211 pp. This sound general introduction is especially useful for its clear definitions and exposition of basic concepts of Buddhist thought.

de Bary, W. T., ed., *The Buddhist Tradition* (Vintage paperback, 1972), 417 pp. The first chapter in this source book provides readings in early Buddhist teachings.

Majumdar, R. C., *et al., An Advanced History of India,* third edition (London, 1967), 1126 pp. The same period is covered here in greater detail.

Thapar, Romila, *A History of India,* Vol. 1 (Baltimore, 1966), 381 pp. Chapter 3 provides a lucid and concise account of social and political change in North India about 600-321 B.C.

3.3 ETHICAL PROTEST AND REFORM IDEOLOGY IN CHOU CHINA

Fairbank, John K., Edwin O. Reischauer, and Albert M. Craig, *East Asia: Tradition and Transformation* (Boston, 1973), 969 pp. Chapter 3 surveys the period of the classical philosophers.

Fung, Yu-lan, *A Short History of Chinese Philosophy* (New York, 1960), 368 pp. The first 16 chapters provide a solid, thoughtful survey of the major schools of classical thought.

McNeill, William H., and Jean W. Sedlar, eds., *Classical China* (Oxford paperback, 1970), 274 pp. This small volume contains a wide selection of translated readings in Chou and Han literature.

Mote, Frederick, W., *Intellectual Foundations of China* (Knopf paperback, 1971), 135 pp. This is a concise and stimulating introduction to classical Chinese thought.

Waley, A., *Three Ways of Thought in Ancient China* (Anchor Book paperback, 1939), 216 pp. Extended translations with perceptive commentary on Confucian, Taoist, and Legalist thought.

Watson, W., *Early Chinese Literature* (Columbia paperback, 1962), 304 pp. This monograph offers a nontechnical introduction to the forms, styles and bibliography of Chou and Han literature.

GLOSSARY

Ahinsa (or **ahimsa**). Commonly translated "nonviolence," was the principle of noninjury to living things. Ahinsa was important in early Buddhist doctrine and strongly emphasized in Jainism.

Ahura Mazda. "The God Mazda," supreme deity and the principle of right and truth in Zoroastrianism. Ahura Mazda stood in opposition to the demonic Anrya Mainyu, who represented evil and untruth.

An-Atta. Literally "non-self," the original Buddhist doctrine that the notion of "I," the self, is an illusion. Instead, it is argued, there is only an unstable coming together of the five *skandhas:* matter and form; sensations; perceptions; psychic constructions; and conscious thought.

Arhat. One who has successfully pursued the eightfold path to the point of enlightenment *(bodhi)* and *nirvana,* or the extinction of suffering.

Baal. General term for the divinities worshipped by the Canaanites, who were one of the peoples who occupied Canaan (roughly modern Israel) when the people of Israel settled there after the Exodus.

Babylonian captivity. Refers to the period during the sixth century B.C. when many of the people of Israel were deported to Babylon by their Chaldean conquerors.

Buddha. The historic Buddha, first formulator of Buddhist doctrine and founder of the school, lived approximately from 563-483 B.C. Buddha means "enlightened," but the meaning of the term was extended in later times in Mahayana Buddhism to include a great number of Buddhist divinities. The historic Buddha is also known by other names or epithets including Sakyamuni, "Sage of the Saka clan;" Gotama Buddha (Gotama was another name for his clan); Suddhodana (his personal name); and Siddhartha, "He Who Has Attained His Goal."

Chaldeans. Probably speakers of a Semitic language, appeared in ninth century B.C. Recorded as the inhabitants of the swampy lowlands at the head of the Persian Gulf. They subsisted on fishing, agriculture, and herding and do not appear to have had any cities. Their mobility and their dispersed small settlements made it relatively easy for them to resist Assyrian control. Between 625-539 B.C., they led the Mesopotamian city dwellers in liberation from Assyrian control and established a large, but short-lived, kingdom.

Chuang Tzu. "Master Chuang," was Chuang Chou to whose authorship the Taoist work entitled *Chuang Tzu* was ascribed. His approximate dates are 369-286 B.C. The *Chuang Tzu* eloquently made the case for spontaneity and naturalness in life in opposition to laws and social conventions.

Confucianism. The term commonly adopted by Western scholars to denote the doctrines held by those men of learning who regarded themselves as the followers of Confucius. "Confucians," who were regarded as a school or as followers of an intellectual tradition, were usually designated in Chinese as *ju* or collectively as *ju-chia,* "ju-school."

Confucius. Latinized version of the name of K'ung Ch'iu (ca. 551-479 B.C.), a native of the state of Lu and possibly the descendant of one of the Shang aristocratic houses that was moved to the state of Sung after the Chou conquest. After an unsuccessful official career, he became a teacher and the founder of the Confucian tradition in Chinese thought. The most important surviving written records of his thought are to be found in the *Lun Yu,* or *Analects.*

Cosmogony. Either the origin of the universe or a theory or myth devised to account for the origin.

David. Founder and king of the monarchy of Israel around 1000 B.C. Under David and his heir, Solomon, the people of Israel were politically organized as a territorial state with a permanent royal capital at Jerusalem.

Elite. A group or element in a society that presumes on some ground or other to hold a superior status or authority. Thus elitism refers to either a claim to such status or to a theory justifying the existence of elites. Elites may be of different kinds, such as political elites or intellectual elites.

Ezekiel. Hebrew prophet who urged patient and sincere observance of the worship of Yahweh while awaiting divine deliverance from the Babylonian captivity.

First Isaish. Prophet in Israel in the late eighth century B.C., who attacked the greed of the great families that had acquired big estates and oppressed the poor. He also joined the prophet Micah in warning of dire consequences if the state of Israel continued to rely upon foreign alliances instead of the will of Yahweh.

Gibborim. The landholding military aristocracy of ancient Israel, roughly analogous to the *shih* of late Chou China and the Aryan *kshatriyas* in India.

Han Fei (lived ca. 280-233 B.C.). Legalist philosopher whose essays comprise the work *Han Fei Tzu.*

Jen. Here translated as "shared humanity," is more commonly translated as "benevolence." *Jen* was the essential principle of the social orientation of human nature as this was understood by Confucius and Mencius.

Jeremiah. Prophet in Israel around 600 B.C., foretold the fall of Jerusalem and urged acceptance of the Chaldean conquest and the Babylonian exile as just punishment visited by Yahweh upon the people for their sins.

Ju. "Weakling," the common epithet for the learned followers of Confucius. The term may also have been used much earlier to denote the learned descendants of Shang nobles who were required to serve in the Chou court.

Karma. The causative principle by which each life in a chain of lives is affected by deeds done in earlier lives in the same chain. Thus good deeds in one life result in good *karma* and a happier condition in the next life.

Lao Tzu. The fictitious person traditionally supposed to have written the Taoist classic *Tao Te Ching, The Way and Its Power.* The real authors of this work have never been identified. It is also uncertain when the work was compiled, but it was probably around 300 B.C.

Legalism. The teachings of the *Fa Chia,* "School of Law," whose early representatives included Shang Yang, Shen Pu-hai, and Han Fei. The name is somewhat misleading because law was only one aspect of this body of political theory.

Literati. Men of learning, especially literary learning. In the context of Chinese history, this term is generally associated with scholarship based on the classical texts associated with Confucius and his followers. Since these same works were the main foundation of official ideology during most of Chinese history, the term literati also points to civil officials generally.

Mahavira. Known also as Jaina, "The Conqueror," Mahavira was the principal founder of Jainism. His approximate dates are 540-468 B.C.

Mencius. Latinized name of Meng K'e, who lived approximately from 372-289 B.C. He was a follower of Confucius and one of his principal interpreters. Like Confucius, he was most successful as a teacher. The principal source for his life and teachings is the book that bears his name.

Mo Tzu. Mo Tzu, "Master Mo," or Mo Ti (ca. 479-381 B.C.). An official of the state of Sung. The book entitled *Mo Tzu* was attributed to his authorship, although much of it is of later date. Mohism denotes the doctrine of Mo Tzu and his followers with its emphasis on the principle of *ai,* "universal love."

Nirvana. Ultimate reality, ultimate truth, and the ground of all existence in Indian thought. To achieve enlightenment in the Buddhist sense is to know and to become one with *nirvana.* In a negative sense, to attain *nirvana* is to escape from the chain of births and deaths, the end of illusion, craving, and suffering.

Orthodoxy. Literally any true doctrine as opposed to an untrue or heterodox doctrine. Orthodoxy also is commonly used as here to denote the doctrines officially held to be true by some religious or political body.

Parochialism. With respect to civilized societies a stubborn attachment to the culture of one's own region and a conviction of its superiority.

Samsara. Usually translated as "transmigration of the soul." In its simplest form the doctrine of *samsara* explained the cycle of birth and death as the eternal migration of souls that entered each living thing at birth, left it at death, and entered another newborn being. *Samsara* is an important concept in Jainism and Buddhism, but in Buddhism it has reference to chains of existence with no distinct or persisting soul.

Sanctification. The attribution of the quality of holiness or sacredness. Thus a royal throne, although made by mortal hands, may be perceived as sacred or as sharing in the transcendent power and authority of a god or gods. This process may be reversed by desanctification, as when a once-sacred royal throne is redefined as simply the seat of the political head of state.

Sangha. In Buddhism, the monastery or convent, the community of monks and nuns.

Shang Yang (d. 338 B.C.). Belonged to a minor lineage of the ruling house of the state of Wei in China. He served his state for a time, then broke with its ruler and defected to the rival state of Ch'in. As a minister in Ch'in he commanded an army against his native state. He was also identified as the source of the program of administrative and legal reforms that strengthened Ch'in for its final drive toward imperial unification of China. Shang Yang was forced into rebellion against Ch'in by a hostile faction, defeated and killed. The *Book of Lord Shang,* attributed to him, is counted as one of the major works of Legalist political thought.

Sogdians. The Iranian inhabitants of Sogdiana (known to the Greeks as Transoxania), the area lying between the Amu Darya and Syr Darya rivers.

Tao. A road, path, or way, and by extension, a "way" of acting. By further extension, the "way" of the universe and, finally, the ultimate reality, the self-existent, transcendant, and therefore indescribable *Tao. Tao* in its many different senses was an important concept in the doctrines of different schools, especially Confucianism and Taoism.

Taoism. Used in at least two very different senses. In the first, it refers to the doctrines of such early quietists as the authors of the *Tao Te Ching* and the *Chuang Tzu,* sometimes called "philosophical Taoism." In the second sense, it refers to the indigenous religious system of China including a vast and complex body of religious, cosmological, and proto-scientific belief and practice, sometimes called "religious Taoism."

Tiglath Pileser III (r. 744-727 B.C.). The ruler who reestablished Assyrian dominance in West Asia and strengthened the Assyrian state by centralization of royal administration. His military victories included the capture of Samaria, capital of the northern kingdom of Israel. This was followed by mass deportations, which gave rise to the legend of the "Ten Lost Tribes of Israel."

4

The Rise of Universal Empires during the First Millennium B.C.

The Rise of Universal Empires during the First Millennium B.C.

539 B.C. to 9 A.D.

The crisis of civilization to which the ethical reformers of the first millennium B.C. addressed themselves was resolved eventually by the formation of great empires that unified rival states under a single, centralized authority. Because they brought together the culture zones of entire civilizations, the new political entities may be termed universal empires. In West Asia the Achaemenid empire ruled approximately 550-330 B.C. In South Asia the Mauryan empire, 321-183 B.C., unified most of the Indian subcontinent, while the Ch'in and Former Han dynasties held sway in China from 221 B.C. to 9 A.D. The impetus for the formation of universal empires was provided by a long period of regional warfare, which served to break down older restraints and increase the scale of militarization. It was on the periphery of the civilized world that militarization and the rationalization of state power found their highest development. Outlying, often semicivilized states developed superior military technologies, which were applied to the conquest of an entire civilized area. In the resulting new polities resources were mobilized and power concentrated on a unprecedented scale. New forms and titles were created to set the rulers, the emperors, apart from the kings of smaller states. Military conquest was extended in all directions, and the resulting peace throughout a broad area resulted in a stimulus to commerce and communication, increasing the scale of civilized society. The bureaucratic structure that universal empires created was used to impose standardized practices—weights, measures, currencies, calendars, and written scripts—throughout the territories under the emperor's control. Ideological forms also were given special attention by rulers who sought to enhance their prestige and secure their positions by promoting religions or ideologies. One result of the social stability that universal empires created was to instill a common set of cultural forms throughout the culture area so that the civilization subsequently came to be defined partly in terms of the universal empires. In this sense, for example, Western civilization came to be associated with Rome, its culture and institutions. The existence of universal empires facilitated communication among civilizations by narrowing the distance between them and making secure trade and travel.

4

PROCESSES

The Founding of Universal Empires

a. Shift of power to the periphery
b. Mobilization of resources
c. Military pacification

The Imperial Order

d. Emperorship
e. Universal imperialism
f. Closure of the ecumene
g. Bureaucracy
h. Communication systems

The Cultural Impact of Universal Empires

i. Standardization
j. State ideology
k. Capital cities

PATTERNS

1. **The Achaemenid Empire in West Asia**
2. **The Mauryan Empire in South Asia**
3. **The Ch'in-Han Universal Empire in East Asia**

4. UNIVERSAL EMPIRES

		1	2	3
	ROME	ACHAEMENIDS	MAURYAS	CH'IN-HAN
600 B.C.				
		Cyrus the Great conquers Babylon 539		
		Darius I, r. 521-486		
500	Athenian victory at Marathon 490	Xerxes I 486-465		
400			Kingdoms and republics in north India	
		Artaxerxes III, r. 359-338		
		Alexander the Great overthrows Achaemenid empire 331-330	Chandragupta Maurya, r. ca. 321-292	
300	Rome unites Italian peninsula			Warring States period 453-222
			Ashoka, r. ca. 272-232	
				Ch'in conquest 221, unification of China Han empire founded by Liu Pang 206
200	Punic and Macedonian Wars make Rome supreme in Mediterranean 264-146			

Date	Rome		India	China
			Pushyamitra Shunga overthrows last Mauryan ruler ca. 183	Tung Chung-shu 179-104, Confucian theorist
			Shunga dynasty 183-73	Princes revolt 154
				Wu Ti, r. 141-87
				Chang Ch'ien missions 139-26, 115, northern campaigns 129-90, conquest of Vietnam 111, conquest of Korea 108
100				
	Julius Caesar 102-44			Hsiung-nu empire divided 60
	Augustus defeats Mark Antony and Cleopatra and becomes supreme 31 B.C.			
B.C./A.D.	Augustus, d. 14 A.D.			Wang Mang's usurpation 9 A.D.
				Later Han dynasty 25-220
	Nero, emperor 54-68			
100	Hadrian, emperor 117-38			
200				
	Diocletian, emperor 285-305, autocracy			

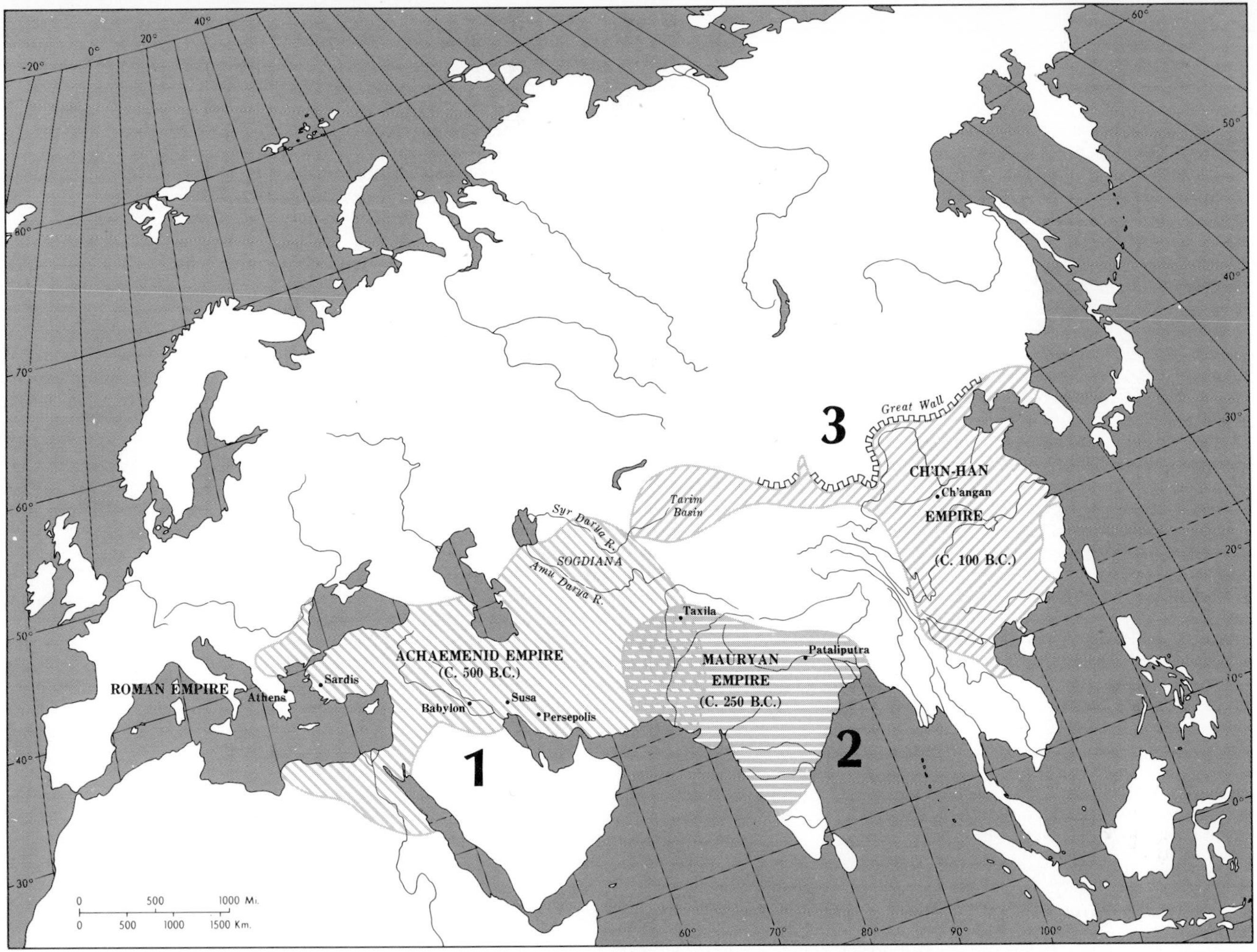

Map 14 Universal empires during the first millennium B.C.

PROCESSES

In the first two chapters we discussed the growth and social and political transformation of civilizations in Eurasia. In the third chapter we considered the emergence of ethical protest and reform ideologies as symptoms of a crisis in civilization precipitated by processes of change. Universal empires, the subject of this chapter, can be regarded as a form of response to the crisis of civilization. The ideologies were reactions to crisis in the realm of values and ideas, while universal empires resulted from action on the level of military power and political organization.

The distinguishing feature of the universal empires was their scale, a scale made possible by the processes of growth in the preceding period. Not only did the size of the universal empires surpass that of earlier states; these vast entities were "universal" in the sense that the political order was at least coterminous with an entire civilized world or culture area. In the usage adopted here the term universal empire will refer specifically to the great empires of the ancient period. In Chapter 9 we will characterize a later set of empires as early modern empires.

THE PERIOD

The period covered by this chapter is 539 B.C. to the beginning of the Christian era. Within that time span the patterns will encompass three different universal empires, one in each of the principal culture areas of Asia. They are. the Achaemenid empire in West Asia (ca. 550-330 B.C.), the Mauryan empire in South Asia (321-183 B.C.), and the Ch'in-Former Han empire in East Asia (221 B.C.-9 A.D.). It should be noted that the corresponding example in the Western cultural area would be the short-lived Macedonian conquest empire or the more enduring Roman empire. Although Rome was the latest of these universal empires to develop, and lay outside of Asia, it is the best known to the Western reader and may occasionally be cited to illustrate some of the processes.

THE FOUNDING OF UNIVERSAL EMPIRES

The formation of universal empires culminated and brought an end to a prolonged period of military conflict.

a. Shift of Power to the Periphery

In the crisis of civilization, the old centers lost their ability to control the outlying areas. A power vacuum in the center led to political instability, fragmentation, and a competition for mastery that produced widespread warfare and chaos. Under these conditions vigorous new leadership came from the periphery of the old civilization. Men of the marches, semiacculturated and semibarbaric, sometimes seminomadic, developed sufficient military power to challenge the old leadership. These vigorous outsiders had partially absorbed the learning, technology, and culture of the old civilizations but were not fully integrated into the social order of the old polities. They were attracted by the wealth and sophistication of the old centers, while at the same time they were relatively free to experiment with new forms of political and social organization which might increase their power. As the crisis of civilization proceeded, rival military forces competed for dominance, and ambitious and gifted commanders emerged who assembled new military machines and conquered the old centers of civilization. The new conquerors benefitted in this undertaking from some civilized institutions and practices already in existence. These they adopted, modified, or rejected as their purposes dictated. Most important, the old centers constituted a precedent for unity and order, and the charismatic hero who finally conquered the center did so with the claim that he was restoring order, albeit in a new form.

b. Mobilization of Resources

The warfare that led to the military unification of the culture area saw an escalation in the scale of military operations. The massive new military machines of the unifiers represented a new scale of organization that could draw on larger areas, mobilize greater manpower and wealth, and apply more sophisticated technologies than had been seen previously. In Chapter 2 it was noted that the practice of agriculture became more productive in terms of crop yield and manpower input and that the diffusion of civilization brought about a great expansion of the cultivated area. These processes in turn resulted in an immense increase in population on the great alluvial plains of Mesopotamia, northern India, and north China. Trade increased, regional specialization in major commodities and luxury goods developed markedly, and nonagricultural technologies such as iron production flourished. The concomitant development of state organization and of administrative techniques for mobilizing these resources provided the foundations of political power on an unprecedented scale. Available manpower for the armies and for public works, revenues for imperial government, food, arms, and equipment for war were necessary preconditions for the formation of the universal empires.

c. Military Pacification

The military leader who was able to eliminate his rivals and control the center was in the best position to establish a new political order. His task was made easier by the claim that he was acting not just for his own interest but in order to restore peace and, in some instances, to preserve the heritage of the old civilizations. This gave his conquest an aura of legitimacy and made it easier for him to convert newly conquered opponents into obedient subjects or even active supporters. But to restore order, he first had to subdue all opposition. The attainment of peace was thus the result of pacification, and the preservation of peace required the maintenance of military superiority.

THE IMPERIAL ORDER

The new imperial order that military pacification brought into being surpassed all previous states in geographical expanse and in elaboration of political organs.

d. Emperorship

Since the new unifying conquerors were not themselves survivors of the old ruling families who had failed to maintain order, it was in their interest to adopt titles and ceremonials different from those of the discredited old regimes. Claiming to be the saviors of civilization, they took on new trappings that reflected the unprecedented scope of their claimed authority. Because their rule spanned a number of kingdoms, they often took titles that elevated them above ordinary rulers—the distinction in English between king and emperor.

e. Universal Imperialism

The universal empire was the product of a prolonged process of conquest in which rival powers were eliminated and a new control was exerted over the old centers of civilization. The peace-keeping function that was central to the purpose and justification of the new order was fulfilled by continuous exercise of military power. Once internal enemies were eliminated, the military might of the conquerors was turned outward for expansion on the peripheries. All the universal empires maintained great armies, which conquered on a continental scale. Ruthless destruction was visited upon competitors who challenged the new state's authority. A notable example of this process is the prolonged struggle between Rome and Carthage in which Carthage was eventually obliterated. The consequence of universal imperialism was to bring an entire culture area under the control of a single political authority.

f. Closure of the Ecumene

As a result of imperial expansion, virtually all of the civilized territory of Eurasia came under the control of a few universal empires. The tendency for these territorially acquisitive powers was to expand until they either ran out of space (Han China reached the shoreline of the Pacific), encountered obstacles (such as the Libyan desert or the Central Asian steppe zone in the case of the Achaemenids), or annexed more territory than they could effectively administer (which happened with the Mauryas). One result of this outward thrust was the closure of the Eurasian ecumene. The empires expanded until the frontiers of the major civilizations made contact with each other. One effect of this process was to increase greatly the range of contacts between civilizations. Diffusion of cultural influences was facilitated, and trade expanded substantially. Trade routes through Central Asia brought China into contact with South and West Asia and even Rome. Eventually Indian and Chinese influences met in Southeast Asia, where their dual fertilization produced the amalgam we characterize by the term Indochina.

g. Bureaucracy

Management of these vast empires required the comprehensive rationalization of the machinery of government. The principal impetus to this administrative rationalization was, again, the scale of the new state. The size of the imperial armies and the extent of the territories to be administered required that human and material resources be mobilized on a scale far greater than had been the case in the past. Differentiation of function thus went far beyond the rudimentary steps discussed in Chapter 2. Politically, the rulers of empires had to find new agents who could manage government affairs and yet who were loyal to the ruler's interests and not tied too closely to rival interests, such as former ruling elites, a religious authority, or local or regional interests. Organizationally, this meant the formation of a governmental bureaucracy, usually through the modification of preexisting priestly or noble offices, and the codification or standardization of regularized procedures for the management of governmental affairs. Administratively, the formation of a bureaucracy was accompanied by the division of the empire into provincial and other units, colonies, and garrisons, each with specified political, economic, and military functions.

h. Communication systems

Essential to the creation and operation of the universal empire was the improvement of communications and transportation. For military and administrative purposes especially, great attention was paid to welding the empire together with a communications network and particularly to tying outlying areas to the decision-making center at the capital. The Roman roads are perhaps the best-known communications network of the pre-Christian era, but every empire had such facilities, including roads, canals, fleets, ports, staging posts, and messenger services. For the state, the communications network made possible essential functions—the movement of troops, the transportation of supplies, and the transmission of messages. These functions could be performed only so long as travel was made secure by the policing of waterways and highways. A supplementary benefit of the imperial communications network was a growth in trade and commercial activity, stimulated in part by the security of travel.

THE CULTURAL IMPACT OF UNIVERSAL EMPIRES

Administrative unification of the empire greatly facilitated intraregional contact and cultural exchange. Over time there was a tendency for common cultural forms to be diffused throughout the empire, often as a result of state policy or of the influence of the imperial establishment. In this way the creation of the universal empires marked an important turning point in the cultural history of the societies they administered.

The actions of the rulers of universal empires had important implications for the fate of the old civilized cultures, particularly in those cases in which the founders were themselves from the periphery of the culture area and had only partially internalized the values of the older culture. This is well illustrated in the Western culture area. Even though Greece may be said to have lived on in Rome, many of the higher ideals of Greek culture were lost on the vigorous and pragmatic Romans. Second, the very nature of imperial institutions demanded a form of political organization that was incompatible with older forms. Roman emperorship had little use for Greek ideals of the independent city-state, just as it outgrew its own republican origins. Third, the growth of an imperial metropolis and the relationship between the emperor and the mass of his subjects favored a vulgar form of mass culture. This was manifested in monumental art and mass pageantry—in practices that debased the refinements of older traditions while emphasizing the universal authority of imperial rule.

i. Standardization

Administrative unification of the empire and centralization of power created strong pressures for standardization in government, commerce, and social life. Where possible, the state administration would enforce uniform practices such as a standard language, a state calendar, universal currency, a standard system of weights and measures, and uniform tax structures and legal codes. The greatest diversity tended to manifest itself in distant territories possessing cultural traditions alien to those of the imperial center, as in the case of Egypt under Achaemenid rule. Thus, in some parts of the Roman empire local affairs might be managed through the use of indigenous languages such as Greek. The attempt to create uniform legal codes, desirable for reasons of equity and administrative efficiency, could lead either to an enunciation of legal principles in abstract form to accommodate local diversity or to an attempt to impose a common imperial standard upon the entire populace. In any case, the imposition of administrative unity upon cultural diversity fostered the diffusion of standard forms.

j. State Ideology

The need for uniformity was also manifested on the ideological level. Prolonged exercise of universal authority eventually led away from early policies of toleration of cultural diversity and toward a common cultural orientation. The temptation to rationalize rule by the resort to ideology led the rulers of universal empires to seek a systematic body of thought that could legitimize their status. Thus it was that the ethical-protest ideologies that had earlier originated in response to a perceived crisis of civilization came to be adapted to the use of the universal empires. The search for ideological justification grew out of changing imperatives. As the state moved from an active phase of conquest and expansion to a later stage of conserving its control over what it held, the exigencies of pacification no longer sufficed to rationalize state power. At this juncture an opportunity was opened up for reform ideology or religion to penetrate the state. Comparable adaptations were made in each case: in the Achaemenid empire it was a modified Zoroastrianism; in the Mauryan empire, Buddhism; in Han China, Confucianism; and in Rome, Christianity. Once this adaptation took place, the formidable communications network of the empire became a transmission device for broadcasting the ideology over a vast area. It should be noted, however, that this spread of ideas was not equally effective at all levels of society but primarily involved the upper class or elite group whose support was most essential to the state. Dissemination of the elite value system among the lower classes was variously limited by the amount of social mobility in each society. In a later chapter consideration will be given to universal religions that did penetrate all strata of society by virtue of a mass appeal.

k. Capital Cities

At the center of the universal empires, great capital cities grew up, grandiose in scale and symbolic in form. The design and layout of the palaces and central spaces were calculated to set the ruler apart and highlight the stage upon which men bearing the concentrated power of the empire exercised their authority. In symbolic terms the capital often represented a microcosm of the empire, the world, or the universe, embodying in physical form some of the most important abstract concepts in the elite world view.

The concentration of political authority and the fact that wealth could be drawn from a vastly wider area meant that imperial capitals surpassed all earlier cities in status, wealth, and grandeur. In some cases there was a distinct tendency for the imperial centers to develop a vulgar cultural style markedly distinct from the refinement of earlier capitals in which aristocratic or elitist styles had prevailed. Consider, for example, the contrast between the participatory athletic contests of the ancient Greeks and the mass spectacle of gladiatorial combat in the Roman Colosseum.

The universal empire marked a new and important stage in the development of civilization in that it brought organizational unity to the civilization for the first time. This experience left an indelible mark on civilization, which from that time forward was defined in part in terms of the scope and style of the universal state. The lingering effects of this experience of cohesion will be explored in the next chapter, which describes persisting classical traditions.

By way of qualification it should be pointed out that the processes discussed here did not necessarily appear in the same configuration in all of the universal states. Certainly, the order of events could vary drastically. A good example is provided by the contrast between the evolution of the Roman empire and that of Ch'in-Han China. In the Chinese case the rulers of Ch'in developed a tightly disciplined, highly militarized state and then set about the business of methodically conquering their neighbors. In Rome, by contrast, the work of conquest was well under way before power became concentrated in the hands of a single, all-powerful individual.

PATTERNS

1. THE ACHAEMENID EMPIRE IN WEST ASIA

The foundation of the empire of the Iranian dynasty of the Achaemenids is usually reckoned to date from 539 B.C., when Cyrus the Great entered Babylon as a conqueror. The end came with Alexander the Great's overthrow of the last Achaemenid ruler, Darius III, in 331-330 B.C., although it is arguable that in certain respects the short-lived empire of Alexander's successors, the half-Macedonian, half-Iranian Seleucids (312–ca. 250 B.C.), constituted a legitimate successor state to that of the Achemenids. In any event, the empire of the Achaemenids survived for well over two hundred years, and its comparative longevity is a testimonial as much to the skill of the first Achaemenids as builders of a sound administrative infrastructure as to their undoubted ability as warlords.

It was Cyrus the Great (r. ca. 550-530 B.C.) who laid the foundations of the empire, while his successors, Cambyses (r. 529-522 B.C.) and Darius I (r. 521-486 B.C.), extended its frontiers until they stretched from Egypt in the west to beyond the Indus in the east. There then followed some loss of momentum under Xerxes I (r. 486-465 B.C.) and his three successors, interrupted by an energetic revival under the exceptionally able Artaxerxes III (r. 359-338 B.C.). After the death of the latter, however, the regime rapidly fell to pieces, and in the years 334-331 B.C. the hitherto impressive military organization of the Achaemenids collapsed in the face of a revolutionary weapon of war, the Macedonian phalanx.

Chapter 2 described the fortunes of a succession of military regimes whose manpower and revenue resources centered upon Mesopotamia, then the undisputed heartland of civilization in West Asia. With the collapse of the Neo-Babylonian empire, the disappearance from the scene of its last ruler, Nabonidus, and the entry of Cyrus into Babylon in 539 B.C., there occurred a dramatic shift of power away from "the Land of the Two Rivers" northeastward into the Zagros Mountains, which separate Mesopotamia from the Iranian plateau. The process had already been under way for a number of decades. During this period the Zagros region, like the rest of the Iranian plateau, was inhabited by an Aryan tribal population, partly pastoral nomadic and partly sedentary, speaking various Indo-European dialects and, in the case of the inhabitants of the southwestern extremities of the plateau, exposed to the acculturating influence of the lowland civilizations of Mesopotamia and, in particular, of Elam, located in what is now the Iranian province of Khuzistan.

Periodically, an exceptionally able chieftain brought together a number of tribes over which he exercised a fairly informal kind of overlordship, thereby forming a tribal confederacy that, in relation to its weaker neighbors, enjoyed a formidable capacity for aggression. Other factors, too, may have provided a stimulus to confederate action, such as a comparatively rapid increase in population in a countryside that, on account of its relative aridity, could sustain only rather small communities. There was also, in all probability, an awareness of the declining strength of the hitherto mighty empires of Assyria and Babylon and of the opportunities offered by that decline. This was certainly the background to the career of Cyrus in the third quarter of the sixth century B.C., but he was by no means the first Iranian warlord to challenge the age-old hegemony of the cities of the plains. This had already been undertaken by the Medes, an Iranian tribal confederacy based in the northern Zagros region in what is now Kurdistan, with its headquarters at Hamadan, the classical Ecbatana. Herodotus gives a colorful account of the fall of the last Median king, brought to bay by the young hero, Cyrus, but notwithstanding its unmistakably legendary character it recalls what must have been the successful challenge to Median supremacy posed by a smaller Iranian tribal confederacy, the Parsua, or Persians, located in the southern Zagros region, with their base in the Iranian province of Fars. Herodotus, notwithstanding the Greek forms he gives to Iranian tribal names, places this challenge to the Medes in a most plausible context. He says that there were many tribes inhabiting Iran, some of them sedentary agriculturists and the rest nomadic pastoralists, but that the dominant tribe was the Pasargadae, of which the chief clan was the Achaemenidae, of which Cyrus was the head. The whole story, shorn of its legendary embellishments, stands out as a straightforward account of the rise to power of a tribal confederacy such as has occurred repeatedly over the centuries throughout the vast and predominantly arid zone stretching from the western extremity of the Iranian plateau to the frontiers of China.

Having challenged Median supremacy and emerged as victor in the ensuing conflict, Cyrus promptly enlarged his military manpower by winning over the recently defeated Medes, who joined the confederacy as junior partners, a relationship reflected in the recurring Biblical coupling of "the Medes and Persians." Thereafter, although some tribes may have resisted absorption, most hastened to join the victorious confederacy in fear of punishment or hope of plunder. Growing numbers of fighting men at his disposal guaranteed fresh victories, and these in turn drew new supporters. Increasingly, the confederates would seek to merge their identity with their leader's tribe, often claiming a spurious common ancestry, and this would be a recurring theme in the history of the pastoral tribes of Eurasia, most clearly documented in the case of the Mongol and Turco-Mongol confederacies of the thirteenth and fourteenth centuries A.D..

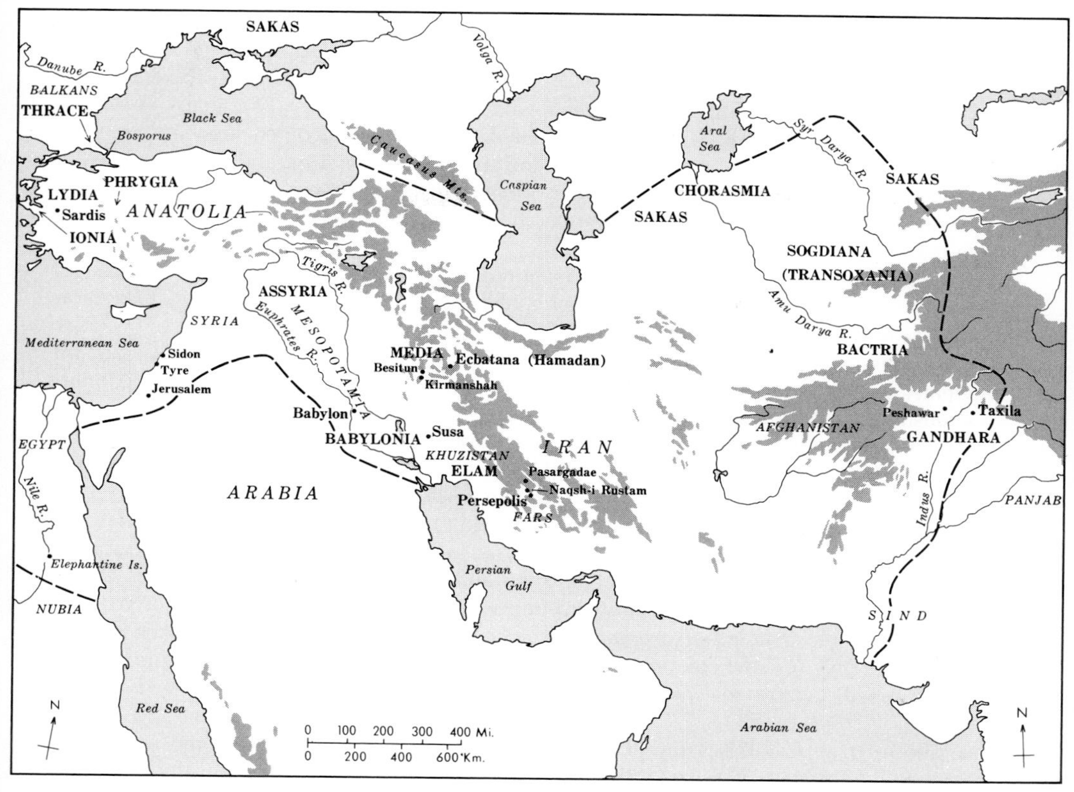

Map 15 The Achaemenid empire, about 550 B.C.

Soon, however, the campaigns of Cyrus brought under his sway areas where the population was neither pastoral nor tribal, as were perhaps the majority of the inhabitants of the Iranian plateau. The subjugation of Mesopotamia, in particular, added a vast population of skilled and disciplined cultivators and artisans whose labor provided a regular revenue base, which in turn made possible the establishment of an elaborate bureaucracy and a splendid court such as no regime confined exclusively to the Iranian plateau could then hope to maintain. Meanwhile, as more and more conquests brought additional territory under the control of a single ruler, the conditions for long-distance trade within the frontiers of the empire became increasingly favorable. Expanding economic activity meant increased prosperity and also additional resources and revenues for the state. Thus, when Cyrus added the surplus agricultural produce of Mesopotamia to the fighting manpower of the Iranian tribes, with their superb horses (for which Media, in particular, was famous) and their fine weapons wrought by the skilled metal workers of the Zagros, he enjoyed a power base such as no ruler had hitherto known. Without it, his immediate successors could hardly have contemplated their grandiose schemes of imperial expansion.

Cyrus' conquests were the achievement of a fairly homogeneous army composed mainly of Iranian tribesmen, but his successors, eager to extend their frontiers and rather uninhibited with regard to combining the role of Iranian confederate chieftain with a more universal concept of monarchy, soon began to enlist troops recruited from the subject population.

Herodotus gives a brilliant account of the great expeditionary force that Xerxes led into Greece in 480 B.C. Among the contingents were Thracians, Lydians, Phrygians, Assyrians, Bactrians, Indians, Arabians, Libyans, and Ethiopians, as well as others less easily identifiable, while the fleet was manned by Phoenician sailors from Tyre and Sidon, as well as Ionian Greeks. The cosmopolitan composition of the army was a reflection both of the diversity of the empire and of the ability of the regime to utilize all the resources available to it.

Achaemenid military expansion did not continue for much more than three-quarters of a century, and thereafter the picture was mainly one of consolidation broken by sporadic revolts and some territorial contraction. Cyrus died in 530 B.C., and at the time of his death the empire already embraced much of West Asia, consisting of the Iranian plateau; the greater part of the Fertile Crescent; and most of Anatolia, including the former kingdom of Croesus, the ruler of Lydia, with its capital at Sardis, not far inland from the Aegean Sea. To the east, Achaemenid rule was acknowledged in the extensive area bounded by the Amu Darya and Syr Darya rivers, an area then known as Sogdiana, because the majority of its sedentary inhabitants were a people of Iranian stock known as Sogdians, and also by its Greek name of Transoxania, the land beyond the Oxus, the name the Greeks gave to the Amu Darya. Sogdiana also sheltered another Iranian people, the Sakas, who then occupied the greater part of the Eurasian steppe zone and whom the Greeks knew as Scythians. Although the Saka tribes living on the frontier marches were coerced into a grudging submission, those living at a greater distance from the area under direct Achaemenid control fiercely resisted attempts to incorporate them into the empire. Cyrus himself was killed in battle against the Sakas, drawn into the steppes beyond the Syr Darya by a cunning ruse.

The reign of Cambyses saw the conquest of Egypt, and the Achaemenid frontier advanced down the Nile as far as the First Cataract. It was, however, under the next ruler, Darius I—Darius the Great—that the empire reached its greatest extent. In the east, the frontier was extended beyond the Indus into the Panjab. In the west, Darius crossed the Bosporus in person and marched through the Balkans to the Danube, penetrating the steppe zone northwest of the Black Sea. Europeans remember his campaigns in the west chiefly on account of his spectacular defeat at Marathon (490 B.C.) at the hands of the Athenians, but in relation to his military exploits elsewhere and his energetic reorganization of the empire, Marathon must have seemed a minor, if humiliating, reverse.

With the death of Darius in 486 B.C. territorial expansion virtually came to an end. The empire was already overextended, and the exertions of the preceding decades began to take their toll. There followed a succession of rebellions, costly in men and resources; the Greeks, whether subject to the empire or living outside it, remained turbulent and unpredictable; and Egypt, in particular, sullenly resisted alien rule, more conscious than any other part of the empire of its unique cultural identity. Nor was there any solution to the problem of the steppe frontier—except perhaps to ignore it. Yet, until the Macedonian counterattack came in the second half of the fourth century, the empire remained indubitably the supreme military power in West Asia. No one was more surprised than Alexander's Macedonian soldiers when, taking the field against the armies of the Great King, Darius III, they found themselves the victors in battle after battle against an enemy whose resources in manpower and money had always seemed to the Greeks to be almost limitless. Here, however, the Greeks were in error. It seems improbable that the Achaemenid armies were as large as their enemies supposed, and after the initial period of conquest, diplomacy became as much a weapon of Achaemenid expansionism as war had hitherto been—as the Greek states found to their cost, seeing themselves set against one another by the Great King's adept and well-informed agents.

The Consolidation of the Achaemenid Empire

The Achaemenids seem to have recognized that they had brought into being a regime that, in extent and diversity of population, was without precedent in their own day. They set no bounds upon their conquests and ruthlessly eliminated opponents, whether foreign foes or disaffected subjects, but they also advanced an articulate justification for their rule, endowing it with a universal validity and expressing it in terms of a sovereignty granted to them by the principal Achaemenid deity, Ahura Mazda, as a reward for their righteousness and sense of justice. Magnificent court ceremonial, elaborate protocol, and the skillful diffusion of propaganda in the form of rock-carved edicts located in prominent positions all stressed the semidivine and universal nature of Achaemenid kingship. At Besitun, near Kirmanshah in northwestern Iran, Darius ordered a bas-relief to be carved on a cliff face above the great highway that ran from Babylon to Hamadan, commemorating in three languages his victories over his enemies. The opening words of the inscription reveal the ruler's self-image: "I am Darius the Great King, King of Kings, King in Persia, King of Countries." At the same time, the last two phrases point to a dichotomy in Darius' own mind: on the one hand, he maintains an ethnic identity as an Iranian warlord; on the other, he is universal monarch. This distinction emerges more clearly in an inscription at Naqsh-i Rustam, near Persepolis, where he is styled "King of countries containing all kinds of men, King of this great earth far and wide," but also "a Persian, son of a Persian, an Aryan, having Aryan lineage." These inscriptions and a number of others that have been discovered, written in Old Persian cuneiform, describing the ruler's achievements and enumerating the peoples over whom he ruled, reflect, as do no other sources for the period, a novel imperial ideology that was both the *post facto* justification for the original Achaemenid conquests and also a tool for reinforcing the obedience of the vast subject population.

In connection with this ideology it should be noted that there existed a concept expressed by the word *hvarnah,* which in Old Persian meant "the imperial glory of Iran." It seems probable that it was during the Achaemenid period that there emerged among the Iranian people for the first time that long-lasting idea that the fortunes of Iran and of its rulers were inextricably bound together, thereby providing a sanctity and a charisma for the monarch, the shahanshah, or "king of kings," which would endure long after the disappearance of the Achaemenids and their successors, the Arsacids and Sasanids, and which would remain a factor to be reckoned with, even after the Muslim conquests had impressed new patterns of political and social organization on the entire region.

The crowning achievement of the Achaemenids was not their vast conquests but the way in which they managed to retain them for so long. During the lifetime of Cyrus the empire seems to have been held together by a comparatively simple institutional mechanism. The monarchy was still, in some respects, a tribal monarchy, with the king seen as the supreme chieftain of a victorious confederacy. The army was composed principally of tribal contingents, and the revenue of the state took the form of tribute. By the time of Darius I, however, important changes had taken place. The person of the ruler had now been elevated to a position far above even the most prominent of his supporters, the great nobles or the tribute-paying underkings. The tribal nobility was being slowly transformed into a nobility of service. The army had assumed a multiethnic composition, reflecting the plural character of the empire as a whole, and an elaborate provincial administration had been set up. The empire was divided into somewhere around twenty units, each of which was governed by a satrap, the Greek form of an office and title that henceforward would be found for several centuries not only in Iran and in the Indo-Iranian borderlands but also throughout northern India. The principal source of revenue that sustained this elaborate administration was a fixed yield from each province, assessed on the basis of prior estimates. Not every part of the empire, however, was included within the satrapies, some areas enjoying indirect rule

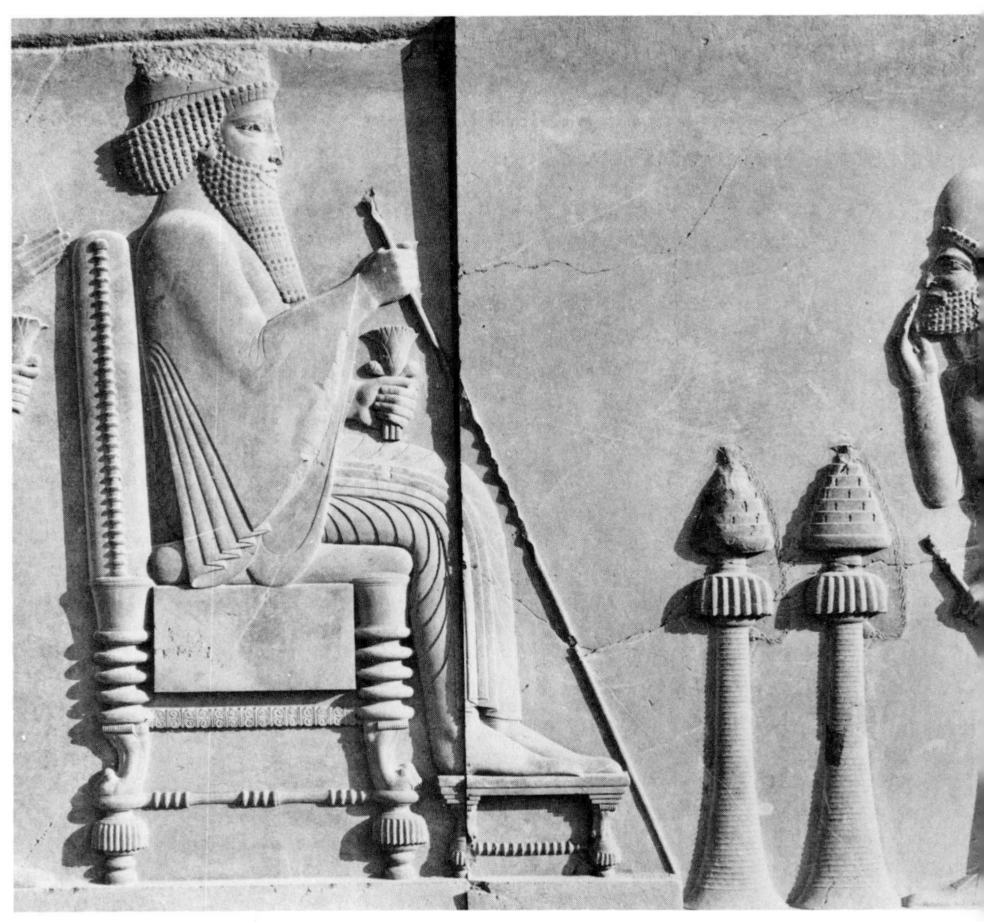

4.1 Darius the Great (522-486 B.C.) giving audience. Bas-relief from the Treasury, Persepolis, now in the Archaeological Museum, Tehran. In front of the king are two fire altars. Courtesy: The Oriental Institute, University of Chicago.

under their own hereditary rulers, who paid tribute to the Great King. The province of Fars in southwestern Iran, the homeland of the Achaemenids, was exempted from paying revenue, in lieu of which it provided the crack troops for the army.

The driving force in the administration was the ruler himself. Everything depended on his personal ability and his capacity for administration. It appears that the Achaemenids had no deputy or chief minister comparable to the *vazir* of later Islamic rulers. Presumably, advice was sought from and authority delegated to a trusted circle of counsellors—close relatives, boon companions, and members of the nobility. The Iranian ruling elite, apart from its principal function of supplying military leaders, provided the backbone of the civilian administration. Most of the satraps were recruited from this source, although occasionally a member of the imperial family or a tribute-paying vassal would be appointed to a satrapy, and so also were the more important subordinate officials. Each satrap maintained a local court modelled on that of the Great King, and hence the headquarters of his administration provided a focal point for the dissemination of Achaemenid imperial culture, as did the garrison towns and the settlements of Iranian colonists, which were widely scattered in various parts of the empire. Little is known about local government within the satrapies, but it seems certain that each satrapy must have been divided into a number of districts and perhaps subdistricts in which the officials, in all probability, were mainly local men.

The distance of most satrapies from the court of the Great King meant that, in practice, the satraps enjoyed a high degree of autonomy. To counterbalance this, the central government kept a close watch over its provincial representatives through an elaborate system whereby messengers were constantly traveling on the highways of the empire, transmitting instructions and bringing back reports. There must also have been an extensive network of spies, such as was likewise a prominent feature of Mauryan rule in India. The Greek writers refer to two officials at court whom they described as "the eye of the king" and "the ear of the king," and it is probable that these officials were responsible for acquiring information as to what was going on throughout the empire and perhaps also for exercising the functions of an inspectorate. In this, as in so much else, the Achaemenid administration served as a prototype for the later regimes of the Arsacids and the Sasanids, who in turn bequeathed at least some elements of their governing institutions and ideology to their Islamic successors.

Control of the satrapies from the center was dependent on the maintenance of regular channels of communication. The Achaemenid rulers attached great importance to developing an effective system of communications, and so they bound the peripheries of the empire to its heartlands with a network of roads along which the messengers of the Great King rode back and forth, changing horses at regular staging posts along the way, where remounts were kept ready for them. The most famous of these roads was one that ran from Susa, in Khuzistan, through Mesopotamia and Anatolia, to Sardis. The prime purpose of these roads was political—to control the provinces effectively and to expedite troop movements—but they also encouraged the growth of the transcontinental caravan trade and, indirectly, the dissemination of knowledge, ideas, commodities, and life-styles. It is probable that the established caravan routes of later centuries first took shape in this period, which was also a period that saw a vast increase in man's geographical knowledge. The Achaemenid rulers seem to have fostered an interest in exploration and commercial expansion. Darius I, whose construction of a canal between the Mediterranean and the Red Sea was perhaps motivated partly by economic considerations, commissioned an expedition to survey the course of the Indus. Other expeditions are known to have explored part of the coastline of Africa.

The formation of the Achaemenid empire probably assisted in the diffusion of both more varied food crops and improved techniques for cultivation. The ingenious Iranian method of using underground water channels for irrigation purposes may well have spread to Libya,

Sind, and the oases of Central Asia during the period of Achaemenid domination, which perhaps also saw the earliest diffusion of the "Persian wheel," a device for raising water from far below the surface of the ground. Rice, brought from China, began to supplement a basic diet of wheat and barley in the eastern provinces of the empire in the late Achaemenid period, although it did not reach Mesopotamia until Seleucid times, and the same was true of peaches and apricots, which, notwithstanding the fact that they were first cultivated in China, were thought of by the Greeks as Iranian fruit. Much concerned with the quality of their cavalry, the Iranians were the first to cultivate alfalfa clover for fodder. They were also much addicted to wine and it was probably in Achaemenid times that viniculture became widely diffused over West Asia, to disappear almost completely with the coming of Islam centuries later.

In general, the unification of West Asia under Achaemenid rule, reinforced by an impressive network of roadways, greatly enlarged men's perceptions of the world in which they lived and of what lay beyond it, provoking a new kind of intellectual curiosity. Herodotus, a Greek through and through, was nonetheless a characteristic product of this age of universalism, with his encyclopedic interests and insatiable curiosity. It must be remembered that the Achaemenid empire was not only a necessary precondition for the conquests of Alexander and the Greek penetration of Central Asia and India, but also the physical setting for much of the later flowering of Hellenistic civilization.

The conquests of the first Achaemenid rulers extended the frontiers of the empire almost to the limits of the known world of West Asia. Beyond those frontiers lay, for the most part, areas hardly worth the effort of conquest for a regime whose lines of communication were already extended to the maximum. Thus, in the southwest, the Achaemenids never attempted to absorb the Arabian peninsula into their empire, remained content (after one abortive invasion of Nubia) to make the First Cataract the extent of their expansion up the Nile, and turned back from the uninviting wastes of the Libyan desert. With regard to the southeastern frontier in the Indo-Iranian borderlands, the inscriptions list two satrapies located in the subcontinent itself, one on the lower Indus in what is now Sind and the other comprising the country around modern Peshawar on the upper Indus and part of the western Panjab, a region to be discussed in the next chapter under the name of Gandhara. It is by no means clear how effective Achaemenid rule east of the Indus can have been, and in all probability the eastern satraps were local rulers whose relationship with the Great King was that of tribute-paying underkings. Nevertheless, according to Herodotus, these provinces were the most valuable in the empire in terms of their revenue yield. Unfortunately, very little is known about the Achaemenid presence in this area, although it is quite possible that future excavations may prove their influence to have been much greater than has hitherto been supposed.

In Europe, the Achaemenids found the Greek city-states an intractable problem, due partly to their failure to retain control of the sea. In terms of a military occupation, the rugged Greek mainland and its innumerable offshore islands posed formidable difficulties for a landpower with its center hundreds of miles away to the east. Thus, the later Achaemenid rulers may well have been correct in thinking that the Greeks could more easily be manipulated by a policy of divide and rule, by kid-glove diplomacy tempered with an occasional display of the mailed fist, than by outright conquest.

It was in the steppe region to the north that the Achaemenids encountered the most formidable resistance. The Sakas, like most pastoral-nomadic peoples, learned how to master a horse and to handle a bow almost as soon as they were old enough to sit in a saddle, and although the Achaemenid army included excellent cavalry contingents, it proved unable to hold its own for any length of time over such mobile and elusive foes. The Saka tribes living closest to the Achaemenid frontier did indeed make what was probably a half-hearted submission, but those at a safer distance remained perpetually hostile, fearful of losing their independence. It was a relationship typical of the age-old struggle between the nomads of Central Asia and their sedentary neighbors, and did not preclude regular commercial and cultural contacts. An inscription of Darius I at Naqsh-i Rustam enumerating the subject peoples of the empire lists three separate groups of tribute-paying Sakas. These have tentatively been identified as occupying the steppe zone bordering the Syr Darya, the steppe zone north of the Aral Sea and east of the Caspian, and the steppe zone northwest of the Black Sea beyond the Danube. Even in the case of these tribes it may be doubted whether Achaemenid control was more than nominal, and there must have been a good deal of sporadic frontier fighting. Nevertheless, throughout the Eurasian steppe zone as a whole, the cultural influence of Achaemenid Iran was very strong, exemplified by the Iranian artifacts and a magnificent Achaemenid pile carpet discovered by Soviet archaeologists in the frozen grave of a nomad chieftain at Pazyryk in the Altai Mountains of eastern Siberia.

The Cultural Impact of the Achaemenid Empire

Under the sway of the Achaemenids there was a tendency for certain distinctive cultural manifestations to be diffused throughout the empire and even beyond it, a process that was accelerated under Alexander and the Seleucids, who, at least in the eastern satrapies, modified their Hellenistic heritage in order to accommodate it to Iranian traditions. An important factor in this cultural diffusion was the attitude of the early Achaemenid rulers, who seem to have deliberately disseminated the cults, institutions, and even forms of official art that they judged to be useful for purposes of imperial propaganda.

Upon the diversity of the empire the Achaemenids superimposed a unifying administrative framework, against which, however, must be set the fact that most subordinate officials were recruited from the indigenous local population and were therefore representatives of regional cultures as well as of the imperial power. Perhaps more important was the Achaemenid policy of imposing Aramaic upon the empire as an administrative *lingua franca,* serving as the language of official communication from the Indo-Iranian borderlands to the island of Elephantine near the First Cataract, where a precious trove of Achaemenid administrative documents has been recovered. Old Persian cuneiform was used for the rock edicts of the dynasty, but these were generally located on the Iranian plateau itself, in the dynastic homeland. Some of these official pronouncements were bilingual and even trilingual, as in the case of the famous Besitun inscription, which was carved in Old Persian, Elamite, and Akkadian.

The Achaemenids also sought to superimpose the idea of a universal law, representing the forces of moral order, over and above the diverse customary law of the various peoples of the empire. Age-old custom no doubt continued to provide the legal framework by which most of the population lived, but due weight must be given to Greek references to the Iranian preoccupation with the concept of justice and Hebrew respect for "the law of the Medes and Persians, which altereth not." Attempts to standardize administrative and legal practice necessitated elaborate record keeping on the part of the bureaucracy. Many administrative tablets have been recovered, especially from Susa and Persepolis, and they confirm the impression left by the account in the Book of Ezra of how, in the reign of Darius II, a search was made "in the house of the rolls, where the treasure was laid up in Babylon," to find the original decree of Cyrus granting the Jews permission to rebuild Soloman's temple, and how it was eventually found in the palace at Ecbatana (Hamadan). In order to improve the revenue system, and perhaps also to encourage trade, the Achaemenids introduced a standard bimetallic currency of gold and silver. Croesus of Lydia was probably the first ruler to experiment with this, but Darius followed his example. Standardization was also extended to weights and measures, although it may be doubted how effective such policies can have been in the more remote areas.

The Achaemenid empire arose in the wake of and partly in consequence of a period of intense rivalry among the various military powers of West Asia, a rivalry that produced widespread dislocation and suffering. Under these circumstances the Achaemenids succeeded in projecting an image of themselves either as liberators, as in the case of the Jews, or as the legitimate successors of spiritually bankrupt regimes, as in the case of the Babylonians. Thus, following the overthrow of the Babylonian ruler, Nabonidus, who had alienated the priests of Marduk, the patron deity of Babylon, Cyrus paid homage to the god and the other Babylonian gods, and in Akkadian documents he styled himself "King of Babylon, King of Sumer and Akkad," stressing continuity with the Mesopotamian past. In general he displayed a remarkable tolerance towards the religious particularism of the subject population, and Achaemenid goodwill towards the Jews, as recounted in the Bible, appears in striking contrast to their sufferings at the hands of the Assyrians and the Babylonians. The Achaemenids sought to provide a moral justification for their rule which would make it acceptable to all their subjects. Thus, in one of his inscriptions, Darius declared that sovereignty had been granted to him by Ahura Mazda, the principal deity of the Achaemenids, because he had always acted righteously and justly to all men. This emphasis on divine support as the reward for virtue and justice is a striking feature of the imperial ethos of Achaemenid Iran and was clearly the foundation for such claims as the dynasty made to universal empire.

The religious life of the Achaemenids remains a subject of considerable obscurity. Ahura Mazda appears to have been the principal deity of the Aryan pantheon, but there were other important deities, such as Mithra and the goddess Anahita. The cult of the latter, in particular, may have acted as a focus for common worship throughout much of the empire but this was a late development, and in the time of Darius I there is no mention of any deity other than Ahura Mazda. The Magians, the priests of the Iranians, have been the object of much scholarly dispute and it is still uncertain whether they were a distinct tribe, like the Jewish Levites, or a functional caste, like the Hindu brahmans. They impinged upon Iranian society in a number of ways, performing religious rituals, including animal sacrifices, practicing magic somewhat in the manner of Central Asian shamans, and acting as judges, officials, and royal counsellors in much the same way as did the brahmans in India. Exactly what role they played in the dissemination of Zoroastrianism is still unclear. In a period characterized by a great deal of spiritual unrest it was necessary to establish some kind of equilibrium between the ethical teachings of Zoroaster and observance of the old Aryan cults, with their emphasis on ritual and sacrifice. From the time of Darius I onward, Zoroastrian beliefs, and also people who may be described as Zoroastrians, must have been drifting into western Iran from the eastern homeland of Zoroaster, and to some extent the Achaemenids harnessed the Zoroastrian ethos, with its stress on truth, justice, harmony, and duty, to the preexisting Magian cults and especially the worship of Ahura Mazda. It should not, however, be supposed that Zoroastrianism under the Achaemenids was in any way a state religion or that there was a Zoroastrian church and priesthood such as would emerge under the Sasanids.

The universalism of the Achaemenids called for concrete expression, manifested in the emergence of a distinctive style in architecture and the arts, eclectic in origin yet fully capable of projecting the desired impressions of enduring power and splendor. Vast palaces and public buildings, monumental sculptures, and dramatically sited bas-reliefs testified to the glory of the ruler. Sometimes, as in the case of the bas-relief at Besitun, these were located on a major highway where they could not fail to impress passing travelers, but it was in the metropolitan centers of the empire that this imperial propaganda found fullest scope for expression.

It seems unlikely that the early Achaemenid rulers, with their tribal antecedents, were particularly attracted to urban life, although they were, for political reasons, great builders and colonizers. They were frequently on the move, accompanied by their court and the central organs of government, living a peripatetic existence in luxurious encampments from which they could easily indulge their traditional pastimes of hunting and horsemanship. In the early years of the empire, Ecbatana, the former Median capital and a summer residence of the Achaemenids, and Babylon were the most important metropolitan centers, with Sardis serving a similar function as a focal center for the western satrapies. Later, Darius resuscitated the old Elamite capital of Susa in Khuzistan ("Shushan the palace" of the Book of Esther), which he made into the administrative capital of the empire and where he built on a most lavish scale.

There remain to be mentioned the two most famous surviving monuments of the Achaemenid period, Pasargadae and Persepolis, situated in the enclosed plain known as Marv Dasht, which stretches northward from Shiraz, in the province of Fars. Pasargadae (the name is possibly connected with the leading tribe of the Persians, mentioned by Herodotus) is especially associated with Cyrus. Here can be seen the remains of a citadel, perhaps intended as a treasury, a pillared hall that must have formerly been part of a larger residential complex, and the structure traditionally known as the tomb of Cyrus. No evidence of urban settlement has been discovered, and presumably this was a royal residence but little else, located in this remote part of the dynastic homeland. Some way to the south lies the great complex of buildings, erected on a monumental platform above the plain, known as Persepolis, while close by, at Naqsh-i Rustam, are located the tombs of most members of the Achaemenid dynasty, carved out of a cliff face in front of which stands a fire temple dating from the same period.

It seems probable that Persepolis and adjacent Naqsh-i Rustam had some kind of sacred associations, perhaps connected with the preservation of the dynasty, and that the ruler visited the site only on ceremonial occasions such as the Iranian new year festivities. It is a strange fact that excavations at Persepolis have revealed no residential quarter beyond an area of workmen's huts belonging to the masons and artisans who labored on the site and that no Greek writer before the time of Alexander, who burnt it to the ground, ever mentioned it, although in general the Greeks were exceedingly well informed about life in the Achaemenid empire. It has therefore been suggested that the site was taboo to all but those who participated in the ceremonies performed there. It seems probable, however, that elsewhere in the Marv Dasht there must have existed in Achaemenid times a sizeable urban settlement, perhaps dating from before the founding of the empire. One possible site has been located toward the northwest extremity of the plain, and it has been suggested that this may be Anshan, the city of which Cyrus and his ancestors were kings.

2. THE MAURYAN EMPIRE IN SOUTH ASIA

Mauryan rule in India did not begin until after the demise of the Achaemenid empire in West Asia being almost exactly contemporary with that of the Seleucids (312–ca. 250 B.C.), the successors of Alexander as masters of the Iranian plateau and of the greater part of the Fertile Crescent. The Mauryan empire was founded by Chandragupta Maurya (r. ca. 321-292 B.C.), was extended by his successor, Bindusara (r. 292-272 B.C.), and reached its greatest extent under Ashoka (r. ca. 272-232 B.C.). Ashoka's reign witnessed the culmination of nearly a century of imperial conquest and consolidation and also the adoption of Buddhism as the official religion of the empire. Thereafter, however, the dynasty declined rapidly, the last Mauryan ruler being overthrown around 183 B.C. by his own commander in chief. Around this time, bands of Greek soldiers from Bactria, the area in northern Afghanistan bounded by the Hindu Kush Mountains and the Amu Darya, began to cross the Indus and infiltrate into the Panjab, marking the beginning of a period of recurring invasions that would continue for at least two centuries.

The Mauryan empire, which now occupies a prominent place in Indian perceptions of the national past, seems to have been largely forgotten in later centuries, and its history has been reconstructed only with considerable difficulty during the past century and a half. Indeed, Ashoka himself was unknown as a historical personality until British Orientalists in the early nineteenth century pieced together a number of references to a hitherto unidentified ruler. It follows from this that much less is known about the Mauryan empire than about the Achaemenid empire, which seems to have served in a number of ways as a model for this first universal empire in the Indian subcontinent. The archaeological evidence is at best fragmentary, although further excavation may do much to extend existing knowledge of the period. The epigraphic material, although of great value, is not as extensive as that of later epochs. Important Greek notices of Mauryan India have survivied, especially in the account of the Seleucid envoy, Megasthenes, but all of them are incomplete and therefore need to be treated with some caution. Most modern accounts of the Mauryan empire rely heavily on a manual of statecraft known as the *Arthashastra,* attributed to a brahman, Kautilya, who was said to have been the adviser of Chandragupta Maurya. The following account is also based partly on material contained in the *Arthashastra,* but it should be stressed that the work took on its present written form long after Mauryan rule had ended, and in any case was as much a blueprint for government as a description of actual conditions.

The Formation of the Mauryan Empire

During the fourth century B.C. the rival kingdoms stretching across northern and central India continued their bitter struggle to establish a single hegemony. Although no single state emerged unequivocally supreme, the most powerful and consistently aggressive appears to have been that of Magadha, where the Nanda dynasty ruled from its capital at Rajagriha, some distance from the Ganges in Southern Bihar. The strength of the Nandas rested on an exceptionally large army and a comparatively elaborate system of taxation. Most of their revenue was derived from confiscating the greater part of the agricultural surplus, but they probably obtained additional sources of income from taxing the flourishing river trade passing east and west through their territory.

Magadha was a great power in eastern India and a thoroughly predatory neighbor, but the area it dominated was relatively circumscribed, consisting for the most part of the lower course of the Ganges (the eastern part of modern Uttar Pradesh, Bihar, and western Bengal). Around 321 B.C. this kingdom succumbed to an assault by a newcomer on the scene, Chandragupta Maurya. The origins of the founder of the Mauryan dynasty remain a matter of dispute, although the various traditions contain elements of the sort usually found in stories about the birth and upbringing of hero-kings, and to this extent they resemble the legends about the early years of Cyrus. They include a distant connection with the Nandas, a claim (almost certainly spurious) that the Mauryan clan belonged to the *kshatriya,* or warrior caste, a childhood of deprivation, and an adolescent encounter with Alexander the Great. In reality, he was probably of humble birth and came from the northern marches of the Magadhan kingdom in what is now the frontier region between India and Nepal, the region that had also been the homeland of the Buddha.

Chandragupta Maurya's overthrow of the Nandas, a process in which he seized their more distant provinces before striking at the heart of the kingdom, led to the foundation of an empire that would eventually include the whole of India north of the Narbada River, beyond which lies the great tableland of the Deccan. He followed the example of the Nandas in making Magadha the center of his empire, but the scale of his conquests resulted in an inevitable shift of power away from the east. Notwithstanding the fact that his capital,

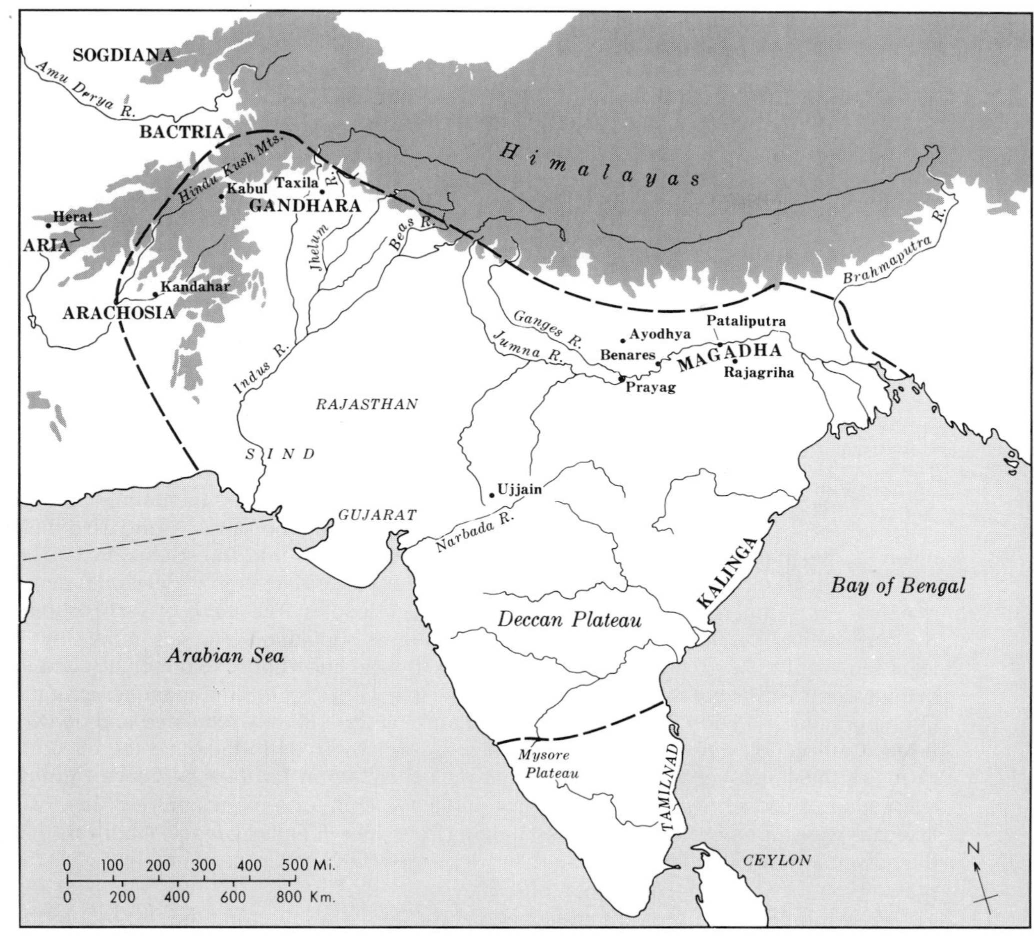

Map 16 The Mauryan empire, 322-185 B.C.

Pataliputra (Patna, in Bihar), was located in the heart of Magadha (in much the same way as the Achaemenid capital of Susa was situated in Elam and relatively close to Babylon), most of his energies as well as those of his successors were directed towards the frontier regions, as in the case of the Achaemenids.

The processes by which Chandragupta Maurya acquired a military establishment capable of overthrowing the Nandas remains a matter for speculation. It may be supposed, however, that, as in the case of the founders of other dynasties, many of his original followers were drawn to him in response to an obvious talent for leadership and a skill in acquiring booty. It is possible that an important element in his forces came from the Panjab, although there is no evidence to support this hypothesis. The story of the meeting with Alexander, however, points to associations with the northwest. Moreover, the destruction of the Achaemenid empire and the termination of Achaemenid rule in Gandhara and Sind, followed by Alexander's advance into the Panjab as far as the Beas River in 326 B.C., must have caused a good deal of unrest in the Indo-Iranian borderlands. Quite possibly there was a drift of refugees eastward, and some of these would have been unemployed or defeated fighting men, eager to seek service with any master capable of assuring them of a livelihood.

With the overthrow of the Nandas, their former military establishment would have been absorbed into the expanding Mauryan war machine, which thereafter grew steadily larger after each new conquest. The Roman writer Pliny, guilty no doubt of some exaggeration, described the Mauryan army as consisting of 9,000 war elephants, 300,000 cavalry, and 600,000 infantry, and although such figures cannot be trusted, they make the point that, so far as foreigners were concerned, the military manpower of India was regarded as enormous. A large proportion of the troops were levies who served on a seasonal or part-time basis, but there was also a standing army. The latter could have been maintained only if the state had at its disposal a stable income derived from regular and efficient taxation.

The Mauryas seem to have mobilized their material resources more effectively than had any previous regime in the subcontinent. The bulk of their revenue came from the land, which was regarded as belonging to the king, while the produce grown on it belonged to the cultivator, who paid to the state approximately one-third of the value of the annual crop. The cultivator was also liable for the payment of various other taxes, including a tax on water wherever the land was irrigated by water provided by the state. To increase their revenue, the Mauryas initiated large-scale hydraulic projects and forest clearance. The manpower for the construction of public works and for the colonization of new lands came mainly from prisoners of war and transported subject peoples. The status of such peoples was little better than that of serfs. There was also a large population of slaves in the strictly legal sense of the word, but most of these appear to have been household menials, and in many cases their slavery was temporary and came to an end after a certain number of years. Of the urban population, both merchants and artisans were closely regulated and heavily taxed. Craft guilds were widespread but their existence served to facilitate the effective taxing of their members, which was perhaps a major reason for their existence. Almost every kind of economic activity, whether a service, a craft, or a manufacturing skill, was taxed, as were virtually all commodities. Judging from the evidence available it appears that the power and wealth of the Mauryan rulers depended on the exercise of unrelenting fiscal pressure on the part of their revenue officials.

Only a most skillful use of the manpower and material resources at the disposal of the state could have made possible, at that early date, conquests on a scale that Indian rulers would find difficult to emulate, even in later centuries. Having overthrown the Nanda regime, Chandragupta Maurya turned in the direction of the northwest and advanced as far as the Indus, beyond which lay the empire of the Seleucids, heirs to the Achaemenid concept of universal empire in the West. Then, perhaps judging the time inopportune for a head-on confrontation with those powerful neighbors, he turned to the south, annexing a vast area that included Gujarat, Rajasthan, and what is now Madhya Pradesh. He thus brought the whole of northern India from the Bay of Bengal to the Arabian Sea under his single rule and in so doing set a precedent for a succession of future north Indian empires based on control of the Panjab and the Gangetic plain. He then turned northwest again to measure his strength against Seleucus I (r. 312-280 B.C.), whom he seems to have defeated or overawed. This probably occurred sometime around 304 B.C. and resulted in the Mauryan annexation of the Seleucid satrapies in what is now Afghanistan, including the Kandahar region (Arachosia) but stopping short of Herat (Aria). From this time onward, however, relations between the two empires became relatively cordial, with diplomatic missions that were also commercial missions passing back and forth across their respective frontiers.

Bindusara, the second ruler of the line, seems to have been no less of an expansionist than Chandragupta Maurya, although very little is known about him. It must have been during his reign, however, that the southern frontiers of the empire were advanced beyond the Narbada as far as the distant Mysore plateau, leaving only the Tamil states, in the southern extremity of the peninsula, and Kalinga (the area of modern Orissa on the east coast) unabsorbed. Tamilnad remained independent but in the case of Kalinga, Ashoka, Bindusara's successor, determined to add it to the empire, which he did at the cost of enormous loss of life. It was apparently his experience during the conquest of Kalinga that led to his conversion to Buddhism, the outcome of his disgust at witnessing such scenes of carnage and misery. In any case, by that stage the Mauryan empire had reached an extent beyond which no Indian regime at that period could hope to expand. The imperial structure was already overstrained, and within half a century of Ashoka's death (ca. 232 B.C.) most of the outlying regions had gone their own way under local dynasties, while the Mauryas themselves were replaced in Magadha by the Shungas (183-73 B.C.).

The Consolidation of the Mauryan Empire

There can be little doubt that the first three Mauryan rulers embarked on their far-flung campaigns and created an elaborate machinery for governing the subject population, unique in India at that time, with an implicit belief in the virtues of a universal world order supported by an expansionist imperialism. The initial model for such aggressive militarism must have been the example set by the Nandas in Magadha but there were other influences at work as well. The Achaemenid empire, with its easternmost satrapies extending across the Indus into the Panjab, must also have served as a model for would-be empire builders in northern India and, likewise, the career of Alexander. Hardly less significant, the Seleucids, heirs to the Achaemenids in their control over the Indo-Iranian borderlands, were exact contemporaries of the Mauryas, and the two regimes maintained fairly close contacts. Seleucus I sent one of his daughters to be a bride of Chandragupta Maurya and it has even been suggested that this half-Macedonian, half-Iranian princess may have been the grandmother of Ashoka. It seems likely that Achaemenid Iran, taken with its Seleucid successor regime, served as a mentor to Mauryan India.

The Mauryas were able to control so vast an area because they created an elaborate administrative structure, which by the standards of the period appears to have been remarkably effective. The cornerstone of the entire system was, predictably, the ruler himself and almost everything was dependent on his energy and ability. He was attended by a council of advisers, whose opinions he sought on matters of importance, while the day-to-day business of the government was directed by a body of officials concerned with the collection and distribution of revenue, commissariat arrangements for the army, and perhaps the administration of justice. In certain circumstances the ruler himself gave judgment in open court, as did the provincial governors, but for most of his subjects, living in virtually self-sufficient village communities, the law under which they lived was the customary law of their own village, administered by a village headman or a council of elders.

The Mauryan empire was divided into provinces in much the same way as was the Achaemenid empire, with each province parceled up into smaller administrative units. The provincial governors were generally experienced officials sent out from the capital, but a few were members of the imperial family or local rulers who had submitted to Mauryan rule and were trusted to remain loyal to the regime. Among these latter would have been figures who may aptly be described as subkings and who would have been, in effect, hereditary governors of the areas over which they had charge. The existence of these subkings is a reminder that there were limits to the centralizing and bureaucratic features of Mauryan imperialism.

In order to watch over the doings of the provincial governors and officials at every level there was an elaborate system of paid spies and informers. The impression left by Kautilya's *Arthashastra* is one of pervasive mistrust and almost totalitarian efficiency. In reality, distance, conflicting personal interests, and sheer inefficiency must have severely curtailed the

4.2 The *stupa* at Sanchi, central India, built by Ashoka (ca. 272-232 B.C.) as part of a program of founding *viharas* (Buddhist monasteries) and *stupas* (shrines containing Buddhist relics) throughout the Mauryan empire to promote the spread of Buddhism. Source: Alexander Cunningham, *The Bhilsa Topes* (London, 1854), Plate 7.

extent of government interference in the lives of most Indians, for whom, over vast areas of the country and for the greater part of the year, it was the decisions taken by their local village council or guild that had the greatest effect on their lives.

As in the case of the Achaemenids, the Mauryas found it necessary to improve communications between the various parts of their empire so as to ensure effective surveillance of provincial officials and to forestall rebellion. They therefore allotted substantial resources to road building and repairing. Most of the highways of Mauryan India must have been ancient tracks, used since time immemorial, which the regime cleared and widened, planting avenues of trees to provide shade, constructing resthouses for the convenience of travelers, and erecting milestones to indicate the distance from place to place.

The main purpose of these highways was to facilitate administrative control and the movement of troops, but they also encouraged the transportation of goods and the migration of peoples from one part of the empire to another, and even beyond it. Of particular importance were the roads that ran from the Panjab across the Indus, either in the direction of modern Kandahar, leading westward to the Iranian plateau, or through the Kabul valley and across the Hindu Kush Mountains to the banks of the Amu Darya River (the region known to the Greeks as Bactria). It was probably via the latter route that large numbers of horses must have been brought annually into India to provide remounts for the Mauryan cavalry. Much of the long-distance trade with the Seleucid empire consisted of luxury commodities—fine textiles, perfumes, precious stones, Indian slave girls, and war elephants, the latter being regarded as of such value to those who acquired them that their sale was strictly controlled. Among the commodities requested in exchange by the Maurvas, the sources mention aphrodisiacs, a philosopher, and Greek slave girls, whose presence in Pataliputra may account for references to Amazonian female guards who protected the king's person and accompanied him on his hunting expeditions. Other imports from the west included precious metals, dried fruits, and high-quality wines.

Long after the Mauryas had disappeared from the scene, their roads remained as reminders of India's first experiment in universal empire. It was along these roads that Buddhism would eventually spread across the Panjab and through Afghanistan, bound for China. They were perhaps the most substantial part of the legacy of Mauryan rule.

No Indian rulers until the sultans of Delhi in the early fourteenth century and the Mughul padshahs of the seventeenth century would bring again so much of India under their control as did the Mauryas. While it lasted, the Mauryan empire embraced, however loosely, the greater part of the subcontinent. Tamilnad in the far south alone remained outside, probably because of the logistical difficulty of incorporating so distant an area into an empire based on the great plains of the north. There must have been, nevertheless, considerable commercial and cultural intercourse between the Tamil states and those provinces of the Mauryan empire that bordered them, although less is known regarding such contacts than in the case of Mauryan relations with Ceylon. To the east, the impenetrable jungles and hills beyond the line of the Brahmaputra River discouraged travel, but to the west the Mauryas maintained relatively close contacts with the Hellenistic world and were apparently well informed regarding various Macedonian dynasties, such as the Egyptian Ptolemies, as well as their Seleucid neighbors.

The Cultural Impact of the Mauryan Empire

After the disintegration of the Mauryan empire, northern India experienced a series of invasions by foreigners of predominantly Iranian stock—Bactrian Greeks, Sakas, Parthians, and Kushanas—all of whom manifested, in various degrees, self-consciously assertive aspirations to empire. Under their rule, the style and substance of the administrative arrangements, which survived in some areas even under the indigenous Gupta dynasty of the fourth and fifth centuries A.D., seem to have followed the model of universal empire provided by the Mauryas. It is therefore interesting to note those enduring aspects of Mauryan imperialism which survived the fall of the empire, serving as examples for the emulation of later conquerors.

As in the case of the Achaemenids, standardization was an important element in the work of imperial consolidation. This was achieved to some extent by creating a framework of administrative uniformity, by the imposition of such universal obligations as the payment of revenue and military service, and, wherever possible, by inculcating loyalty to the dynasty. Naturally, there were formidable problems of communication, given a subject population of such ethnic and linguistic diversity. Thus while in India proper imperial edicts were inscribed in the Brahmi script, which was intelligible wherever Brahmanism prevailed, in the northwestern provinces these were inscribed in Kharoshthi, a script derived from the Aramaic of the Achaemenid empire, sometimes in conjunction with a Greek version. In theory, at least, the state controlled every aspect of economic life. In Pataliputra, the capital, for example, boards of officials watched over the commercial and manufacturing life of the city, imposed a standard currency, weights and measures, and issued some kind of certificate guaranteeing the quality of the goods for sale.

Like the Achaemenids, the Mauryas sought to impress their subjects with the splendor of universal kingship. The ruler was described as "The King, Beloved of the Gods," and his pronouncements were carved on conspicuously sited rocks in much the same way as the edicts of Darius had been. Living through a period of intense spiritual ferment, the Mauryas seem to have felt a disinclination to link their fortunes with the traditional brahmanical formulation of a political system in which the king, at least in theory, fulfilled his *dharma* (the moral duty imposed upon each living person by his or her caste and circumstances) by upholding a socioreligious order conceived by brahman ideologues. Moreover, in that age rulers could hardly avoid being affected by the prevalence of syncretic cults and of new patterns of religious expression, which everywhere challenged the traditional order and which were perhaps most conspicuous in an urban setting, especially in those cities that serviced a cosmopolitan court.

It is interesting to note that a late tradition asserts that Chandragupta Maurya became a Jain, that he renounced his throne in favor of a monk's begging bowl, and that he eventually starved himself to death in the ultimate act of renunciation sometime around 292 B.C. Bindusara, his successor, was associated with the Ajivikas, a sect that combined philosophical determinism with extreme asceticism. Ashoka became a Buddhist, propagating a new concept of *dhamma* (the Prakrit, or vernacular, form of the Sanskrit word *dharma*) that extended far beyond the traditional Hindu perception of individual duty to encompass a new kind of social responsibility, which included tolerance and nonviolence. Ashoka's rock inscriptions and edicts, erected throughout the empire, served as a means of publicizing this new Buddhist *dhamma*. Whether, indeed, Ashoka's conversion was as sudden as he claimed (revulsion against the slaughter that he had brought about in Kalinga) is not as important as the long-term consequences of his decision. By converting to Buddhism, Ashoka linked his fortunes to the most dynamic movement of the age, and although his decision did nothing to postpone the collapse of his dynasty, it contributed to the territorial expansion of Buddhism and to its survival in northern India for several centuries. Yet even in Ashoka's lifetime the overwhelming majority of his subjects must have continued to observe the rituals of Brahmanism, even if Buddhism was exercising a pervasive influence among certain classes, especially the urban traders and craftsmen. It may also be questioned whether, in adopting Buddhism as the official religion of the empire, Ashoka himself necessarily abandoned all the observances of Brahmanism, other than the bloody animal sacrifices, which he endeavored to abolish. Neither then, nor for several centuries afterwards, was it always necessary to choose one way or the other. At all events, as an imperial cult, the Buddhism of Ashoka's time failed to thrust its roots deep enough to deflect a fierce brahmanical reaction under the Shungas (183-73 B.C.). That Buddhism continued to flourish and spread for at least another five centuries was due less to the patronage of the Mauryas than to the appeal it exercised over a succession of foreign invaders, soon to begin penetrating the Panjab, and also to its ability to discard its pristine austerity and to assume forms that were at one and the same time eclectic, colorful, and infinitely adaptable.

It seems probable that the Mauryan period was an age of vigorous urban growth, exemplified by the prosperity of such cities as Ayodhya and Benares in eastern Uttar Pradesh, Prayag (Allahabad) at the confluence of the Ganges and the Jumna, and Ujjain in Madhya Pradesh, later to become great centers of Hindu religious life and culture. Excavations at Pataliputra, the Mauryan capital, have not proved particularly rewarding due to the site being waterlogged, but uncovered sections of the outer defenses confirm the accuracy of Megasthenes' impressive description of the city in its prime. One of the greatest centers of the empire, which has been extensively excavated, was Taxila, between the Indus and the Jhelum. Taxila faced westward as much as eastward, its prosperity linked to the caravan cities of Afghanistan, at this period the crossroads of Asia. In these cosmopolitan trading centers—Alexandria-in-Arachosia (Kandahar), Alexandria-in-Aria (Herat), and Alexandria-of-the Caucasus, at the northern extremity of the Kabul valley—as in Taxila itself, there was already taking place an intricate fusion of cultures derived from a mingling of peoples, Indian, Iranian, Bactrian Greek, and Sogdian from beyond the Amu Darya. It was in these cities that the future invaders of India would first encounter the dying traditions of Mauryan universalism.

3. THE CH'IN-HAN UNIVERSAL EMPIRE IN EAST ASIA

The successive efforts of the Ch'in and Former Han dynasties (221 B.C.-9 A.D.) brought a large measure of peace and political unity to the wartorn world of late Chou China. With occasional interruptions, this continued to be the case until the last decades of the Later Han dynasty (25-220 A.D.). The changes in social structure and governmental practice that marked the political and military struggle among the independent states of late Chou were now used in the cause of empire. By around 100 B.C. a new ideology, imperial Confucianism, had taken form. This comprehensive world view, which tied dynastic history and, indeed, all human experience to a unified cosmic order, was a synthesis of many elements of late Chou thought, even though its canonical texts were the so-called Confucian classics, works associated with Confucius and his school. In its external relations the Chinese empire under Ch'in and Han combined political, economic, and military strategies to expand the area of Chinese dominance. At its greatest extent, the empire now reached about three thousand miles from the east coast of Korea westward to the headwaters of the Indus and the Jaxartes (Syr Darya) and about two thousand miles from eastern Mongolia southward to near modern Hue in Vietnam. The maximum land area of about 2.5 million square miles bore a maximum population of just under 60 million (census of 2 A.D.), with some non-Chinese people probably not counted. These four centuries of unity also saw important advances in technology, trade, communications, and urbanization.

Although the Chou dynasty was seen in later perspective as having established a single sovereign rule as the Chinese political norm, this claim is clouded historically by the relatively loose form of the early Chou kingdom and by the fact that some great states, such as Ch'u and Yueh, were sovereign and independent from their origins. Despite the traditional veneration of feudal Chou, therefore, it was the bureaucratic Ch'in and Han that furnished the basic institutional and ideological models for later imperial dynasties. The impact of the Han imperial image on Chinese culture is also reflected in the fact that

Chinese afterwards often called themselves "men of Han" (*Han jen*) in contradistinction to non-Chinese. Even today, "Han people" (*Han tsu*) is the ethnic term used to designate the culturally Chinese majority population of the People's Republic. The entire Chinese world was unified in 221 B.C. by the western frontier state of Ch'in, which had emerged in the mid-fourth century B.C. as a great power and during the third century conquered its last rivals in rapid succession. But Ch'in failed to achieve the permanence and stability of a universal empire. Its leaders relied heavily on the sanction of military power because they had had to overcome formidable resistance from the beginning. Once their victory had been attained, they forced the pace of administrative and cultural unification and provoked a great rebellion by riding roughshod over the strong regional traditions of the defeated states. The Ch'in imperial rule, therefore, scarcely survived the death of the founding emperor, and the task of consolidation was left to the more politic and subtle leaders of the immediately succeeding Former Han dynasty (206 B.C.-9 A.D.).

At first, the Han founder gained political support and popular acquiescence by granting large fiefs to leading generals in a partial and temporary reversion towards feudalism and by promising to abolish some of the more unpopular measures of Ch'in. Han imperial ideology, like that of Ch'in, depended heavily on cosmology and on sacrificial rites but gradually incorporated ethical and ceremonial prescriptions of Confucius and his followers, which pleased many literati and gave the regime a benign image. The Han empire entered an expansionist phase during the reign of Emperor Wu (Wu Ti), 141-87 B.C. This was followed by a period of retrenchment, and the last decades of the pre-Christian era saw a precipitate decline in the fortunes of the dynasty, with the central government virtually paralyzed by factional disputes and by an erosion of central government authority in the provinces, where a new class of landowning families had become strong enough to defy the prefectural magistrates and to influence the selection of imperial bureaucrats. Wang Mang, a fundamentalist Confucian reformer, usurped the throne in 9 A.D., established the Hsin ("New") dynasty, and instituted a program of reform that was nothing less than utopian in its implications. While the reforms were directed at real problems, the new regime was too weak to carry out more than a few of them before Han loyalists seized the opportunity offered by disastrous floods in the north China plain, peasant uprisings, and Hsiung-nu invasions and reestablished the Han in 25 A.D. The Later Han (25-220 A.D.) continued the dynasty and its tradition but was unable to arrest the forces of social change.

Founding of the Chinese Empire

With the rise of the state of Ch'in in the Wei valley, the center of political power moved once again to the periphery. The core of the Shang state had been the western margins of the north China plain in Honan and Hopei, but Chou had arisen on the frontier in the Wei valley. The Chou remained in the west until the invasions of 771 B.C. forced the move eastward to the plain. During the fourth and third centuries B.C., the state of Ch'in, under the guidance of Legalist ministers, reorganized its administration, fully mobilized for war, and became the most powerful of all the states. A decisive factor in this second westward shift of power was the Ch'in program of waterworks. In the late third century B.C., Ch'in completed the Cheng Kuo irrigation canal, which became the core of a vast irrigation system north of the Wei River between the Ching and Lo rivers. This system irrigated and virtually drought-proofed nearly 700,000 acres of land. This vast agricultural resource enabled Ch'in to compete economically with the major states of the north China plain, where large-scale irrigation had been underway throughout the Warring States' period. The Wei irrigation works also provided the reliable agricultural surplus that was needed for the construction and support of the huge Ch'in and Western Han imperial capitals. While the Wei valley was the key area of Ch'in and Western Han, another peripheral area began rapid development at about the same time. Near the end of the fourth century B.C., Ch'in

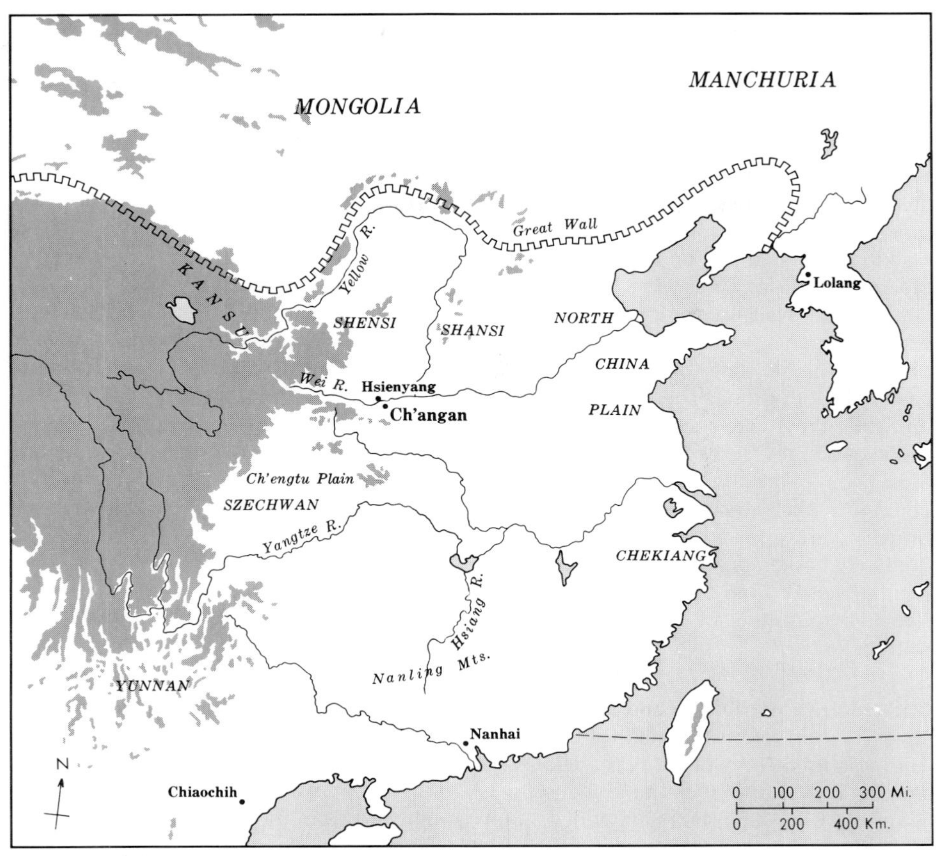

Map 17 Han China, about 100 B.C.

conquered the southwestern states of Shu and Pa (modern Szechwan) and constructed an irrigation system in the Ch'engtu plain, an area that was destined to gain in importance in Eastern Han and, eventually, became one of the great population centers of modern China, far outstripping the Wei valley itself in economic importance. The Western Han not only made strenuous efforts to maintain the Wei valley irrigation system but even made major additions to it. It was not until the first collapse of Han rule and the destructive warfare of the Wang Mang usurpation and Han restoration that the imperial center retreated eastward once more to the plain.

The fact that the formation of the Ch'in-Han universal state occurred in two stages reflects the difficulty of social pacification in the Chinese case. Powerful though Ch'in had become by mid-third century B.C., the unification by conquest was possible only because the other great states failed to coordinate their defense. Han fell in 230, Chao in 228, Yen in 226 (but survived nominally until 222), Wei in 225, Ch'u in 223, Yueh in 222, and Ch'i in 221. The prestigious old states of Lu and Sung had been absorbed earlier by Ch'u. Each of these states had its own proud traditions, its remembered victories in war and diplomacy, and its local cults and customs. The conquerors proceeded to divide the empire into forty regional administrative and military units, or commanderies. Although some of the capital cities of the defeated states retained importance as seats of commanderies, each state was divided among several administrative offices, and these were directly responsible to the Ch'in capital at Hsien-yang. Thus, the old states were divested of all marks of sovereignty and were split up among smaller jurisdictions, so that there remained no institutional focus for old loyalties. That such measures were in order became apparent as soon as the revolts against Ch'in got underway. The rebels legitimized their uprisings and gained followings by proclaiming the restoration of the states of Ch'u, Ch'i, Chao, Wei, Yen, and Han (a different Han than that of the imperial Han dynasty). Of these states, all but Yen found heirs of their old ruling houses to assume the thrones. When Liu Chi, founder of the Han dynasty, defeated his rivals, he compromised with regionalism by creating eight great principalities, which he granted to his leading supporters. Four of these, Ch'i, Chao, Han, and Yen, were based on the old states of the same name, while the other four encompassed large areas of east and south China. The new princes, however, were not heirs of the old ruling houses, and even they were soon replaced by relatives of the imperial Liu clan. Subsequent emperors gradually curbed the independence of the princes by splitting their states among their heirs and sending out administrators from the capital. Fearing the final loss of their autonomy, the princes revolted in 154 B.C. but were utterly defeated. From this time on, princes were allowed only to share in the tax revenues from their lands, which were gradually broken up and reorganized as commanderies, and they were forbidden to leave their estates or hold office in the central government. The lesser nobility, the marquises, had no administrative authority at all over their marquisates but were allowed to hold office in the capital.

The Empire Under Ch'in and Han

Over its short term of unified rule, the Ch'in dynasty set a course of imperialism that the Han also followed when it was able. Owing to the great strength of the Turkic Hsiung-nu empire in the north, the main direction of Ch'in expansion was toward the south. The first emperor, Ch'in Shih-huang-ti, sent an army southward from the middle Yangtze region, formerly the heart of the state of Ch'u, up the Hsiang River valley, over the Nanling divide, and down the other side to the Canton delta. Some of the troops continued west and south to occupy part of what is now northern Vietnam. New commanderies were organized to incorporate these new territories permanently within the empire, and government seats near the modern cities of Canton (Nan-hai), Hanoi (Chiao-chih), and elsewhere, with their soldiers and administrators, became sites of cultural interaction between Chinese and the surrounding majority population of Yueh (Viet) people. Communications with the far south were improved by the construction of a canal through the Nanling Mountains, which linked the Hsiang and Hsi Kiang (Canton) watersheds.

Ch'in Shih-huang-ti undertook to sweep the Hsiung-nu from the northern frontiers, but he did so in the face of contrary advice from his Legalist minister, Li Ssu. Li's argument is a classic statement on the northern strategic problem and deserves our attention:

> The Hsiung-nu have neither towns nor caches of supplies; they are nomads who move about in all directions. They are difficult to overtake and difficult to hold in obedience. If you send light forces, they will easily penetrate this region, but they will die of hunger there. If you send well-supplied troops, they will be unable to move ahead or to pursue the tribes in their maneuvers in the desert. Even if you were to conquer this region, it would avail you nothing, because you would never force these people to stay in fixed habitations. So after conquering them, you would have to exterminate them and Your Majesty, as father and mother to the people could never do such a thing. You will only burden your army, to the great satisfaction of these savages, and all for an ephemeral undertaking![1]

[1] A. Tschepe, *Histoire du Royaume de Ts'in* (*Variétés Sinologiques*, No. 27, Imprimerie de la Mission Catholique, 1909), p. 272.

Li Ssu's estimate of the situation proved quite correct, and after years of fruitless skirmishing in the steppes of Inner Mongolia, the First Emperor adopted a defensive strategy. During the Warring States' period, boundaries had been fortified by massive walls, both within and on the outer frontiers of the empire. Ch'in now linked up and reconstructed walls originally built by individual states before unification. An army of about a third of a million laborers was assigned to the task, which was undoubtedly the most grandiose of all the construction projects undertaken by the First Emperor. The wall, when finished, ran from the northwestern coast of Korea across the Liaotung peninsula of southern Manchuria, then westward across the top of the great loop of the Yellow River. Another wall ran southwestward across modern Shensi to Lin T'ao in eastern Kansu. The fact that this latter frontier was drawn in such a way as to expose roughly the northern half of modern Shensi to the Hsiung-nu testifies both to the might of the nomadic federation and to the tenuousness of Chinese occupation of the northwest.

Ch'in's construction of the Great Wall by no means resolved the dilemma of the northern frontier; the northern peoples beyond the wall, adapting their way of life to the Inner Asian habitat of desert and prairie, could not be converted into subject Chinese farmers and townsmen, and the Chinese could choose only between a costly policy of frontier defense and an even costlier and often disastrous forward policy. Roughly speaking, we may see an alternation between defensive and offensive strategies during the entire Han period, strategies that seem to correspond to fluctuations in the military and financial resources held by the imperial regime, on the one hand, and to the Chinese perception of conditions among the Inner Asian peoples favorable to political and military initiatives against them, on the other hand. Whatever the policy of the moment, two basic motives seem to have been present throughout: one was the security of the northern frontier and the other was the control and profitable exploitation of the overland trade involving China, the nomads, Central Asian city-states, India, and the Roman empire.

Soon after he had founded the Han dynasty, the emperor Kao Tsu engaged the Hsiung-nu in a great battle within the wall in northern Shansi. He was not only defeated but very nearly captured, and the imperial capital at Ch'angan was endangered. Chastened by this experience, he and his successors adopted the "peace and intimacy" policy, which euphemistically denoted a policy of appeasement. From 198 to 133 B.C. the Han empire bought peace in the north by providing princesses to marry the *shan-yu* (precursor of the Turkish and Mongol khan), making annual payments of silk, rice, and other commodities, and granting to the Hsiung-nu empire a status of formal equality. Moreover, the Great Wall (as constructed by Ch'in) was recognized as the boundary between the empires.

This state of affairs was felt by many Han officials to be an unbearable humiliation, and in 133 B.C. the emperor Wu Ti, himself an ardent expansionist, considered that the time had come for his armies to take the offensive. He refused to pay the customary tribute and, between 129 B.C. and the end of his reign, mounted some sixteen expeditions into Mongolia and the far west (as far as Sogdiana, between the Syr Darya and Amu Darya). The cost of these offensives in men, horses, and materials was enormous, with some of the Han armies numbering more than 100,000 men. Moreover, despite their many defeats, the Hsiung-nu armies were never destroyed. The main positive result of these military operations may have been to keep the pastoral peoples on the defensive and to facilitate their later incorporation into the Han tributary system.

Less spectacular than the great campaigns but of much greater importance for China was Wu Ti's establishment of a protectorate over the Central Asian trade routes out of the Kansu panhandle and around the Tarim basin westward toward India and the Mediterranean. The basic issue here was a growing competition between the Chinese and the nomadic peoples living in the steppes north of the trade routes for control of the trade. The nomads would strike southward against the trading cities, plunder them, and depart. The oasis dwellers, mostly Iranians, lacked the means to defend themselves and were, therefore, favorably disposed towards the Chinese, at least in the beginning. The Han were able to establish permanent garrisons in the cities and made the local farming and trading population bear the expense. During most of the Former and Later Han from the reign of Wu Ti, this long westward salient remained in Chinese hands.

Fortunately for the Han, the great tribal federations of the steppes were inherently unstable, and from 60 B.C. the Hsiung-nu empire was divided among two or more rival *shan-yu,* except for a brief period of restored unity from about 20 to 47 A.D. This made possible the establishment of a new version of the "peace and intimacy" policy in external relations, the tribute system, which, in elaborated form, was maintained by the Chinese empire down to the late nineteenth century. Under the tribute system, foreign rulers accepted a formal status of vassalage, which they acknowledged by sending tribute missions at stipulated intervals to the Chinese court. The tribute, which was not of much commercial value, was requited by gifts of greater value from the emperor to the visitors. The advantages on the foreign side were that the tributary state enjoyed the privilege of trading, both in connection with the missions and at other times at frontier trading stations, and that the titles and symbols of authority bestowed by the emperor were often valuable to the recipient in affirming his political legitimacy. The advantages on the Chinese side were that the barbarians were less inclined to break the peace when this would result in the loss of privileges and that the nominal acceptance of inferior status on the part of the foreigners permitted the emperor to imagine that his authority was universal in fact as well as in theory. As we will see in later sections of the text, however, the proper functioning of this system depended on the maintenance of adequate military and political sanctions by the empire and on the failure of the barbarians to cooperate effectively in their own interests, and these conditions were not always met.

Two other fields of imperial expansion demand our attention. In an attempt to outflank the Hsiung-nu on the east, Wu Ti conquered the Korean kingdom of Chosen in 108 B.C. and established a Chinese colony and garrison at Lo-lang (near modern Pyongyang), which grew and flourished for two centuries as a commercial center until its absorption into a new Korean state, Koguryo, in 313 A.D. In the far south, when the Ch'in dynasty was overthrown, the three southern commanderies broke away and became the independent kingdom of Southern Yueh (Nam Viet), with its capital at Nan-hai near modern Canton. In modern Vietnamese perspective, this is seen as a Vietnamese regime and a forerunner of their own national state. Wu Ti conquered Southern Yueh in 111 B.C. and established prefectural offices to administer it. Chinese rule was not intensive at first, however. At the time of the internal conflicts of the Wang Mang period, large numbers of officials and their families took refuge in the far south and the Chinese presence was more strongly felt and resented. In the first reign of the Later Han, an uprising by Vietnamese nobility (led by the Trung sisters, who have since been sanctified as national heroines) against the Chinese was suppressed by the Han general, Ma Yuan. Ma then instituted a more rigorous administration and a Confucian school system for the indoctrination of Chinese culture. Vietnam was to remain under Chinese rule until the attainment of independence in 939 A.D. Although both Korea and Vietnam eventually broke away, they were subject to such intensive cultural influence as integral regions of the empire that they continued to develop as distinct cultural variants within the greater Chinese culture area.

From the standpoint of Chinese imperialism, the closure of the Eurasian ecumene may be said to have begun in the early years of Han Wu Ti, when he undertook the destruction of the Hsiung-nu empire, which at its greatest extent stretched three thousand miles across the steppes from southern Manchuria west to the Aral Sea. He also dispatched a court attendant, Chang Ch'ien, on two diplomatic missions, 139-126 and 115 B.C. Chang was not wholly successful as a diplomatist, but on his return he was able to add to the emperor's information about the western regions and about the Central Asian trade routes. The establishment of Chinese control over the oasis cities under the tribute system and the disintegration of the Hsiung-nu empire were accompanied by an increase in Sino-Western trade, which reached its highest level during the Later Han. The most important commodity in the trade with Rome was Chinese silk, prized by traders because it was light, easily

4.3 Han dynasty monumental sculpture. The horse is trampling a barbarian who holds a bow in his left hand and a spear in his right. This piece is one of several associated with what was probably the tomb of Ho Ch'u-ping, one of Han Wu Ti's favorite generals and a successful campaigner against the Hsiung-nu.

Source: Peter C. Swann, *Chinese Monumental Art* (New York, Viking Press, 1963).

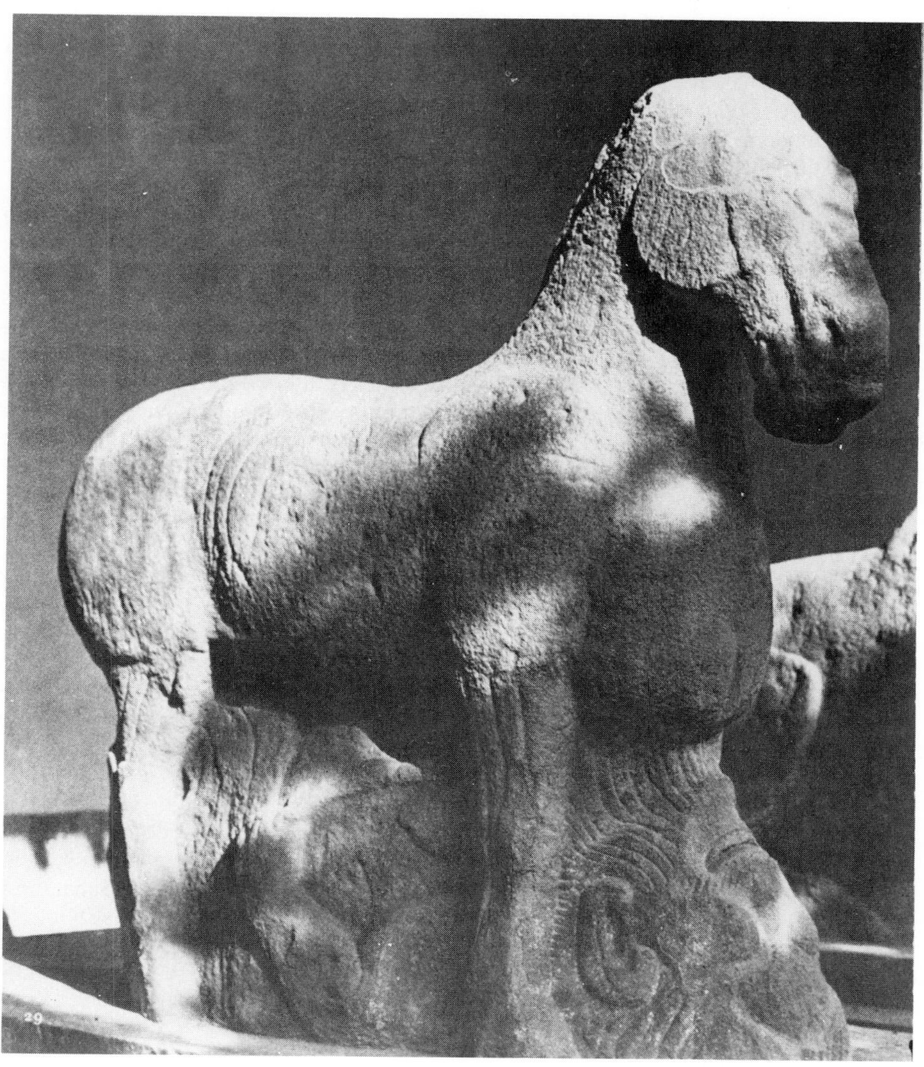

carried, and brought a high price in Western markets. Other goods were carved jades, bronze mirrors, lacquer ware, and possibly some ironware. Entering China from Central Asia and farther west were fine horses, rugs, woolen textiles, linens, amber, Roman glass, and Red Sea pearls and coral. These goods were not traded directly from producing to market area but, for the most part, were passed along in stages from one middleman to another. Indeed, many of the Chinese goods were originally included among the gifts presented to representatives of tributary states and only later found their way into commercial channels. The trans-Eurasian trade also involved India. Although the Han tried and failed to gain political and military control of the southwest (modern Yunnan province), a flourishing trade persisted between the Chinese cities of Szechwan and eastern India by way of Burma. Other routes, branching off the Inner Asian silk route, connected China with northwest India. Finally, one ought not to overlook the sea trade, which proceeded down to the Persian Gulf and the Red Sea across the Arabian Ocean to India, the Straits of Malacca, southern (modern) Thailand, Chiao-chih, and the China coast. While this route was less important than the land route, by late Han it became the foundation of commercial prosperity on the Vietnamese coast and the Canton area.

Imperialism and the enjoyment of luxury appear from time to time as major themes in the records of Ch'in and Han, but the professed aims of the founders of both dynasties were purely altruistic; each after his own fashion saw himself as the savior of (Chinese) civilization. After his assumption of the title of emperor, Ch'in Shih-huang-ti traveled about his domain and had inscribed tablets of stone set up on the peaks of the sacred mountains he visited. In these, he boasted of having brought peace and harmony to the world. He also claimed that he had improved on the imperfect rule of the sage kings so dear to the Confucians. But it is important to note that he did not present himself as an innovator or cultural iconoclast, nor did he set the customs of his own state of Ch'in against those of the rest of China. Rather, he saw himself as having taken up the task of clarifying and universalizing what he believed to be the essential principles of civilization.

Han Kao Tsu's circumstances, as an obscure commoner, were quite different from those of the Ch'in First Emperor, and his political style was marked by a seeming modesty, but he, too, had to justify himself, first as a rebel against Ch'in and then as dynastic founder. After his conquest of the Ch'in capital in 207 B.C., he promised the assembled leaders of the city that he would abolish the harsh laws of Ch'in, which was consistent with his efforts to present a relatively benign image. In fact, however, he and his heirs made little change in Ch'in law, administration, or ideology during the first century of their rule. Major changes did not occur until the period of retrenchment, which began around 68 B.C., and even these left the state essentially intact.

The formal structure of government and the written laws and ordinances under the Ch'in and Han established a norm for later emulation. Even though Han Kao Tsu presented himself as the deliverer of the empire from the tyranny of Ch'in and distributed some two-thirds of the area of the empire to his generals as fiefs, it should be borne in mind that he retained the richest and strategically most important regions for himself and that these and the fiefs were governed internally through a system taken over from the Ch'in. His commitment to the centralization of authority and to bureaucratic rule was stronger than any tendency he may have had towards feudalism and the sharing of sovereignty, and it was only a matter of time (about fifty years, in fact) before all of China was once again subject to the authority of the emperor's appointed officials.

At the center of Han government and living in closely guarded seclusion was the imperial household, including the emperor, his near relations, his empress and secondary wives, his personal attendants and servants including eunuchs, and all the servants of his immediate family. Sharply distinguished from this intimate setting was the central civil administration, comprised of appointed officials, who had more or less clearly defined governmental responsibilities and whose salaries were kept in correspondence with their official ranks.

The emperor was perceived as the sole earthly source of political authority, but it was also understood that his authority was derived from his possession of Heaven's mandate, much in the manner of the Chou kings. He was, therefore, not expected to be an arbitrary despot (although he might act like one), but rather a kind of steward, managing the world on behalf of Heaven. It also followed from this that the ruler was not the personal owner of the empire. Indeed, in an absolute sense, no one could own the land, because in the last analysis the land was the basic resource by which Heaven provided for the sustenance of the people. The ruler's legitimate function was to see that the land was used in a manner conducive to the general welfare, whether this meant forced migration of people from overpopulated areas to underutilized lands or the confiscation of privately owned land for redistribution. As the sole sovereign, the emperor was also the final source of all law; he commissioned the compilation of codified law subject to his own ratification and amendment, and his edicts and ordinances and his judicial decisions were all incorporated into the legal system. And, finally, all officials were subject to appointment or dismissal by authority of the emperor, although the emperor naturally found it necessary to delegate much of the work of screening and evaluating his personnel.

An important consideration in political stability was the handling of the imperial succession. Normally, the eldest son of the principal wife was named heir apparent, but the emperor for good or bad reasons might prefer a younger son or a son by a secondary wife. This uncertainty left the door open to attempts by the relatives of imperial consorts to try to manipulate the succession in their own interests. This problem became particularly acute when the emperor died young either without heirs or with no heirs old enough to assume the throne. Another way in which the imperial clan was vulnerable was in its isolation from the world outside the walls of the palace grounds. On the one hand, a certain distance had to be maintained between the emperor and the outside world if he was to guard his sovereign authority, but that very distance, over a period of generations, made it increasingly difficult for the emperors to make intelligent judgments on political and policy matters. This, in turn, made possible the usurpation of imperial authority by cliques of consort families, officials, generals, or palace attendants.

The central administration grew in authority and prestige during the first Han reigns and became a stronghold of scholar-officials who believed that the emperor should leave policy initiatives and the active direction of the government to his ministers. This was all very well so long as the emperors were willing to concur or, as in the case of Wen Ti, were subtle enough to have their way without appearing to be despotic. But Han Wu Ti initiated a bitter struggle with his central government and undermined its authority by creating new instruments of imperial rule.

The central administration was formally headed by a chancellor, a chief censor, and a grand commandant. The chancellor was the chief administrative officer of the empire, and in some reigns of Han he was the virtual ruler. The chief censor headed a staff of capital and provincial officials, who monitored the conduct of administrators and reported their findings to him. The grand commandant was a temporary military office and was relatively unimportant. On the next lower level were the nine ministers, who were assigned to specific administrative functions including ceremonial, revenues, economic controls, military procurement, external relations, and imperial clan affairs.

Under the system inherited from Ch'in, the administration of local government was carried on mainly on two levels. The basic unit was the county *(hsien),* of which there were from 1,100 to 1,400, varying according to need. A hundred-odd commanderies *(chun)* each supervised between ten and twenty counties. The counties and commanderies were organs of imperial government, headed by officials recruited and assigned by the emperor and his chancellor. Beneath the counties stood a subbureaucratic hierarchy: townships, small towns, and the wards and hamlets into which the large and small towns were subdivided. Physically, this hierarchy was expressed by walls: within the town walls were ward walls and within the ward walls were walled family homesteads. Each level had its head, a local man, whose status was ratified by the county authorities and who was responsible for the enforcement of the laws and the administration of tax and service obligations within his unit. The cultivated fields were allotted by the local authorities to the peasant families, who lived in the towns. These allotments were the basis for the assignment of tax and service responsibilities. One must suppose that there were also villages and hamlets in many places which did not fit neatly into this pattern, but the concentration of most of the population in and near the walled towns (37,844 in all, by one count) may have resulted from the endemic warfare of late Chou times. It is also clear that both Former and Later Han saw an erosion of the common holdings of the free peasantry, as locally powerful families, official families, and titled nobility used their economic and political power to build up large private holdings and correspondingly large followings of tenants and other dependents. The general picture of local government when the Han was near its peak of efficiency, however, is one of regularized central authority penetrating Chinese society to great depth.

The local administrations were controlled by the central government not only through the appointment and transfer of the chief officials but also by requiring the commanderies to submit annual summary reports on the counties under their supervision. These reports were drawn up under seven headings: finance, economy, education, criminal proceedings, condition of the people, banditry, and natural disasters. Copies of these documents were filed with the chancellor and the imperial secretary, and officials closer to the emperor also had access to them. In the interest of even stronger control, thirteen censorial inspection circuits were established to organize the work of the investigative officers, who scrutinized the performance of officials within the areas for which they were responsible.

The Former Han period made one of its greatest contributions to the art of political organization in the matter of recruiting officials for civil administration. The basic elements of the Chinese system (fully developed during the T'ang, 618-907)—public education, recommendation, qualification by written examination, and practical training—all were present. A typical pattern might be as follows: A student in the imperial university (or a provincial college) upon completion of his studies and a satisfactory examination was sent to serve as a minor functionary in local government. His prefect might then recommend him to the central government, where he would submit to a written examination and then, perhaps, be assigned to serve as a court attendant. If he found favor with the emperor, he might then be appointed to a high office in the central government or a commandery.

Quite apart from the presence of an imperial bureaucracy, the recruitment of officials from an empirewide class of land-owning, educated families also contributed to the political unification of China. Leading families in all parts of the empire could hope that they might place their members in the government, with all that that implied for legal privilege and social prestige. Moreover, even as early as the Han, the "rule of avoidance" was adopted whereby officials were forbidden to administer their native commanderies or counties. This made it more difficult for them to use their offices to promote their personal interests at the expense of the state and fostered their obedience to the central government by separating them from their local political bases. Such measures of political centralization were limited, however, by the fact that the head officials of the commanderies and counties had to work through administrative staffs that were locally recruited from leading families and were inclined to serve their private interests.

Although voluntary obedience was necessary for political stability in the long run, the sanction of military force was always in the background and was often invoked. The Ch'in lost no time in asserting an imperial monopoly of armed might; one of the first acts of the First Emperor was to conduct a house-to-house search and confiscation of arms. The collected weapons were brought to the capital and melted down and recast in the forms of gigantic statues and sets of bells. Although the Han army's most obvious continuing responsibility was to man the hundreds of small forts that stood a few miles apart across the entire length of the Great Wall, each commandery, interior regions included, had its own military officers who were responsible for the handling and training of conscripts. When banditry, revolt, or invasion required the mobilization of large numbers of troops, the commandery would have to await specific authorization from the central government to take the field. If it were a question of a major, sustained campaign, then the central government would give the command to a general of its own choosing. By such means the imperial regime guarded its monopoly of large-scale military power. Most of the needed military manpower was provided directly or indirectly by a system of conscription. At the age of twenty-three, all able-bodied peasants registered on the tax rolls became liable for two years military service: one year in the capital region, one year of local garrison duty. In addition, they were theoretically obliged to serve three days each year on the frontiers until they reached the age of fifty-five. In practice, of course, they were not intended to serve for such short periods, but to pay an annual tax exempting them from service. The proceeds from the tax were then applied to the cost of maintaining a force of long-term professional soldiers on the frontiers.

Han imperial authority was most powerfully centralized during the reign of Wu Ti. In order to overcome the gulf between the imperial palace and the central administration, the emperor wrested control of the empire from his chancellors and ministers and placed it in the hands of low-ranking palace functionaries. Chancellors were dismissed or executed in rapid succession while an elaborate imperial secretariat took shape in the palace. The imperial secretariat of Wu Ti originated as a document-drafting office within the obscure ministry of the privy purse. Officials of this office were originally of no great influence or political importance, and they had access to the palace, where they aided the emperor in drafting documents. This personal staff channelled communications to the emperor, organized information, and made policy recommendations. With their assistance Wu Ti was able to make his own policy and to reduce the once powerful office of chancellor to a mere administrative organ obedient to his will. Since only women and eunuchs were allowed into the emperor's private quarters at the rear of the palace area, Wu Ti experimented with the appointment of eunuchs to the secretariat. Most eunuchs were uneducated, however, and this proved impracticable.

Han Wu Ti not only took the reins of the central government into his own hands, but also proceeded to use his authority to dominate the entire society. The great families in the countryside and the flourishing merchant class represented a long-term threat as well as a short-term source of revenue. Wu Ti used ruthless censorial circuit inspectors and commandery officials to break up estates, expropriate merchant wealth, and forcibly remove many wealthy families to the vicinity of the capital, where they could be controlled. He also instituted heavy commercial taxes and established state monopolies of salt and iron in order to divert commercial profits into the imperial treasury. In later reigns, the dominance of the society by imperial power declined, and the growth of local centers of wealth and power began once again.

Good communications were a necessary condition of enduring unity, and Han inherited and then expanded a system of imperial highways built by Ch'in. From the capital at Ch'angan, four major highways ran in different directions. One followed the north bank of the Wei River upstream and then continued out the Kansu panhandle into Central Asia. (This was the eastern section of the silk route.) Another followed the south bank of the Wei about a hundred miles upstream, then turned south over the western end of the Ch'inling divide and ran down into the Szechwan basin, already a rich area owing to the Ch'in irrigation works. A third highway ran southeastward to the middle Yangtze region and on over the Nanling divide to the Canton region. A branch ran westward to the Hanoi region. Still another highway ran eastward across the north China plain and, bending toward the south, crossed the lower Yangtze by ferry and continued on down into modern Chekiang. A fifth highway connected the capital with the vicinity of Peking and continued across southern Manchuria into northern Korea. Other highways ran northward to the frontier, serving the garrisons along the wall. The imperial highways and the post houses built along them were originally intended for official use only, but in time they served private transport as well. North China was also covered with a network of lesser roads maintained by local authorities. Officials traveled in horse-drawn two-wheeled carriages, while common people used wagons pulled by oxen or donkeys. By Han times the efficiency of land transport had been much increased by the use of a breast harness that enabled draft animals to pull heavier loads than had been possible with the primitive neck harness.

For movement of bulk commodities, water transport was still, and would remain, far cheaper than land transport, and much of Ch'in and Han hydraulic engineering was intended to serve barge traffic as well as to prevent flooding and to furnish water for irrigation. As the Former Han capital rapidly outgrew even the rich resources of the Wei valley region, ever greater quantities of tax grain had to be delivered from the commanderies of the north China plain. The Yellow River and canals connected to it made it possible for much of the grain to be transported by boat. In the reign of Wu Ti, the route was shortened by the construction of a canal that connected the capital with the Yellow River at a point near the confluence with the Wei. By this means it was possible to raise annual grain deliveries to the impressive total of nearly 400,000 tons.

Private trade tended to integrate the empire economically. Merchants already constituted an important social class in late Chou times. During Former Han they gained in wealth and number in the face of considerable opposition and competition from the government, especially under Wu Ti. Merchants were a legally inferior class and forbidden to purchase land. Especially in Former Han, their activities were hampered by compulsory registration and rental of stalls in the government-controlled marketplaces and by the requirement that they carry passports and bills of lading as they went about their business. They were also subject to tolls along the highways. At times, the establishment of state monopolies in important commodities cut into their commercial profits. It was impossible for the state to present anything like a united front against commerce, however, because the very people who should have been most anticommercial, civil and military officials and wealthy families, often succumbed to the temptations of quick profits and became part-time merchants themselves. Merchants and their goods therefore continued to circulate and to provide a small measure of economic integration.

Cultural Impact of Ch'in and Han Rule

Standardization was a consequence of bureaucratization. Since members of the imperial service were expected to serve in whatever region they might be assigned to, they needed uniform regulations to guide them. Centralized regulation and administration of agricultural and commercial taxes and the effort to control commodity prices all required uniform weights, measures, and units of account. Such standards were defined and imposed by the Ch'in after the unification and were continued by the Han. The effects of standardization of the writing system were especially important for subsequent Chinese history. Ch'in made mandatory the use of the so-called small-seal script in order to obviate confusion arising from regional variations that had arisen among the states of late Chou. In the course of the Han dynasty, the hundreds of thousands of government clerks in the daily performance of their "paperwork" (actually writing on slips of wood, in most instances) evolved simplified forms of characters, even as the number of characters was increasing. (A Han dictionary contains nine thousand.) The Han clerkly style came into general use and survives to this day with little change. The common heritage of Chinese literature was easily shared by learned people in all parts of the empire, despite the persistence of mutually unintelligible languages and dialects, and the same heritage has remained accessible to successive generations of Chinese for some two thousand years.

The Ch'in-Former Han universal state produced two imperial capitals: Ch'in's Hsien-yang, Former Han's Ch'angan. Ch'in Shih-huang-ti began with a capital that had been constructed by an earlier king in the fourth century B.C., and after the beginning of his imperial rule he expanded it to immense proportions. In at least one sense there was a point of continuity with the cities of Shang and Chou: the ceremonial complex of ancestral temples, sacrificial altars, palaces, and parks. In addition to providing the necessary setting for the conduct of the religious-ceremonial aspect of imperial rule, Ch'in Shih-huang-ti also constructed replicas of the ancestral temples and palaces of all the defeated rulers and, according to a later account, provided estates near the capital to accommodate the 120,000 wealthy families he forced to settle in the capital region. He not only created a city of great size, but he also achieved a fitting symbol of the universality of his empire by concentrating there all the great families and their ancestral cults. It was the fate of Hsien-yang to be utterly destroyed by Hsiang Yu, Han Kao Tsu's great rival, and a new Han city had to be built nearby at Ch'angan. The Former Han capital seems to have been built rather haphazardly, irregular in form (as defined by its fourteen miles of outer walls and gates) and in internal organization, but it did preserve the basic distinctions between the ceremonial complex, the nine official markets, and some one hundred sixty residential wards. Both of these urban centers of empire were of great size, connected to the provinces by good land and water routes, and provided with the appropriate religious and symbolic structures. Both, finally, were richly endowed with the high culture of the empire, as represented by the great concentration of wealthy families, estates of the nobility, and institutions of higher learning.

In approaching the question of Han culture we may begin by returning to the point that the establishment of the universal state involved a shift of power to the periphery. The Ch'in state was essentially a newcomer in the political world of late Chou and had been created out of the Jung barbarian society of the loess uplands. When faced with the need to legitimize their imperial rule, the Ch'in quite naturally perceived the Chou-centered traditions of the conquered area and the regional loyalties and cultures of the states as potentially dangerous. In the edicts of the new regime we may see a selective program of cultural transformation. As the traditionalists of the old order, the Confucians were regarded as dangerous subversives; their stubborn loyalty to the doctrines they attributed to the founding kings of Chou and their habit of resolving present problems in terms of ancient precedents brought down upon their heads the wrath of the First Emperor. Many of them were executed and their books banned. The basic social institution of the clan, or lineage group, with its focus on ancestral worship, was undermined by the legal principle that all persons were simply imperial subjects, irrespective of their descent. This point was dramatically brought home by its application even to the ruling house, whose members were, at least in theory, subject to the full rigor of the law. The banning of the *Book of Songs (Shih Ching)* and the ritual texts added to the difficulty of maintaining the common-descent groups by making illegal the songs and ceremonial manuals used in their rites.

To be sure, the Ch'in dynasty, with its anti-Confucian bias, did not last long, and the succeeding Han gradually shifted from opposition to patronage of Confucian learning. But the Han scholars were now looking back at Chou across such a gulf of social and cultural change that they were unable to understand the traditions they espoused. Even the task of reassembling the late Chou texts was only partially completed, so great was the physical destruction of books in the course of the Ch'in persecution and the anti-Ch'in revolution. Moreover, the shift toward centralization, bureaucratization, and standardization was not reversed by Han, despite the dynasty's pragmatic spirit and willingness to compromise, and this made any revival of the aristocratic and feudal principles of Chou a practical impossibility.

The cultural transformation of China during the third and second centuries B.C. is dramatically registered in the state ideologies of Ch'in and Han. The ideologies may be approached from two directions: from that of literary exposition and that of imperial ritual. Both Ch'in and Han produced ideologies that were based on the new systematic theories of the cosmic order as an integral, organic system, with the principal difference that Ch'in combined cosmology with legalism (and a little Confucian moralism), while Han eventually combined cosmology with Confucian principles (but in practice continued the Legalist focus on the bureaucratic state and its interests). The Ch'in First Emperor adopted the theories of the five-element school of cosmology, according to which all phenomena are produced by the cyclical interactions of the five elementatal forces of earth, wood, metal, fire, and water, each of which dominates, or "rules," the universe in its turn. This cycle was associated with the succession of dynasties: earth and the Yellow Emperor; wood and the Hsia dynasty; metal and the Shang dynasty; fire and the Chou dynasty; and water and the Ch'in dynasty. The water element was also associated with the color black and the number six. Ch'in regulations, therefore, required that the imperial carriage be drawn by six black horses, while the standard measurements were a base-six system, and black gowns were to be worn by all participants in religious ceremonials. The common term *blackheads* to denote the people generally appears to have resulted from a Ch'in order requiring commoners to wear black headbands. By such measures, the new regime sought to create a new order that would be in perfect harmony with the element water, which was thought to have succeeded the element fire, dominant in Chou times. The First Emperor also prepared a list of eight principal gods who became objects of state worship, including those representing Heaven, Earth, War, Yin (the female cosmic principle), Yang (the male cosmic principle), Moon, Sun, and Four Seasons. Further to make his rule effective he assiduously served a multitude of local cults of the gods of mountains and rivers, and we have already noted that he made his capital the site of the continuing ancestral cults of the defeated houses, whose members had been uprooted from their own sacred places. The Legalist side of Ch'in ideology was most clearly expressed in the debate between Li Ssu and a traditionalist adviser at the court of the First Emperor. The latter insisted that the only way to make the new regime secure was to divide it into large fiefs, after the fashion of the early Chou. It could be assumed that the grateful vassals and their heirs would ever stand ready to come to the defense of the imperial house in time of need. Li Ssu, however, won the argument by insisting that, on the contrary, it was just this division of sovereignty that had undone the Chou and that the triumph of Ch'in had ushered in a new and unprecedented age that called for the universalization of the latest and most scientific principles of statecraft.

The Han dynasty continued for a long time to rule under the cover of Ch'in ideology. Han emperors ruled by virtue of the cosmic power of water until 104 B.C., when Wu Ti first honored earth, the next power in the cycle of destruction, and adopted the corresponding color and number: yellow and five. The principal Ch'in state cult of the four cosmic powers (five in Han) was not replaced by the allegedly Confucian cults of Heaven and Earth until 31 B.C. It was during the reign of Han Wu Ti, however, that a new ideology was formulated which later became the Han imperial orthodoxy. The author of the new system, Tung Chung-shu (ca. 179-104) in effect synthesized a slightly altered version of the Ch'in cosmology with Confucian ethical principles and *li* ceremonial. This in effect completed the search for a more benign image and at the same time reinforced the social status of the *li*-oriented literati. Another significant feature of Tung Chung-shu's system was that it provided the basis for a science of reading portents. It was asserted that unusual natural phenomena were signs sent by a benevolent Heaven to warn the ruler that he must correct some fault in his own or a subordinate's conduct. The reporting and reading of omens became a means by which officials could exercise some measure of control over an emperor.

The new Han ideology was intellectually satisfying in that it provided plausible answers to questions about the universe. Also, and of great importance to the state, the organic theory of the universe, with its matching of different kinds of phenomena, made it possible for the ideology to absorb and confirm many old practices dear to the traditionalists, such as divination, sacrifice, and the moralistic interpretation of portents in unusual natural phenomena. Indeed, in both Ch'in and Han ideology one may see how in the realm of intellectual speculation men sought the same kind of certitude, permanence, and psychological comfort that they sought in the realm of action by building a universal state upon the ruins of the Chou order. Confucius' willing acceptance of doubt and anxiety as the price of honesty and the pursuit of truth required more stamina and devotion than most people, including many of his followers, were capable of.

There were differences in culture from region to region and from class to class. One effect of the long survival of the Han may have been to somewhat lessen these cultural variations, but one should bear in mind that even today differences persist in such obvious matters as cuisine, dress, speech, and religion. But certain uniformities should be considered. It has already been noted that the empire was provided with a common literary medium. The adoption of a state ideology and the associated formation of public and private schools led to a standardization of formal education for the social and political elite. The growth of trade in Han times led to the emulation of upper-class style by the wealthy plebians, despite the existence of sumptuary laws that often forbade this. The bronze mirror, once an elegantly adorned and inscribed piece of aristocratic paraphernalia, was popularized in Han and the content of the inscriptions was reduced to an appropriately popular level. Likewise, Han potters turned out glazed ceramic wares that appear to have been cheap facsimiles of aristocratic family-heirloom bronzes. The very existence of sumptuary laws, to say nothing of contemporary complaints about their violations, reveals the extent to which the striving for higher status in a competitive society fostered a certain degree of cultural uniformity. Finally, it should be noted that in the course of the Han, millions of peasants were conscripted or hired for corvee and military service and often transported to the farthest corners of the empire to build or fight. The stories that they could tell on their return must have given their fellow villagers a vivid sense of the larger world and encouraged them to think of themselves as "men of Han."

CONCLUDING REMARKS

The formation of universal empires in the first millennium B.C. was a dramatic phase of human history. The strife and suffering of regional states severely tested the fabric of civilized society, and the protests of the ethical thinkers and reformers discussed in the preceding chapter were symptomatic of the distress that people felt. The universal empires, by exerting control over an extended cultural area, sharply reduced the level of interregional conflict. Ironically, the pacification that accompanied the formation of a universal empire was possible precisely because the rulers of the new order had rationalized and enlarged their war-making powers to the point where they were able to overcome all opposition. The founders tended, as well, to come from marginal areas of the civilized world, where the arts of war were honored more than civil virtues. In light of these circumstances one can ask how the unification of the civilized world by a militarized power affected the course of cultural development. To what extent did the imposition of a centralized control and the suppression of resistance discourage the independent development of regional cultures and by so doing restrict the number of potential lines along which the civilization might grow in the future? Certainly the co-option and assimilation of the ideas of previous ethical reformers into a new state ideology needs to be studied here. On the positive side, one might ask how the organizational accomplishments of the empire, such as the creation of communications networks and currencies and law codes, facilitated growth and innovation in trade, industry, technology, and even perhaps art and literature.

The empires considered here were separated from one another by both time and space. The Achaemenid empire had already come to an end before the Mauryan empire was founded, yet it probably exerted some influence on the latter both directly through the example of its satrapies in the Indian subcontinent and indirectly through the impact of Alexander the Great, whose conquests drew heavily on the Achaemenid experience. The Ch'in-Han empire, by contrast, was far enough removed from West Asia and South Asia and sufficiently distinct in style that there is no reason to believe that its formation was influenced by the Achaemenid or Mauryan achievements. In each case, the most important influence of each of these empires was to be felt within its own area, for which, in subsequent ages, it could serve as a model and a precedent for the amassing of political power.

The requirements of centralized administration obliged each empire to solve the same problems in ways that were unique, yet comparable. Thus one can examine such institutions as the military forces or the provincial administration to see the similarities and differences that characterize the unique patterns of a universal process. While the creation and preservation of a universal empire posed the same kinds of problems for rulers in different cultures, it is not so clear why such comparable empires came into existence. Why did empires of great magnitude arise within a few centuries of each other? What were the elements in each case that were unique? Did the preexistence of powerful states in Egypt, Mesopotamia, and Assyria oblige the Achaemenids to adapt their rule to greater cultural diversity than was the case in other areas? Did the terrain of northern India prove an obstacle to the Mauryan empire in firmly consolidating its conquests? What accounts for the relative stability and cultural uniformity of the Ch'in-Han universal empire in contrast to the Achaemenid and Mauryan cases? Related to this last question is the problem of explaining the persistence or disappearance of patterns established under universal states in later periods, which is the subject of the next chapter.

BIBLIOGRAPHY

4.P THE RISE OF UNIVERSAL EMPIRES DURING THE FIRST MILLENNIUM B.C.: PROCESSES

Eisenstadt, Shmuel N., *The Political Systems of Empires* (Free Press paperback, 1969), 524 pp. An elaborate sociological comparison of empires; difficult to read but filled with analytical insights.

Parsons, Talcott, *Societies: Evolutionary and Comparative Perspectives* (Prentice-Hall paperback, 1966), esp. pp. 69-95. A highly abstract discussion of the developmental stages of society with one chapter devoted to "historic" intermediate empires.

Starr, Chester G., *The Emergence of Rome as Ruler of the Western World* (Cornell University Press paperback, 1950), 122 pp. A brief outline of the rise of a universal empire on the eastern end of the Eurasian landmass; useful for comparative purposes.

Toynbee, Arnold J., *A Study of History,* Vol. 7A, *Universal States* (Oxford University Press paperback, 1963), 379 pp. A richly suggestive treatment of empires in the context of a great metahistorian's overview of human history.

Wittfogel, Karl A., *Oriental Despotism* (Yale paperback, 1963), 556 pp. An ambitious and provocative theory about the evolution of despotic political institutions in the setting of a "hydraulic economy" requiring control of river systems; widely criticized.

4.1 THE ACHAEMENID EMPIRE IN WEST ASIA

Culican, William, *The Medes and Persians* (New York, 1965), 260 pp. The best introduction to the subject, with a good bibliography and illustrations.

Frye, Richard N., *The Heritage of Persia* (Cleveland, 1963), pp. 1-177. A far-ranging survey that draws on a wealth of source material, literary and linguistic, archaeological and numismatic, and traces the Iranian impact far beyond the bounds of the Iranian plateau.

Ghirshman, Roman, *Iran* (Penguin paperback, 1954), pp. 73-242. A survey of the period which is both scholarly and readable, by a leading archaeologist.

———, *The Arts of Ancient Iran, From Its Origins to the Time of Alexander the Great* (New York, 1964), 439 pp. A lavishly illustrated survey of the Iranian achievement in the visual arts, down to the close of the Achaemenid period.

Herodotus, *The History,* trans. by A. de Selincourt (Penguin paperback, 1954), 599 pp. An indispensable source for the study of the Achaemenid empire.

Phillips, Eustace D., *The Royal Hordes* (McGraw-Hill paperback, 1965), 126 pp. An illustrated account of the steppe peoples bordering the Iranian and Greek culture zones with emphasis on the Sakas (Scythians).

4.2 THE MAURYAN EMPIRE IN SOUTH ASIA

Basham, Arthur L., *The Wonder That Was India* (Evergreen paperback, 1959), 568 pp. An indispensable reference work on ancient Indian civilization, organized under subject headings.

Drekmeier, Charles, *Kingship and Community in Early India* (Stanford, 1962), pp. 189-226. An important discussion regarding the *Arthashastra* of Kautilya.

Nikam, Narayamrao A., and Richard McKeon, *The Edicts of Ashoka* (University of Chicago Press paperback, 1966), 68 pp. Currently the most accessible translation.

Thapar, Romila, *A History of India,* Vol. 1 (Penguin paperback, 1966), pp. 70-91. The most accessible account of the period by a leading authority.

———, *Ashoka and the Decline of the Mauryas* (Oxford, 1961), 270 pp. Likely to remain the definitive account for many years.

Wheeler, Sir Mortimer, *Flames over Persepolis* (New York, 1968), 171 pp. An archaeologist's explanation of the diffusion of Iranian culture throughout Afghanistan and northern India following the collapse of the Achaemenid empire.

4.3 THE CH'IN-HAN UNIVERSAL EMPIRE IN EAST ASIA

Ch'u T'ung-tsu, *Han Social Structure* (Seattle, 1972), 550 pp. Analysis of Han society with extensive documentation.

de Bary, William T., ed., *Sources of Chinese Tradition* (Columbia University Press paperback, 1960), 976 pp. Part 2 presents source material on Han intellectual history.

Fairbank, John K., Edwin O. Reischauer, and Albert M. Craig, *East Asia: Tradition and Transformation* (Boston, 1973), 969 pp. Chapter 4 presents a concise history of the Ch'in and Han dynasties.

Loewe, Michael, *Everyday Life in Early Imperial China* (Harper Perennial paperback, 1968), 208 pp. Topical chapters cover the Han culture, state, and society.

Yu Ying-shih, *Trade and Expansion in Han China* (Berkeley, 1967), 251 pp. This monograph deals broadly with economic, institutional, and political aspects of Sino-barbarian relations during the Han.

Watson, Burton, trans., *Records of the Grand Historian,* 2 vols. (New York, 1961), 563, 543 pp. Translation of portions of the great general history of Ssu-ma Ch'ien pertaining to the Former Han.

GLOSSARY

Arthashastra. A Sanskrit treatise on government of uncertain date but traditionally attributed to the brahman Kautilya, chief minister of Chandragupta Maurya.

Aryans. The common term used to describe the Indo-European invaders of northern India during the second and first milleniums. Strictly speaking, a linguistic description.

Bactria. The area in northern Afghanistan bounded on the south by the Hindu Kush Mountains and on the north by the upper Amu Darya River. Originally inhabited by the Iranian Bactrians, it became, during the Seleucid period, the northeastern outpost of Hellenism and the location of the important Graeco-Bactrian kingdom.

Brahman. The highest of the four castes into which traditional Hindu society was divided.

Ch'in Shih-huang-ti (259-210 B.C.). Hereditary ruler of the state of Ch'in, he terminated the Chou dynasty in 249 and completed the conquest of China in 221. By imposing his strongly centralized and bureaucratic regime on all of China, he created the first Chinese universal empire.

Cosmology. A branch of learning which assumes that the universe can be understood in terms of regular processes and which attempts to identify these processes and the manner in which they interact. Historically, it may be regarded as a less personal or anthropomorphic equivalent of the mythology of ancient times and tends toward a more detached or scientific method.

Deccan. The great tableland of central India. The Narbada River was traditionally regarded as constituting the dividing line between northern India and the Deccan plateau.

Dharma. A Sanskrit word conveying the sense of duty or right conduct in relation to the social order. The Prakrit form, *dhamma,* was given an extended meaning by the Buddhist emperor Ashoka to convey a sense of social as well as individual responsibility.

Fars. The homeland of the Achaemenid and Sasanid dynasties; a province in southwestern Iran, with its present capital at Shiraz.

Gandhara. The region of the western Panjab and the trans-Indus country centering upon the modern city of Peshawar. The great metropolitan centers of Taxila and Purushapura were both located in Gandhara, which appears as Gadara in the lists of the provinces of the Achaemenid empire.

Han Kao-tsu (248-195 B.C.). The temple name of Liu Chi, founder of the Han dynasty. Han Kao-tsu was born a commoner and rose in the ranks of one of the rebellions against the state of Ch'in. While retaining most of the laws and institutions of Ch'in, he achieved greater political stability by means of limited concessions to the feudal form of political organization.

Han Wu-ti (r. 141-87 B.C.). The Han dynasty emperor whose reign was marked by the vigorous expansion of Chinese political power into Korea, Vietnam, and Central Asia. He also strengthened and centralized political control within China.

Hsiung-nu. Pastoral-nomadic peoples first organized in a great tribal federation in Mongolia in the third century B.C. They remained formidable antagonists of the Chinese empire until the fifth century A.D., when they were finally absorbed into other ethnic groups.

Kharoshthi. A script derived from Aramaic and used in the Indo-Iranian borderlands.

Khuzistan. A province in southwestern Iran, bordering modern Iraq and the Persian Gulf, with Ahwaz as its capital. The Elamite and Achaemenid metropolis of Susa was located in Khuzistan, as were the important Sasanid centers of Shushtar and Gondeshapur. Today, Abadan, one of the world's largest oil refineries, is located in Khuzistan.

Kshatriya. The warrior caste, ranking second to the brahman in the caste hierarchy of Hindu India.

Li Ssu (ca. 280-208 B.C.). Legalist minister to Ch'in Shih-huang-ti, argued for the establishment of a bureaucratically controlled imperial regime and suggested the suppression of the books and doctrines of the followers of Confucius.

Marches. Borderlands or frontiers.

Prakrit. A colloquial form of Sanskrit which served as a popular language of communication at the time when Sanskrit was becoming increasingly the language of the brahmans and brahmanical learning.

Sakas (Greek, **Scythians).** The nomadic-pastoral people occupying the Eurasian steppe zone from around the sixth century B.C. to the fourth century A.D., and who spoke an Iranian language or languages. The Sakas had close cultural contacts with the Greeks of the Black Sea region and with the Iranians, and played a great part in the history of northwestern India.

Sanskrit. The classical language of Hindu civilization derived from Vedic. The parent-language of a number of modern Indian vernaculars, including Hindi, Bengali, Gujarati, and Marathi.

Satrap. An Achaemenid provincial governor. The word is derived from the Greek form of the Old Persian *kshatrapa,* which also found its way into India, where it was widely used during the Saka and Kushana periods.

Shahanshah (Persian, "king of kings"). The title of the pre-Islamic rulers of Iran and also of the present-day Pahlavi dynasty. Some Islamic dynasties, notably the Buyids, adopted the title to stress continuity with the pre-Islamic past.

Shaman. A worker of magic among the Central Asian and Siberian tribes. Shamans claimed to possess supernatural powers and to pass into ecstatic trances. Their social functions were somewhat similar to those of the witch doctor of sub-Saharan Africa.

Sogdians. The Iranian inhabitants of Sogdiana (known to the Greeks as Transoxania), the area lying between the Amu Darya and Syr Darya rivers.

Sumptuary laws. Prohibition on the possession of certain kinds of goods. Such laws may be intended to curb extravagance in general or, as often was the case, to preserve distinctions of rank by requiring different life-styles for people of different status.

Tribute system. Han Wu-ti's campaigns against the Hsiung-nu and the breakup of the Hsiung-nu federation resulted in the establishment of a new form of relationship between this pastoral-nomadic people and the Chinese state. In return for tribute missions and court attendance by foreign rulers or their representatives, the Chinese state gave lavish gifts. The effect was to create at least the appearance of barbarian submission to the Chinese empire while keeping the peace on the frontiers.

Vazir. The minister of a Muslim ruler. In fact, a ruler might appoint concurrently two or more *vazirs* to have charge over different areas of administration but the term is usually applied in the sense of a chief minister, as with the Ottoman "grand vizier."

The Persistence of Empire in the Face of Change

350 B.C. to 650 A.D.

The first universal empires of West, South, and East Asia—the Achaemenid, the Mauryan, and the Han—achieved brilliantly the task of pacifying and organizing their respective societies. Each spread its rule over vast areas and diverse peoples. The mobilization of human and material resources enabled the rulers to spread military and political power until their states were almost in direct contact with one another. Intoxicated with their triumphs, the rulers of the first empires patronized new religious and political ideologies and gave them the standing of official orthodoxies.

But neither the empires nor the ideologies invoked to justify their rule could survive forever. They depended upon an abundance of people and tilled land not subject to the control of insubordinate regional authorities or aristocratic establishments. They also depended upon a corps of loyal and efficient administrators. These necessary conditions could not be maintained indefinitely. The private ambitions of great families led them to expand their landholdings and their local political power, while officials who had no overriding private interests became increasingly difficult to find. As political power came to be less effectively exercised from the center, the empires lost control over the subject peoples along their cultural frontiers. Barbarian states were then formed in frontier regions and sent invading armies deep into the heartlands of the civilized societies. Such factors as these in different combinations brought an end to the early empires.

Despite these failures, however, new empires were raised on the ruins of the old. If particular empires proved to be mortal, the empire as an idea and an institution enjoyed sufficient prestige to ensure its continued use as a model to guide the political ambitions of later dynasties. Changed circumstances and the varied origins of the new empire builders worked against the exact reproduction of past regimes, however, and the later institutional and ideological patterns became highly complex. Old ideologies were sometimes revived by new regimes, but they were subject to mounting criticism for their sterility and their growing irrelevance to a changing world. New or reformed ideologies were developed by reworking ancient traditions into classical models. New eclectic ideologies evolved from both indigenous and alien traditions. Still other reformers rejected the authority of the past and advocated reform on pragmatic grounds.

In all the major civilized areas, however, the efforts of later rulers to coerce their subject populations by means of an imperial framework tended to be less effective than those of their precursors, until at the end of the period covered in this chapter the civilized societies were undergoing major crises that left them vulnerable and responsive to new messages of hope borne by the universal religions.

5

PROCESSES

The Disintegration of Universal Empires

a. Private control of wealth and resources
b. Regional organization of political and military power: feudal tendencies
c. Popular unrest
d. Formation of frontier states

Tradition and Innovation

e. Imperial successor states
f. The hardening of imperial traditions
g. Unorthodox alternatives

PATTERNS

1. **The Parthians and Sasanids in West Asia**
2. **The Kushanas and Guptas in South Asia**
3. **China during the Later Han, Three Kingdoms, and Western Chin**

5. PERSISTENCE OF EMPIRE

		1	2	3
	ROME	PARTHIAN/SASANID	KUSHANA/GUPTA	LATER HAN/THREE KINGDOMS
300 B.C.	Rome unites Italian peninsula		Diodotus I establishes Greek kingdom in Bactria ca. 247-235	Warring States
		Parthian empire founded ca. 248		
200	Punic and Macedonian wars make Rome supreme in Mediterranean 264-146			Ch'in conquest, 221, unification of China
				Former Han dynasty, 206-9 A.D.
		Mithradates I, r. ca. 171-138	Shunga dynasty 183-73	
			Menander, ca. 155-ca. 145, Indo-Greek ruler	
100		Mithradates II, r. ca. 123-87		
			Maues, 97-ca. 77, Indo-Saka ruler	
		Battle of Carrhae 53 B.C.		
	Julius Caesar d. 44 B.C.			
B.C./A.D.	Roman empire		Satavahana dynasty 28 B.C.-250 A.D.	Hsin dynasty, 9-23 Later Han dynasty, 25-220
	Augustus d. 14 A.D.		Gondophares, r. 20-46, Indo-Parthian ruler	Ming Ti, r. 57-75
		Vologeses I, r. 51-80 A.D.		
100			Possible date for the accession of Kushana ruler, Kanishka, ca. 78	Invention of paper, announced 105
				Classics carved on stone 175-183 Yellow Turban Rebellion 184

Date				
200	Era of military conflict and disunion in Roman empire	Mani, b. ca. 216 Ardashir establishes Sasanid empire 224, r. 224-ca. 239 Shapur I, r. 239-272	Vasudeva d. ca. 227, disintegration of Kushana empire	Three Kingdoms 220-280, division of China
300	Diocletian r. 285-305, autocratic imperial rule, administrative reform, persecution of Christians Constantine wins control of entire empire 324, Constantinople made capital 330	Shapur II, r. 309-379	Gupta dynasty 320-467 Samudra Gupta, r. 330-379	Western Chin 265-317 Chin unification 280 Hsiung-nu Han 304-330
400	Division between Eastern and Western halves of empire becomes permanent Visigoths sack Rome 410 End of emperorship in the West		Chandra Gupta II, r. 380-413	
500		Kavad, r. 488-496 and 499-531 Mazdak	Early Chalukya dynasty, 453-757	
	Justinian, r. 527-65, Eastern emperor, retakes Italy, Africa, part of Spain; codification of Roman law	Khusru I Anushirwan, r. 531-579	Toramana, Hun ruler, d. ca. 510 Mihirakula, Hun ruler, d. ca. 542	
600		Khusru II Parviz, r. 590-628		Sui reunification of China 589 T'ang dynasty
700		Arabs capture Ctesiphon 636 Arabs defeat Sasanids at Nihavand 642	Harsha of Kanauj, r. 606-648 Pulakeshin II, r. ca. 610-ca. 642, ruler of Early Chalukya dynasty	

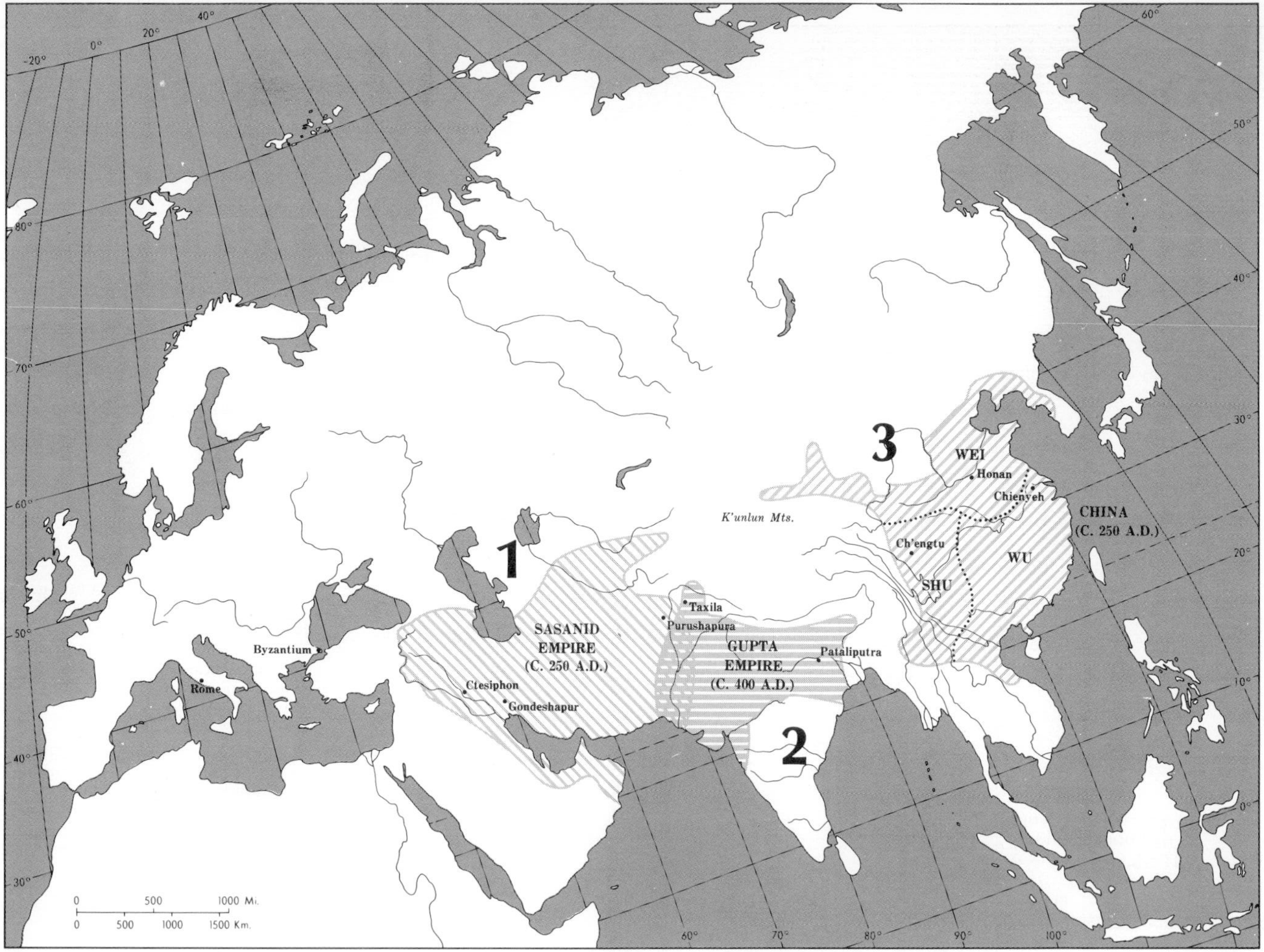

Map 18 The persistence of empire in the face of change

PROCESSES

The social and cultural crisis of the middle of the first millennium B.C. was resolved with the formation of the universal empires. This resolution proved to be only temporary, however, as the imperial order was undermined by social forces beyond its control. Internally, the expanding agricultural and commercial economies of the civilized societies presented opportunities for the creation of aristocratic estates and these, in turn, lent themselves to the formation of independent centers of regional political and military power. The empires, which had been built on the foundation of bureaucratic control over the peasantry and the markets and had been backed by their monopoly of armed force, were now gradually deprived of the means to maintain themselves. Externally, the empires relinquished control over their outer frontiers as they shifted the burden of defense from conscript armies to mercenary troops, who were often of the same ethnic origin as the enemies they were hired to fight against, as in the case of the Greek mercenaries of the Achaemenids. Societies of mixed nomadic and civilized origins then grew up on the margins of the empires and prospered on the profits of continental trade. Weakened by internal social and economic changes, the empires were vulnerable to attack by the strong, independent states that formed in these distant frontier regions. Each of the first empires was eventually destroyed by some or all of these factors in combination.

The ideologies and institutional forms of the first empires survived in the successor states that undertook the political reorganization of the civilized societies. The new regimes that were the political heirs of the Achaemenid, Mauryan, and Former Han dynasties tried to restore the old empires, and strengthened their claims to legitimacy by adopting their ideology, ceremonial, protocol, and titles with certain more or less deliberate changes. They were sometimes successful in temporarily overcoming the entrenched aristocracies or in integrating them into the imperial state, so as to get control of revenues and manpower once again. But the processes that had brought the empires down were not easily reversed, and behind the outward appearance that little had changed, the new rulers had to compromise and innovate in order to hold on to effective power. Reformers under these conditions tried to make their proposals more authoritative by identifying them with the classical models they claimed to have found in the sanctified literature of antiquity. Among those who succumbed to this tendency, however, the habit of investing traditions with classical status led to intellectual sterility and blind imitation. Fortunately, this tendency invited challenge by people of independent and innovative mind. Thus a period that was marked by pedantic classical scholarship also saw renewed speculation on social, political, and general philosophical issues. This was reflected in new approaches to statecraft, technology, the natural sciences, and metaphysics. Ultimately the decline of interest in the classical traditions opened the civilized societies to the influence of the universal religions, which will be the subject of the chapter following this one.

THE PERIOD

For West Asia the period covered in this chapter runs from about 350 B.C. until 651 A.D. This span of a thousand years includes the declining decades of the Achaemenid dynasty, the conquests of Alexander and the Seleucid successor state, the restoration of Iranian rule by the Parthian Arsacids, and finally the Sasanid empire, which ended with the conquest of Iran by the Arab Muslims. For South Asia the period covers the eight and a half centuries from the fall of the Mauryan dynasty, in 183 B.C., until the middle of the seventh century A.D. and includes the northern Indian empires of the Kushanas and the Guptas. In East Asia the period begins around 50 B.C., in the declining years of the Former Han dynasty, and runs to 317 A.D. This period of more than three and a half centuries includes the unsuccessful attempt by the Hsin dynasty (9-23 A.D.) to restore effective imperial control, the Later Han, the fragmentation of the empire into three rival kingdoms, and the ephemeral reunification under the Chin.

THE DISINTEGRATION OF UNIVERSAL EMPIRES

a. Private Control of Wealth and Resources

Although the early empires achieved power by a combination of military domination, administrative efficiency, and persuasive ideology, they were secure only so long as they could prevent the formation of independent aristocracies in the provinces. In the long run, this proved to be an impossibility. The imperial bureaucracies were spread thin, the populations subject to their authority were diverse and very large, and they had to operate over great distances. Units of local administration had therefore to obtain the cooperation of influential landowning or commercial families in order to carry out their functions of taxation, conscription, and preservation of order. In this situation, local elites gained in power at the expense of imperial authority, and they used this power in their own interest to refuse to contribute their proper share of taxes and services. The burden of supporting the state was shifted to those towns and villages that were still accessible to the tax collectors, and this in turn encouraged the residents of these communities to place themselves under the protection of locally powerful families, still further eroding the economic foundations of the state. The concentration of wealth in private hands was accelerated by the expansion of trade within and across imperial frontiers. Profits made in trade could be invested in land and in agricultural manpower. The exploitation of peasants and artisans by wealthy families was worsened by the state's inability to protect them, and this contributed to mass unrest.

b. Regional Organization of Political and Military Power: Feudal Tendencies

Armed might was the ultimate sanction of political authority. When military power escaped from official control and passed into private or independent hands, then the government was powerless to override local resistance to its laws and commands. Great families, or groups of families, used their wealth and their economic control over large segments of the population to develop private armies. These in turn were used both to defy the central government and to engage one another in struggles for regional domination. In these circumstances, competition among independent military leaders sometimes resulted in the breakdown of imperial regimes and the reorganization of the old empire on the basis of a feudal or semifeudal distribution of authority among agencies of imperial government and regional groupings of entrenched power holders. The balance between imperial and local power will be seen to have varied, however, between regions and in different periods.

c. Popular Unrest

The difficulty with which imperial governments were faced in attempting to control local elites was sometimes matched by the difficulty with which both of these groups maintained control over the peasants and artisans. The common people normally had the alternatives of maintaining themselves on small private plots or allotments and bearing a disproportionate share of the tax and service burden of the state or placing themselves under the protection of great private households. In the latter case, they paid for the gain in security by land rents, sharecropping, usury, enserfment, or the sale of their labor. Private estates and peasant villages were not always able to employ all the labor available, however. New areas might be brought under cultivation, but this required heavy investment of manpower and resources. As a result, large numbers of people, especially in periods of natural disasters, left their villages and towns to live as bandits or rebels. Sometimes they made common cause with foreign enemies of the state in frontier areas. The presence of large numbers of uprooted people with no secure place in the social order enlarged the scope and increased the intensity of disorders within the empire. At times, however, it played into the hands of the central government when imperial authorities were able to settle them in agricultural colonies on virgin or abandoned lands, thereby enlarging the tax base.

d. Formation of Frontier States

The long-term establishment of civilized society based on agriculture and town life in areas suitable for agriculture had gone hand in hand with the development of pastoral nomadism in the areas of natural grasslands that were either too deficient in rainfall and surface and underground water or too steeply pitched for successful farming. The longest frontiers between these contrasting kinds of economy and society were in northeastern Iran and northern and northwestern China. Because neither geography nor the techniques of agriculture and husbandry lent themselves to precise delineation of boundaries between settled and pastoral society, the frontiers tended to become zones of interpenetration and interaction between farmers and townsmen on the one hand and the herdsmen on the other. Through trade, politics, and war, one group or another might take advantage of the great distance from the centers of imperial power to establish frontier states. The frontier states constituted a formidable threat to the empires when they were able to combine the military skills and manpower of a large section of the pastoral population in the frontier region and in the steppes beyond with the economic resources of a large agricultural population. At the very least, the frontier states confined the empires within constricted borders, and in some cases they were able to conquer and reorganize entire civilized societies.

TRADITION AND INNOVATION

e. Imperial Successor States

The notion of the successor state implies something more than the mere fact that one regime followed another in a given society. The term also implies that the founders of the later regimes regarded themselves as having restored legitimate political authority and that they were the proper inheritors of the old order. It is important to understand that this was the case whether the new regime was created by conquest, rebellion, or palace coup, and whether the founders were indigenous to the inner regions of the empire or were foreigners moving in from the frontier regions. Moreover, a unified empire might be dismembered among a number of rival successor states, all claiming exclusive right to legitimate authority throughout the empire, and conversely, once divided in this fashion among several rival legitimacies, an empire might be reunified by still another successor state. In the course of restoring political authority, the founders of the new regimes often undertook widespread reforms. These might be frankly innovative or, more often, would be presented as a return to the forgotten ways of a past golden age.

f. The Hardening of Imperial Traditions

During the decline of the first empires and under the rule of their successor states, the formal aspects of government, such as official terminology, law codes, court ceremonial, and ideology, came to be sanctified and made orthodox. Some of the scholarship patronized by the rulers or by ecclesiastical hierarchies was committed to the copying, editing, and explanation of important texts with the aim of getting the imperial tradition into its "correct" form and transmitting it to succeeding generations without further change. In such cases, the idea of a golden age that existed long before the establishment of the first empires now was transformed into an anachronistic and pedantically detailed blueprint. This represented one possible response to the challenge of social and economic changes taking place within the civilized societies. Although this was doomed to fail in the long run because mere verbal or symbolic assertions of tradition could not arrest the course of change, the tradition continued to have a distinct, if limited, value in politics. New regimes and new policies were more readily accepted by people who were unable to imagine any alternative to the dispensation of the universal empire when they were presented to them as a restoration of the old order rather than as novel improvements. Even the leaders of some popular rebellions legitimized their movements in terms of traditional ideology.

g. Unorthodox Alternatives

Before the formation of the first empires, the major civilizations had produced a wide range of intellectual perspectives and philosophical systems. As the first empires declined and then gave way to successor states, thinkers who were not committed to the orthodoxies of their time had rich and varied resources to draw upon in their efforts to find alternatives. Some were engaged in the search for new or more useful principles of government and social order, while others turned aside from society and withdrew to speculate on the human condition, unencumbered by public responsibilities.

The intellectual and aesthetic excitement of this period may have been in part a consequence of the course of empire in the Asian civilizations. The very scale of political organization and the constant movement of great numbers of people—officials, armies, colonists, merchants, and fugitives—from one region to another all combined to break down cultural parochialism. At least in the more urbanized settings, a cosmopolitan spirit flourished and traditional concepts and values were examined from new perspectives, criticized, and refined. Even the vicissitutes of imperial dynasties, including their overthrow and their replacement by new regimes, inspired deeper examination of the principles of social and political order and of the nature and destiny of man.

PATTERNS

1. THE PARTHIANS AND SASANIDS IN WEST ASIA

The Achaemenid empire was overthrown by Alexander the Great in 331-330 B.C. After his death, the majority of the former imperial satrapies passed into the hands of one of his Macedonian generals, Seleucus, who, like Alexander himself, had taken an Iranian wife and who now began to construct a new imperial edifice founded upon a combination of Macedonian and Iranian traditions. The short-lived Seleucid empire lasted from 312 B.C. to sometime around 250 B.C. Its long-term impact was not very great but under the rule of the Seleucids, Hellenistic civilization did penetrate farther east than ever before. Alexander had founded Greek colonial cities wherever he had gone, including at least three within the frontiers of what is now modern Afghanistan, and the Seleucids followed his example.

The Seleucid empire was overthrown by the Parthians, the first of two exceptionally long-lived dynasties that dominated the Iranian plateau and the greater part of Mesopotamia for almost nine centuries. The Parthians ruled from around 248 B.C. down to 224 A.D., when the last of their many kings was killed in battle fighting the founder of the Sasanid dynasty, Ardashir. The Sasanid empire was one of the most powerful and belligerent regimes ever to control the Iranian plateau and the eastern part of the Fertile Crescent, ruling from 224 A.D. to 651 A.D., when the dynasty succumbed to the Muslim Arabs.

The Parthians were a nomadic people of Iranian stock, culturally akin to the Saka tribes then occupying the greater part of the Eurasian steppe zone. Their most recent homeland prior to their conquest of the Seleucid empire seems to have been the region south of the Aral Sea along the lower Amu Darya, where they had been horse and cattle breeders, but during the middle decades of the third century B.C. they began to advance southwestward into the Seleucid satrapy of Parthia, the area now comprising southern Turkmenistan and the Iranian province of Gurgan, due east of the Caspian. They were led by two brothers, Arsaces and Tiridates, and although the former (from whom the Parthian royal house was known to the Greeks as Arsacids) was killed in battle around 248 B.C., Tiridates continued the advance across the Elburz Mountains, establishing his headquarters at Hecatompylos (the site of which has been tentatively identified near Damghan) east of Tehran. From this vantage point he began the systematic conquest of the Iranian plateau, a task completed by Mithradates I (r. ca. 171-138 B.C.), whose rule eventually extended from the Euphrates in the west as far as the vicinity of Herat in modern Afghanistan and Marv in Soviet Central Asia. His successors, recognizing the fiscal, commercial, and strategic importance of Mesopotamia, established the Parthian winter capital at Ctesiphon on the Tigris, close to the flourishing commercial entrepot of Seleucia, while Ecbatana (Hamadan) was retained as a summer capital.

During the 360 years that followed the death of Mithradates I, the Parthian empire experienced violent fluctuations in its political history, periods of vigorous expansion being followed by periods of foreign invasion, bloodthirsty struggles for the throne, and protracted civil wars. One brilliant phase of consolidation and expansion occurred during the reign of Mithradates II (ca. 123-87 B.C.), who succeeded to the throne after a period of acute internal dislocation and who managed to drive off the waves of Saka invaders who at the time were threatening the northeastern marches of the empire. Another such period occurred during the second half of the first century B.C., a period that opened with the destruction of the Roman legions at Carrhae in 53 B.C., one of the greatest defeats ever inflicted upon the Romans by any of their foes.

During the first two centuries of their rule, the Parthians appear to have been greatly attracted towards Greek culture. Greek was used as an administrative *lingua franca* and was inscribed on the coinage, and must have been widely spoken by the ruling elite. Later, the long conflict with Rome seems to have diminished the Parthians' appetite for Hellenistic civilization, causing them to turn back to the Iranian part of their heritage, and this trend can be clearly seen from the reign of Vologeses I (51-80 A.D.), who seems to have inaugurated a deliberate policy of Iranicization. During the last century and a half of Parthian rule, a period of disastrous wars with the Romans in which Ctesiphon was three times captured by the enemy, even greater stress was laid on identification with the Iranian past. But the policy must have been initiated too late or have been undertaken too halfheartedly, for the dynasty was eventually overthrown by a revolt that stressed both the alien nature of Parthian rule and the indigenous origin of the leader of the uprising, Ardashir.

Ardashir's family was closely associated with the province of Fars, the homeland of the Achaemenids. His grandfather, Sasan (hence the name of the dynasty), had been a hereditary priest in the temple of the goddess Anahita at Istakhr, near Persepolis, and his father, Papak, had married the daughter of a local ruler, had then engineered a coup against his father-in-law, and had eventually taken his place. Ardashir himself was thus a person of considerable local importance, a warrior-leader sprung from a family enjoying great prestige on account of its sacerdotal background. His rebellion against his Parthian overlord was expressed in terms of a narrow particularist patriotism and a harking back to Achaemenid times.

The rule of the Sasanids, although far more stable than that of the Parthians, also alternated between periods of spectacular military success and great material affluence and periods of foreign invasion, internal rebellion, and national humiliation. The reigns of Ardashir (224–ca. 239 A.D.) and his son, Shapur I (ca. 239-272 A.D.), were periods of territorial expansion and vigorous internal consolidation. Another great period was the long reign of Shapur II (309-379 A.D.). Later, from the middle of the fifth to the middle of the sixth

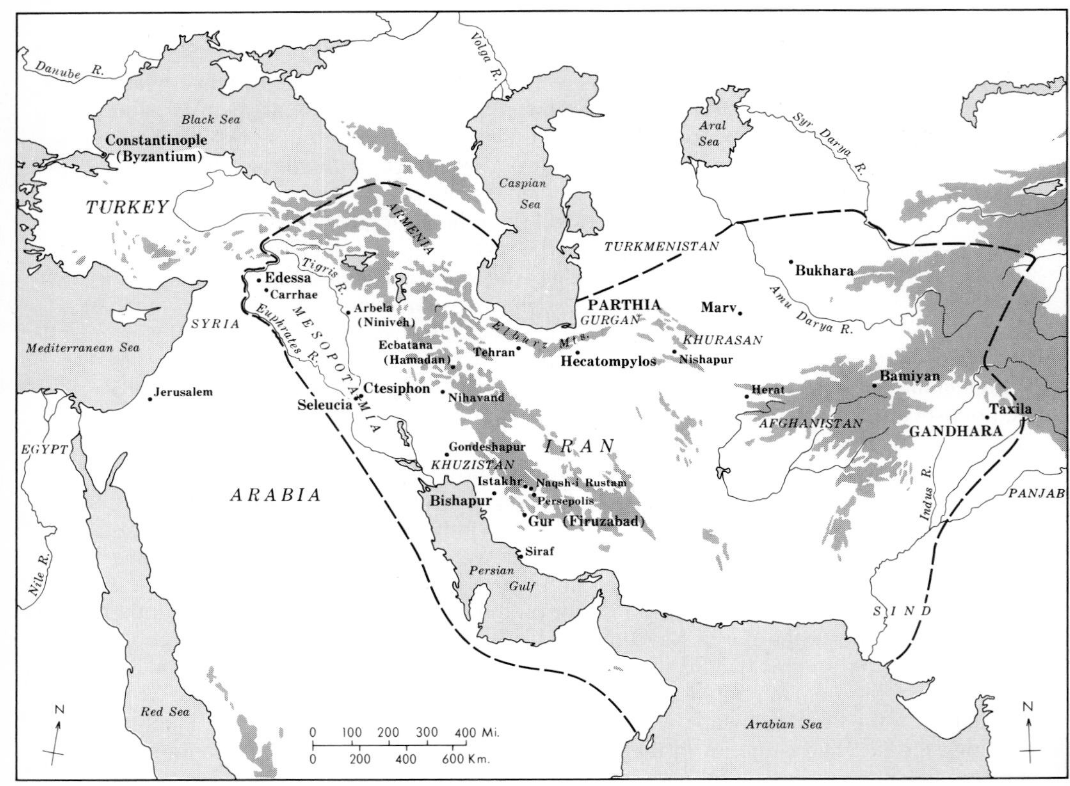

Map 19 The Sasanid empire under Shapur I, about 239-272 B.C.

century, the empire lay more or less at the mercy of the Hephthalites, or White Huns, who threatened its frontiers from the northeast, across the Amu Darya. Then, during the reign of Khusru I Anushirwan (531-579 A.D.), there was a short-lived revival of past glory under the rule of the man who became, for later ages, a byword for magnificence, wisdom, and justice.

The death of Khusru's successor was followed by one of those recurrent struggles for power at court that characterized the political life of the Sasanid empire no less than that of the Parthian. The central figure in this particular upheaval was a military commander of outstanding talent, Bahram Chubin, who later became a figure of folklore and was claimed as an ancestor by the Muslim Samanid dynasty in tenth century Bukhara. Another and much more famous figure in later literature and legend was Khusru II Parviz (r. 590-628 A.D.), the last great figure in the history of the Sasanid dynasty. During his reign, Iranian armies advanced westward to within sight of Constantinople itself, in addition to capturing Jerusalem and invading Egypt. But these triumphs were followed by no less spectacular disasters—a crushing defeat at the hands of the Byzantine emperor, Heraclius, at Arbela on the site of the ancient Nineveh, the siege of Ctesiphon by a Byzantine army, and the deposition and murder of the shahanshah, or "king of kings," by his outraged nobles. For centuries afterwards, Islamic writers would continue to evoke the name of Khusru Parviz, the mighty infidel ruler whose reign had spanned the lifetime of the Prophet Muhammad, as an example of the mutability of human affairs. Even more famous was the legend of his love for his beautiful Christian wife, Shirin, which gave him a place among the celebrated lovers of Islamic folklore. By the beginning of the seventh century A.D., however, the empire itself was utterly exhausted as a result of disastrous foreign wars and grinding taxation and was disintegrating from within as a result of acute social tensions. In consequence, resistance to the Arab invaders was halfhearted and not very effective. Ctesiphon fell in 636, and in 642 the Arabs won a resounding victory at Nihavand, near Hamadan, which opened the entire Iranian plateau to their armies. In 651 the last ruler of the Sasanid dynasty, a refugee in Khurasan, was murdered by one of his own subjects and Iran became an appanage of the Arab empire of the caliphs.

Organization of Political and Military Power

A striking feature of Parthian and, to a lesser extent, of Sasanid rule was the emergence of what may loosely be termed feudal tendencies, not in the medieval European sense of a system of land tenures linked to military service, but in the sense of a decentralized royal authority competing with a nobility, whether landholding and sedentary or pastoral and nomadic, which enjoyed substantial local autonomy because it provided the military infrastructure without which the central government would have collapsed. For this reason, if for no other, the nobility or a part of the nobility intervened in the affairs of the empire whenever the central government seemed suitably ineffective, in order to further its particular local or class interests. It would, however, be unwise to contrast the feudal tendencies of Parthian and Sasanid times with the supposedly centralizing policy of the Achaemenids. Under all three dynasties, strong rulers strove to impose their will upon a refractory nobility, while weak ones made what terms they could with the various combinations of the great families, in order to survive.

At the time when the Parthians entered Iran, the traditions of pastoral-nomadic life must still have been very strong among them. The Arsacids themselves were not so much the leaders of a people as of confederate tribes and clans ruled by their own chieftains. These latter, who probably regarded any growth of Arsacid power and influence with mixed feelings, came to form the turbulent higher nobility, among whom seven great families, generation after generation, monopolized the great offices of state, the provincial governorships, and the military commands. So far as it can now be reconstructed, the internal history of the Parthian empire down to the close of the first century B.C. took the form of a constant oscillation between a throne bent on consolidation of its authority and a nobility determined to prevent that consolidation at almost any price. Thereafter, however, the centrifugal forces seem to have won the day. In any case, the loose structure of Parthian provincial government encouraged an excessive devolution of authority, especially in the frontier regions. Like the Achaemenids before them and, to a lesser extent, the Sasanids after them, the Parthians permitted the survival of client kingdoms, of which Armenia is probably the best known because of its contacts with the Romans. Client rulers were required to recognize Arsacid overlordship, pay tribute or revenue, and contribute military levies, but otherwise they did very much as they pleased.

The Parthian army was made up exclusively of cavalry, well suited either for rapid offensive raids into enemy territory or for harrying defensive tactics over vast tracts of arid wasteland. The cavalry consisted of both heavy and light units, the former wearing laminated armor and therefore presumably recruited from among the nobility and their retainers. The heavy cavalry carried a long lance as chief weapon, although probably most of these troops were also armed with bows. The light cavalry consisted of mounted archers who wore no armor and who were dressed in a long tunic, baggy trousers, and a flowing cape. These were the famous Parthian archers so feared by the Romans; their favorite tactic was to advance to the attack, feign a retreat, and then, when the enemy was in full pursuit, shoot flights of arrows at their pursuers from across the backs of their horses as they rode off at a gallop. Probably only a fraction of the army in the field at any one time was made up of

5.1 Shapur I (ca. 239-272 A.D.) receiving the submission of two Roman emperors, from a bas-relief at Naqsh-i Rustam, near Persepolis. Philip, who was forced to make a humiliating peace with Iran, kneels at Shapur's feet while the captive Valerian stands before his conqueror, who firmly grasps him by the wrist. Source: G. Rawlinson, *The Seventh Great Oriental Monarchy* (London, 1876).

troops directly under the command of the king. The rest were in the service of members of the nobility, towards whom they probably felt far closer ties than they did towards the king. It followed, therefore, that their performance against the enemy depended very much on the attitudes and interests of their own leaders.

The weaknesses of Parthian rule, with its decentralized administration and its turbulent ruling elite, were fully understood by Ardashir and Shapur I when they set about consolidating their hold over the empire. Their prime concern was to introduce centralization, both in the civil and military aspects of government, and they set out to establish a relatively elaborate bureaucratic structure, both at the center and in the provinces. A hierarchy of officials was created, answerable to separate secretariats for finance, justice, military affairs, and so forth, with the whole organization in the charge of a chief minister, whom some historians have seen as the prototype of the later Muslim *vazir.* The revenues of the empire were obtained from several sources, including the taxation of commerce and income derived from crown lands and mines. The principal source of revenue, however, was the produce of the land, of which the state claimed an annual share. For most of the Sasanid period it appears that the method of collection was crop sharing at harvesttime, but the system was overhauled during the reign of Khusru Anushirwan, who ordered fixed assessments based on prior estimates of the annual yield. This, in turn, involved the introduction of cadastral surveys and the maintenance of elaborate records. On the basis of the available evidence, it appears that Sasanid fiscal administration achieved a high degree of efficiency and, like other aspects of Sasanid government, served as a model for later Islamic regimes.

Sasanid provincial administration reverted more to the pattern of Achaemenid times than to anything known under the Parthians, and there appears to have been a conscious attempt to avoid depending on the great families for the government of outlying areas, just as there also appears to have been an attempt to diminish the number of client rulers and subkings. During the reign of Shapur I the empire was divided into twenty-seven provinces, and these were administered either by officers personally appointed by the shahanshah or by members of the imperial house. In the east, however, a great viceroyalty had been formed during the reign of Ardashir as a result of the victories won by the heir apparent, the future Shapur I, over the Kushanas. Thereafter it became customary for the Sasanid crown prince to administer this area as an appanage, taking the high-sounding title of kushanshah. His charge consisted of the country bordering the upper reaches of the Amu Darya and the greater part of modern Afghanistan, extending perhaps to the Indus. Elsewhere, the command of exposed frontier regions was given to an official known as a *marzban,* a warden of the marches, whose importance seems to have increased progressively during the later Sasanid period.

The military decentralization of Parthian times was also countered by the Sasanids in the appointment of a single commander in chief, who was invariably a member of the imperial family. Later, Khusru Anushirwan replaced the single commander in chief by four regional commanders with the intention of reducing the concentration of power, but the cure proved worse than the complaint. Unlike the Parthian army, the Sasanid army did not consist exclusively of cavalry but included infantry units and war elephants, the latter indicative of close contacts with the Indian subcontinent. The cavalry, however, remained the most important arm, being divided between heavily armed horsemen carrying long lances and wearing laminated armor and lightly armed, highly mobile mounted archers. The heavy cavalryman, despite his lack of stirrups, must have been a most formidable opponent and has often been described as the forerunner of the medieval knight of Christian Europe, with his powerful horse and his costly armor. The Sasanid army in the field was often accompanied by contingents provided by the various client rulers, such as the king of Armenia, or by subsidiary allies, such as the king of the Chionite Huns in the reign of Shapur II.

It would probably be fallacious to suppose that the Sasanid empire achieved a high degree of centralization. In practice, the higher nobility, whether tribal chieftains or great landholders, continued to play a very active part in imperial affairs, while the lesser nobility, the *dihqans,* steadily consolidated and expanded their position at a local level throughout the period. One explanation for the continuing predominance of the nobility in the face of concerted efforts at centralization must be attributed to the fact that the shahanshah needed the nobility more than the nobility needed the shahanshah. As in the Parthian period, this was because the empire's relations with neighboring regimes and the problems of frontier defense necessitated frequent military operations costly in revenue and manpower.

Foreign Relations and Frontier Problems

The Parthian and the Sasanid dynasties were expansionist and predatory, and both were surrounded by equally belligerent foes. One significant factor in their external relations was the geographical position of Mesopotamia and the Iranian plateau lying athwart the trade routes that linked East Asia, Central Asia, and South Asia to the basin of the Mediterranean and the surrounding regions. Commercial intercourse between the Chinese and Roman empires, for example, involved either crossing territory belonging to the shahanshah or bypassing it by taking a much longer route across the steppes north of the Caspian Sea or across the Arabian Sea from Sind to Egypt. Naturally, the rulers of Iran endeavored to turn this favorable geographical location to their own advantage by levying tolls on the goods passing through their territories, especially the silk bound for the Roman world, which was brought from China along the famous Silk Road through Central Asia. This policy of taxing the transit trade through Iran provoked deep resentment and a search for alternative trade routes. The Iranian government responded by establishing an indigenous silk industry in Khuzistan, not without considerable success.

Due presumably to commercial considerations, the Sasanids also sought to establish their hegemony in the Persian Gulf and to acquire a predominant position in the commerce of the coastal areas bordering the Arabian Sea. Thus Khusru Anushirwan regarded an Ethiopian invasion of the Yemen as being so detrimental to Iranian interests that he even sent an expedition to southern Arabia to expel the invaders. A growing amount of evidence, much of it derived from recent excavations at the site of the port of Siraf on the coast of Fars, suggests that maritime trade was of very great importance in the economic life of the Sasanid empire. It is possible, although at the present time still unproved, that the Sasanids were hardly less of a great power at sea than they were on land.

The land frontiers of Parthian and Sasanid Iran were of enormous length, and they were undefined in the modern sense. These open frontiers constituted no barrier to the pastoral nomadic groups who seasonally crossed them in search of pastures and who acknowledged no ruler other than their own chieftains, except out of necessity or short-term expediency. On the Mesopotamian frontier, where the Iranian sphere of influence adjoined the Roman sphere of influence, or on the northeastern marches with the steppe world, there were broad stretches of country that offered no favorable terrain on which to confront an invading foe.

For the Parthians the major foe was Rome, with whom they engaged in direct conflict in Mesopotamia and Syria. In the mountainous country to the north, however, where the frontiers of modern Turkey and Iran converge with the Soviet Union, they sought to advance their own frontier or to withstand further Roman probing by means of client kingdoms, such as Armenia, which invariably bargained with both sides for the most favorable terms. On the northeast frontier the Parthians were at first confronted by the nomadic Saka tribes advancing from the steppe zone of Central Asia. Mithradates II at the beginning of the first century B.C. deflected them so that they turned southeastward in the direction of the Indus, but at the close of the same century a powerful nomadic confederacy, that of the Kushanas, established a vast empire stretching from the southern shores of the Aral Sea as far as Bihar in northern India. This constituted a permanent threat to the Parthians at the very time when their struggle with Rome was beginning to take an unfavorable turn.

Under the Sasanids, external threats diminished somewhat in seriousness, largely because the new dynasty was better able to cope with them. Against both the Kushanas and the Romans the early Sasanids won impressive victories, which also assisted them in consolidating their hold over the former Parthian territories and in legitimizing their seizure of power. In the case of the Kushanas, their empire was already in decline by the third century A.D. and Ardashir's son, the future Shapur I, seems to have been able to annex all the remaining Kushana territory west of the Indus without much difficulty. In the west, Shapur's achievements were even more impressive. He inflicted humiliations on the Romans far exceeding anything achieved by the Parthians. One Roman emperor was murdered in camp, another was compelled to sue for peace, and a third (Valerian) was actually taken prisoner. In later reigns the fortunes of war fluctuated between spectacular successes and ignominious failures, but the long-term consequences of these interminable wars was to sap the vigor of both antagonists—of the Sasanids in holding back the Huns and other steppe peoples to the north, of the Byzantines (after Constantinople replaced Rome as the capital of the Roman empire in 330 A.D.) in dealing with the Germanic and other invaders of Italy and the Balkans, and of both in confronting the Arabs.

Internal Unrest

Conspiracies and revolts by the nobility of the Parthian and Sasanid empires were all too frequent. Evidence for lower-class uprisings centers on the so-called Mazdakite movement of the first half of the sixth century A.D., which seems to have been a reaction to the oppressive and exploitive character of late Sasanid society. This was due not only to the heavy cost of foreign wars, of keeping the Huns at bay, and of maintaining the imperial court, the nobility, and the Zoroastrian church, but also to the basic structure of Sasanid society. It seems probable that the Sasanids, reacting from the outset to the recognizable weaknesses of late Parthian society, endeavored to establish a social system in which the entire population (excluding, presumably, slaves) was divided into four orders, or estates. These consisted of (1) the Zoroastrian priesthood, including judges; (2) the military; (3) officials, scribes, physicians, and men of learning; and (4) merchants, artisans, and cultivators. This division, reminiscent of the Hindu caste system but also of the functional division of society in the later Roman empire, is described in a major source, the *Letter of Tansar,* which has survived only in much later Persian and (partial) Arabic recensions. The *Letter of Tansar,* which is attributed to the reign of Ardashir but more probably reflects conditions under Khusru Anushirwan, declared that every person in the empire was born into a particular class or caste and that without the shahanshah's permission there could be no change of status or occupation. Undoubtedly the intention was to freeze society into formal divisions, but in practice Sasanid society, although strongly hierarchical, must have been, like Hindu society during the same period, much more flexible and complex than official spokesmen for the regime cared to recognize.

Throughout the Sasanid period there appears to have been a steady deterioration in the condition of the free cultivator, who, especially during the final two centuries of Sasanid rule, was being inexorably reduced to the status of a serf, no longer working on his own land but on land belonging to the king, to a great nobleman, to the Zoroastrian clergy, or to a *dihqan.* Taxation grew increasingly burdensome, while at least during the last phase of the empire the nobility enjoyed complete exemption. It was against a background of grinding fiscal extortion and the involuntary transfer of land from cultivators to landholders that there occurred the movement of social upheaval associated with the name of Mazdak. He remains an obscure figure, but seems to have preached a new religion, probably a variant of Manichaeanism, which contained powerful undercurrents of social protest against the greed and selfishness of the ruling classes. Apparently he won the confidence of the long-reigning Kavad (488-496 and 499-531 A.D.), who as a child had been a hostage with the Huns and who, when temporarily driven from his throne by rebellious nobles, fled to them again and returned with their support. At some period in his reign and with Mazdak beside him in the role of confidential adviser, he began to introduce radical reforms to alleviate the sufferings of the lower classes, allegedly at Mazdak's instigation and presumably in response to broad-based manifestations of discontent. The outcome of this was a widespread uprising against the throne by the nobles and clergy, with the heir apparent, Khusru Anushirwan, at their head. Kavad was compelled to reverse his former policies and to pursue a more conventional line of territorial aggrandizement. Mazdak was executed, his followers massacred, and the Mazdakite books burned.

Like other revolutionary movements that have threatened the established order, the

Mazdakites were accused by their foes of attempting to destroy the basic fabric of society. In particular, they were accused of confiscating land belonging to the nobles and distributing it to the peasants, and also of seizing the women in the nobles' harems and sharing them communally. The emphasis on these two activities in the few surviving notices of the Mazdakite movement indicates two major grievances of the period: the consolidation of small holdings into great estates accompanied by the imposition of serfdom upon cultivators who formerly tilled their own fields, and the incarceration of large numbers of women in the households of the nobles. Khusru Anushirwan, although he proved a ruthless persecutor of the Mazdakites, endeavored to introduce a more efficient and equitable system of land revenue administration. The long-term success of these measures may not have been very great. Nearly a century and a half separates the Mazdakite movement from the Arab conquest of the mid-seventh century, yet the kind of social distress manifested during the reign of Kavad was probably endemic during the century preceding the fall of the empire. This would go far toward explaining why the Arabs met with so little resistence when they eventually occupied the Iranian plateau.

The Tradition of Empire

Both the Parthians and the Sasanids saw themselves as heirs to the imperial tradition of the Achaemenids and as heirs to a mystique of kingship in which the fortunes both of the shahanshah and of the kingdom itself were traced back to legendary dynasties that had preceded the Achaemenids. It was the achievements ascribed to these legendary dynasties that occupied so much of the folklore of Iran and of the national epic written in the early eleventh century, the *Shah-nama* of Firdawsi. In all the heroic tales of ancient Iran, including those describing the exploits of Rustam, a warrior with attributes similar to Hercules, the institution of monarchy was given a prominence unusual even in societies similarly constituted to that of pre-Islamic Iran. There was, for example, a special word, *farr,* which connoted a ruler's inherent qualities of kingliness and his enjoyment of divine favor, attributes that were applied to such figures as Ardashir, Shapur I, and Khusru Anushirwan.

As foreign invaders the Parthians were somewhat slow to identify with Achaemenid traditions of monarchy and empire, and it does not appear that the title of shahanshah was used extensively before the second half of the first century A.D., a period of self-conscious identification with native Iranian, as opposed to Hellenistic, traditions. The Parthian royal house was also surprisingly slow to invent a spurious genealogy linking it with the Achaemenids. The Sasanids, however, went out of their way to stress imperial continuities, as was to be expected of a dynasty of priestly origin coming from the homeland of the Achaemenids. They assumed the title of shahanshah, claimed blood relationship with the Achaemenids from centuries before, and did everything possible not only to discredit the former Arsacid dynasty but even to erase all memory of it.

More significant than genealogy was the way in which the Sasanids self-consciously identified with the Achaemenid empire and sought to preserve its traditions. There was an almost antiquarian respect for the past and for the "golden age" of Darius the Great. Sasanid rock carvings and architecture were a propagandist art, especially in the way in which they glorified and idealized the ruling dynasty, and they owed much to Achaemenid example. The Sasanids, like the Achaemenids, seem to have attached great significance to the vicinity of Naqsh-i Rustam, near Persepolis, where most of the Achaemenid rulers had built their tombs, and it was at that site in particular, as well as in other less prominent locations, that Ardashir and Shapur I ordered the carving of bas-reliefs in which the former was shown being invested as shahanshah by Ahura Mazda and in which the latter was portrayed triumphing over his Roman enemies. Not surprisingly, Sasanid promotion of the traditions of earlier times led them to support and encourage Zoroastrianism, which from the very beginning of the Sasanid period was deliberately molded into a state church responsive to the needs of the dynasty.

The Crystallization of Tradition

The Sasanids showed a marked tendency towards pursuing traditionalist policies, partly perhaps as a reaction to the anarchy of the late Parthian period and partly, too, in consequence of their own sacerdotal origins. It has already been stressed how they endeavored to establish an immobile hierarchy of functional castes. Likewise, they patronized Zoroastrianism, presumably on the grounds that the Zoroastrian clergy was the most cohesive and influential group able to provide legitimation for the new dynasty, and also perhaps because the new regime regarded the priesthood as an obvious source of manpower from which to recruit judges and officials.

Under the Parthians, who appear to have been distinctly eclectic in religious matters, Iranian religion in general displayed a thoroughly syncretistic character. Zoroastrianism, still in all likelihood a fairly amorphous set of beliefs and rituals, continued to be less important than the cult worship of Ahura Mazda, Mithra and, most important of all, the goddess Anahita. Under the Sasanids, however, a change took place, Zoroastrianism becoming a ferociously aggressive state church, preoccupied with the power and prestige of its priesthood and determined to eliminate would-be rivals. This process seems to have occurred early in the Sasanid period, the key figure in the transformation being a Zoroastrian priest named Kartir, who, during an extended period of great influence, served as royal adviser, supreme judge and, eventually, high priest. In an important inscription of his, uncovered at Naqsh-i Rustam, his ecclesiastical policy can be seen to have been the extirpation of all rival religions, the building of fire temples and fire altars throughout the empire, and the establishment of regional hierarchies of priests. From this time forward the emphasis was on traditionalism accompanied by fear of innovation, and for the lay population, conformity and obedience to clerical authority reinforced by considerable missionary activity and the vigorous persecution of all other sects. Much energy was also expended in compiling an orthodox canon of sacred texts.

Alternative Orthodoxies

Sasanid Iran was a plural religious society, which, apart from the official Zoroastrian church, sustained Christian, Jewish, Manichaean, and Buddhist communities as well as remnants of much older sects. Nestorian Christianity, in particular, constituted a formidable threat to Zoroastrianism and was regarded as such by the Zoroastrian clergy, which savagely persecuted what must have been a substantial minority. The conversion of the Roman empire to Christianity during the fourth century A.D. further undermined the position of the shahanshah's Christian subjects, who could now be presented as agents of a foreign power, and under Shapur II, in particular, many were massacred at the shahanshah's instigation. Later, when the Nestorian church asserted its independence from Constantinople towards the close of the fifth century, the status of the Christian subjects of the empire improved. An ecclesiastical hierarchy headed by a Catholicos in Ctesiphon gave the community an institutional framework, and it is a measure of the vitality of the Nestorian church that much energy was spent in missionary activity in Central Asia. Even at the imperial court Christian influences at times manifested themselves regardless of the political situation, partly because several rulers had Christian women in their harems, some of whom enjoyed a visible political ascendancy.

Another challenge to Zoroastrianism was posed by Manichaeanism, a dualistic faith founded by the prophet Mani, who was born around 216 A.D., his father originating from Hamadan in western Iran and his mother allegedly being related to the Arsacids. Mani's teachings centered on a dualistic concept of human life as a ceaseless struggle between the forces of good and evil, the light and the dark, and, like the original Zoroaster, he was apparently more concerned with ethics than with ritual or belief. Shapur I seems to have been very favorably disposed towards him, permitting him to travel through the empire propagating his beliefs and to send his missionaries far beyond the frontiers of Iran. After Shapur's death in 272 A.D., however, the Zoroastrian clergy began a concerted assault upon the Manichaeans, who were apparently growing in number. Mani himself died in prison, presumably murdered, and his followers were massacred wherever they could be found. Many, however, managed to flee beyond the frontiers of the empire and those who escaped along the caravan routes into Central Asia established Manichaean communities in the remote oasis settlements bordering the Takla Makan desert, where they developed a distinctive literature and art and where they remained vigorous enough to bring about the conversion to Manichaeanism of the khaqan of the Uigur Turks and his entourage sometime around 783 A.D. Isolated Manichaean communities may even have survived down to the time of the Mongol conquests of the thirteenth century.

Mazdakism has already been referred to as an offshoot of Manichaeanism and as a vehicle for social protest, and it, too, persecuted in the land of its birth, found its way into the steppes and deserts of Central Asia, where it seems to have had a small following among the Western Turks. Notwithstanding the fierce intolerance of Zoroastrian orthodoxy, Sasanid Iran clearly possessed a remarkable spiritual vitality, exemplified not only in the missionary activities of Nestorians, Manichaeans, Mazdakites and, in all probability, other long-forgotten sects, but even within the Zoroastrian church itself.

Cultural Achievements

Under the Parthians and the Sasanids, Iran was a melting pot of civilizations in which indigenous traditions interacted with influences converging on West Asia from the Hellenistic world to the west, the steppe zone to the north, and the Indian subcontinent to the east. One of the many legends associated with the name of Khusru Anushirwan describes how an Indian raja sent the shahanshah a chess set without indicating how the game should be played. Khusru's physician, Buzurgmihr, a famous figure in Iranian folklore, solved the problem and invented the game of backgammon in order to baffle the raja's brahman ministers. Buzurgmihr is also said to have had a hand in bringing from India to Iran the famous cycle of tales known as *Kalila va Dimna,* which was translated from Sanskrit into Pahlavi (Middle Persian) and eventually into Arabic. This vogue for collections of tales originating in India and translated from Sanskrit into Pahlavi is some indication of the extent to which Sasanid Iran was open to Indian influences.

Official translations were not restricted to pleasure reading but extended to works on medicine, mathematics, and astronomy. In addition to translations from Sanskrit, translations were made from a number of other languages, especially Greek and Syriac. Shapur I founded in Khuzistan the city of Gondeshapur, which throughout the Sasanid period enjoyed a preeminence as a center of learning, especially in medicine. By the time of Khusru Anushirwan in the sixth century, Gondeshapur possessed a full-fledged academy, due partly to the enlightened patronage of the shahanshah himself and partly to fortuitous circumstances—the closing of the Nestorian schools of Edessa in 489 and the flight of the Neoplatonists from Athens after 529. In any event, in the late Sasanid period Gondeshapur was a flourishing home of cosmopolitan culture, which, notwithstanding the upheavals resulting from the Arab conquest of the empire, transmitted an invaluable legacy to the new centers of Islamic learning.

Apart from Arabic and Persian recensions, very little has survived of the original corpus of Pahlavi literature. Such fragments as we have indicate a literature reflecting the tastes of the imperial court and the nobility. One form of composition that seems to have been very popular was the *andarz-nama,* a collection of sayings and anecdotes relating to government, statecraft, and worldly wisdom, which was doubtless a traditional Iranian genre of great antiquity but came to be associated in particular with the period of Khusru Anushirwan. This was a form of literature that helped to shape the later Islamic genre of *adab* literature, or "mirrors for princes." There must also have been a great tradition of epic poetry, now totally lost.

In the arts, the Sasanid achievement, as exemplified in the surviving palaces and fire temples, in the famous bas-reliefs, and in an astonishingly beautiful range of metalware, was a spectacular one. Unfortunately the sumptuous Sasanid textiles have almost all long-since disappeared, although small fragments survive in a few European cathedrals and churches where they were brought in the early Middle Ages, often accompanying precious relics from the East. The Sasanids were also great builders of cities. Ardashir built a circular city at Gur (Firuzabad) in Fars, and although Parthian Ctesiphon was retained as the Sasanid winter capital, Shapur I set an infectious example to his successors with his numerous foundations, including Gondeshapur in Khuzistan, Bishapur in Fars, and Nishapur in Khurasan. During the Islamic period and down to the present day there have been very few major urban settlements on the Iranian plateau whose origins cannot be traced back to Sasanid times, if not earlier.

2. THE KUSHANAS AND GUPTAS IN SOUTH ASIA

The period to be discussed in this section stretches o er eight centuries, from approximately 183 B.C., when Mauryan rule expired in northern India, to 648 A.D., when the great emperor Harsha of Kanauj died without an heir and his empire disintegrated almost immediately. Although the detailed history of this period, including the basic chronology, is a matter of great uncertainty due to the relative paucity of sources, a significant comparison can be made between the course of events in northern India and on the Iranian plateau during almost exactly the same time span.

The Mauryas were overthrown by the short-lived Shunga dynasty (183-73 B.C.), which followed the Mauryan example in choosing Magadha as the core area of its north Indian empire. Unlike the Mauryas, however, the Shungas rejected Buddhism as an imperial ideology and became ardent patrons of Brahmanism. The first ruler of the new dynasty, Pushyamitra Shunga (183-151 B.C.), whose name suggests that he may have originally been an Iranian soldier of fortune, had been the commander in chief of the last Mauryan ruler before he murdered him and seized his throne. Perhaps because he needed the support of the brahmans to justify his usurpation, he restored the old Vedic sacrifices, persecuted the Buddhists, and, indicative of his imperial pretensions, twice performed that greatest of all Vedic rituals, the horse sacrifice (*ashvamedha*), which in addition to being an ancient fertility rite was also an assertion of imperial hegemony over other rulers. Yet even within the lifetime of the first Shunga a new epoch was beginning in the history of northern India, an epoch that was to last for some 470 years and during which the ruling dynasties and ruling elites would be predominantly foreign.

The newcomers came in a succession of waves—Bactrian Greeks, Sakas, Parthians, and Kushanas—entering the subcontinent from the general direction of Central Asia as the Aryans had done centuries before. The languages they brought with them—Greek, Saka, Pahlavi (in the case of the Parthians), and Tocharian—all belonged to the Indo-European group, and it appears as if, after the initial hostile encounter, each overlay of invaders easily assimilated with the preceding one. Once established in India, the newly founded regimes drew strength both from the political heritage of Mauryan times and also from imperial traditions outside the subcontinent—Macedonian, Iranian and, in the case of the Kushanas,

Chinese. Culturally the invaders were very eclectic in their tastes, dress, life-style, religious practices, and patronage of the arts. The civilization that emerged under their rule was exceptionally syncretic and cosmopolitan, with native Indian elements mingling with influences from as far away as Greece and Egypt. Some of these invaders were drawn to Buddhism, and it was partly on account of their political support that Buddhism flourished for so long in northern India and was able to hold its own for so long against the Brahmanism, which always remained the religion of the majority of the population.

In 320 A.D. a native dynasty, the Guptas, founded a north Indian empire that extended from the Arabian Sea to the Bay of Bengal and from the foothills of the Himalayas to the Narbada River and even beyond it. The Gupta empire lasted until 467 A.D. (Gupta rule in a truncated form survived much longer) and can be viewed as an indigenous reaction to centuries of foreign domination in much the same way that the establishment of the Sasanid empire in Iran can be seen as a reaction to centuries of Parthian rule. However, in the last decades of the fifth century and the early decades of the sixth, invading Huns ravaged the northern and western parts of the empire and in so doing brought to an end a period of great material prosperity and cultural achievement. The expulsion of the Huns by a confederacy of Indian rulers was followed by half a century or more of intense rivalry among the various dynasties that endeavored to establish themselves in the vacuum created by the fall of the Guptas and the disappearance of the Huns. Eventually the Gupta empire, at least in outward appearance, was reconstructed by one of the greatest figures in Indian history, Harsha of Kanauj (r. 606-648 A.D.), but his achievement ended with his death, and from the middle of the seventh century until the beginning of the thirteenth century, when the sultanate of Delhi was founded by the Muslim Turks, northern India knew no more universal empires of the kind that had emerged under the Mauryas, the Kushanas, and the Guptas. Instead there followed century after century of ceaseless rivalry among local dynasties too equally balanced in resources to be able to overwhelm each other and so mutually antagonistic that when, in the early eleventh century, invaders once more began to penetrate the Panjab from beyond the Indus, they were incapable of combining in the face of a common threat to their survival.

Foreign Invasion and Imperial Consolidation

The first invaders were Bactrian Greeks, who began to make their way into the Panjab during the reign of Pushyamitra Shunga. The origins of these invaders go back to the second half of the third century B.C., when a powerful Greek kingdom was established by Diodotus I (r. ca. 247-235 B.C.) in Bactria, the area in what is today northern Afghanistan lying between the Hindu Kush Mountains and the upper reaches of the Amu Darya. This was, at that time, the most remote outpost of Greek civilization anywhere in the world, but although the Bactrian Greeks and their descendants, the Indo-Greeks in the Panjab, retained with great tenacity a large measure of their Hellenistic heritage, they were far from being of pure Greek or Macedonian stock, having intermarried with the Iranian Bactrians, who were the indigenous inhabitants of the region, as well as with the Iranian Sogdians, who lived beyond the Amu Darya.

The Bactrian Greeks, although torn by dynastic feuds and internecine rivalries, were strong enough to keep at bay both the Seleucids and, after them, the Parthians. They also advanced across the Hindu Kush Mountains and occupied the Kabul valley, where there were probably already several Greek colonies dating from the time of Alexander. From the Kabul valley their line of advance led either south toward Alexandria-in-Arachosia (Kandahar) or east into Gandhara, the country around modern Peshawar on the upper Indus and the western districts of the Panjab. Probably the first Greek ruler to cross the Indus was Apollodotus 1 (r. ca.167-160 B.C.), whose advance into the Panjab halted the westward probing of Magadhan troops under the command of Pushyamitra Shunga's grandson. Dur-

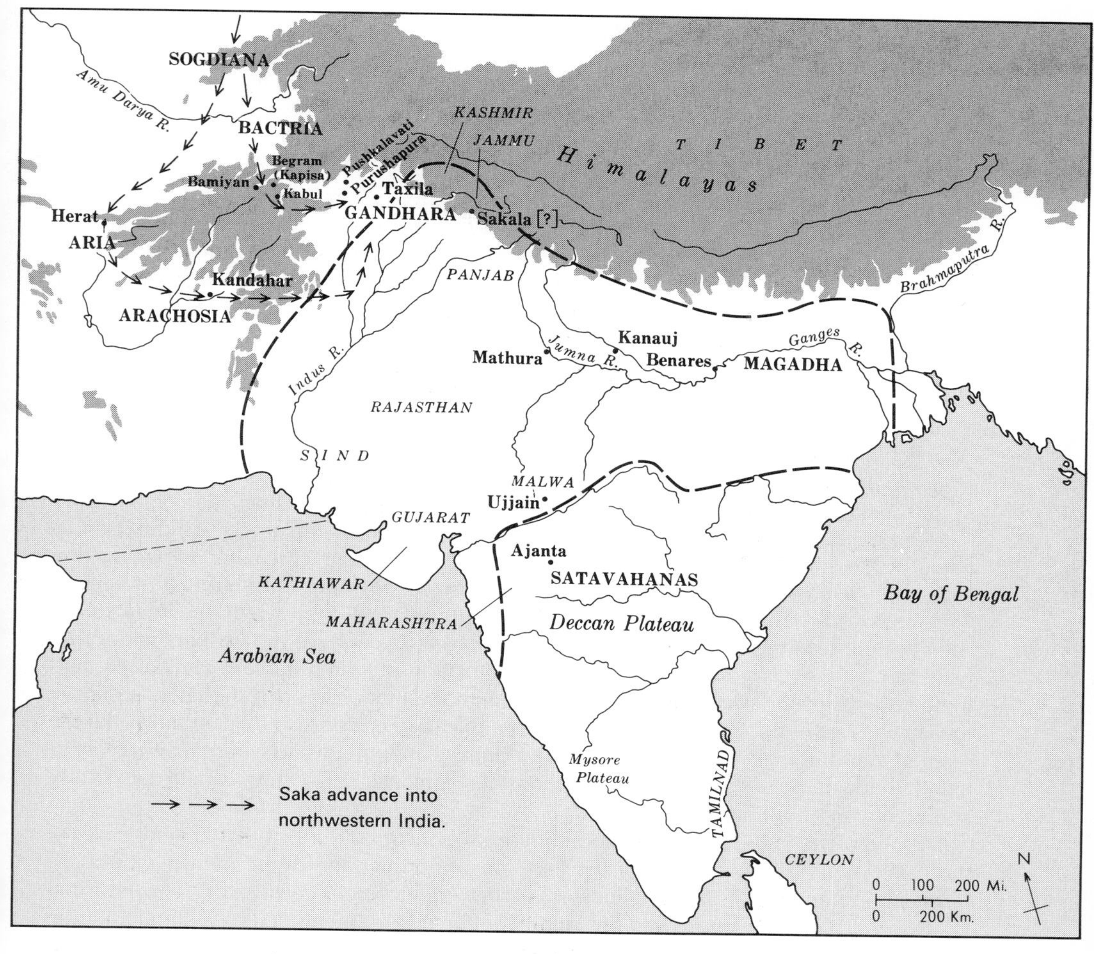

Map 20 The Gupta empire, late fourth century A.D.

ing the next two decades a powerful Greek kingdom was established in Gandhara. The most famous of the Indo-Greek kings was Menander (r. ca. 155-ca. 145), who apparently became a convert to Buddhism (he appears as King Milinda in a celebrated Pali work, the *Milindapanha,* describing how the king was converted by a Buddhist monk from Ceylon) and under whose rule the Indo-Greek kingdom reached its greatest extent. Greek traders and soldiers, however, must have traveled far beyond the frontiers of Menander's kingdom since the Yavanas, as the Greeks were known to the Indians, appear by no means infrequently in the Sanskrit and even Tamil literature of this and the succeeding period.

The Greeks in Bactria were powerful enough to repulse their Seleucid and Parthian neighbors but they could not withstand the pressure applied by the nomadic Sakas to the north, who began advancing south out of Sogdiana and across the Amu Darya during the second half of the second century B.C. Entering Bactria, the Sakas turned southwestward toward the Iranian plateau but were driven off by Mithradates II in the marches of the Parthian empire. They then began a circuitous migration through what is now western and southern Afghanistan, passing through Alexandria-in-Aria (Herat) and Alexandria-in-Arachosia (Kandahar), until they reached the Indus, perhaps somewhere in upper Sind.

Meanwhile, it seems likely that other bands of Sakas had begun to infiltrate into the Kabul valley as auxiliaries in the service of rival Greek rulers. During the first half of the first century B.C. the Sakas swept aside the Indo-Greek kingdom in the Panjab and replaced it with an Indo-Saka kingdom of much greater extent. The first Indo-Saka ruler known from his coinage was Maues (r. 97-ca. 77 B.C.), who may have begun his career as a mercenary of an Indo-Greek king but who, by the time of his death, controlled an area extending from Kandahar eastward to Mathura on the Jumna, with Taxila as his capital. Under his successors—among whom Azes I must have been especially prominent, since a Saka calendar is dated from his first regnal year—the Sakas spread themselves far and wide in northern and western India, presumably in quite considerable numbers. Although they must have intermarried with their Indo-Greek predecessors and also taken Indian women as concubines, they managed to retain a distinct identity for far longer than did any other invaders of this period. This may have been due to the fact that they entered the subcontinent not only in war bands, like the Greeks and the later Parthians, but also as tribal communities. In any event, there can be no doubt that, especially in Gujarat and Malwa, the Sakas survived as a ruling elite throughout the entire period of Kushana and Gupta rule.

At the beginning of the Christian era a new wave of invaders replaced the Indo-Sakas as rulers of the Panjab. These were Parthians, presumably led by chieftains belonging to a cadet line of the imperial Arsacids, who advanced across the Indus from the general direction of Kandahar and eastern Iran. Like the Indo-Sakas, they rapidly assimilated the eclectic culture of the Gandhara region. Excavations at Taxila have shown that their capital was the center of a thoroughly syncretistic civilization in which Iranian, Hellenistic, and Indian elements mingled indiscriminately. As with the Indo-Sakas and the later Kushanas, the chronology of the Indo-Parthians remains a matter of considerable uncertainty, but the reign of the best-known of the Indo-Parthian kings, Gondophares, to whom a Syriac Christian tradition ascribes conversion at the hands of the apostle St. Thomas, can be dated fairly confidently to about 20-46 A.D.

The end of the Indo-Parthian kingdom must have occurred during the middle decades of the first century A.D. as a result of the invasion of northwestern India by a people more formidable than any of their predecessors. These newcomers consisted of a great tribal confederacy, probably composed of a number of diverse elements, led by a dominant tribe or clan known in India as Kushanas. It seems likely that the Kushanas were the ruling group in the nomadic confederacy known to the Chinese as the Yueh-chih and to Western sources as the Tochari. These latter, expelled from their ancestral grazing grounds close to the frontiers of China by the more powerful confederacy of the Hsiung-nu, migrated westward and by the time they reached the area between the Syr Darya and the Amu Darya had absorbed a substantial Saka element and had also undergone some degree of Iranicization (i.e., Sogdianization). Around the time that Gondophares was reigning in Taxila, the Kushanas controlled a vast steppe empire extending from the southern shores of the Aral Sea to the Indus. They soon entered the Panjab and advanced eastward down the Ganges to the vicinity of Benares, their conquests being rounded off and consolidated by Kanishka, one of the most famous names in the history of ancient India. The year of Kanishka's accession remains a subject of heated debate, with the hypothetical date ranging from 78 A.D. to 144 A.D., although the lower figure seems the more probable. Of the later Kushanas, and of their decline as an imperial power, little is known for certain. The process of fragmentation may have been relatively gradual, but its beginning can be dated to around the time of the Sasanid conquest of the Kushana territories west of the Indus, which occurred around 227 A.D. Kushana rule in a truncated form survived the loss of the outlying provinces. A line of Kushana kings continued to reign at Mathura for the best part of a century and to control the western part of the Gangetic plain, although without asserting any serious pretensions to universal empire.

Meanwhile, for the first time since the fall of the Mauryas, an indigenous dynasty set about the task of bringing the whole of northern India under a single imperial rule. Like the Mauryas and the Shungas, the Guptas began the process of empire building from Magadha, where none of the preceding foreign dynasties had held sway, and although they were not unfriendly towards the Buddhists they supported Brahmanism in a way that none of their predecessors between the Shungas and the later Kushanas had done. Like a number of other important Indian dynasties, the Guptas appear to have been of relatively low caste, since they contracted marriages with tribal women and foreigners beyond the pale of the caste system. In other respects, however, they identified with the Hindu great tradition to such an extent that some modern Indian historians regard the Gupta period as constituting the "classical" phase of Hindu civilization.

The first of the Gupta rulers, Chandra Gupta I (r. 320-328 A.D.), laid the foundations upon which his two successors were to build, by establishing a strong power base in what is now Bihar and eastern Uttah Pradesh. With this to support him, his son, Samudra Gupta (r. 330-379 A.D.) advanced eastward into Bengal and westward as far as the Jumna, in addition to bringing an extensive area of central India under his rule. His son, Chandra Gupta II (r. 380-413 A.D.), rounded off these conquests by annexing a substantial part of the Panjab and by subjugating the surviving Saka principalities in Malwa, Gujarat, and Kathiawar. Both Samudra Gupta and Chandra Gupta II appear to have crossed the Narbada and campaigned in the Deccan. The sources mention a number of southern rulers who acquiesced in Gupta suzerainty, but it seems unlikely that the country beyond the Narbada was ever directly administered by the Guptas, who regarded the fairly nominal submission of these subkings and their payment of tribute as preferable to the responsibilities of formal empire in a region so difficult to control from the Gangetic plain.

Kumara Gupta I (r. 415-455 A.D.), the son of Chandra Gupta II, reigned at the very apogee of the empire but within a decade of his death the Huns began their devastating raids into the Panjab, and although his immediate successor had some success in holding them back, later Gupta rulers were unable to resist the pressure. The Huns were the most savage and destructive of all the invaders who ever entered India across the northwest frontier, and much of the Gupta empire had been laid waste before they were eventually confined to Kashmir by a confederacy of local rulers led by a Saka prince from Malwa. The Huns disappeared even more completely than the Indo-Greeks and the Indo-Parthians had done, presumably becoming one element in the formation of the future Gurjara confederacy and of the Rajputs of Rajasthan. Early in the seventh century a local ruler from Kanauj on the upper Ganges, Harsha (r. 606-648), was able to recreate the Gupta empire to an extent more or less resembling what it had been two centuries before. Certainly the spirit that pervaded Harsha's court and administration reflected the finest achievements of Gupta times. He died, however, without leaving an heir to consolidate his work, and northern India was thereafter divided among local dynasties incapable of achieving the kind of imperial unity towards which the Guptas and Harsha had aspired. The death of Harsha marks a distinct break in the history of northern India in the pre-Muslim period. The age of universal empires was definitely over.

The Organization of Political and Military Power

Under the foreign dynasties that succeeded the Mauryas in northern India the pattern of administration became increasingly feudal in much the same way as it had in Parthian and Sasanid Iran. Yet even under the Mauryas centralized bureaucratic control had never been quite as complete as a reading of the *Arthashastra* would imply. The fact is that in almost all periods of Indian history prior to the nineteenth century, administrative decentralization and the devolution of authority were the rule rather than the exception. The somewhat more diffuse patterns of authority to be found under such dynasties as the Kushanas should

5.2 A representation of a *bodhisattva* in the Gandhara style, showing the features and dress of an Indo-Saka or Indo-Kushana chieftain. Courtesy: Museum of Fine Arts, Boston, Helen and Alice Colburn Fund.

be viewed not as being in contrast to Mauryan or Gupta practice but rather as being different in degree.

In the light of what little is known regarding administrative practice under the Indo-Greeks, the Indo-Sakas, the Indo-Parthians, and the Kushanas, it can be assumed that the mark of their rule was adaptability, the result of their exposure to more than one tradition of government. There can be little doubt that they were acquainted, at least to some extent, with the bureaucratic structures of Mauryan times, which themselves owed something to Achaemenid and possibly Seleucid precedents. Iranian influences also came in with the invaders themselves, all of whom had experienced some degree of Iranicization before crossing the Indus. The Indo-Greeks also retained remnants of a distinctly Hellenistic heritage. Apart from the latter, all the invaders belonged, directly or indirectly, to the nomadic world of the Central Asian steppe zone, where the exercise of political authority tended to be widely diffused and where major decisions were often reached on the basis of mutual consensus among a ruling elite of interrelated tribal and clan leaders. Conceivably, the councils of nobles that acted as royal advisers in the India of the Guptas and of Harsha were in part derived from the informal gatherings of tribal and clan leaders around their supreme leader which must have been characteristic of the foreign dynasties of the preceding period.

Provincial government under all these dynasties took the form of a division into satrapies, following the practice established long before on the Iranian plateau by the Achaemenids and continued thereafter by the Seleucids, the Parthians and, to a modified extent, by the Sasanids. The officer usually in charge of a province was known as a *kshatrapa,* or "satrap," a title that long endured in northwestern India, as in the Indo-Iranian borderlands, but the survival of other titles such as *strategos* ("general") and *meridarch* ("governor") indicates the long-lasting influence of the Indo-Greeks. The successive invaders of northwestern India during this period were probably rather few in number and lacked both local knowledge of the country and bureaucratic traditions of government. At the lower levels of administration this compelled them to rely heavily on the cooperation of traditional indigenous elites—just as, centuries later, the Muslims and the British had to do—while at the higher levels they were forced to establish some kind of a modus vivendi with the foreign elite that had immediately preceded them. At the same time, the cultural affinities between successive waves of invaders allowed for a considerable amount of fraternization and intermarriage.

Under the Guptas there was a trend towards greater centralization and bureaucratization. This was partly because the reigning dynasty enjoyed indigenous roots such as the invaders had lacked and also because they had at hand in the brahmans ready instruments for consolidating and extending their authority. At least at the higher levels, the various invading dynasties had been so eclectic in their religious patronage that even when they honored Shiva and the other gods of the Hindu pantheon they did so along with Iranian and Greek deities. Nor did they grant an especially privileged position to brahmans as such, whereas under the Kushanas, in particular, Buddhist monks enjoyed the generous support of the royal house and, presumably, of the ruling Kushana elite. Under the Guptas, however, the position was reversed, since although the Gupta rulers displayed a broad tolerance towards their Buddhist subjects they were nonetheless Hindus and upholders of the brahmanical social order.

The relative ease with which invading armies, both during the period under discussion and in later centuries, conquered extensive tracts of northern India is a problem of great interest to the historian of the subcontinent. One contributory factor was geography. The northern plains stretching from the Panjab across Uttar Pradesh to the frontiers of Bengal present no natural obstacles to an army advancing from across the Indus and in this way are quite different from the Deccan plateau, which has only rarely come under the effective control of regimes based in the north. Another significant (although negative) factor may be termed the process of propulsion. Some of the invaders who at various times forced their way across the Indus and occupied the Panjab were under pressure from more powerful peoples in their rear—as in the case of the Bactrian Greeks, who had the nomadic Sakas pressing them from the north. Yet even when due allowance is made for these factors, it is surprising to note the comparative ease with which these invaders, in some cases not very numerous, made themselves masters of vast areas of the subcontinent. Clearly, superior military techniques had much to do with it. Apart from the Indo-Greeks, most of the invaders consisted of mounted archers who possessed much the same kind of advantage over Indian armies, made up chiefly of infantry, as did the Muslim Turks centuries later. Among the nomadic peoples of the Central Asian steppe zone it was normal for all adult males in a tribe to be warriors, trained to ride and to handle a bow from an early age, as well as to supervise their livestock. When a group like the Sakas began to migrate into new territory all the male members of that society were, in a sense, professional fighting men, in contrast to the people of the sedentary agricultural societies of the subcontinent, in which only the *kshatriyas* were warriors and the great majority of the population consisted of cultivators and artisans unskilled in the use of weapons and accustomed to thinking of fighting as the business of the high caste *kshatriyas*.

Apart from the Indo-Greeks, it is unlikely that any of the invaders maintained units other than cavalry. The Guptas, however, like the Sasanids, preferred to employ a combination of infantry, cavalry, and war elephants. The effect of centuries of invasion by mounted archers had long since made the war chariot redundant as a weapon, but because war horses bred in India tended to deteriorate after one generation, the Guptas, like Indian rulers for centuries after them, were confronted with the problem of how to ensure a regular supply of fresh cavalry mounts from Central Asia. Against their indigenous opponents, the Guptas were able to bring a most formidable military machine to bear, since within the subcontinent itself there existed no regimes of comparable strength. It was their tragedy that, later, they were compelled to face wave upon waves of invading Huns, more mobile and more ferocious than perhaps any other invaders in Indian history. Against such foes neither traditional Indian methods of warfare nor the resolution of Gupta generals could achieve any permanent success.

Foreign Relations and Frontier Problems

The short-lived rule of the Indo-Greeks, the Indo-Sakas, and the Indo-Parthians consisted largely of a struggle for survival, of penetrating as far as possible into the subcontinent while keeping a wary watch on the Indo-Iranian borderlands to their rear. However, under the Kushanas, who possessed a vast area of territory stretching from the Aral Sea to Bihar, there developed a much more complex pattern of relations between northwestern India and the adjacent regions.

The Kushanas played a very special role in relation to the network of caravan routes extending across much of Asia. In Central Asia, in particular, that long stretch of the Silk Road which passed westward out of Kansu as far as the Amu Darya lay within the frontiers of their empire, which meant that they controlled the principal trade routes linking East Asia with South and West Asia. In the case of West Asia, however, a complicating factor to be reckoned with was the deep-rooted enmity of the Parthians towards the Kushanas, derived partly from a natural suspicion of the intentions of a powerful nomadic confederacy hovering on the marches of northeastern Iran and partly because the Parthians themselves were determined to profit from their highly favorable location vis-à-vis the east-west trade routes. Furthermore, there usually existed an endemic state of warfare between the Parthians and the Romans, towards whom the Kushanas were favorably disposed. From the Kushana point of view, trade with the West, and especially a share of the carrying trade between

China and the Roman empire, was of the greatest importance. Hence, the Kushanas reacted to what, from their point of view, was Parthian obstructionism by attempting to find alternative routes that avoided traversing the Iranian plateau, such as those crossing the steppes north of the Caspian Sea. Far more important, however, was the sea route from the ports at the mouth of the Indus to Roman Egypt across the Arabian Sea, which came to be increasingly used during the Kushana period. This increase may have been partly due to the discovery by a Greek, Hippalus, of how to use the monsoon winds to make the direct crossing of the Arabian Sea and thereby avoid the time-consuming and dangerous voyage along the pirate-infested shores of the Makran coast and the Arabian peninsula, a discovery probably made during the second half of the first century A.D.

From all this it is clear that, notwithstanding their nomadic antecedents and their claims to universal empire, the Kushanas derived much of their wealth from their control of the trade routes, and it is likely that the Kushana ruling elite not only protected merchants but also invested directly in mercantile activities. Certainly, the principal urban centers of their empire—Kapisa (Begram), Pushkalavati (Charsada), Purushapura or Kanishkapura (near Peshawar), Taxila, and Mathura—served, in addition to their political and sacral functions, as great commercial marts. Excavations at Begram have uncovered an extraordinary range of artifacts and objects d'art from this period which make clear that this summer capital of the dynasty was also a major entrepot to which, to take a single example, glassware from Alexandria in Egypt was brought in large quantities for onward transmission to China.

Unlike the Kushanas, the Guptas, as befitted a native north Indian dynasty, displayed much interest in the course of events in the Deccan, while conditions in the Indo-Iranian borderlands gave them little incentive for expansion in that direction. At first they had as neighbors on their northwestern frontier the aggressive empire of the Sasanids, and when that declined it was superseded by the dreaded power of the Hephthalite Huns, with their headquarters at Bamiyan in central Afghanistan, near enough to be within striking distance of the Indus. In the Deccan and the south generally, the situation was much more propitious. It seems probable that the most powerful Gupta kings did exercise a distant overlordship over many of the petty rulers of central and perhaps even south India. This situation, however, changed radically during the later Gupta period, when there arose in the Deccan the exceptionally powerful and long-lived dynasty of the Early, or First, Chalukyas (453-757 A.D.), which put an end to any further question of domination from the north. The general course of events during the period under discussion (and, indeed, in the ensuing period between the middle of the seventh century and the expansion of the Delhi sultanate at the close of the thirteenth century) tended to confirm the geographical, logistical, and cultural barriers to the effective unification of the subcontinent, whether from a base in the Gangetic plain or elsewhere.

Traditions of Empire

It appears that all the invaders of northwestern India, whether Indo-Greeks, Indo-Sakas, Indo-Parthians, or Kushanas, thought imperially: not only did they embark upon predatory expansion at the expense of their neighbors, but they also rationalized the process through the use of suitably impressive titles, forms, and symbols of authority that they took over from their predecessors or invented themselves. Unquestionably, the Mauryan tradition of universal empire continued to be influential, a tradition already shaped, at least in part, by Achaemenid and Seleucid example, but there were also the contemporary models of the Parthian and Sasanid empires. In the case of the latter, indirect Sasanid influence may have been felt throughout the Gupta period, since the evidence points to much intercourse between Iran and northern India during these centuries. The influence of Iranian traditions of monarchy and empire, perhaps reinforced by Hellenistic concepts of divine kingship, was widely felt in the Indian subcontinent. The Kushana rulers, to take a striking example, took for themselves the title of maharajatiraja, which was a precise equivalent of the Iranian title of shahanshah, or "king of kings." Another Kushana title, daivaputra, was equivalent to the Chinese title meaning "son of heaven." In later times, such titles, which in Kanishka's day reflected the splendor of the great Kushana empire and its ruler, came to be widely used by local chieftains and petty dynasts to inflate their overblown and often parochial pretensions, but this was symptomatic of a more general institutional malaise that gripped northern India after the fall of the Guptas. The Guptas themselves pressed the quasi-divine concept of monarchy that prevailed under the Kushanas to its logical conclusion—a divine kingship in which the ruler came to be co-opted into the Hindu pantheon, in some instances as an incarnation of Vishnu. Several Gupta monarchs also performed the *ashvamedha,* or horse sacrifice, sure evidence of their universalist pretensions.

Crystallization of Tradition

As successive invaders advanced into India they found it increasingly necessary to establish a basis of support from among the indigenous population. To the higher castes and to the brahmans, in particular, the newcomers were all *mlechchhas* (meaning "impure") and therefore outside the caste system, yet it was necessary to face the realities of political power, which if not exercised by foreigners, was likely enough to be exercised by groups of fairly low-caste status, such as the Guptas. Thus in much the same way that Pushyamitra Shunga, although probably of foreign origin, acquired brahmanical status, perhaps as a quid pro quo for his support of the brahmans against the Buddhists, so also were the Yavanas (Greeks), Sakas, Pahlavas (Parthians), and Hunas (Huns) co-opted into the caste system as *kshatriyas.* In general the regimes of this period, even when they displayed an unmistakable proclivity for a particular cult, as did some Kushana emperors for Buddhism, maintained a conciliatory attitude towards Hinduism and made generous grants for the support of brahmans. In this they demonstrated a religious eclecticism that is vividly exemplified by the religious iconography of their coin series. Thus, the Kushana coins carry figures of Shiva and his Nandi bull, Greek deities such as Athena, Zeus, and Heracles, the Iranian Mithra and Anahita, Egyptian Serapis, a Zoroastrian fire temple, and even one of the earliest representations of Buddha. Excavations at Taxila show the city to have been throughout this period the home of a number of syncretic cults derived from both West and South Asia. Syncretistic patterns of worship also characterized the Buddhism of the Kushana period.

Buddhism under the Kushanas changed from what it had been at the time of the Magadhan kingdoms and under the Mauryas in much the same way that Zoroastrianism during the centuries of Parthian and especially Sasanid rule changed from what it had been under the Achaemenids. Traditionally, these changes have been associated with the reign of Kanishka, but this attribution surely telescopes what must have been a lengthy and gradual process. Moreover, if Kanishka himself was a Buddhist, he was not a Buddhist as that term would be understood in later centuries in other parts of Asia, since he continued to honor other faiths. A Zoroastrian fire temple erected by him has recently been uncovered in northern Afghanistan, and there is a presumption that he must have worshipped the various deities whose figures appear on his coinage. His reign does, however, seem to mark the culmination of a distinctive trend in the history of Indian Buddhism, a trend of the greatest importance for the future development of that religion.

Kanishka himself was a great patron of Buddhism in the sense that his generosity did much to promote the institutional life of Buddhism, in particular by the construction of *viharas,* or "monasteries," and *stupas,* which were hemispherical structures erected over relics of Buddha or of a Buddhist saint. This kind of patronage naturally stimulated a distinctive Buddhist iconography leading to the emergence of the Gandhara style, in which Indian and Romano-Hellenistic influences mingled with superb effect, and of a related but more truly indigenous style associated with the Mathura region. The emergence of this iconography gave Buddhism visual forms of expression that contributed greatly to its diffusion along the caravan roads of Central Asia, where it was carried by monks and merchants who were, like those whom they converted, subjects of the vast Kushana empire. It was during Kanishka's reign too that there assembled in Kashmir the Fourth Buddhist Council, an event that marked the distinct emergence of Mahayana Buddhism, with its deification of Buddha, his association with a host of supernatural beings, and the acceptance of the concept of *bodhisattvas* (those who forego *nirvana* in order to be of service to suffering humanity). Hereafter the differences between Mahayana and Hinayana Buddhism (the Buddhism of Ceylon and Burma) hardened into dogma. Buddhism as the Kushanas knew it was moving in the direction of one of two alternative orthodoxies.

The establishment of the Gupta empire did not bring about any appreciable decline in the status of Buddhism, since the new dynasty maintained a genuine policy of toleration and even extended some support to the Buddhists, an attitude that also characterized the half century of Harsha's rule. But meanwhile Buddhism itself was showing evidence of a failing spirit, its original teachings becoming diluted by institutionalization and the pursuit of ritual. In the days of the Mauryas, Buddhism had been taken up by the rising mercantile and urban classes, which had continued, century after century, to be its most loyal and generous supporters, even more so than the invaders who also patronized it. But this association with wealth and with the mercantile classes had changed the character of Buddhism so that it became less and less the faith of the poor and the oppressed. Eventually the foreigners who supported Buddhism became submerged in the caste system (the Huns in India were always antagonistic towards Buddhism), while the mercantile classes with which it had become so closely identified declined in importance after the fall of the Gupta empire. Only in eastern Bihar and Bengal did Buddhism survive, under the Pala dynasty (760-1142 A.D.), developing the Tantric form of Vajrayana Buddhism that would eventually spread into Tibet and, much later, Mongolia. With the coming of the Muslims, to whom Buddhism appeared as a rival proselytizing faith, Buddhism was finally rooted out of the land of its birth. Not until the twentieth century did it reappear, when, as a consequence of caste oppression, large numbers of untouchables in Maharashtra and Mysore have recently become Buddhists.

Cultural Achievements

The cultural eclecticism and religious syncretism of the age of invasions, taken with the presence of significant foreign elements, have tended to obscure the course of indigenous development in the period preceding the emergence of the Gupta empire in northern India. Clearly, where Buddhism was concerned the achievements were extraordinarily impressive, whether judged in terms of canonical literature or popular folk literature, the art of the cave shrines and monasteries of central India, or the better-known art of Gandhara and Mathura. Yet it is easy to overlook the fact that during this period of foreign rule in which Buddhism, in particular, flourished, Hinduism too was evolving new forms and new responses to changing situations. The older Vedic religion and, most conspicuously, the elaborate Vedic sacrifices were tending to give way to patterns of worship that suggest a renewed process of acculturation between the Brahmanism of northern India and the older religious life of the non-Aryan populations of the peninsula. Most striking was the emergence in this period of the worship of the great gods, Vishnu and Shiva, who now and ever afterwards would occupy a commanding position in the Hindu great tradition. The worship of Vishnu and Shiva and their various manifestations and consorts involved a degree of personal commitment and devotion to a particular deity which was very different from the service of the old Aryan gods.

With the formation of the Gupta empire, Sanskrit, although still restricted to a very small proportion of the population, achieved its apogee as one of the world's great literatures.

The Gupta rulers and their nobles and courtiers were to prove munificent and discriminating patrons of culture and learning, and it is Sanskrit poetry and drama with which Gupta patronage is most immediately associated. Kalidasa, perhaps the best-known Sanskrit poet, was probably a contemporary of Chandra Gupta II. The intellectual achievements of the age also extended to music, medicine, mathematics, and astronomy, as well as to traditional religious scholarship. It is a misfortune that the wealth of Sanskrit literature surviving from the Gupta period is not matched by a comparable heritage in the visual arts. Splendid pieces of Gupta sculpture have survived, but painting and architecture have suffered from the passage of time. Much of what is now regarded as the finest work of Indian architects, sculptors, and painters dates from the post-Gupta period or from areas in the peninsula where the Guptas never ruled.

3. CHINA DURING THE LATER HAN, THREE KINGDOMS, AND WESTERN CHIN

The Chinese universal state of Ch'in and Han resolved some of the social and ideological issues of late Chou times, but forces of cultural growth and social change soon overtook the new imperial order and precipitated a new crisis. The present section will be devoted to examining the causes of the crisis and the efforts of several regimes to cope with it during the years from about 50 B.C. to 317 A.D. The idea of a unified empire, as represented in the institutions of the Han dynasty and in the classical texts of late Chou that were given their definitive form and canonical status in the Han, retained its ideological force in some degree during the two millennia ending in the twentieth century. But that idea was not always realized in practice. The year 317 A.D. saw the collapse of the most nearly successful effort at imperial reunification between the Later Han and the conquest of south China by the Sui in 589. The centuries following 317 in China saw the fragmentation of the empire among many ephemeral states, widespread adoption of Mahayana, the Buddhist universal religion, and the deep interpenetration of Chinese and other Asian civilizations. The successful restoration of the universal state in Sui and T'ang was presently followed by a renaissance in which the classical works of Chou and Han once more provided the staple fare of Chinese intellectual life, albeit now seen in a new perspective and differently understood. In this long scale, the years ca. 50 B.C. to 317 A.D. appear as a period of official adherence to obsolescent forms, the classical mode, in the face of rising intellectual challenge and irrepressible change.

In 220-222 A.D. the disintegrating empire of the Later Han dynasty lost even the appearance of unity when first two, and then three, states divided its territories, each claiming to be the sole rightful sovereignty. In 264 the strongest of them, the state of Wei in north China, conquered the state of Shu in modern Szechwan. In the following year the now enlarged state of Wei was ended by a coup which led to the founding of the state of Chin in its place. In 280 Chin subjugated Wu in the east, thereby restoring the empire to a single sovereignty. This reunification proved ephemeral, however—a mere ghost of the Former Han. Unable to cope with the internal forces that had undermined both Han dynasties, the Chin succumbed in 317 to the invading armies of the semibarbarian frontier state that presumptuously called itself "Han" and had to reestablish its rule over a truncated southern empire from a new capital at Chein-k'ang, modern Nanking, south of the lower Yangtze (whence the retrospective designation Eastern Chin). Thousands of leading families now fled to sanctuaries in the south, leaving the north open to several centuries of barbarian infiltration and domination.

Change in Economy, Technology, and Science

Economic growth continued despite the vicissitudes of empire. In the agricultural sector, still by far the most important, migrations during the Later Han accelerated progress in the exploitation of the Yangtze valley and the far south. Owing to the facts that the central government was markedly weaker than in Former Han and that the capital had been transferred eastward out of the Wei valley and onto the great plain, the old capital area in the Wei valley declined in population and production. Also, the instability of the northern frontier and the settlement of barbarians within the Great Wall spurred a considerable Chinese southward migration. Striking increases in population were recorded in the Hsiang and Kan river valleys (modern Hunan and Kiangsi). Farther to the west, the population of the Ch'engtu plain in Szechwan flourished, swelled by immigrants from Shensi crossing the Ch'inling Mountains. Other colonists pushed still farther into the Tali region of western Yunnan, where overland trade with India added to the local expansion of agriculture as the basis of prosperity. Finally, the southward flow continued into the Hanoi region, where the southernmost reaches of the empire shared in the general development of the south. To keep this southward shift in perspective, however, it should be understood that the growth of Chinese society in the south, while remarkable in comparison with earlier times, was still very far from balancing that of the north, which would remain the political and economic core of the empire until late in the T'ang dynasty, five hundred years later.

During the Three Kingdoms period once again, as in the late Chou, interstate rivalries provided another spur to economic growth. Despite its short duration, this interval of political division was marked by governmental promotion of large-scale flood-control, irrigation, and water-transport works. The state of Wei aggressively pursued a policy of strategic development across the great plain of the Yellow and Huai rivers. The state of Shu Han exploited the resources of the irrigation works around Ch'engtu, and Sun Ch'uan, founder of Wu, moved eastward with his troops into the vicinity of Nanking, where he employed them in the construction of canals and the establishment of agricultural colonies. Later, during the weak and troubled reign of the Western Chin dynasty, there was a new southward migration far exceeding that of Later Han. Hsiung-nu conquests in the north during the first two decades of the fourth century sent the great families flooding into the undeveloped land south of the Yangtze. Various estimates suggest that 60 or 70 percent of the great families were involved and that the number of individuals may have totalled one or two million. The effect of this migration was to give another strong impetus to the economic development of the south, partially offsetting the depletion of the north.

As the agricultural base expanded, internal and external trade boomed during the Later Han. Governmental controls over commerce had reached a high point in the reign of Wu Ti, when the salt and iron monopolies were instituted and rich families were subjected to heavy taxation or confiscation. After this period, government pressure on private economic enterprise diminished, and the Later Han was a period of laissez-faire. Whereas most trading had taken place in the markets of the *hsiang* and *t'ing* walled towns subject to regulation by the local subbureaucracy, much of this activity was now shifted to the estates of the great families, which in some cases operated their own local markets. The growth of interregional trade was noted by contemporary observers who complained that the highways were choked with commercial traffic and that agriculture was being neglected as the commoners rushed into trade to try to make their fortunes. The commercial fever even affected the imperial court, where there was a vogue for exotic imported goods. The emperor Ling (r. 168-189) favored foreign fashions in dress, furnishings, and entertainment.

The whole period, Hsin and Later Han through Western Chin, also saw marked development and spread of improved agricultural technology. Although ox plowing had been known since late Chou times, the practice took centuries to spread through the empire and

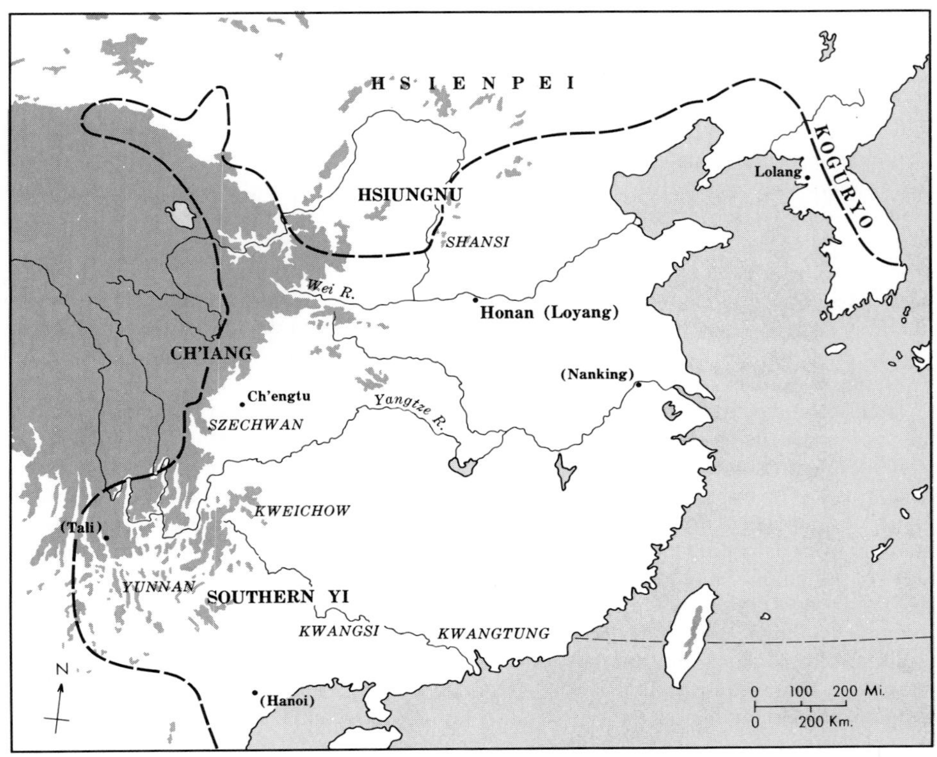

Map 21 The Western Chin empire, about 300 A.D.

became general in Later Han and the Three Kingdoms. A critical factor in the increased use of animal power was the rise during Han of the great landed estates. The landowners, with their hundreds of slaves and thousands of peasant dependents, had the means and the economic incentive to build up herds of draft animals and acquire expensive equipment. The estates also were the setting for the invention of a mechanical drill for sowing seed grain, the wheelbarrow for light transport along the footpaths that fed the highways, and machinery for milling grain that was powered by treadmills, draft animals, or waterwheels. A water-powered trip-hammer for making flour became common on the estates of Szechwan, and rotary fans were used for winnowing. Such machinery presupposed skill in mechanics, and this is attested to both by literary sources and by archaeology. Ratchets and gear wheels were made of bronze and iron. Some of these were highly ingenious, including a set of double-helical bronze gears excavated in Shensi.

Technology was advancing in nonagricultural fields as well. The production of salt from underground brine in west China required the drilling of wells and the installation of bamboo well casings to a great depth—as much as two thousand feet. Natural gas was found and tapped to provide fuel for boiling the brine. In iron metallurgy, by 31 A.D. small blast furnaces were provided with water-powered piston bellows, a practice that became common four centuries later. In Western Chin times, coal had been substituted for wood in some areas to heat crucibles. The market for ersatz valuables led to the production of glass as imitation jade, crystal, and pearls. Glass was also used for drinking vessels and for lenses to make fire by focusing the sun's heat. The Han was also an important chapter in the long history of experiments with, and applications of, magnetism. The crude, ladle-shaped lodestone that turned on its rounded bowl was superseded by the floating needle, forerunner of the mariner's compass that later would be perfected in China and widely used. In some communities, at least, the problem of a supply of fresh water was solved by the installation of ceramic pipelines, remains of which have been found in great abundance.

One more instance of technology must be mentioned because of its obvious relation to processes of growth: the invention of paper. The formation of a large and growing wealthy class, the expansion of trade and urbanization, the spread of learning, the founding of public and private schools, and the growth of the bureaucracy all created a great demand for writing materials. By Former Han, the costly silk scrolls and the clumsy wooden books were supplemented by a kind of protopaper made of matted waste-silk fibers. In 105 A.D. a palace official announced the invention of a new process for making true paper out of a mixture of cheap and abundant fibers. By the end of the Later Han, the techniques involved in brush and paper writing had been so perfected that already an aesthetic tradition of connoisseurship of fine papers, brushes, and inks had appeared. Papers were sized (glazed with paste, etc.) for good writing qualities and were treated with an insecticide extracted from a certain tree bark to protect it from worms. Although book printing was not invented until the eighth century, the large-scale production of paper by the end of Han did result in a great increase in the availability of manuscript literature. According to a contemporary account, the popularity of one "best-seller" of the third century, Tso Ssu's poetic trilogy of the capitals of the Three Kingdoms, was said to have driven up the price of writing paper in Loyang.

Mathematics, usually with a utilitarian bent, continued to develop during our period. Han and early post-Han mathematical texts reflect a great interest in arithmetic, number theory, and algebra but less interest in geometry. They include problems familiar to modern schoolchildren: mixture problems, pursuit problems, and what appears to be the first worked-out problem in indeterminate analysis. By the beginning of the Christian era, the value of *pi* had been calculated, not very accurately, as 3.154. A mathematician of the Three Kingdoms period, pursuing accuracy far beyond any practical requirement of that time, arrived at a value of 3.14159 by means of a 3,072-sided polygon. (In the fifth century it was calculated to seven places!) The cosmological basis of Han ideology ensured a continuing interest in astronomy. By Han times the astronomers used the system of twenty-eight "lunar mansions" (segments of a celestial sphere having as axis a diameter passing through the polestar), which served the same purpose as the twenty-four hour circles of modern astronomy. Any star or constellation could be located by its "mansion" and by its angle of declination from the polestar (the celestial sphere was divided into 365.25 degrees). On this plan, star maps were compiled containing all named constellations. The accuracy of astronomical measurement is indicated by the fact that the phenomenon of precession (the slight westward movement of the intersection between the planes of the ecliptic and the earth's equator) had been discovered in Han, though not yet understood.

Instability of the Frontiers

Although the Han passed its peak of military expansionism in the reign of Wu Ti (141-87 B.C.), the forward policy of the reign of Ming Ti (57-75 A.D.) restored the empire to its former size. Even during the Three Kingdoms period and Western Chin, Chinese outposts were maintained in the regions of modern Vietnam and Korea, and Wei and Western Chin held on to the Kansu corridor leading along the Inner Asian trade route from the Wei valley northwestward to the eastern margins of the Tarim basin. The outward diffusion of Chinese culture also continued through this troubled period. The southern Hsiung-nu tribes became economically and politically dependent on the Eastern Han regime, a development that facilitated Chinese control of the north and west but that eventually also led to the formation of the independent Hsiung-nu state of Han within the Great Wall and the subsequent loss of north China. Moreover, the Koreans and Vietnamese attempted to throw off Chinese rule; the former succeeding in 313 A.D., but the Vietnamese only in 939. This should remind us of the way in which the spread of Chinese culture in Chou times contributed to the disintegration of the unified monarchy, with new barbarian or semibarbarian states forming on the frontiers and playing an aggressive role in Chinese politics. In Korea and Vietnam, the Chinese colonies grew in population and in their power to affect the local inhabitants because of their role as places of refuge for Chinese who lost out in the factional and military conflicts of Later Han and Three Kingdoms time. Internally, the imposition of order by the Han regime and the maintenance of improved communications afforded new opportunities for private wealth. Ambitious families enlarged their holdings in land, invested in trade and industry, and fostered important advances in Chinese material technology. But as agents and beneficiaries of economic and technological growth, the new aristocrats gained in power and independence at the expense of the governmental principles of centralized and bureaucratic administration, and thereby contributed to the decline of the imperial regime. Moreover, former peasants dispossessed of their lands by the great families constituted an internal proletariat ready for violent revolution. Growth also occurred in the spread of learning to a much enlarged class of literati, larger, indeed, than could be given employment in government. The presence of an immense number of unemployed educated men in the capital contributed to the scale and intensity of the fatal factional struggles within the central government of Later Han times.

In considering the process of barbarian-civilized interaction in this period, a distinction again must be made between the hard frontiers in the west and north and the soft, or moveable, frontiers in the south and northeast. The eastern margins of the Tibetan plateau from Kansu southward past the Szechwan basin into Yunnan were a region of rugged mountains and steep valleys. This was the habitat of the Ch'iang people. This relatively permanent cultural frontier still, some two thousand years later, divides the Chinese from Tibetans. The Ch'iang did not form large tribal federations or states but remained in smaller family or tribal units. Pressed by the Hsiung-nu in the northwest and by the Chinese from the east, they were compelled to fight or submit to one enemy or the other. During and after the Later Han, fighting frequently occurred between the Ch'iang and the Chinese settlers, and imperial forces were sent to try to pacify the region. Gradually some of the Ch'iang were drawn into the Chinese political and economic system and fully absorbed, while others either stayed in place and preserved their customs or moved deeper into the Tibetan pleateau, contributing to the formation of the Tibetan people.

During and after the Later Han, the northern frontier became highly unstable. Around 100 A.D. the Hsien-pi and another people associated with them, the Wu-huan, moved out of their Manchurian homeland, displaced the northern Hsiung-nu westward, and established their dominance over the southern Hsiung-nu along the Chinese frontier. The Hsien-pi federation of tribes mounted devastating raids into Chinese territory. Through the Western Chin period the Chinese rulers of the north lacked sufficient strength to defend their territory by military means alone and so relied heavily on political and economic inducements to encourage the barbarian tribes to fight among themselves. Frontier commanders also were able sometimes to detach small groups of disaffected Hsiung-nu to serve in their own armies. This was a dangerous practice, however, since the foreigners did sometimes defect to the enemy along with associated Chinese units. The dangers inherent in the use of foreign troops were increased when their numbers were very large. The Later Han general Ts'ao Ts'ao successfully paved the way for his son's usurpation of the Han throne and the establishment of the state of Wei by admitting nineteen tribes of Hsiung-nu, as his allies, to good land far south of the Great Wall in Shansi in 180 A.D. It proved impossible to absorb the foreigners, however, and in 304 they established the independent state of Han (later called Chao), which proceeded to overrun the heart of north China from the Wei valley to the Shantung peninsula during the following decade.

The Korean and Vietnamese provinces of the Han empire proved less resistant to the diffusion of Chinese culture. The northwestern part of Korea remained subject to the great Chinese colony in Lo-lang until the Hsiung-nu conquest of the north cut off communications with the home country. The native state of Koguryo fell heir to the Chinese regime as ruler of the north. During the four centuries of Chinese rule, the Chinese and their Korean subjects were in a clearly marked colonial relationship. The Koreans, reduced to servile status, were, for the most part, little influenced by the culture of the conquerors, but some of them were absorbed into the colonial establishment as minor functionaries in the service of Chinese officials and others were involved in private trade. After the conquest of the north by Koguryo, the Lo-lang community, with its mixed Chinese and Korean elite population, provided a major cultural and economic resource for the new state and contributed to the early stages of the Korean adaptation of Chinese literature, ideology, and political institutions. The origins of the state of Koguryo in the northeast around the end of the Former Han may be seen as an instance of stimulus diffusion. During the period of Chinese political domination, Koguryo evolved beyond the reach of the colonial government from clan and tribal organization to territorial monarchy. The population was engaged mainly in hunting, and the pattern of government was essentially feudal and therefore antithetical to the Chinese. Yet the stimulus for large-scale and relatively stable political organization was probably provided by the challenge presented by the Chinese conquest of the western part of the peninsula.

The case of cultural diffusion in Vietnam shows both similarities and differences in comparison with that of Korea. Chinese governors during Wang Mang's Hsin dynasty and the first years of the Later Han pursued a policy of active sinicization, promoting the southern Chinese style of irrigated agriculture and the use of the plough drawn by ox (or water buffalo) and trying to impose Chinese customs and ceremonials. As the Chinese colonists occupied and developed the best lands and drew Vietnamese into the colonial service as functionaries and militiamen, the native aristocracy became increasingly hostile. In 40 A.D. the execution of a Vietnamese nobleman touched off a rebellion led by his widow and her sister, the famous Trung sisters, who to this day have remained popular symbols of national resistance (against the Chinese and, more recently, the French and Americans). The Trung monarchy was quickly suppressed by a massive invasion force under the general Ma Yuan. After this second conquest Vietnam was more intensively administered than before, and there soon developed a substantial mixed Sino-Vietnamese elite, trained in the Chinese classical literature. By the end of the Han, Vietnamese scholars were entering the Chinese bureaucratic class both in Vietnam and in other parts of the empire as well. The villages of Vietnam, then, as now, remained the stronghold of the indigenous Yueh culture, in contrast with the sinicized culture of the literati. So committed to the Chinese classical world view were the Vietnamese scholars that at the end of Han, when the southern provinces might have broken away entirely, the native Vietnamese governors continued to accept the nominal authority of Wu and Western Chin and to promote Chinese learning and bureaucratic institutions. Thus there was no Vietnamese counterpart of Koguryo to displace Sino-Vietnamese authority and sever the region from the empire. In the extreme south, however, in the vicinity of Hue, Chinese influence and control were more tenuous, and a combination of land and sea invasions from other parts of Southeast Asia and the strong diffusion of Indian culture coming by sea from India and overland from the Indianized state of Funan (in modern Cambodia) resulted in the formation of the Buddhist kingdom of Champa. Champa diverged sharply from the Chinese model and, pressed into the narrow coastal strip between the mountains and the sea, became predominantly a mercantile, rather than an agricultural, society. Consequently, from soon after the Han period, this southernmost fragment of the Vietnamese provinces did break away and pursue its own very different course of development until its conquest by the Vietnamese in the fifteenth through seventeenth centuries.

In the immense territory extending from the Yangtze valley southward to Yunnan and modern Kwangtung and Kwangsi, much the same processes were at work. Much of the population of the Yangtze valley from Szechwan to the delta were Man barbarians, hardly affected by Chinese culture despite a long exposure going back well into Chou times. Still farther south in modern Yunnan and Kweichow were the still more exotic southern Yi barbarians. Through both Han dynasties, imperial officials and the Chinese colonists dependent on them strove by force and by schooling to transform the native populations into Chinese. During the Three Kingdoms period, Chu-ko Liang, the famous statesman and leader of Shu Han, proved particularly aggressive in the conversion of the natives of southern Szechwan. Accounts of the time, while reflecting the great effort made by Chinese to convert the barbarians, nevertheless imply that the task was barely begun and that it was sometimes even a question of whether the Chinese settlers could be prevented from assuming native dress and customs. However, the continued immigration of Chinese from the north and the suitability of the southern regions for intensive agriculture ensured that eventually some of the non-Chinese peoples would be absorbed, with the rest retreating deep into the remotest mountains.

Social Change and the Breakdown of Imperial Government

Chinese civilization and its imperial institutions were perceived as part of an unchanging universal order. A cyclical procession of dynasties was ordained, but the imperial order itself, under its succession of dynasties, was eternal. But from our perspective in time we know what the Chinese of Han could not have known: that their civilization and universal state were subject not only to cyclical changes in dynasty but also to complete breakdown. After the Former Han, attempts to revive the imperial unity were largely unsuccessful for nearly four hundred years. The perfect harmony of man in society and of society in the universe that was thought to prevail when the imperial regime was in its most flourishing early phase was an imperfectly realized ideal. The imperial government was a system of sovereign authority generated within Chinese society and, therefore, subject to forces of growth and change that were constantly present within that society. The founders of Ch'in and Han successively crushed the major political and military interests arrayed against them, but they could not arrest the formation of new antagonistic groups. The downward turning point for Han probably came in the reign of Wu Ti, who lacked the balance and universal perspective of most of his predecessors and used his great authority in a vain attempt to satisfy his ambitions for world conquest. Toward the end of the Former Han, the imperial throne became the object of a factional power struggle that culminated in Wang Mang's usurpation and the short-lived Hsin dynasty. The subsequent overthrow of the Hsin, the overthrow of the succeeding Later Han, the usurpation of the state of Wei and the founding of Chin, and finally, the collapse of Chin all were the results of the rise of powerful social forces beyond the imperial governments' control as well as of episodes of personal incompetence on the part of the rulers themselves.

Of all the disintegrative forces at work in the empire, the most important was competition among families for control of the land and its products, resulting in a tendency toward a new feudalism. Land was still, and would long remain, the principal form of capital investment and the economic foundation of the great families. Although Han had continued the Ch'in laws that required separate domicile of married brothers and despite the fact that family property was usually divided about equally among sons, families within the same lineage group were able to cooperate effectively in their common economic and political interests. A few old lineages surviving from late Chou times, others prominent from the Han founding, and a much greater number of new families together formed an aristocratic class that reached a high level of power and maturity in the later decades of Former Han. The great families acquired land by a variety of means, including foreclosing on loans secured by land, receiving gifts of land from the imperial government, and illegally expropriating their neighbors' land. The expansion of private trade accelerated the concentration of landed wealth in the hands of the great families by affording them new opportunities for profits, which could then be invested in land and agricultural development.

The creation and maintenance of great estates was closely connected with the holding of bureaucratic office. On the one hand, possession of wealth enabled a family to obtain a good education for its more talented members so as to qualify them for office and to enable them to gain access to the society of locally powerful and influential people, which was necessary in order to have one's relatives recommended for official appointment. On the other hand, possession of public office greatly facilitated a family's efforts to build up an estate. Officials and their near relatives enjoyed such eminent social status and were so favored by the law that they were less vulnerable than commoners to injury either by government or by private rivals. Moreover, most high-ranking officials were awarded the hereditary noble rank of marquis, which carried with it the tax-free award of the income from lands donated as fiefs. Whether legally by use of the privileges of officials and nobility or illegally by submitting false tax returns and by browbeating the local tax collectors, the great families were able to evade most of their land and poll taxes and their military and corvée responsibilities. Under the shelter of office and rank, the estates flourished.

For the imperial government, the consequences of the concentration of land ownership were uniformly bad. The government as a whole was being corrupted by its conversion into a fortress of entrenched privilege. The administration of tax and corvée regulations became increasingly difficult, and revenues declined. The burden of tax and service was shifted to the steadily shrinking sector of village lands cultivated by ordinary peasants without benefit of official connections. The number of tax-paying *hsiang* and *t'ing* communities fell to about half its Former Han level. The increasing tax and service pressure on the free peasants forced them ever more deeply into debt and dependence on the great families until they were forced to give up their land altogether and become tenants. The estates, becoming richer and more powerful, increased their profits by adopting more efficient agricultural techniques and by engaging in commercial and industrial ventures. Their growth in size and complexity involved the formation of a new class of private retainers and soldiers. To assist in the expansion and management of their operations, the great families attracted retainers (literally "guests") to their service, men with useful skills or strength who were willing to work in return for protection and pay. They also built up private armies to guard their property and houses against robbers or bandits and, frequently, to fight in vendettas with rival families. On occasion, an aristocrat on imperial military service might even bring his private army along with him and keep it under his command. Completing the vicious circle, as the estates became armed and fortified camps, the imperial monopoly of the legitimate use of force was challenged, and people increasingly sought the protection of the great families instead of the government. The imperial regime was thus rendered ineffectual at the local level even while it was undermined at the center by families or cliques of families who tried to control it for their own advantage. Thus, despite the persistence of the machinery and ideology of empire, Chinese society was moving once again in the direction of feudalism. It should be borne in mind, however, that enough of the imperial forms and ideals remained to prevent a full restoration of feudalism, and even when the society was most divided, during the fourth through the sixth centuries, it was governed through a mixture of feudal and bureaucratic institutions and practices.

Internally the Han government revealed certain inherent weaknesses that contributed to its eventual collapse. In many cases, the attempt to remove the imperial family from

5.3 Pottery model excavated in 1969 from a Later Han dynasty tomb in Kansu. The wealth, pride, and independence of the great families of this period are suggested by the lofty central tower and the fortified exterior walls. Source: *Wen Wu,* 1972, No. 2.

intimate contact with the outside world was all too successful. In the seclusion of the palace the princes grew up in the company of women and eunuchs, and these childhood companions sometimes proved to be the closest and most influential of the emperors' friends. Doubtless, the reputation of the eunuchs has suffered at the hands of their bureaucratic and aristocratic enemies, but there is no doubt that some of them were thoroughly corrupt and used their influence with the throne for their great personal gain. The eunuchs were able, at times, to organize as a powerful court faction with extensive connections with certain political or commercial interests throughout the empire.

While local control was passing into the hands of the great families, the central government itself was being torn apart by rival factions. One formidable group in the capital, in addition to the eunuchs, was the consort families—the relatives of the empresses and secondary imperial wives. Except for the early decades of Han, the consorts were chosen from wealthy and prestigious families. Once in the palace, their families made the greatest possible use of their presence there to advance their own interests. Most powerful within this group were the relatives of those consorts who were fortunate enough to see their sons on the throne. The mothers of the emperors, the dowager empresses, were in a strong position owing to the traditionally required respect on the part of any man, the emperor not excepted, towards his widowed mother. Sharp political struggles were waged at court, therefore, among rival consort families trying to manipulate the imperial succession. One such family, the Wang, achieved so much power that it was able to obtain the throne for a young child and have one of its number, Wang Mang, appointed regent. From this position, in a carefully graded series of steps, Wang Mang finally set the young emperor aside and assumed the throne in the name of his "New" (Hsin) dynasty in 9 A.D.

Another group at court was the regular scholar-bureaucrats. Once the real managers of imperial government, their role had declined relative to the eunuchs and consort families. In the last years of the Later Han they, together with a veritable army of students and "street people" centering around the imperial university, fought a spectacular but losing struggle of pamphlets, propaganda, and intrigue against the eunuchs and the consort families. With the central government falling apart and the countryside laid waste by the Yellow Turbans, a Taoist-inspired popular rebellion, effective political and military power rapidly passed into the hands of a few generals and their loyal retainers. The generals and statesmen, constituting a new center of power in the empire, continued to be a major factor in imperial politics through the Three Kingdoms period and Western Chin. Wei, Shu Han, and Wu were founded by such families, and another family, the Ssu-ma, established the Chin by executing a successful coup against the Ts'ao family, rulers of Wei.

While the government was losing its power to govern, the conditions of the mass of the population became ever more insecure. The great families had no responsibility for the general welfare and, in any case, were mainly interested in increasing their private wealth. Small-holding peasants, tenants, and landless laborers could no longer rely on the government as a strong guarantor of public order and the possibility of survival; aristocratic vendettas, banditry, deteriorating dikes, and empty public granaries created a general sense of insecurity. The proletarianized peasants, having no community in which to live, wandered about and often turned to banditry. Ominously for the future of the Han regime, they began to draw on the religious resources of rural cults and to form widely ramified secret societies. In the year 3 A.D., for example, the authorities became aware of an ecstatic religious movement in Shantung based on worship of the Queen Mother of the West, a goddess thought to inhabit the K'unlun Mountains and to possess the power of conferring immortality upon the faithful. Encouraged by beliefs in supernatural powers that favored their cause (though not necessarily in the cult of the Queen Mother), growing numbers of peasants turned to armed rebellion or simple banditry. Wang Mang, for all his overt concern with social reform, inadvertently contributed to the tide of mass disorder both by undermining the legitimacy of imperial authority when he usurped the throne and by further demoralizing an already corrupt government by enacting radical and unenforceable laws. The largest of these uprisings, that of the Red Eyebrows in the eastern provinces, contributed to the collapse of Wang Mang's Hsin dynasty, destroyed one of the several Liu family attempts at the restoration of the Han, and was largely suppressed only in 27 A.D., after about ten years of fighting.

The general improvement in the peasants' economic condition after the founding of the Later Han was a temporary phenomenon resulting mainly from the drop in population during the wars of the Hsin period and the resulting scarcity of labor relative to cultivated land. The basic social problem of equitable distribution of land and of the products of the land remained unsolved, however, and an increasingly cynical and corrupt imperial regime proved incapable of coping with the reemergence of mass unrest. Roughly, the last fifty years of Han witnessed a ruthless and absorbing struggle for power among several factions in the imperial capital. The emperors, now quite helpless, turned to one group after another to help them escape control by one or more rival factions, only to become the pawns of their allies. The nouveau-riche families of imperial consorts, empresses, secondary wives and palace eunuchs, with their far-flung networks of political ties outside the capital; provincial generals and their military cliques; and frustrated civil bureaucrats all played their roles in a round of purge and counterpurge that left the central government of the empire in ruins. Under these conditions, masses of disaffected peasantry with the aid of frustrated intellectuals undertook to supply the ideological and organizational essentials of order that the empire could no longer provide. In 184 A.D. there began a rebellion that still provides a classic example of mass revolution in China, based on the two main principles of spiritual salvation and communal social utopia. In two similar, if not politically connected, movements, the Yellow Turbans and the Five Pecks of Rice, rebellious peasants undertook to reorganize Chinese society in a hierarchy of religious communities having such characteristics as communal, instead of private, property, puritanical ethical standards enforced by strong social pressures, and the cure of disease by public confessional. In their attempt to make their utopia real they raised armies and commenced the obliteration of the Han government at every level. The rural militarists reacted with a vigor born of crisis and, at the head of their private armies and in the name of the empire, proceeded to slaughter the rebellious peasants. When the threat of rebellion had been turned back, a few victorious generals had become the masters of what remained of the empire and initiated the Three Kingdoms period by dividing it among themselves.

The Imperial Tradition and Its Critics

The recurrent crises of the Chinese universal state, from the decades preceding the Wang Mang usurpation in 9 A.D. until the collapse of the Chin unification in 317, inspired a renewal of the great philosophical debates of the first crisis period, late Chou, the period we have associated with ethical protest. But this second crisis period differed significantly from the first. Whereas the establishment of the universal state of Ch'in and Han, completing the transition from a manorial to a market economy, from an aristocratic to a competitive society, from a feudal to a bureaucratic polity, offered a novel resolution of the first crisis, statesmen and intellectuals facing the second crisis, the disintegration of the universal state, found themselves without novel solutions. The main thrust of Later Han and early Six Dynasties intellectual activity was directed not only towards the clarification of the main lines of Chinese thought as these had been laid down in late Chou but also towards the reform and reinvigoration of the universal state.

In the preceding chapter on the universal empire we saw Tung Chung-shu's exuberant formulation of a new and highly eclectic ideology, designed to match the political achievements of the imperial order and to distinguish Han rule from that of Ch'in. One of the first manifestations of a classical reaction, an attempt to return to the Chou dynasty roots of Han ideology, came to the fore in the closing decades of the Former Han dynasty. The official ideology formulated by Tung Chung-shu and the state-salaried imperial professors asserted an intimate and indissoluble connection between the processes of the cosmic order and events in the realm of man. The emperor in this scheme was flatteringly assigned the stupendous role of regulator of the cosmos, responsible for maintaining the right relationship between the human and cosmic orders. The basic texts employed by the government scholars were the so-called New Text classics *(Book of Changes, Book of History, Book of Poetry, Spring and Autumn Annals,* and the *Ritual Classic).* These texts had been recited from memory by learned Confucians and transcribed in the current script (whence the term New Text). To these works were appended voluminous commentaries that constituted officially approved interpretations of the basic texts. These apochryphal writings *(wei,* or "woof," by contradistinction to the *ching,* "classic," or "weaver's warp") increasingly burdened textual scholarship with far-fetched speculations. For example, Confucius was first perceived simply as an ordinary mortal man who was also a great teacher, then as an uncrowned king, a predestined sage, and finally as a miraculously conceived demigod. Confucian scholars who were offended by some of the grosser absurdities of the New Text ideologues and who were usually not favored with government offices closed ranks around a rival set of classics, the so-called Old Texts, written in ancient-form characters. More important than either the differences between New and Old Text versions or their relative authenticity was the fact that the Old Text school, animated by a spirit of skepticism and a zeal for reform, undertook to recover the basic ethical and social teachings of Confucius but without abandoning the basic assumptions of Tung Chung-shu's cosmology. Although the Old Texts were put forward as the authentic classics around 90 B.C., it was not until 51 B.C. that the imperial government was finally persuaded to organize a learned conference for the purpose of hearing the claims of the rival schools. The Old Text scholars failed in this attempt to break the New Text monopoly on official scholarship, but in the reign of P'ing-ti (1-6 A.D.) several professorships for Old Text classics were established for the first time.

When Wang Mang established his new regime, he found it convenient to turn out the New Text establishment scholars altogether and install the Old Text school, thereby staking out a new ideological foundation. The Old Text scholars lent their authority to his attempt to devise a program of reform allegedly based on Chou dynasty precedents. When Liu Hsiu founded the Later Han dynasty on the ruins of the Hsin, he reinstated the New Text scholars. But the debate continued. A new round of court discussions in the White Tiger Hall in 67 A.D. reconfirmed the official standing of New Text scholarship. As official ideologists, the New Text scholars now complacently gave themselves up to sterile and pedantic glosses on the canonical texts, leaving it to their Old Text rivals to play a more creative role.

The greatest figure of the Old Text school, Wang Ch'ung (d. ca. 100 A.D.), composed his famous critique of New Text superstition, the *Lun Heng,* and inexorably the Old Texts and their scholars gained in intellectual prestige despite their failure to obtain official endorsement. The dissident scholars, who came to include a great number of minor functionaries, frustrated office seekers, and some thirty thousand students, assumed the role of a party of opposition from about 150 A.D., attacking the court aristocracy, palace eunuchs, and leading bureaucrats as the principal agents of corruption and incompetence in the empire. Some of their number, organized in a League of Literati, produced a great volume of muckraking literature of a new genre, called "righteous criticism" by its authors. The charges were written from a Confucian ethical perspective and implied that the salvation of the empire depended on a return to the classical principles of ceremonial *(li)* and righteousness. Their energy and the sharpness of their criticism provoked a swift reaction on the part of the palace eunuchs, who succeeded in having the entire membership of the League forever banned from holding office and caused many of the members to be arrested and punished. The compulsion to keep up an appearance of Confucian orthodoxy still dominated the demoralized court, however, and the official scholars were set to the task of completing one last emendation of the classical texts (New Text version), and these were then engraved on hundreds of stone tablets, a task that occupied seven years of toil (175-183 A.D.). Inasmuch as the regime was now past reforming and on the point of final collapse, the tablets appear in retrospect to have been not so much a new legitimation as an epitaph. Yet such was the prestige of the classics that the Three Kingdoms' state of Wei, striving, no doubt, to legitimize its usurpation of Han, carefully gathered up and repaired the Han tablets that had been broken and scattered in the struggle and flight of the defeated dynasty and proceeded to engrave a new set, this one of three Old Text versions of the *Book of History* and the *Tso Chuan* (commentary on the *Spring and Autumn Annals).* These works were laboriously inscribed in three scripts: the great seal (archaic), small seal (Ch'in), and clerical (Han). From the time of the Three Kingdoms, the Old Text school was orthodox and the New Text school passed from the scene.

Another way to look at the persistence of the canonical traditions is to consider those occasions on which imperial regimes incorporated classical formulae in their programs of reform. An important case in point was the repeated invocation of the *ching-t'ien,* or "well-field," system of land tenure. Mencius' description of this system has already been noted. The well-field system appears frequently in Han literature with the implication that this was the correct way to distribute rights of land use. Han statesmen were fully conscious of the agrarian problem, the concentration of fields in the hands of a few aggressive families, leading to the destitution and unrest of the peasantry. The well-field system was commonly pointed out as the undoubted solution to the problem. When Wang Mang usurped the throne in 9 A.D., one of his first acts was to institute the well-field system exactly as it was thought to have functioned in antiquity. In order to clarify the legal implications of this measure, he declared all lands to be "king's lands," by which he meant to replace private by feudal tenure. All land then was to be allotted according to the classical formula. This attempt at reform was terminated soon after by Wang Mang's inability to put it into effect. This was by no means the end of the matter, however. The Wei and the Western Chin again tried to bend social realities to fit the classic mold and once more instituted standardized land allotment systems. This effort made due allowance for the claims of aristocracy and confirmed the great families in possession of ample estates, while trying to reserve the rest of the land to the peasants and allotting it to them according to a plan.

Some thinkers of the Later Han and Three Kingdoms periods despaired of finding in any version of the Confucian ideological heritage the answers to the social and political problems of their time. The breakdown of order naturally inspired efforts to strengthen legal restraints. Some went so far as to frankly adopt the Ch'in Legalist prescriptions and principles. Ts'ui Shih, active in the mid-second century A.D., saw his own troubled time as comparable to the period of the breakdown of the Chou kingdom and therefore called for the rejection of the Confucian tradition of benevolent kingship in favor of the model of the *pa,* or "hegemon," who reestablishes order in the world by military and political power. He also asserted that restraint in the execution of the laws and humanity in the imposition of punishments could only play into the hands of the forces of disorder. The romantic military hero Ts'ao Ts'ao, who with his son Ts'ao P'ei founded the Three Kingdoms' state of Wei, was in the Legalist tradition at least in his sense of having been liberated from the ethical scruples so dear to Confucians, and their administrative reforms in Wei, though ultimately unsuccessful, showed a Legalist rigor.

During the Three Kingdoms and Western Chin periods, there was also a vigorous revival of interest in the reinterpretation of the Taoist classics of Chuang Tzu and Lao Tzu. Where the Legalists threw off the restraints of Confucian ethics and historical precedents in their search for rational and timely solutions for present problems, so the neo-Taoists rejected both Confucian convention and Legalist political activism in favor of spontaneity and naturalness. Some, such as Kuo Hsiang, late-third-century supposed author of a great interpretive commentary on the *Chuang Tzu,* tried to reconcile spontaneity with life in society. In a modification of Chuang Tzu's doctrines he denied to the Tao the status of the metaphysical absolute and source of all being. Tao for him was simply *wu,* "nothing." All things arose and underwent continual transformation spontaneously and in accord with their own natures, rather than as a consequence of the transforming operations of the Tao. This represented an extreme position on the Taoist principles of individuality and spontaneity. At the same time, however, Taoists of this persuasion took account of the social order by holding that the elements of the society and culture were also spontaneously self-created and transformed, whereas for Chuang Tzu they had been regarded as wholly artificial. Thus, to live spontaneously and happily on principles stated in the *Kuo Commentary* required spontaneous accord in thought and action with the one's own nature, but not necessarily the rejection of all convention. What was held to be harmful was deliberately to imitate any conventional model in disregard of one's own feelings. Taoists of another sort engaged in a form of dialogue called "pure conversation," by which was meant conversation dissociated from social and political realities. They represented a tendency to withdraw from society and pursue a life of heightened sensitivity to nature and to their inner states.

The period 9-317 A.D. presents many instances of the stubborn persistence of elements of classical ideology and governmental and legal forms, all against a background of social and cultural change and ideological debate. The inability of successive regimes to arrest change and restore the classical order left the way open for the widespread adoption of an alternative ideology and way of life, the alien faith of Mahayana Buddhism.

CONCLUDING REMARKS

The first Asian empires were torn apart by unmanageable concentrations of power within their societies and were subjected to invasion or infiltration by alien peoples along their Inner Asian frontiers. All of them while they lasted achieved a balance between political power at the center and in the provinces beyond. This was a precarious balance, and in each case it was disrupted by the steady erosion of imperial control over human and economic resources as these were acquired by thriving aristocracies. Weakening at the center made defense of the frontiers more difficult and it also prevented the state from protecting the peasantry from exploitation and domination by local elites. Under these circumstances, frontier peoples and oppressed peasants looked to new leaders for protection and by invasion or rebellion brought down the imperial regimes. The idea and the goal of imperial unification outlived the empires, however, and new political structures were erected again and again on the ruins of the old. The successor regimes, or their founders, selected elements of the received traditions—law, ideology, state cult, and official hierarchies and procedures—as material from which to fashion new states. However, these processes of renewal could not continue indefinitely in the face of relentless change, and eventually they ran their course.

There were marked differences, however, in the course of empire in the different Asian civilizations. The Iranian empires showed a striking diversity in the contrast between the Iranian plateau east of the Zagros, with its mixed agricultural, pastoral, and commercial economy, and the more urbanized and intensively cultivated western provinces in Mesopotamia. Since the peoples of the plateau were politically dominant they shaped the overall structure of the empire. The relatively greater importance of pastoralism on the plateau and the openness of the Inner Asian steppe frontier to the north and east imparted a more military and aristocratic character to the empires of Iran than was found in the other civilized societies of Asia. At the other extreme, the Chinese empires were substantially based on a relatively homogeneous "Han" population of farmers and townsmen, and the northern and western frontiers were somewhat more sharply defined, although this region did support a modest development of Chinese and foreign aristocratic militarism. The empires of South Asia, after the Mauryan, were not only based on the north but were mainly confined to that region. Northern India, the Indo-Gangetic plain, was more solidly agricultural than was the Iranian pleateau, but the northwest frontier was wide open to invasion from the steppes. Invaders here played an important role, and the weight of aristocratic militarism in India was greater than in China, but less than in Iran.

As a result of these differences in environment and adaptation, the empires of Iran were compelled to go the furthest in political compromise with the indigenous aristocracy, and imperial government was less effectively centralized and bureaucratic than was the case in China. Both Iran and India were subject to foreign conquest, however, and the successor states of the first empires were commonly established by outsiders. As a consequence, the indigenous political traditions, Achaemenid in the one case and Mauryan in the other, had to survive in the face of challenges by alternative traditions such as the Hellenic and possibly the Chinese and had to come to terms with such religious ideological alternatives as Zoroastrianism, Buddhism, Brahmanism, Manichaeanism, and Nestorian Christianity. In China, on the other hand, the successor states down to the end of the Western Chin in 317 A.D. were of indigenous origin, and their political and religious ideological alternatives—such as imperial Confucianism, Legalism, neo-Taoism, and popular messianism—were largely home grown, although external influences may have contributed to the latter.

Comparison of the first empires with their successor states thus raises challenging questions about the definition and measurement of centrifugal and centripetal political forces, bureaucratic and feudal institutions, and the persistence, adaption, and interaction of established and newly emerging traditions and ideologies.

BIBLIOGRAPHY

5.P THE PERSISTENCE OF EMPIRE IN THE FACE OF CHANGE: PROCESSES

Eisenstadt, Shmuel N., "Intellectuals and Tradition," *Daedalus* 101.2:1-19 (1972). A sociological analysis of the formation of traditions.

————, ed., *The Decline of Empires* (Prentice-Hall paperback, 1967), 180 pp. Selected material for comparison in different areas and periods.

Kroeber, Alfred L., *An Anthropologist Looks at History* (University of California Press paperback, 1962), 213 pp. Chapter 4, in particular, considers the role of tradition in the identity of civilizations through time.

Toynbee, Arnold J., *A Study of History*, Vol. 7A, *Universal States* (Oxford University Press paperback, 1963), 379 pp. This volume, and especially pages 1-52, presents the author's views on the uncreative character of societies organized in imperial polities.

5.1 THE PARTHIANS AND SASANIDS IN WEST ASIA

Bivar, David, "Sasanians and Turks in Central Asia," in Gavin R. G. Hambly, ed., *Central Asia* (New York, 1969), pp. 49-62. A concise account of developments on the eastern and northeastern marches of the Sasanid empire.

Colledge, Malcolm A. R., *The Parthians* (New York, 1967), 243 pp. A readable account of what is perhaps the most obscure period in the pre-Islamic history of Iran, with a good bibliography and illustrations.

Frye, Richard N., *The Heritage of Persia* (Cleveland, 1963), pp. 178-255. A far-ranging survey that draws on a wealth of source material, literary and linguistic, archaeological and numismatic, and traces the Iranian impact far beyond the bounds of the Iranian plateau.

Ghirshman, Roman, *Iran* (Penguin paperback, 1954), pp. 243-357. A survey of the period which is both scholarly and readable, by a leading archaeologist.

———, *Persian Art: The Parthian and Sassanian Dynasties, 249 B.C.-A.D. 651* (New York, 1962), 401 pp. A lavishly illustrated survey of the Iranian achievement in the visual arts during a little known but intensely creative period.

Whitehouse, David, and Andrew Williamson, "Sasanian Maritime Trade," *Iran, Journal of the British Institute of Persian Studies* 11:29-49 (1973). A preliminary analysis of the evidence for the existence of extensive Iranian contacts with the countries bordering the Indian Ocean, offering an entirely new perspective on the Sasanid period.

5.2 THE KUSHANAS AND GUPTAS IN SOUTH ASIA

Auboyer, Jeannine, *Everyday Life in Ancient India, from Approximately 200 B.C. to 700 A.D.* (New York, 1965), 294 pp. Although the author draws on source material covering many centuries, the emphasis is primarily upon the Gupta period.

Basham, Arthur L., *The Wonder That Was India* (Evergreen paperback, 1959), 568 pp. An indispensable reference work on ancient Indian civilization, organized under subject headings, with the emphasis on the Gupta period and the succeeding centuries down to the Turkish invasions.

Hallade, Madelaine, *The Gandhara Style and the Evolution of Buddhist Art* (London, 1968), 266 pp. Monograph in which the content extends far beyond the visual arts. Superbly illustrated.

Rosenfield, John M., *The Dynastic Arts of the Kushans* (Berkeley, 1967), 131 pp. An important monograph, which ranges far beyond the limits of art history, with an excellent bibliography and fine illustrations.

Thapar, Romila, *A History of India*, 2 vols. (Penguin paperback, 1965, 1966), Vol. 1, pp. 92-166. The most accessible account of the period by a leading authority.

Woodcock, George, *The Greeks in India* (London, 1966), 199 pp. A most readable account of a complicated and fascinating period.

5.3 CHINA DURING THE LATER HAN, THREE KINGDOMS, AND WESTERN CHIN

Balazs, Etienne, "Political Philosophy and Social Crisis at the End of the Han Dynasty," in Balazs, *Chinese Civilization and Bureaucracy* (New Haven, 1964), 309 pp. Analyzes the intellectual response to the disintegration of the Han state.

Dubs, Homer H., trans., *History of the Former Han Dynasty*, Vol. 3 (Baltimore, 1955), 563 pp. This translation from the first century classic of Pan Ku provides a detailed account of the career of Wang Mang.

Eberhard, Wolfram, *A History of China* (University of California Press paperback, 1971), 367 pp. Chapter 7 surveys the period of the Six Dynasties with particular attention to the role of elites of non-Chinese origin.

Fung Yu-lan, *A Short History of Chinese Philosophy* (New York, 1960), 368 pp. Chapters 18-20 survey the intellectual history of Later Han and early Six Dynasties.

Loewe, Michael, *Crisis and Confict in Han China* (London, 1974), 340 pp. This new monograph provides an account of ideological controversy and change during the Former Han.

Yang Lien-sheng, "Great Families of Eastern Han," in E-Tu Zen Sun and John de Francis, eds., *Chinese Social History* (New York, 1966), 400 pp. An important study of social change that contributed to the disintegration of the Han state.

GLOSSARY

Ashvamedha. The horse sacrifice, which was the most important and elaborate of all Vedic sacrifices and which combined a fertility cult with an assertion of political paramountcy.

Bactria. The area in northern Afghanistan bounded on the south by the Hindu Kush Mountains and on the north by the upper Amu Darya River. Originally inhabited by the Iranian Bactrians, it became, during the Seleucid period, the northeastern outpost of Hellenism and the location of the important Graeco-Bactrian kingdom.

Deccan. The great tableland of central India. The Narbada River was traditionally regarded as constituting the dividing line between northern India and the Deccan plateau.

Dihqan. Originally, a member of the lesser nobility in Sasanid Iran. The *dihqans* remained the principal landholding class down to the eleventh century but their status as a class deteriorated after the Seljuk conquest of the Iranian plateau.

Firdawsi (d. 1020). Iranian poet, author of the *Shah-nama,* or *Book of Kings,* the national epic of Iran. The *Shah-nama* preserved the memory of the pre-Islamic past of Iran, strengthened the Iranian sense of cultural identity, and helped to establish the primacy of New Persian *(Farsi)* over other Iranian dialects.

Khurasan. Formerly a vast area extending northeastward from the central Iranian desert to the Amu Darya River, with its metropolitan centers located at Nishapur, Marv, Herat, and Balkh. Today Khurasan consists of a province in northeastern Iran, bordering the U.S.S.R. and Afghanistan, with its capital at Mashhad.

Khuzistan. A province in southwestern Iran, bordering modern Iraq and the Persian Gulf, with Ahwaz as its capital. The Elamite and Achaemenid metropolis of Susa was located in Khuzistan, as were the important Sasanid centers of Shushtar and Gondeshapur. Today, Abadan, one of the world's largest oil refineries, is located in Khuzistan.

Kshatriya. The warrior caste, ranking second to the *brahman* in the caste hierarchy of Hindu India.

Kuang-wu Ti (r. 25-57 A.D.). The imperial title of Liu Hsiu, founder of the Later Han dynasty (25-220 A.D.). Liu Hsiu was a member of the imperial house of the Former Han dynasty. His regime therefore constituted a dynastic restoration.

Kushanas. Perhaps the ruling clans among the Tochari, or the Yueh-chih. Of uncertain ethnic origin, they controlled an area stretching from the Aral Sea to the Indus by the close of the first century B.C., and during the first century A.D., conquered a large part of northern and central India. Tolerant of religious and cultural diversity, they stood out as munificent patrons of Buddhism, which, under their protection, spread across Central Asia until it reached the frontiers of China.

Kushanshah. Following the Sasanid conquest of the Kushana territories west of the Indus ca. 225 A.D., the latter were incorporated into a single viceroyalty, which became the traditional appanage of the Sasanid heir apparent, who held the title of kushanshah.

Mlcchchha. "Unclean," a term of opprobrium applied to those outside the caste system, such as the tribal populations or foreigners.

Neo-Taoism. The revival of interest during the late Han and early Six Dynasties periods in philosophical Taoism. This was a decidedly syncretic school, however, which attempted to clarify Taoist metaphysics and reconcile it with the ethical and social imperatives of Confucianism.

Old Text School. An eclectic but essentially Confucian school that undertook to free Confucian doctrine from its entanglement with the cosmological system adopted by Tung Chung-shu under the patronage of Han Wu-ti. Wang Ch'ung (27-100 A.D.) and others also denounced many of the supernatural beliefs that had been incorporated into the Confucian tradition since Tung Chung-shu. The school derived its name from the fact that it made use of texts written (and possibly forged) in ancient characters, in contradistinction to the New Text version employed by Tung Chung-shu.

Sakas (Greek, **Scythians**). The nomadic-pastoral people occupying the Eurasian steppe-zone from around the sixth century B.C. to the fourth century A.D. and who spoke an Iranian language or languages. The Sakas had close cultural contacts with the Greeks of the Black Sea region and with the Iranians and played a great part in the history of northwestern India.

Sanskrit. The classical language of Hindu civilization, derived from Vedic. The parent language of a number of modern Indian vernaculars, including Hindi, Bengali, Gujarati, and Marathi.

Satrap. An Achaemenid provincial governor; the word is derived from the Greek form of the Old Persian *kshatrapa,* which also found its way into India, where it was widely used during the Saka and Kushana periods.

Shahanshah (Persian, "king of kings"). The title of the pre-Islamic rulers of Iran and also of the present-day Pahlavi dynasty. Some Islamic dynasties, notably the Buyids, adopted the title to stress continuity with the pre-Islamic past.

Sogdians. The Iranian inhabitants of Sogdiana (known to the Greeks as Transoxania), the area lying between the Amu Darya and Syr Darya rivers.

Stupa. A shrine of hemispherical shape erected over a relic of the Buddha or of a Buddhist saint.

Uigurs. A Turkish people who in 744 founded an empire in Mongolia centered on the Orkhon River; in 762 their kaghan was converted to Manichaeanism. With the overthrow of the Uigur empire in 840, the Uigur tribes were dispersed, the majority fleeing into the Tarim basin in what is now Sinkiang, where they eventually displaced the indigenous Indo-European population and where they have remained ever since.

Vazir. The minister of a Muslim ruler. In fact, a ruler might appoint concurrently two or more *vazirs* to have charge over different areas of administration but the term is usually applied in the sense of a chief minister, as with the Ottoman "grand vizier."

Vihara. A Buddhist monastery.

Wang Mang (?-23 A.D.). Nephew of the empress of the Han emperor Yuan-ti (r. 49-33 B.C.). He used the influence of his family at court to organize a coup against the throne in 9 A.D. In that year he founded the Hsin ("New") dynasty and instituted a drastic but impractical program of reform. His regime ended with his death in 23 A.D. at the hands of rebel forces.

The Rise of Universal Religions

300 to 900 A.D.

Civilizations are often identified in terms of the dominant religious traditions associated with them. Thus a term like Christendom is paralleled by the terms Dar al-Islam, the Hindu World, or the Buddhist World. This, of course, can be misleading, both because these civilizations all had a past that extended far back beyond the emergence of these universal religions and because religion in the sense of theological beliefs and ritual behavior is but part of the complex patterns that distinguish one civilization from another.

Nevertheless, it is clear that the dramatic rise and spread of Islam, the development of Hinduism, and the dissemination of Buddhism represented fundamental transformations in the history of civilizations in Asia. In the latter half of the seventh and the early part of the eighth centuries a new faith inspired the Arabs to expand throughout West Asia and into North Africa and Europe, establishing an Islamic world on the ruins of the Byzantine and Sasanid empires. In the same period Mahayana Buddhism, an elaboration of the teachings of the Indian Gautama Buddha which had been spreading gradually for some centuries through Inner Asia and into China, became firmly established in China as well as in Japan on the fringes of East Asia. In South Asia during this same era the Hinduism of the brahman elite acquired the distinctive forms that were to characterize it down to the present period.

In each case these religions provided a new cultural unity, replacing the political unity lost with the collapse of the old universal empires and their successors. The changes brought about by the permeation of these new types of religious beliefs and institutions were to leave a lasting impression on both elite and popular culture. The task of this chapter, therefore, is to distinguish these universal religions from each other and earlier types, analyze the processes by which they spread, and compare the initial phases of their impact upon the areas in which they took root.

6

PROCESSES

The Formation of Universal Religions

a. Universal theism
b. Salvation through an intermediary
c. Immortality in paradise
d. Popularization of traditions

The Spread of Universal Religions

e. Initial diffusion of universal religions
f. Adaptation of indigenous culture
g. Domestication of foreign elements

PATTERNS

1. **Islam in West Asia**
2. **Hinduism in South Asia**
3. **Mahayana Buddhism in East Asia**

6. UNIVERSAL RELIGIONS

		1	2	3	
	CHRISTIANITY	ISLAM	HINDUISM	MAHAYANA BUDDHISM	
				(CHINA)	(JAPAN)
	Julius Caesar, r. 46-44 B.C.				
B.C./A.D.	Crucifixion of Jesus, ca. 30 A.D. St. Paul and St. Peter, d. 64 Gospel of St. Mark in written form ca. 70			Early Mahayana in Kushana empire in South and Central Asia	
100	Destruction of Jewish community in Palestine Growing consensus on form of New Testament				
200					
300	Rise of monasticism Constantine calls Council of Nicaea 325 Constantinople capital of Eastern Roman empire 330; Christianity state religion 393		Brahmanism widespread in South and Southeast Asia Gupta empire 320-467; Hinduism, Buddhism and Jainism coexist	End of Western Chin in China 317 Elite acceptance of Mahayana in China Kumarajiva translates texts Fa Hsien, pilgrimage to India 399	Japanese involvement in Korea 369
400	Visigoths attack Rome 410 St. Augustin, d. 430 Last Roman emperor in West deposed 476 Franks converted to Christianity 496		Pallavas, ca. 300-888, in Tamilnad; patronage of Brahmanism in the south		
500	Byzantine conquest of Italy 533-552 Lombards invade Italy 568 Pope Gregory 590-604	Muhammad, Prophet of Islam ca. 570-632	Huns in northern India Chalukyas in western Deccan	Sui reunification of China 589; imperial patronage of Mahayana Hsuan-tsang's pilgrimage to India	Buddhism introduced into Japan ca. 538 Japanese driven from Korea 562
600					

		Flight from Mecca to Medina 622, start of Muslim calendar Caliphate of Ali 656-661	Harsha of Kanauj, 606-647, in northern India Political fragmentation in northern India		Taika reforms in Japan 645
700	Muslim invasions of Spain 711-18 Battle of Tours, 733, Muslims defeated Franks support papacy against Lombards 754	Umayyad caliphate 661-750 Abbasid caliphate 750-1258 al-Mansur, caliph 754-775; Baghdad founded	Rashtrakutas, ca. 760-970, in western Deccan Palas in Bengal ca. 760-1142	An Lu-shan's Rebellion 755, decline of T'ang	*Kojiki* 712 *Nihonshoki* 720 Todaiji temple 752 *Man'yoshu*, c. 760 New capital at Heian 794
800	Charlemagne crowned emperor 800 by Pope Leo III	Harun al-Rashid, caliph 786-809 al-Mutawakkil, caliph 847-61 Eighth Imam of the Shiis disappears 873	Shankara ca. 788-820 Pratiharas in Kanauj ca. 800-1000 Chola revival in Tamilnad ca. 850-1260	Intensified opposition to Mahayana	Last Japanese mission to China 838
900		al-Razi, physician, d. 925 al-Farabi, philosopher, d. 950	Second Chalukya dynasty, ca. 980-1180, in western Deccan		
1000		Ibn Sina (Avicenna), philosopher, d. ca. 1036 al-Biruni, polymath, d. 1048			*Tale of Genji* ca. 1012
1100		al-Nasir, caliph 1180-1225	Ramanuja d. 1137		End of Heian period 1185
1200		Mongols sack Baghdad 1258			
1300					

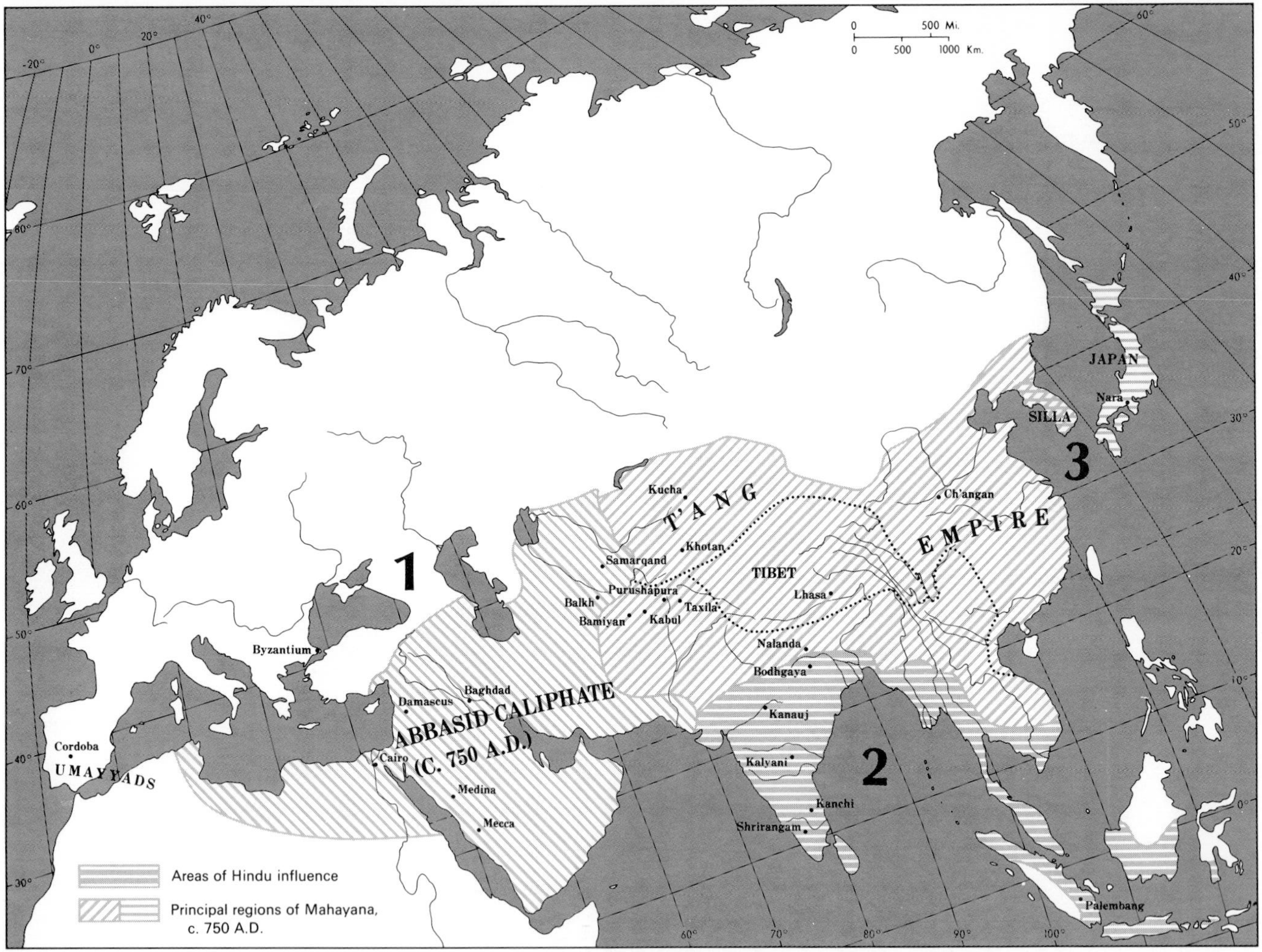

Areas of Hindu influence

Principal regions of Mahayana, c. 750 A.D.

Map 22 Universal religions

PROCESSES

The rise of new types of religions in the centuries following the breakdown of the classical patterns of the universal empires was to have far-reaching significance for the history of civilizations in Asia. The conversion to Islam in West Asia, to Hinduism in South Asia, and to Mahayana Buddhism in East Asia produced profound changes both because of the nature of these religions themselves and because of their role in the diffusion of culture across the boundaries of these civilizations. Much of the entire range of human life became permeated with a god-centered spirituality, as a new ethos of divine purpose came to pervade artistic endeavor, economic practices, political principles, social customs, and man's view of his own past and future. Human history itself was sanctified by the concept of divine providence. Not only did the classical heritage of each of these civilizations undergo complex alterations, but each was infused with new elements from outside this tradition. As in the case of Christianity, the universal religion of medieval Europe, each of these religious ideologies was in some sense alien in origin; each arose in one cultural area and had its greatest success and most enduring influence in another. As they spread they served as vehicles for the diffusion of social institutions and cultural values that were often foreign in style and substance as well as in origin. Thus two general questions will be considered in this chapter: First, what constituted the central aspects of these religions? Secondly, how were they integrated into the life of the recipient civilizations?

THE PERIOD

The startlingly rapid expansion of Islam in West Asia is conventionally dated from 622 A.D., the year that the prophet Muhammad left Mecca for the city of Medina, where his message was to gain new support. This first era in the history of Islam can be said to have closed by the end of the tenth century, when Arab hegemony in West Asia, as exemplified by the rule of the Abbasid caliphs in Baghdad, was superseded by that of various Iranian and Turkish dynasties.

In South Asia, Hinduism as a universal religion is a more elusive historical phenomenon. Although it appears to have spread northward in India during the Gupta period (320-535 A.D.), its adoption is difficult to date precisely, for the Hinduization of the north varied from region to region. One of the slowest to feel the full effects was the Bengal region in the twelfth century.

In East Asia, Mahayana Buddhism was entrenched in both the north of China and the Yangtze valley by about 300 A.D. This Buddhist era in Chinese history reached its apogee in the early T'ang dynasty (618-907) and then suffered a marked decline in the ninth century. This was not before, however, it had played an integral part in the expansion of Chinese cultural influence and the stimulation of new centers of civilization on the Korean peninsula and the Japanese archipelago.

THE FORMATION OF UNIVERSAL RELIGIONS

The religions that emerged in Asia in the first millennium A.D. were in many crucial aspects a departure from the religious creeds and practices of earlier periods. Thus throughout the following discussion particular emphasis is placed on what was essentially new and especially on contrasts with key tenets in the ethical philosophies of the moral reformers treated in Chapter 3.

a. Universal Theism

These new religions shared with earlier moral reformers a belief in the universality of truth and claimed a message valid for all mankind. Unlike those ethical philosophers, however, these new salvation ideologies were unequivocally god centered. To be sure, the Hebrew prophets had preached an ethical monotheism (although the covenant was with a particular people), and the existence of deities was not denied by most of the reformers. Nevertheless, if not atheistic, such teachers as Confucius and Buddha were at least unconvinced of the need for theism in their ethical systems. Their tone had been humanistic and existential. In the era of universal religions the tone changed and man was no longer at the center, for there stood the Allah of Islam, the Shiva or Vishnu of Hinduism, the Cosmic Buddha of Mahayana teachings, who, like the Deus of Christianity, essentially transcended the world of man. Salvation was attainable only through devotion and obedience to god's divine will.

b. Salvation through an Intermediary

The gap between man and god, however, was not unbridged. In these religions it was believed that god did intervene in this world in order to advance his divine purpose. Of particular importance was the belief that out of compassion god offered salvation through the agency of saints, *avatars,* or *bodhisattvas.* In some cases, as in Christianity, the manifestation of the divine in a particular figure was central to the new faith. Gautama Sakyamuni, the moral reformer who lived at the turn of the fifth century B.C., thus became the historical Buddha, a manifestation of the Cosmic Buddha, who had appeared in this form to offer a path to salvation. The strict monotheism of Islam resisted the attribution of divine characteristics to Muhammad; yet as the one true prophet he was to have a key place in that religion. Over time numerous historical personages and holy men acquired this charismatic aura and were placed alongside other saints in the hagiography. This was a radical departure from older salvation ideologies, which, except for the Messiah principle in Judaism, did not lay great stress on saintly or divine intervention.

c. Immortality in Paradise

The concept of salvation in these new universal religions was formulated in far more concrete terms than common in older doctrines or ethical teachings. Whereas, for example, the concept of *nirvana*—the final extinction of suffering—was quite abstract in Buddha's ethical thought, in Mahayana sects there developed elaborate descriptions of intermediary paradises where the faithful might abide after death. Islamic preachers in similar fashion focused attention on the rewards of the godly and the punishments of the ungodly in a future life beyond the grave. Thus, in these religions human life with its earthly misery could be viewed as but an interlude, and the promises of immortality for the righteous were made in terms understandable to all.

d. Popularization of Traditions

What is quite striking about these religions is the degree to which they reflected the sentiments, anxieties, and concerns of the common man. Although each was to develop a highly sophisticated theology, the central message remained capable of direct expression in terms meaningful to those outside of the literate elite. Theism and savior worship seemed particularly attractive to the masses, who saw in god's beneficence a hope that their state of degradation would ultimately end—if not in this world then in the next. Ordinary people could orient their religious lives toward the divine by personalizing their relationship with a deity, demonstrating their devotion through reverence for holy images or the relics of the saints. In this process practices of the older agrarian religions were infused with new ethical ideals, classical mythological stereotypes took on new spiritual meaning within the framework of a sacred history, and traditional philosophical systems were reinterpreted to accommodate faith in a divine will. Thus, for example, Indian fertility rites came to be identified with faith in the supremacy of the deity Shiva, and reverence for the phallic lingam to be symbolic of personal devotion to that god. On the other hand, abstract metaphysical concepts, such as *karma,* once the sole possession of priestly elites, were now available in popularized versions to the Buddhist faithful. In a similar fashion, the historical legends of West Asia, such as the Hebraic story of Joseph in Egypt, were incorporated in Muhammad's message about divine providence. The openness of these universal religions to popularization and synthesis with preexisting traditions was itself an important factor in their spread from one cultural area to another.

THE SPREAD OF UNIVERSAL RELIGIONS

For those within the faith the diffusion of Islam into West Asia, of Hinduism northward into the older centers of Indian civilization, or of Mahayana Buddhism into China is most often explained in terms of the intrinsic superiority of the new message. By the same token, those outside the faith have seen the conversion to an alien religion as the result of foreign conquests and the power of the sword. For the historian, however, the picture is more complex. Without denying the powerful appeal of these new salvation ideologies in and of themselves (especially when combined with new techniques of medicine, impressive artistic forms, and other attractive elements) or ignoring the role of political force in spreading the faith, adequate explanation must begin with an analysis of why older civilizations were open and receptive to universal religions formulated outside of the preexisting tradition. Here it needs to be stressed again that each of these civilizations was experiencing major crises within itself at the time of the introduction of the new faith. Politically, the universal states of the preceding era had collapsed, and efforts to revive their administrative institutions and to reestablish stability in the social organization and order in the economic system had been unsuccessful. The intellectual and religious orthodoxy of the classical period, having been closely identified with the universal states, suffered a similar fate. The result was a widespread sense of crisis, a loss of confidence in the validity and relevance of indigenous institutions, which thereby rendered these civilizations permeable to new influences even where these were clearly alien in origin.

e. Initial Diffusion of Universal Religions

New waves of nomadic intruders and the establishment of political dominance by aliens were both a causal factor in shattering the self-contained equilibrium of ancient civilizations and a means by which new religions were introduced. In West Asia there was a clear example of a universal religion, Islam, being introduced by the armed force of conquering Arabs. In China the initial contact with Mahayana Buddhism came over trade routes through the agency of traveling monks and merchant laymen. Yet there, too, the patronage Buddhism was to receive from regimes originally established by conquerors from outside the Chinese tradition provided a powerful stimulus for Buddhism to take root in Chinese soil. The process of conversion to the new universal religions and the adoption of associated cultural institutions and values, however, involved different factors for different strata or groups within society. For the oppressed, brotherhood within the new faith offered enhanced social status and the hope at least of escape from oppression. For new political elites it could both justify the displacement of the previous ruling class and serve as a means of circumventing and undercutting the entrenched position of older intellectual or cultural elites. Thus, for example, Buddhist monks afforded the alien Toba rulers in northern China with a means to break the hold of the native nobility and yet staff the upper echelons of government with men competent in administrative skills. Again, for merchants the advantages of religious ties in facilitating economic exchange could be a powerful and tangible incentive to conversion and the acceptance of new institutional arrangements.

f. Adaptation of Indigenous Culture

Neither the weaknesses within the recipient civilizations nor the strength of the new forces associated with the universal religions should lead us to overlook the obvious fact that traditional attitudes, norms for social behavior, institutionalized roles, and other aspects of the classical heritage had very deep roots. Far from being swept away by the floodtide of religious zeal or alien intrusion, core institutions and traditional values continued to exist and exert their influence on human life. Typically, however, these underwent a process of adaptation. Preexisting political principles such as the concept of emperorship were reinterpreted in order to accommodate to the new religious theology. Legal and bureaucratic institutions were reordered and patterns of economic behavior altered to adjust to the new religious ethos and the prominent position of religious institutions. The manner in which monasteries, for example, came to function in providing educational and charitable services did not destroy older patterns of family and community relations but did produce changes within them. Continuity with the past was thus preserved not merely by a passive coexistence of the old with the new but through a more dynamic process of adaptation.

g. Domestication of Foreign Elements

At the same time that the indigenous culture was being altered by the impact of universal religions, the complex sets of beliefs and patterns of behavior associated with the new faiths were themselves modified to be compatible with their new settings. Often the adjustments to and borrowing from the recipient environment seem superficial, and certainly they appeared so to many contemporary observers. But the use, for example, of native philosophical terms to translate the new message into the vernacular had far-reaching implications for the development of religious beliefs in the new cultural context. The elevation to the status of state religion, moreover, required new consideration to be given to the relationship between God and Caesar—that is, between the dictates of dogma and the requirements of political reality—as, for example, in the case of the caliphates in West Asia.

These processes of adaptation and domestication often worked to produce totally new cultural mixtures—artistic forms, institutional arrangements, and value systems—in which elements drawn from foreign and indigenous sources were combined in such a way as to lose their separate identities in the new synthesis. Islamic architecture is an example of how the inspiration of a universal religion interacted with preexisting artistic traditions to produce strikingly new styles. On the other hand, it is also important in conclusion to underline the fact, sometimes obscured by terms such as "Hinduization," "Indianization," sinicization, that it was often possible for the new foreign and the old indigenous patterns to retain their separate identity while coexisting. One of the more significant aspects of this is that the process of integration was therefore sometimes reversible. For example, the monastic institution of Buddhism had, by the early T'ang period in China, been closely integrated into the workings of central government and the life of the capital. By the end of the T'ang period, the political and cultural role of the Buddhist clergy had been drastically reduced and monasticism was no longer at the center of Chinese political or cultural life. Chinese civilizations continued to be permeated by Buddhism in the late T'ang, but as Confucian-oriented bureaucrats reasserted themselves and state Confucianism in a new form became dominant again, the church as a secular institution was to lose its tightly integrated position. Nevertheless, even in the case of Buddhism in China, universal religions were to make indelible impressions on civilizations in Asia.

PATTERNS

1. ISLAM IN WEST ASIA

The period covering the rise and dissemination of Islam in West Asia extended from the early seventh to the late tenth century. The beginning of the Muslim calendar dates from 622 A.D., when Muhammad, the Prophet of Islam (ca. 570-632), fled from his birthplace, Mecca, and sought sanctuary for himself and his followers in the neighboring city of Medina. The Islamic world order established by the caliphs, his successors as leaders of the Muslim community, began to disintegrate during the tenth century, when Iranian dynasts and Turkish warlords asserted their *de facto* independence over extensive areas of West Asia, just as the Berbers were to do later in North Africa and Spain. The caliphate itself survived until 1258, when Baghdad was sacked and the last reigning Abbasid caliph was killed by the Mongols, but long before that time Arabo-Islamic civilization as it had emerged during the seventh, eighth, and ninth centuries had been deeply permeated by non-Arab, and especially Iranian, influences.

Muhammad died in 632. His role as leader of the Muslim community, although not his unique prophetic role, was assumed by a succession of four caliphs (from the Arabic word *khalifa,* meaning "successor"), chosen from among his former companions, under whose direction the Arabs extended their conquests to include the eastern provinces of the Byzantine empire and the greater part of the Sasanid empire, and the newborn Muslim polity began to take shape. The last of these caliphs was the Prophet's cousin and son-in-law, Ali (656-661). Following his assassination, a political opponent, Muawiya, established the dynasty of the Umayyad caliphs. Distantly related to the Prophet, the Umayyads transferred the capital of the expanding Arab empire from Medina to Damascus, where they became exposed to the lure of Syrian and Hellenistic influences. The Umayyads ruled from 661 to 750 and extended the frontiers of the Islamic world from Spain to the Indus. In 750, however, a revolt in the eastern provinces of the empire resulted in the establishment of a new line of caliphs, the Abbasids, descendants of the Prophet's uncle, Abbas. The Abbasids, whose military supporters were drawn mainly from the Arab garrisons stationed in Khurasan, fell increasingly under the influence of Iranian culture and especially of pre-Islamic Iranian traditions of government and statecraft. They abandoned Damascus, with its Umayyad associations, and built a new capital, Baghdad, founded by the caliph al-Mansur (754-775) on the Tigris, close to the ancient metropolitan centers of Babylon, Seleucia, and Ctesiphon. The Abbasids survived until 1258, reigning for a span of five centuries, but it was only during the first two centuries that they effectively ruled as well as reigned. Thereafter, their authority was greatly reduced by the turbulence of the people of Baghdad, the mutinous conduct of their own bodyguards, the ambitions of provincial governors, the aspirations of Iranian dynasts in the east and, finally, the penetration of much of West Asia by a succession of Turkish invaders from Central Asia.

For most Muslims, the caliphs, even when they were known to be incompetent and worldly, were still regarded as possessing a unique kind of charisma. There were, however, two groups of Muslims who consistently denied the legitimacy of the caliphs, whether Umayyad or Abbasid. The first of these was the Kharijites, a community of fundamentalists originating among the tribal population bordering the sedentary zone of southern Iraq, the name the Arabs gave to Mesopotamia. The second group comprised the supporters of Ali, Muhammad's cousin and son-in-law, who believed that the leadership of the Muslim world lay with Ali and his descendants. In their view, these latter should have succeeded Ali as caliph but for the treachery of Muawiya, which led to the usurpation first of the Umayyads and then of the Abbasids. To the partisans of Ali (known as Shiis), all the caliphs since 661 were illegitimate since sovereignty was invested in Ali and his descendants, the twelve Shii

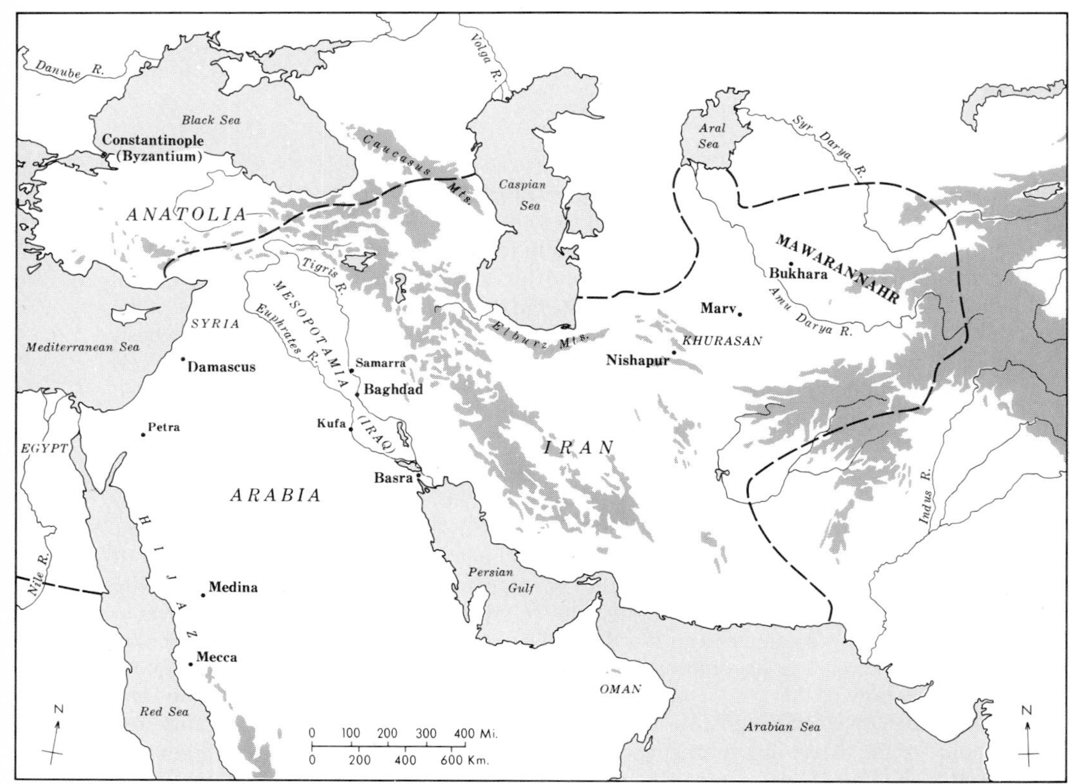

Map 23 The Abbasid caliphate, about 800 A.D.

imams (*imam* meaning the head of the Muslim community), most of whom fell foul of the government of the day, which was fearful of their potential charisma as political leaders. The Shiis ascribed to the imams the role of divine comforters and attributed to them the quality of perfectability; some even regarded them as emanations of the Godhead. The twelfth and last of the imams, Muhammad al-Mahdi, disappeared in the cellar of his house in Samarra in 873. The Shiis believe that although he is now hidden from the world, he continues to watch over its affairs and that he will emerge again from his concealment on the Day of Judgment.

Islam as a religious system is primarily associated with the Arabian peninsula, one of the most arid and sparsely populated areas on the surface of the earth. It is important to recognize, however, that Arabia, although vast and remote, was very far from being cut off from the ancient centers of civilization in West Asia. Although much of the center of the peninsula consists of desert, its northern and northwestern fringes are adjacent to the relatively densely populated lands of the Fertile Crescent, bringing its inhabitants into direct contact with the ancient civilizations of Mesopotamia, Syria, and even Egypt. These pre-Islamic Arabs consisted not only of nomadic pastoralists, the bedouin, but also of townsfolk and agriculturists. An important trade route, passing through the Hijaz, linked southern Arabia, famous in Roman times as a source of frankincense and other aromatics, to the ports of the eastern Mediterranean, and long before the preaching of Islam, caravan cities such as Mecca itself and Petra, in the present-day kingdom of Jordan, were flourishing commercial centers. In the far south of the peninsula, the Yemen sheltered important agricultural communities. Arabian archaeology is still in its infancy but it can be assumed that a century from now knowledge of pre-Islamic Arabia will have expanded far beyond what is known today. If so, much new light may be thrown not only on material living conditions but also on the antecedents of Islam itself.

Although Arabia is thought of mainly in terms of its vast deserts, the sea has always been a significant factor in the history of the region. The peninsula itself possesses an enormous coastline, with many excellent harbors. Some of the most fertile parts of Arabia, such as the Yemen, Hadramawt, and Oman, lie close to the sea, while both the Persian Gulf and the Red Sea are conveniently narrow stretches of water which have been major trade routes since the earliest times, giving easy access to the ancient centers of civilization in West Asia—lower Mesopotamia and Egypt. In those comparatively safe waters experience in the construction and handling of boats probably developed at much the same time as on the Nile and on the eastern Mediterranean seaboard, and it seems likely that from very early times the Arabs of the coastal regions were inveterate mariners and traders.

As a way of life, Islam, youngest of the world's great religious systems, appears deceptively simple. The most important injunctions placed upon a Muslim are: affirmation of belief in Allah as the one true God and of Muhammad as His Prophet; prescribed daily prayers; almsgiving; fasting during the month of Ramazan; and, when practicable, pilgrimage to the holy cities of Mecca and Medina. Obviously, during the course of many centuries Islam has elaborated its teachings and broadened its theological horizons far beyond these initial five pillars of the faith, but they remain, nonetheless, the core of Muslim belief and worship.

The Formation of Islam as a Universal Religion

Perhaps the most striking aspect of the new religion preached by Muhammad to the pagan population of the Hijaz was its unswerving monotheism: there were no two ways of serving God; there were no alternative paths to follow. Truth was absolute. It knew no qualification. It was also universal in its application. Islam was for all men who were prepared to believe in the teachings of Muhammad. It was not restricted to a particular people, as was Judaism. Nor was it the product of a socio-religious system confined within a particular geographical area, as was Hinduism. Its truths had been enunciated in part over many centuries by a succession of earlier prophets sent by God, including Abraham, Moses, and Jesus. The last and greatest of these messengers from God was Muhammad, who was the Seal of the Prophets because his teachings, embodied in the Quran, were the fulfillment of all that had gone before him. Never again would God have need to send another prophet.

What mattered above all else in Islam was faith, which meant unquestioning obedience to the will of God. God was all-knowing and all-merciful, but His intentions were inscrutable and His purposes unknown. He was seen most often as a judge who rewarded the virtuous and punished the wicked, and hence there were ascribed to Him those attributes of a father figure already familiar to the Abrahamic tradition. Because what mattered most was to have faith in God and to obey His word, the Muslim world view necessarily projected a division of human society into two categories, those who believed in God and endeavored to do His bidding, and those who did not. This division of the world into believers and nonbelievers , Muslims and non-Muslims, pervaded the Muslim psychology at all levels. It meant that the world was divided into two regions: the *Dar al-Islam,* which consisted of all those lands where Muslims lived under the law of Islam, protected by a Muslim ruler, and the *Dar al-Harb,* which was the land of the infidels. Within the *Dar al-Islam,* non-Muslims were permitted to reside but only on sufferance as a protected community, living in accordance with their own laws in all matters relating to their religion and customs but severely circumscribed in the overall range of their activities. Originally conceived as a means for regulating the life of those Christian and Jewish communities

6.1 The Great Mosque at Mecca. Ottoman Turkish miniature, early eighteenth century. Pilgrimage to Mecca and Medina, the Holy Cities of the Hijaz (Arabia), is incumbent upon all Muslims who are able to undertake the journey. Courtesy: Chester Beatty Library, Dublin.

encapsulated within the Arab empire of the caliphs, the concept of a non-Muslim as a protected person (*dhimmi*) was eventually extended beyond the so-called Peoples of the Book—Christians and Jews—to include the Zoroastrians of Iran and even, following the Muslim conquests in northwestern India, the Hindus.

India presented a peculiarly difficult case because there the majority of the subjects of the Muslim state were, and remained, infidels and, far worse, idol worshippers. Was India, therefore, truly *Dar al-Islam,* even when an indubitably orthodox Muslim sultan ruled in Delhi? Most thinkers were inclined to stretch the definition in these circumstances, but a further difficulty in defining what constituted the *Dar al-Islam* arose following the establishment of European colonial rule during the late eighteenth and nineteenth centuries. If India under the sultans of Delhi and the Mughul padshahs was regarded as part of the *Dar al-Islam,* was it still to be so regarded when the Muslims of India had passed under infidel rule, even when the new regime was meticulous in avoiding interference in religious matters? In this, opinion was divided, even among those regarded as leaders of the community. There was, however, not much doubt that it was highly undesirable for Muslims to live within the *Dar al-Harb,* against which, at least in theory, ceaseless warfare should be waged until the whole earth acknowledged the one true God and the words of His prophet. Holy warfare against unbelievers (*jihad*) was held to be a religious act of the highest merit, and the *ghazi,* the soldier who fought on the frontiers of the Muslim world against the foes of his faith, believed that if he was killed in battle in the course of *jihad,* he would be transported straightaway to paradise.

To the Muslim, the human soul (and also, in some sense, the human body) was immortal, with the prospect, therefore, of life beyond the grave. Obedience to God's will brought reward in a future life, if not in this one, and no less certainly, disobedience brought retribution. The Muslim, like the Christian, possessed a very vivid perception of what to expect in the afterlife. Accustomed to living, for the most part, in arid lands, where water is precious and the heat can be unbearable, the first Muslims conceived of paradise as a garden, shaded by trees and made cool by running water, where the faithful were to be forever served by moon-faced *houris* ("maidens"). The image of the garden suggests Iranian influence, while the *houris* (proof to nineteenth century European traducers of Islam of incorrigible Muslim sensuality) may be in part derived from the female attendants of the Zoroastrian afterlife. Hell, naturally enough, was conceived of as a place of torment where the damned suffered in agony as punishment for their sins in this world.

As in the case of other religious systems, Islam was confronted by that fundamental problem of human suffering when the sufferer is clearly not guilty of any sin—the problem posed in the Book of Job. Such cases could not be justified on the grounds of divine retribution, and since Islam knew no doctrine of reincarnation there could be no question, as in the case of Buddhism, of punishment for sins committed in a previous existence. The Muslim, therefore, concluded that the suffering of the innocent was a test of faith. In the last resort, it was evidence of the inscrutable will of God.

Islam offered men and women salvation if they obeyed God's will and avoided sinful conduct. Sin was disobedience to God's will. God's will was made known to the world through the words of His prophet, and in particular through the Quran, the Muslim sacred text that was believed to be, quite literally, the word of God given to Muhammad by the angel Gabriel. Because it was held to be God given, there was little or no possibility of modifying or stretching its injunctions. Glosses could be made on the meaning of obscure passages but its origin meant that, in all essentials, it was inviolable. The Quran, however, was a relatively short book and there were extensive areas of social behavior and belief with which it failed to deal. These omissions were, in course of time, met with by the *Hadith,* or *Sayings of the Prophet,* which, with the passage of several generations, multiplied enormously. Thus it became necessary to weed out those that were spurious from those that were genuine, and so the authentication of *Hadith* became a major intellectual pursuit among Muslim scholars. Yet even the Quran and the *Hadith* together were not sufficient in themselves to determine every aspect of life in the new society, and so there took shape the *Sharia,* or *Law of Islam,* which, together with the Quran and the *Hadith,* has ever since determined the prevailing configuration of life-style, behavior, and psychological attitudes throughout the Muslim world. Like the Quran, the authority of the *Sharia* emanates ultimately from God, and so it has proved, even in the present century, extraordinarily difficult for Muslim reformers and innovators to bypass it.

The Divisions of Islam: Shiis and Sufis

Together, the Quran, the *Hadith* and the *Sharia* provided the Muslim with all that he needed in order to serve God and follow the path of salvation. At least such was the view of those Muslims—at all periods, the overwhelming majority—who observed the custom of the community *(sunna)* and who were consequently known as Sunnis. Yet from very early times there were always some Muslims who felt that the *sunna* was not enough, that it was too rigid, too impersonal, or too austere to meet the entire range of their emotional needs. Such people sought a more personal relationship with their Creator, needing to express their faith not only through obedience but also through love. One such group was the Sufis, the mystics of Islam. Another was the Shiis, the largest minority sect in the Muslim world, who are now restricted mainly to the Yemen, Iran, and parts of Iraq and northern India but who in the past exercised an influence on the evolution of Islam out of all proportion to their numbers.

During the early Islamic period Shiism possessed elements that were eschatological, dynastic, and social. In theological terms, Shiism met a deeply felt need for divine intercession in the affairs of men. This was provided by the Twelve Imams, of whom the twelfth, the Hidden Imam, would return as the Mahdi, or "rightly guided one," on the Day of Judgment. But this conception of the imam as divine intercessor was joined with a powerful desire on the part of some Muslims to have the leadership of the community invested in the family of Ali as charismatic, hereditary rulers, and hence Shiism attracted those who were hostile to the rule of caliphs, whether Umayyads or Abbasids, and who rejected their claim to be the legitimate leaders of the community. Thus, again and again in the early Islamic centuries, political revolts were headed or initiated by leaders claiming descent from Ali. Prior to the successful revolution of the Fatimids in North Africa during the tenth century, virtually all these revolts proved abortive, due either to inept leadership or to a lack of widespread popular support. They were, however, regarded with the greatest apprehension by the authorities. Shiism was attractive not only to those with political grievances. It also exercised a subversive appeal for those peoples occupying areas remote from the main course of events in West Asia, such as the Elburz Mountains of northern Iran, always a rich breeding ground for sectarian movements, although it was not until the sixteenth century that Iran itself became a bastion of Shiism, which it remains to this day.

Not all Muslims who felt the need for a more personal faith turned to the emotionally charged doctrines of Shiism. The majority followed the mystical path of the Sufis (so-called from the Arabic word for wool, *suf,* from which their robes were made), seeking to establish a personal relationship between God and man. There has been much controversy as to the origins of the mystical and esoteric elements in Islam. Some scholars have stressed the preponderant influence of Christian, Gnostic, and even Hindu elements, while others have drawn attention to indigenous strands of mystical and esoteric thinking extending back to the Quran itself. But, whatever its origins, Sufism as the term is generally understood was a comparatively late development that appears to have appealed mostly to non-Arabs—Iranians, Turks, and Indians. It also provided the impetus for forms of institutionalized religion of a kind hitherto unknown in Islam—brotherhoods of Sufi dervishes, organized into orders (*tariqa*); chains of authority (*silsila*) passed down through each order from generation to generation by a *murshid,* or "spiritual director" (popularly known as a *shaykh*), to a favorite disciple, who was often his son or grandson; and convents (*khanqah*) where the dervishes meditated, taught, undertook charitable activities, and lived a life of communal worship. The essence of Sufism was love of God, expressed at its highest level in the passionate outpourings of the mystical poets, wherein the worshipper addressed God in the language of a lover approaching his mistress, frequently using phrases of thinly concealed eroticism. Nor was the imagery of the lover the only borrowing from everyday life which the Sufis adopted to stimulate the intensity of their faith: music and dancing, frowned upon by the pious, were also enlisted in the quest for spiritual exaltation.

These various paths to salvation—the *sunna* for the orthodox, the imamate for the Shiis, and the mystical way of the Sufis, who might be either orthodox or heterodox—were largely matters of personal faith, determined by the place and the time. But in a broader sense the Muslim saw the entire span of human history as a ceaseless striving for salvation, history being, in its purest essence, the record of God's purpose for mankind, or how He had sent a succession of prophets who were His messengers, each one of whom revealed a part of His divine will. Among these prophets were to be found figures from the Jewish and Christian experience, including Noah, Abraham, Moses, Elisha, John the Baptist, and even Jesus, since both the Jews and the Christians had been chosen to be agents of God's will and were monotheists who possessed a sacred scripture and who had foresworn idolatry, the most loathsome of offenses in the sight of God. But at the end of this chain of prophets, He sent a final prophet, Muhammad, who revealed His will in its entirety, thus rendering superfluous the revelations of his predecessors. With his coming and the dissemination of his message there was no longer any excuse for men to disregard God's will, since Muhammad was the Seal of the Prophets, the last messenger, whose teaching superseded the partial revelation of earlier prophets. As a messenger he had done no more and no less than to pass on the divine will, and his utterances, preserved in the Quran, were held to be, in the most literal sense, the Word of God. Once his teachings had been passed on to a sufficient number of people, the spread of the new faith, whether by force or persuasion, became incumbent upon all believers, and as the Arab armies swept across three continents it seemed as if the new age that was dawning, the age of Islam, was the culmination of the human experience. Assured of rewards in the life to come, Muslims were also to be rewarded with the good things of this life as well. If this sense of history being on their side was inherent in the Muslim psyche during the first Islamic centuries, it immediately becomes apparent how painful and perplexing to thinking Muslims were to be the great misfortunes of later centuries—the Christian crusades in Syria and the Iberian *Reconquista,* the Mongol holocausts of the thirteenth century and the humiliations of European imperialism.

In practice, Islam was not spread mainly by the sword. There were plenty of enforced conversions among the recently conquered peoples, but in general the process was one of gradual acculturation to the Islamic life-style, in which many motives, including self-interest, played a part. Moreover, throughout the first two or three Islamic centuries there remained within the framework of the empire of the caliphs substantial minorities of non-Muslims—Zoroastrians, Jews, and Armenian and Nestorian Christians—while in some of the more remote areas older cults proved extraordinarily resilient. In general, Islam spread rapidly because it possessed a deep and pervasive appeal that went far beyond anything West Asia had known prior to that time. In the seventh century A.D. official Christianity meant for most of the Christian communities of Asia the intolerant orthodoxy of the Byzantine emperors. For the subjects of the Sasanid shahanshah, Zoroastrianism had become a state church with an exclusive priesthood intent on enforcing religious conformity. By way of contrast, the new faith of Islam was a religion open to all people, irrespective of race, color, sex, or social background, who thereby became part of the *umma,* the "community of believers." It is true that in later centuries Muslims would be compelled to submit to despotisms as ruthless and exploitive as in any other society, but Islam itself as a way of life always retained an egalitarian component, not always very obvious to the outside observer yet a factor of some importance in determining the nature of social relationships. This was due partly to the awesome distance separating man from God, which made both sultan and slave alike seem as mere grains of sand before the throne of Allah. The most devout Muslim aspired only to become "the slave of God."

Islam knew no priesthood, and in this it stood in striking contrast to Christianity, Zoroastrianism, or Hinduism. Islam possessed no sacramental or truly ritual elements involving the participation of priestly intercessors, but the social function and leadership roles undertaken by the clergy in Christian society were filled in Islam by the *ulama* (from the Arabic *alim,* meaning a person learned in the Islamic sciences), who were scholars and teachers educated in theological exegesis and jurisprudence, especially the Quran, the *Hadith,* and the *Sharia*. Their social significance lay not so much in their theological expertise, since theology per se occupied a less prominent position in Islam than in Christianity, but in their knowledge of the law. This was because the *Sharia* pervaded every aspect of daily life, regulating patterns of behavior, of diet and dress, and, more especially, relationships between kindred, neighbors, and the community at large. Not to obey the *Sharia* was to live the life of an infidel, but to live strictly in accordance with its injunctions called for guidance and the ultimate sanction of coercion. Thus, it was the *ulama* who had the responsibility for determining whether a particular community observed the *Sharia* correctly and hence whether it was a community composed of pious and God-fearing Muslims.

Apart from the fees and emoluments attached to certain offices, the *ulama* were provided for mainly out of endowments granted in perpetuity and known as *waqfs*. The less prestigious among them looked after the local mosque or shrine, announced the prescribed hours of prayer, preached the Friday sermon in the principal congregational mosque of the town or city, and taught children the basic tenets of the faith at a mosque school. The most prestigious among the *ulama* included scholars and teachers of Islamic learning (who in later times were generally attached to a *madrasa,* or "theological college"), consultant jurists and, most important of all, *qazis,* or "judges." Usually appointed to his post by the caliph or sultan, the *qazi,* once in office, exercised authority more or less independently of the ruler, and since it was upon him that the responsibility rested for ensuring that the community lived in accordance with the *Sharia,* his importance as a social force can hardly be exaggerated. In passing, it should be noted that the lack in Islam of an official church or clergy made it much harder than in Christianity to enforce orthodox belief other than by the intervention of the *qazi* or other leading members of the *ulama,* acting on behalf of popular consensus. There was no ecclesiastical hierarchy and there were no ecclesiastical jurisdictions, so that inquisitorial processes such as those familiar to Christian Europe were hardly possible. In matters of faith, the *ulama* could coerce dissidents by threats of legal action, perhaps reinforced by mob violence, but the advocate of heterodox opinions, once he had quitted the city in which his views were unpopular, might reside unmolested in a neighboring city if the local *ulama* happened to be indifferent to his views or if he could acquire a powerful protector.

In watching over the welfare of the community, the *qazi* was assisted by another important local figure, the *muhtasib,* whose functions were to enforce the law with regard to what was forbidden and what was permitted to Muslims. Since he was also an inspector of markets, his tasks included such diverse matters as preventing wine drinking and prostitution, regulating the conduct of the *dhimmis,* and keeping a check on all commercial transactions. Thus, it was his responsibility to ensure, for example, that flour was not adulterated, that animals were killed by the butchers in the prescribed manner, that slaves were not abused in the slave market, and that the shopkeepers' weights and measures were accurate. For the most part, both the *qazi* and the *muhtasib* carried out their duties without reference to whatever was the formal political authority above them. Rulers and governors might come and go, but the enforcement of the *Sharia* had to be maintained whenever practicable, and it was the *qazi* and to a lesser extent the *muhtasib* who provided continuity in the form of legitimate authority. This goes a long way to explaining why Islamic society as a whole could remain so fundamentally stable, even during periods of dynastic upheaval. Men lived under the authority of the *Sharia* quite as much as, if not more, than they lived under the rule of caliph or sultan, and the *Sharia* was enforced by the *qazi*, who taken with the *ulama* in general was regarded by the urban population as the natural head of the local community.

This also goes far toward explaining an important aspect of Islamic civilization, the apparent indifference with which the greater part of the population observed the political comings and goings of dynasty and court. Most Muslims were well aware that much of the public or private life of the ruling elite accorded very little with the injunctions of the *Sharia* and so they came to regard political life as a whole as something outside their own experience, attuned to goals and values different from their own. The reasons for this development were largely fortuitous. During his own lifetime Muhammad had been both the Prophet of Islam and the political leader of the new community. At his death his prophetic function died with him, but the community still needed political leadership, and this was provided by Muhammad's *khalifa* (caliph), or "successor." The first four caliphs had been close associates of the Prophet, while the fourth, Ali, was his cousin and son-in-law. They enjoyed not only the prestige that accrued to the office of caliph but also a special kind of reverence and even charisma due to their having been among the companions of the Prophet. After the murder of Ali, however, the caliphate passed to the Umayyads, who transferred the capital of the empire to Damascus in Syria, where they held court as worldly potentates, influenced by the imperial traditions of Byzantium and to a lesser extent Iran, so that they came to be regarded both in their own day and ever afterwards as self-indulgent and unrighteous. After 750, when the Abbasids replaced the Umayyads, this trend continued. The Abbasids, although more concerned than the Umayyads with promoting an image of themselves as spiritual leaders of the entire Muslim world, contributed even further to the transformation of the caliphate into a traditional type of universal empire. Whereas the first four caliphs had lived lives of patriarchal simplicity, the Abbasids maintained a brilliant and extravagent court, where they were surrounded by foreign slaves and bodyguards, were supported by a vast bureaucracy of officials, and enjoyed the company of large numbers of slave concubines, watched over by eunuchs. Originally the caliph had been known simply as the Commander of the Faithful, a title reflecting his role as military leader of the Muslims, but to this came to be added other honorifics such as the Shadow of God on Earth, which reflected his transformation into an Iranian shahanshah, heir to centuries of Achaemenid and Sasanid absolutism. The bureaucracy, whether residing in Baghdad or stationed throughout the provinces, was supervised by the caliph's deputy and chief minister, the *vazir*, and his office too was ultimately derived from a Sasanid model.

Historians have long pondered over the extraordinary rapidity with which the Arab armies overran within the span of three or four generations an area stretching from the Atlantic Ocean and the Pyrenees to the Indus and the Syr Darya, and also the fact that they encountered so little effective opposition. Obviously, among the factors to be reckoned with were the religious zeal and the thirst for plunder of predominantly bedouin troops, whose nomadic background gave them the advantage of maximum mobility as compared to their sedentary foes and who were frequently commanded by leaders possessing remarkable tactical skills. Yet these factors alone are not sufficient to explain what happened. Account must also be taken of the internal dissensions of their enemies. Both the Byzantine and Sasanid empires were suffering from internal exhaustion, partly as a result of their recent mutual conflicts, and both contained communities that were fiercely oppressed by their respective governments. In the Asian and African provinces of the Byzantine empire many Christians—Copts, Nestorians, Armenians, etc.—had long been alienated from the regime by the persecuting activities of the Orthodox church. The Sasanid empire was divided by deep and bitter social cleavages and harsh oppression of the lower orders. In both empires, official Christianity and Zoroastrianism displayed a withering of the spirit consequent upon their identification with the authority of the state and the interests of the ruling classes. Islam, by way of contrast, possessed all the immediate appeal of a new ideology that combined with the proselytizing zeal of its missionaries a degree of tolerance that, at least at first, was in sharp contrast to the persecuting policies of Byzantine Orthodoxy and Sasanid Zoroastrianism. The first generations of Muslim conquerors did not insist on the total conversion of the newly conquered population. Indeed, for them to have done so would have been somewhat injudicious, since apart from war booty the principal source of revenue for the Muslim state in its early years was derived from taxing non-Muslims.

In Sasanid Iran and Byzantine Syria there had been much social oppression—crippling taxation and, in the former, rigid social stratification, which included, for example, the exemption of the nobility from paying taxes. Many, although not all, of these disabilities were now swept aside. The Arabs remained a privileged group but the non-Arab subject peoples, who in any case greatly outnumbered their conquerors, were gradually co-opted into the system, first by becoming Muslims and then by becoming clients *(mawali)* of a particular Arab tribe, a privilege that extended to the client's entire family and even, in some instances, community. The *mawalis* were to some extent second-class citizens, but they were usually no worse off and were often much better off than they had been before. The rapidity of the diffusion of Islam meant that almost within the span of a single generation the opportunities for personal advancement available to the *mawalis* increased enormously, and most conspicuously in the sphere of commercial life. The new universal empire of the caliphs brought into being a marketing area of a size such as the world had never seen before, stretching from Morocco and Spain to China, a marketing area straddling three continents wherein a common religion, a common life-style and, above all, a common medium of communication (Arabic) for the upper classes released the potentialities of economic activity over immense distances of the earth's surface. Arab caravans penetrated the Great Wall of China, Arab *dhows* furrowed the seas beyond Ceylon and even the Straits of Malacca, and Arab merchants frequented the trading marts on the frontier marches of the lands of the Franks and the Slavs, while in the dark forests of the north, Viking warriors traded slaves, furs, amber, and walrus ivory for the golden *dinars* and silver *dirhams* on which were inscribed the name of the one true God and of his deputy on earth, the Commander of the Faithful.

Throughout the *Dar al-Islam* a new religion, a new pattern of legal institutions, and new forms of government imposed some degree of uniformity over lands of great ethnic and cultural diversity. Below the surface, however, more ancient ways continued to survive relatively intact, exemplifying long-standing regional traditions and particularist identities. Despite the pervasive role of Islam in everyday affairs, the dominant features of social life in, say, urban Syria remained different from those of urban Iraq or Khurasan. Established centers such as Damascus in Syria, Marv or Nishapur in Khurasan, or Bukhara beyond the Amu Darya did not acquire their later Islamic characteristics overnight. Even the new cities that were founded as garrison headquarters and administrative centers in Iraq, such as Kufa, Basra and, at a somewhat later date, Baghdad, can never have been wholly Arab in their ethnic composition since, apart from the military, the majority of their populations would from the outset have consisted of non-Arab *mawalis.* In the eyes of at least some, perhaps most, of the latter, the Arabs must have appeared as barbarous and uncouth while, by way of contrast, the *mawalis* at their best embodied centuries of practical wisdom in the economic utilization of the resources available to them as well as in matters of statecraft and government and in the quest for the good life. It followed, therefore, that not the least of the problems facing the new rulers was how to prevent both their followers and themselves from being wholly assimilated by their subjects. Hence their concern to retain traditional Arab ties of tribe and clan and to maintain, as far as was practicable, a segregated camp life designed to prevent the Arab tribesmen from being seduced by the attractions of alien ways of life.

Inexorably, however, the Arabs found themselves absorbing substantial elements in the indigenous cultures of the *mawalis.* For example, the court life and administrative arrangements of the early Umayyads and even the architectural style of their mosques and palaces showed unmistakable Byzantine derivation. In Abbasid Baghdad, on the other hand, the traditions of ancient Iran overshadowed all other influences, taking concrete form with al-Mansur's Round City, the caliph's residential quarter in Baghdad, which was probably inspired by Sasanid prototypes. Slavery and polygamy, both endemic in pre-Islamic Mesopotamia and Iran, were regulated and to some extent humanized by the injunctions of the *Sharia,* but they also may have become more widespread. Certain of the least attractive features of Sasanid times—the unrestrained despotism of the shahanshah, the confinement of large numbers of women in the harems of the ruler and his nobles, and the ubiquity of eunuchs and executioners at the royal court—proliferated in Abbasid Baghdad in an atmosphere of debilitating luxury and fearful insecurity. All this was alien to the traditional life-style of the desert Arab.

At the same time, the caliphs adopted many practical measures from their predecessors in matters ranging from chancellery protocol to the definition of land tenures and irrigation rights. The bureaucratic families that had for generations served former regimes were enlisted in the service of the new state, and for a surprisingly long time the pre-Islamic coin types remained in circulation, Arabo-Byzantine gold *dinars* (derived from the Roman *denarius)* in the west and Arabo-Sasanid silver *dirhams* in the east. In such ways continuities with the pre-Islamic past were maintained, especially in the Iranian culture zone. There, the Iranians, possessed of a profound sense of their historic achievements, tenaciously treasured the memory of the kings and heroes of ancient times, a memory that under their influence infected even the Arabs themselves.

While the Arabs were adopting and adapting elements of *mawali* culture, Islam itself was undergoing modification in the course of adjusting itself to a wider world. In Syria and Mesopotamia it felt the impact of Hellenistic and Christian influences; on the Iranian plateau, the influence of pre-Islamic Iran. Perhaps the most significant change of all may be termed the urbanization of Islam as a way of life. It is true that Islam itself had originated in an urban setting—first in Mecca and afterwards in Medina—but during the initial Muslim conquests the faith had been disseminated by means of Arab armies composed mainly of nomadic bedouin of the desert, and there would always remain certain aspects of Islam that betrayed its Arabian origins. Despite all that, however, there grew up the conviction that the ideal Muslim society was an urban one, in which one lived one's life as a member of a community of fellow believers, with a congregational mosque serving as a place for communal worship and assembly and with such amenities as running water and a bathhouse to enable one to carry out the prescribed ablutions that preceded the act of prayer. Propriety required the seclusion of women, and this in turn called for maximum privacy and special domestic arrangements that were practicable only within an urban setting. Neither the cultivator, who needed to use his women for manual labor, nor the nomad, whose women assisted him in the tending of his livestock, could effectively maintain such a system, and for this, as for much else, they were judged to be indifferent Muslims. To put it another way, only in an urban environment could the *Sharia* be enforced in all its rigor, with the commands of the *qazi* and the views of the *ulama* in general enjoying the full force of popular support. Thus, irrespective of its size, the city came to be seen as a natural repository of religious values and ultimately of civilization, the only place where the ordinary Muslim who was neither dervish nor hermit could be sure of living in accordance with the injunctions of the *Sharia*.

In intellectual terms, Islam imbibed a wide range of alien influences, although not without much heart searching and dissension. In particular, the process of assimilating Hellenistic philosophy and scientific knowledge called for a most strenuous readjustment of intellectual horizons, so that some turned aside rather than face the full implications of that confrontation. Yet, notwithstanding the presence of the intellectually pusillanimous and the downright obscurantist, West Asia, together with Spain and North Africa, experienced during the centuries of Arab domination one of the most exhilarating epochs in the history of the human mind, as the new ideology and the dynamic forces that Arab domination had unleashed grappled with and endeavored to synthesize old knowledge and new experience. It is difficult to categorize precisely the great thinkers of the Abbasid period—al-Kindi (*fl.* tenth century), al-Razi (d. 925), al-Farabi (d. 950), Ibn Sina (d. 1036?), or al-Biruni (d. 1048), among many others—since their intellectual curiosity was so eclectic that they dabbled in many fields. True wandering scholars, passing from city to city and from court to court seeking patronage wherever they could find it, they have frequently come down in history as, say, philosophers or mathematicians, although in their own lifetimes they were better known as physicians or astronomers or even men of affairs. Nor is it easy to label them in a geographical or ethnic sense, since although they were as likely to be of Iranian or even Turkish descent as of Arab, they invariably wrote their treatises in Arabic and were representatives of a highly cosmopolitan culture that was as much at home in Cordoba or Fez as it was in Herat or Bukhara. Muslim scholars were attracted to certain well-defined areas of knowledge—medicine, mathematics, astronomy (with astrology), chemistry (with alchemy), natural history, and geography. This was partly a matter of the immediate concerns of the society in which they lived, but it was also partly due to the fact that they were better acquainted with the speculative and scientific literature of Classical Antiquity than with the writings of its poets, dramatists, and men of letters. They knew Plato, Aristotle, Plotinus, Ptolemy, and Galen, for example, but not Sophocles or Thucydides. Those classical writers to whom they did have access, however, they mastered to the limits of their capacity, passing on their knowledge through the translators of Palermo and Toledo and thereby making possible the Aristotelian renaissance of thirteenth century Europe.

The assimilation of alien elements necessarily involved some modification of Islamic society, in some instances of a most extensive kind. If, for example, the Abbasid caliph's court in tenth century Baghdad bore little resemblance to the Prophet's patriarchal household in seventh century Medina, much the same might be said of many other aspects of Islamic life over a comparable time span. Among these changes, perhaps none was more striking than the transformation that took place in the ethnic composition of the ruling elite over the same three centuries. There were several stages in this process: the increasingly influential role of the indigenous populations of Syria, Iraq, and Iran, former *mawalis,* in the affairs of the caliphate; the intermarriage of Arabs with *mawalis* and with slave women drawn from all the known regions of the world; the regional and cultural particularism of the Iranians, manifested in the emergence of breakaway regimes on the Iranian plateau; and the penetration of the *Dar al-Islam* by the Turks, whether as mercenaries, slave-soldiers (*mamluks*), or tribal auxiliaries. By the close of the tenth century the Arabs were no longer in any position to exercise political authority over wide stretches of West Asia, and with the loss of political authority went a diminution of their influence on cultural life. The Arab component of Islamic civilization was beginning to contract. For all that, however, there would always remain among non-Arab Muslims an acute awareness of the uniqueness of the Arab contribution to Islamic civilization. Whatever fate held in store for the Arabs, there was no denying that the Prophet of God and his companions had all been men of Arab stock and that God had made known His will through the medium of the Arabic language.

2. HINDUISM IN SOUTH ASIA

Hinduism makes no claim to have been revealed to a single prophet in the sense that Christianity or Islam do, nor can its origin be traced back to an historical founder like the Buddha. Hinduism evolved slowly from various cults, and from the Vedic tradition of the Aryan brahmans in the first century B.C. until early in the Christian era it had become the religion we know as Hinduism. It flowered in northern India in the fourth and fifth centuries and in the south somewhat later, reaching its full development in the ninth century, coinciding with the decline of Buddhism in the Indian subcontinent. The word Hinduism derives from Arab usage of the eighth century; the Hindus themselves had no name for their religion. Among Hindus no sharp distinction was recognized between the sacred and profane; rather, life itself was viewed as a rite. Various spiritual orientations could lead one to "liberation" from the world of illusion, including such alternatives as study, selflessness, the practice of austerities, yoga, and devotional practices. For the purposes of this chapter the cults of the two principal Hindu deities, Vishnu and Shiva, and the appearance of devotional (*bhakti*) worship, which came to fruition between the seventh and the ninth centuries, will offer in comparison with Islam and Mahayana Buddhism the most fruitful instances of the processes under discussion.

The Emergence of Hinduism within Indian Civilization

In discussing the spread of Hinduism it is useful to distinguish between Brahmanism, the religious cult of the Vedic sacrifices as perpetuated by the brahmans, and later Hinduism, a broad spectrum of religious practice that included both popular and elite beliefs and in which many indigenous cults were linked theologically to the Vedic beliefs of the Aryan invaders. Because the brahman caste continued to be prominent in later social and religious life, the distinction between Brahmanism and Hinduism is not a hard and fast one. In general, Brahmanism was diffused from northern India to the south as Aryan culture extended its impact, while Hinduism developed in various parts of the subcontinent as Vedic doctrines were reinterpreted or fused with local religious cults. Some of the most important innovations in devotional worship took place first in the south.

Brahmanism was an important element in the formulation of Hinduism. Its history began when the Aryans entered northern India around 1500 B.C. Despite the later influx of other peoples from Central Asia, Iran, and even Greece, the Aryan conquest of northern India left a permanent impact in the form of a stratification of society into castes, with the Aryans occupying the higher positions. The *kshatriyas* (warriors), brahmans (priests), and *vaishyas* (cultivators who later became traders and landowners) constituted the "twice born," the second birth being the religious initiation undergone in boyhood. The twice born practiced the Vedic rituals from which the *shudras* (the lowest class, later to become cultivators) were excluded. Outsiders entering Indian society as conquerors, or indigenous groups on the peninsula coming into contact with the Aryans could be accommodated into the caste system by assuming an appropriate status. As the centuries passed, the brahmans, by virtue of their position as ritual specialists and custodians of the oral literary tradition, elevated their own position in society at the expense of the warriors, whose preeminence in tribal society was lost with the advent of a sedentary style of life. As monarchies were formed on the Indo-Gangetic plain, tribal republics continued to maintain the older Aryan traditions in the foothills of the Himalayas. In Chapter 3 it was noted that some *kshatriyas* who found themselves at a disadvantage in the centralized political order of the great states of the plain withdrew to seek new roles in outlying areas, in some cases to pursue a religious avocation. The brahmans meanwhile adapted to the evolution of kingship by filling ministerial posts and providing ritual services to the rulers. They also dominated the field of education. The brahmans fostered their favored position in society by stressing the importance of ritual purity and by reinforcing caste barriers. The codification of sacred law in works like the *Manava Dharmashastra* (or *Manu-Smriti*) early in the Christian era was indicative of a tendency in Brahmanism to make the laws of society more explicit, more rigid, and more favorable to their own ascendancy. As we shall see, *dharma* represented sacred ideals for the stratification of society into castes but also for the regulation of the individual life at its various stages.

In the first and second centuries A.D. economic and religious developments unrelated to Brahmanism hastened the transformation of Indian society. The expansion of commerce within the Indian subcontinent and trade by sea with Southeast Asia and the Roman world stimulated the emergence of new classes of merchants and craftsmen, which were organized into guilds along the lines of subcastes. Brahmans were discouraged by their social regulations from taking part in trade or traveling by sea, and so they had little to do with commercial expansion, although some brahmans did manage to reach Southeast Asia. Those groups that participated in trade tended to support Buddhism, which flourished in the second and third centuries. Thus it was trade and the missionary activities of Buddhism and Jainism that acted as vehicles in carrying many Aryan cultural elements such as the Sanskrit language to southern India and Southeast Asia.

In contrast to Brahmanism, which had tended to be diffused in conjunction with northern Indian institutions of caste and kingship, Hinduism as a religion tended to spread on two levels. On the popular level it developed in the form of religious cults in which Vedic gods occurred as the objects of worship, often identified with older indigenous deities. On the elite level the cults came to be linked with the philosophical and literary traditions borne by the brahmans, who also continued the old ritual practices as a priestly class while adopting the new orientations.

On the elite level the service of brahmans in the courts of rulers, the preservation of Vedic literature, and the performance of sacrifices guaranteed the survival of much of the early Vedic tradition, but new elements were continuously being added to form the new theistic religion we know as Hinduism. As early as the Mauryan period, some two centuries before Christ, the caste system had developed and worship of new deities in temple settings was established practice. By the era of the Guptas (320-535 A.D.) the major Hindu sects of Shiva and Vishnu had found acceptance in northern India. Little evidence is available on religious conditions in the subcontinent at that time, but what little information there is, including the testimony of Chinese Buddhist pilgrims who traveled to India in search of sacred texts, indicates that Buddhism, Jainism, and Hinduism existed side by side. Hinduism may well have been tied more closely to the state than were the other two faiths because of the usefulness of the brahmans and their rituals in making secure the position of the ruler. Already most of the people were vegetarians and refrained from drinking liquor, and strong measures were enforced to prevent the pollution of the twice born by contact with outcaste groups. On the level of mass religion, the Hindu texts knows as *Puranas,* which embodied monotheistic doctrine in popular terms, took their final form. By the beginning of the sixth century pressure from invading Huns contributed to the decline of Gupta rule, and northern India entered a period of political fragmentation that was to persist for centuries.

A briefly successful effort to revive the Gupta empire was carried out by Harsha of Kanauj in the first half of the seventh century, after which time northern India experienced a prolonged period of political fragmentation. It was not until the early thirteenth century, when Muslim Turks formed the Delhi sultanate, that a unified empire was reestablished with its seat in the heartland of Indian civilization. The centuries following the Gupta collapse were characterized by tendencies toward feudalism and the chronic rivalry of regional states. Long-distance trade declined, as did the importance of urban centers, with the result that parochial tendencies appeared in intellectual and cultural life. The political events in northern India may be noted briefly. North of the Gangetic plain in Kashmir a strong regional power emerged by the seventh century and a series of local dynasties managed to preserve the independence of their territory until the Muslim conquest of 1339. East of the Gangetic plain the powerful Pala dynasty was formed in Bengal in the eighth century. In the ninth century the Palas extended their power briefly to the west as well as to Assam and the southern coastal region, but by the eleventh century Pala rule was weakened, and in the twelfth century the Bengal region came under the power of the Senas. By the middle of the ninth century Kanauj, the old center of Harsha's empire, came under the control of the Pratiharas, a branch of the Gurjara peoples who had been powerful in the north and west since the sixth century. The Pratiharas contested territory with rival kingdoms to the east and south but their most important role was their defense of northern India against invaders from the northwest. By the end of the tenth century Pratihara vigor had ebbed and in 1018 Kanauj was taken by Sultan Mahmud of Ghazni. These events, which are prefatory to the founding of the Delhi sultanate, will be taken up in the next chapter.

South of the Narbada River and stretching nearly across the peninsula from coast to coast was the territory of the Chalukyas, whose dynasty lasted from the sixth century until the middle of the eighth century, when they were succeeded by the Rashtrakutas. The Rashtrakuta dynasty was brought to an end in the late tenth century by a feudatory who claimed descent from the Chalukyas, whose name he revived. The second Chalukya dynasty, with its capital at Kalyani, ruled the Deccan until the twelfth century. In the south, on the eastern side of the peninsula along the Coromandel coast, the Tamil-speaking region was ruled by the Cholas, whose origins can be traced back to the time of Ashoka. The fact that Tamil is a Dravidian language and that non-Aryan religious practices were maintained in this region points to the possibility that these southerners may have been descended from the pre-Aryan ruling elite of northern India. In any case, the transition from tribe to kingship took place under the early Cholas who presided over the emergence of a Tamil culture. The Cholas were eclipsed from the fifth to the ninth centuries by the Pallavas, a ruling group that was probably of northern origin. The Pallavas facilitated the southward diffusion of elite Brahmanism and the assimilation of its concepts and institutions with Dravidian culture by claiming descent from the Hindu deity Brahma, by taking titles in the northern style, and by making Vedic sacrifices. Brahmans were patronized with the award of prominent positions and gifts of land, and the Pallava capital at Kanchi became an important religious center. Hindu colleges were established where Sanskrit, the court language, was used in instruction. Royal patronage aided the Hindus in a prolonged period of theological debate as they challenged the Buddhists. A revived Chola kingdom displaced the Pallavas at the end of the ninth century and controlled the Coromandel coast for three hundred years, until Islam penetrated to the far south.

Whereas elite, or court, Hinduism was first favored in the north, the first development of a popular Hinduism, propagated by traveling teachers and saints from all classes of society, took place in the south, in the Tamil country during the period of Pallava rule. Gradually this movement spread northward from the Tamil-speaking area, affecting first the Kannada-speaking population of the Mysore plateau, then Maharashtra, and finally the Hindi-speaking regions of the north. In terms of the development of a universal religion, this

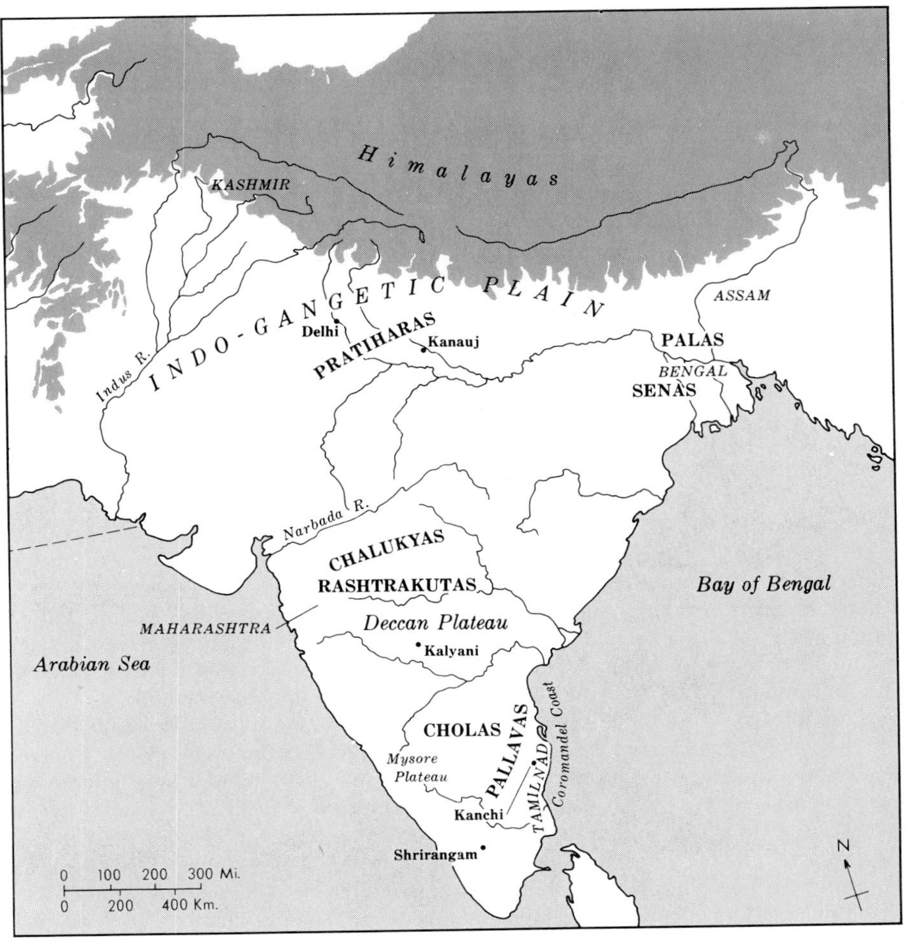

Map 24 Hindu India, to 1000 A.D.

growth of popular theism marked the adaptation of Hinduism to indigenous cultures. In Hindu literature, Sanskrit gave way to vernacular languages, such as Tamil in the south. The spread of this popular faith infused with local customs and beliefs was the philosophical reconciliation of Hindu theism with older Vedic traditions. Shankara in the late eighth century and Ramanuja in the early twelfth century were both southerners who contributed greatly to this accommodation, especially when their teachings were carried to the north. In this sense one can speak of certain elements in Hinduism, particularly devotional worship, spreading from south to north. Still, this trend took place within a culture zone already characterized by Aryan institutions. If there was a spread of Hinduism comparable to that of Islam and Mahayana Buddhism it was probably to be found in the diffusion of Hinduism to Southeast Asia, where it followed in the path of Buddhism as a natural component of prolonged contacts by sea from which the developing societies of Southeast Asia selectively appropriated for their own use the most appealing elements in Indian civilization.

The Later Evolution of Hinduism

The growth and development of the Hindu religion cannot be traced with great accuracy, due to a lack of historical documentation. However, the broad outlines of Hinduism's development can be discerned through the various texts that have propounded its central doctrines. The earliest Aryan literature, the Vedas, took the form of hymns to the gods. No temples or idols were involved in Vedic religion, but priests performed ceremonies that made use of fire and of animal and plant (especially the intoxicating soma) sacrifices. Sacrifices, it was believed, forged a propitious link between the sacrificer, the victim, and the gods. Indra, whose warlike deeds protected the Aryans, ranked first among the gods, but the gods were many and varied. Also worthy of note was Varuna, an all-knowing and omnipresent god who punished sin and who evoked fearful supplication in the hymns. In the more than one thousand verses of the *Rig Veda,* the oldest and most sacred of the texts, there are references to *brahman,* a generalized force or magical power, like *mana,* which was possessed by priests; whence the designation of those who handled religious matters as brahmans. *Brahman* was also linked to the breath, a familiar instance of an unseen vital force with spiritual power, and from this notion flowed other assumptions about hymns and chanting and even the notion that simple respiration was a sacred act. Complementing the Vedas were two other types of texts, the *Brahmanas* and the *Upanishads,* which were later in origin and which carried on the work of building a system of ritual practice and religious theory on the essentially mythological foundation of the Vedas. The *Brahmanas* were detailed explanations of ritual practice written in prose. Their name derived from the word *brahman,* meaning either "prayer" or the "ritualist who offers prayers." The *Upanishads* (meaning "sessions between master and disciple") date from around the seventh century B.C. and reflected the philosophical speculation of a class of forest hermits. The concern of the *Upanishads* was no longer with the correct forms of ritual and sacrifice but with the meaning of ritual and the knowledge of various spiritual forces. In the speculations of the *Upanishads* great emphasis was placed on the brahman, the universal cosmic principle, which was now identified with the individual self, or soul *(atman).*

It became customary in Indian usage to distinguish between revealed literature of divine origin (*shruti*) and the somewhat less sacred "traditional" literature of human origin (*smriti*). In historical terms, the *Upanishads* marked the end of the Vedic period and of the body of revealed wisdom. The subsequent period, spanning roughly the millennium from 500 B.C. to 500 A.D., was characterized by traditional *smriti* works. Included in this category were the *Dharma Sutras* (law codes or manuals of human conduct), the later *Dharma Shastras* (expansions upon the *sutras* in verse), the epics (the *Mahabharata,* which included the *Bhagavad Gita* and the *Ramayana*), and *Puranas,* which constituted a sort of historical record linking the mythical past with historical times.

The *Dharma Shastras,* the most famous of which was the *Code of Manu,* the *Manava Dharma Shastra* (or *Manu-Smriti*), specified in detail the norms of behavior for all sections of society. *Dharma,* which has no precise English equivalent and includes such notions as duty, natural law, an ethical ideal, and a way of life, might be rendered "ordained duties." The two central conceptions in the prescriptive *Dharma Sutras* were a hierarchy of four castes and a division of life (for males at least) into four stages. The caste system has already been referred to, but it is significant that emphasis was placed on maintaining the purity and security of those highest in the hierarchy. Attention was given in the *sutras* to the classification of persons of mixed caste parentage, but they made no provision for one rising within the caste system. Stratification was measured in terms of relative impurity, with excluded castes at the bottom, whose touch, shadow, or even sight could pollute. Such persons were restricted in their movement, and in some cases were obliged to carry a noise-making device to give warning of their approach. The stages of life were four: student, householder,

6.2 View of the main shrine of the Kailasanadha Temple to Shiva at Kanchipuram, a ninth century example of Pallavan architecture in the Deccan. The Pallavas were an important cultural link between the north and the Dravidian south. Source: Alexander Rea, *Pallava Architecture,* Architectural Survey of India, New Imperial Series (Madras, 1909), Vol. 34, Plate 10.

hermit, and ascetic. At the appropriate time boys were assigned to teachers for a period of spiritual instruction, the duration of which varied depending on whether the youth was a brahman, *kshatriya,* or *vaishya.* This crucial event marked the beginning of social maturity and entry into ritual practice. It was regarded figuratively as a spiritual birth, hence the term twice born (*dvija*) to refer to the members of the top three castes. The stages of life, in which a man first underwent a spiritual apprenticeship as a student and then engaged in a full spectrum of social relations as a householder before withdrawing progressively from society in old age, constituted an accommodation to social reality. The student stage provided for socialization into the brahmanical tradition through training in Sanskrit literature, the householder stage brought the productive years of life within the purview of orthodoxy, and the last two stages enabled Brahmanism to encompass forms of withdrawal from society which became especially popular in the first millennium B.C.

With the epics Hinduism came into its own, as heroic tales were given a religious interpretation and God emerged in a new relationship to man. The *Mahabharata,* a poem of more than 90,000 stanzas, is the story of a prolonged power struggle centering on the area around Dehli and culminating in an heroic eighteen day battle that destroyed all the protagonists except the five brother heroes. Discourses on many subjects have been sandwiched into the text, a fact that makes it far more than an account of historical events. The most important of these later interpolations, the *Bhagavad Gita* (*Song of the Lord*), takes the form of an address to Arjuna, one of the heroes, by his comrade and charioteer Krishna on the eve of the great battle. Krishna speaks to Arjuna's doubts about the slaughter soon to take place, assuring him that death is unimportant and does not involve the destruction of the soul. In the course of this exposition Krishna reveals himself as the Supreme Being. Thus the *Bhagavad Gita,* which was probably composed in the early Christian era, marks the emergence of a popular Hinduism in which Krishna supersedes the Vedic god Indra and transcends a declining Brahmanism by offering men a new relationship to God. The doctrine of the *Bhagavad Gita* is compatible with that of the *Upanishads* in that it accepts the essential unreality of the world, yet the *Gita* endorses an active disposition in the world in which one "acts without acting" by engaging in an action without becoming involved in its results. (Thus Arjuna could play his role on the battlefield without being concerned about the outcome.) Also present in the *Gita* is the notion that all persons, regardless of status, can have a direct relationship with God by means of personal devotion. Here perhaps is an example of Hinduism responding to the challenge of Buddhism and Jainism.

The other major epic, the *Ramayana,* also began as a secular tale and was later modified and reinterpreted as a sacred Hindu text. Its story recounts the adventures of a prince named Rama and his faithful wife, Sita. So colorful is the story that it has been retold in many forms, and versions of the *Ramayana* are still popular in distant Java and Thailand as well as in India itself. Rama, the rightful heir to his father's throne, found his succession blocked by the ambitions of his stepmother and so withdrew with his wife to the wilderness. There Rama's aid was solicited by sages of the forest who were being harassed by demons. The king of the demons even kidnapped Sita, but the heroic Rama together with his allies, the monkeys, finally won her back. Subsequently Rama regained his kingdom, and his reign, the *ramarajya,* or "reign of Rama," became an ideal period of virtuous rule, invoked in this century by Gandhi as a model of good government. The characters in the *Ramayana* represent embodiments of *dharma.* Rama himself is the ideal husband and ruler, his wife a model of feminine virtue; even the demon king is a stereotypical villain. In later interpretations Rama was seen as the incarnation of a god (Vishnu) who descended to earth to restore order, and by the beginning of the Christian era he was the object of a devotional cult. Thus through theological interpretation the *Ramayana* became another link forged between popular devotional theism and the older ideals of the brahmanical tradition.

Part of the genius of Hinduism was its capacity to encompass many elements and to reconcile diverse values and purposes. One device that facilitated this was the notion of the four ends of life: virtuous duty *(dharma),* material gain *(artha),* pleasure *(kama),* and spiritual liberation *(moksha).* These terms gave the appearance of unity to many forms of literature and knowledge within the purview of Hindu doctrine. The first and last of these four ends were concerned with morality and spirituality, which tend to be associated with religion in the Western tradition. In the Indian tradition the lines were not so clearly drawn. Thus there evolved in addition to the *Dharma Sutras* and *Dharma Shastras* works that dealt with practical affairs. The *Artha Shastra (Treatise on Material Gain),* attributed to Chandragupta Maurya's minister, Kautilya, is a handbook of statecraft, advising the ambitious ruler how to conduct his affairs and get ahead in the world. A work better known to contemporary Americans is the *Kama Sutra,* a text dating from the Gupta period. This work offers practical advice on the pursuit of pleasure in sexual relations both in and out of marriage. The popularity of the English translation of the *Kama Sutra* is due more to the fact that it contains explicit advice on sexual technique than to the existence of any widespread interest in premodern Indian society. A more specifically religious class of texts deserving of mention is the *Puranas (Ancient Tales).* Compiled by the brahmans, these texts gave an account of historical events beginning with the mythological past, included the events of the epics, detailed the genealogies of dynasties, and explained religious doctrines in simple terms. The eighteen principal *Puranas,* none of which predates the Gupta period, were the popular texts of Hinduism.

Another unifying device in Hinduism was the classification of various intellectual positions into six schools of philosophy. The effect of this designation, which came about early in the Christian era, was to recognize a majority of the divergent philosophical trends of the preceding period as valid alternative paths to salvation. The six schools were: (1) the School of Analysis, which was concerned with logic and epistemology, tools developed in disputation with the Buddhists; (2) the School of Particular Characteristics, which expounded an atomic theory; (3) the School of Enumeration, which was atheistic and propounded a dualism of soul and matter; (4) the School of Application *(Yoga),* which emphasized bodily and psychic training as a means to salvation; (5) the School of Inquiry *(Mimamsa),* which was supported by orthodox brahmans and expounded the law of the Vedas; and (6) the Vedanta School (meaning "end of the Vedas"), which also claimed origin in the Vedas and refuted nonbrahmanical theories. The Vedanta School soon became the most important system of Indian philosophy and it remains so today. Its doctrine was based on the *Brahma Sutras,* a text of the early Christian era, and the *Upanishads,* and it addressed itself to elaborating on the identity between the individual self, or soul *(atman),* and universal being, or consciousness *(brahman).* The most important thinker of the Vedanta School was Shankara, who gave Hindu philosophical doctrines a classical formulation during the first years of the eighth century.

Hinduism as a Universal Religion

Universal theism found its expression in Hinduism in the concept of monism or nondualism. Shankara (788?-820), a brahman thinker from southern India, addressed himself to this problem. According to Shankara, plurality and causality were illusion *(maya).* The ultimate reality was the *brahman*—the universal and impersonal world soul of the *Upanishads.* The *brahman* was also identical with the individual soul. Salvation or liberation from the world of illusion was to be gained through knowledge of this identity. Using this conception of liberation, which resembled the Buddhist idea of *nirvana,* Shankara gave Hindu doctrine a rational elaboration. But Shankara was flexible enough to recognize that devotional activities of the type currently in practice in the temples were not devoid of value. Religious actions, while insufficient in themselves for the attainment of salvation, could help to turn the mind towards knowledge. Devotion also could play a subordinate role. Thus Shankara created a theoretical foundation for a link between the individual and a Supreme Being which could accommodate a variety of religious practice. In practical terms he took steps to spread his doctrine. He wrote commentaries on the important texts, traveled about India preaching, reorganized temple worship at many centers, and founded an order of Hindu monks.

Some three centuries later, Ramanuja (d. 1137) carried the Vedanta School another step forward in the direction of an explicit theism. A brahman who taught at the great temple of Shrirangam in southern India, he based his teachings on the *Brahma Sutras,* the *Upanishads,* and the *Bhagavad Gita.* Ramanuja's monism was qualified in the sense that although souls were part of *brahman* and returned to reside in perfect communion with the Supreme Being, they retained a distinct identity. Furthermore, in contrast to Shankara's abstract intelligence, the Supreme Being was personalized and identified with Vishnu. The relationship between the individual and God was characterized by grace and love and marked by reciprocal need. Although the utility of ritual was still recognized by Ramanuja, the primary path to salvation lay through intense devotion to God. This marked the opening of Vedantic thought to popular religious practice by giving a philosophical basis to devotional worship *(bhakti).* After his death, Ramanuja's ideas gained acceptance throughout India. Later, in the thirteenth century, Madhva was to develop Ramanuja's doctrine to the point where there came a break with the teaching of the *Upanishads,* claiming that souls were individual and distinct. Madhva's throught deserves mention here primarily because it constitutes a probable case of Christian influence on a Hindu thinker and thus an instance of the domestication of foreign elements in Hinduism.

In Hinduism, salvation was to be achieved by a union with God which would remove the soul from the cycle of rebirth. Hinduism shared with Buddhism the notion of transmigration *(samsara),* which bound the soul to repeated births in an endless and meaningless repetition. The nature of each incarnation was bound by the law of *karma* (deed), by which actions in the world of matter determined the relative degradation of each subsequent rebirth. Escape, or salvation, lay in release *(moksha,* "spiritual liberation") from transmigration. This view of life, which reflected deep disillusionment with the world, gained wide acceptance by the middle of the first millennium B.C. The pessimism of this world view contrasted sharply with the attitudes found in early Brahmanism in which man's environment was subject to positive improvement through the proper application of ritual and sacrifice. The later view, which underlay both Hindu and Buddhist thought, was a negative one that regarded striving in this life as futile and consequently tended to renounce worldly life in theory and to limit commitment to mundane goals in practice. The trend in Hindu theology was to minimize the importance of the physical world by viewing human events in a cosmic span of time. Time was measured in *kalpas,* or "cycles," each of which constitues a day in the life of God, who lives for a span of 100 years. In each of these cosmic days the God creates the universe and again absorbs it. Each *kalpa* consists of 4.32 billion years and is divided into 14 periods, which are further divided into 71 great intervals, which in turn consist of 4 *yugas.* The world is currently in the fourth *yuga* of an interval, a *yuga* consisting of 1,200 god years, each the equivalent to 360 human years. The fourth *yuga,* known as the *kali yuga,* is an era of degeneration when the world is full of evil. At the end of the era Kalkin, a manifestation of the God Vishnu will appear to pass judgment on the world.

The intermediary who was to make salvation possible for the Hindu worshipper could be any one of a number of individual deities, each of whom represented an aspect or a manifestation of a single god. In mature Hinduism the multiplicity of deities was merged together and each identified with one another. In the simplest scheme there was a trinity of gods who represented aspects of the same elemental force, like the faces of a diamond.

These were Brahma, Vishnu, and Shiva. Brahma was a god of creation, a personalized form of the very abstract *brahman* of the *Upanishads,* but he was very rarely the object of cult worship. Most popular was Vishnu, the god who preserved the world and who embodied many other deities. The Vaishnavites, or worshippers of Vishnu, comprised the most numerous group of Hindus, while the next most numerous was the Shaivites, those who belonged to the cult of Shiva. Shiva was a destroyer god who also had female manifestations. The Hindu God, in whatever manifestation, bestowed grace upon the believer in exchange for devotion *(bhakti). Bhakti* appeared first in northern and western India in the worship of Vasudeva, a god who later came to be identified with Vishnu. In the south, *bhakti* found its fullest development in Tamilnad. The *bhakti* movement, characterized by a passionate love of God, spread throughout India between the seventh and ninth centuries. A school of *bhakti* developed with its own devotional texts and many regional cults. Surrender to God could take many forms, among which were prayer, confession, repeating his name, wearing his insignia, singing or writing in his praise, worshipping his image, and communing with fellow worshippers.

It was noted above that the doctrines of Ramanuja reconciled devotional worship with the teachings of the *Upanishads.* Thereafter, a Hindu monotheism emerged in which every individual could attain salvation through a direct personal relationship with a chosen deity and in which priestly intermediaries did not necessarily play a significant role. What remained unsettled was the question of the extent to which salvation was dependent upon the efforts of the individual. In a sense, this question was inherent in the formulation of the ends of man. The concept of *dharma* required moral behavior in this life, while the goal of *moksha,* or "spiritual liberation," seemed to imply an abnegation of the world. Hindus took differing positions on the relative importance of knowledge, action, and devotion in the attainment of salvation. The followers of Ramanuja divided on the question into two groups, which came to be known as the southern and northern schools. The difference between their positions was explained in terms of analogies, using cats and monkeys. The northern school maintained that just as a baby monkey must cling to its mother's back, so must the believer make a positive effort to achieve salvation, while the southern school saw salvation as a matter of God's will alone in the same way that a mother cat picks her kittens up by the skin of the neck. Immortality in the Hindu religion must be understood primarily as escape from mortality, or rather from recurring mortality, rather than a conscious state of happiness in an afterlife. The Hindus did possess the notion of heavens and hells, but the union with God which *moksha* entailed was not described in terms of sensory experience.

Vishnu and Shiva

Vishnu, whose cult was most extensive in northern India, represented the positive and creative elements in Hinudism. His portrayal in figures and paintings was symbolic rather than representational, depicting his qualities and powers more than his appearance. He was shown as a dark figure with four arms, holding in his hands a conch symbolizing the origin of existence, a discus or wheel representing the cycle of existence, a lotus signifying the universe, and a mace, which is the power of knowledge. On his breast he wore a jewel, one of the treasures churned from the cosmic sea, which represents consciousness, and a lock of hair, which was interpreted as the source of the natural world. Many other objects were associated with Vishnu and his various manifestations including a chariot, which represents the swift power of the mind, and symbols of royalty such as the whisk, the fan, the flag, and the parasol. In sleep he was depicted as lying on a thousand-headed snake, and awake he sometimes rode on a great bird with a human face. Vishnu's consort, Lakshmi, was also worshipped as an important goddess.

The identity of Vishnu evolved from earlier gods such as Vasudeva and Krishna. When Vishnu gained ascendance and came to be regarded as the Supreme Deity in a monotheistic system, other gods were identified with him as *avatars,* or incarnations of Vishnu. There were ten principal incarnations: the Fish, which gave warning to the primeval man of the great flood; the Tortoise, which dove into the cosmic ocean and brought up treasures; the Boar, which probably represents the absorption of a non-Aryan sacred pig; a Man-lion; a Dwarf; Rama-with-the-ax, a mythological figure who destroyed a rebellious *kshatriya* class and thus represents the ascendancy of brahman rule; Rama, the hero of the *Ramayana* and a major incarnation; Krishna, who aided the heroes of the *Mahabharata* and is the most important incarnation of Vishnu; Buddha, an incarnation that reflects the desire to assimilate other cults into the Hindu pantheon; and Kalkin, the future incarnation who would appear on a white horse with a flaming sword. Rama, as was mentioned above, represented an embodiment of *dharma* and righteousness which gave a tangible form to brahmanical norms. In Rama's wife and his brother and in their monkey-headed demigod helper, Hanuman, the devotee could find familiar roles to identify with.

In the case of Krishna, Vishnu is portrayed in a more complex form. A god of recent historical origin, he displaced some of the older Vedic deities. Krishna is often portrayed as a child who works miracles as well as mischief and who thus appeals to women as a child god. In another aspect he is associated with herding and is depicted as an amorous cowherd who enjoys seducing the wives and daughters of the herdsmen, especially his favorite lover, Radha. The two of them, Krishna and Radha, are the subject of a vast body of romantic literature. In his romantic aspect Krishna may have evolved from a fertility god in southern India. In theological interpretations, this amorous dimension, Krishna playing his flute to call the women from their beds, was characterized as God calling men to divine love.

Whereas Vishnu represented the positive and creative side of Hinduism, Shiva was an incarnation of all that was negative and destructive. In the most abstract sense he represented disintegration; he was the lord of sleep and was associated with darkness and death, with evil and with time—the destroyer of all things. In some cases Shiva was represented as a bull and as the lingam, or male sex organ, a fact that indicates the survival of pre-Aryan fertility cults going back to the time of the Harrapans. The female counterpart of Shiva was particularly revered in some parts of India and took many forms, including that of a mother goddess; of a consort to Shiva; of Durga, who is beyond reach; or of Kali, the power of time. Kali was depicted as a bloodthirsty black figure wearing a necklace of skulls and holding swords and severed heads. Some extreme Shaivite sects practiced human sacrifice and others carried on magical rites in secret nocturnal meetings. In the popular literature and imagery Shiva had both a terrifying and a lovable aspect. He was a father figure, a destroyer of demons, a yogi in meditation, and a dancer. Although Shiva was worshipped throughout India, his cult was most prevalent in the south.

Surviving sculpture from the early Christian era provides some information about the forms in which Hindus worshipped their gods. The development of temples was probably influenced by the institutional practices of Buddhism, shrines excavated out of hillsides being as characteristic of Hinduism as of Buddhism. Hindu temples typically consisted of a gateway, a terrace, and a courtyard leading to an inner shrine in which a dark chamber, symbolizing a cave, contained the principal image of the deity. Not only at large religious centers but also in little village shrines priests carried out elaborate rituals that involved awakening the god (i.e., the statute in the shrine) with music, bathing him, dressing him, and offering food in appropriate ceremonial forms. Such activities were intensified at the time of religious festivals. Although ritual specialists, monks, and teachers (*gurus*) played important roles in holy places, it must be stressed that Hinduism did not develop an organized church hierarchy. Worship was essentially an individual matter allowing an unlimited number of approaches to God. Temples and other holy places were particularly important for pilgrimages, which became a popular mode of religious expression and in the south, in particular, were important factors in the economic life of a region. Ritual bathing played a major role in Hindu practice, and in many instances rivers were employed in sacramental cleansing. When temples were not close to natural bodies of water they often included man-made tanks for bathing, a feature that may have existed in the ceremonial centers of the pre-Aryan civilization of the Harappans. Ideally the devout Hindu performed rituals daily, at dawn, at dusk, and before meals, but his practice could involve many forms of yoga and the repetition of religious texts (*mantras*), which could range from the single syllable *om* to lengthy verses believed to have magical potency.

To sum up, it may be noted that Hinduism evolved gradually from Aryan roots and that its doctrinal contents conformed to the social structure of Indian society. The nomadic origins of the Aryans were suggested in the persisting pastoral elements in Hinduism, including the bucolic portrayal of Krishna, the sacred bull, and the use of clarified butter and other bovine products in rituals. Brahmanism survived in the special place accorded the Vedas and in the theoretical justifications given to the caste system. The absorption of local cults and non-Aryan religious elements of many kinds is evident in the manifold incarnations of the gods, Hinduism itself finding unity primarily in the assertion of the common identity of all gods, particularly in the monotheistic tendencies of Vaishnavism and Shaivism. Devotional Hinduism achieved its greatest development in the middle centuries of the Christian era, prior to the imposition of Muslim rule on most of the subcontinent. The facts that Hinduism did not have an authoritarian organizational structure and that it was not tied closely to the state meant that its development as a universal religion was unimpeded by the political division of India, but also that it was unable to assert or enforce a strict orthodoxy in questions of theology and religious practice.

3. MAHAYANA BUDDHISM IN EAST ASIA

Mahayana Buddhism, despite its South Asian origin, has been the universal religion of the societies of eastern Asia. Throughout China, Tibet, Mongolia, Korea, Japan, and Vietnam the landscape has been transfigured by the presence of monasteries, minor temples and shrines, and pagodas. The collective life of family and village has been expressed at least in part by Buddhist ceremonies and served by monks and nuns. The prayers and simple offerings of hundreds of millions of country people, to say nothing of the lavish patronage by the wealthy, have testified to their belief in the power and grace of their favorite Buddhist divinities. So pervasive are the visible manifestations of Mahayana in East Asia that the casual observer might easily be led into the error of mistaking it for the whole sum and essence of the culture and civilization of the culturally varied peoples among whom it has so greatly flourished. In point of fact everywhere in East Asia Mahayana began and remained in a complex relationship with indigenous, pre-Buddhist traditions. The Chinese classical tradition with its intellectual focus in the Confucian canon and its functional association with the institutions of imperial bureaucratic rule never lost its clear identity and eventually survived the Buddhist deluge to become once more the exclusive official orthodoxy of the ruling classes. To make the picture more complicated still, one must also remember that Mahayana, in each of the societies that adopted it, was itself naturalized and modified by the indigenous, pre-Buddhist culture. Thus, for example, if one may say that China was to a certain extent Indianized by the spread of the originally Indian religion of Mahayana, it is no less true that the Mahayana religion was sinicized in its Chinese forms and became, to that extent, a domesticated Chinese religion. The very fact that Mahayana was highly adaptable to alien cultural traditions offers a clue to our understanding of it in its historical role as a universal religion.

Mahayana Buddhism was formulated in the cosmopolitan setting of the Kushan empire in northwest India during the first three centuries A.D., followed by its diffusion and domestication among the peoples of East Asia. Buddhist temples and clergy existed in a few urban enclaves in China as early as the first century A.D., but they were still largely, if not altogether, a feature of non-Chinese mercantile settlements. The critical last decades of the Han created conditions more favorable to the penetration of Buddhism among Chinese literati and commoners, and the foreign religion slowly gained native adherents during the third century. It was the fourth century, however, following the collapse in 317 of the Western Chin's attempt to reunify the empire, that the initial diffusion of Buddhism, especially of Mahayana, finally occurred on a large scale. During the fourth and early fifth centuries, corresponding to the period of the Sixteen Kingdoms of north China (317-439), political fragmentation and social disruption reached their greatest extent. Although the ideology and the institutional model of the Han empire still enjoyed a measure of official patronage, the old order commanded less respect than before, and Buddhism was enthusiastically received by widening circles of Chinese adherents.

By the time that the course of political events in China turned from political fragmentation towards imperial reunification, Buddhism was already rooted in Chinese society. Northern China was brought under the unified rule of the Northern Wei dynasty in 440 A.D. and the foundations were then laid for the empires of Sui (581-618) and T'ang. During the period from the second half of the fifth century until the mid-eighth century, strong sovereigns and their aristocratic supporters joined in lavish patronage of the Buddhist clergy and their temples. These three hundred years were the time of the greatest prosperity of Chinese Buddhism.

Formation of Mahayana in Northwest India

Mahayana Buddhism developed in northwest India during a period marked by political instability followed by the rise of the Kushan empire. The disintegration of the Mauryan and Seleucid empires opened northwestern India to invasions from the north and west, and that region became the scene of successive barbarian attempts to build empires on the Achaemenid and Seleucid model. Early in the second century B.C., Greek militarists liberated themselves from Seleucid control and, taking advantage of the absence of strong indigenous resistance, moved south and west establishing independent Hellenistic kingdoms in Kashmir and the Indus region. A century later, Iranian nomads, the Scythian Sakas, were driven southward from their Aral pastures and into northwestern India, where they displaced the Greek rule and established a short-lived empire modeled at least superficially on the Achaemenid. They, in their turn, were subjugated by a new wave of Iranian tribes led by the Yueh-chih, once the rulers of Chinese Turkistan but now driven westward by the Hsiung-nu. Yueh-chih leaders soon transformed their victorious tribal federation into the Kushan state, a great empire lying athwart the Inner Asian trade routes passing east and west between China and the Roman empire and running southward into India.

The chronology of the Kushan empire is obscure, but its first imperial reign began about the middle of the first century A.D. and attained its greatest wealth and power in the reign of Kaniska, probably in the second half of the second century. Under Kushan rule, trade flourished and the commercial cities of Kabul, Purushapura, Bamiyan, and Taxila were the scene of a prosperous cosmopolitan culture. Although early Hinduism was in decline, Buddhism flourished under the generous patronage of wealthy merchant families and guilds. Not only did Buddhism gain by the addition of great numbers of temples and *stupas,* but it also underwent rapid artistic and doctrinal development under the influence of its cosmopolitan setting. Buddhism found a new and splendid aesthetic expression in the Gandharan style, which placed Hellenistic sculpture at the service of Buddhist iconography. At the same time, Buddhist teaching began to develop in the direction of theism and devotional cults, a change that was to culminate in the Mahayana religion of universal salvation.

Mahayana Buddhists adopted the name of their religion (which means "Greater Vehicle") in contradistinction to the older teachings, which they disparagingly called Hinayana ("Lesser Vehicle"). Because Hinayana is an unfriendly and partisan term, we shall use instead the name Theravada, which is accepted by the followers of the more conservative tradition themselves. The principal issue that distinguished Mahayana from Theravada was the great Mahayana emphasis on universal salvation through the mediation of devotional cults that were accessible to ordinary people not gifted with great spiritual or intellectual powers. Whereas Theravada, though not necessarily atheistic, continued to concentrate on the disciplines of renunciation, spiritual self-cultivation, and meditation, theism, or the belief in gods and especially the Universal Buddha, became a prominent characteristic of the Mahayana.

The origins of Mahayana go back at least to the times of Ashoka (268-231 B.C.), when a major division arose between the stricter, more conservative Sthaviravadins in Eastern India and the Mahasamgikas in western India, who were more liberal and democratic in their tendency to encourage even humble lay people and members of such a disparaged category as women to hope and work for their salvation. The Mahasamgikas were therefore particularly responsive to the growing popularity of the idea of *bhakti,* or "salvation through faith," during the last centuries B.C. and culminating around the time of Christ. Mahayana developed around a core that consisted of the basic early teachings. What is important is not so much the uniqueness or originality of the Mahayana doctrine as the different doctrinal emphasis and religious spirit. With this reservation in mind, we may attempt to summarize the main outlines of Mahayana doctrine.

Mahayana retained the idea that the common-sense, visible world was illusory and that only the Buddha-nature, immanent in all things, was real. Also shared with Theravada were the doctrines of the Four Noble Truths and the Eightfold Path. Mahayana differed mainly in that it offered a great variety of specific paths to salvation suited to people of different levels of understanding and different conditions of life. Among the distinctive features of Mahayana were the vividly imagined *buddhas* and demons and the heavens and hells over which they presided, and the ideal of the *bodhisattva,* "enlightenment being." The *buddhas* and the *bodhisattvas* were conceived of as compassionate beings who would assure salvation to all who sincerely invoked their aid. Nothing less than universal salvation was their goal.

Buddhist thought avoided a clear distinction between gods and men, since both kinds of being were part of the phenomenal world and therefore not wholly real entities. Moreover, a Buddha stood at the end of a series of existences in the cycle of birth and death in the world of living things. Thus every *buddha* presupposed a succession of creatures on the road to the enlightenment and *nirvana.* In Theravada, this aspiration was expressed in the ideal of the *arhat,* one who had so perfected his understanding that he had reached the threshold of salvation. The corresponding ideal in Mahayana was that of the *bodhisattva,* who was more perfected than the *arhat* in the sense that he had transcended his idea of self and could think of salvation only in terms of universal salvation, salvation for all.

But the creation of a host of compassionate *buddhas* and *bodhisattvas* raises a question: Since the Buddha is one and immanent in the universe, how can there be a plurality of beings worthy of belief and devotion? One answer to this question was supplied by the doctrine of *trikaya,* the "three bodies of the Buddha." The "body of essence" was the real Buddha, the ultimate reality. The body of essence, however, had the power to project emanations, which were called the "bodies of bliss." The bodies of bliss included the many Buddhas in their supernatural splendor, and they could be seen only by the spiritually perfected beings. The bodies of bliss in turn had the power of manifesting themselves in the form of ordinary mortals, and under this aspect they could be seen by anyone. Thus the historical Buddha appeared in the world as the young Sakya prince. Since the historical form of the Buddha was relatively unimportant to the doctrine, however, Buddhist sculptors represented the Buddha as they imagined him in the form of the body of bliss. Figures of the Buddha are often of colossal size, and a supernatural radiance is suggested by the use of gold leaf. Thus even though the *buddhas,* as bodies of bliss, were part of the transitory phenomenal world, they were still accepted as manifestations of the body of essence and invested with great spiritual power.

The popularization of Mahayana, both in India and in the societies that adopted it, was accomplished in part by the adaptation of the religion to the continuing everyday needs of ordinary people and to ancient forms of religion, which now often assumed an outwardly Buddhist appearance. In India, the *samgha,* or "monastic community," soon took up the task of providing for the material as well as the spiritual needs of the lay community. As the monasteries, despite the monks' vow of personal poverty, became wealthy through pious donations, they often accepted responsibility to provide charitable assistance to the poor, hungry, and friendless. They often assisted in famine relief and in medical services, for example. Moreover, lay believers did not limit their prayers for divine assistance by the Buddhist divinities to spiritual matters but also prayed for mundance favors, such as the birth of sons, success in business ventures, cure of disease, and so forth. Moreover, some of the principal Buddhist divinities appear to have been of pre-Buddhist origin, as the trinity of Amida, Avalokitesvara, and Mahasthamaprapta, may have been an Iranian Mithraic trinity now in Buddhist form. Thus, both the cults of Buddhism and the purposes to which they were sometimes put were familiar and therefore readily acceptable to ordinary people, and this in turn made possible the rapid popularization of the religion, even while it invested everyday life and old cults with a new religious significance.

The Spread of Mahayana Buddhism in China: Initial Diffusion

In an earlier chapter we saw the Chinese imperial order of the Han dynasty and its successor states undergo a series of crises and partial restoration during the period from 9 A.D. to 317 A.D. The causes of this decline were seen to be in part social—the concentration of wealth in a developing economy, a deepening conflict between the great families and the increasingly proletarianized masses—and in part political—the shattering of the central government by bitter factional struggles and the preemption of regional governmental authority by the great families in the provinces. Associated with the decline of empire was the Old Text challenge to the official New Text orthodoxy and the popularity of philosophical and religious Taoism. All of these factors facilitated the introduction and spread of Mahayana among all levels of the Chinese population.

The growing threat of political disintegration that began near the end of the Former Han became a reality about three centuries later with the collapse of the Western Chin in 317. The first decade of the fourth century saw the government of the Chin torn apart by wars of succession among the princes, and the defense of the north was no longer possible. Northern China remained in a state of almost total political disintegration during most of the period of the Sixteen Kingdoms (317-439) when Turkic, Tibetan, and Chinese warriors established states that lasted only a few decades. Southern China during the fourth through sixth centuries was essentially a developing colonial region. Perhaps a majority of the population was still non-Chinese. Dominating and exploiting them were successive layers of gentry who had come as entrepreneurs or as refugees from the north, forming a rigidly stratified aristocracy. A series of four short-lived dynasties—Sung, Ch'i, Liang, and Ch'en—succeeded the Chin, ruling from the area of modern Nanking. None of these four regimes was able to control the aristocratic estates or collect taxes from them, despite the rising agricultural and commercial prosperity of the region. The lower classes, in the absence of a strong government to protect their interests, engaged in military coups and Taoist-inspired rebellion.

The political fragmentation and continuous warfare during the period of the Sixteen Kingdoms in north China brought about important changes in the social pattern there. The walled agricultural towns of the free peasantry, with their hierarchy of local heads, had already been badly eroded. Most of the towns that remained appear now to have been abandoned, their inhabitants either fleeing to the south or, more often, taking refuge in village settlements around the estates of the great families. The great families themselves, together with their private armies, were no match for the armies of the new barbarian or semibarbarian states and could protect their position only by collaborating with the new rulers. Such collaboration led to the fusion of old and new leading families in a Sino-barbarian aristocracy. In the north, as in the south, the society became deeply stratified and the hereditary status of the great families was eventually spelled out in genealogical compilations. In the south, the power of the aristocracy and the inability of weak governments to protect the interests of the people led to widespread rebellion by the fifth century.

Conditions throughout China were now peculiarly favorable to the widespread diffusion of new doctrines. The classical tradition of Han, the gentry orientation towards professional careers in civil bureaucracy, and the intellectual commitment to the official ideology of Han Confucianism had now been undermined. The ethics of public service was meaningless when bureaucratic careers were seldom possible, and the cosmological theories of the New Text school were hardly credible when the imperial order justified by them seemed now to have collapsed beyond hope of restoration. Although classical learning did not vanish—many rulers patronized Confucian schools on a small scale because they felt it necessary for the perpetuation of even the most rudimentary forms of government—it could no longer pose an insurmountable obstacle to rival systems of thought and belief as the dominant element in official ideology. At the same time, the alienated lower orders of society continued to provide fertile ground, as they had since the declining stages of Han, for the propagation of doctrines of salvation and utopian ideologies.

Another factor in the diffusion of Buddhism in China was the state of relations between Chinese and other Asian civilizations. Since Chinese imperial expansionism was no longer a serious possibility, the most important kind of relationship was that of trade. If political disintegration in north China often proved a disaster for old gentry families, it was not always so for merchants. The removal of the imperial regime with its mercantile controls allowed private trade to flourish, despite interruptions by war. Cities from Loyang and Ch'angan westward out the Kansu panhandle still functioned as centers of international trade, and the states of western Kansu depended mainly on commerce as the basis of their economy. Nearly all of the Sixteen Kingdoms, moreover, established their capitals in cities along the main trade routes. Sea trade kept pace. By the fourth century Indian merchants had developed maritime commerce in South and Southeast Asia far beyond the level of Han and Roman times. Indian-influenced commercial states were forming on the southern margins of the Chinese world, such as Funan in modern Cambodia and Champa in modern central Vietnam. Northern Vietnam and the Canton region were also developing as major centers of sea-borne trade. The capital region of the southern dynasties was linked by sea to the Southeast Asian centers. Although the Kiangsu and Chekiang area did not at this time have large colonies of foreign merchants, the northern cities did—a point of great importance for the differences that developed in northern and southern Buddhism.

Such, in general terms, were the conditions under which Buddhist doctrines, forms of worship, and institutions began to spread rapidly throughout China. Chinese-Buddhist contacts had occurred for at least three centuries, albeit on a small scale and without attracting much official notice. The Kushan empire, as we have noted, was a flourishing

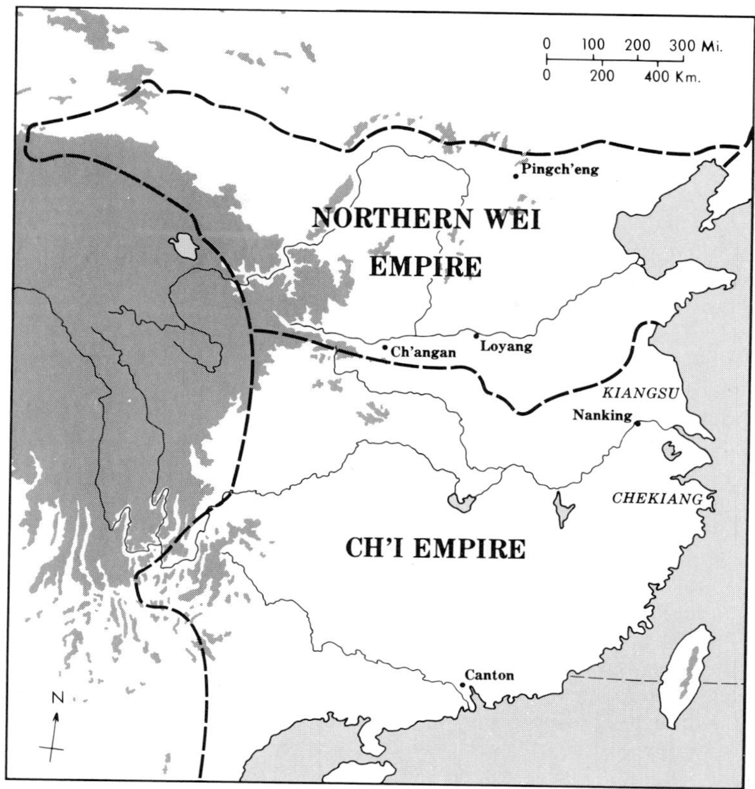

Map 25 China, about 500 A.D.

center of overland trade involving East, West, and South Asia. Inner Asian trade between China and West and South Asia moved by stages from one trading city to another, from Loyang and Ch'angan through Kansu to the Tarim basin, then on the northern route around the desert by way of Kucha or the southern route by way of Khotan and thence towards Balkh or Samarqand. The oasis cities of the Tarim routes were better watered than now (many are desert ruins), with intensive agriculture and substantial populations, mainly of Iranian peoples. Here caravans would pause, rest, reequip, and do business. Since many of the merchants engaged in this trade had already become Buddhists in their home cities of northwest India or Central Asia, they were often accompanied on their journeys by missionary monks, who in turn established monasteries in cities along the way. The establishment of the first monasteries in north China undoubtedly occurred in this way.

Already in the second half of the first century certain common Sanskrit Buddhist terms made their appearance in Chinese transcription in official and private writings. A private Buddhist translation project under the leadership of a Parthian nobleman, An Shih-kao, was evidence of growing interest in the religion among literati in Loyang at the end of the Han. Among the other nationalities represented in the group were Scythians (Yueh-chih), Sogdians, and Indians. This marked the beginning of the long and laborious process of making Sanskrit and Pali scriptures intelligible to Chinese audiences. An Shih-kao's translations appear to have been of a kind most likely to be attractive to aristocratic court intelligentsia and stressed material concerning *dhyana* ("meditation") practices, which had obvious resemblances to Taoist quietism. At the other end of the social scale, the potential popularity of Buddhism among the masses was demonstrated in 194 A.D. when an official-turned-rebel used his lavish patronage of the Buddhist community in Kiangsu to attract a large and devoted personal following. It was reported that tens of thousands flocked to his temple to hear instruction in the Mahayana doctrines and to partake of the public feasts that were set out for them.

As Buddhist clergy began to pass over from the role of serving mainly foreign urbanites to a more active proselytizing among the Chinese, the task of justifying the faith to its critics was also begun. Around 200 A.D. a certain Chinese monk, Mou Tzu, composed a tract in the form of skeptical questions and justifcatory answers. Here, even so early, may be seen some of points of conflict between Buddhist and classical Chinese teachings. For example, asked how Buddhist doctrine could be valid when it was not expounded in the teachings of the sages Yao, Shun, the Duke of Chou, and Confucius, he parried the question by asserting that the teachings of the Buddha were of such transcendent and universal worth that the sages, good men that they were, would have adopted them had they had the opportunity.

For all of this, however, at the end of Western Chin in 317 A.D. Buddhism was still of marginal importance. But after the capture and sack of Loyang and Ch'angan by the Hsiung-nu, many of the great families of these regions, some Buddhist converts among them, fled southward, where they joined in the establishment of the Eastern Chin state. The north then passed under the control of the Sixteen Kingdoms. North and south, the adoption of Buddhism then proceeded at a much faster pace.

In the north, non-Chinese rulers who were determined not to capitulate culturally to the Chinese needed an ideology to justify their permanent domination. Long before his founding of Later Chao (329-352), Shih Lo had become an enthusiastic patron of Buddhism. The agent of his conversion was Fo-t'u-teng, a missionary monk who had arrived in Loyang from the west in 311, just after it had fallen to the Hsiung-nu. The visitor was presently introduced to Shih Lo, then still a general. Fo-t'u-teng refrained from discoursing to the general upon the deeper truths and, instead, awed him by feats of magic. The association between these two lasted for some twenty years. With learned monks at his disposal, Shih had less need for Chinese literati, and he had access to a new ideology, which was important for his political ambitions. Shih Lo's new-found guide encouraged him in his dreams of empire by telling him of a prophecy he said he had heard long before, that he would one day be ruler of China. From the time of its founding, the state of Later Chao was a faithful patron and protector of Buddhism.

Important consequences followed from such official endorsement of Buddhism. Rich merchants, aristocrats, and noblemen furnished money for the construction of new temples. By doing so, they served the ends of their own salvation and of their increase in wealth as well. Grateful monks would say prayers for the patrons' and their ancestors' everlasting bliss, and at the same time they established a profitable relationship with rich and powerful institutions that enjoyed imperial favor. Conditions in the north had made it extremely difficult for the great families to protect their estates. Now, by the simple expedient of donating the right to collect rent from their lands and serfs to the temples, they placed them under official protection. The temples reciprocated by sharing with the donors the profits derived from the lands. Some of the aristocrats, usually those in a condition of relative poverty, left their homes to take up the monastic life. They were to provide the principal source of an educated native clergy. Great numbers of destitute commoners also turned to the temples, offering themselves (with their land, if any) as slaves or serfs in return for a small measure of material security and spiritual consolation. Although Later Chao was soon to be supplanted by the Tibetan dynasty of Former Ch'in, the expansion of Buddhism under state protection continued. The work of translation that had been begun on a large scale by An Shih-kao was now greatly advanced by the Kuchean aristocrat Kumarajiva. A man of immense learning and many talents, he raised the standards of translation to a high level of sophistication, and doctrines once misleadingly offered in Taoist terminological disguise could now be better understood by learned Chinese.

By the time the Toba state of Wei and its successor states early in the fifth century began the task of politically reintegrating the north, Buddhism was already widely popular and the pattern of its adjustment to Chinese state and society already well established. The monasteries, under their economic aspect, had assumed the function and, in some respects, the form of the estates of the great families. They had become useful both to aristocrats and to commoners. At the same time, because they had developed under imperial protection, they had to pay the price of subordination to public authority. Because the rulers saw themselves as Buddhist patrons and leaders, they insisted upon exercising at least formal regulation of the Buddhist clergy.

The adoption of Buddhism in the south during the fourth century progressed at about the same pace as in the north, but under rather different conditions. First, the south was not subject to non-Chinese domination of most of its territory, and although wealthy aristocratic families might rise and fall in their political position, they were at least relatively secure in their possession of lands and serfs and in their social status. Moreover, the intellectual climate was very different. On the one hand, there were both the time and the resources to permit many scholars to continue to study the classical texts of Confucian and Taoist thought, and on the other hand, the impact of Buddhism here was less direct than in the north, mediated as it was largely by Chinese monks rather than by foreign missionaries.

Among the northern refugees who gathered in the south at the capital of Eastern Chin (317-419) at the beginning of the fourth century were Buddhist monks and laymen. Moving in the intellectual and literary circles of the aristocracy, they presented and defended their doctrines and sought ways of making them acceptable. The Chinese Buddhists, well versed in Chinese classical literature before their training in Buddhist doctrines, were quick to discover resemblances between Buddhist and classical ideas, especially those of Taoism. Some adopted the method they called *ke-yi*, or "matching the meaning," by which Buddhist concepts were matched, one at a time, with superficially similar classical concepts and explained in terms of them. This process of adaptation of indigenous cultural traditions involved distortions of classical and Buddhist concepts alike, but had the effect of providing for the introduction of some Buddhist teachings in disguised form and thereby domesticating them. Works were written to demonstrate the compatibility of indigenous and Buddhist teachings, and growing numbers of aristocrats combined Buddhist with classical scholarship. The leadership and patronage of the wealthy and powerful commended the foreign religion to widening circles of aristocracy. But the growth of the monastic communities involved great numbers of commoners as well. The number of monasteries in Eastern Chin reached 1,768 and the number of monks, 24,000. By the sixth century these figures had reached 2,846 and 82,700, respectively. Without in the least impairing the highly stratified character of the society, the monasteries provided models of egalitarianism. Monks of every level of aristocracy and commoners as well were required to live and dress alike, in accordance with the *Vinaya* (monastic rules). While great families, secure in their social eminence, lost nothing by having some of their members ordained as monks, members of poor families undoubtedly were drawn to the monasteries in part by the opportunity they offered of associating with and studying in the company of monks of high social origin.

Buddhist institutions in the south profited by the strong position of their aristocratic sponsors vis-à-vis the government. Whereas northern Buddhism grew up under the protection of the state and in a condition of subordination to it, the southern clergy remained remarkably independent of governmental control. The presence of Buddhist Monks not only in the scores of monasteries ringing the capital but on the very palace grounds forced a ceremonial issue of the greatest importance: Should monks be required to prostrate themselves before the emperor in the manner of subjects generally? In the north this was unquestionably the case, given the ruler's direct command over the clergy. In the south, however, the weakness of the rulers and the might of the aristocratic patrons of Buddhism resulted in the opposite decision being made. Monks were allowed to omit the usual act of obeisance on the grounds that their devotion to the way of transcendent truth removed them from the sphere of the emperor's authority.

Dramatic evidence for the active role played by Chinese in the diffusion of Buddhism in their own society is to be found in the travels of some two hundred Chinese monks who made the incredible journey by sea or by land to foreign centers of Buddhist learning in Southeast Asia and India. It also cannot be emphasized too strongly that the deliberate pursuit of religious wisdom in foreign lands especially during the fourth through eighth centuries reflected an astonishing reorientation of Chinese literate culture, an opening to the world around. An early pioneer traveler to India was the monk Fa-hsien, who left his native land in the year 399 to search out an authoritative version of the *Vinaya* so as to elevate the standards of monastic discipline. Many others were inspired by his heroic example, including the great Hsuan-tsang of early T'ang times, whose journey became the subject of popular stories and, eventually, of the novel *Record of a Journey to the West (Hsi-yu chi,* portions translated as *Monkey).* Several of the monks wrote accounts of their travels and these offered to their readers an unprecedented source of accurate information on other civilizations. Learned Chinese were now aware of the fact that their own was but one of several civilized societies, a lesson that was largely forgotten in time, and had to be learned again.

If Mahayana Buddhism was the most important vehicle for the diffusion of alien culture in China, other forms of influence were apparent and had enduring effects. The Iranian culture centers of the Tarim basin mediated the diffusion of Indian music and dance, and Iranian merchant colonies in the commercial centers of north China, including Ch'angan, implanted Nestorian Christianity, Mazdakism, and Manichaeanism, the last being the most important in the long run. The style of the Chinese aristocracy of northern China was heavily influenced by "barbarian" dress and preoccupation with horses. Toba and T'ang ceramic human and animal figurines convey the exotic and cosmopolitan flavor of life among the upper classes.

Imperial Reunification in Sui and T'ang

The adoption of Buddhism in China appears, for the most part, to have been a response to the fourth century crisis in Chinese civilization. The Chinese universal state had passed over from decline to disintegration, and the claims of the classical tradition upon the exclusive loyalty of the literati could no longer be sustained. But in the course of the fifth and sixth centuries the empire was politically reintegrated by the Toba states (386-581), the Sui (581-618) and T'ang (618-907) dynasties. This restoration of the Chinese universal state did not, however, bring with it a restoration of Han society and the elimination of the originally alien religion. Instead, it resulted in a new form of the universal state, both institutionally and ideologically. The aristocratic and quasi-feudal pattern of post-Han society was not greatly disturbed but became, instead, the foundation of a new empire that adjusted its administrative forms and its policies to the changed social conditions. Buddhist clergy and doctrines, far from constituting an obstacle to reintegration, were skillfully employed by Sui and early T'ang rulers to reinforce the social and ideological solidarity of their regimes. The reunified empire used the northern model of governmental dominance over the Buddhist clergy and joined in the emperor's person two roles, that of Chinese emperor in the classical tradition and, at the same time, that of Cakravartin (like Ashoka Maurya), the lay Buddhist sovereign and patron and protector of the faith. This new pattern, however, was highly unstable. In the long run, the reestablishment of the empire was incompatible with the aristocratic rule of great families and with the Buddhist dominance of the intellectual and aesthetic life of China.

The reunification of the empire occurred essentially in two stages. In the first stage, the state of Northern Wei, founded in 385 by a Turkish group, the Toba, occupied first the northeast, then the northwest. All north China was under unified rule by 439. The Toba rulers were strongly influenced by Chinese culture and allowed governmental administration to pass into the hands of Chinese officials. While Chinese aristocratic families reestablished their fortunes, acquired large estates, and managed local government, Toba tribesmen who had remained in the grasslands with their herds became resentful, and in 530 they undertook a great rebellion against their government. After a brief period of disunion, Yang Chien, a Chinese official who had married into the ruling family of one of the northern states, established the Sui dynasty in 581. Eight years later, in the second stage, Sui conquered the feeble Chinese state in the south and thereby brought the entire empire under one rule for the first time since 317. Sui, like Ch'in eight hundred years before, pursued the task of reunification with such energy as to provoke a mass revolt, which resulted in the founding of the T'ang dynasty (618-907) by Li Yuan and Li Shih-min, a dynasty that was destined to preside over a brilliant revival of imperial rule for three hundred years.

It is not easy to say why Sui and T'ang were able to reunify the Chinese empire when other states had tried and failed over a period of nearly three centuries since the collapse of Western Chin. Some economic and institutional factors may be cited, however, as having made this achievement more possible. First was a trend toward development and integration of the economy. Improved techniques in northern dry farming and the expansion of southern rice cultivation added to the productivity of Chinese agriculture. The fifth and sixth centuries also saw an increase in commercial activity. The still-underpopulated south led the way in this development, but trade also prospered in the north, where Buddhist monasteries served as important centers of capital accumulation, finance, and commercial enterprise, especially around the political centers. Interregional trade, probably on a small scale, had also begun to provide some economic unification of north and south. When political unification was achieved, it began in the north and was completed by the conquest of the south. While the southern states at Nanking were too weak politically to make effective use of the wealth of their region, the Northern Wei state skillfully mobilized the material and manpower under their rule. In doing so, it laid the foundation upon which the imperial regimes of Sui and T'ang were later raised.

When the Northern Wei was established at P'ingch'eng (modern Tat'ung) in northern Shansi in 386, north China had been ravaged by the wars of the Sixteen Kingdoms and large areas of potentially productive land were left unused. The Wei ruler then undertook the first in a series of forced migrations that moved hundreds of thousands of Chinese peasant households to the region of the capital and other strategic areas. The agricultural colonists were subjected to effective bureaucratic control and the government adopted schemes for the allotment of land and draft animals in order to maximize their agricultural output. The population of the colonies was organized into a subbureaucratic hierarchy arbitrarily imposed on the village settlements. By this means, the population could be taxed and conscripted, and the state thereby placed on a solid foundation. These measures were continued and elaborated by the Toba successor state of Chou (557-581) and by the Sui. At the same time, these northern regimes were able to secure the acquiescence, if not the active support, of the entrenched Chinese and barbarian aristocracy by leaving them relatively undisturbed in the possession of their estates and their hereditary official titles. (The governments were strong enough to deprive some of the aristocrats of their lands, but this may not have occurred on a large scale.)

An important factor in the imperial reunification was the popularity of Buddhism and its use by the Sui founder, Yang Chien, to strengthen his authority. His ancestors had been aristocratic Chinese collaborators with Hsien Pei states in the north for generations and were subject to Buddhist influence. He spent his childhood in the care of a nun, and his strong-willed empress was a devout lay Buddhist. Although he made use of the Han dynasty model in organizing his regime and patronized Taoists, he cultivated Buddhism as his strongest bond with his subjects. He presented himself as a Cakravartin king who, like Ashoka, was a divinely inspired protector of the true law and a model of Buddhist ethics. After an initial period of hostility when the Sui conquerors broke the political power of the southern clergy, Yang Chien pursued a successful policy of conciliation, which combined patronage with control and thereby promoted the integration of the south into the northern-dominated empire. Everywhere he displayed his Buddhist commitment by building temples. The quick overthrow of Sui by T'ang in 618 did not result in any major change in the Buddhist policies of Sui. The T'ang founders came from the same Buddhist Sino-barbarian aristocracy as their predecessors, and they integrated Buddhist institutions and clergy even more fully into the political organization of the state.

Sui and T'ang made a great, and largely successful, effort to bring north and south together under effective imperial rule. The greatly expanded resources of the southeast were now tapped (for the benefit of the immense capital city at Ch'angan) by the canal system constructed by the Sui and improved by T'ang. Highway construction was undertaken on an unprecedented scale. Empirewide recruitment of some officials through a civil-service examination system contributed to solidarity and cultural uniformity. Sui and T'ang inherited from northern Wei a more rational central administrative structure, including the six ministries (civil office, rites, revenue, war, works, and punishments), a Secretariat of State Affairs, an Imperial Secretariat, and an Imperial Chancellery, the last of which was a stronghold of leading aristocratic officials and had the power to review and criticize imperial policy.

Externally, the Sui and T'ang extended Chinese imperial authority farther than ever before. The Sui and T'ang made effective use of alliances with Turkish tribal federations in order to control the far west with minimum military costs. At its greatest extent the T'ang empire reached westward into modern Afghanistan. Regional protectorates were also established over Vietnam, southern Manchuria, and Mongolia. The T'ang ruling house had originally been linked by descent and by politics with the Turks, and subsequent expansion of the empire into Central Asia reinforced the cosmopolitan character of the regime and its great capital in the Wei valley.

Domestication of Mahayana in China

The reunification of China that began under the Toba states and was completed by Sui and T'ang provided conditions favorable to the integration of Buddhism with the indigenous culture and society. Cities, now safe from the ravages of war, grew rapidly in size and became increasingly commercialized. The government-managed markets in the cities were of unprecedented size and activity, and once again, as in Later Han, one finds anticommercial tracts warning against luxury and waste and the neglect of agriculture. Closely associated with this growth in trade and in commercial wealth, the number of Buddhist monasteries and of monks and nuns doubled and redoubled. By the end of Northern Wei, there were about four to five thousand large temples, with an average of fifty monks each, and about forty thousand village temples with two or three monks each. Quite apart from the abundant literary evidence of religious fervor, including the practice of self-immolation, this immense investment in buildings and clergy testifies to the success with which Buddhism had become domesticated in its Chinese setting and to the extent to which Chinese cultural orientation had been modified. A substantial part of the fortunes made in commerce was invested in the temples. Although donations to temples may have been more or less inspired by the intention of gaining salvation by the merit of sacrificing one's wealth for the advancement of the truths of the Buddha, we have already noted that the privileged status of the monasteries made them useful to the wealthy who felt a need to protect their property against taxation or confiscation. Quite apart from this, the monasteries, once they were adequately capitalized, engaged in a wide variety of profitable enterprises. They milled grain, loaned money at interest, assisted in the organization of loan societies, established agricultural colonies farmed by temple slaves, and rented and operated stalls in the city markets. Such worldly activities could be justified as nurturing the monastic endowment. Because monks were forbidden by the *Vinaya* to engage in business or farming, however, they had to get around the rules by having these functions performed by lay dependents or servants of the monastery.

Even as the Buddhist monastic communities were settling into the preexisting pattern of Chinese society and economy, they also had to accommodate themselves to the Chinese political pattern. Chinese imperial government did not admit the possibility of any legitimate rival center of authority. All who lived in the empire were the emperor's subjects and he bore ultimate responsibility for their material, moral, and spiritual welfare. By the time of the founding of the Sui dynasty, the basic terms of the institutional relationship between the state and the Buddhist *samgha* had been established. The Buddhist monasteries were allowed to hold large estates without being subject to most kinds of taxation. In return, however, they had to submit to state regulation. The government fixed limits on the number and size of monasteries and temples in the administrative subdivisions of the empire, set standards for the ordination of monks, and issued certificates of ordination. From time to time, the government demonstrated its power over the monasteries by carrying out large-scale expropriations of monastery estates. The acceptance of this relationship implied a weakening of the principle that the *samgha's* whole reason for existence was its removal from the corrupt and transitory realm of society and the state.

The successful propagation of Mahayana in China presupposed accommodation to indigenous values and religious beliefs. A few instances will serve to illustrate the point. Given the importance that had always been attached to the perpetuation of the family and its ancestral cult, the separation of the monk from his family was not easily accepted in China. One Buddhist answer to this dilemma was to institute religious services for the benefit of the deceased. A monk could justify his vocation to the family he had left behind by having prayers read for the safe repose of the ancestral spirits. Another answer was to search the voluminous scriptures for every shred of evidence that would tend to show that love of parents was a Buddhist virtue. Accommodation to the indigenous religion was most marked in the small rural temples, which may often have originated as local cult sites that were converted to the use of a village Buddhist monk. In such places, local spirits were given places in the Buddhist pantheon and were served by the temple.

Indigenous values also shaped the formation of different schools of Buddhist doctrine and practice and contributed to their success or failure. The most popular form of Buddhism was that of the Pure Land (Ch'ing-tu, Japanese Jodo). The Pure Land sect was based on the cult of Amida and Avalokitesvara (known to the Chinese as Kuan-yin and to the Japanese as Kwannon). Amida and Avalokitesvara presided over the Western Paradise and their devotees were assured of eternal bliss in their realm. The chief canonical work of this school was the *Lotus Sutra,* which in translation became the most popular Buddhist text throughout East Asia. The *Lotus* is simple and moving in its language, vivid in its images, and conveys a welcome message of hope for all seekers of salvation. The absence of any indigenous religion of spiritual salvation had left a need that had now been filled.

Another sect that gained great popularity among literati in T'ang times was the T'ien-t'ai (Tendai in Japanese). The late sixth century founder of the school, Chih-i, demonstrated by his subtle metaphysics that the phenomenal world was really the absolute misperceived and that all phenomena, as all teachings, may ultimately be identified with the absolute. It was thus possible for him to argue that apparently contradictory teachings ascribed to the Buddha were all true and had been expressed by the Buddha intentionally on different levels of truth. Apart from the importance of his metaphysical contributions to later Chinese thought, his teaching represents an adjustment of the manifold quality of the Indian doctrines to the tendency of Chinese thought towards harmonization and reconciliation of real or apparent contradictions. Because of this, T'ien-t'ai was usually favored by the emperors in Sui and early T'ang. One might finally mention Ch'an (Zen in Japanese). Although the name Ch'an is a transcription of *dhyana* (Sanskrit for "trance" or "meditation") and the Chinese use of the term implies a debt to Indian Buddhist teachings on meditation, Ch'an techniques, with their reliance on startling paradox and their avoidance of conventional instruction, seem to owe more to classical Taoist inspiration. The subtlety of its philosophical basis and the difficulty of its discipline limited the popularity of Ch'an largely to people of leisure and therefore of means.

Adaptation of Indigenous Culture

While Mahayana underwent extensive changes in the Chinese cultural setting, Chinese culture itself was modified under the influence of the foreign religion. Certain basic Mahayana concepts and institutions such as those of *samsara, karma,* monasticism, paradise, and the *bodhisattvas* became embedded in Chiese popular religion. The indigenous Chinese religion of Taoism, which has survived as a distinct tradition, was greatly modified, as for example in the development of monastic institutions, an ordained priesthood, and an immense canonical literature. As will be shown in the following chapter, Confucian tradition also came to be deeply reinterpreted under the influence of Buddhist ideas. Moreover, the assumption of charitable functions by the monasteries inspired the imperial government to establish certain new welfare services, such as care for the aged and free medicines for the poor.

One of the characteristics of Mahayana that appears to have had a certain influence on Chinese culture was its egalitarian spirit. The *Vinaya* established a kind of internal democracy in the governance of the monastic communities, and the association of laymen and monks of all classes of Chinese society in the communal activities of the monasteries cut across the rigid class lines that characterized Chinese society until late in the T'ang. In this sense, the monasteries and village temples may have provided a kind of social cement, helping to bind Chinese society together.

Consistent with its egalitarian spirit, Mahayana encouraged the development of a popular literature. Popular tracts, including *sutras* and versions of the *jatakas,* or "birth stories" of the Buddha, were reproduced in immense numbers, thereby giving rise to the fateful Chinese invention of the art of printing. At the same time, folk songs and stories were collected and written down. Many have survived in the great monastic library discovered a few decades ago sealed in a Tun-huang rock temple. Among literati, simplicity and the common touch were often favored in prose and poetry instead of the artificiality exemplified by the parallel-prose form of Han times. Liberated from traditional formalism and inspired both by folk culture and by foreign music and literature, Chinese poetry in the Six Dynasties and T'ang was at the height of its expressive powers.

By mid-T'ang the diffusion, adaptation, and domestication of Mahayana in China were well underway. The clergy and their temples had become a familiar feature of the Chinese urban and rural scene. Distinctively Chinese forms of Buddhism had evolved, with their own literature and clergy. Buddhist iconography, Indian or Central Asian at first, had become aesthetically Chinese in feeling and execution. The village temples had often assumed the functions and even many of the forms of the indigenous local or Taoist cults, so that it was difficult to say that a given country shrine was Buddhist or not, despite its having certain obviously Buddhist features. But the blending of Buddhist and pre-Buddhist elements was not and would never be complete. The classical tradition had begun to revive in the north in the fifth century, while it had survived in the south. In the reunited empire, linked to the splendor of the Sui and T'ang regimes, classical learning was pursued with greater confidence than before. Religious Taoism, for all its debt to Buddhist models of organization and doctrine, retained an identity of its own. When at a later time the imperial court was to return unambiguously to a classical ideological orientation, the survival of Buddhism was in no way threatened. Rather, it was officially tolerated as a religion appropriate to the ignorant masses and as a means of encouraging them to responsible and obedient behavior.

The Spread of Mahayana Buddhism to Japan

Up to this point the focus of this study of Asian civilizations has been on developments in the heartland of the Eurasian landmass, the great inner crescent of fertile river valleys extending from the Tigris-Euphrates in the west through the Indus and Ganges in South Asia and up to the Yellow and Yangtze rivers in China. Historical developments during the latter half of the first millennium A.D. in another area outside of this original heartland warrant attention: the spread of Buddhism and Chinese civilization to the northeast corner of Asia where Korea and the Japanese archipelago are situated. Like Southeast Asia, the northeast was a rimland, or peripheral area, on the fringe of the major sphere of the city-centered, more highly differentiated and organized Chinese empire. This geographical isolation meant that stimuli from the older Chinese civilization were received only very gradually in the initial stage, which in the case of Japan extended down to the end of the fourth century A.D. During the fifth and sixth centuries, however, contact through the Korean peninsula became more frequent, and by the beginning of the seventh century Japan had entered a period of intensive borrowing which was to last until the mid-ninth century.

The fact that the new civilization in Japan, as in Korea and Southeast Asia, was in many ways a variation on an outside pattern makes it of particular interest. The diffusion of cultural patterns outward from centers of civilization to noncivilized areas or from one civilization to another is part of the recurring phenomenon of human interaction from the earliest times and will be the central theme again in the analysis of the modern era. This phenomenon of diffusion in the case of early Japan, as is so often the case elsewhere also, is obscured by the often contradictory documentary materials, and there is by no means consensus on the meaning of the archaeological and linguistic data. Nevertheless it is possible to outline the processes involved.

The agricultural and technological revolutions associated with the type of surplus economy essential to the development of civilization had their beginnings in Japan during the so-called Yayoi period—roughly five centuries between 250 B.C. and 250 A.D. It was in this period that the majority of the inhabitants of the Japanese islands, themselves originally migrants from the Asian mainland and having absorbed from the continent the techniques of irrigated acriculture, became a settled agrarian people. Techniques and tools for the production of food are, of course, usually prime candidates for diffusion, since they can be easily observed or transmitted without the extensive contact necessary to acquire a broader knowledge of the donor culture and, moreover, have immediately recognizable advantages for increased well-being. The pattern of wet-rice agriculture required a somewhat complex system of diking, channeling, and leveling of fields necessitating intensive use of labor, but it was one that produced very high yields. In this same span of time a knowledge of weaving of textiles and the working of both bronze and iron were acquired through contact with the continent.

This early cultural diffusion from the Chinese civilizational sphere does not appear to have been accompanied by any sudden large-scale migration or armed intrusion, at least not prior to the fourth century A.D. Rather, the Japanese islands had become populated in a long and gradual series of movements. The approximately one-hundred-mile-wide strait between the island of Kyushu and the tip of the Korean peninsula, and the five hundred miles of open sea between Japan and China were formidable obstacles to easy contact with continental Asia, and it is probable that innovations in agriculture and technology, like the people themselves, came in trickles rather than torrents. Evidence from the so-called Tomb, or Tumulus, period (ca. 300-600 A.D.) does suggest, however, the possibility of an invasion by a coherent group of outsiders utilizing the horse and superior armor and weaponry.

Whether or not the Tumulus culture was an indigenous development, it would seem evident that a clearly differentiated and stratified society was taking shape on the more fertile coastal plains of southwestern and central Japan. The huge burial mounds that came to dot the landscape, stocked with bronze and iron utensils and other symbols of wealth and requiring very large expenditures of coordinated labor, are indications of a steep social pyramid of wealth, prestige, and power. At the top of this division of labor and status were aristocratic lineage groups (the *uji*), which, as an elite, controlled both land and labor. The heads or patriarchs of these lineage groups apparently combined the roles of political, economic, and religious "managers." The topographical characteristics of the volcanic islands of Japan—small coastal plains formed from swift-flowing rivers separated one from another by hills and mountains—were not conducive to the type of coordinated water control that may have aided the emergence of a single cohesive managerial elite in other areas of the world, but the heads of the regional *uji* did perform the tasks of coordinating the labor as well as the religious life of the local communities.

Basic to the latter role were the beliefs, myths, values, and symbols that later came to be termed Shinto. As was typical of agrarian religions elsewhere, Shinto was primarily concerned with fertility and the continual renewal of the agrarian cycle. The godhead, or the divine, was viewed as a force diffused throughout nature, including both earth and the cosmos, and manifested itself in such phenomena as the sun, thunder, trees, rocks, and in anthropomorphic deities as well as in perhaps the charisma of exceptional personalities. The realm of the *kami,* or the "divine," was thus not separate or transcendent from that of man; the world was pervaded by spiritual forces. Individual families venerated the spirits of at least the most recently departed ancestors, while communities paid collective deference to local guardian forces that protected them as a whole. The primary rituals consisted of acts of purification (from the polluting influences of such natural occurrences as disease or antisocial behavior) and actions intended to propitiate the divine powers.

In the Tumulus period important political changes had been taking place, and by the fifth century A.D. recurring power struggles between competing networks of regional *uji* elite had led to the establishment of a loose hegemony under one particularly successful group of families known as the Yamato—the progenitors of the imperial line in Japan (and a term that, like Han in China, came later to be applied generically to the Japanese as a whole). This lineage group and its allies may have originally gained their position of prominence through military force during the course of moving northward from Kyushu to the Yamato plain in central Honshu (near the present city of Nara). The continuing efforts of the Yamato to expand and consolidate their hegemony as a central aristocracy are crucial to the story of the creation of an urban-centered civilization in Japan, for it was under their leadership and in large part because of their political ambitions that intensive borrowing from China began in the early seventh century.

Contact with Chinese civilization, although stretching back into the prehistoric period, had been previously intermittent. Geography made the Korean peninsula the major channel for Chinese influence. Chinese patterns of government and culture had taken root in the north of that peninsula by the second century B.C. There was, however, a sharp division between the northern and southern halves of the peninsula and the latter remained substantially outside of the sphere of Chinese influence and therefore something of a breakwater between Japan and the semi-sinicized northern states. But during the fourth century A.D., a northern kingdom, Koguryo, utilized Chinese bureaucratic techniques to mobilize its resources behind expansion. This pressure brought about a major reaction in the south, as a kingdom known as Paekche emerged to counter the north by itself borrowing political institutions from the Chinese, and the Paekche king, in search of military help, enlisted Japanese support. Around the year 369 this struggle came to involve more and more inhabitants of Japan and as result the flow of cultural element from China increased down the Korean peninsula and across the Tsushima Straits. Around the year 405 the king of Paekche sent the Yamato court what today would be termed technical advisers—a number of educated scribes capable of writing the Chinese language and thereby assisting in the keeping of administrative records. While these immigrants were to be joined by artisans skilled in metal working, sericulture, and other material techniques, it was the adoption of a written script that was to have the most far-reaching consequences, constituting as it did a major step in an intellectual revolution with profound ramifications for the future political and social life of the Japanese. Another major step came in the following century (the most usual dates given are either 552 or 538) when Paekche's role as a cultural broker culminated in the formal introduction of Chinese Buddhism.

The cumulative effect of these two instances of cultural borrowing was immense. First of all, the mere use of a written script gave a previously nonliterate society a new medium for social communication and artistic creation as well as a means of preserving a consciously intellectualized tradition. The historical myths of earlier ages were eventually compiled and systematized. Native poetry (an indigenous tradition that has continued down into the modern era to possess a vitality and appeal rivaling any among world literatures) could now be permanently recorded. Access to the poetry of T'ang China, moreover, provided new stimulus at the same time that classic Chinese essay forms and the didatic but imaginative Buddhist *jataka* tales encouraged the development of new prose genres. Nor were the stimuli confined to literary forms; the Chinese language was a medium for acquiring familiarity with Chinese social philosophy and ethical thought, with their highly articulated concepts concerning man's relationship to the natural and social orders.

The major vehicle for the importation of Chinese culture was the institution of monastic Buddhism. It is not difficult to imagine some of the excitement and appeal this highly developed universal religion had for members of the Japanese elite, despite our distance in time and culture today. There was little in the native religious life to rival the cosmopolitan learning of the Buddhist clerics, the intricate theology, the systematic canon, the pomp and mystery of the esoteric ritual, the exotic imagery and artistic brilliance of the iconography, or the sheer material display inherent in the monumental architecture of its temples. For those moved by practical concerns, the monks and artisans attached to these temples afforded a fund of more mundane skills in carpentry, bridge building, urban planning, and an applied knowledge of medicine and calendar making. These, combined with the pseudoscientific or magical claims for influencing natural phenomena such as drought or pestilence, gave Buddhism a this-worldly appeal not unlike that which aided the efforts of Christian missionaries in Asia in the nineteenth century. But perhaps the single most easily

Map 26 Korea, about 500 A.D.; Japan, about 800 A.D.

identifiable motive for many of the Japanese elite during this period of intense borrowing was a political one. Of course, the lines should not be drawn too distinctly, since the prestige of a patron of new religious, artistic, and intellectual activity can itself be translated into authority, as the central aristocracy of the Yamato were well aware. Indeed, the initial patronage given to Buddhism by one prominent court family, the Soga, immediately aroused the suspicions of its chief rivals and led to a stormy beginning for the new faith. In a mixture of zealot reaction and power politics, the Soga and the handful of Buddhist clergy in the mid-sixth century were berated for causing natural calamities, temple images were thrown into canals, and nuns were defrocked. The Soga reasserted their influence, pointing to a new series of abnormal happenings that followed these irreligious acts, and pushed for expanded contact with China. Although the Soga themselves were eventually eliminated from power in 645, their successors manipulated the throne to carry out a series of changes (known collectively as the Taika Reforms) inspired by the T'ang model. Politically, Japanese society would appear to have been groping toward a more clearly monarchical form of rule for some centuries. The exposure to the Chinese model of centralized imperial government—a model whose efficacy had been concretely demonstrated in 562 when the Japanese were driven out of Korea by the superior forces of a sinicized Korean kingdom and again in the mid-seventh century when T'ang naval power dealt the Japanese several defeats—gave new impetus and shape to this existing trend.

It is evident that the Soga, the Taika reformers, and their immediate successors were, in borrowing from China, engaged in an attempt to transform the loose and often ineffective hegemony of the Yamato throne into something more closely approaching central rule. In 604 the Soga clique then in control of the throne proclaimed the emperor single sovereign lord over the diverse lineage groups throughout Japan and asserted that all the people were his subjects. Beginning in 607, increasing numbers of the most loyal and able courtiers were sent on the hazardous open sea journey to the Chinese metropolis to study. Such returning students were to aid in laying out a grandiose capital at Nara in 710 (Japan's first true city) and, beginning in 702, to draft a series of comprehensive codes aimed at creating the type of bureaucratic control they had observed in the T'ang government. As in the case of the T'ang, these reformers intended the new bureaus to oversee a wide range of social and economic life, including the promotion of education and morality and the creation of a communications system encompassing roads, bridges, post stations, and lighthouses. But at the heart of these late seventh and early eighth century reforms was an attempt to radically alter the land tenure system. Seeking to create a broad-based, rational tax structure, the imperial government sought to bring areas of arable land and the labor necessary to cultivate it under central rule. An administrative structure divided into provinces and counties was created and an elaborate land survey and census was undertaken to provide the information needed to establish an allotment system by which fields would be assigned and periodically reassigned to household groups. If this plan had been fully implanted and maintained, it would have ensured both the more efficient use of land and labor, on the one hand, and vastly enhanced the power of the throne, on the other, by funneling revenues directly to the central government. In the long run it proved overly ambitious, as did other political aspects of these Taika innovations.

Domestication of Buddhism: The Heian Period

This attempt at a thorough overhauling of political institutions through the massive diffusion of Chinese culture has sometimes misleadingly been referred to as the sinicization of Japan. In reaction, historians who have investigated this period in depth and discovered the limits of the displacement of indigenous patterns have emphasized the failure of Chinese institutions to take root in the less advanced environment of Japan. What needs to be stressed, however, is the fact that original intent was seldom to produce an exact replica of the T'ang model. The process of borrowing from China in these centuries was to a high degree one of conscious and controlled selection. It was not a case of an alien pattern being imposed wholesale by Chinese invaders. The major borrowing in the sixth through ninth centuries was controlled by members of the Japanese elite itself, who were consciously selecting among foreign institutions and ideas those that might serve as solutions to problems created by indigenous developments. Those that were imported were most often soon domesticated—that is, carefully shaped in order to integrate them into the Japanese context. Certainly, one of the clearest features of the new bureaucracy was the manner in which the hereditary privileges of the leading lineage groups were preserved. The reformers did not directly challenge the principles of aristocracy. Rather, the fundamental importance of lineage groups and the aristocratic principles in general were reaffirmed, as rank within the administrative hierarchy was automatically equated with the hereditary patents of nobility. The goal of the reformers lay not in approaching a Confucian ideal of meritocracy but in consolidating the dominant position of the aristocrats surrounding the central throne vis-à-vis the powerful magnates in the local regions. In this they had considerable success.

Related to the last point is the often-noted Japanese modification of the Confucian concept of the Mandate of Heaven. Compelled to account for the cyclical rise and fall of imperial houses in Chinese history, Confucian scholars had in a sense stretched the concept of merit to fit the extraordinary case of dynastic change. Where a corrupt and impotent ruling dynasty had proven undeserving by failing to fulfill its proper function, then the Mandate might pass to more worthy hands. In Japan by the seventh century familial authority and the sanctity of bloodlines had given the imperial house a routinized charisma that was to aid in its preservation as the single dynastic line down to the modern era, despite recurring struggles between branches of the imperial house and later centuries of vicissitudes and absence of real decision-making power. The reformers, bent as they were on enhancing imperial prestige, were understandably uninterested in doctrines that might even theoretically qualify that prestige. Although not totally ignored by Japanese students of Confucianism, the rejection of the concept of dynastic change is an example of how Chinese political philosophy was domesticated to fit its new home.

In a similar fashion, aspects of the indigenous culture, rather than being swept aside, were reshaped to permit integration with the newly borrowed institutions. The evolution of the Shinto religion in the period of intensive borrowing is rich with examples of this process of adaptation. Whereas some elements—for example, the veneration of ancestral spirits—were in basic harmony with the new, others presented a challenge. Best studied is the reorganization of the pantheon of deities and the myths concerning the origins of the elite lineage groups. The *uji* had apparently long traced their ancestry back to descendants of particular figures in the Shinto pantheon, among which there is no evidence that the sun goddess, the progenitor of the Yamato *uji,* was by any means universally accepted as preeminent. In the hands of the imperial scribes who worked to compile these myths in the *Kojiki* (*Record of Ancient Matters,* 712) and the *Nihonshoki* (*Chronicles of Japan,* 720), however, the sun goddess emerges clearly at the head of the pantheon. The remainder of the pantheon was ordered hierarchically in close correlation with the contemporary hierarchy of aristocratic families. To the same end these compilers presented a version of earlier history that systematically enhanced the prestige of the imperial line in a process comparable to the early political organization of civilizations elsewhere (see Chapter 2). Moreover, the priestly functions of the lineage patriarch—for example, ritual purification in preparation for spring planting, the thankful celebration of the autumn harvest—were extended to give the emperor a sacerdotal role on behalf of society as a whole.

The written compilation of what came to be the canon of Shinto was clearly a response to its new rival, Buddhism. By the same token, shrine organization and the functions of a full-time priesthood underwent a parallel elaboration. The overall trend in this period, however, was toward integration. The outstanding example of conscious efforts in this direction was the creation with official patronage of Ryobu, or "Dual Shinto." Described most simply, this version of Shinto rationalized the existence of the two religious by explaining that the foreign and native deities were one and the same, having merely manifested themselves at different times in different countries in diverse forms. Hence, the sun goddess of the *Kojiki* and *Nihonshoki* was in reality Roshana (Vairocana), the Lord of Light and the chief figure in the Kegon sect of Buddhism. Lesser Shinto deities were equated in the same fashion with appropriate members of the Mahayana pantheon. Although this attempt at synthesis was not totally successful and theological disputes continued to arise in later times over the sticky question of which had primacy—Was the sun goddess merely a guise adopted by a deity whose true essence was that of the Buddhist Vairocana or was it the other way around?— this response to the problem, by preserving the possibility of some separate identity for each, permitted the elite to patronize the two religions simultaneously. Even prior to the full development of Dual Shinto, a huge, fifty-three-foot cast-bronze image of Roshana became the chief object of worship in the Todaiji, a Nara temple founded in the eighth century to serve as the core for a network of subordinate temples planned for each province, symbolizing Buddhism's new status as a state religion. It is significant that when difficulties were encountered in the formidable task of casting the statue, an official appeal was made to the Shinto powers for aid, and in 752 at the celebration of the completion of the figure, a ceremonial cart symbolizing the Shinto god Hachiman was transported from the distant southern island of Kyushu in order to be present.

Language, a cultural phenomenon of critical importance to the total cultural system of a society, offers further examples of the processes of adaptation and domestication. Japanese does not belong to the Sinitic language family and its highly inflected verb forms, multisyllabic vocabulary, and distinctive syntactical construction (characteristics that have led comparative linguists to group it with such Altaic languages as Turkish and Finnish) resisted easy synthesis with Chinese. Yet, there were strong pressures toward some degree of synthesis. In the first place, because of the paucity of native vocabulary for much, if not most, of the borrowed culture, the adoption of a very large number of loan words was to be expected, but the widely divergent phonemic structure of Chinese created tongue-twisting problems for the Japanese speaker. Secondly, whereas a phonetic script such as the Roman alphabet could be modified to represent sounds in languages quite distinct from Latin, the Chinese written character, or logograph, was not adaptable in the same manner. The solution to the first problem was commonplace enough: Japanese systematically mispronounced or domesticated Chinese consonants and vowels while simultaneously adapting the native language to expand the range of meaningful sounds, thus incorporating the new vocabulary. The cumulative effect of such domestication and adaptation was, over time, to produce many new syncretic features within spoken Japanese, although the language retained its essential identity. The problem of writing this language was a much more formidable one. One solution was simply to become bilingual and compartmentalize—that is, utilizing Chinese in written communication while retaining the Japanese for spoken. The *Nihonshoki (Chronicles of Japan)* mentioned above was thus written entirely in Chinese, although the subject matter was native history. But from very early in the process of creating a literate civilization, the Japanese proved unwilling to sacrifice the ability to represent in written form the vocabulary of native religious, poetic, and other cultural elements that had no acceptable counterpart in Chinese. A temporary compromise was hit upon in the compilation of the *Kojiki (Record of Ancient Matters)*. Chinese characters were utilized not for their intrinsic meaning but primarily for their sound. The monumental compilation of native poetry known as the *Man'yoshu (Collection of Myriad Leaves*, ca. 760) was a further refinement of the same technique. This initial compromise, however, was extraordinarily cumbersome and time consuming. A much more satisfactory solution took the form of selecting the minimum number of Chinese logographs necessary to render Japanese syllables and then simplify these to the point where they could serve as an effective writing system, in the process of which their original Chinese meaning was lost. It thus became possible to write native Japanese entirely in a new phonetic, or syllabic, script known as *kana* ("borrowed names"). Eventually, a combination of factors (e.g., the exceedingly large number of homonyms, the utility of characters in representing Chinese loan words, the prestige of Chinese itself) was to make the chief form of written Japanese a mixture of logographs and syllabic signs integrated into a distinctive whole.

These developments took place as the intense borrowing from China that began in the sixth century had slowed. By the ninth century attitudes toward borrowing from China changed very markedly. The last of the large-scale cultural missions sailed in 838, and after this date the Heian-period Japanese elite were no longer to place a high priority on the introduction of innovations from abroad. From the mid-ninth century on, the tide of Chinese influence began to recede, as both foreign developments (the T'ang empire was entering its death throes) and domestic conditions were at work to produce a lessening of interest. The last major signs of enthusiasm for the Chinese model were the building of a new capital at Heian (modern day Kyoto) on the street plan of the Sui capital of Ch'angan and the founding with imperial patronage of two new sects of Chinese Buddhism—Tendai (T'ien-t'ai) and Shingon, both newly imported from the mainland. But the removal of the court to Heian in 794 itself symbolized a new sophistication on the part of the elite toward the instituions they had borrowed, for the chief motive for moving the capital from Nara was the mounting friction between the court and the Nara temples that dominated that city. Having borrowed to bolster their political power and prestige, the court aristocracy had no

6.3

6.4

The spread of Buddhism was a powerful force for cultural diffusion.

6.3 T'ang dynasty pagoda near the capital city of Ch'angan (near modern Sian). The pagodas and rock temples of India were adapted to Chinese architectural tastes as Buddhism in China assumed a Chinese form. Source: O. Siren, *Histoire des Arts Ancienne de la Chine*, les éditions G. Van Oest (Paris and Brussels, 1929).

6.4 The pagoda at the Horyuji Temple, founded in 607 A.D. under the patronage of the Empress Suiko and her regent Prince Shotoku. The present buildings on the outskirts of Nara, which date from the eighth century, are excellent examples of Japanese adaptation of architectural forms borrowed from China and Korea. Courtesy: Japan Information Service, Consulate General, San Francisco.

intention of allowing foreign influences to overshadow its own position. Important court families were particularly outraged by the ambitions of a monk named Dokyo, who had become a fixture in the ruling empress' council and bed chambers and contrived to have himself appointed grand minister of state in 765. The Buddhist establishment of Nara, as well as the newer Tendai and Shingon sects, continued throughout the Heian period to possess considerable temporal power by virtue of large landholdings and the development of armed corps of men attached to the temples, but the clergy was effectively shut out of the inner circles of imperial government at the new capital.

The ninth century also marked the beginning of a long decline in the importance of Chinese-style political institutions. The functions of the central government were gradually usurped by aristocratic families. The most important of these, the Fujiwara, achieved such a deeply entrenched position in the court that through skill at intrigue and a private military force held in reserve they were able to completely control the imperial throne and dominate the central aritocracy. The role of the emperor was reduced to a largely ceremonial and symbolic one shorn of any real power (a position in which emperors were to remain, with very brief exceptions, throughout later Japanese history). For over three centuries, from the mid-ninth down to the mid-twelfth centuries, the main Fujiwara family, with the support of its branches, manipulated the throne and filled the more important bureaus within the imperial government. Increasingly, however, the Fujiwara tended to bypass the central government machinery. Having used their official position to secure further legal and tax immunities for land and peasants under their control, their major administrative task became the supervision of these private domains—a task for which they developed a simpler, more efficient system of institutionalized control within the framework of familial authority and outside the framework of the imperial codes. Similar practices were adopted by other court families, including the imperial family itself. When combined with the holdings of the Buddhist temples, the cumulative effect was to put larger and larger acreage and numbers of people outside the sphere of the government, thus rendering the official hierarchy more and more of a paper facade. Posts within the bureaucratic hierarchy continued to be sought for the prestige they symbolized, but the levers of political power, like the sources of material wealth, now lay elsewhere.

The loss of dominance suffered by the central aristocracy as a group and the emergence of a provincial elite that eventually shouldered the older court families aside will be considered in the next chapter. Here it should be noted that although the decline of the Chinese-style administrative system was certainly an important factor in the failure of the Heian aristocracy to maintain its hold on the country as a whole, the two historical trends should not be confused. Fujiwara-style control over private estates in outlying regions remained an effective means of siphoning wealth from the provinces into the capital city for several centuries despite the collapse of the old land allotment system and the drying up of taxes gathered through the imperial bureaucracy. So long as the stewards on the private estates remitted rents to the central aristocracy, the court remained the political as well as cultural center of the society as a whole. Indeed, under the Fujiwara there developed in the city of Heian during the tenth and eleventh centuries a style of life whose level of elegance and refinement must be said to rival any in world history.

The city itself in this period perhaps reached a population of 100,000, of which a tenth or less would have been participants in the culture of the court. The economic and social life of the city was almost entirely subordinated to the aristocratic families—a very tight-knit subsociety closely interrelated by marriage and blood ties yet rigidly ordered into a hierarchy of minutely defined distinctions. Prestige within this tight circle was increasingly associated with aesthetic sensitivity. Extraordinary stress was placed on the capacity for literary expression, accomplishment in music, and facility with the brush, while very close attention was paid by both sexes to wardrobe fashions, personal ornamentation, and the complex ballet of court etiquette. The most characteristic art of this period is to be found in its poetry, for even the various genres of prose featured poetry as a medium peculiarly appropriate for the expression of the many moods evoked by romantic love, the beauty of the natural world, or the vicissitudes of human life. It is this classical court poetry with its unique imagery that has since received the most attention from Westerners and given the Heian Japanese a special place in the history of world literature. By the end of the period a distinctive prose style had also developed—a style marked by not only the beauty of its form but also in content by its sharp insights into the human personality and the complexities of human relations. The outstanding example, the early eleventh century *Tale of Genji, the Shining Prince (Genji Monogartari),* has been considered by some worthy of the claim to be the world's first true novel.

The authors of the most notable prose works as well as much of the memorable poetry of the late Heian period were women. This feminine domination has often been attributed to the preoccupation with Chinese literature on the part of the male courtiers; but it is also evident that Heian court life, within rigid limits, permitted women to participate rather fully. Indeed, women in Japan were never, not even in the modern era, to regain roles within elite society comparable to those played by their predecessors in the Heian court. The significant factors here may have been the great premium placed on the aesthetic—a realm in which Heian males were willing to recognize female contributions—and the strategic function of matrimonial alliances in court power struggles. The combination of physical charm and artistic ability were highly valued for the male as well as the female, but they were absolutely crucial for daughters if a family was to hold its own in court intrigues. Nevertheless, it would be mistaken to speak of social freedom for either sex in the Heian court. The very ingrown quality of court society that permitted the art of human communication and hence literature to reach such extraordinary heights of refinement also restricted acceptable behavior and made courtiers extremely sensitive to the scorn of their peers. Moreover, prevailing beliefs concerning the pervasive influence of spirits and demons produced for both sexes an atmosphere fraught with anxieties and insecurities.

In this atmosphere Buddhism remained an important influence on both art and life in the Heian period. It was not, however, the metaphysical subleties of Mahayana theology that most appealed to the elite. Rather, the most popular form of Buddhism within the court from the tenth century on was Amidism—salvation through devotion to Amida (Amitabha). The present world, it was believed, has passed into the last of a series of epochal cycles or eras—an era too corrupt and degenerate for man to achieve enlightenment through his own efforts. Thus, blocked from salvation through mere virtuous conduct or assiduous study, the layman could trust only in Amida, who had vowed to share his grace with others so that all sentient beings might find ultimate release. The attractiveness of Amida's Western Paradise was matched only by the repulsiveness of the graphically depicted hells of late Heian preaching. The most popular form of worship at the court became the ritual incantation of Amida's name. It would be an exaggeration, however, to describe Heian court life as permeated by a god-centered spirituality. G. B. Sansom was much nearer accuracy when he suggested that the predominant cult was a cult of beauty which he characterized as "poetic emotion touched with ritual," deriving as much from Shinto as from Buddhism.

Thus, Japanese culture at Heian exhibited a persisting duality as Chinese influences coexisted with elements obviously indigenous in origin. Much interaction took place between the two and some resulted in patterns that were clearly the product of synthesis. There was another duality in Japanese civilization during the Heian period—a duality created by the gap between the life-style of the elite and that of the masses. The style of life we have been considering, it should now be stressed, was very largely the monopoly of the elite in the capital and the uppermost strata of the provinces who had contact with the capital. While the Taika Reforms of the seventh century did have impact on the political and economic life of the provinces, they did not necessarily reach into the social life of lower classes to anywhere near the same degree. The effect of intensive borrowing from China was nowhere as great as it was in the areas surrounding Nara and Heian, and the general populace outside of that area participated very little in it. It is particularly essential to note that Buddhism, while possessing in the Japanese context those characteristics associated with universal religions elsewhere, did not inspire mass conversion in the provinces during these early centuries. Neither the Buddhist clergy nor their aristocratic patrons in the capital demonstrated much concern with the salvation of the common man. Shinto remained the religion of the agrarian masses, and it was not until the late twelfth and turn of the thirteenth centuries, when newer forms of Amidism, evangelistic in content and popular in style, spread rapidly throughout the society that one can speak of a mass Buddhist movement. By this time, the court at Heian had lost its dominant political position to a new class of military nobles who gradually gained control of the provinces and then, in 1185, created a new governmental structure located at Kamakura. Civilization in Japan was at this point moving into a different era in which a new cultural synthesis was also to be formed.

CONCLUDING REMARKS

There are two major foci for the comparative study of salvation ideologies: (1) the similarities and contrasts in the content of the religious message and (2) the differing historical contexts in which these universal religions arose and spread. The messages of the Islamic, Hindu, and Buddhist faiths each centered on rather clearly defined concepts of the nature of the godhead and divine intervention into human affairs. Allah, Shiva, Vishnu, and the Buddha were most often conceived of as personal deities to whom the common man as well as the elite owed ultimate devotion and strict obedience. Nevertheless, each of these religions and even the various sects within them held different views on many questions concerning the nature of the divine. Is the deity omnipotent or subject to cosmic law? How is one to describe the rewards or punishments of a life after death? Can salvation be achieved through one's own efforts or is man totally dependent upon the divine grace of the lord? How is the nonbeliever to be treated?

The theological doctrines of these religions also assigned different roles to the laity as opposed to the *ulama,* priesthood, or monks, and this raises questions for the historian of social and political institutions. In many ways the relationship between religious specialists and the political elite is quite comparable; Buddhist monks served as advisers to emperors in East Asia, influencing legal and economic policy, much in the manner that the *ulama* were accorded positions as guardians of the faith and interpreters of the Quran as applied to everyday life in West Asia. But the political position of the *ulama* and monks varied over time within these civilizations and was often the subject of intense conflict. Yet another rich field for study is the contrasting social functions of Buddhist monastic orders, Sufi brotherhoods, or other priestly organizations. In China, Japan, India, West Asia, and elsewhere such religious organizations were often intricately involved in systems of land tenure, commercial trade, social welfare, and even political action.

The historical study of these religions is of particular interest to the comparativist because of the many opportunities it affords for exploring the permutations and variations of their central themes in very different cultural contexts. Buddhism, South Asian in origin, clearly manifested very distinct patterns in Japan as compared with China, or indeed in southern China as contrasted to northern China. Much more remains to be said about how preexisting regional patterns within separate civilizations influenced and were influenced by the doctrines and institutions of these universal religions. There is also the complex problem of how different social classes or indeed the different sexes received and understood these religious messages. Finally, the historian might explore further the question of why these civilizations experience peaks in religious creativity in certain periods.

BIBLIOGRAPHY

6.P THE RISE OF UNIVERSAL RELIGIONS: PROCESSES

Eliade, Mircea, and Joseph M. Kitagawa, eds., *The History of Religions: Essays in Methodology* (University of Chicago Press paperback, 1959), 163 pp. Provocative approaches to comparative study of religions over time.

Odea, Thomas F., *The Sociology of Religion* (Prentice-Hall paperback, 1966), 120 pp. An introduction to the subject influenced by the functionalist school, with good bibliography.

Robertson, Roland, ed., *Sociology of Religion* (Penguin paperback, 1969), 473 pp. Selections from important writings on general approaches and more specific aspects by a wide range of scholars.

Toynbee, Arnold J., *A Study of History,* Vol. 7B, *Universal Churches* (Oxford University Press paperback, 1963), 782 pp. An extremely influential if often obscure treatise on the place of universal religions in the history of civilizations.

6.1 ISLAM IN WEST ASIA

Cahen, Clarke, "Economy, Society, Institutions," *The Cambridge History of Islam,* 2 vols. (Cambridge, 1970), Vol. 2, pp. 511-38. A reliable overview by a leading French Islamicist.

Gabrieli, Francesco, *Muhammad and the Conquests of Islam* (World University Library paperback, 1968), 241 pp. A relatively short and highly readable account, with excellent illustrations.

Gibb, Hamilton A. R., *Mohammedanism: An Historical Survey* (Oxford paperback, 1970), 131 pp. The best among a number of introductions to the field, despite an outdated title.

Levy, Reuben, *The Social Structure of Islam* (Cambridge University Press paperback, 1969), 505 pp. A fine compilation, especially useful as a reference work.

Von Grunebaum, Gustave E., *Classical Islam: A History, 600 A.D.-1258 A.D.* (Chicago, 1970), 201 pp. An outstanding work of synthesis by a scholar of great learning and perception. The bibliography provides a first-rate guide to further reading.

Watt, W. Montgomery, *What Is Islam?* (New York, 1968), 234 pp. A sensitive and sophisticated enquiry by a scholar who is also the author of the best biography of Muhammad written by a non-Muslim.

6.2 HINDUISM IN SOUTH ASIA

Archer, W. G., *The Loves of Krishna* (Evergreen paperback, n.d.), 127 pp. and 39 plates. A delightful survey of Indian prose, poetry, and painting depicting the exploits of Krishna, a major incarnation of Vishnu.

Basham, A. L., *The Wonder That Was India* (Evergreen paperback, 1959), Chapters 3, 5, 6, and 9. A vivid portrayal of the essential features of Brahmanism and Hinduism in the context of Indian society and culture.

Danielou, Alain, *Hindu Polytheism* (New York, 1964), 537 pp. Extensive quotation from sources characterizing the principal deities; with limited explanation, but rich illustration and original Sanskrit texts appended.

de Bary, William Theodore, ed., *Sources of the Indian Tradition,* Vol. 1 (Columbia University Press paperback, 1964), pp. 1-361. Translations of important texts from Brahmanism and Hinduism with commentary.

Renou, Louis, ed., *Hinduism* (New York, 1962), 255 pp. A brief overview of Hinduism with selected texts and introductory remarks by an authority.

Walker, Benjamin, *The Hindu World,* 2 vols. (New York, 1968). An encyclopedia composed of alphabetically arranged entries about many aspects of Hindu literature and religion.

6.3 MAHAYANA BUDDHISM IN EAST ASIA

de Bary, W. Theodore, ed., *Sources of Chinese Tradition* (Columbia University Press paperback, 1960), 976 pp. Chapters 16 and 17 provide extensive readings in Chinese Buddhist literature.

Fairbank, John K., *et al., East Asia: Tradition and Transformation* (Boston, Houghton Mifflin, 1973), 969 pp. Chapter 5 surveys the period of the Six Dynasties and early T'ang.

Kitagawa, Joseph M., *Religion in Japanese History* (New York, Columbia University Press, 1966), 475 pp. Chapters 1 and 2 survey the introduction of Buddhism, the nature of its accommodation with the indigenous religious tradition, and its significance for ancient Japanese culture.

Morris, Ivan, *The World of the Shining Prince: Court Life in Ancient Japan* (Peregrine paperback, 1969), 349 pp. A very readable description of the values and social institutions of the nobility in the late Heian period, particularly of interest on the position of women, the nature of religious beliefs, and the synthesis of Chinese and indigenous culture.

Sansom, George B., *A History of Japan to 1334* (Stanford University Press paperback, 1958), 510 pp. The standard general history, especially strong on the cultural patterns that result from borrowing from Chinese civilization.

Thapar, Romila, *A History of India,* Vol. 1 (Penguin paperback, 1966), 381 pp. Chapters 5 and 6 cover the formation of Mahayana Buddism in its historical setting.

Wright, Arthur F., *Buddhism in Chinese History* (Stanford University Press paperback, 1959), 144 pp. Penetrating and readable analysis of the role of Buddhism in Chinese history.

GLOSSARY

Aryans. Speakers of an Indo-European language who invaded India from the northwest in the second millennium B.C.

Bhakti. In India, devotion to a personal god. This theistic religious orientation was probably most common among the lower orders of society. Mahayana Buddhism in the course of its development in India was strongly influenced by *bhakti,* which was now held to provide a means of salvation accessible to ordinary lay believers—salvation through faith. Among Hindus this form of worship spread in the first millennium A.D.

Bodhisattva. The *bodhisattva* in Mahayana Buddhism was the alternative to the early Buddhist model of the *arhat.* Instead of pursuing one's own salvation to the extinction of suffering and the attainment of *nirvana,* the *bodhisattva* was a perfected being who stopped short of *nirvana* in order to share his great store of merit with fellow creatures on the path to salvation. The *bodhisattvas* in Buddhist practice were gods, some or all of whom had existed earlier in other contexts and were the objects of devotional cults, such as those of Avalokitesvara and Maitreya.

Brahmanas. Prose texts detailing ritual practice which complemented the Vedas.

Brahmanism. The religious cult of the Vedic sacrifices perpetuated by the brahmans, as opposed to either non-Vedic religion or the broad spectrum of later Hinduism which developed far beyond its Vedic origins.

Brahmans. The priestly caste in Aryan society. Originally ritual specialists, they rose to become the highest stratum of Indian society.

Caliph (Arabic, **khalifa**). Originating with the title of the Prophet Muhammad's successor, Abu Bakr, Khalifat Rasul Allah, "Successor of the Messenger of God." The caliph was the head of the Islamic umma, "the community of believers," and was referred to as *amir* al-muminin, "commander of the faithful."

Dar al-Harb. "The abode of war," that is, those regions not under the sovereignty of a Muslim ruler.

Dar al-Islam. "The abode of Islam," that is those regions under the sovereignty of a Muslim ruler and where the Sharia was enforced.

Dervish. A Sufi; either a religious mendicant or a member of a Sufi brotherhood *(tariqa)* attached to a dervish convent *(khanqah).*

Dhimmi. A member of a non-Muslim religious community (e.g., a Christian or a Jew) living under the protection of a Muslim ruler in accordance with the requirements prescribed by the Sharia.

Dinar. A Muslim gold coin.

Dirham. A Muslim silver coin.

Fujiwara. A family of Heian court nobles who as regents controlled court politics in Japan from the mid-ninth to the mid-twelfth centuries; hence the latter part of the Heian period is often referred to as the Fujiwara period.

Ghazi. A warrior living in the frontier areas of the Muslim world and engaged in holy warfare *(jihad)* against non-Muslims.

Guptas (320-535 A.D.). The dynasty that presided over a period of political unification in northern India when Buddhism, Hinduism, and Jainism existed side by side.

Hadith. An orally transmitted saying attributed to the Prophet Muhammad.

Heian (Kyoto). The imperial capital in Japan, built in 794 A.D. Although it served as the site of the imperial court until 1868, the end date of the Heian period is usually put at 1185, when real political power was shifted to the city of Kamakura.

Hijaz. The central and northern coastal region of western Arabia, in which the Muslim pilgrim cities of Mecca and Medina are located. The ancient overland trade route linking southern Arabia to the Mediterranean world passed through the Hijaz.

Hsuan-tsang. Chinese pilgrim monk who journeyed across Central Asia to India. On his return to Ch'angan in 645 after an absence of sixteen years, he was given a hero's welcome. He devoted the remaining years of his life to the translation of sutras he brought back with him.

Jihad. The holy warfare that Muslims were enjoined to wage against non-Muslims.

Khanqah. A dervish convent.

Khurasan. Formerly a vast area extending northeastward from the central Iranian desert to the Amu Darya River, with its metropolitan centers located at Nishapur, Marv, Herat, and Balkh. Today Khurasan consists of a province in northeastern Iran, bordering the U.S.S.R. and Afghanistan and with its capital at Mashhad.

Kshatriyas. The warrior or aristocratic caste in Aryan society.

Kumarajiva. Native of the Central Asian city of Kucha, he was raised as a Buddhist and educated in India. His fame as a master of Mahayan metaphysics led to his being brought to the Ch'angan court of the Tibetan Ch'in state in 401. There he headed a huge translation project. The quantity and quality of the work made a substantial contribution to the growth of Chinese Buddhism.

Kushanas. A people of uncertain but probably predominantly Iranian stock who invaded Afghanistan and northwest India during the first century A.D. The Kushan empire provided the commercialized and cosmopolitan setting in which Mahayana Buddhism developed as a universal religion.

Mahabharata. An epic poem recounting power struggles in north India in the first millennium B.C.; an important religious allegory.

Mamluk. A slave-soldier, generally although not exclusively a Turk, a Georgian, or a Circassian.

Mawali. Non-Arab converts to Islam who were attached as clients to particular Arab tribes.

Muhtasib. The official in the Islamic city responsible for regulating the markets and for enforcing public morality.

Murshid. A Sufi teacher, also known as a *shaykh* or *pir.*

Nara. The first true Japanese city, built as the imperial capital in 710 A.D. on a Chinese model; hence the name of the historical period 710-784. Although the imperial court moved to Heian (Kyoto), Nara continued to be an important Buddhist center.

Puranas. Popular Hindu texts that embodied monotheistic doctrine.

Qazi. The Islamic judge who administers the Sharia.

Quran (or **Koran**). The Muslim "Holy Book," which is held to be the Word of God, transmitted to the Prophet Muhammad by the Angel Gabriel.

Ramanuja (d. 1137). A brahman thinker in southern India who identified the universal soul with Vishnu, thus personalizing the trend toward monism.

Shankara (?788-820). Brahman thinker from southern India who preached the identity of the individual soul and the world soul and that salvation was to be obtained through knowledge of this identity.

Sharia. The Law of Islam, derived from the Quran, the *Hadith,* or *Sayings of the Prophet,* and the analogical interpretations of the jurists.

Shaykh. Sufi teacher, also known as a *murshid* or *pir.*

Shiis. Those who follow the *shia* (or "party") of Ali, Muhammad's son-in-law and the fourth caliph of the Muslims. The Shiis, although subdivided into a number of sects, constitute the largest minority group (as opposed to the Sunni majority) within Islam, and are today chiefly to be found in Iran and Iraq.

Shudras. The lowest of the original four castes of Aryan society, they were excluded from Vedic rituals; later they became cultivators.

Silsila. The chain of authority passed down from one *shaykh* or *murshid* to the next in a Sufi order *(tariqa).*

Soga. A family of Japanese court nobles in the sixth and early seventh centuries who used their dominant position to sponsor Buddhism and other imported culture from Korea and China.

Sufi. A dervish or mystic. Hence, Sufism, Islamic mysticism.

Sui Wen-ti. Founding emperor of the Sui dynasty in 581. By conquering the southern state of Ch'en, he reunified China politically for the first time since the Chin dynasty in 280 A.D. Raised as a Buddhist, he joined Buddhism to Taoism and Confucianism in an eclectic ideology. Buddhism in China was now so widely popular that Wen-ti sought support for his rule by presenting himself as a generous patron of the *sangha.*

Sultan. A ruler, "one who exercises power"; the title adopted by territorial rulers in the Muslim world from the eleventh century onwards.

Sunnis. Those who follow the *sunna,* or practice of the Prophet Muhammad; the majority community in the Islamic world.

Taika reforms. A series of Japanese reforms inspired by Chinese models of imperial government begun after a coup d'etat in 645 A.D. and extending into the eighth century.

Tariqa. A Sufi order or brotherhood.

Twice-born. The three highest castes—*kshatriyas,* brahmans, and *vaishyas*—who were allowed to practice the Vedic rituals; the second birth was the initiation of religious instruction in boyhood.

Uji. The elite lineage groups or extended familial networks, sometimes translated as "clans," that dominated Japanese society in the period prior to the emergence of an imperial state.

Ulama. The Arabic plural of *alim,* meaning a scholar trained in the Islamic "sciences." Collectively, the *ulama* enforced the Sharia and determined the social norms that governed the life of the Muslim community as a whole.

Umma. The Islamic "community of believers."

Upanishads. Texts of the first millennium B.C. containing philosophical speculations on spiritual forces and the nature of the universe; the name implies a discussion between a master and a disciple.

Vaishyas. Originally the cultivator class in Aryan society, the caste later included many traders and landowners.

Vazir. The minister of a Muslim ruler. In fact, a ruler might appoint concurrently two or more *vazirs* to have charge over different areas of administration but the term is usually applied in the sense of a chief minister, as with the Ottoman "grand vizier."

Vedanta. The most important of the traditional six schools of Hindu philosophy, it based itself on the Vedas, refuting nonbrahmanical theories.

Vedas. Religious hymns and texts dealing with both ritual and philosophical speculation transmitted for generations among the Aryans through memorization and recitation; subsequently the oldest sacred texts of Hinduism.

Waqf. A religious endowment, generally of land, granted bythe donor in perpetuity.

Yamato. Originally a place-name, it is used to refer to the lineage group that established the imperial dynasty in Japan and also, later, simply the Japanese people as a whole.

Yun-kang. The place near the Northern Wei capital at modern T'ai-yuan where a complex of Buddhist rock temples was hewn from the face of cliffs. Comparable rock temples were cut at Lung-men after the capital was moved to the nearby city of Loyang.

The Regional Fragmentation of Civilizations

750 to 1500 A.D.

Over the millennia, beginning with the appearance of the first urban centers, each of the major civilizations of Asia had expanded to include within it a wide range of peoples speaking various languages, living in diverse geographical environments, constituting separate communities, and maintaining distinct subcultures within the basic unity of the civilization. At times that unity had been fostered by huge empires that worked to centralize economic and cultural activities as well as political institutions. At other times, religious patterns and identification with a common faith provided a unifying force even in the absence of a central political structure. But in the period between the tenth and the sixteenth centuries the unity of each civilization was severely challenged.

In some cases the most serious challenge was posed from the outside as new waves of invaders threatened to carve up the areas of civilization into disparate entities. Thus, invaders from Inner Asia once again made their impact felt in China, northern India, and parts of West Asia. More often, the challenge was as much internal as external. The divisive dynamics of ethnic, regional, and class differences were continually at work within all of these civilizations. When centrifugal forces overcame the forces that made for unity, the equilibrium was lost and the civilization fragmented into its component regions. Thus, for example, China became divided into north and south while also losing much of its position of dominance in East Asia as Vietnam, Korea, and Japan developed more autonomy culturally as well as politically.

To describe these phenomona entirely in terms of the decline of older forms, however, would overlook the creative aspects involved. Freed from centralized control and stimulated by new contacts both overland and by sea with distant lands, the separate regions often experienced a revitalization in the religious, artistic, and intellectual spheres. This, then, is a particularly confusing era in the history of civilizations in Asia and one that warrants close study by the comparative historian.

7

PROCESSES

a. Fragmentation of the religious culture area
b. Formation of regional political entities
c. Renaissance of regional cultures
d. Growth of maritime centers
e. Steppe-sown interaction

PATTERNS

1. **Regional Fragmentation in West Asia**
2. **Regional Fragmentation in South Asia**
3. **Regional Fragmentation in Southeast Asia**
4. **Regional Fragmentation in China**
5. **Regional Fragmentation in Japan**

7. REGIONAL FRAGMENTATION

	1	2	3	4	5
700	WEST ASIA	DELHI SULTANATE	SOUTHEAST ASIA	CHINA	JAPAN
800	Tahirids rulers of Khurasan 821-873 Buyids rulers of western Iran ca. 832-1055		Nanchao invades China		
	Samanids rulers of Mawarannahr 819-1005			Huang Ch'ao Rebellion 874; decline of T'ang	
900				Five Dynasties in China 907-960 Liao state, north China, 916-1125	
	Buyids capture Baghdad 945		Vietnamese independence 939	Koryo dynasty, Korea, 935-1392	
	Fatimid conquest of Egypt 969	Rajaraja I, Chola ruler 985-1014		Sung dynasty in China 960-1127, at K'aifeng	
1000	Sultan Mahmud of Ghazni, r. 998-1030 Nizam al-Mulk, Seljuk *vazir* 1017-92	Sultan Mahmud of Ghazni 998-1030 Rajendra I, Chola ruler 1014-42	Li dynasty in Vietnam 1009-1225		
	Firdawsi, poet, d. 1020 Toghrïl Beg, Seljuk sultan1038-63 Seljuk Turks capture Baghdad 1055		Pagan dynasty in Burma 1044-1287	Hsi Hsia empire 1038-1227 Wang An-shih 1021-1086	Rebellion in Kanto region 1051
	Independent Seljuk sultanate in Anatolia ca. 1077				Rebellion in Kanto region 1083-87
1100	al-Ghazali of Tus, theologian, 1054-1111	Ghurids sack Ghazni 1115		Chin State, north China, 1115-1234	

	Hasan-i Sabbah, founder of Nizari Ismaili sect in Alamut, d. 1124 Caliphate of al-Nasir, patron of the *futuwwa,* 1180-1225	Qutb al-Din Aybak captures Delhi 1193	Angkor Wat constructed	Southern Sung, 1127-1279, at Hangchow Chu Hsi neo-Confucian thinker, 1130-1200	Honen's Jodo sect 1133-1212 Fighting in capital 1156 Taira displace Fujiwara control 1160 Kamakura shogunate created 1185
1200	Chingiz Khan captures Bukhara 1220 Seljuk sultanate in Anatolia submits to Mongols 1243 Hülegü captures Baghdad 1258 Nasir al-Din Tusi, mathematician and philosopher, d. 1274	Dynasty of the "Slave Sultans" of Delhi 1206-90 Amir Khusru, poet, 1253-1325 Khalji dynasty of Delhi 1290-1320	Conquest of Nan Chao 1253 End of Srivijaya empire Decline of Khmer empire Majapahit 1294-ca. 1500	Mongol conquest of south China 1279	Death of Eisai 1215 Shinran's Shin sect 1224 Death of Dogen 1253 Mongol attacks 1274, 1281 Nichiren, d. 1282
1300		Khalji army south to Madurai under Malik Kafur 1311 Tughluq dynasty of Delhi 1320-1414 Bengal independent sultanate 1336 Bahmanid sultanate in Deccan 1347 Timur sacks Delhi 1398	Ayuthia, Thai kingdom 1350-1767		Ashikaga period begins 1333 Yoshimitsu as shogun 1368-94
1400		Sayyid dynasty of Delhi 1414-51 Lodi dynasty of Delhi 1451-1526	Islam in Malacca ca. 1400 Abandonment of Angkor		Noh playwright Zeami, d. 1443 Onin War, beginning of Sengoku period, 1467
1500		First Battle of Panipat 1526; Mughuls conquer Delhi sultanate Battle of Talikota 1565; Vijayanagar overthrown by Golkonda, Bijapur, and Ahmadnagar			

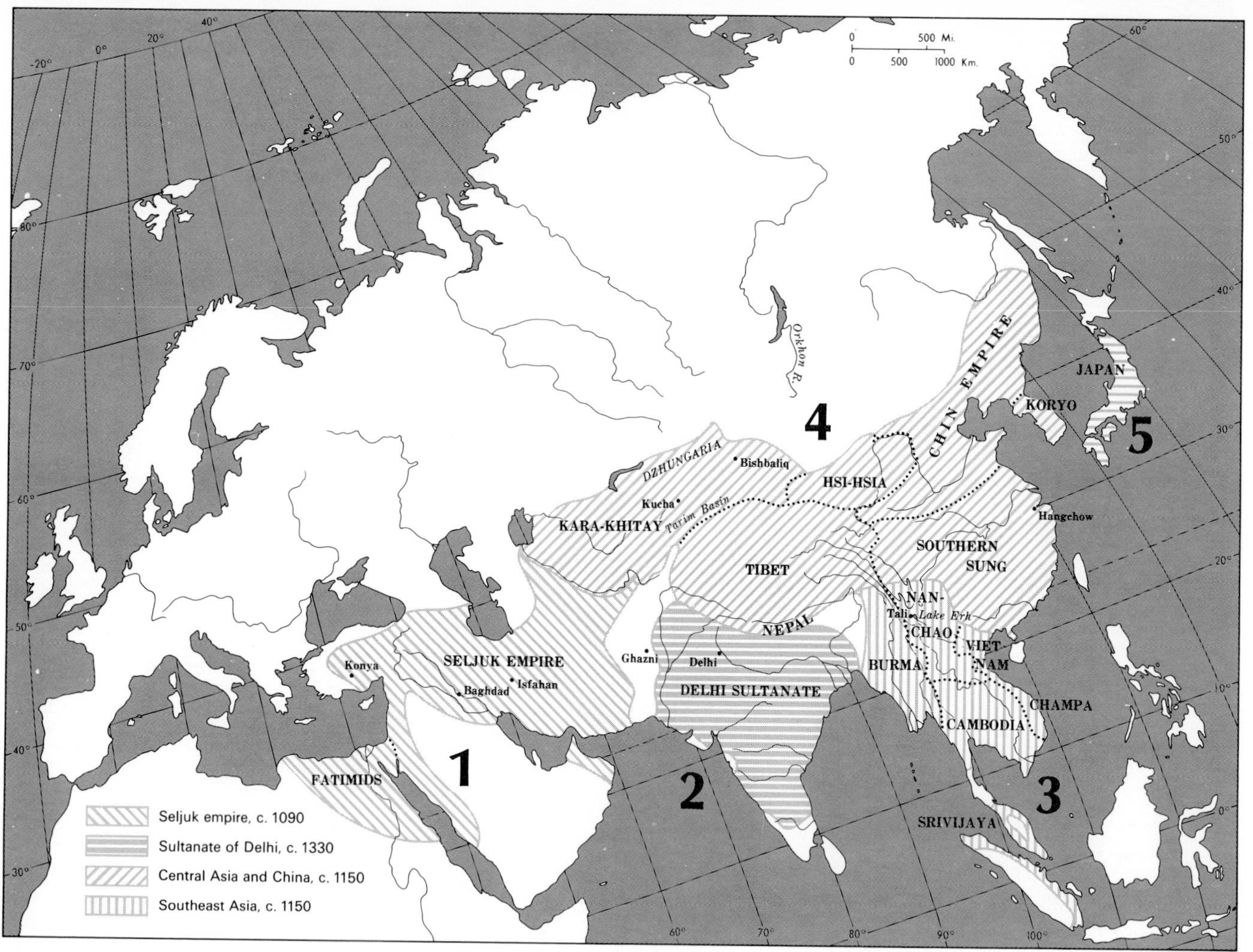

Map 27 The regional fragmentation of civilizations

PROCESSES

In the preceding chapters we have been concerned primarily with tracing the growth and elaboration of distinct civilizations in three principal regions of Eurasia—West Asia, India, and China. These major civilizations, following the experiences of territorial unification under a universal empire and cultural transformation by a universal religion, had come to possess many of the characteristics that were to continue to distinguish them down into the modern period. Thus, with the beginning of the second millennium A.D. we have come to yet another new era in Eurasian history, and our attention in this and subsequent chapters will be focused less on the accretion of new elements than on the viability of these ongoing, maturing civilizations. It is an era in which they were to face two particular types of challenges. One was the test of unity among the various cultural and geographical subdivisions of the civilization, the challenge of maintaining internal integration in the face of centrifugal forces that often led to regional fragmentation—the breakup of a civilized region into subregions. This is the main topic of the present chapter, which covers the period between the spread of the universal religions and the dramatic conquest by the Mongols. Related to this, however, was a second challenge, a test of the integrity of each civilization in the face of contact with forces from outside. The most familiar instances of this are the intrusion by the Mongols from along the Inner Asian land frontiers in the thirteenth and fourteenth centuries and later the expansion of the European maritime powers that seized control of the sea in the modern period. These external challenges will be treated at length in Chapters 8 and 11 (see Volume 2), but here we will be concerned with earlier cases when interaction with outside areas affected these civilizations in important ways.

There are four principal developments in this period. First, the integration each civilization had achieved politically through the model of a universal state and culturally through the adoption of a universal religion was shattered by centrifugal forces that undermined its unity, diminished its vitality, and weakened its ability to control interaction with the societies of Central Asia. Second, the growing diversity, disunity, and dissension within these once highly integrated civilizations were paralleled by the rise of new civilized cultures in the heartland of Central Asia, where the processes of steppe-sown symbiosis had transformed centers of caravan trade into sophisticated cities whose sedentary populations existed on irrigated agriculture as well as east-west commerce. Third, accompanying the weakening of the older civilized centers inland there emerged newly civilized societies on the coastal periphery of the Eurasian continent—independent societies such as those in Japan and in Southeast Asia that demonstrated vigorous cultural as well as political and economic growth. Fourth, the growth of these peripheral areas marked the culmination of long-term developments in maritime activity which now, long before the expansion of Western European seapower, had come to transform the Arabian Sea, the Persian Gulf, the Indian Ocean, the Strait of Malacca, and the China Sea into well-traversed avenues of interregional trade and communication.

THE PERIOD

In West Asia this chapter begins with the decline of the Abbasids during the ninth and tenth centuries and extends through the periods of Turkish hegemony during the eleventh and twelfth centuries. In South Asia fragmentation will be discussed separately in northern India and southern India. Northern India came under the control of Turkish invaders from Central Asia, and the period 1193-1526 is commonly, if inaccurately, referred to as that of the Delhi sultanate. In southern India there was considerable political, economic, and cultural change in Tamilnad under the Hindu Cholas (ca. 900-1200) followed by the rise of the Hindu empire of Vijayanagar (1336-1565), which extended its control over much of the south.

In East Asia also there was a marked pattern of fragmentation. From about 750, the T'ang empire lost control over its frontiers. Subsequently, northern China fell under the control of Central Asian regimes such as the Khitan (the Liao dynasty, 947-1125) and the Jurched (the Chin dynasty, 1115-1234), which greatly facilitated cultural diffusion across the Inner Asian frontier of China. In the south an embattled Sung dynasty experienced a brilliant cultural flowering that produced a revived Confucianism, now enriched in scope and subtlety by the synthesis of many Buddhist elements. After 1126 the Sung faced seaward since difficulties in the north caused it to move the capital to the maritime port of Hang-chou.

On the periphery of these older civilized regions, Japan emerged from the shadow of Chinese influence to develop a distinctive cultural style of its own during the late Heian (tenth and eleventh centuries), Kamakura (1185-1333), and Ashikaga (1333-1573) periods. Although Southeast Asia continued to be too culturally diverse to speak of a common civilization, by the fifteenth century a number of vital cultures came to maturity as the earlier Indian and Chinese elements were synthesized with new elements of Islamic origin.

a. Fragmentation of the Religious Culture Area

To understand the history of Eurasian civilizations following the rise of the universal religions it is necessary to recognize that in this period they cannot be considered as unified and integrated units. The cultural unification that the universal religion had imposed over vast territories during its early spread—a unification often facilitated by the networks of the universal empires—lasted only as long as popular enthusiasm for the new faith was strong enough to bridge the gap between the masses and elites and to bind together different sectional and linguistic groupings. As these religions became more highly institutionalized their early dynamism and flexibility were often lost. Doctrine that had once carried a message of social change became sterile and dogmatic as resistance to further reform mounted. Religious leaders long in positions of power became distant from the masses and tended cynically to seek to enhance their own elite position. It must be noted, however, that because of the great diversity within any given civilizational area it is common to find that one part enjoyed economic prosperity and a creative efflorescence while simultaneously another region suffered economic depression and cultural stagnation. The fact that the older empires were in disarray or dormant and the universal religions were becoming rigid does not mean that creative change was absent. Creativity was indeed often greatest in periods of disunity precisely because orthodoxy could not be enforced and the need for new solutions was intensely felt.

b. Formation of Regional Political Entities

As the integrating force of universal religions weakened, regional diversity asserted its influence. The older political centers lost control over large portions of territory and people, which were then regrouped into new political entities. Sometimes the fragmentation followed the contours of the old fissures dividing north from south. This was especially marked in India and China, where nomadic intrusion from the north was an important factor in the division. In other cases the configuration was much more complex, but the new states formed during this period differed from the older universal empires in that they controlled only parts of a culture area. Even these smaller regional states often found it difficult to assert centralized control within their own borders and relied heavily on feudal arrangements to maintain political stability.

c. Renaissance of Regional Cultures

While regional regimes could not aspire to embody the scale of cultural unity once achieved by universal empires, they often did act as the vehicles for new religious and cultural movements. These in turn often took the form of a renaissance of the subcultures of the area. Thus, in the Iranian plateau area of West Asia there seems to have taken place a renaissance of Iranian culture values hitherto submerged beneath layers of Arabo-Islamic civilization. In Sung China, neo-Confucianism represented both a philosophical fusion of Confucian and Buddhist ideas and a reaction by literate elites within Chinese society defending a parochial Chinese identity against the foreign values and universal claims of Mahayana doctrine and practice.

d. Growth of Maritime Centers

For some centuries prior to this period Eurasia had experienced an increase in interregional contact by sea. The rise of the universal religions on the one hand and the decline of inland political capitals on the other combined to facilitate the development of coastal cities as centers for maritime trade and interaction. Religious pilgrims such as the Muslims from Southeast Asia bound for Mecca mingled with merchants and pirates from many lands on the well-traveled searoutes that stretched all the way from Japan and Korea to the Red Sea. Arab traders established Muslim enclaves in the ports along the China coast, while Chinese merchants fanned out among the islands of the South Pacific and plied the carrying trade between India and East Asia. Advances by the Chinese in nautical technology, such as the compass, watertight compartments on ships, improved sails, rigging, and rudders, greatly enhanced the capabilities of ocean-going transports. In the West, European participation in religious crusades and the establishment of footholds in Syria and Palestine served to link together a truly Eurasian network of maritime trade. It should be noted, however, that the Atlantic states lagged behind Arab and Chinese maritime achievements until the fifteenth century.

e. Steppe-Sown Interaction

Contemporaneous with this further development of maritime contact along the Eurasian coastline was a change in the pattern of interaction along the land frontiers of Inner Asia. Agriculturally based urban societies had long coexisted in Central Asia with the pastoral-nomadic peoples, but now the importance of the latter for the history of West, South, and East Asian civilizations was to increase. Islam played a crucial role in Central Asia both as a vehicle for the diffusion of institutions from these civilizations and as a factor facilitating trade and contact along the inland trade routes. Where nomadic or seminomadic peoples pressed against the borders of these older civilizations there was a tendency for hybrid regimes, such as the Kara-Khitay, the Liao, and the Chin, to the north of China, to flourish by combining pastoral traditions with borrowed institutions. By creating precedents, enhancing communications, and developing political and technological skills among nomadic peoples these states laid the groundwork for the great Mongol federations that were to attempt the unification of Eurasia in the next era.

In view of the fact that in the modern period European maritime power was to dominate all of Eurasia accessible from the sea, it is instructive to look back at this earlier era of balance between civilizations and ask how the seeds of later European divergence were sown. The growth of maritime activity in Europe in the late medieval period in the Mediterranean which led in the fifteenth century to the rise of the Atlantic seaboard powers was not unique, since it was paralleled by equally vigorous seafaring activity in Islamic West Asia and along the coastlines of East Africa, India, and China, as well as the extended islands of Southeast Asia. The most obvious difference between Europe and the culture areas of Asia was that in Europe this innovation in maritime technology continued unabated, while in these other parts of Eurasia it tended to be inhibited once regional unity was reestablished by land-based early modern empires (see Chapter 9). In Europe the tendency toward regional fragmentation was extremely pronounced. The various states based on linguistic and ethnic frontiers emerged early and competed so vigorously among themselves that they resisted reunification under any would-be successor to the Roman empire. Such diversity contrasts most sharply with China at the other extreme, which underwent repeated political reunification. West Asia, too, despite great diversity, was united in the early modern period by the Ottoman and Safavid empires, although Turkish, Arab, and Iranian cultural elements were never permanently fused together. In South Asia there were a number of cultural and linguistic regions that could potentially have developed as states and nations of the type that were to appear in Europe, but, down to the present at least, the sharpest divisions have been along religious lines. Thus India is predominantly Hindu, Pakistan almost exclusively Muslim, and Sri Lanka (Ceylon) mainly Buddhist. The Bengali Muslims of Bangladesh (formerly East Pakistan) have broken with their coreligionists of Pakistan but still remain separate from the Bengali Hindus of India. In Europe, however, the Holy Roman Empire proved far weaker as a unifying agent than the local interests that supported the emergence of modern nation-states, although as in Ireland religious sectarianism continues to be a divisive issue.

In summary, then, the fragmentation that followed the expansion of the universal religions proceeded unhindered in Europe and can be viewed as the beginning of the nation-state configuration that characterizes our own time. In the civilizations of Asia, however, the Mongol domination tended to stimulate the formation of new empires in the early modern period—empires that sought, albeit with varying degrees of success, to reunite the major civilizations politically. In the course of events power was once again concentrated in landlocked cities oriented toward inland frontiers, while coastal centers and maritime commerce were subordinated to continental interests. In Europe circumstances were such that maritime activity continued to expand, first in the Mediterranean and then on the Atlantic, until in the fifteenth century the West Europeans attained the capacity to extend their activities on a global scale.

PATTERNS

1. REGIONAL FRAGMENTATION IN WEST ASIA

The preceding chapter described how West Asia became integrated into a single Arabo-Islamic culture zone extending eastward from the Atlantic shores of Morocco and Portugal to the Syr Darya and the Indus, a culture zone in which the Muslim religion had implanted a fairly uniform pattern of beliefs, behavior, and life-style, although modified, where appropriate, by local conditions. It had also implanted a political order centering on the institution of the caliphate, notwithstanding the fact that almost from the time of Muhammad's death there had been profound disagreement as to precisely who was the legitimate caliph. During the period from the middle of the ninth century to the first half of the thirteenth century, when the Mongols of Chingiz Khan imposed a new set of patterns on the Muslim societies of much of West Asia, the political unity of the Arabo-Islamic world-state and the cultural unity of Arabo-Islamic civilization, exemplified by the philosophical, scientific, and literary achievements of Abbasid Baghdad, were both eroded. New centers of political power and regional culture arose, often located towards the fringes of the *Dar al-Islam,* to challenge the former primacy of the Islamic heartlands of the Fertile Crescent and, in particular, of Iraq. The Arabs found themselves compelled to relinquish power to non-Arabs, generally Iranians or Turks. The Arabic language ceased to enjoy its former monopoly as the language of learning in the face of the revival of Persian. The emergence of the idea of a sultanate, essentially a secular authority although expected to enforce the

Sharia, diminished the prestige formerly accruing to the caliphate. Most significant of all, a new people, the Turks, entered the Muslim world, either as slave-soldiers or as tribal invaders, and permanently changed the course of history in these ancient lands. Seen from one angle, these centuries were characterized by acute political instability, savage dynastic and tribal struggles for power, and the meteoric rise and fall of kingdoms. Seen from another, they were characterized by exceptional diversity in creative achievement, by the growth of sophisticated regional cultures sustained by refined and vigorous urban patriciates, and by major innovations, whether in statecraft and government, in the speculative sciences, or in the mystical outpourings of the Sufis.

Fragmentation of the Religious Culture Area

At first sight it would appear rash to describe this period of Muslim history as one of religious fragmentation since, during the four centuries covered by this chapter and for long afterwards, the sense of the Muslim world being a single society, shaped by a common set of religious beliefs, values, and behavioral patterns, was far stronger than any awareness of the pressures of centrifugal diversity. Muslims still, in the main, divided mankind into two categories—believers and nonbelievers—and the majority understood the righteous and godly life to mean obedience to the *Sharia* and to the will of the orthodox Sunni caliph in Baghdad. Below the surface, however, Islam was undergoing complex and profound transmutations, although these transmutations were not felt everywhere at the same time or with an equal degree of intensity. Nor were they necessarily perceived by contemporaries in the way historians, wise after the event, perceive them. It was perfectly possible for a man to live in Baghdad during the late ninth or early tenth century and not appreciate how greatly times were changing. It was even possible to live in eleventh century Baghdad and not recognize the significance of the revolutions that had so altered the face of the world one's forefathers had known.

These centuries witnessed a decline not only in the political authority of the caliphs (to be described in the following section) but also in spiritual authority. Among the factors that contributed to this decline, the most spectacular was the gradual transformation of the caliphs' household and government into a luxury-loving court and a greedy, corrupt bureaucracy where material wealth, the pursuit of power, and an ostentatious life-style had long since expelled the puritanical ideals of pristine Islam. A similar transformation had occurred with the *ulama,* among whom the pursuit of status, wealth, and material security cast them, as a class, in the role of an "establishment" clergy, even when exceptional individuals among them continued to enjoy reputations for scholarship and sanctity. It might be logical to assume that, in consequence, they found it increasingly difficult to communicate with the Muslim masses, yet the evidence points to the *ulama* in later Abbasid times involving themselves in bitter sectarian strife into which the ordinary inhabitants of the major urban centers followed them with fervor. Islamic historians are still baffled by the extent and the intensity of this faction fighting and urban violence, especially in the cities located in the eastern provinces of the caliphate, and suspect that behind the religious slogans may be discerned profound social and economic grievances. Yet the evidence remains inconclusive and contemporaries certainly saw these struggles almost exclusively in sectarian terms, of Sunnis versus Shiis, of fundamentalists versus latitudinarians, or, most often, of the followers of one particular *madhhab*, or "school of law" (Hanafi, Hanbali, Maliki, or Shafii) versus another. The destructiveness of these confrontations can scarcely be overstressed. In 1162, for example, Nishapur, after decades of intramural strife, was quite literally destroyed, not by tribal invaders, but by the supporters of rival *madhhabs.* As late as the second quarter of the fourteenth century the Moroccan traveler Ibn Battuta found much of Isfahan desolate in consequence of civil violence between Sunnis and Shiis.

One highly significant development in this period was Sufism, the term commonly applied to Islamic mysticism and derived from the Arabic word for the coarse woolen garment worn by those who, as mendicant dervishes, chose to pursue the mystic's quest for knowledge of the unknowable and of communion with the incommunicable. It should not be assumed, however, that every Sufi was a person gifted with unique insights. Sufis could be ordinary men or women who, without necessarily rejecting the everyday world in which they lived and worked, sought the mystical path as a means to spiritual and psychological fulfillment or as inner consolation in a world overflowing with suffering and cruelty—which probably explains why the period of Mongol devastation in the thirteenth century coincided with the finest flowering of the Sufi spirit. There is also a danger of assuming that Sufism, by its very nature, was at all times a challenge to orthodoxy, a kind of heretical alternative to the Sunni way. The Sufi, however, was not necessarily bound to place himself outside the Sunni tradition, and although some forms of Sufism certainly were heterodox and even heretical this was not invariably the case. One could be an orthodox Sunni believer and a Sufi at one and the same time. Having made this point, it still remains true that Sufism, like Shiism, tended to become a vehicle for movements of social protest and political activism concealed beneath the cloak of religion and that it appealed to almost all sections of the population, to highly educated scholars and officials, to merchants and craftsmen, and even to the nomadic tribesmen. A Sufi did not have to be a professional dervish or religious mendicant. Frequently he was an urban artisan or petty trader who was a part-time member of a Sufi brotherhood *(tariqa),* somewhat in the manner of a modern Free Mason, and his membership gave him not only a heightened spiritual experience but also a sense of community with his fellow members, and perhaps even an increased feeling of security. Where the poorer classes in the cities were organized into guilds, as they often were in later centuries, the Sufi brotherhoods frequently established close affiliations with them.

In Baghdad itself and in the cities of Iran and Anatolia the guilds and, even more, the solidarity groups known as *futuwwa,* composed in the main of young, relatively poor urban males, could be factors of the greatest social significance, providing a viable social framework when the city administration had broken down (e.g., by acting as an auxiliary police force) or, by way of contrast, becoming the sponsors of organized violence against the existing regime or against those whom they perceived to be their enemies. The connection of the Sufi brotherhoods with the *futuwwa* dates from the eleventh century, and frequently individual dervishes were among the ringleaders in the recurring outbreaks of urban violence characteristic of this period. In the countryside, dervishes often ministered to the spiritual needs of predatory tribesman or even to roving *banditti*. The period is one in which religion and politics were closely interconnected in communal organizations, often of a semisecret character and of which the true objectives are no longer discernible. Some decades prior to the fall of Baghdad to the Mongols in 1258 a shrewd caliph, al-Nasir (r. 1180-1225), attempted to place himself at the head of all the *futuwwa* and to use the ideological and chivalric elements embodied in these fraternities to restructure both the caliphate and the spiritual life of the community. The attempt failed, for the caliphate as an institution was moribund and the Mongol incursions were already beginning.

If Sufism, both in terms of its potential for the dissemination of heterodox beliefs and as a rallying point for social and political unrest, contributed towards the disintegration of Islamic solidarity, this was even more true of Shiism. The origins of Shiism were discussed in the preceding chapter, where it was stressed that as a form of protest against the status quo, Shiism presented several distinctly attractive features, theological and messianic, dynastic and political. Shiism was frequently a cover for movements of social protest, as in the case of the ninth century rebellion of the *zanj,* East African slaves employed on the salt flats downstream from Basra, which was led by an Alid pretender. Under the Umayyads and the early Abbasids, Shiism had been essentially an Arab movement, composed of those who, whatever their motives, upheld the cause of the Alids, the descendants of Ali and Fatima. Later, Shiism appears to have spread rapidly among the predominantly Iranian population of the eastern provinces of the caliphate. The Iranian plateau, in particular, proved peculiarly congenial for Shii missionaries, presumably on account of the pervasiveness of pre-Islamic Iranian sectarian eschatology. Shiism flourished in just those areas where the manifestations of the religious life of pre-Islamic Iran survived longest—in mountainous regions where isolated communities could maintain their cultural identity relatively intact while making minimal concessions to the conquering Arabs who dominated the open country. One such region was located in the mountainous tract of country south of the Caspian Sea dominated by the Elburz Range and centering on the provinces of Gilan and Mazandaran, of which the latter was then known as Daylam. The Daylamis were devoted adherents of Shiism. They were also much in demand as mercenaries, even in distant Baghdad. During the tenth and eleventh centuries a Shii dynasty from Daylam, the Buyids (ca. 932-1062), first conquered western Iran and became masters of Ray, Isfahan, and Shiraz and then in 945 seized Baghdad itself, where for over a century they ruled unchallenged in the capital of Sunni Islam, overawing, deposing, and even murdering successive caliphs. It cannot be stressed too strongly how deleterious for the self-image of Sunni Islam was the knowledge that the Abbasid caliph, the Commander of the Faithful, was a puppet in the hands of Shii heretics.

Buyid rule in Baghdad was eventually brought to an end by the Seljuk Turks, who captured the city in 1055 and who prided themselves on being rigid Sunnis, but already Shiism had begun to manifest itself in a new and much more dangerous form. In 969 Egypt had been conquered by the Fatimids (909-1171), descendants of Ali and Fatima, who were exponents of an extreme messianic form of Shiism known as Ismailism and whose North African Berber troops carved out for them a vast empire that included, in West Asia, Syria, Palestine, the Hijaz, and the Yemen. As early as 910 they had assumed the title of caliph, thereby rejecting the legitimacy of the Abbasids, and with their great military and financial resources they posed a most formidable challenge to the unity of the Muslim world, a challenge far greater than that posed by the Umayyads in distant Spain, who followed the Fatimid example by assuming the title of caliph in 928.

The threat posed by the Fatimids to the Abbasids, especially after 1055, when Iraq passed under the control of the Seljuk Turks, was not so much the danger of external invasion as of conspiratorial infiltration. The Fatimids directed against the Abbasid provinces a campaign of intense propaganda conducted by secret missionaries who established networks of Ismaili supporters not only in major urban centers such as Isfahan but also in the mountainous regions of Syria, northern Iran, and western Afghanistan. Ismaili Shiism, which was quite different from the Shiism of the Buyids or of the later Iranian Safavids and is now mainly to be found among the Indian and East African followers of the Agha Khan, was peculiarly suited to dissemination by means of secret cells and furtive emissaries, since at that time it was characterized by esoteric and hermetic doctrines that placed great stress on hidden knowledge and initiation. Under the dynamic leadership of Hasan-i Sabbah (d. 1124), who founded the breakaway sect of the Nizari Ismailis and who formed an independent state in the Elburz Mountains north of Qazvin and Tehran, they became a very real threat not only to Sunni orthodoxy but also to the survival of the Seljuk empire itself. The activities of the Ismaili *dais,* or "missionaries," extended over a vast area of West Asia, and contemporaries, including the European crusaders and, later, Marco Polo, were duly awed by their alleged practice of procuring the deaths of those who opposed them by employing "self-sacrificers." "Self-sacrificers" were drugged with hashish (from which is derived the word *assassin)* and, as a result of carefully manipulated hallucinations, were assured of the delights of Paradise, even if they were killed in attempting to assassinate their victims. Of

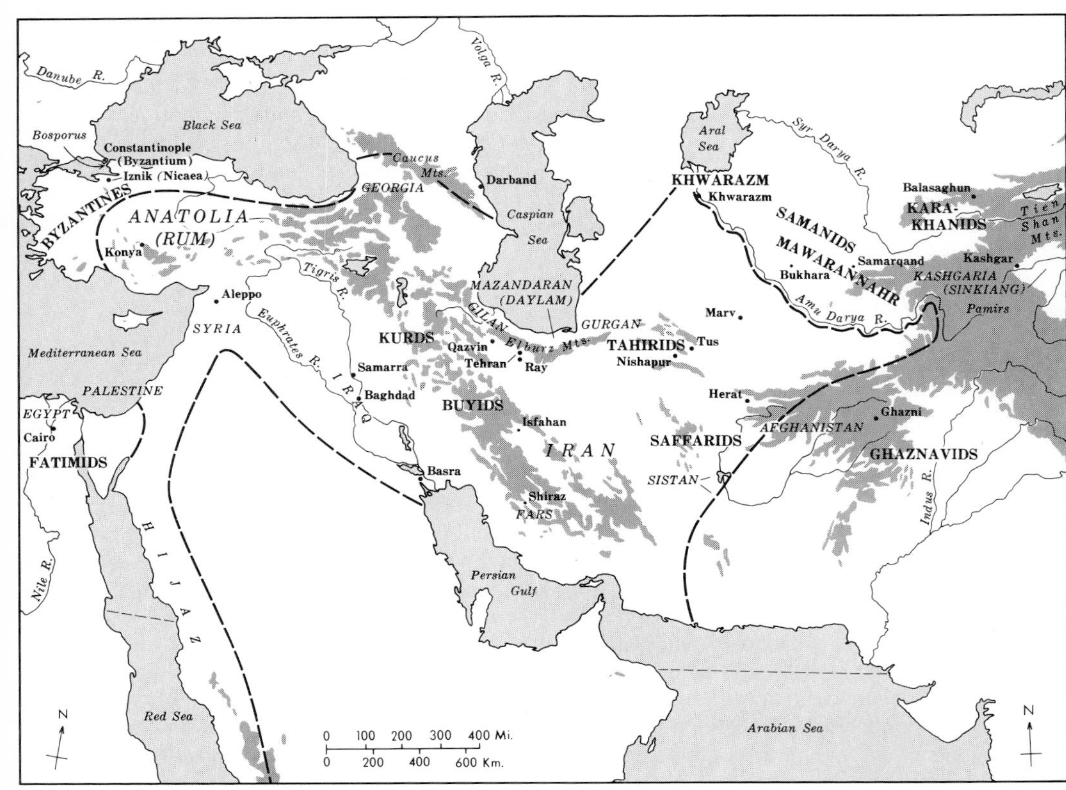

Map 28 The Seljuk empire, about 1090

greater interest today is the question of what drew men to this sect, which recruited not only the poor and the oppressed but also several of the greatest scholars of the age, including Nasir al-Din Tusi (d. 1274), philosopher, mathematician, and astronomer. Some scholars have interpreted Ismailism, especially in its urban setting, as a lower-class movement composed mainly of artisans and craftsmen oppressed by the fiscal exactions of the Seljuk administration. Others, emphasizing its rural aspects, have suggested that it should be seen as the final attempt of the dying society of the *dihqans,* the traditional Iranian landholding class, to resist ever-increasing domination by the cities and by urban-based elites. Others again, while not necessarily rejecting these explanations, see it as a self-consciously Iranian reaction to the rule of a Turkish tribal elite bent on enforcing Arabo-Islamic Sunni orthodoxy. Whatever the explanation, there can be no doubt that the Ismaili movement in this period constituted a formidable challenge to the basic tenets of Sunni Islam, a challenge with which even the mighty Seljuk sultans of the late eleventh century were unable to deal and which persisted until the middle decades of the thirteenth century, when it was eliminated by Hülegü and his infidel Mongols, who had their own grievances against the Ismailis.

Fragmentation of the Abbasid Universal Empire

The fragmentation or diversification of Islam as a universal religion cannot be treated in isolation from the political fragmentation of the Abbasid caliphate as an imperial power and as the institutional framework that, at least in theory, bound together the Muslim *umma,* or "community of believers." The loss of the caliph's spiritual authority was linked to the decline of his prestige as the head of that community and the concomitant establishment of the office of sultan, which, while imposing on its holder the obligation to maintain and defend the *Sharia* and the Muslim way of life, embodied a concept of secular monarchy that the office of caliph did not.

A number of quite distinct factors contributed to the political decline of the Abbasids. The most obvious factor was the steady degeneration in the character and abilities of successive caliphs, notwithstanding isolated exceptions such as al-Nasir (r. 1180-1225), whose connection with the *futuwwa* has been mentioned in the preceding section. Another factor was the increasing size and ineffectiveness of the central bureaucracy, which was no longer able to exercise adequate control over its agents in distant provinces, where widespread disorders and civil strife were becoming endemic. In Baghdad, the greatest metropolitan center of the Muslim world, urban violence and military mutinies by the caliph's household troops were occurring with increasing frequency. From a strictly military point of view the Arab tribal levies, which had originally composed the greater part of the caliph's military establishment, had long possessed an ugly reputation for insubordination and intertribal feuds, so that successive caliphs had sought to replace them by units supposedly more loyal and more susceptible to control. In consequence, the caliph's household troops and the greater part of the army consisted of either non-Arab mercenaries or slave-soldiers, known as *mamluks,* recruited from several different ethnic groups—Daylamis, Georgians, Slavs, Berbers, Nubians, and Turks—although the Turks were regarded as the most warlike and therefore the most desirable *mamluks.* These Turks came from the steppe region of Central Asia lying to the north of the Black Sea, the Caspian Sea, the Aral Sea, and the Tien Shan Mountains, and since Islam had not yet penetrated the steppe region beyond the Caucasus or the Syr Darya, these Turks were still non-Muslims and were therefore, in Islamic law, legitimate objects of enslavement. From the early ninth century onwards there developed an extensive slave trade in young Turkish *mamluks,* which was channelled to Baghdad through the great entrepots of Bukhara and Khwarazm in Central Asia and also through Darband, an important depot for the slave trade on the southwestern coast of the Caspian Sea. The caliphs of the mid-ninth century who first recruited bodyguards of Turkish slaves must take the blame for setting the caliphate on a downhill course, since these turbulent praetorians rapidly established themselves as the real masters of the imperial city. From this time forward the institution of slave-soldiers became virtually ubiquitous throughout West Asia and remained so down to the sixteenth and seventeenth centuries, when the Ottoman Janissaries were recruited from Balkan Christians who possessed the juridical status of slaves and who, having been converted to Islam, were trained to man the sultan's army and bureaucracy.

While successive caliphs struggled to curb their ambitious troops and to quell the rising tide of factional violence in the metropolis, the more distant provinces of the empire were drifting into virtual independence. Egypt, always apt to go its own way in view of its peculiarly self-sustaining economy and its great distance from the heartlands of the caliphate, became more or less autonomous from the second half of the ninth century under the rule of a succession of recalcitrant Turkish governors. In Khurasan, half a century earlier, the caliph had appointed an Iranian, Tahir, as his local representative, and although the latter thereafter proceeded to act as an autonomous ruler the caliph acquiesced in the arrangement, since Tahir was well able to keep order in that traditionally unruly province. When Tahir died his son was recognized as the new governor. In this way the Iranian Tahirid dynasty established itself in the important regional center of Nishapur. Exactly the same happened in Mawarannahr, the vast province northeast of Khurasan extending from the Amu Darya to the Syr Darya. There, another gubernatorial dynasty, the Samanids, established a powerful regime on the fringes of the Muslim world and made Bukhara, their capital, the brilliant center of a distinctive regional culture while continuing to maintain an appropriately deferential attitude in all their formal communications with the caliph's government in Baghdad.

The Samanids in Mawarannahr, the Tahirids in Khurasan and, to a certain extent, the rebel governors of Egypt nominally upheld the caliph's prestige by recognizing his titular suzerainty, but even this formality was not universally adhered to. In the province of Sistan, the now desolate wastes of eastern Iran and southwestern Afghanistan that then were still comparatively fertile and well populated, there occurred a popular insurrection under the leadership of a local coppersmith, Yaqub al-Saffar (867-879), and his brother, Amr (d. 900), which seems to have included ideological elements that stressed an Iranian cultural identity and were, in consequence, anti-Arab. Yaqub al-Saffar and his brother for a time extended their conquests to include Fars and part of Khurasan and even threatened Baghdad, since unlike the Tahirids and the Samanids they showed scant respect for the caliph's authority. Even more striking was the course taken by the Shii Buyids from Mazandaran, mentioned earlier, who openly rejected the Sunni caliphate and in 945 seized Baghdad, which they occupied thereafter for more than a hundred years.

While all these events were occurring in the late ninth and early tenth centuries it was, of course, quite possible for a worldly-wise citizen of Baghdad to disregard upheavals in distant Cairo, Nishapur, or Bukhara and to dismiss a person such as Yaqub al-Saffar as a glorified bandit. For such a person, Baghdad was still the center of the world. Yet within the city itself, the signs of the times were clear enough. Since the reign of al-Mutasim (833-842) most caliphs had been virtual prisoners in the hands of their Turkish or Daylami troops, and it was partly to escape from their control and partly to elude the violence of the Baghdadis that first al-Mutasim, and then al-Mutawakkil (r. 847-861), followed by several of his successors, transferred their residence to a new capital at Samarra, higher up the Tigris, which was not finally abandoned until 892, when the court returned to Baghdad. The return, in itself, settled nothing. Mayhem and massacre continued in and around the metropolis, reaching a climax with the Buyid occupation of the city in 945. This occupation lasted until the Buyids were finally ejected in 1055, when the caliph was transformed from the helpless puppet of his Shii foes into the relatively tractable pawn of the much more powerful, albeit orthodox, Seljuks. Whatever Baghdad, with the Abbasid court at its center, had hitherto contributed to the shaping of Islamic civilization (and that contribution had undoubtedly been very great), it passed during the tenth and eleventh centuries into an intellectual, no less than a political, backwater. Military might, intellectual vigor, and artistic creativity had definitely shifted toward the peripheries of the Muslim world and away from the heartlands.

Formation of Regional Political Entities

The breakway provinces of the caliphate, whether or not they openly declared their independence or chose to retain a formal link with Baghdad, tended to acquire distinct regional personalities resulting partly from the exigencies of local geography and partly from the survival in each region of pervasive cultural traditions predating the rise of the Arabo-Islamic universal empire. Thus the Samanids, in establishing their rule between the Amu Darya and the Syr Darya, took possession of a region (the ancient Sogdiana, or Transoxania) that had long possessed a distinct cultural personality. Similarly, the Saffarids in Sistan consciously or unconsciously identified with the legendary past of that isolated region. These regimes—the Samanids in Mawarannahr (819-1005), the Saffarids in Sistan (ca. 867-ca. 1495), the Tahirids in Khurasan (821-873), the Buyids in western Iran (ca. 932-1062), and several more localized powers—all possessed a distinctly Iranian character. In each case the ruling house was of Iranian stock and, except where military establishments of Turkish slaves were maintained, as in the case of the Samanids, it was the indigenous

Iranian population of each region, both urban and rural, that provided the ruler with the necessary support to maintain himself against neighboring rivals or would-be contenders for his throne. To justify their *de facto* usurpation of the caliph's authority these rulers developed patterns of legitimation that had an obvious appeal to their Iranian subjects, so that although the Buyids alone assumed the lofty Sasanid title of shahanshah, or "king of kings" (the rest being generally content with the more modest and ambiguous title of *amir*, or "commander"), all stressed genealogical links, whether genuine or spurious, with the pre-Islamic past.

Relatively stable, wealthy, and enlightened in their dealings with their subjects, these rulers enjoyed the active support of the two classes that mattered most, the *dihqans*, or local landholders, who had survived the upheavals of the initial Arab conquest and were the living embodiment of pre-Islamic Iranian traditions, and the more recent urban patriciates of such cities as Isfahan, Ray, Nishapur, Tus, Herat, and Bukhara. The latter were a somewhat diverse group composed of the leading *ulama*, the more prosperous merchants, and those local landowners who had been drawn into urban politics by intermarriage and economic interest. Most of the time these patricians were able to dominate the life of their respective cities without being greatly affected by dynastic upheavals, but their local support could be vital to a ruler on account of their wealth, their presumed influence over the urban population as a whole, and the fact that they staffed much of the bureaucracy that administered these states. Ultimately, however, the capacity of the new dynasties to survive and expand depended on their military resources. In some instances these were local in character, as in the case of Buyid reliance on their Daylami followers or Saffarid use of local Sistani levies, but for the most part they relied on Turkish slaves imported from the Central Asian steppe zone whose supposed loyalty, coupled with their great reputation as fighters, made them seem highly desirable. The Samanids, in particular, located nearest to the source of the supply, acquired large numbers of these *mamluks*, who eventually monopolized the highest military and civilian offices in the state. Eventually, Sebüktigin, a Turkish *mamluk* of the Samanids who was a local governor with his headquarters at Ghazni in eastern Afghanistan, felt himself sufficiently distant from Bukhara to conduct himself as if he were his own master. When he died his son, Mahmud, succeeding to the command of a large army and the possession of ample resources, declared himself independent of the Samanids and assumed the title of sultan. In 1019, in gratitude for Mahmud's campaigns against the Buyids in central and western Iran, the caliph granted him the title of Right Hand of the State.

The establishment of the empire of Mahmud of Ghazni (r. 998-1030) in eastern Iran, Afghanistan, and northwestern India (his Indian career will be discussed in a later section) marked the end of what has been called by some historians the "Iranian Intermezzo" in the history of the eastern part of Muslim West Asia and the beginning of a phase, lasting until very recent times, when the greater part of West Asia was under the physical domination of Turkish or Turco-Mongol military elites. While Mahmud of Ghazni was occupying the Samanid territories south of the Amu Darya, the surviving Samanid regime in Mawarannahr itself was being attacked by a Turkish dynasty from beyond the Syr Darya and the Pamirs, the Karakhanids. Unlike the Ghaznavids, originally Turkish *mamluks* who had been exposed to a fairly intensive process of Iranicization, the Karakhanids appear to have been the dominant clan of a tribal confederacy that controlled the steppe region north of the Tien Shan Mountains as well as Kashgaria to the south, having a northern capital at Balasaghun and a southern one at Kashgar. In 992 they captured Bukhara, the Samanid capital, and within a few years had occupied the whole of Mawarannahr. Highly successful in their ability to combine older Turkish tribal traditions with the Irano-Islamic culture of their new possessions, the Karakhanids were the first Turks to enter the Muslim world as a conquering tribal confederacy and then to assume the functions of traditional Muslim rulers.

7.1 Regional Fragmentation: West Asia

The first half of the eleventh century saw the Ghaznavids and the Karakhanids uneasily partitioning vast tracts of the eastern fringes of Muslim West Asia, while western Iran and Iraq continued to be controlled by the Buyids, now a decaying power. To the west, Palestine and much of Syria were under the rule of the Fatimid caliphs, based on Egypt, while in Anatolia the Byzantines were still an infidel regime to be reckoned with. Separating the possessions of the Buyids, the Fatimids, and the Byzantines lay an enormous area of rugged, mountainous country centering on northern Syria and western Anatolia, where local chieftains struggled to retain their independence in the face of more powerful neighbors, an area soon to be fought over by Kurds, Turks, and Frankish Crusaders. Here, as in the lands to the east, a new imperial order was about to be established by one of the most dynamic groups ever to impose themselves on West Asia, the Seljuk Turks.

The Seljuks were a branch of the confederacy of the Oghuz, or Western Turks, who, while still pastoral nomads and only partially Islamicized, pressed into Mawarannahr from the steppes zone, swept aside the Karakhanids, and advanced into Khurasan, then a part of the Ghaznavid empire. Under the leadership of Toghrïl Beg (r. 1038-63), first of the so-called Great Seljuks (to distinguish them from later cadet lines), they advanced across Iran, occupying Marv, Nishapur, Ray, and Isfahan, until they finally entered Baghdad in 1055, where an agreement between the Abbasid caliph and the Seljuk sultan restored the former's tarnished spiritual prestige while providing orthodox legitimation for the newcomers' conquests. Toghrïl Beg's successors continued to press westward into Anatolia, where, after defeating the Byzantines, they established an empire that extended over much of West Asia and remained relatively intact until around 1157.

The Seljuk regime was the most complex and impressive exercise in Islamic empire building between the decline of the Abbasid caliphate in the early ninth century and the rise of the Mongol il-khanate and its rival, the Mamluk sultanate of Egypt, in the thirteenth. During the period of its greatest extent (the second half of the eleventh century) Seljuk rule extended from the shores of the Mediterranean to the deserts of Sinkiang. A well-trained army of predominantly mounted archers, composed of both Turkish tribal levies and of *mamluks,* maintained the sultan's authority over this vast area, which was administered by officials who were either Iranians or were acculturated to Iranian traditions of administration. Most were drawn from families that, generation after generation, had served whatever had been the dominant regime in the area, and they were the living embodiment of ancient Iranian concepts of autocratic and bureaucratic government, which, surviving the fall of the Sasanids, had been adopted first by the Abbasids and later by the Samanids, Buyids, and Ghaznavids. The most conspicuous figure in the Iranicization of Seljuk rule was Nizam al-Mulk (1017-92), who was a native of Tus in Khurasan and whose father had been a revenue official under the Ghaznavids. He himself rose up to become the all-powerful *vazir* of Malik-Shah (r. 1072-92), for whom, towards the end of his life, he wrote a manual of statecraft, the *Siyasat-nama,* or *Book of Government,* which in addition to being an important source for certain aspects of the history of the period offers a unique insight into the mentality of the Iranian bureaucracy that served the Seljuk sultans. Through its pages can be seen the way in which the empire was perceived by its master organizer and also the methods by which the Nizam al-Mulk and like-minded persons tamed the invading Turks by persuading them to adopt the seasoned and stabilizing techniques of government already in operation in the Irano-Islamic world.

Another preoccupation of Nizam al-Mulk, as of successive Seljuk sultans, was the imposition of orthodoxy. With the capture of Baghdad in 1055 the Seljuks had become the official protectors of the Abbasid caliphate and also of Sunni orthodoxy, threatened from outside by the territorial ambitions of the Fatimids and from within by the Nizari Ismailis of Hasan-i Sabbah, who may have been responsible for the assassination of both Nizam al-Mulk and of Malik-Shah himself. Nizam al-Mulk was rightly obsessed by the threat to internal stability posed by the Ismailis, and one way in which he attempted to ensure that the bureaucracy and the *ulama* should be orthodox, and therefore loyal, was by establishing a chain of theological colleges *(madrasas)* in the major cities of the empire wherein Ismaili doctrines and heterodox beliefs in general were to be vigorougly rebutted. Each college was known as a *Nizamiya,* so named after its founder, who provided a generous endowment. Some of the ablest teachers of the age held appointments in these colleges, among them al-Ghazali of Tus (1054-1111). One of the few truly original minds to emerge from the later Islamic scholastic tradition, he showed himself relentless in his hostility to Shiism in whatever form he encountered it, while at the same time laboring to harmonize the Sufism of his time with the basic theological propositions of Sunni orthodoxy.

It is important, however, not to overestimate the extent of Seljuk integration into Irano-Islamic society, since in one important respect the Seljuk period marks a fundamental break with the past through the introduction of a new and characteristically Turkish form of land tenure, the *iqta.* An *iqta* was an assignment of revenue-exempted land made to a military commander in lieu of salary. In theory, such lands were not permanently alienated by the central government because an *iqta* was not a private possession to be sold or disposed of at will. Nevertheless, in practice, the state rarely exercised much control over the revenue or even over the population occupying an area included within an *iqta.* Since the holder of an *iqta* expected to exchange it sooner or later for another and, with luck, more productive one, there was a strong temptation to exploit it to the maximum by means of short-term fiscal exactions for so long as one held it. This system constituted a break with the Abbasid and pre-Islamic Iranian tradition of centralized authority and has been regarded by some historians as a process of feudalism, although it is obvious that the Seljuk *iqta* as such bears no relationship to the feudal tenures to be found in contemporary Western Europe.

The Seljuk empire began to disintegrate when provincial governors realized that the central government was no longer able to control and coerce its more distant agents, a process that was accelerated by pressure on the northeastern frontier by further waves of fresh tribal invaders, Oghuz Turks and Buddhist Kara-Khitans, the latter a branch of the Tungusic people who had dominated northern China between the tenth and the twelfth century. The Seljuk provincial governors were generally either tribal chieftains or trusted *mamluks,* as in the case of the governors of Khwarazm, a remote but rich province south of the Aral Sea. Others were cadets of the ruling house, and when such was the case it was customary for them to be placed in the charge of an experienced counsellor and military commander, who held the title of *atabeg.* In course of time these *atabegs,* and indeed almost all military commanders located far enough away from the central government to escape retribution, either proclaimed their independence or quietly behaved as if the empire no longer existed. The result was rapid fragmentation.

The most impressive and enduring successor state to the empire of the Great Seljuks was the cadet line that established the Seljuk sultanate of Rum, the name then used by Muslims to describe Byzantine Anatolia. The initial penetration of this region by the Turks began in the mid-eleventh century and was the work of Turcoman tribes functioning as *ghazis,* warriors dedicated to waging holy war against the infidels on the frontiers of Islam. The Turcomans themselves were turbulent and unpredictable subjects and it seems probable that the Seljuk sultans, whose empire was centered in Iran and Iraq, were only too glad to deflect the energies of the Turcomans westward against the Byzantine frontier. Then, in about 1077, Süleyman, a kinsman of Malik-Shah, established an independent sultanate in Anatolia, making Konya his capital and in the same year capturing the Byzantine city of Iznik (Nicaea), which brought him within striking distance of the Bosporus. In this way was founded a powerful Turkish regime that survived for nearly three centuries (1077-1307), withstanding the combined attacks of Byzantines and Crusaders and, in consequence of the great revenues accruing to the state on account of its favorable location on the intercontinental trade routes, providing the conditions for the evolution of a hybrid Turco-Iranian culture of great brilliance. Compelled to submit to Mongol overlordship after 1243, the Seljuk court at Konya remained a sanctuary to all who could escape the Mongol fury in the lands to the east, and even in decline, Seljuk rule ensured the ongoing Turkification of Anatolia and the consolidation of a society and a civilization that would provide the infrastructure for the future rise of the Ottomans.

In the history of West Asia as a whole, the Seljuk Turks, tribal warriors from Central Asia and only recent converts to Islam, played a somewhat analogous role to the contemporary Normans in Western Europe. They imparted a new vision and fresh energies to a weary world and to an overripe civilization, their genius as soldiers and as proconsuls enabling them to establish a political order in which they stood forth as champions of orthodoxy and as renovators of the caliphate rather as the Normans in Sicily and south Italy posed as the protectors of the papacy against the Hohenstaufen emperors. They beat back the Crusaders from the West and imposed a measure of discipline on a society that had long been a prey to anarchy.

The Renaissance of Regional Cultures

The fragmentation of the Arabo-Islamic universal state into regional successor states, with their seats of government often located far from the heartlands of Arabo-Islamic civilization in the Fertile Crescent, greatly stimulated the emergence of regional cultural centers that signified a realignment of both military and economic power throughout West Asia. The economic importance of regional capitals such as Nishapur and Bukhara or of commercial entrepots such as Herat was due in large measure to their location on the elaborate network of transcontinental caravan routes that covered the entire area, but their importance as centers of culture was due to the fact that they were also, as windows onto a wider world, natural centers for cultural cross-fertilization. Thus Ghazni, in eastern Afghanistan, looked out beyond the Indus towards India. Bukhara, itself an ancient regional capital, faced the Central Asian steppe zone. Konya and the other Seljuk cities of Anatolia enjoyed continuous contacts of every kind with the Byzantine empire and sheltered large Christian populations. Even more important, the emergence of these regional cultural centers, often sustained by traditional local elites such as the *dihqans* in Khurasan and Mawarannahr, encouraged the preservation and even the resuscitation of indigenous cultural values that had been partly or wholly submerged by the floodtide of Arabo-Islamic civilization.

These new centers of wealth, power, and higher culture were scattered over a vast area of West Asia and were often located at great distances from each other, but they had this in common: they all tended to serve as focal points to which was drawn the economic and cultural life of whatever region they dominated. Often they served as the permanent headquarters of independent dynasties, each of which endeavored to outbid its rivals in maintaining what passed for a sophisticated court and in dispensing funds to scholars and men of letters. The outlook, tastes, and life-style of these Iranian or Iranicized Turkish rulers and their followers have been preserved in a most interesting literary genre, manuals on statecraft and courtly manners written specifically for the benefit of the ruling elite and characterized by a distinctly pragmatic outlook and by lavish exemplification from past history, especially from the legendary history of pre-Islamic Iran. The most famous of these "mirrors for princes" was the *Qabus-nama,* written by Kay Kavus ibn Iskandar, an eleventh century ruler in Gurgan, southeast of the Caspian Sea, for the edification of his son and heir, which is available in English translation and which perfectly exemplifies the prevailing courtly milieu.

With the establishment of these local capitals, the men who had formerly made their way to Baghdad in quest of fame and fortune—scholars, scientists, poets, doctors, adventurers, and soldiers of fortune—now gravitated from one regional court to the next, for a time in

7.1 Coins of the Seljuk sultans of Rum (Anatolia). *Upper:* Suleyman II (1196-1204), copper, no mint. The Seljuk horseman, armed with a mace, must represent the sultan, since the head is encircled by a nimbus. *Lower:* Kay Khusru II (1237-1246), silver, Konya. The device of the Lion and Sun, now the official emblem of Iran, is said to have been the horoscope (the Sun in Leo) of Kay Khusru's Georgian wife. Author's collection.

the service of the Buyid ruler of Shiraz, then moving on to try that of the Samanid *amir* of Bukhara or the Ghaznavid sultan far to the southeast. But the new centers held out opportunities not only for this ostentatiously peripatetic elite. Their needs, material and spiritual, called for the services of merchants and purveyors, craftsmen and artisans, theologians and saints on a scale hitherto unknown outside the metropolitan cities of the caliphs—Damascus, Baghdad, Cordoba, and Cairo.

These regional capitals aroused deep sentiments of loyalty among those who lived in them. In this period a person did not normally identify with an area, or even with a particular ethnic group unless his immediate background was tribal, and he rarely felt any profound ties with a ruling dynasty subject to sudden and precarious fluctuations in fortune. Rather, for the urban trader or artisan no less than for the cleric or official it was his birthplace or the city he had made his home, together with his religious affiliation within that city, that commanded his loyalty and with which he identified himself, so that a man from Nishapur felt deep pride in calling himself a Nishapuri, as did a man from Isfahan in calling himself an Isfahani. For the bourgeoisie, in particular, the good life meant the urban life. Beyond the walls of the city or the encircling girdle of orchards and gardens lay a wilderness inhabited by boorish peasants and treacherous, unpredictable tribesmen. Psychologically, the cities were regarded as oases of civilized behavior and relative tranquility in what was felt to be a harsh and alien environment.

It is a curious fact, for which no satisfactory explanation has yet been offered, that in the period under discussion and even to some extent in the preceding period the turbulent cities of the northeastern zone of the Muslim world sheltered some of the most original minds in the entire history of Islam. Thus, to mention only four of the most significant thinkers of the tenth and eleventh centuries, al-Farabi (d. 950) came from beyond the Syr Darya, Ibn Sina (d. 1036?) was born in Bukhara, al-Biruni (d. 1048) was a native of Khwarazm, and al-Ghazali (d. 1111) was born in Tus, the birthplace also of Nizam al-Mulk and of the Iranian national poet, Firdawsi. Yet, irrespective of their origins, Islamic scholars and men of letters continued to think and write in Arabic, and even so Iranian a dynasty as that of the Tahirids in Nishapur was as well known for its patronage of Arabic as of Persian literature. A change, however, was beginning. One of the most striking characteristics of the period under discussion was the rise of Persian, not in place of but complementary to Arabic throughout those areas of West Asia where the indigenous populations were not Arabic speaking. In the eastern provinces of the caliphate, despite the Arab conquests, Persian had continued as the speech of the great mass of the population, but now, in this age of Iranian dynasts, it was being adopted increasingly as the language of court culture, polite learning, and high-level administration, encouraged by regimes such as those of the Samanids and the Buyids. A simplified New Persian was evolving from the cumbrous Middle Persian spoken in Sasanid times, and especially in Khurasan and in Mawarannahr poets such as Rudaki (d. 940) and Firdawsi (d. 1020) were moulding it into a literary tongue as fresh, as flexible, and as sophisticated as the English language Chaucer was to mould three hundred years later. Among the great masters of Persian literature—Rumi, Sadi, Hafiz, and the rest—Firdawsi, as the national poet *par excellence,* occupies a very special place. Born in Tus in Khurasan, Firdawsi passed much of his life in the territories of the Samanids and his outlook and temperament were perfectly attuned to the cultural milieu of the Samanid court, although late in life he was compelled to enter the service of Sultan Mahmud of Ghazni, who proved a somewhat insensitive patron. Perhaps this insensitivity was hardly surprising, in view of the fact that the sultan was a Turk and that the poet was the mouthpiece for the expression of an age-old Iranian pride in the glories of a past that knew neither Arab nor Turk. Indeed, Firdawsi's masterpiece, the *Book of Kings (Shah-nama),* had little or nothing to say to the Ghaznavids or any other Turkish dynasty. Rather, it was addressed to the Iranian *dihqans,* now in the twilight of their long history, celebrating the chivalry and courage of their ancestors and of the monarchs and heroes whose names and deeds had become part of the warp and woof of Iranian identity.

Much of the Persian literature written before the coming of the Seljuks has been lost, but that which has survived fully justifies the use of the term renaissance to describe this revival of New Persian (the language that has continued to be spoken in Iran down to the present day) and the literary masterpieces written in it. To Iranians, it seems in retrospect as if their forebears in the centuries between the fall of the Sasanids and the rise of the Samanids and the Buyids had been asleep, reawakening to seize again their ancient primacy, only to be overwhelmed by the onrush of the Turks. But to put the process another way, Irano-Islamic civilization, an already rich amalgam of traditional Iranian and Arabo-Islamic civilization, now acquired a new and valuable addition, the Turkish component. To Muslims, whether Arabs or Iranians, living in the heartlands of Islamic culture, the Turks were barbarians, although, as in the case of Roman perceptions of the Germanic invaders of their empire, the Turks were also seen as the repositories of specifically barbarian virtues as well as barbarian vices. What was overlooked by contemporaries, and by the historians who have seen the past largely through their eyes, was the fact that the Turks themselves were part of yet another complex society, that of the Central Asian steppe zone. Even at the time when the Karakhanids were becoming integrated into the *Dar al-Islam,* their language, Khakani, spoken by the Karakhanid ruling elite of Kashgar and Bukhara, was chosen as the vehicle of expression for two unique literary monuments to the Turkish perception of their own cultural identity. These were the *Kutadgu bilig,* a lengthy didactic poem written for an eleventh century ruler of Kashgar, which contains much precious information regarding Karakhanid society, and the *Divan lughat al-Turk*, a dictionary of Khakani written in 1074. A dialect of Khakani seems to have been the base for another Turkish language, Khwarazmi, spoken in the territory ruled in the twelfth and early thirteenth centuries by the Khwarazmshahs and later adapted for use in the Mongol khanate of Kipchak. Khwarazmi seems to have developed fast as a literary language, deriving its religious vocabulary and thought from Arabic literature and its courtly and profane poetry from Persian, a process repeated by Chaghatay Turkish in the fifteenth and sixteenth centuries. Paradoxically, the Seljuks, most powerful of the pre-Ottoman Turkish rulers of West Asia, seem to have contributed little or nothing to the development of the Turkish languages, since they employed Persian exclusively as the language of government and the court, while Arabic remained the language of science and religion. Their contribution to an Irano-Turkish cultural synthesis can be seen most strikingly in their textiles, metalware, and decorated pottery, as well as in the distinctive Seljuk style of architecture.

The Extension of Maritime and Overland Communication Networks

In the preceding chapter it was stressed that the Arabs in the course of their extraordinary expansion during the seventh and eighth centuries became masters of the seas encircling West Asia as well as of the great wastes of desert and steppe, plying their ships over the Mediterranean and venturing down the Red Sea and the Persian Gulf to trade with the coastal settlements of East Africa and the west coast of India. Sinbad, dropping downstream from the great entrepot of Basra at the start of one of his voyages, was as quintessential a figure of Arabo-Islamic civilization as was the caliph Harun al-Rashid in his palace in Baghdad. The fragmentation of the Islamic world which followed the decline of the Abbasid caliphate did not involve any loss of maritime skill or daring and later generations of Sinbads continued to set sail from Basra on hazardous trading expeditions. The Fatimid and Ayyubid rulers of Egypt were much preoccupied with seapower and maintained formidable naval establishments in the eastern Mediterranean, and the coastal cities of Syria and Anatolia continued to be the scene of great maritime and mercantile activity, although exposed from the close of the eleventh century onwards to raids and even permanent occupation by European crusading armies and their commercially minded allies and paymasters, the republics of Venice and Genoa. Even the Seljuks of Rum, notwithstanding their Central Asian antecedents, were well aware of the benefits conferred on those who could acquire some kind of maritime and naval hegemony, possessing as they did a long Mediterranean and Black Sea coastline, and at Alanya, on the southern coast of modern Turkey, can still be seen the naval dockyard built by a thirteenth century sultan beneath the great citadel that served as his treasury and winter quarters.

Yet then, as always, the maritime trade routes were less important to the Muslim world as a whole than were the overland trade routes, which gave West Asia its special significance as the crossroads of three continents. The Iranian and Turkish dynasts of Inner Asia—and the thirteenth century Mongol conquerors who succeeded them—well understood the value of this overland commerce and usually fulfilled the function of protectors to the merchants who conducted it and who were among the few groups in an emergency capable of providing them with ready cash or credit. The transcontinental caravan trade involved a large number of persons—the merchants themselves, guards, guides, the men who looked after the animals, and those who maintained the bazaars, the watering places, and the caravanserais along the way. In matters of insurance, credit, bills of exchange, and market information it was a highly complex business and, as was to be expected, very cosmopolitan, involving great profits, some danger, much time and labor, and travel over immense distances by slow-moving beasts of burden. Of the routes themselves, the ancient Silk Road between China and the Mediterranean, referred to in previous chapters, was only the most celebrated of several major trade routes, such as those that linked Egypt and the Mediterranean with sub-Saharan Africa or that great passage down the Volga that brought Russian slaves, honey, furs, amber, and mammoth ivory to the bazaars of Khwarazm and Darband and for which evidence survives in the hoards of Samanid silver coins discovered in the Baltic lands and even Scandinavia. This commerce across hundreds of miles of often bleak and forbidding territory was sustained partly by the enlightened self-interest of those rulers through whose territory the caravans passed and partly by a network of market towns, which often consisted of little more than a makeshift bazaar, and of caravanserais, the latter generally erected by local rulers and notables as an act of charity similar to the construction of fountains, bridges, and colleges. The modern traveler in West Asia can still see the remains of these often monumental structures—sometimes located in what appears to be the midst of a wilderness—which marked the staging points on the regular caravan trails. Anatolia, in particular, was provided by the Seljuk sultans of Rum with a comprehensive network of caravanserais, and some of them were so enormous and so well provisioned as to be able to give ample shelter to large numbers of men and beasts seeking protection from the elements and from marauding bandits. Some were so effectively fortified that they withstood even the ingenious assaults of the Mongol invaders.

The fact is that even in this age of political and cultural fragmentation, the *Dar al-Islam* was still, in certain respects, a single entity across which a man could travel from Morocco to the frontiers of China, as did Ibn Battuta in the fourteenth century, and find a common faith, a common outlook, and even a common life-style. Consequently, and perhaps to a greater extent than other traditional societies, the Muslim world was full of wanderers—merchants, craftsmen, soldiers of fortune, scholars, saints, slaves, entertainers, vagabonds, and rogues—and in Damascus or Mecca a traveler from Bukhara or Ghazni would not find it surprising to be rubbing shoulders with a man from Marrakesh or Granada. Typical of this relative disregard for distance is the story of how the Seljuk *vazir* Nizam al-Mulk one day crossed the Amu Darya with his entourage and paid the boatmen with bills of exchange made out in Aleppo. It follows, then, that in this period Islam had not yet turned in on itself in thwarted pride and confusion, as it was to do in later centuries. Muslims maintained regular contacts with the Byzantine Greeks when they were not actually engaged in fighting them. They served the enlightened Norman kings of Sicily, as in the case of the great Arab geographer Idrisi (d. 1154). They shared their knowledge with the Jewish and Christian scholars of Toledo. Al-Biruni in the eleventh century probably knew more and wrote more about Hinduism than any other foreigner in India down to the end of the eighteenth century, and he achieved this by his willingness to penetrate what was then an unknown land and to try to understand very alien beliefs and attitudes. Shaykh Sadi, an inveterate wanderer of the thirteenth century, also made his way to India and penetrated the secrets of the great temple at Somnath, from which he barely escaped with his life. Al-Biruni and Sadi were poles apart in the way they looked at Indian society, but they both exemplified that intellectual curiosity and love of travel that among some Muslims at least, and especially among the wandering scholars, was a feature of this period, when the desert road and the seashore were invitations to adventure rather than barriers to human intercourse.

Steppe-Sown Interaction

Throughout this period, West Asia as a whole was brought into an increasingly intimate relationship with the steppe zone of Central Asia, whether in consequence of the pressure of tribal invasions or of the movements of traders and missionaries. The relationship was a truly symbiotic one, which increased in intensity with the Mongol invasions of the thirteenth century but diminished steadily after the widespread introduction of firearms among the peoples who inhabited the peripheries of Central Asia ended forever the age-old advantage of the mounted archer of the steppes over the sedentary cultivator of the oases and the arable zone. It was not, however, a new relationship. Rather, it was a reenactment of an ongoing struggle, dating from ancient times when the armies of the Achaemenids, the Macedonians, and the Arsacids battled with the fierce Saka tribes beyond the Amu Darya and the Syr Darya, and which had been repeated by the Sasanids, fighting to withstand the onslaught of successive Hunnish confederacies, and by the Arabs in Mawarannahr, holding back the infidel Western Turks along the line of the Syr Darya. In this age of fragmentation, however, the pressures from the steppes intensified. At first, there emerged regimes that served as barriers to penetration, such as the Samanids and even the Karakhanids, but with the coming of the Seljuks there began a succession of truly nomadic invaders—the Oghuz, the Kara-Khitans and, finally, in the thirteenth century, the Mongols of Chingiz Khan.

The situation on the northeastern fringes of the Muslim world was not comparable to that on the frontiers of northern China since nowhere, except in the Caucasus region, was there the kind of separation of steppe and sown prevailing in Inner Mongolia. Instead, there was a vast indeterminate zone of territory extending from the Syr Darya southwestward across Mawarannahr to the Amu Darya and on, across Khurasan, until it disappeared into the wastes of the central Iranian desert. This area was one where true desert, scrub desert, steppe, and mountain merged into each other and into riverine tracts and oases capable of sustaining a considerable sedentary population. Here cultivators and pastoralists could and did live side by side in a symbiotic relationship. Apart from the river line of the Syr Darya and the Amu Darya there was no strategic frontier at which to bar the advance of the nomads and no man-made barrier such as the Chinese Wall, although the Sasanids, centuries before, had built a defense line in Gurgan, consisting of walls and garrison forts of which impressions can still be seen from the air. Because of this vast indeterminate zone extending southwest from the Syr Darya, nomad invaders leaving the steppe zone to the north did not immediately find themselves in an area of intensive cultivation such as confronted nomadic invaders of north China or bedouin invaders of Iraq approaching from the south. Instead, they began a process of steady infiltration into an area that already contained a pastoral-nomadic element among which they might find kinsfolk or at least potential allies. Often the nomads entered this zone in the role of auxiliaries of the dominant elite, as the Özbegs were to do during the fifteenth century. The swift and sudden invasions of the thirteenth century Mongols were rather exceptional, and certainly the Turkish invaders of the eleventh and twelfth centuries followed closely the pattern of infiltration. Neither infiltration as a means by which nomadic pastoralists entered this area nor the symbiotic relationship between nomad and cultivator was a new pattern. It is clear, for example, that in the Achaemenid and Macedonian periods Mawarannahr, then known as Sogdiana or Transoxania, sustained a mixed agrarian and pastoral population, and did so ever after.

In the relations between pastoralists and nonpastoralists there was mutual dependence as well as mutual antagonism. In the eyes of the sedentary population, the nomads were barbarians, at worst predators, at best troublesome neighbors all too willing to turn a blind eye when their flocks strayed onto the cultivated land; but for all that, they needed the meat, wool, hair, hides, beasts of burden, and even breeding stock that the nomads had to offer. For their part, the nomads needed many commodities obtainable only from the settled population or the townsmen—utensils, weapons and metalware of all kinds, rice or flour, tea, and luxury commodities for the tribal elite. Thus, when not in actual conflict, they had to maintain the semblance of a modus vivendi, so that after the harvest had been cut a farming community would permit the local nomadic group to graze its flocks on the stubble, or an urban community, not unwilling to enlarge its trade, warily allowed the nomads to camp close to the town at market time. Virtually nothing is known of the traders and peddlers who made their way from the settled areas to the nomad encampments deep in the steppe zone. In Abbasid and Samanid times these must have included many slave traders, since at that time slaves were, with horses, the two most valuable commodities indigenous to the steppes. How this slave trade operated is a matter for speculation, although certain aspects of it (in a reverse direction) must have been reenacted by the nineteenth century Turcoman slave raiders in Khurasan. In the western part of the steppe zone the slaves were either indigenous Turks, or Slavs brought from the areas to the north or northwest, but in the eastern part of the steppe zone they were mainly Turks from the northern steppe region or Tungusic tribes from the Siberian forest zone. They were captured by kidnapping expeditions or in the course of conflicts arising out of tribal feuds and disputes over grazing rights, and were then sold to merchants who brought them to the slave markets of the *Dar al-Islam*. Nowhere is there any evidence to suggest that once they had become converted to Islam and acculturated to the norms of Irano-Islamic society these slaves showed much desire to return to the harsh life of their fellow tribesmen on the steppes, and there is a hint or two in source material originating in thirteenth century India which implies that slaves who "made good" sometimes persuaded free members of their families to join them in luxurious bondage.

Religion was another factor linking steppe and sown. Although shamanism, such as the Mongols were to retain down to their conversion to Tibetan Buddhism in the seventeenth century, prevailed over the entire steppe zone down to late Abbasid times, the steppe peoples had long been exposed to various faiths—Zoroastrianism, Mahayana Buddhism, Nestorian Christianity, and Manichaeanism. Some of these influences had been swiftly assimilated into older shamanist cults, while others had survived in a somewhat less adulterated form. Nestorian Christianity was prevalent among two important tribes in twelfth century Mongolia, the Karaits and the Naimans, while Manichaeanism had been adopted by the Uighur Turks in what is now Chinese Sinkiang as early as the eighth century. The spread of Islam into the steppe zone was not the least of the major developments that occurred in the period under discussion. As political power and cultural vigor shifted from the heartlands of the Muslim world to its peripheries, a concomitant impetus was given to the conversion of the Central Asian Turks and the other infidel peoples living on the fringes of the *Dar al-Islam*. The missionaries themselves, who were sometimes heterodox refugees fleeing from the bastions of orthodoxy and whose teachings were already tinged with Sufi,

Shii, and other esoteric beliefs, were generally dervishes and it was therefore the Islam of the dervishes that won the steppe peoples for the faith, just as it was later to win the peoples of India and Southeast Asia. The dervish who lived among the nomads soon found that, consciously or unconsciously, he had to mould his religion to his congregation's expectations so that often he appeared less of a mulla and more of a shaman, a worker of magic and miracles, evoking the primeval spirits of nature that ruled the steppe. It was a process similar to that of the dervish in India who adopted vegetarianism, who abhorred the killing of cattle, and whose mystical teachings acquired a peculiarly pantheistic tinge.

In the early Islamic centuries it must have seemed as if intercourse between steppe and sown was largely a one-way process, exemplified by the aggressive role of Abbasid viceroys and their Samanid successors as wardens of the marches. With the coming of the Seljuk Turks all this changed. Once exposed to the Irano-Islamic culture of West Asia, the Turks enthusiastically adopted the faith and, to some extent, the life-style of their Arab and Iranian subjects, but they remained what they had been from the beginning, masters of horse and bow who were feared by all who came into contact with them for their courage and skill in warfare. Inevitably, they imparted new elements into the amalgam of the civilization of West Asia—their ruthlessness and discipline in battle, their skill as effective, if rapacious, administrators, their concepts of sovereignty and world domination, which were to be shared by the later Mongols and Tatars. Contemporaries attributed to them a thirst for empire and for mastery over men which then seemed unique, and if those contemporaries were correct, it was a state of mind the Turks took with them wherever they went, whether to Bukhara and Baghdad as freeborn warriors or to Cairo and Delhi as nominally submissive *mamluks*.

2. REGIONAL FRAGMENTATION IN SOUTH ASIA

In South Asia the period from the opening of the eleventh century to the second half of the sixteenth century, when the Mughul empire gained control over most of northern and central India, was one of divergence from the prevailing pattern elsewhere in Asia. In West Asia, for example, these centuries saw the political and cultural fragmentation of the universalist Abbasid caliphate of Baghdad, followed by a series of devastating Mongol or Turco-Mongol incursions. In South Asia the period opened with the establishment of Muslim rule over much of northern and central India, which led to the emergence of an Islamic empire, the sultanate of Delhi, closely modeled on West Asian prototypes. This phase reached its culmination in the late thirteenth and early fourteenth century. By the close of the fourteenth century, however, the processes of political and cultural fragmentation were in operation and in the far south the Vijayanagar empire, centered on the valley of the Tungabhadra River, embodied a vigorous Hindu reaction. The course of events in South Asia was also markedly different from elsewhere in that, apart from raids into the Panjab and Timur's sack of Delhi in 1398, the subcontinent was spared the ravages of Mongol armies although Mongol expansionism indirectly affected the course of Indo-Islamic history.

Having stressed these divergences, it is important to note the similarities between developments in West and South Asia. First, the Islamic penetration of India was yet another aspect of Turkish expansionism, a process at work in Central Asia, West Asia (including parts of Europe and Africa), and South Asia between the eleventh and the seventeenth centuries. Second, the Turks in South Asia, as in the case of the Turks in Iran, Iraq, and Anatolia, remained separate and aloof from the subject population of the territories that they had conquered, although in West Asia there was a common cultural affinity between fellow Muslims and a degree of mutual comprehension between the Seljuks and their

Christian subjects in Anatolia which was hardly conceivable in the case of the idol-worshipping Hindus. In fact, Turkish rule in India can be considered, from at least one angle, as a colonial situation in which only very limited interaction was possible between rulers and ruled. Third, Islamic civilization in India was not so much an offshoot of classical Arabo-Islamic civilization as of the later Irano-Islamic synthesis. This synthesis, which flourished in Iran, Anatolia, and Central Asia under Seljuk and Mongol rule, included Sufi cults, which, once planted in the soil of the subcontinent, assumed distinctly heterodox and exotic shapes. Fourth, in some areas of South Asia there occurred among certain social groups a remarkable degree of cultural syncretism, notwithstanding the general prevalence of a colonial-type relationship between Muslims and Hindus.

Fifth, by threatening the northwest frontiers of the subcontinent throughout much of the thirteenth and the first decades of the fourteenth century, the Mongols, as elsewhere in Asia, made a significant impact on the course of events. They caused the sultans of Delhi to maintain a very large military establishment on a permanent war footing, compelling the infant state to stand on its own feet by forcing it to recognize that between threatening Mongols and unsubdued Hindus it was ringed by foes, which in turn encouraged the growth of a defensive mentality. More important in the long run, by their destruction of urban life in Iran and Central Asia, the Mongols set in motion a migration into northern India of scholars, saints, and bureaucrats which introduced into the rather uncouth frontier society of thirteenth century Delhi the manners, attitudes, and life-style of the ravaged Iranian lands beyond the Indus.

The Expansion of Islam into South Asia

Historians are in the habit of speaking about the Muslim invasions of India, yet the phrase, although unlikely to disappear, is not altogether accurate. It would be more correct to refer to the invasion of India by Turks who happened to be Muslims and whose chief motive for entering the subcontinent was the opportunity for plunder but whose exploits, as in the case of the contemporary European crusaders in Palestine and Syria or of the later Spanish conquerors of the New World, were subsequently justified by clerical apologists as having been undertaken for the glory of God. In fact, the Muslim raids into India during the eleventh and twelfth centuries and the political consolidation that followed later can be interpreted as part of a larger movement of Turkish peoples which took the Seljuk Turks as far as the Bosporus and other Turkish tribes to the westernmost limits of the Eurasian steppe zone. Islam itself, moreover, was not entirely unknown in India before this time. As early as 711 an Arab army had advanced into Sind, which for a century and a half had been a nominal province of the caliphate. Muslim traders and seamen were also familiar figures in the cosmopolitan ports of Gujarat and Malabar, and on the latter coast marriage with local women had resulted in the growth of local Muslim communities, ancestors of the present-day Moplahs, and the peaceful dissemination of Islam among some of the local seafaring folk.

India on the eve of the Turkish invasions of the early eleventh century was passing through a recurring phase of regional fragmentation, in which Hindu kingdoms that enjoyed unequal resources and varying degrees of centralized control fought one another across vaguely defined frontiers for territorial gains, which as often as not were lost again within a matter of years or even months. Ethnic, linguistic, and cultural diversity, together with competing caste interests, prevented combination against the common foe. Even the warrior Rajputs, who held a broad band of territory extending from Gujarat to the Ganges and who might have established a *cordon sanitaire* against the invaders, were largely preoccupied in fratricidal feuds among themselves. In encounter after encounter with the invaders they fought heroically but always as individuals in quest of personal glory, while against this chivalric tradition of Rajput warfare was pitted the hard professionalism of the

Turks. The Turks were probably at a disadvantage as regards numbers but they were the most renowned horsemen and archers in Asia, although the Rajputs handled such horses as they had well enough and Indian bows were highly esteemed, even among the steppe peoples. What gave the Turks the overwhelming advantage, however, was their military organization, for their armies were composed mainly of *mamluks,* purchased as slaves and then disciplined as perhaps no troops in Asia had been disciplined before. They combined the training and morale of professionals with the greed of mercenaries, and in the service of former *mamluks* who were the living embodiment of their own aspirations, they fought for a share in this vast land that was now theirs. As reward, they sought to secure its fabled wealth, a legend in their own homelands since ancient times, and its teeming population, to be sold as slaves or enjoyed as concubines.

Formation of Regional Political Entities

As described in the previous section, Sultan Mahmud of Ghazni (r. 998-1030), the son of a *mamluk* in the service of the Samanid ruler of Bukhara, carved out an extensive empire for himself in eastern Iran and Afghanistan. From Ghazni, his capital in eastern Afghanistan, he led a succession of forays into northwestern India, penetrating eastward as far as Kanauj on the Ganges and southward to the shores of the Indian Ocean, where he destroyed the great temple of Shiva at Somnath. These expeditions produced enormous profits for both him and his followers, who returned to Ghazni loaded with plunder and accompanied by vast numbers of slaves, but resulted in no permanent occupation of the ravaged territory. After his death, however, his successors were expelled from the Iranian plateau by the Seljuks and, as a result, set about the consolidation of their Indian conquests, with Lahore as a second capital to Ghazni. Thus in the garrison towns of the Panjab there evolved a new, raw Muslim society composed of the occupying troops and officials, their female slaves and the children of those slaves, brought up as Muslims, as well as the traders, artisans, and menials who serviced their needs and who, in many instances, converted to Islam.

The Ghaznavids faced an open frontier to the south and east, inviting further penetration, but they were themselves threatened from the rear. The Seljuks, as it happened, showed no interest in Indian conquests but in central Afghanistan Ghaznavid rule was brought to an abrupt end by the Ghurids, a dynasty originating from Ghur in the mountains east of Herat, who in 1115 sacked Ghazni itself with the utmost ferocity. The Ghurids were of Iranian stock but in supplanting the Ghaznavids they adopted the characteristically Turkish institutions of the latter and co-opted into their service the bulk of the latter's Turkish followers. During the final quarter of the twelfth century the last of the Ghurid sultans, Muizz al-Din Muhammad, dispatched a succession of expeditions deeper and deeper into northern India leading some in person and delegating the leadership of others to his handpicked Turkish *mamluks,* whom he himself had purchased and brought up in his household. The greatest of these was Qutb al-Din Aybak, who in 1193 conquered the Rajput stronghold of Delhi for his master, while a rival commander, Ikhtiyar al-Din Muhammad, pressed onward into Bihar and western Bengal, where he established his headquarters at Lakhnawti in Malda district. For the next three centuries Lakhnawti remained the greatest Muslim metropolis in eastern India.

Muizz al-Din Muhammad was assassinated in 1206 and since he had no sons his slave commanders fought among themselves for control of the empire. From his base in Delhi Qutb al-Din Aybak swiftly asserted his primacy and eliminated his rivals but he did not live long enough to enjoy his triumphs, for he died in 1210 from an accident while playing polo. Qutb al-Din Aybak and his successors down to 1290 are traditionally known as the Mamluk, or "Slave," dynasty, although only Qutb al-Din Aybak, Shams al-Din Iltutmish (r. 1211-36), and Ghiyas al-Din Balban (r. 1266-87) were technically *mamluks*, the remaining rulers being descendants of these three. The real architect of the Delhi sultanate was Shams

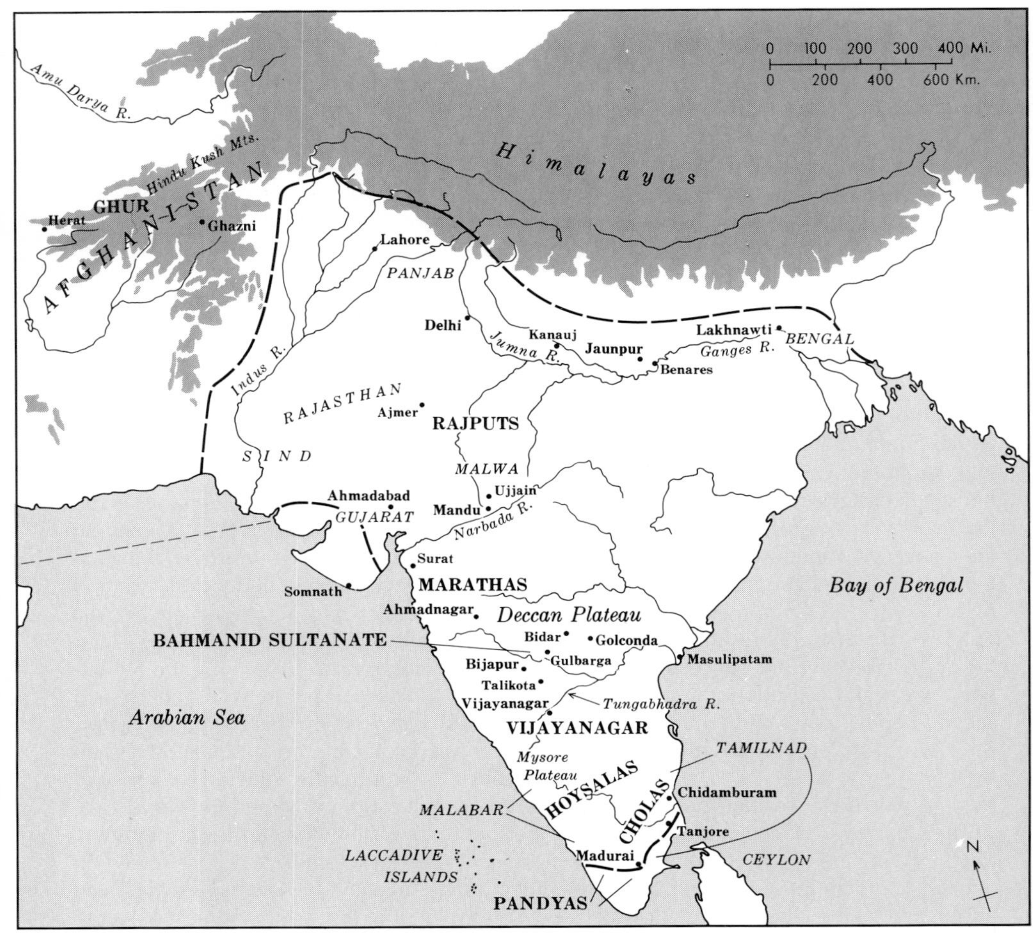

Map 29 The Delhi sultanate, early fourteenth century

al-Din Iltutmish, a Turkish slave brought up in the household of Qutb al-Din Aybak and an outstanding soldier and administrator as well as a learned and pious Muslim. Prior to his death he attempted to secure the throne for his daughter, Raziyya (r. 1236-40), being well aware of the mediocrity of his male offspring, but the Turkish slave commanders could not stomach the rule of a woman, however able. Raziyya was overthrown and the throne passed in quick succession to the sons and a grandson of Shams al-Din Iltutmish, all of whom were first manipulated and then thrust aside by competing factions among the *mamluks*. Finally, the most powerful among the latter, Ghiyas al-Din Balban, mounted the throne in 1266 and ruthlessly imposed his will on his former peers. His descendants, however, lacked his formidable powers and after a short period of anarchy a new dynasty, the Khaljis (1290-1320), seized the throne.

The Mamluk sultans of Delhi provided the institutional framework by means of which their successors, including the later sultans of Bengal, Gujarat, and the Deccan, and even to some extent the Mughuls, would exercise control over their vast possessions. Their rule was essentially foreign in the sense that every post of responsibility was filled by a non-Indian who was almost always a Turk or the son of a Turk, and usually a slave. The Turkish ruling

Muslim Rule in Pre-Mughul India
Sultanate of Delhi
Mamluk (or "Slave") dynasty, 1206-90
Khalji dynasty, 1290-1320
Tughluqid dynasty, 1320-1414
Sayyid dynasty, 1414-51
Lodi dynasty, 1451-1526
Principal Successor States of the Delhi Sultanate
Sultanate of Bengal (capital: Lakhnawti), 1336-1576
Sharqi Sultanate of Jaunpur, 1394-1479
Sultanate of Malwa (capital: Mandu), 1401-1561
Sultanate of Gujarat (capital: Ahmadabad), 1391-1583
Bahmanid Sultanate of the Deccan (capital: Gulbarga; later, Bidar), 1347-1527
Principal Successor States of the Bahmanid Sultanate
Nizam-Shahi Sultanate of Ahmadnagar, 1491-1633
Adil-Shahi Sultanate of Bijapur, 1490-1686
Qutb-Shahi Sultanate of Golconda, 1512-1687

elite of thirteenth century Delhi was a service nobility. Status within that nobility was conferred solely by service in the upper echelons of the sultan's government and, with few exceptions, promotion was through the ranks of the slave army. Skilled Iranian officials supervised the revenue administration and Indian-born Muslims and even some Hindus occupied subordinate posts, but the racial exclusiveness of the Turks and the intimate network of relationships that controlled the sultan's slave household made it virtually impossible for any who were not Turks and *mamluks* to acquire or retain real power. Following Chingiz Khan's appearance on the banks of the Indus in 1221 successive sultans judged it necessary to maintain a substantial part of their armed forces in the Panjab, in readiness in the event of a Mongol attack. In consequence, the ruling elite had only limited opportunities for enriching themselves through plundering expeditions into Hindu-held territory, and the government was compelled to find alternative means of retaining the loyalty of its followers and also of maintaining a sufficient number of troops on a war footing in case of need. The sultans therefore followed the Ghaznavid and Seljuk practice of assigning land that was exempt from payment of land revenue to high-ranking military officers in lieu of salary, from the income of which they were required to maintain a specified number of troops. As in the Seljuk case, such lands were never, in theory, permanently alienated from the crown, although in practice constant vigilance was needed to ensure that they did not become hereditary fiefs.

The government of the Delhi sultanate followed the characteristic pattern of Turkish regimes in West Asia. The sultan, who recognized the spiritual suzerainty of the Abbasid caliph in Baghdad, exercised an unlimited authority, the only restraint on his conduct being the necessity of retaining the loyalty of his military followers and a genuine, or affected, concern to observe the *Sharia*. In attendance upon the sultan was his *naib*, or "deputy," and under him the administration consisted of three more or less separate hierarchies. The first consisted of the sultan's household, composed of trusted slaves responsible for the welfare and safety of their master. Under the supervision of a principal chamberlain, they held such posts as those of cupbearer, robe-bearer, standard-bearer, chief huntsman, and master of the horse. These posts conferred great influence and power because the men who filled them had daily access to the sultan. The same was true of the eunuchs, who had charge of the sultan's women. Unlike the household slaves, however, these were not Turks but Indians or Ethiopians. The second hierarchy consisted of the military commanders, the *amirs* and *maliks,* who were also available for appointment as governors in the provinces. They, too, like the members of the sultan's household, were mainly Turks and slaves. The third hierarchy, with the *vazir* at its head, constituted the civilian administration, of which the main function consisted of assessing and collecting the land revenue and other sources of income and of disbursing funds to cover government expenditure. In this branch of government Turkish slaves were apparently little used and the *vazir's* subordinate staff consisted mainly of Iranians or Indian-born Muslims, among whom the latter possessed much-needed local knowledge. The *vazirs* of the sultans of Delhi rarely exercised the kind of authority enjoyed by the Abbasid *vazirs* or, much later, by the *vazirs* of the Ottoman sultans, due largely to their nonmilitary functions but also to the long-established supremacy of the *naib.*

Rough-and-ready order was maintained throughout the empire by scattered military garrisons. In everyday matters the small Muslim population, mainly confined to the larger towns except in the Panjab, looked to the *qazi* for leadership and guidance, as an arbitrator in disputes between fellow Muslims and, to some extent, as an intermediary and intercessor between them and the brutal *amirs* and *maliks,* the military commanders. The Hindus, mainly cultivators, were left entirely to themselves so long as they paid the land revenue regularly. The agents of the central government were indifferent to their existence and certainly made no sustained effort to bring about their conversion, provided they kept the peace and did what they were told. Fairly early in the course of the establishment of Muslim rule the invaders realized that there was no possibility of converting the mass of the Hindu population. The government seems to have accepted this, just as the Ottoman government later accepted the resilience of Christianity in its Balkan provinces, but the situation involved compromises and inconsistencies. It was often difficult to follow the injunctions of the *Sharia* in so plural a society, especially with regard to the status of the non-Muslims, and it was difficult, even where the population was solidly Muslim, for the *muhtasib,* the official who endeavored to enforce Islamic precepts of morality, to carry out his duties of enforcing the rules as to what was permissible and what was nonpermissible for his coreligionists.

As a minority, even a ruling minority, the Muslims had to be constantly on their guard, everywhere surrounded by an overwhelming majority of infidel subjects who presumably hated them and who were on the lookout for the opportunity to rise up against them. As in a European colonial society, there grew up an exaggerated sense of communal solidarity. Among the Muslims ruling elite, in particular, tensions and rivalries were always near the surface—*mamluk* versus non-*mamluk,* Turk versus non-Turk, foreign Muslim versus Indian-born Muslim—but ultimately even these antipathies had to be subordinated to the need for the community to hang together. This forced men to acquiesce in acts of tyranny or impiety by their rulers which, in the older Islamic lands, would have aroused a protest from among the more courageous of the *ulama* and perhaps demonstrations in the bazaar. It was the price that had to be paid for the wealth and ease of India, so different from the frugal existence lived in the oases and nomadic encampments of Central Asia. Furthermore, for those Muslims who lived in the Panjab and even for the citizens of Delhi there lingered the old fear of the Mongols, passed on from generation to generation. A ruler such as Ghiyas al-Din Balban, who compelled his erstwhile *mamluk* comrades to perform the humiliating Iranian ceremonial of prostration and who was never seen to smile for twenty years, might be regarded by the ruling elite and the *ulama* as a grim tyrant, but if he could keep the northwestern marches free of Mongol raiders few would want to see his authority challenged.

The rule of the Khalji dynasty (1290-1320), followed by that of the Tughluq dynasty (1320-1414), although the latter declined rapidly after 1388, constituted the culminating phase in the history of the Delhi sultanate. Each of these two dynasties produced at least one ruler of exceptional talent, Ala al-Din Muhammad Shah (r. 1296-1316) and Muhammad ibn Tughluq (r. 1325-51). Both were great warriors who advanced the frontiers of Islam far into peninsular India and both, in the view of contemporaries, possessed a wayward and inscrutable personality. The Moroccan traveler Ibn Battuta, for example, pondered the paradox that Muhammad ibn Tughluq was the most generous but also the most bloodthirsty of rulers: that he was openhanded to all strangers who came into his presence but that it was impossible to approach the palace gateway without seeing fresh evidence that the executioners had been at work.

During the first three or four decades of the fourteenth century the sultanate of Delhi may have been the most powerful state in the entire Muslim world, the only regime with comparable military and fiscal resources being the Mamluk sultanate of Egypt. An authority on the period, Simon Digby, has recently hazarded a guess that the population of Delhi during the lifetime of Muhammad ibn Tughluq should be estimated at around 400,000, making it second in size only to Cairo among contemporary Muslim capitals. Figures assembled by the same authority suggest that, at its greatest, the sultan's army may have reached around 300,000 men. Of the wealth and luxury of the court and of the ruling elite and of the manner in which the sultan distributed costly gifts to his followers and to the newcomers to his kingdom, Ibn Battuta provides impressive evidence, while the surviving monuments of the Tughluqid period in and around Delhi are indicative of lavish state expenditure on public works of various kinds.

Much of the wealth of the Khaljis and the Tughluqs came from plunder. With a century of consolidation behind him, with the Mongol threat receding, and with an enormous military establishment available for employment, Ala al-Din Muhammad Shah embarked upon the systematic conquest of the Deccan and the far south. Under the command of a eunuch, Malik Kafur, the sultan's forces advanced into central India and overwhelmed the Hindu kingdoms of Devagiri in modern Maharashtra and Warangal in modern Andhra Pradesh, both in 1307. Then, in 1310, Malik Kafur overthrew the Hoysalas on the Mysore plateau and in the following year attacked the Pandyas of Madurai in southern Tamilnad. After each of these expeditions the Khalji armies returned to Delhi carrying enormous quantities of gold, pearls, and precious stones and accompanied by large numbers of slaves, horses, and war elephants. At the same time an attempt was made to establish a permanent foothold in the south. Muslim governors were appointed to some areas, including distant Madurai, while submissive Hindu rulers were co-opted into the empire as tribute-paying vassals. Inevitably, however, the distance of the new provinces from Delhi and the inadequacy of communications tempted both Muslim governors and Hindu tributaries to throw off their allegiance, so that the successors of Ala al-Din Muhammad Shah, and especially Muhammad ibn Tughluq, were compelled to undertake strenuous campaigns in an effort, largely unsuccessful, to reassert control. One side effect of this expansion southward was the spread of Islam into areas hitherto exclusively Hindu. This missionary movement owed little or nothing to the example of the predatory Khalji and Tughluqid armies but to the Sufis, who, together with some Muslim traders and artisans, followed in the wake of the armies and established themselves in the new garrison towns of the Deccan. A thin veneer of Irano-Islamic court culture spread over these local centers of Muslim power and influence, and by frequenting them Hindu chieftains in the neighboring countryside acquired a knowledge of Muslim administrative methods and, more significantly, of Muslim methods of fighting. On the negative side, however, expansion southward, although profitable in the short term, resulted in the dispersal of the military resources of the sultanate over too wide an area, and the consequence everywhere was loss of control by the center. Like other empire builders from the north before and after them, the sultans of Delhi discovered that crossing the Narbada and advancing into the Deccan weakened rather than strengthened their hold over their older possessions. Even before the death of Muhammad ibn Tughluq, who died during the course of quelling a revolt in Sind in 1351, the process of fragmentation had set in. As early as 1335 the Muslim governor in Madurai had rebelled and had gone unpunished. Then, in the following year, the great Hindu kingdom of Vijayanagar was founded, which for the next two centuries and longer dominated the greater part of southern India. In 1336 the Muslim governor of Bengal threw off his allegiance and that province remained for all practical purposes independent of Delhi until the Mughul conquest of the late sixteenth century. In 1347 the Muslim governor of the Deccan proclaimed his independence and founded the powerful Bahmanid sultanate, and his example would be followed half a century later by the Muslim governor of Gujarat (1391). This process of fragmentation was exacerbated by the weakness and incompetence of the Tughluqid sultans who succeeded Firuz Shah (r. 1351-88), the last able ruler of the dynasty. It was completed by the invasion of the Panjab by the ferocious Turco-Mongol conqueror Timur, who in 1398 sacked Delhi, massacring most of its male inhabitants and carrying off large numbers of women and skilled artisans to Samarqand, his Central Asian capital.

During the century and a half that followed Timur's sack of Delhi the subcontinent presented a confused picture of political fragmentation accompanied, as has so often been the case in such periods, by striking manifestations of spiritual and cultural creativity. Reviewing the scene from south to north during the fifteenth century, almost the entire peninsula as far north as the Tungabhadra River had been incorporated into the Hindu Vijayanagar kingdom, beyond which lay the Bahmanid sultanate, straddling the Deccan plateau from coast to coast. Both these regimes fought each other sporadically in a series of exhausting wars of attrition, in which their respective resources were fairly equally balanced, with the advantage tilting slightly in favor of the rulers of Vijayanagar. North of the Narbada the principal successor states of the Delhi sultanate were the sultanate of Gujarat, with its capital at Ahmadabad; the sultanate of Malwa, with its capital at Mandu, near Ujjain; the Sharqi sultanate, with its capital at Jaunpur in the eastern part of modern Uttar Pradesh; and the sultanate of Bengal, with its capital at Lakhnawti. Delhi itself was ruled for the first fifty years of the fifteenth century by the undistinguished Sayyid dynasty, which sought initially to legitimize its unsteady grip over the surrounding countryside by claiming to exercise authority on behalf of Timur's son, Shah-Rukh (r. 1405-47) ruling far away in distant Herat. It was eventually replaced by the Afghan Lodi dynasty (1451-1526), which steadily extended its frontiers to include both the Panjab and the greater part of Uttar Pradesh, overthrowing the sultans of Jaunpur to the east (1479) and engaging in protracted conflicts with the sultans of Malwa to the south.

The triumph of the Lodi Afghans indicated new forces at work in fifteenth century India, forces that were an outcome of the process of fragmentation but that also intensified it. A characteristic feature of the fifteenth and sixteenth centuries (as also, to a limited extent, of the early eighteenth century) was the migration into northern India of considerable numbers of Afghan tribesmen, perhaps in consequence of a sudden increase of population in their barren mountain homeland. Unlike their Turkish precursors, these Afghans brought with them their families and a tightly knit tribal organization, which assisted them in preserving a more distinct cultural and ethnic identity. Fierce fighters, they encountered little difficulty in taking over both the sultanates of Delhi and Malwa, while those with ambitions still unsatisfied passed down the Gangetic plain to establish strongholds of Afghan power in Bihar and Bengal. Another element that contributed to the prevailing instability was the Habshis, or Ethiopians, brought into India as *mamluks* after the supply of Turkish *mamluks* had dried up with the Mongol conquests of Central Asia and the conversion of the Turks of the steppe zone to Islam. Habshis were to be found mainly in the sultanates of Gujarat, the Deccan, and Bengal, all of which had access to the sea. The Khalji commander Malik Kafur was a Habshi, as was the founder of the Sharqi dynasty of Jaunpur, and so were several short-lived sultans of Bengal.

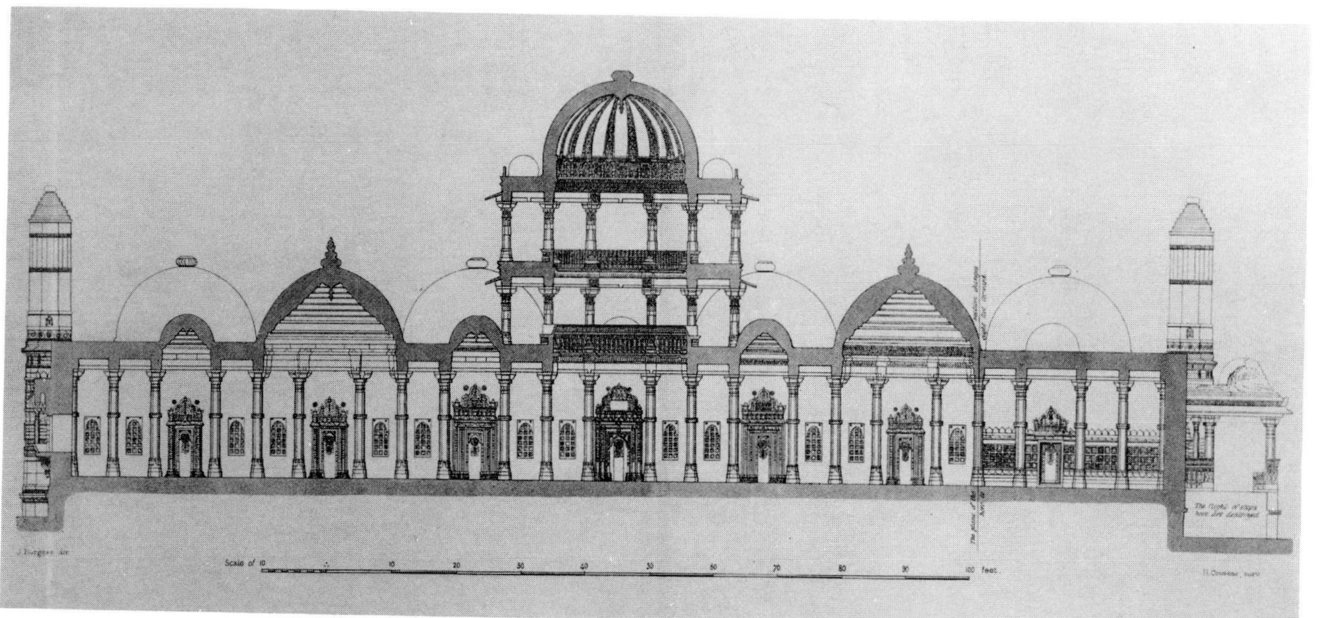

7.2 Cross section of the congregational mosque at Mahmudabad (Champanir) in Gujarat, built by Sultan Mahmud Begra (1458-1511). The architectural style patronized by the sultans of Gujarat (1391-1583) was a fine blending of Muslim and Hindu traditions of building. Source: James Burgess, *Archaeological Survey of Western India* (London, 1896), Vol. 23.

Perhaps even more striking than the role of the Afghans and Habshis in the warring states of fifteenth century India was that of the Hindus, now becoming familiar with Muslim methods of warfare. The confrontations between the rulers of Vijayanagar and the Bahmanid sultans have already been mentioned. No less remarkable was the military activity of the Rajputs in Rajasthan, where warrior chieftains held their own, and more than held their own, against the neighboring sultanates of Malwa, Gujarat, and Delhi. Significantly, none of the regional sultanates that emerged with the decay of the Tughluqs possessed the military resources enjoyed by the Delhi sultanate in the days of its prime, and so they endeavored to bring in outsiders to fulfill the same functions as the former Turkish *mamluks*. The numbers of these outsiders, whether Habshis, Iranians, or Arabs from the ports of the Red Sea and the Persian Gulf, were never sufficient, so that the sultans were compelled to enlist recruits from among the Hindu population of their own territories, led by Hindu feudatories who could no longer be treated in the contemptuous way their forefathers had been treated by Khalji and Tughluqid conquerors. Hindus were also much in demand in order to carry on the civil administration, especially the assessment and collection of the land revenue, and so a kind of modus vivendi grew up between the Muslim and Hindu elites in the regional sultanates to an extent that would have been impossible in the former Delhi sultanate. These regimes were acculturated to the Indian environment in a way the Delhi sultanate had never been, and out of the balance of political forces within them there emerged a mutually enriching exchange of elite attitudes, manners, and culture.

This period of political fragmentation and of cultural fusion continued in northern India into the second half of the sixteenth century, when the Mughuls, having overthrown the Lodi sultanate (1526), conquered first the sultanate of Malwa (1561), then Bengal (1576), and finally Gujarat (1583). In the south, the regional sultanates survived far longer. The Bahmanid sultanate disintegrated in the early sixteenth century, to be replaced by three successor states, which in 1565 overthrew the kingdom of Vijayanagar at the so-called battle of Talikota. Of these three successor states, the sultanate of Ahmadnagar was located in the northwestern Deccan in what is now Maharashtra, with its capital at Ahmadnagar, not far from Poona. The sultanate of Bijapur, with its capital at the city of the same name, straddled southern Maharashtra and northern Mysore. The sultanate of Golconda, with its capital, also of the same name, close to Hyderabad, extended over much of Andhra Pradesh and Tamilnad. The first survived down to the first half of the seventeenth century, the last two into the second half, but all were eventually conquered and annexed by the Mughuls. Following the example of the Bahmanids, these sultanates in the Deccan utilized the services of local Hindu elites to maintain their hold over their extensive but rather loosely held possessions. Under the sultans of Ahmadnagar, for example, the Hindu Marathas were the real rulers in the countryside, although foreign Muslims visiting the sultan's court may well have missed this point. Maratha soldiers and brahman officials also served the sultans of Bijapur and Golconda, forming new local elites that gained so tenacious a hold on the administrative structure at the lower levels that they were able to maintain themselves unscathed in the ensuing dynastic upheavals, serving in succession the Mughuls, the Nizams of Hyderabad, the French, and the British as usefully as they had formerly served the sultans of Golconda or Bijapur.

Evolution of Regional Cultures

In cultural terms, the most significant development in South Asia during the centuries under discussion was the dissemination of Islam and of Irano-Islamic civilization in areas where hitherto the Muslim way of life had been virtually unknown. During the first two centuries of Muslim penetration, the period of the Ghaznavids and the Ghurids, Islam were seen by the inhabitants of India as primarily, although not quite exclusively, the religion of predatory raiders, who were hated and feared wherever they went. When, in the thirteenth century, the Delhi sultanate came into existence, the sultans and their military followers showed little enthusiasm for the propagation of the faith, while such of the Muslim *ulama* as had made their way into India resided chiefly in Delhi or the larger garrison towns, where they were employed in the service of the state as judges and legal consultants or were attached to mosques and colleges. Thus the *ulama* as a whole constituted a part of the ruling establishment, and although the Mongol holocausts in Central Asia and Iran had the effect of driving many pious and learned men to seek sanctuary within the frontiers of the Delhi sultanate, these newcomers were also, for the most part, co-opted into the establishment. The *ulama* derived their income from fees and gifts received in return for services rendered, from salaries or pensions paid by the state, or from religious endowments that were, in many cases, set up by the ruler or one of his predecessors. Many, if not civil servants in the accepted sense of the word, were nevertheless maintained out of state revenues. Few felt much of an urge to undertake missionary activities or to move away from the main concentrations of Muslim population, and they were apparently not encouraged to do so by their rulers.

Islam in pre-Mughul India was not, therefore, disseminated by the *ulama* but by the Sufis, who here, as elsewhere, included both mendicant dervishes, who were very much their own masters, and members of *tariqas,* or Sufi "orders." These orders were mainly Iranian or Central Asian in origin and their presence in Muslim India meant that the spiritual life of that country would be more akin to that of Iran and Central Asia than to that of Iraq or Egypt. In a Sufi order spiritual authority was invested in a leader known as a *murshid.* At his death his authority passed to his designated successor, who in some cases was a son, since the Sufis rarely practiced celibacy, but in other cases was a favorite disciple. The chain of authority that ran through a succession of *murshids* was called a *silsila,* and it was by means of the *silsila* that each order maintained its own traditions, preserved an internal consistency in its teachings, and established a basic pattern of responses in its dealings with the outside world—the representatives of government, the *ulama,* and the other orders. The most influential Sufi order in pre-Mughul India was that of the Chishtiya, founded by Shaykh Muin al-Din (d. 1236), whose birthplace was Chisht, a small town to the east of Herat. Shaykh Muin al-Din Chishti emigrated to India and finally settled in Ajmer, in the heart of Hindu Rajasthan. In choosing to pass his days among infidels in what was still a Rajput stronghold, instead of in Delhi or some other center of Muslim political power, he was setting an example that many other Sufis would emulate. Some of his disciples established themselves in remote villages of Rajasthan and the Panjab, adopted the dress and diet of Hindu peasants and, in some instances, supported themselves by cultivating the soil. Many became vegetarians and abjured cow killing. A few undertook ordeals of self-inflicted pain and mortification of the flesh in the manner of Hindu *yogis* and *sannyasis.*

The Sufis were far from popular with the *ulama,* partly because of the great influence they exercised over the masses, both Muslim and Hindu, and partly because in their way of life, their teachings, and their quest for divine inspiration they followed heterodox and even forbidden paths, experimenting with breath regulation, seances, and hallucinatory drugs, as well as utilizing music and dance to induce a state of ecstasy. Living among the poor and the outcast, they unconsciously imbibed Hindu religious attitudes and pantheistic assumptions, while at the same time they propagated a faith that was both more tolerant and more selfless than that of the orthodox *ulama.* Even during their own lifetime the Sufi *murshids* acquired a charisma that was felt by the entire population, from low-caste Hindu cultivators to the mighty Turkish *amirs* at the sultan's court, and following their deaths, their tombs became places of pilgrimage and the scenes of miracles and wonders. They contributed immeasurably to the Indianization of Islam in the subcontinent, but they also contributed to the revitalization of Hinduism through the impact that Sufism in general made on the *bhakti* cults of devotional worship to a single god. Indeed, for some seekers after truth, such as Kabir, the fifteenth century weaver of Benares, Allah and Rama were only different names for the one universal Deity.

The Sufis were sometimes objects of suspicion for certain Muslim rulers, just as they were for the orthodox *ulama,* since they avoided contact with the court and maintained that government service was incompatible with a life of piety and virtue. Sufi literature includes many variants on the theme that those who attend on the thresholds of the palaces of kings will find the Gate of Paradise closed to them. At the same time, when they chose to settle in the vicinity of the capital or a major urban center their presence often proved disturbing to those in authority, since they tended to acquire a large following of disciples and clients, even among the *amirs* and *maliks,* thereby causing rulers acute unease at the knowledge that some of their most powerful and perhaps least trustworthy subjects were assembling at some Sufi convent, often in a group and at night, beyond the formal protocol of the court and the observation of the spies who haunted the palace. In consequence, there was a continuous pressure, both friendly and less than friendly, to draw the *murshids* and other prominent Sufis into a closer relationship with the government by offering them gifts of money, pensions, endowments of land and, occasionally, a daughter of the reigning sultan. Such pressures were hard to withstand, and not all Sufis were immune to temptation, but the greatest of them met the challenge face on, as when Shaykh Nizam al-Din Awliya (d. 1323), learning that the sultan planned to visit him unannounced, declared that his house had two doors and that should the sultan enter through one door he would immediately leave through the other. The sultans did, however, have some justification for their anxiety. Whether they wanted to or not, the Sufis were invariably drawn into public affairs since few of their visitors sought exclusively spiritual guidance. Their reputations as saints and as workers of miracles attracted many in search of help—seeking the whereabouts of a missing valuable or a cure for leprosy or sterility—while others sought counsel in confabulations that often had political overtones. Moreover, the very reverence with which the great *murshids* were regarded aroused the jealousy of the sultans, as when the famous poet and disciple of Nizam al-Din Awliya, Amir Khusru (1253-1325), described his spiritual master as an emperor without throne or crown, before the dust of whose feet emperors stand in awe. In fact, the *murshids* of the Chishtiya order constituted almost a rival source of authority in the sultanate, a source of authority available for the disaffected to manipulate for their own purposes. Relations between the Sufis and the state grew increasingly strained under the Khaljis and the Tughluqs, until finally Muhammad ibn Tughluq resolved to end the tension once and for all by forcibly integrating the Sufis into the government hierarchy by making them recipients of state pensions. The Sufis recoiled from this obvious snare, and the sultan, outraged at their defiance, drove them from their old-established centers into the recently conquered lands to the south. One consequence of this action, which was probably not lost on the sultan, was to send these God-intoxicated men into areas where hitherto Islam had scarcely penetrated and thereby enlist them in strengthening and disseminating the faith far from the politically overcharged atmosphere of the capital.

Unlike the Sufis, the Muslim ruling elite was not greatly influenced by the Indian environment so long as it could maintain contact with the Islamic lands beyond the Indus. From the time of the thirteenth century Mongol invasions of Central Asia and Iran, if not before, the flow of theologians, scholars, and officials, all seeking their fortunes in India, ensured that Irano-Islamic civilization as it existed in Shiraz, Herat, or Bukhara would be the main component of elite culture. This was true even of the later Muslim regimes in the Deccan, where the ruling dynasties, engaged in perpetual confrontation with the north Indian states, where the Muslim military elite was predominantly Turkish or Afghan, maintained close contact with Iran by sea. As a result, Muslim society in the Deccan acquired pronounced Iranian and Shii overtones. In general, however, the farther the Muslims were from Delhi and the northwest, the greater the likelihood of cultural interaction between Muslims and Hindus. This interaction could assume unusual forms, such as rulers in the regional sultanates becoming patrons of local vernaculars. Among the Muslims themselves, Turkish soon gave place to Persian as the *lingua franca* of the ruling elite, Persian also being well spoken and well written by those Hindus—and there were many of them—who served in Muslim administrations. Persian enabled the Muslims of India to retain their contacts with Iran and Central Asia, but it also served as a vehicle of communication between Muslims and Hindus at a certain social level and as a link language for geographically diverse elites in much the same way that English does today. It was to remain the common language of administration, diplomacy, and court culture down to the second quarter of the nineteenth century.

Urdu did not emerge until long afterwards, but an interesting controversy centers on whether the vernacular spoken by Amir Khusru, the famous disciple of Shaykh Nizam al-Din Awliya and the greatest of the Persian poets of India, was proto-Hindi or proto-Urdu. Either way, it was presumably the patois of Delhi and the surrounding countryside in the early fourteenth century, and it is evidence of at least some degree of cultural interaction that this Indian-born Muslim who so admirably exemplified the Irano-Islamic literary heritage on Indian soil should have shown such unfeigned delight in his command of his local vernacular.

It is in the visual arts, and especially architecture (little Indo-Islamic painting has survived from the pre-Mughul period), that Hindu-Muslim cultural interaction can be seen most distinctly. Such interaction was already implicit at the beginning of the thirteenth century, when the Muslim conquerors of Delhi erected their first mosque with material taken from demolished Hindu temples but without succeeding in effacing the evidence of its origins. Thereafter, the near contemporary Qutb-Minar and the supposed mausoleum of Shams al-Din Iltutmish close by, as well as the shrine of Shaykh Muin al-Din Chishti at Ajmer, reveal a partial capitulation to Hindu surface decoration, a trend in Indo-Islamic architecture that reached its climax over two centuries later in Gujarat and Bengal, where the employment of Hindu craftsmen to decorate, and perhaps even of Hindu architects to design, the tombs and mausoleums of Ahmadabad and Lakhnawti resulted in masterpieces of stylistic synthesis different from anything to be found elsewhere in the Islamic world.

Growth of Maritime Centers

At no time in recorded history has the Indian Ocean acted as a barrier to intercourse between Southeast Asia, South Asia, West Asia, or East Africa. During the eleventh and twelfth centuries, when the Ghaznavids and Ghurids were penetrating India from the northwest, the Tamil kingdom of the Cholas, with its capital at Chidamburam, was at the height of its power and prosperity in south India. Rajaraja I (r. 985-1014), who ordered the building of the great temple of Shiva at Tanjore, exercised his sway over Tamilnad itself, Ceylon, the Maldives, and the Laccadives, while Rajendra I (r. 1014-42), dispatched a fleet against the Srivijaya empire of Sumatra, which had been interfering with Chola shipping passing through the Straits of Malacca en route to China. These maritime traditions survived the coming of the Turks from landlocked Central Asia. As soon as the invaders penetrated to Bengal and to Gujarat they actively encouraged the growth of oceanic trade, especially in the case of Gujarat, where so much of the carrying trade was already in the hands of their Arab coreligionists. In the far south the Chola kingdom had disappeared long before the raids of Malik Kafur. It had been weakened by a protracted struggle with the powerful Chalukya kingdom in the Deccan, which left it too feeble to withstand pressure from the Hoysalas of Mysore, who annexed much of the former Chola territories around 1216, or from the Pandyas of Madurai, who followed the example of the Hoysalas around 1257. Isolated pockets of Chola rule, however, survived long enough to be incorporated into the fourteenth century kingdom of Vijayanagar, which owed much to surviving traditions of Chola rule in the area. Chola traditions of seafaring and ocean commerce were also taken over by Vijayanagar, so that, on the eve of the arrival of the Portuguese at the close of the fifteenth century the south Indian states—Vijayanagar itself, the principalities of the Malabar coast, and the sultanates of Ahmadnagar, Bijapur, and Golconda—were all deriving great profit from their flourishing seaports, crowded with Malay, Arab, Iranian, Armenian and, soon, European traders. This oceanic trade was not only highly lucrative but also essential for survival, for while the trade with East Africa brought much-needed Habshi *mamluks,* that with Egypt brought bullion and weapons of war, and that with the Persian Gulf ports, cavalry mounts. But the importance of the ports did not lie exclusively in their commerce, for with foreign commodities came foreign sects, foreign manners, and foreign life-styles so that the Malabar coast, for example, continued to be, as it had always been, one of the most cosmopolitan areas in South Asia. The tradition of tracing the course of Muslim fortunes in India from the standpoint of Delhi and the northwest tends to conceal the true importance of coastal India in the precolonial period. It is easy to forget that Lakhnawti, the greatest Muslim metropolis in eastern India, traded with the lands bordering the Bay of Bengal as much as with its own hinterland; that Masulipatam, the main port of the sultanate of Golconda, and Surat, the principal port of the Mughul empire, owed their wealth exclusively to maritime trade; and that Ahmadabad, possibly the largest manufacturing city in sixteenth century India, looked to its outlets on the Gulf of Cambay for access to the distant markets of the Persian Gulf and Egypt. Not for nothing did a sixteenth century chronicler observe that while the revenues of the sultans of Delhi were paid in grain, those of the sultans of Gujarat were paid in pearls.

3. REGIONAL FRAGMENTATION IN SOUTHEAST ASIA

To this point, Southeast Asia has been treated as marginal to the civilizations of South and East Asia. This does not imply the judgment that Southeast Asia was unimportant, nor that the region was merely a cultural extension of the Indian and Chinese societies. The documentation of early Southeast Asian history is mainly archaeological or second hand (based on reports of Chinese and Indian travelers) before the fifth century A.D., when the first indigenous written documents appear. Even from this time, the record improves only gradually and unevenly, some areas being better known than others. The emphasis in this section will be on the period from 900 to 1500 A.D., but it will begin with a summary of the earlier development of civilization in the region.

Early Civilization in Southeast Asia

Although some of the earliest evolutionary steps towards the human species may have been taken in Southeast Asia, the region appears to have received its modern population as the result of a persistent southward drift of peoples coming from, or through, south and southwest China. These population movements began long before historic times and have never ceased. This fact should serve to remind one of the common cultural roots shared by the wet-rice regions of southern China and Southeast Asia. Throughout historic times and into the present, the basic ethnic and linguistic substratum of Southeast Asia has been Austronesian, principally Malay, and to a lesser degree Austro-Asiatic, principally Mon and Khmer. (The main modern representative of the Khmer are the Cambodians.) The basic similarity of these peoples has resulted in both groups being designated Indonesian. Overlying this basic ethnic foundation are such later arrivals in northern Southeast Asia as the Burmese, Thais, and Vietnamese, but the modern cultures of these peoples reveal the profound influence of the Indonesians among whom they settled.

Civilization in Southeast Asia was built on the twin economic foundations of intensive irrigated agriculture and maritime trade, and in both of these activities the peoples of the region were notable pioneers. By the time that Indian cultural influence can first be discerned (around the first century A.D.), both the mainland and island realms of Southeast Asia were already characterized by a fairly homogeneous Bronze Age civilization. Among the shared elements were the following: irrigated rice cultivation, domestication of the water buffalo, some use of bronze and iron (supplementing continued use of stone tools), boat building and navigation, and matrilineal descent groups. The high bronze culture that had regional expressions in the Dongson culture of northern Vietnam and the Tien culture of southwestern China during the fourth and third centuries B.C. was probably the center from which bronze metallurgy was disseminated throughout the entire region. Another possible such center was in northern Thailand, where recent finds show that bronze casting began at least as early as in north China. Some of the utilitarian bronzes cast by the Dongson and Tien artisans were of Chinese type, but the ceremonial bronze vessels and drums reveal by their style and decoration the presence of a strong and distinctive regional culture. Chinese influence here was adapted to the indigenous religious values and artistic traditions.

Indian influence on the development of civilization in Southeast Asia is obvious, but many questions remain as to the way in which it was exerted and how it was related to the indigenous cultures. Mainly on the basis of archaelogical evidence it is apparent that the older view, which holds that the process was simply an eastward projection of Indian society and culture, has to be discarded. The rice growers, mariners, and merchants of Southeast Asia played the commanding role in their own cultural development, making selective use of elements of Indian culture and altering these to conform to their own tastes and needs. Moreover, although the first links between India and Southeast Asia were undoubtedly commercial, Indian cultural influence did not become significant until economic development, formation of major cult centers, and urbanization in the region had begun to lead into political organization and the formation of states. The first states in Southeast Asia were based mainly on intensive agriculture, although trade was also an important factor. Contact with Indian traders and with native merchants returning from voyages to India made political and military leaders aware of the ideological and symbolic resources of kingship in India. Probably by the first century A.D., local rulers found it useful to import and patronize Indian brahmans and monks to assist in the organization of administration and court ceremonial. Some aspects of Indian practice never caught on, however, such as the institution of caste. On the other hand, different rulers invested heavily in the construction and maintenance of Hindu or Buddhist temples and monasteries. The earliest written documents of the region were composed in Sanskrit, and the royal titles adopted by the rulers were derived from Indian political tradition. These first courts and capitals, however, with their outward display of foreign influence, were culturally remote from the great mass of the population in the villages, where the indigenous, pre-Indic culture lived on and exerted a steady influence on the Indianized upper classes. The long-term effect of this interaction was the formation of a distinctive Southeast Asian civilization with regional variations.

The first important Southeast Asian state known to history was the kingdom of Funan, which was centered in the lower Mekong valley (within modern Cambodia). *Funan* is a Chinese rendering of the Khmer *phnom,* meaning "mountain." The rulers of this state were called King of the Mountain, with reference to the local state cult of the sacred mountain marking the center of the Khmer universe. According to the Hinduized royal tradition, the state was founded by a brahman in the first century A.D. Funan was subjugated by the new Khmer state of Chenla in the sixth century and disappeared as a distinct entity soon afterwards. For about five centuries Funan dominated intraregional Southeast Asian trade and the trade with India and China. Politically it extended its control westward to include

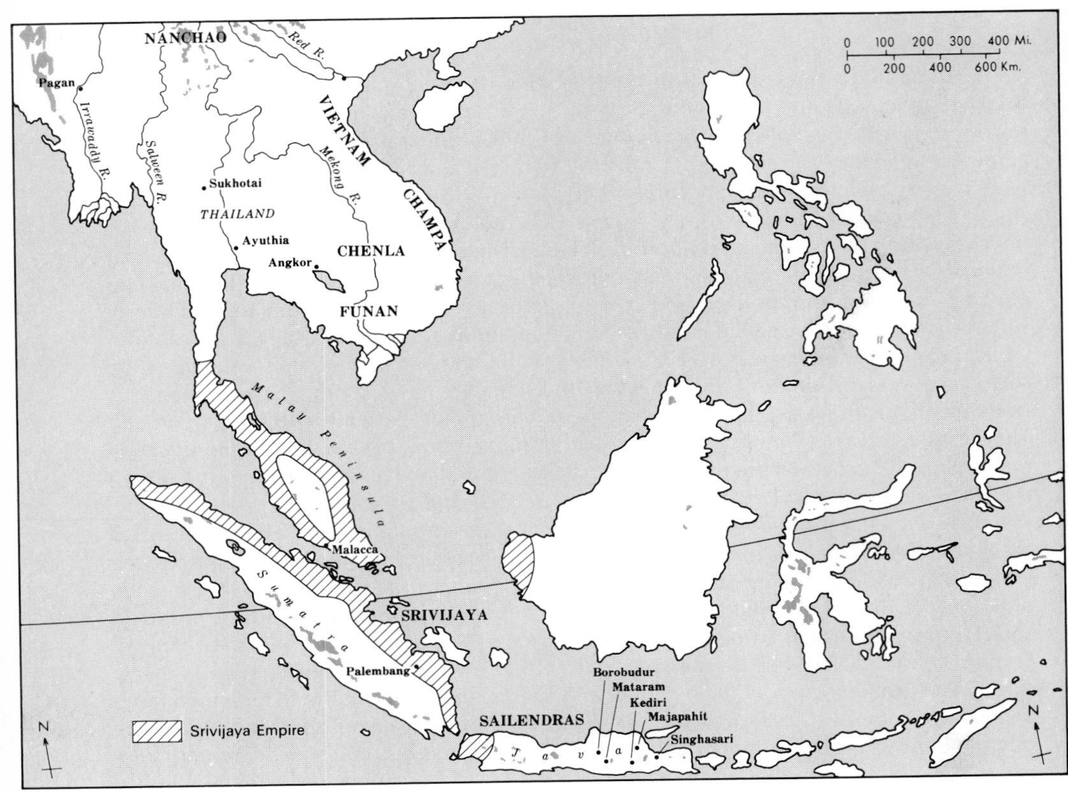

Map 30 Regional fragmentation in Southeast Asia

the upper portion of the Malay peninsula. Chinese visitors were impressed by the size of the capital city and by the dense network of canals that were used for drainage and irrigation as well as to link together the principal cities of the realm.

While the kings of Funan were adapting elements of Indian culture to their needs, the region of modern northern Vietnam was firmly incorporated into the expanding Chinese empire. In 218 B.C. the Ch'in dynasty conquered and colonized the far south including the areas around modern Canton and Hanoi. These southern commanderies broke free in 207 B.C. during the general anti-Ch'in rebellion and were organized until 111 B.C. as an independent kingdom. Chinese control was reasserted in 111 B.C. and a full-scale Chinese civil and military administration was installed in the first century A.D. With this there began the intensive introduction of Chinese culture, but again, as in the case of Funan, the most important elements of the culture that were introduced were those associated with the political system and these, then, interacted over about two millennia with the deeply rooted indigenous culture of the countryside. Southward expansion of Chinese political power and cultural influence down the coast was checked for a time, however, by the formation of the maritime trading state of Champa in the second century A.D. The Chams were Indonesians and their state, like that of Funan, was organized in the light of Indian high culture, in this case in its Buddhist form.

The next major states in order of appearance were those of the island realm. The Buddhist kingdom of Srivijaya profited by the decline of Funan to become the principal maritime power in Southeast Asia. Srivijaya was situated on the southeast coast of Sumatra with its capital near modern Palembang. Its origins are obscure, but it may have been raised on the foundations laid by the still earlier state known only from Chinese sources as Kan-t'o-li, a tribute paying trading partner of the Six Dynasties' state of Sung. Srivijaya extended its political power by reducing other states in Sumatra and the Malay peninsula to vassalage. Its rulers promoted trade and, at the same time, were munificent patrons of Mahayana Buddhism. The Chinese pilgrim-monk I-Ching in the eighth century found at Palembang one of the great centers of Buddhist learning and spent many years there in study. Except for a brief period of subordination to the maritime empire of the Indian Cholas in the eleventh century, Srivijaya maintained its primacy against all rivals until the mid-twelfth century. The neighboring island of Java also was the scene of state building. In the eighth and ninth centuries the kingdom of the Sailendras flourished in central Java. Sailendra kings built the Borobudur Mahayana temple complex, one of the largest and most elaborate structures of its kind in Asia. Surrounding the central structure are miles of galleries with hundreds of sculpted Buddhas and thousands of reliefs. The reliefs especially are as rich in the expression of the indigenous culture and style as they are in Mahayana iconography. Some of the other states on Java used Hindu iconography and ceremonial, but in time there appeared a syncretic tendency leading toward a fusion of Buddhism and Shaivism.

Southeast Asia from the Tenth to the Fifteenth Centuries

In the tenth century, Southeast Asia was a region of considerable cultural uniformity. The empires that dominated the mainland and island realms, the Khmer kingdom of Angkor and the maritime empire of Srivijaya, respectively, represented Indonesian and Indian cultural syntheses. Moreover, Sanskrit provided a courtly *lingua franca* throughout most of the region, despite some development of vernacular literatures for secular purposes. In the succeeding several centuries, however, this cultural region underwent a deep and possibly permanent fragmentation. On the mainland, the southward drift of Burmese and Thais accelerated and modified the old Mon cultures even while being themselves much influenced by them. The formation of the new Burmese and Thai kingdoms, Pagan, Sukhotai, and Ayuthia, coincided with the decisive period for the popularization of Theravada Buddhism in those countries and in neighboring Cambodia. Farther to the east, Vietnam broke away from its integral place in the Chinese empire and became independent. For about two centuries after independence, the Vietnamese gave cultural expression to their freedom from the Chinese trend toward neo-Confucianism by relying to some extent on Mahayana Buddhism and learned monks in organizing and managing their state.

Meanwhile, in the island realm a tremendous increase in trade with India and the West, and with China, brought a seaward shift of wealth and power away from the older inland political centers and created strains on the old empires such as Srivijaya and, in Java, Mataram and Kediri, that contributed to their disintegration. In the late stages of this disintegration an important factor was the spread of Islam, which became, among other things, a political weapon in the hands of the restive leaders of the booming mercantile communities on the coasts. Islam was not new to the region at this time. Arab and Persian Muslims had been conspicuous among the foreign traders for centuries, but they do not appear to have had a significant cultural impact. When Islam was successfully propagated in Southeast Asia, the agents were Indian converts—Gujaratis and Bengalis. The establishment of Islam in India principally by the Turks from the thirteenth century thus may have been a necessary condition for the spread of the faith into the Indian-influenced culture area in the east. During the fifteenth century, especially, local rulers began to call themselves shahs or sultans, patronized Indian Muslim teachers, built mosques, and encouraged others to do likewise. This had the effect of further strengthening the coastal mercantile interests against the old Buddhist and brahmanical establishments and contributed to the political decline of the latter.

In consequence of these changes, on the eve of the expansion of European activity into the East, Southeast Asia had become politically fragmented among a great number of rival states and, more important perhaps, had come to the parting that left the island portion, including the Malay peninsula, under Islamic influence while retaining its Indonesian languages (chiefly Malay) and the mainland area mostly committed to Theravada Buddhism (excepting Vietnam) and dominated linguistically by the more northerly languages of Tibetan and Chinese affinities (chiefly Burmese, Thai, and Vietnamese).

Cambodia

After the disappearance of the state of Funan, Cambodia was ruled for about two centuries by several rival monarchies. Khmer political unity was restored by a new dynasty founded by Jayavarman II in 802. He and his successors restored the royal cult (usually Shaivite, but sometimes Vaishnavite and even Mahayana Buddhist). Canals and irrigation works were expanded. Retention of runoff from the monsoon rains in great man-made reservoirs permitted year-round rice cultivation and huge increases in annual yields. Several capitals were built successively in the vicinity of Angkor and provided with immense temple complexes to serve the state cult. At the height of its power, the kingdom reached from the Annam coast westward almost to the Salween in eastern Burma and included the northern portion of the Malay peninsula. The kingdom appears to have been based on a rich and closely regimented core area under direct administration by some thirty governors and a large number of vassal states farther from the capital. In the central area at least, the population was subject to compulsory labor and military service. Slaves, including war captives and captured non-Khmer mountain people, were also employed.

Full mobilization of wealth and population was necessary for the extravagant construction projects undertaken especially during the twelfth and thirteenth centuries. The Vaishnavite temple of Angkor Wat, the Mahayana Bayon temple, and the new capital city of Angkor Thom were all built during a period of about a hundred years. At the same time the state assigned enough peasant villages as religious endowments to support some 300,000 clergy and servants in 20,000 temples and shrines. Despite the immense scale of state enterprises, workmanship in construction, and scholarship in official literature were both maintained at an extremely high level.

The kingdom precipitously declined in power from the end of the thirteenth century. Some of the contributory factors were invasions by the Chams, who were hard pressed in the north by Vietnam, and by the Thais of Sukhotai and Ayuthia. Perhaps equally important was the exhaustion of Cambodian human and material resources by the Angkor kings. The capital area around Angkor was finally abandoned in the fifteenth century because it could no longer be defended against the Thais, and it was reclaimed by the advancing jungle. A much diminished Cambodian state survived along the Mekong, hemmed in on the south by the Chams and later the Vietnamese, and in the north by the Thais. With the passing of the imperial style of rule Theravada Buddhism was popularized and provided the basis for a less authoritarian and elitist society.

Burmese, Thais, and Vietnamese

In and near modern Yunnan province of southwestern China the major rivers of mainland Southeast Asia descend from the southeastern corner of the Tibetan plateau and fan out east and south towards the sea. These include the Red River of northern Vietnam, the Mekong,

7.3 Angkor Wat, the enormous Vaisnavite temple built by the Cambodian emperor Suryavarman II in the twelfth century. Suryavarman's wars and building projects marked an extreme point in the formation of the Khmer state. Source: G. Maspero, *L'Indochine,* editions G. Van Oest (Paris and Brussels, 1930), Vol. II, Plate 22.

the Salween, and the Irrawaddy. This southwest border region of China was long a stronghold of Thai and Burmese as well as other peoples and a source of southward migration down the river valleys. This was also a region important for overland trade between central China and South and Southeast Asia. The heart of this region was a high, fertile plain around Lake Erh. Here the city of Tali developed on the basis of a heavy local production of rice and the profits obtained from the trade route coming from Szechwan and running westward to the upper Irrawaddy and down into Burma. In the seventh century the rulers of Tali were unwisely encouraged by the T'ang to organize a provincial regime to control the southwest on behalf of the Chinese empire. From this beginning there soon developed the powerful and independent kingdom of Nanchao under Thai leadership. All Chinese efforts to conquer this region failed until the thirteenth century. Nanchao imperialism in the ninth century resulted in the Thai political and military penetration into central China, central Burma, and northwestern Vietnam.

Out of this border region came the Pyus, who settled among the indigenous Mons and established several states in Burma only to be ruined by attacks from Nanchao and submerged by new migrations of Burmese. During the eighth through eleventh centuries, the Burmese established their control over the Irrawaddy valley down to the delta and organized a major kingdom based on the capital city of Pagan. The Burmese achieved a cultural synthesis through interaction with the Mon, adopting Theravada Buddhism and adapting the Mon script for literary Burmese. Also from Nanchao territory, Thais moved southward during and after the tenth century into the region that now bears their ethnic name and into upper Burma (where they are known as Shans). By early in the thirteenth century a number of small Thai states had appeared, one of which, Sukhotai, threatened the declining Khmer Angkor kingdom farther south.

The southward movement of Shans and Thais was sharply increased in the second half of the thirteenth century as a result of events in China. A new dynasty, the Yuan, had been established by the descendants of the Mongol conqueror Chingiz Khan. This inaugurated a vigorous expansionist phase in Chinese history. In the course of their conquest of south China the Mongol armies destroyed the kingdom of Nanchao, and some decades later they invaded Burma in strength, where they destroyed the kingdom of Pagan. This both provided a new impulse to the southward movement and weakened the resistance to it. Burmese political unity was shattered for centuries after with the formation of rival Shan, Burmese, and Mon states. Thailand, on the other hand, came under the control of the powerful new Thai state of Ayuthia (1350-1767).

In Vietnam, independence from China in 939 was followed by a period of political rivalry among military leaders. Unity was achieved and maintained by the Li (1009-1225) and Tran (1225-1400) dynasties. During this period large-scale hydraulic engineering projects under royal direction controlled the Red River floods and extended the acreage of irrigated rice lands. Major steps in administrative reform, such as regularization of administration of a professional civil service recruited by competitive examinations, moved the monarchy towards a closer approximation of the Chinese model. On the other hand, a strong local tradition, protonationalist, developed through the years of repeated Chinese attempts to reassert imperial control. Vietnamese historical literature (written in literary Chinese and usually modeled after the form of Chinese works) provided a vehicle for Vietnamese political tradition and national pride. Late in the period of the Tran dynasty the *chu nom* script was divised, adapted from the Chinese, which made it possible to write in the Vietnamese vernacular. This medium was especially important for the preservation of the indigenous Vietnamese drama. By the fifteenth century Vietnam had grown in population, wealth, and political organization to such an extent that it was able to play a major role in Southeast Asia. Under the Le dynasty (1428-1788) a last major Chinese effort at reconquest was defeated and the southward expansion of Vietnam was furthered by the destruction of Champa in the fifteenth century.

The Island Realm

The empire of Srivijaya began a slow disintegration during the eleventh century, a process that continued into the thirteenth century as former vassal states detached themselves or came under the domination of rival states. The center of political power during this time shifted to eastern Java, where Kediri (ca. 1050-1222), Singhasari (1222-92), and Majapahit (1293-ca. 1520) successively played leading roles in the control of trade in and around the islands. Majapahit, however, passed its peak during the fourteenth century, and a new power, Malacca, appeared on the southwest coast of the Malay peninsula. The consort of a Majapahit princess established a trading port here, prospered, and laid the commercial and diplomatic foundations on which his heirs built a modest empire that by about 1500 incorporated a number of states on the peninsula and on Sumatra. The situation of Malacca enabled its rulers to control shipping through the straits, and it also became the major entrepot for traders from East, North, and West Asia dealing in the trade goods of China, the spice islands, and India.

From the outset, Malacca also was the principal local center for the dissemination of Islam throughout Southeast Asia. The founder accepted conversion and his heirs, despite their contradictory simultaneous adherence to brahmanical court ritual, were enthusiastic promoters of their new faith. The Malacca sultans furthered their interests by marriage alliances with other princely merchants and thereby helped to introduce Islam into their families. Brotherhood in Islam reinforced the marriage connection and so was politically useful. Moreover, there developed at Malacca a large colony of Javan residents engaged in trade. There in the Malacca sultanate they were subject to Islamic influence, which they extended through their connections with their home ports. The introduction of Islamic religious practice was actively assisted by Indian merchants, who did a lively business providing religious articles such as tombstones bearing appropriate inscriptions in Arabic.

The effects of Islamic influence on the culture of the islands was initially superficial, as had been the case earlier with Hinduism and Buddhism. By 1500 there were scores of commercial enclaves where Islam had taken root among the leading families, but many cities held fast to Hindu or Buddhist practice and the mass of the population occupying the agricultural villages had not yet been affected by the new religion.

One aspect of Southeast Asian history that remains to be considered is the incorporation of some of its states into the "world order" of the Chinese empire through the establishment of tributary relations. During the Sung period, despite the great expansion of trade and the increasingly active role of Chinese ships and merchant enterprise throughout East and Southeast Asia, the imperial regime did very little to convert commercial connections into political ones, although from time to time some tributary missions were sent by trading states and imperial policy sometimes favored one or another party in local conflicts, as in the Sung support of Champa against Vietnam. The advent of the Yuan dynasty brought an altogether different policy. The Mongol rulers at first were earnestly bent on completing their mission of world conquest and accordingly dispatched fleets into Southeast Asia, as well as land forces across the frontiers into Burma and Vietnam. This extension of Chinese naval power beginning in the late thirteenth century was a factor of relatively minor importance to the history of the region, but some effects should be noted. Naval interventions by the Yuan and later by the Ming early in the fifteenth century did result in a great increase in the number of tributary missions going to the Chinese court and offered opportunities for Chinese political influence to work. One of the more important instances involved Malacca, which quickly became a favorite tributary of the Ming if only because it was valued as a counterweight to the formidable Thais of Ayuthia. The expansion of the Malaccan state was probably aided to some degree by its special relationship with China.

4. REGIONAL FRAGMENTATION IN CHINA

The diffusion and domestication of Mahayana Buddhism from India to Southeast, Central, and East Asia resulted in the inclusion of Chinese civilization within a vastly larger world of common religious belief and practice. Chinese civilization, however, despite the profound influence of Buddhism, retained its cultural identity. An expression of that identity in political terms was the T'ang empire, which at its height in the seventh and early eighth centuries came to exercise some degree of control or suzerainty over most of the Mahayana realm outside of India.

During the following five centuries, ending with the Mongol conquests in the thirteenth century, centrifugal political forces proved far stronger than the forces of unity, and the Chinese empire fragmented into a number of strong and independent states, which in most cases corresponded to distinct ethnic identities. Everywhere Buddhism survived this fragmentation, so that even as late as the present century a Buddhist monk might feel quite at home in a monastery in any country of Asia, but everywhere also the Buddhist clergy was so clearly subordinated to or identified with the state that regional political interests prevailed over considerations of universal religion.

Eventually, the process of fragmentation went so far during the tenth through thirteenth centuries (the Five Dynasties and Sung periods) that some inland territories populated by Chinese were incorporated into expansive alien frontier states. This in turn contributed to the inability of the Sung empire to make an effective defense against the Mongol empire in the thirteenth century. The astonishing reversal of fortunes that led the Chinese empire from dominion over much of Asia in T'ang to its subjugation to alien rule in the Mongol Yuan (1279-1368) is difficult to understand. This section will be concerned with the decline of the Chinese empire down to the eve of the Mongol conquest, and some possible explanations will be offered.

Fragmentation of the Mahayana Religious Culture Area

In the course of time, Buddhism became politically less important both as a common element among different societies and as a unifying element within those societies. With regard to the first point, the founders of Sui and T'ang, for example, made effective use of Buddhist institutions and ideology as means to the goal of political integration. Unfortunately for the Chinese empire, however, this practice was one that could be used equally well by non-Chinese rulers who wished to strengthen their hand against Chinese or other foreign domination. A striking case in point is that of Tibet. Thinly scattered across the immense area of the Tibetan plateau, the Tibetans faced west and south toward Kashmir and north India, east toward western and northwestern China, and north toward the Iranian oasis cities of the Tarim basin. A land of mixed pastoral nomadism and agricultural oases, Tibet had long remained politically disorganized. The Ch'iang and Ti, Tibetan peoples of the most populous eastern region, had fought almost continuously with their Chinese neighbors without ever having achieved large-scale political organization even within their region. The fourth century state of Ch'in created by a tribal federation under Tibetan leadership collapsed almost at once. It was not until the seventh century that the peoples of Tibet were brought under a single sovereignty, and in this Buddhism was an essential factor. The first Tibetan king, Srongtsan Gampo, faced the problem of overcoming the entrenched localism of the Tibetan aristocracy and the mutual antagonism between herders and farmers. He proceeded to make marriage alliances with Nepal and with the T'ang court, and through these marriages he imported Indian and Chinese Buddhist teachers. This initiated a three-cornered contest between the rival Buddhists and the intransigent nobles, who justified their opposition to the king by defending the native shamanist Bon religion against the foreign teachings. Ultimately, the Indian-sponsored Tantric Buddhism and Mahayana (Madhyamika) metaphysics won out over the Chinese Ch'an teachings. The Lamaist Buddhism of Tibet evolved later from a mutual accommodation of Tantrism and Bon. Although the diffusion of Buddhism in Tibet was still in an early stage, it had apparently gone far enough by the eighth century to contribute to the integration of a state that was able to wrest the southern oases of the Tarim basin and the Kansu panhandle from T'ang control. Among other cases that might be mentioned, Silla, the first Korean state to unify the peninsula, made Buddhism the state religion in the sixth century, and the Vietnamese, after breaking away from Chinese rule in the tenth century, made good use of Buddhist clergy and doctrines in forming their state. Tibetan and Turkish control of the west and northwest contributed to the fragmentation of the Mahayana realm by interrupting the international travels of Chinese monks.

While Buddhism was bent to the service of state builders on the frontiers of China and thereby contributed to the fragmentation of the Chinese empire, it also lost much of its ability to unify Chinese society against forces that tended to pull it apart. The most important causes of the decline of Buddhism in China are to be found in economic, social, and political changes. These, to be discussed at length elsewhere in this section, are briefly as follows: In the course of their domestication in China, Buddhist values and institutions had adapted to the aristocratic social order of Six Dynasties and early T'ang. The great monasteries, which were also the centers of Buddhist learning, were *par excellence* institutions of the aristocratic lineages, and their patterns of landownership, business enterprise, and control of manpower assimilated, and improved upon, the model of the aristocratic estates. Likewise, at the other end of the social scale the rural temples fitted themselves to the communal mores of the peasant villages. In the course of the T'ang and Sung, however, the progressive commercialization of the urban and rural economy and the concomitant professionalization and expansion of the bureaucracy undermined both the aristocracy and the communal solidarity of the villages. The shift of bureaucratic power from the hands of the aristocrats to increasing numbers of wealthy *parvenus* through the Confucian-oriented civil-service examination system politically weakened the patrons of Buddhism while strengthening the hands of the growing numbers of non- or anti-Buddhist literati. The aristocrats suffered their *coup de grace* at the hands of the new class of professional militarists who dominated the political scene in late T'ang and the Five Dynasties period. The reintegration of China by the Sung in the context of a new social order and under the auspices of a revived Confucian ideology left Buddhism with little in the way of vigorous or influential patronage. It was thus left to survive mostly as a highly variable and localized amalgam of Buddhist and indigenous beliefs and practices in the countryside. Only the Taoist-influenced Ch'an Buddhism retained its freshness and vitality among the literati. Such monasteries as continued to be active in scholarship were not usually vital centers of religious thought but rather were occupied with preservation of existing doctrine and with writing histories and collective biographies of their faith in happier times.

The decline of Chinese Buddhism among the literari was not entirely the result of social forces beyond its control, however. When the Buddhist clergy claimed and obtained exemptions from taxation, corvée and military conscription, it went on to allow its monasteries to be used as tax shelters for the aristocrats. Donations of lands and valuables to the monasteries were not always, or perhaps even usually, for reasons of simple piety, and the great urban monasteries became immensely wealthy. This pleased neither the landless rural and urban poor nor the imperial revenue officials. Under these conditions it was difficult to uphold Buddhist spiritual authority and to justify the tax losses suffered by the state. When the T'ang state underwent a succession of calamities, including An Lu-shan's rebellion in the mid-eighth century, the notion gradually gained currency that the root cause of the empire's troubles was to be found in monastic corruption and parasitism as well as foreign subversion. This in turn provided a climate of opinion favorable to a decree of 845 closing all the monasteries, confiscating their wealth, and returning their clergy and dependents to the tax rolls. Although the decree was rescinded before it could be fully executed and the clergy soon recovered approximately its former numerical strength, the blow was a heavy one and its effect on the morale of the clergy was irreversible.

The fragmentation of the Buddhist world within Chinese society was also reflected in the role of Buddhist clergy and its doctrines in the leadership of popular rebellions. Whether out of political frustration or a genuine sense of social injustice, dissident monks appeared from time to time among the leaders of popular uprisings. The egalitarian implications of Buddhism conformed to the ideological requirements of social revolution, and the eschatalogical doctrines of the cult of Maitreya, the Buddhist messiah, were a suitable reinforcement for the indigenous revolutionary tradition as represented by the Yellow Turban rebellion of late Han times. The Buddha Amida was also invoked in revolutionary causes, and the syncretic West Asia religion of Manichaeanism made contributions to rebel ideologies as well. The enrichment of Chinese revolutionary ideology by foreign sources reached an early culmination in the White Lotus Society, which was formed from indigenous, Buddhist, and Manichaean elements in late Sung and emerged from underground in the fourteenth century to play a leading role in the great rebellion that overthrew the Yuan.

Fragmentation of the Chinese Empire: Formation of New Political Entities

The most important achievements of Sui and T'ang imperialism were those related to the reestablishment of effective control over the Inner Asian trade routes through the Tarim basin and Dzhungaria. This was made difficult by the strength of the competing forces in these regions: Turks in the north and Tibetans in the south. During the period of the Toba states in north China, a vast federation of steppe peoples was formed in Mongolia. The federation broke apart around 550. One of the groups that constituted this loosely organized empire was that of the Turks. Turks now appeared for the first time under that name (T'u-chueh in Chinese transcription). The Turks swiftly organized a new federation that dominated most of Inner Asia and interferred in Chinese politics by playing one north Chinese state against another. This regime also proved ephemeral, however, and the constituent tribes in 582 divided into two lesser federations: the Eastern Turks, based on the Orkhon valley in northern Mongolia, and the Western Turks, based in the Altai. Thus, when the Sui reunified the Chinese empire by conquering the south, the new regime was able to make an alliance with the Eastern against the Western Turks. This policy was resumed by the early T'ang rulers and it so magnified Chinese political and military power that the Tarim basin was brought under imperial control for the first time in about five hundred years. Successful campaigns were also waged against the largely Tibetan federation of the T'u-yu-hun and broke their control of the trade routes passing through Kansu.

At the other end of the northern frontier the Sui emperors repeatedly tried and failed to conquer the northern Korean state of Koguryo. This effort may have been occasioned by the threat of a Korean-Turkish alliance directed against the Sui. The T'ang, probably for the same principal reason, continued the campaign against Koguryo until at last in 668 victory was achieved. The T'ang armies in the end were supported by those of the Korean state of Silla. Silla, aided by popular resistance to the Chinese conquest, promptly expelled the T'ang armies and unified the peninsula for the first time. Although they were now effectively independent, the Koreans accepted the nominally inferior role of tributary to the T'ang court in order to reap the economic benefits of this relationship. On the southern frontier of China the reconquest of the south by Sui carried imperial arms and administration into the southern provinces now corresponding to northern Vietnam. In early T'ang new administrative units were organized and Chinese control of the region reached an unprecedented intensity. In the southwest (roughly modern Yunnan province), the ethnically variegated population of valley farmers, mountain dwellers, and mercantile townsmen had come under Buddhist cultural influence from northern Burma. The principal cultural centers were in the rich agricultural plains, a large one around Lake Tien (near modern Kunming) and a smaller one near Lake Erh (near modern Tali). The early T'ang rulers exerted both cultural and political influence on this region by establishing suzerain relations with local tribal heads and granting them titles. In the interest of more efficient control, they gave superior regional rank and authority to one of these, who ruled from Tali. In the far west, Tibet was effectively beyond the reach of T'ang political and military power, but the T'ang court might have been able to flatter itself that it had brought Tibet within the empire by means of the marriage alliance with the Tibetan kings.

The immense size of the T'ang empire made it necessary for imperial authority to be established in high-level regional offices on the frontiers. Six protectorates-general were organized. Two were in the critical Tarim region: Western Pacification near modern Kucha and Northern Palace near modern Beshbaliq. Two were in the north: Northern Pacification, originally in the Orkhon valley in the heart of the Eastern Turks' territory but later in Inner Mongolia, and Shan Yü (title of the rulers of the ancient steppe empire of the Hsiung-nu) near Ta-t'ung. The Eastern Pacification office was situated in southern Manchuria east of the Liao River. The sixth office was that of the Southern Pacification (An-nan, from which comes Annam, denoting northern Vietnam) near modern Hanoi.

The T'ang empire depended for its existence on the willing cooperation of a considerable proportion of the non-Chinese peoples on the frontiers. Such cooperation in turn depended partly upon T'ang prestige, which was measured chiefly in terms of military strength. During most of the seventh century both the military strength, based on the *fu-ping* militia system, and the extension of political power into the frontier regions were successfully maintained despite occasional reverses at the hands of Koreans, Tibetans, and Western Turks. Subsequent centuries, however, saw the decline of Chinese military power and the progressive loss of control over the frontiers. In the northeast the Korean state of Silla followed up the expulsion of the T'ang armies by adapting the T'ang political model to the Korean state. From their capital at Kyongchu, roughly a miniature Ch'angan, they proceeded with the bureaucratic patterning of royal administration. By the middle of the eighth century the T'ang administrative hierarchy from province and prefecture down to the lowest subbureaucratic level had been reproduced. Politically, the state was dominated by Silla aristocratic lineages organized into aristocratic ranks, and even more than was the case in early T'ang, offices were distributed hereditarily to the leading families. The T'ang-style government, however, served very well the centralizing aims of the royal court. North of the Korean frontier a new political entity, the state of Pohai, was formed among the Tungusic peoples of Manchuria. Here, in the meeting ground of Inner Mongolian steppe nomadism, hunting and fishing exploitation of the northern forests, the well-established Chinese agriculture of the Liaotung region, and pockets of agriculture in the Manchurian plain, political organization was beginning a career that would lead to the formation of powerful states.

In the southwest the kings of Tali pursued their task of political unification with such vigor that the king Ko-lo-feng not only rebelled against T'ang authority but inflicted spectacular defeats on two Chinese expeditionary forces sent south in 751 and 754. For more than a century thereafter the kingdom of Nanchao (also called Tali), strengtened by an influx of Chinese administrators captured or invited to the kingdom, became a major power, extending its frontiers until they included southern Szechwan, the western half of

Kweichow, and northern Burma, as well as the entire province of Yunnan. Although lack of a single sufficiently strong economic base area doomed the state to eventual subjugation from the north, it retained its independence until the Mongol conquest in the thirteenth century. Meanwhile, the Tibetan monarchy turned from amity to aggression during the second half of the seventh century and became a formidable power on the western frontier, sometimes acting against China in alliance with Nanchao. Weakened by the An Lu-shan rebellion, 755-763, the T'ang frontiers crumbled at a more rapid rate. The Uigur Turks, based originally in the Orkhon region within the territory of the Eastern Turks, emerged as the leading power in Mongolia. The T'ang had to turn to them for aid against An Lu-shan and paid the price of Uigur harassment and interference for about a century afterwards. Moreover, the Tibetans took advantage of the T'ang dynasty's troubles to invade the Ch'angan capital region and to occupy large areas of Kansu and Shensi, thereby terminating T'ang control of the northwest. When both the Tibetans and the Uigurs declined militarily in the mid-ninth century, the T'ang state was too weak to take advantage of the fact, and new powers emerged on the northern frontier: the Sha-t'o Turks in the Ordos and the Khitan in eastern Inner Mongolia.

Despite a good recovery after the An Lu-shan rebellion based on a new tax structure and a steady flow of revenues from the flourishing southern provinces, the T'ang regime disintegrated during the last quarter of the ninth century. The court, dominated by palace eunuchs, torn by factionalism, and despised by the military governors who had achieved *de facto* independence in the regions they administered, was unable to offer effective resistance to a wave of mass uprisings by the impoverished peasantry of the north. The greatest of these (874-884), led by Wang Hsien-chih and Huang Ch'ao, was suppressed only with the aid of the Sha't'o Turks and by the defection of a rebel general, Chu Ch'uan-chung. Chu obtained a high military post and used this position in 906 to dethrone the emperor and install a puppet, who was used to legitimize his termination of the dynasty and the establishment of the first of the Five Dynasties of north China (907-960). Chu, of peasant origin, was hostile to the aristocracy, and his assumption of power was accompanied by the extermination of many leading families. The leader of the Sha-t'o Turks, supported by Chinese aristocrats, founded a new regime. In rapid succession there followed two more dynasties of Turkish origin and one of Chinese origin. The south meanwhile was fragmented among ten kingdoms, of which as many as six were in existence at one time. In one last coup in the north, the Chinese general Chao K'uang-yin ended the Chou and founded the Sung (Northern Sung, 960-1127, and Southern Sung, 1127-1279).

The empire suffered even more costly losses of territory during the Five Dynasties and Sung than in T'ang. Annam revolted against Chinese rule as the T'ang regime disintegrated, and in 939 the state of Southern Han failed in its last effort to restore its control there. The year 939 subsequently was taken to be the first year of Vietnamese independence from China. Despite Chinese attempts at reconquest and long periods of formal tributary relations, that independence has proved to be permanent. Of far greater consequence strategically, however, was the formation of new states on the northern frontier. A pastoral nomadic people related to the later Mongols, the Khitan, occupied a region in the northern part of modern Jehol where there was a mixed settlement of agriculturalists (including Chinese) and herders. In 916, the Khitan leader of a tribal federation founded the state of Liao. Within ten years he had broken up and absorbed the Pohai state in the east and invaded territory of the Tibetans in northwest China. In 936 the Liao ruler was granted sixteen northern Chinese prefectures, including the vicinity of modern Peking, in return for supporting the Chinese state to the south. The large Chinese population and agricultural resources of this area provided Liao with a base on which to build a powerful frontier realm that eventually reached from eastern Manchuria to the T'ien Shan Range north of the Tarim basin. Farther east, Liao expansion was checked by the second unification of Korea. The

Map 31 China during the Southern Sung, about 1200

disintegration of Silla led to a division of Korea from 891-935, when political unity was reestablished under the Koryo dynasty. Koryo continued to use institutional forms of early T'ang type, joined to a predominantly Buddhist (T'ien-t'ai) ideology. Although in the twelfth and thirteenth centuries the Koryo kings became the instruments of a military dictatorship based on personal armies and administration, the dynasty survived until 1392. Frequently accepting a tributary relationship with China or one of the north Chinese states, Korea successfully resisted all attempts at conquest until the Mongol invasion of the thirteenth century, and even then the Koryo kings held on to the outward forms of sovereignty. The maturation of a Korean great tradition is indicated by the completion of a major history of Korea by Korean scholars in the twelfth century.

A third major northern state, the Hsi Hsia, took shape in Kansu and the Ordos during the late tenth century. A mixed population of Toba and Uigur remnants, long-established Chinese urban settlements, and the leading group of Tangut Tibetan pastoralists was organized into a unified state, which assumed the status of an empire in 1038. Bolstered economically by its firm hold on the overland trade route through Kansu, Hsi Hsia played an important role in East Asian politics until its destruction by the Mongols in 1227.

7.4 Regional Fragmentation: China

The Sung regime after its establishment in the north China capital city of K'aifeng in 960 made several unsuccessful attempts to dislodge the Khitan from its Chinese territories and then turned its main attention to the reconquest of the southern states, a task that was accomplished in 979. Even within its greatly reduced frontiers, the Sung was immensely rich and populous, but with its major resources now in the south, it was difficult and costly to bring them to bear on the northern frontier. Despite bitter opposition on the part of the advocates of reconquest, the prevailing policy was one of appeasement. Treaties with the Khitan in 1004 and the Hsi Hsia in 1044 obliged the Sung to pay a substantial annual tribute to each, thereby reversing what to the Chinese was the normal relationship with barbarian states. The rise of yet another state, created by rebellious Jurchen Tungusic subjects of the Liao in central Manchuria, seemed to offer the Sung an opportunity to recover the lost northern prefectures. The new state of Chin (1115-1234) quickly entered into an alliance with Sung against the Liao. Liao was destroyed in 1125, with some of the surviving Khitan nobles fleeing westward to found the state of Kara-Khitay. The Khitan fugitives unified the mainly Turkish populations of the region from the Oxus valley eastward, including the Tarim basin, where the Uigurs were now the dominant element. Victory immediately turned into disaster for the Sung, however, because their Jurchen allies turned on them and Chin armies pushed deep into the south. The Sung capital was taken, compelling the survivors of the Sung court to flee across the Yangtze into Chekiang in 1127. Not satisfied with this, the Chin armies continued southward in pursuit and devastated the cities of the lower Yangtze region. Some of the lost territory was regained in a Sung counteroffensive and the war was concluded by treaty in 1141. The Sung had purchased peace at immense cost: all of north China south to the Huai valley was surrendered to Chin. The Sung capital was reestablished in the modern Hangchow (1138) and the dynasty's territory was now reduced to the prosperous Yangtze valley and the regions to the south of it. China remained divided between the Jurchen Chin in the north and the Southern Sung in the south until both were destroyed by the Mongols; Chin in 1234 and Sung in 1279.

This fragmentation of the Chinese empire in late T'ang and Sung is probably best understood in terms of the political consequences of economic and social change. The early strength of the empire depended, on the one hand, on the ability to mobilize economic and military manpower resources for war on the northern and northwestern frontiers and, on the other hand, on the ability to incorporate non-Chinese aristocratic leaders, such as Turkish militarists, into the imperial political system without loss of control over them. Mobilization was achieved through the centrally controlled taxation of the free peasantry on the allotments granted them under the equal-field *(chun-t'ien)* system and by organizing some of the peasants in a trained military reserve under the *fu-ping* system. The ability of the T'ang regime to secure cooperation of the Turks depended to some extent on the continued domination of the T'ang imperial government by the Kuan-chung (Wei valley) aristocracy, which was deeply intermarried with Turkish families long established in the same area. As early as the eighth century these favorable conditions no longer obtained with the same force as in the century before.

The most basic cause of this deterioration was the progressive commercialization and urbanization of the Chinese economy. Commercialization resulted in the erosion of the social position of the aristocracy by partially replacing the vertical links of personal master-client relationships that gave medieval Chinese society its manorial character, with the economically more rational relationships between landlord and tenant, merchant and bureaucrat, and among members of voluntary trade or commercial associations. The once rigidly stratified aristocratic society was opened up to individual or family enterprise and newly rich families emerged from the lower ranks of the aristocracy and the commoners. In these circumstances, the aristocracy was on the defensive in two senses. First, in order to check the rise of the new wealthy urban class, aristocrats endeavored to use the authority of the imperial government to maintain close regulation of trade but not to suppress trade, since they themselves were engaged in it. Secondly, in order to uphold the effective authority of the state, which they largely dominated through hereditary official privileges, they tried to preserve the equal-field and *fu-ping* systems against the economic forces that were undermining them. As commerce expanded and new fortunes were made, investment in land for reasons of profit and social status became increasingly common, and as a result allotment land of the free peasantry passed illegally into private hands. This change in the pattern of land tenure was accelerated by a vicious circle in which the growing private estates shifted the burden of taxation and military service to the remaining free peasants, thereby encouraging them to sell or abandon their lands and migrate into the south, where the *chun-t'ien* system and the taxation based on it had never been effectively implemented.

Control of trade in early T'ang was facilitated by the fact that marketing was confined largely to administrative seats of the rank of county or above. Outside the cities, at least in the north, the population lived in agricultural villages that were largely self-sufficient. Within the cities, T'ang retained the ancient practice of confining trade to designated marketplaces that were under government management. The market supervisors controlled hours of business, prices, and the quality of goods. In order to do business, a merchant had to rent a stall or shop and register with the authorities. Since merchants were easily identified by the appearance of their names in the registers, they were subject to effective enforcement of the laws specific to their occupation. These laws included commercial taxation and sumptuary laws forbidding them to acquire such status symbols as large and elegant houses, horses, horse-drawn vehicles, and clothing such as might properly be worn by gentlemen of rank. Moreover, merchants and their sons were legally barred from entering the government through the civil-service examinations, and they were subject to severe limitations with respect to land ownership. The development of private trade was also limited in early T'ang by the government's success in absorbing most of the agricultural and textile surpluses through taxation and disbursements, thereby keeping these major commodities out of commercial channels.

Government regulation of land tenure and trade was weakest in the south, where the labor- and capital-intensive irrigated agriculture and a relatively high level of commercialization made the officially ordained pattern (which had originated in Toba and Sui times in the north) difficult to enforce. The peculiar problems of the south became much more serious a matter as the population of that region increased relative to that of the north. Probably by the tenth century, the south's proportion of the total population, which had been about a fourth in early T'ang, exceeded one-half; and in Southern Sung, it became much greater still. It was from the south, therefore, that the aristocratic order was most threatened. During the latter half of the seventh century, Kao Tsung's empress, Wu Tzu-tien, used her great political influence to promote her own and her family's interests. From the time of Kao Tsung's death in 683, Empress Wu was the effective ruler of the empire. In 690 she terminated the T'ang dynasty, assumed the imperial throne, and proclaimed the establishment of the Chou dynasty. She reigned as emperor until her overthrow and the T'ang restoration in 705. As a usurper and as the first woman emperor in Chinese history, she was vulnerable to a countercoup by the imperial Li family and its aristocratic supporters. The empress drew her support from two distinct elements. As an ardent and generous patroness she won the support of the Buddhist clergy of the great monasteries, who acclaimed her as a divine manifestation of the Buddha and provided her with favorable omens to legitimize her assumption of rule. At the same time, she undermined the aristocratic opposition by admitting larger numbers of wealthy southerners to the civil service through increased reliance on the civil-service examinations as a means of recruitment. She also relaxed somewhat the enforcement of the legal restraints on trade and landownership. Despite efforts by the imperial government under aristocratic influence to reverse the changes that had occurred under Empress Wu, it proved to be impossible to restore the *chun-t'ien* and *fu-ping* systems to their original level of efficiency. By the middle of the eighth century it had become difficult to obtain sufficient tax revenues, and the *fu-ping* militia system had become so ineffective that it had been found necessary to reorganize the defense system. The northern frontier was divided into several large military commands on a provincial scale. Here, the regional commanders took charge of their own civil administration and replaced militia men with their own mercenary armies. Many of the frontier forces and, in many instances, their officers were of non-Chinese origin. For the aristocracy this meant that control of the major military forces had passed from them into the hands of professional militarists of doubtful loyalty.

Governmental attempts to maintain the regulations of early T'ang were finally shattered by the rebellion of An Lu-shan. An, the son of Turkish and Iranian parents, had risen through the ranks in frontier service to high military office. As the favorite of a court faction, he was permitted to gain control over several of the regional military commands in the northeast. The rise of a rival group in the capital threatened his political position and he responded by raising his army in rebellion. He occupied Loyang, had himself proclaimed emperor, and proceeded to occupy Ch'angan. The T'ang loyalist forces recovered from their early defeat, and with the crucial assistance of the Uigur cavalrymen they eventually destroyed the rebel armies. Nine years of war had devastated the north, sent waves of refugees into the south, and made a shambles of local administration.

Several important consequences followed from the An Lu-shan rebellion. One was that regional military commanders appointed in many interior provinces to deal with the emergency refused either to disband their armies or to surrender their offices. Some regional commands became hereditary in the families of the original incumbents. Similarly, garrison commanders at the prefectural level became too well entrenched to be removed. Another consequence was that the central government was compelled to recognize that the *chun-t'ien* system and the corresponding tax and services systems could not possibly be restored. Henceforth, the principal form of tax was to be the "double tax," so called because it was levied in two annual installments. The significant feature of the new tax was that it was based on a land survey that determined the amount of land actually in the possession of each tax-paying household. This also meant that the long-standing legal restrictions on purchase and sale of land were now removed and land was freely marketable. In practice, the independent provincial authorities were left to develop their own revenue systems so long as they forwarded acceptable amounts to the central government. Third, the decentralization of political authority and rivalry among governors resulted in a reversal of state commercial policies; trade was now freed from the original controls, allowed to expand, and was tapped for revenue by means of a wide variety of commercial taxes. Even in the case of the highly profitable state salt monopoly, private merchants were admitted to an active role in the trade and allowed a generous share in the profits. Finally, the reorganization of local and provincial government during and after the rebellion had the effect of opening up government service to more commoners and petty aristocrats than ever before. The imperial government had some success in recovering the power of appointment and removal of governors and prefectural officials in the independent provinces and in gaining control of tax collection, especially in the more cooperative southern provinces, but this limited recovery was achieved at the cost of accepting and adjusting to changed social and political realities.

The balance between central and provincial power remained precarious during the century after the An Lu-shan rebellion, and when the empire was torn by a rebellion led by Huang Ch'ao a new generation of regional commanders, mostly professional soldiers of plebian origin, reasserted its independence. When Chu Ch'uan-chun usurped the T'ang throne, his ambition to reunify the empire under his rule was frustrated by the creation of rival states by his fellow regional commanders in the southern provinces. When imperial reunification was achieved by the Sung annexation of the last southern state in 978 and the last northern state the following year, it represented the triumph of the military and civil organization and the pragmatic politics of the regional commanders. It was not, therefore, a T'ang restoration in any significant sense, but a new regime generated by the class of plebian provincial militarists who had contributed to the destruction of the aristocratic empire.

Despite the devastation wrought by rebellions and wars, the entire period from mid-seventh century to the Mongol conquest in the thirteenth century was one of rapid economic growth and technological advance. The extent to which this was so is suggested by the fact that the Chinese population increased during those five hundred years from about 53 million to about 100 million. Commercialization was a leading factor in social change. Gradually during late T'ang and Sung, trade broke out of the pattern of government regulation. The inner walls that had divided the cities into cellular structures were broken through or knocked down. Merchants and artisans circulated freely and kept their own hours. K'aifeng in the Sung, probably the largest commercial center in the world at that time, never slept. Markets and street vendors did business at all hours of day and night. Networks of markets formed around the great cities, and some markets that had begun as periodic fairs in open fields became permanent markets, and eventually towns.

Agriculture in late T'ang and Sung proved highly responsive to the stimuli of commercialization and urbanization. If there had not been a great increase in the output of agricultural products, neither the overall population increase nor the growth of cities could have occurred. Greater output was achieved only partly by expanding the acreage under cultivation. Increased per-acre yields were probably more important. Southern agriculture was transformed by the introduction of fast-ripening and drought-resistant varieties of rice from Southeast Asia. This made it possible for two or three crops to be harvested annually in the same fields. Millet, wheat, and barley, all of which had already been intercropped in the north, were now grown on southern hillsides not suited to irrigated rice cultivation. These advances were supported by the steady improvement of agricultural equipment and of techniques of planting, cultivation, and manuring. By the adoption of new seeds and techniques, landowners were able to take advantage of the opportunities for profit in the great urban markets. Agricultural production for urban markets was refined in Sung to such an extent that whole counties specialized in cash products such as citrus fruits, tea, or silk and had to import food grains. Nonagricultural technology was equally affected by the growth of trade. Double locks were installed in canals, which enabled barges to be floated from one level to another instead of having to be hauled up or down ramps. The combination of abundant supplies of cultivated hemp fibers and an expanding market for textiles inspired advances in spinning machinery. The iron and steel industry, already impressive in scale in Sui and T'ang, attained heights not to be reached again until the nineteenth or twentieth century. Iron was produced in such abundance that it was used to make iron-chain suspension bridges and as a building material in pagodas. Large amounts of iron and steel were also consumed by the armaments industry for weapons and armor.

China's commercialization in late T'ang and Sung also could not have occurred at least in the same degree without a great expansion in the supply of money and credit. In the absence of a good monetary system, marketing would have become difficult. Shortages of copper cash in the Nanking area became acute as early as the Six Dynasties period. The T'ang dynasty currency included copper cash and gold and silver in ingot form. The new form of taxation in late T'ang increased the proportion of money relative to commodities in revenue collection, which exacerbated the currency shortage just at a time when trade was expanding. The need for a new medium of exchange was met to some degree by the use of "flying cash." Great quantities of tea grown in the south were consumed in the capital area.

7.4 Anonymous Sung dynasty painting of a market village. The ease of water communications in south China contributed to the expansion of trade in that region and the formation of a pattern of local and regional markets. Courtesy: Editions D'Art Albert Skira, from James Cahill, *Chinese Painting,* Geneva, 1960.

A tea merchant in Ch'angan who wished to remit money to a supplier in the south took the money to the capital branch office maintained by the province to which it was to be sent. Officials there would receive the money and issue a voucher guaranteeing payment of the same amount in the province. This made it unnecessary for the merchant to risk the shipment of cash, and it also provided the provincial administration with an efficient means of remitting taxes. In the Sung another medium of exchange became available when protobanks, or deposit shops, issued bank notes of standard denomination against metallic currency deposited with them. The notes were redeemable at the shop. This service was taken up and monopolized by the government, and the first true paper currency system had been established. Unfortunately, when the government was hard pressed by rising military expenses, it resorted to inflationary overissue of the currency.

Progressive commercialization and urbanization and the growth in population created a new social and cultural situation in China in place of the aristocratic order of masters and their clients, serfs, and slaves and of personal obligations of free peasants with respect to taxation and service. A more "rational," profit-oriented society was integrated economically in the expanded marketing system, tenant-landlord relations tended toward conflict over economic advantage, and taxation was based on impersonal calculations of land and other quantifiable standards. Financial experts in imperial service made advances in economic theory and systematically collected and analyzed economic data. In a distinct but related sphere, mathematics, especially algebra, developed to its highest premodern level of sophistication. Learning was disseminated by greatly increased production of printed books. Competitive recruitment of the civil service and the objective measurement of merit were hallmarks of Sung government. Voluntary associations of tradesmen and merchants cut across the familiar boundaries of family and neighborhood. While it seems certain that this "modernization" of society was uneven, being most advanced in the most urbanized areas, and that even there it could hardly have gone as far as it did in the twentieth century, the change was highly significant, and it was noticed by contemporary observers and critics. At least from early Sung times the decline of the extended family, or clan, was deplored, and several leading reformers undertook to promote a revival of clan property, ancestral cult, and social solidarity.

The character of Sung government was shaped by the altered social context. At the summit of power, the emperor in Sung times was not *primus inter pares,* leader of a stable group of illustrious aristocratic families with their own bases of regional power as in early T'ang, but rather an autocrat able to make policy decisions very much on his own. This was no less true for the fact that the emperors ordinarily consulted and even deferred to their chosen advisers, because the advisers could easily be dismissed and replaced at the emperor's pleasure. The formation of a large class of highly educated, well-to-do families, especially in the south, provided a large pool of bureaucratic talent. This was effectively exploited by the expanded and refined systems of personnel recruitment and control. The commercialization and monetization of the economy and the relative depersonalization of the urban society encouraged the achievement of unprecedented centralization and thoroughness of financial administration. Finally, the great wealth and productivity of the Sung economy presented the state with relatively large and easily tapped sources of revenue, thus adding to the independence of the state in formulating and pursuing its goals. The prime illustration of this may be found in the reform program of the eleventh century statesman Wang An-shih. Wang won the support of the emperor and was allowed to make some important administrative innovations. He established a powerful policymaking body, the Finance Planning Commission, and reformed the civil-service examinations to make them more immediately practical and less literary in content. In view of heavy losses suffered in fighting against the Hsi Hsia and the immense cost of maintaining the swollen and inefficient professional army, he reinstituted a militia system inspired by the T'ang precedent. His economic measures generally struck at the vested interests of commercial and official groups. A new land survey was undertaken to end tax evasion by the wealthy, and wealthy families were also taxed to provide funds for the costs of subbureaucratic local administrative functions that had become a burden on the poor. In order to prevent profiteering by large-scale wholesale and warehousing companies, he set up government offices to provide competitive services. Similarly, the practice of usury was undercut by the provision of government loans at less than current rates. This and other features of the program aroused opposition from those adversely affected by them, and ultimately much of his work was undone, but his reforms were nonetheless an impressive demonstration of the economic power that the Sung government was able to exercise when it chose.

The Neo-Confucian Renaissance

In the sphere of philosophy and ideology, the late-T'ang and Sung periods were characterized by the declining interest in Buddhism among the intellectuals, a corresponding revival of interest in Chinese pre-Buddhist thought and, in Sung, the neo-Confucian reinterpretation of the classical canon in the light of philosophical issues and concepts that had been introduced with Buddhism. In the wake of the An Lu-shan rebellion there was a period of vigorous and creative intellectual activity directed toward the identification of the causes of the current crisis and the search for solutions. The spirit was remarkably eclectic, with debate polarizing around Confucian and Legalist principles. At one extreme were ideological fundamentalists who called for a literal reestablishment of the idealized institutions of the Chou dynasty. At the other extreme were rigorous Legalists who rejected the models of antiquity in favor of powerful measures of rationalization and political centralization. Advocates of these positions were not necessarily anti-Buddhist; indeed, some were masters of Mahayana metaphysics. The return to pre-Buddhist sources of Chinese political tradition, however, was indicative of the decline of literati Buddhism in the eighth century. An early enemy of Buddhism in T'ang, Han Yü (768-824), launched what proved to be a somewhat premature campaign to purge China of the contagion of Buddhist doctrine and practice. An undercurrent of xenophobia, which was present in his anti-Buddhist writings, was more apparent in the ninth century, when it contributed to the great assault on the monasteries in 845. Hostility towards foreigners and things foreign fed on the antagonism aroused by Turkish and Tibetan invasions, the treachery of the semibarbarian An Lu-shan, and the presence of rich foreign merchants reaping great profits under the protection of arrogant Uigur militarists. Furthermore, eastern and southern literati who increasingly filled provincial and central government offices were offended by the alien style and manners of the northern aristocratic families, who were often at least partly of non-Chinese descent and had long associated with foreign militarists. Under the circumstances, it was only too easy to believe that all might yet be well with the empire if it could return to its own ancient principles.

The revival of Confucian studies suffered from a lack of originality in interpretation, for the most part, until the Sung, when neo-Confucian *li-hsueh,* "study of principles," was formulated. The *li-hsueh* in the field of formal philosophy, which was to become the official ideology of the Chinese empire from the thirteenth century to the twentieth, was mainly the work of classical scholars of the eleventh and twelfth centuries. The culminating and authoritative formulation of *li-hsueh* was embodied in the classical commentaries of Chu Hsi (1130-1200). The main points to be noted for our present purposes are these: first, *li-hsueh* preserved the classical goals of a harmonious, hierarchical society, personal self-perfection in social ethics, and the aesthetic ideal embodied in the traditional Chinese music, ceremonial, and dress; second, it anchored these values in an integrated system of metaphysics and cosmology of such persuasive elegance as to make it a successful rival of Buddhist thought; and third, it provided a powerful ideological justification for conservatism in the society and politics by arguing for the basis of the classical norms in eternal, absolute principles. By applying Buddhist metaphysical subtlety to the reinterpretation of classical texts, the neo-Confucians of Sung cut the ground from under their Buddhist rivals. About the only field on which the literati Buddhists were not strongly challenged at this time was in the subitist, or meditative, route to enlightenment. Ch'an (in Japanese, Zen) Buddhism continued for two or three centuries to enjoy a large following among literati who were beguiled by direct, intuitive means of apprehending truth. Although the beginnings of a subitist (sudden enlightenment), intuitional form of neo-Confucianism can be found in Sung times, this beginning did not come to maturity until the popularization of the school of Wang Yang-ming (1472-1528).

To the landowning literati, whether in or out of public office, the *li-hsueh* would prove in the long run to be as reassuring as Wang An-shih's dynamic bureaucratism was upsetting. The metaphysical foundation of the *li-hsueh* was the *li-ch'i* dualism. All observable phenomena in the universe were to be correctly understood in terms of matter *(ch'i)* and principle *(li)*. For example, both carts and boats might be constructed of wood and both were employed in transportation, but their principles were different in that one traveled by land and the other by water. Moreover, *li,* or "principles," were eternal, as the principle of the boat was logically, if not temporally, prior to any material embodiment of the principle in an actual boat. The conservative implications of Chu's system become apparent when one considers that fact that not only material things were so constituted, but roles and relationships as well. As certainly as there was a principle of the chair, or boat, so was there a principle of man and a principle of the state. Since the principles governing social relationships, like principles generally, were rational principles, that is, were accessible to the universal human faculty of reason, one could discover them by the exercise of the rational faculty on the data provided by observation. The sages of antiquity, who had formulated the classical social norms, had done just this. Consequently, the *li-hsueh* barred the door to radical innovation and left only the possibility, or rather the obligation, for each, by study, observation, and reflection, to discover the unchanging principles for himself. The hierarchical ordering of society, with its unequal distribution of responsibilities and rewards, was justified by the argument that although all men were formed of *ch'i,* or "material," in conformity with an identical human principle, their material embodiment was not uniform in the content of impurities. The more impure, the murkier, the material endowment, the more obscured and obstructed was the ideal form, the human principle, embedded in it. Thus, all men shared a common humanity in their identical ideal constitution, or principle, but they were unequal in that in their understanding and in their actions they were not equally perfect. It followed then that some were more fit to rule, others to be ruled.

The metaphysical dualism of the *li-hsueh* had been anticipated in the discovery (by the sophists, such as Kung-sun Lung of late Chou) of universals, that is, of qualities (such as whiteness or hardness) that could be conceptually separated from the objects to which they were attributed. But this line of thought was not pursued and became a dead end in the growth of Chinese philosophy. This distinction between abstract principles and their material embodiment was reintroduced in the Later Han or the Six Dynasties period by the translation of Buddhist philosophical literature, whence it found its way into the neo-Confucianism of the Sung. *Li-hsueh* also owed a debt to Taoist cosmologists of the Six Dynasties and T'ang who had continued to try to map out the stages and processes by which the universe was formed and kept in being. As refined by Chu Hsi, material in its essential form is differentiated by the operation of the principles of motion and rest into the active and passive forces of Yin and Yang. These, in turn, interact to give rise to more differentiated forms, the five material forces of earth, wood, metal, fire, and water. These, in their turn, interact, under the control of the more specific principles, to produce all possible phenomena. Lastly, we may turn to a final, and important, Buddhist contribution to the *li-hsueh:* its mystical aspect, in which there appears to be a transcendental concept of enlightenment in Confucian disguise. Quite apart from all the specific principles, such as those that we have so far referred to, there was one supreme principle, *t'ai chi,* or "the supreme ultimate." The supreme ultimate was the master principle according to which the entire universe was formed. Chu held that this master principle was immanent in all phenomena, along with the principles specific to each. To explain the seeming paradox of this distribution of the indivisible principle, he used the simile of the ubiquitous moon on a clear night, repeated by reflection on the surface of every lake and pond. In view of the presence of this treasure within every being, the reward for the purification of one's material embodiment through painstaking study and self-discipline was not just the full realization of one's perfect human principle, but the joyous discovery of the principle of the entire universe—enlightenment of an order that stood comparison with the *nirvana* of the Buddhist seekers after salvation.

During the period of the development of neo-Confucianism, the mainstream of Chinese intellectual life shifted from the great monasteries into the growing numbers of Confucian academies where the curriculum was based mainly on historical and classical Confucian literature. By the time of Wang An-shih, issues of state policy were debated in Confucian terms, and although the influence of Legalist concepts might be discerned, they were not openly avowed. While Buddhism was officially tolerated (and regulated), the suggestion of Ou-yang Hsiu (1007-1072) may have been fairly typical: the people should be won away from the alien faith by the thoroughgoing reformation of Chinese society on Confucian principles. If this were done, they would have no difficulty in seeing the superiority of the indigenous values.

The Growth of Chinese Maritime Trade

The growth of maritime trade to Southeast, South, and West Asia kept pace with the economic development of the eastern and southern Chinese coasts. During the T'ang, most of the sea trade to the south and west was in non-Chinese hands. Colonies of Malayans, Indians, Persians, and Arabs were established in the foreign quarters of Canton. Although the foreigners were largely independent in their internal affairs, their trade was subject to a superintendency of merchant shipping. Hainan Island may also have become a commercial base for Persians and Arabs, preferred by them because it was less effectively controlled than the mainland port. Canton was devastated in 758 by a raid by Arabs and Persians probably based in Hainan. The port recovered its former prosperity only to be destroyed in 879 by the army of Huang Ch'ao, and the foreign colony was wiped out. When Sung T'ai-tsu occupied Canton in 971, he established a new superintendency there. From this beginning, Sung policy was unprecedentedly favorable to maritime trade. New ports were opened in modern Fukien and Chekiang provinces. Local authorities improved port facilities by dredging silted channels and building warehouses. Foreign merchants were wined and dined and Chinese merchants were given bonuses for generating trade that yielded specified amounts of government revenue.

The booming coastal ports were linked to the expanding system of waterways and markets in the interior. Chinese merchants increasingly engaged in overseas operations to such an extent that they relegated the foreigners to a minor role in the Chinese ports. The surge of Chinese maritime enterprise that sent Chinese ships and sailors into the ports of Southeast and South Asia was made possible in part by the superiority of Chinese shipbuilding and ocean navigation in the Sung. Oceangoing Chinese junks were of immense size, capable of accommodating a thousand persons in some instances. For safety, they were provided with watertight compartments. The design of sails and rigging permitted the junks to sail closer to the wind than competing foreign vessels. Control of the ships was facilitated by the sternpost rudder. Navigation was revolutionized by the Chinese invention of the mariner's compass, and Chinese cartography produced the best nautical charts of the time. As maritime trade grew, piracy also prospered. This and the need for coastal defense against the Chin state led to the organization of naval forces, including prefectural coastal defense bases and an imperial navy. To the advantages of size and sailing qualities, the Chinese vessels added an array of gunpowder weapons to set fire to enemy vessels.

The maritime orientation of the Sung, apparent from the beginning, was intensified by the transfer of the imperial capital to Hangchow in 1127. For the first time the empire was ruled from a city served by oceangoing ships. Since Sung trade across the northern frontiers now took the unprofitable form of annual deliveries of tribute goods to Chin and Hsi Hsia and uncontrolled contraband trade in salt and other monopoly goods, sea trade was actively promoted to compensate for the disruption of overland trade. Maritime commercial taxes rose to an impressive five percent of imperial revenues in the twelfth century.

Steppe-Sown Interaction on the Northern Frontiers

The terms and the consequences of the interaction of Chinese and the steppe peoples in Sung presented some differences from the circumstances of early T'ang, despite the obvious similarities. There was still the basic contrast between the pastoral nomadism of the Inner Asian grasslands and the agricultural and town life of the Chinese within the Great Wall. The zone of interaction in which these ways of life were mixed was relatively narrow in comparison with the West Asian frontiers. The Tibetan, Turkish, Mongol, and Tungusic pastoralists still required grain and textiles and other goods that they obtained by trade and war. But in T'ang, most of the Chinese population lived in the north and was dominated politically by a mixed Sino-foreign aristocracy. As long as the T'ang central government was intact and strong, the aristocrats of the frontiers could more easily be accommodated as allies. Moreover, the diffusion of effective political power among the T'ang aristocracy gave the regime great resiliency in the face of foreign invasions or domestic upheavals.

In the Sung, the aspect of the northern frontier had significantly changed. The center of wealth and population within the Chinese empire had shifted southward toward the Yangze valley, far from the northern frontier. In place of the aristocratic empire of T'ang, the Sung represented a highly centralized autocracy managed by a professional bureaucracy. Buddhism among the official class had yielded to a neo-Confucian renaissance. Concentration of defense policy on the northern frontier was weakened by the new interest in the maritime region.

In some respects these changes were strategically advantageous to the Sung. The economic development of the south, together with a more efficient and centralized administration, enabled the imperial government to invest immense sums in arms, provisions, and pay for the land and naval forces. Military technology advanced rapidly, with gunpowder being used in explosive projectiles thrown by catapults, small rockets, and probably, before the Yuan conquest, the first cannon. Iron plates were used in the construction of armored wagons. The technological advantage was all too easily nullified, however. Once they had conquered frontier areas populated by Chinese and provided with developed mines and workshops, the Khitan and Jurchen lost no time in providing themselves with equipment of comparable quality. Moreover, centralization and bureaucratization may have contributed to the military might of the Sung empire, but it may also have made it easier for invaders to establish their control of an occupied area. The relatively impersonal administrative machinery was made to work for the conquerors.

Finally, the decline of Buddhism relative to the indigenous tradition in China could only widen the cultural gap between the literati officials and the leaders of the pastoral peoples. Where once the Chinese aristocracy had adopted some aspects of their style, values, and religion, and so met them part way, the vigorous revival of indigenous traditions in China made such accommodation more difficult to achieve. While it was the case that leading members of the Khitan and Jurchen regimes adopted Chinese culture to some degree, they did so in the course of taking over and operating for their own benefit some part of the Chinese state. It was perhaps for such reasons as these that the Chinese empire, for all its wealth, efficiency, and technological sophistication, was unable to prevent the loss of the north to foreign rule.

5. REGIONAL FRAGMENTATION IN JAPAN

In the late eleventh century the central imperial regime created in Japan on the model of T'ang China entered a period of sharp political decline. The shift of the economic center of the society away from the Heian (Kyoto) area to the Kanto plain on what had been the northeast frontier, and the growth of the military power of the provincial warrior groups finally destroyed the dominant position of the Heian court nobility. This shift in political and economic power was accompanied by highly significant changes in the religious, artistic, and social life of both the elite and the general populace during the Kamakura (1185-1333) and Ashikaga (1333-1573) periods. These changes eventually resulted in a new cultural synthesis in which many of the forms from the classical Heian period were to survive only in altered form patterned by the influence of new elements. The broader significance of these developments for the history of Asian civilizations as a whole lies in the fact that they represent the fragmentation of the sphere of East Asian civilization formerly unified under Chinese domination. True, the Japanese islands—unlike parts of Southeast Asia and Korea—had never been an integral part of a Chinese empire, but the absence of political hegemony did not belie the reality of Chinese cultural dominance during the early development of civilization in Japan. Now, in the medieval period, civilization in Japan was to develop much more autonomously, albeit with occasional new stimuli from the continent. The term fragmentation describes also the main political process at work within Japan itself during these centuries—the steady erosion of central authority and the devolution of power to the provincial and local levels.

The Breakdown of Heian Authority

One of the most important developments in the late Heian period was the opening up of the Kanto plain to intensive cultivation. Once wet-rice cultivation in this northeastern region—the largest and richest single bloc of arable land in the Japanese islands—became fully developed, it tended to overshadow the area around the old capital. Neither the Chinese-style imperial bureaucracy nor the system of administration developed by such private families as the Fujiwara was able to gain effective control over this key area, and their failure to do so contributed greatly to the decline of the central aristocracy. But the failure to gain control over the Kanto region was only one part of a more general loss of control over land and labor suffered by the old Heian court elite. The organs of bureaucratic government steadily atrophied from lack of any real function as the amount of land and labor subject to imperial taxation and legal jurisdiction shrank. Throughout the Heian period the prominent aristocratic families and the Buddhist monasteries they patronized had ursurped power and wealth in the form of private estates that were immune from government taxes or bureaucratic intervention. Since the owners of these landed estates resided for the most part in the capital, management was delegated to branch families or local nobility. So long as the court aristocrats possessed sufficient prestige and the potential force to maintain a hold on their land stewards and managers, revenue continued to flow into the court and it mattered little whether it came as government taxes or as aristocratic rents. By the eleventh century, however, the hold of the Fujiwara and other aristocratic elite at Heian had slipped disastrously. No longer were they providing the means of ensuring law and order in the prov-

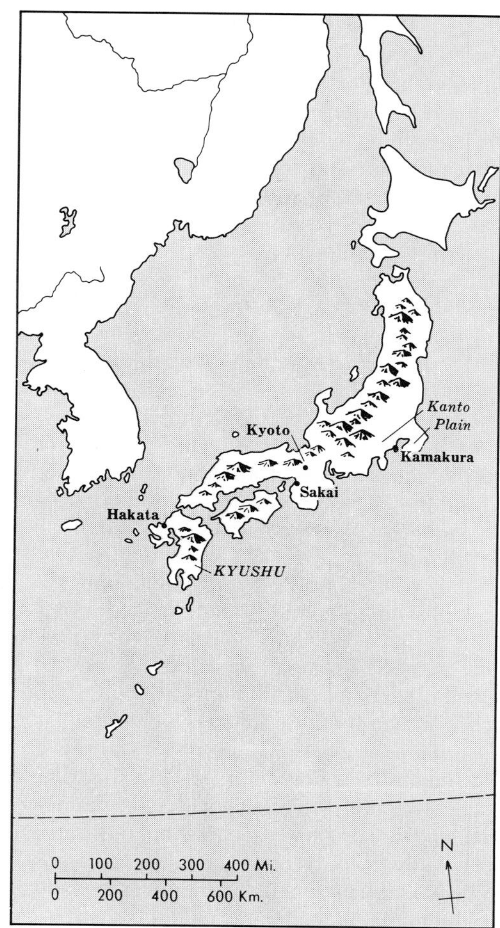

Map 32 Japan during the Kamakura (1185-1333) and Ashikaga (1333-1573)

inces, as central military potential dwindled to insignificance. Moreover, the elitism and arrogance of the great court families apparently blinded them to the gradual enervation in the court culture that was undermining their prestige outside the sphere of the imperial city. Increasingly, real economic power passed into the hands of those in the provinces who actually oversaw the operations of collecting the produce from the cultivator and storing, shipping, and exchanging it on behalf of the aristocratic owner. With the decline of the means to enforce order, the protection of these estates fell to a new class of armed men whose loyalties were eventually transferred to leading members of the provincial elite.

The breakdown of order and authority in the tenth and eleventh centuries led to a fierce competition for power which spread from the outlying provinces into the area of the capital itself. Disputes over land, political position, and other such interests were increasingly settled only after resort to arms. The Nara and Heian Buddhist monasteries themselves organized corps of armed monks or retained the services of laity skilled in violence. In 968, for example, the priests of the Todaiji and the Kokufuji, two of the largest temples in Nara, took up arms in a dispute over possession of some rice land. A dozen years later, the imperial selection of a new abbot for the Enryakuji monastery on Mount Hiei precipitated an incident that culminated in the burning of one of the temples in an attempt to murder the candidate. The Enryakuji, one of the wealthiest and most powerful of the Heian establishments, was frequently involved in this type of struggle during the tenth and eleventh centuries, struggles that sometimes reached the level of pitched battles. In 1081 a dispute between the Enryakuji and a nearby monastery led to an encounter in which it is recorded that the Enryakuji forces set the torch to thousands of buildings belonging to the rival monastery and the surrounding town. Peace was restored only when some three thousand secular warriors were called in from the provinces.

Armed conflict on a large scale was common in the provinces from the beginning of the tenth century; the attempts during the Nara and Heian periods to create an armed force under the control of the central government had proven a complete failure. Social control, like other governmental functions in the country at large, increasingly passed into the hands of the leaders of extended networks of mounted military men organized along quasi-feudal lines. The two most successful of these networks, which were held together by a combination of family ties, shared territorial interests, and bonds of personal loyalty, were the Taira and the Minamoto. Both were involved in numerous and sometimes prolonged conflicts with each other and with other similar groups during the tenth and eleventh centuries. By 1160 the Taira succeeded in taking control of the capital city and the remnants of central government. Perhaps because they did mistake control of the court city for effective control of the country, the Taira were soon unseated by the Minamoto. The Minamoto sensed rightly that real power lay in maintaining a hold on the provinces themselves and therefore established an administration located in the northeastern plain at the town of Kamakura.

The Kamakura shogunate (1185-1333), as it is called, formalized a new pattern of political authority in Japan. In choosing the title of shogun, or generalissimo, the Minamoto symbolized their attachment to the ghost of the old Heian imperial regime, for the title of shogun had a long tradition as chief military agent of the throne. Far from attempting to usurp the throne itself, the Minamoto drew on the remaining prestige of the imperial house to legitimize a dominant position that ultimately, however, depended on their military successes and the allegiance given them by the new provincial elite. There were thus created two originally separate but now interwoven hierarchies—the new feudal order built on relationships of vassalage to the Minamoto lord in return for confirmation of the *de facto* power of the provincial warrior over the land and cultivators, and the remaining shell of the old imperial bureaucracy and the system of private aristocratic estates that had evolved in the Heian period. Until the late thirteenth century the Kamakura shogunate maintained a delicate balance by appointing its supporters to offices and titles within the older system. Eventually, however, this compromise failed to satisfy the more powerful of the military lords, who steadily consolidated their direct control over their regions and began to withdraw their allegiance to the titular overlord in Kamakura. The overthrow of the Kamakura leaders by the Ashikaga and the removal of the shogunate back to the city of Kyoto in the early fourteenth century did little to remedy the situation. Rivalry between the provincial lords became increasingly heated and the Ashikaga shoguns proved unable to put together an alliance stable and strong enough militarily to assert even the limited central authority that the Kamakura shogunate had enjoyed. Japan was by the mid-fifteenth century entering an extended period of political fragmentation in which even those provincial lords who had previously maintained order over relatively large regions now exhausted themselves in bloody civil wars, and authority came to be equated with whatever small plain or series of valleys that a mounted warrior and his allies could defend against neighboring bands.

As a type, the provincial military noble who seized power from the court aristocracy in the Kamakura period is strongly reminiscent of the *uji* elite who dominated political life in the period before the borrowing of Chinese political forms. Thus, the Kamakura and early Ashikaga periods have sometimes been thought of as the rejection of the Chinese bureaucratic model. Certainly, familial authority—power legitimized by patterning it after the model of the extended kinship ties—was of very great importance in the bonds that held

7.5 This section from a late thirteenth century scroll painting depicts one of the many market fairs held at regular intervals in the Japanese countryside where economic activity was stimulated by the decline of the Heian system of aristocratic estates and trade with the Asian mainland. Courtesy: Tokyo National Museum, from George B. Sansom, *A History of Japan, 1334-1615*.

together the political system in the Kamakura and early Ashikaga. This pattern of familial authority also had much to do with the routinized charisma of the imperial house. Emperors might be manipulated with considerable cynicism by the Kamakura and Ashikaga shoguns and by the late fifteenth century were reduced to a poverty so severe that they were dependent upon handouts from competing warlords. Yet, the sanctity of the imperial lineage prevented the throne from either disappearing or being usurped. On the other hand, the concept of a centralized bureaucratic government that had been adopted under Chinese stimulus was not entirely lost. The survival of the imperial throne was at least in part due directly to the memory of the former grandeur of the old Heian government and the throne was to remain a symbol of a past unity, a time when there had existed a stable order with a clear hierarchy of authority, a ghost of an imperial order that was a latent ideal in the minds of some even in the period of extreme political fragmentation following the mid-fifteenth century. In practice, the Kamakura shogunate can be seen as a synthesis of the bureaucratic style with that of the provincial warrior. Although the Minamoto had established it by force of arms, they exercised authority by means of a hierarchically ordered series of bureaus and offices operating within a system of rules and precedents that owed a considerable debt to the concepts of bureaucracy and law introduced originally from China. During the early Ashikaga period, this synthesis of familial authority and bureaucracy began to lose its dominant place within the political culture of Japan as a more clearly feudal pattern emerged. Yet, it was to reemerge in the Tokugawa period (1600-1867).

Religious Developments following the Decline of the Heian Court

Concomitant with the political and economic decline of the Heian aristocracy was the decline of the Heian Buddhist establishment. The Buddhist clergy in the capital, too often preoccupied with the competition for temporal power amidst the intrigues of court, became mired in metaphysical obscurantism and an ossified orthodoxy. The more creative religious responses to these troubled times took place outside the more prestigeful monasteries and tended to be sharply critical of them. Thus the history of Buddhism from the late Heian through the Kamakura and early Ashikaga periods also reflects the dramatic changes that were taking place in Japanese culture. Whereas Buddhism had penetrated the life of the general populace only very slowly following its adoption by the Heian elite, from the end of the twelfth century it became a mass movement, eventually merging with the folk beliefs and practices of the preexisting agrarian religion, Shinto, to form a new religious synthesis.

The most important sects in carrying Buddhism to the people, sects that were to remain the dominate forms of Buddhism down into the modern era, were the Jōdō, or "Pure Land," sect of Hōnen (1133-1212), the Shin, or "True," sect of Shinran (1173-1262), and the Hokke, or "Lotus," sect of Nichiren (1221-82). These three evangelistic preachers, although often in bitter rivalry with each other, personified a number of characteristics common to this popular form of Buddhism. First, they shared a disdain for the Buddhist establishment of the Heian court and its elitist approach to religion. Both Hōnen and Shinran were Amidists, but unlike the teachers of Amidism in the late Heian period, they broke with the powerful monasteries of the capital region, which they perceived as hopelessly entangled in a sterile orthodoxy. They therefore established separate sects that carried the message to the commoner, preaching to whomever would listen in a language comprehensible to all. The message was one of salvation by faith—faith in the divine grace of Amida, Lord of the Western Paradise, through which even the lowly could be saved. Shinran, the more radical of the two, broke with Hōnen over the theological issue of whether the frequent repetitions of calling upon Amida were in effect an accumulation of merit through good works. Shinran took the position that this type of self-help was beyond man, and therefore sincere devotion—in the extreme case, a single calling upon Amida for mercy as a declaration of faith—was the only path to salvation. Nichiren, as much as he scorned his Amidist rivals, shared with them both the hostility toward the metaphysical obscurantism of the older clergy and this second theme, the stress on faith to the exclusion of other paths to enlightenment. For Nichiren, however, it was faith not in Amida but in the efficacy of the Lotus Sutra. The careers of Shinran and Nichiren illustrate the fervor of their commitment to preaching to the masses. Breaking with the older monastic forms, Shinran denied the sharp distinction between clergy and laity and renounced celibacy in favor of marriage. For this heresy he was banished from the capital. He accepted exile in a distant province, where he lived among the common people. Nichiren was constantly in disfavor with the Kamakura authorities for his attacks on those who "do not smite the offender . . . [and] acquiesce in the propagation of a false faith. Woe unto them! It can lead nowhere but to the lowest Hell." At one point Nichiren was actually sentenced to death for such evangelistic preaching, which included predictions that Japan would be punished by foreign invasion for its godless ways. When, in 1274 and again in 1281, Mongol fleets launched abortive invasions on the coast of Kyushu, Nichiren was vindicated.

These forms of Buddhism were also to have impact among members of the provincial warrior class, for whom the more complex doctrines and elitism of the Heian establishment held little appeal. Thus, in religious matters as in others, the new dominant class was closer to the peasantry than the old court aristocracy had been. On the other hand, the leaders of this military class in the Kamakura and Ashikaga periods did become patrons of a new elite cultural style that was in some facets to become as far removed from ordinary life as that of their predecessors. Here the primary religious stimulus derived from yet another new Buddhist sect, that of Zen. The central tenet of Zen was its stress on meditation and intuitive understanding to the exclusion of other paths to enlightenment. Meditation had long been a part of the teachings of Japanese Buddhism, as in the case of the Amidist doctrine of faith, but it was not until the turn of the thirteenth century that Zen began its independent growth as a separate sect in Japan. Again, as with the Amidists, the early Zen teachers attacked the abstract theology, ritual pomp, and aristocratic preoccupations of the Heian clergy. The priest Eisei (1141-1215), who founded the first Japanese Zen sect, had initially chosen to live in Kyushu, while Dogen (1200-53), a disciple who later split with his master over the question of whether enlightenment could be achieved without long experiences in the technique of meditation, traveled to China itself for fresh inspiration. Zen beliefs and practices were to have particular appeal to the military class. For the tough, semiliterate swordsman who typified the early Kamakura period, as well as for the lower echelons of warrior society throughout the middle period in Japan, Zen offered a simple message of solace in the face of death and the need for rigorous mental discipline. For the upper echelons, who acquired a taste for the artistic as well as material symbols of their new status, the Zen quest for the true essence behind the illusion and impermanence of this world inspired new styles in literature, drama, and painting.

Much of what today is thought to be distinctive in Japanese traditional culture had its origins in the society of the military elite of the Kamakura and Ashikaga period. It was the ethic of this warrior class, with its insistence upon honor, valor, and loyalty, that was to dominate much of the thinking about human morality in later periods. This ethic was clearly reflected in the new literary forms, the military romances, that chronicled the careers of proud, courageous leaders whose perserverance brought them victory and of faithful retainers who sacrificed their lives rather than accept shameful defeat or fail in their obligations to their lord. The heroes of such romances bore little resemblance to the ideal courtier of the Heian period, and women were relegated to lesser roles as their status declined in a society preoccupied with martial virtues. Nevertheless, the aesthetic sensitivity of the preceding age was not entirely lost. It was particularly apparent in the new drama form, the *noh,* favored by the Ashikaga shoguns who had moved their political base back to the capital in the fourteenth century. A mixture of dance, mime, music, and lyrical recitation, the *noh* combined a sense of grace and elegance derived from the older court culture with plots and themes closer to the interests of a military elite, the whole infused with the spirit of Zen teachings. Zen Buddhism was also an important element in other new artistic forms that typify the culture of the Ashikaga elite: for example, formal gardens, the tea ceremony, and flower arranging.

Thus, as with the synthesis of Chinese political concepts and patterns of familial authority deriving from the pre-Chinese periods, and as with the synthesis of court Buddhism with the religious urges of the mass populace, the overall style of Japanese civilization in the middle period was an intricate and subtle mix of disparate elements. As a whole, it was a cultural synthesis that remained remarkably viable despite the political anarchy of the late fifteenth and sixteenth centuries.

Maritime Trade

Zen monks had yet another role in the early Ashikaga period. Leading monks served as advisers on foreign relations with China, and the large monasteries built with the patronage of the Kamakura and Ashikaga elite became involved in the commercial trade with the Asian continent. The upsurge of maritime trade that characterized this era in other parts of Asia did not have as strong an influence on Japan, situated on the extreme eastern periphery, as elsewhere, but there were important economic consequences for Japanese society. Toward the end of the twelfth century there was a resurgence of demand for Chinese products and contacts with China increased. Sung porcelains, silk brocades, art objects, and other goods, including books, swelled the volume of trade. In turn, this stimulated Japanese handicraft production in order to meet export demand for swords, fans, lacquer ware, and folding screens. The Japanese economy was still primitive compared to that of its more affluent neighbor and much of its exports consisted of raw materials such as timber, mercury, or gold. Yet the level of domestic economic activity was such that foreign trade was an important stimulus and internal commerce grew steadily. One indication of growth was the increasingly large amounts of minted coins imported from China in the twelfth and thirteenth centuries to serve the need for a standard medium of exchange within Japan. This combination of foreign and domestic factors fostered the emergence of hundreds of small towns situated along improved routes of communications and transportation. The urban inhabitants of Kyoto, Nara, and Kamakura—the only areas that had warranted the label of city—were joined by Japanese living in these small towns and involved in the shipping, storing, and financing coastal and overland trade. By the late fifteenth century, some of the port towns, in particular Hakata (in Kyushu) and Sakai (today part of Osaka), were to become important urban centers.

Despite Japan's isolation, it is possible to speak of an increased cosmopolitanism stimulated by this increased contact with China. Zen monks, in addition to their financial and diplomatic roles, also served as transmitters and interpreters of Chinese developments in the intellectual and artistic spheres. Thus, Japan maintained limited communication with the wider world. Equally important from the point of view of the history of Japanese society, the cultural gap between the culture of the capital and that of the outlying regions of the country was steadily closed. The new cultural synthesis of the Kamakura and Ashikaga periods was not the monopoly of a small elite at the apex of society, as it had tended to be during the Heian period. Economic growth, improved communications, and a more fluid political situation meant that both horizontal and vertical mobility increased over these centuries and cultural participation became more diffuse, thus actually reducing the differences between the subcultures of local regions. The society was undergoing a transformation of great significance for later Japanese history.

CONCLUDING REMARKS

This chapter has dealt with the phenomenon of political disintegration, of breakdown in unity, as another in a series of crises that periodically threatened the stability of the several Asian civilizations. Once again the historian is challenged to explain how integrated political empires such as the T'ang in China and the Abbasids in West Asia lost their capacity to cope with centrifugal forces and fragmented into smaller governing units. What are the processes that undermine centralized political institutions not only in the large empires but even in the smaller, more homogeneous states such as Heian Japan? How do ruling houses lose control over bureaucratic mechanisms for maintaining the status quo? How do aristocratic groups come to challenge central power and under what conditions does the central military establishment become a force for instability rather than stability? This military aspect is of special interest here because the breakdown of internal unity was accompanied by new incursions across the frontiers separating the agricultural civilizations from the peoples of the Central Asian steppe. Turkish peoples established separate regimes in West and South Asia, while other former nomads gained political control in large areas of northern China. Later this would culminate in the great Mongol invasions described in the following chapter.

In this era, however, there are parallel questions regarding the breakdown of established Buddhist, Islamic, and Hindu religious institutions that had been so significant in the maintenance of cultural unity in these universal empires. At times, as in Islamic West Asia, this can be seen in terms of divisions within a universal religion. In South Asia it clearly involved the interjection or superimposition of one religion, Islam, into the world of another, Hinduism. In China, the ruling elites (as distinct from the common people) gradually turned away from Mahayana Buddhism in favor of a newly revitalized form of Confucian ideology. This neo-Confucianism, with its debt to Buddhist philosophy, can be seen as one example of the cultural renaissances that were taking place despite or perhaps because of political disunity, since such cultural developments often entailed considerable synthesizing of old and new or of foreign and indigenous elements into innovative syncretic patterns. These processes of synthesis are even more evident in those areas of Southeast and Northeast Asia where civilizations had originated under the direct stimuli of South Asian or Chinese models. Vietnam, Korea, and Japan are three examples of such areas asserting their cultural independence and creating new political, social, and artistic styles through synthesis.

The attention of the social and economic historian is especially directed toward the development of more extensive maritime contact throughout coastal Asia during this period. What effects did this commercial activity have on social structure and economic value? Since this network of sea routes and ports was to serve later in the modern era as the framework for European expansion, it can be asked in comparative perspective why this maritime activity was ultimately to prove a far greater stimulus to change in European than in Asian societies.

BIBLIOGRAPHY

7.P REGIONAL FRAGMENTATION OF CIVILIZATIONS: PROCESSES

Ganshof, F. L., *Feudalism* (Harper Torchbook paperback, 1961), 170 pp. A short overview of medieval European feudalism which is sufficiently analytical to permit comparison with similar phenomena in Asia.

Hall, John W., "Feudalism in Japan—A Reassessment," *Comparative Studies in Society and History* 4.1:15-51 (October, 1962). A careful analysis of stages in Japanese feudalism with a good introductory section on the problems of comparison.

Lattimore, Owen, *Inner Asian Frontiers of China* (Beacon Press paperback, 1962), 585 pp. Wide-ranging and provocative essays on steppe-sown interaction in Chinese history.

Von Grunebaum, Gustave E., *Medieval Islam, A Study in Cultural Orientation* (University of Chicago Press paperback, 1969), 378 pp. Deals with Islam during a period when both the Islamic and Christian culture zones were facing the stresses of regional fragmentation.

7.1 REGIONAL FRAGMENTATION IN WEST ASIA

Arberry, Arthur J., *Sufism: An Account of the Mystics of Islam* (Harper Torchbook paperback, 1970), 135 pp. A good introduction by an acknowledged authority in the field of Islamic mysticism.

Bulliet, Richard W., *The Patricians of Nishapur: A Study in Medieval Islamic Social History* (Cambridge, Mass., 1972), pp. 3-81. A brilliant interpretation of the distribution of elite status and influence in a medieval Iranian city.

Frye, Richard N., *Bukhara: The Medieval Achievement* (Norman, Oklahoma, 1965), 195 pp. A most readable account of the Samanid period and of social life in tenth century Bukhara. Strongly recommended.

Lewis, Bernard, *The Assassins: A Radical Sect in Islam* (New York, 1968), 140 pp. A lucid discussion of one of the most important Shii sects.

Rice, Tamara T., *The Seljuks in Asia Minor* (New York, 1961), 187 pp. A popular account of life in Seljuk Anatolia, with the emphasis on the arts, illustrated and with a useful bibliography.

Spuler, Bertold, "The Disintegration of the Caliphate in the East," *The Cambridge History of Islam,* 2 vols. (Cambridge, 1970), Vol. 1, pp. 143-60. A succinct overview of a confused period.

7.2 REGIONAL FRAGMENTATION IN SOUTH ASIA

Ahmad, Aziz, *Studies in Islamic Culture in the Indian Environment* (Oxford, 1964), pp. 3-21 and 119-66. Scholarly essays on Indo-Islamic civilization, stressing the religious factor, Sufism and Hindu-Muslim acculturation. Strongly recommended.

de Bary, William Theodore, ed., *Sources of Indian Tradition,* 2 vols. (Columbia University Press paperback, 1970), Vol. 1, pp. 362-520. A useful selection of readings on Indo-Islamic civilization, including some dating from the Mughul period.

Gibb, Hamilton A. R., trans., *The Travels of Ibn Battuta,* A.D. *1325-1354,* 3 vols. (Cambridge, 1958-1971), Vol. 2 (1971), pp. 593-767. An invaluable description of life in the fourteenth century sultanate of Delhi, seen through the eyes of an observant Moroccan traveler.

Hardy, Peter, *Historians of Medieval India* (London, 1960), 131 pp. A unique attempt to probe the facade of Indo-Islamic civilization by asking penetrating questions about the motives and methods of the chroniclers whose works constitute the basic sources for this period.

Ikram, Sheikh Mohamad, *Muslim Civilization in India* (New York, 1964), pp. 3-132. The best general account.

Mujeeb, Mohammad, *The Indian Muslims* (London, 1967), pp. 9-235. A leisurely narrative by a scholar of great learning and perception. Strongly recommended for the advanced student.

7.3 REGIONAL FRAGMENTATION IN SOUTHEAST ASIA

Cady, John F., *Southeast Asia: Its Historical Development* (New York, 1964), 657 pp. Chapters 1-8, pp. 1-169, provide a solid introduction to the period covered in this section.

Coedes, Georges, *The Making of South East Asia* (Berkeley, 1969), 268 pp. Most of this study by a leading French scholar pertains to the period covered in this section. Especially authoritative on the cultural history of the mainland portions of the region.

Fitzgerald, C. P., *The Southern Expansion of the Chinese People* (New York, 1972), 230 pp. Chapters 1-4, 78 pp., provide an account of the shifting Chinese frontier with Southeast Asia.

Hall, D. G. E., *A History of Southeast Asia* (New York, 1970), 1019 pp. The first 12 chapters, 234 pp., survey the early history of the region in considerable depth and incorporate recent scholarship.

Pym, Christopher, *The Ancient Civilization of Angkor* (New York, 1968), 224 pp. A readable study of the society and culture of the Khmer empire.

Vlekke, Bernard H. M., *Nusantara: A History of the East Indian Archipelago* (Cambridge, 1945), 439 pp. The first 4 chapters (90 pp.) present a concise history of Indonesia before the Portuguese domination.

7.4 REGIONAL FRAGMENTATION IN CHINA

Birch, Cyril, ed., *Anthology of Chinese Literature*, 2 vols. (New York, 1965, 1972). Translation of all genres of T'ang and Sung literature may be found in Volume 1.

de Bary, William Theodore, ed., *Sources of Chinese Tradition* (Columbia University Press paperback, 1960), 976 pp. Chapters 18 through 21 provide readings in neo-Confucianism through the Sung.

Fairbank, John K., Edwin O. Reischauer, and Albert M. Craig, *East Asia: Tradition and Transformation* (Boston, 1973), 969 pp. Chapter 6 surveys the late T'ang and Sung.

Fung Yu-lan, *A Short History of Chinese Philosophy* (Macmillan paperback, 1960), 368 pp. Chapters 23-25 present Chinese intellectual history during the Confucian revival.

Gernet, Jacques, *Daily Life in China on the Eve of the Mongol Invasion* (Stanford University Press paperback, 1962), 254 pp. A richly detailed presentation of thirteenth century Chinese culture and society.

Meskill, John, ed., *Wang An-shih: Practical Reformer?* (Heath paperback, 1963), 99 pp. Selections of translations and periodical literature on the eleventh century statesman.

7.5 REGIONAL FRAGMENTATION IN JAPAN

Duus, Peter, *Feudalism in Japan* (Knopf paperback, 1969), 116 pp. A very readable introductory survey with good bibliography comparing and contrasting feudalism in Japan and Europe.

Hall, John W., *Government and Local Power in Japan, 500-1700* (Princeton, Princeton University Press, 1966), 446 pp. A very detailed analysis of the changing bases of political power with special attention to the problems of comparative feudalism.

Kitagawa, Joseph M., *Religion in Japanese History* (New York, 1966), 475 pp. Chapter 3 treats the emergence of popular Buddhism in the Kamakura and Ashikaga periods.

Sansom, George B., *A History of Japan, 1334-1615* (Stanford University Press paperback, 1961), 462 pp. Still a standard history of medieval Japan.

Varley, H. Paul, *Japanese Culture: A Short History* (Praeger paperback, 1973), 227 pp. Chapters 4 and 5 give a general account of literary and artistic developments by a specialist in medieval Japanese history.

Varley, H. Paul, *et al.*, *Samurai* (Dell paperback, 1970), 135 pp. A lively but reliable treatment of the origins, life-style, and historical role of the warrior class.

GLOSSARY

Amir. Generally, a military commander or governor; occasionally a sovereign title, as in the case of the amir of Bukhara.

An Lu-shan. The T'ang frontier general of Turkish and Iranian descent whose rebellion in 755 shattered the imperial administrative system in north China and inaugurated a period of militarism and regionalism in imperial politics.

An-nan. Corresponding to northern Vietnam, An-nan (or Annam) was the T'ang protectorate-general in the far south of the empire. The fragmentation of the T'ang empire allowed Vietnamese separatist tendencies to culminate in the establishment of a Vietnamese state in 939. The Vietnamese maintained their independence from that time until the French conquest in the nineteenth century.

Ashikaga. A family of military aristocrats who seized power in Japan from the Kamakura shoguns and gave their name to the period 1333-1573 (the early half of the period is also known as the Muromachi, while the years between 1467 and 1573 are also called the Sengoku).

Atabeg (literally, "father commander"). The title held by a military commander who also acted as tutor and mentor to a Seljuk prince exercising titular authority as a provincial governor.

Caliph (Arabic, **khalifa**). Originating with the title of the Prophet Muhammad's successor, Abu Bakr, Khalifat Rasul Allah, "Successor of the Messenger of God." The caliph was the head of the Islamic *umma,* "the community of believers," and was referred to as *amir al-muminin,* "commander of the faithful."

Chao K'uang-yin. The military leader who overthrew the Chou state, last of the Five Dynasties, and founded the Sung dynasty in 960. He proceeded to bring most of China under his unified rule, but was unable to reestablish the outer frontiers of early T'ang times.

Chu Hsi (1130-1200). Building on the work of earlier neo-Confucians, he redeveloped a comprehensive new ideology, *li-hsueh,* or "study of principles," which drew on Buddhist and Taoist as well as Confucian inspiration. Chu Hsi's philosophy in the fourteenth century became the official imperial ideology for the training and qualification of civil officials.

Dais. Missionaries sent by the Fatimid caliphs of Egypt to spread Ismaili Shiism throughout West Asia, especially during the eleventh century.

Dar al-Islam. "The abode of Islam." that is, those regions under the sovereignty of a Muslim ruler and where the Sharia was enforced.

Daylam. Mountainous region south and southwest of the Caspian Sea consisting of the present-day provinces of Gilan and part of Mazandaran; the homeland of the Daylami tribes. The Buyid dynasty, which ruled western Iran during the tenth and eleventh centuries, was Daylami.

Deccan. The great tableland of central India. The Narbada River was traditionally regarded as constituting the dividing line between northern India and the Deccan plateau.

Dihqan. Originally, a member of the lesser nobility in Sasanid Iran. The *dihqans* remained the principal landholding class down to the eleventh century but their status as a class deteriorated after the Seljuk conquest of the Iranian plateau.

Fars. The homeland of the Achaemenid and Sasanid dynasties; a province in southwestern Iran, with its present capital at Shiraz.

Firdawsi (d. 1020). Iranian poet, author of the *Shah-nama,* or *Book of Kings,* the national epic of Iran. The *Shah-nama* preserved the memory of the pre-Islamic past of Iran, strengthened the Iranian sense of cultural identity, and helped to establish the primacy of New Persian *(farsi)* over other Iranian dialects.

Fujiwara. A family of Heian court nobles who as regents controlled court politics in Japan from the mid-ninth to the mid-twelfth centuries; hence the late Heian period is often referred to as the Fujiwara period.

Futuwwa. Associations or solidarity groups, generally composed of young Muslim males drawn mainly although not invariably from the poorer elements of the urban population.

Ghazi. A warrior living in the frontier areas of the Muslim world and engaged in holy warfare *(jihad)* against non-Muslims.

Heian (Kyoto). The site of the imperial court from 794 to 1868 and a cultural center throughout this period, although between 1185-1333 and 1600-1868 the political center of Japan was in the Kanto plain region.

Hsi Hsia. A state established among Tibetan and Ural-Altaic pastoralists. Hsi Hsia dominated the western portions of Inner Mongolia from the Ordos to the western end of the Kansu corridor.

Huang Ch'ao. Rebelled against the T'ang in 874. His armies moved rapidly through the richest provinces of the empire, causing immense destruction and loss of life. One of his former followers ended the T'ang and in 907 established the state of Liang, first of the Five Dynasties.

Iqta. The revenue assignment of a certain area, generally granted in exchange for military service.

Jurchen. A Tungusic people of Manchuria, who revolted against their Khitan overlords with Chinese encouragement and established the frontier state of Chin in 1115. The Jurchen state of Chin proceeded to destroy the Khitan Liao state and then expanded its control southward over north China, compelling the Sung dynasty to abandon its capital at Kaifeng and relocate in Hangchow in 1127.

Kamakura. A city on Tokyo Bay in eastern Japan built as the headquarters of the Minamoto shoguns and hence gave its name to the political period from 1185 to 1333.

Kashgaria. The name applied to the region of the Tarim basin in what is now Chinese Sinkiang (formerly Chinese Turkistan), centering on the cities of Kashgar and Yarkand. Bounded on the west by the Pamirs, on the north by the Tien Shan range, on the east by the wastes of the Takla Makan desert, and on the south by the Kun Lun range, Kashgaria was the fulcrum of the caravan routes across Central Asia.

Khanqah. A dervish convent.

Khitan. The great Mongolian tribal federation that founded the frontier state of Liao in 916. The state of Liao included Manchuria, Mongolia, and the Tarim basin as well as a number of strategically important Chinese prefectures in the vicinity of Peking. The state of Liao survived until its conquest by the Jurchen in 1125.

Khurasan. Formerly a vast area extending northeastward from the central Iranian desert to the Amu Darya River, with its metropolitan centers located at Nishapur, Marv, Herat, and Balkh. Today Khurasan consists of a province in northeastern Iran, bordering the U.S.S.R. and Afghanistan and with its capital at Mashhad.

Koryo. Heir to Silla as the ruling state in the Korean peninsula from 936; the Koryo dynasty survived until it was supplanted in a coup of 1392 by the Yi dynasty.

Madhhab. One of the four legal systems or "schools," of orthodox Sunni Islam.

Madrasa. A theological college where the *ulama* were trained in the Islamic "sciences."

Malik. King; in the Muslim East, and especially India, the title was often given to military commanders and provincial governors.

Mamluk. A slave-soldier, generally although not exclusively a Turk, a Georgian, or a Circassian.

Mawarannahr (literally, "that which lies beyond the river"). The Arabic name for the area lying between the Amu Darya and Syr Darya rivers, and including the cities of Samarqand and Bukhara. Known in ancient times as Sogdiana, "the land of the Sogdians," and to the Greeks as Transoxania, "the land beyond the Oxus" (i.e., the Amu Darya), it was generally referred to in the nineteenth century as Russian Turkistan.

Muhtasib. The official in the Islamic city responsible for regulating the markets and for enforcing public morality.

Murshid. A Sufi teacher, also known as a *shaykh* or *pir.*

Nan Chao. The great kingdom established in southwestern China among the T'ai and other non-Chinese peoples in the eighth century. From that time until the Mongol conquest in the thirteenth century, Nan Chao resisted Chinese attempts at conquest.

Nara. Japanese city built as the imperial capital in 710 A.D., which continued as an important Buddhist center after the capital was moved in 784; hence the name of the period 710-784.

Nizam al-Mulk. An honorary title in Persian meaning "regulator of the state." The most famous holder of this title was the *vazir* of the eleventh century Seljuk sultan, Malik-Shah. The Nizams of Hyderabad derive their title from the fact that the eighteenth century founder of the dynasty was given the title Nizam al-Mulk by the Mughul emperor Muhammad Shah.

Pohai. A state founded on the ruins of the kingdom of Koguryo around 700 A.D., Pohai dominated Manchuria and northern Korea from a capital modelled upon T'ang Chang-an. Pohai was absorbed into the Ch'i-t'an Liao state in the tenth century.

Qazi. The Islamic judge who administers the Sharia.

Sannyasi. A Hindu religious ascetic.

Shahanshah (Persian, "king of kings"). The title of the pre-Islamic rulers of Iran and also of the present-day Pahlavi dynasty. Some Islamic dynasties, notably the Buyids, adopted the title to stress continuity with the pre-Islamic past.

Sharia. The Law of Islam, derived from the Quran, the *Hadith,* or *Sayings of the Prophet,* and the analogical interpretations of the jurists.

Shiis. Those who follow the *shia* (or "party") of Ali, Muhammad's son-in-law and the fourth caliph of the Muslims. The Shiis, although subdivided into a number of sects, constitute the largest minority group (as opposed to the Sunni majority) within Islam, and are today chiefly to be found in Iran and Iraq.

Shogun. Originally a title given to the commander of imperial armies in Heian Japan, it came to be adopted in the Kamakura and subsequent periods by the leaders of aristocratic military families to signify their hereditary hegemony (see Kamakura, Ashikaga, and Tokugawa for more on shogunate governments).

Silla. The ancient state in southern Korea, which aided T'ang China in the defeat of the northern state of Koguryo in 668. Silla unified the Korean peninsula under its rule and became independent of the Chinese empire from 675.

Silsila. The chain of authority passed down from one *shaykh* or *murshid* to the next in a Sufi order *(tariqa).*

Srongtsan Gampo. Tibetan king and founder of the monarchy at Lhasa in the seventh century. He married Chinese and Indian wives and invited Buddhist teachers from both countries to his court in an effort to create a regime that would transcend the narrow rivalries of the Tibetans.

Sufi. A dervish or mystic. Hence, Sufism, Islamic mysticism.

Sultan. A ruler, "one who exercises power"; the title adopted by territorial rulers in the Muslim world from the eleventh century onwards.

Sunnis. Those who follow the *sunna,* or practice of the Prophet Muhammad; the majority community in the Islamic world.

Syncretism. The reconciliation or combination of beliefs from different ideological systems. Syncretism led to the formation of new cults when Mahayana Buddhist and indigenous religious beliefs were joined in new combinations.

Tariqa. A Sufi order or brotherhood.

Uji. The elite lineage groups or extended familial networks, sometimes translated as "clans," that dominated Japanese society in the period prior to the emergence of an Imperial state.

Ulama. The Arabic plural of *alim,* meaning a scholar trained in the Islamic "sciences." Collectively, the *ulama* enforced the Sharia and determined the social norms that governed the life of the Muslim community as a whole.

Umma. The Islamic "community of believers."

Vazir. The minister of a Muslim ruler. In fact, a ruler might appoint concurrently two or more *vazirs* to have charge over different areas of administration but the term is usually applied in the sense of a chief minister, as with the Ottoman "grand vizier."

Yogi. A Hindu religious ascetic.

Eurasian Integration under Central Asian Dominance

1100 to 1500 A.D.

Interaction between civilized and pastoral-nomadic societies has been a recurrent theme in the history of civilizations in Asia. This process was important for the initial political organization of civilized societies, for the formation of universal empires, and for the diffusion of the universal religions. The present chapter concerns the climactic event in this historical relationship: the formation of the Eurasian empire of the Mongols in the thirteenth and fourteenth centuries.

Early in the thirteenth century, Chingiz Khan unified most of the steppe nomads and conquered the urban trading centers of Inner Asia. Drawing upon this population of herders and townsmen, he organized a powerful state that served as a foundation for the even greater empire carved out by his heirs. All of the major civilizations at this time were in a state of political fragmentation and were vulnerable to attack from across their frontiers. The Mongols were able to gain control over frontier regions of several civilized societies simultaneously and, by utilizing the resources obtained thereby, continued their expansion until whole civilizations were brought under their rule.

In order to bind their immense empire together, the khaqans (supreme khans) relied in part upon the skills, experience, and learning of the mercantile and religious communities that were spread throughout Eurasia, but the empire's political and administrative unity eventually gave way under pressure from the centrifugal forces that were generated in the regional khanates. The khaqans who ruled China and the subordinate khans who ruled Central Asia, West Asia, and Russia were preoccupied with the management of their own great states and with their mutual rivalries. Moreover, the unity of the pastoral-nomadic political core of the empire was eroded as the Mongol and Turkish conquering elites gradually adopted the urban life-style and culture of the conquered peoples. This opened a breach between them and their ethnic cousins who continued to live as herdsmen in the steppes. In the course of the fourteenth and fifteenth centuries the empire gave way to a revival of imperial polities in the conquered areas: the early modern empires. The collapse of the Mongol empires however, did not bring about the restoration of preconquest conditions. The conquering Mongols and those chieftains, like Timur, who sought to emulate them caused such extensive devastation and depopulation over once prosperous regions that recovery in some areas took centuries. On the other hand, the exchange of administrators and artisans among different regions of the empire and the improvement of overland communications led to an acceleration of cultural diffusion within Eurasia. Finally, the new, post-Mongol empires inherited something of the expanded vision of world dominion and imperial despotism that motivated the original Mongol expansion.

8

PROCESSES

Formation of a Eurasian Community of Civilizations

a. Trade
b. Religious community

Formation of Hybrid Barbarian-Civilized Empires

c. Differential adaptation: steppe and sown
d. War and trade: barbarian-civilized frontiers and symbiosis
e. Adaptation of political institutions by nomadic societies
f. Steppe imperialism
g. Mixed feudal-bureaucratic polities

Reassertion of Indigenous Political Control in the Civilizations

h. Transformation of transplanted steppe societies

PATTERNS

1. **Formation of the Mongol Empire in Central Asia**
2. **The Mongol Empire in West Asia**
3. **Mongol Domination in East Asia**
4. **West Asia under Timur**

8. MONGOL DOMINATION

	1	2	3	4
	FORMATION OF MONGOLS	WEST ASIA	EAST ASIA	TIMUR
1100	Formation of Mongol federation ca. 1125			
	Defeat of Mongols by Tatars ca. 1160 Birth of Chingiz 1167		Southern Sung, capital at Hangchow	
1200	Election of Chingiz 1206			
	Khanate of Ögedei 1229-41 Conquest of Chin 1234	Chingiz Khan attacks Khwarazmshah's empire; Bukhara and Samarqand sacked 1220 Death of Chingiz Khan 1227 Death of Chaghatay Khan 1241 Death of Batu Khan of the Golden Horde, 1255 Hülegü destroys Ismaili fortresses in north Iran 1257; sacks Baghdad 1258 Hülegü, first Il-khan of Iran, d. 1265	Conquest of Chin 1234 Subjugation of Korea 1241 Conquest of Nanchao 1253 Khanate of Kubilai 1260-94 Yuan dynasty 1271-1368 Conquest of Southern Sung 1279 Second invasion of Japan 1281	
1300		Ghazan Il-khan of Iran 1295-1304 Öljeitü Il-khan of Iran 1304-17 Rashid al-Din, Il-Khanid *vazir* and historian, d. 1318 Özbeg Khan of the Golden Horde 1313-40	Civil service exams 1315	Timur 1336-1405

Date				
			White Lotus Society Rebellion 1351-68 Founding of Ming dynasty 1368	
1400			Ming campaigns into Mongolia, sea voyages to Africa	Timur invades Khurasan, takes Herat 1380; captures Baghdad 1393; sacks Delhi 1398; defeats Ottoman sultan at Battle of Ankara 1402 Shah-Rukh 1407-47 Ottoman sultan Mehmed II takes Constantinople 1453 Özbeg chieftain Abul Khayr d. 1468, Özbegs and Kazakhs separate
		Khan of the Crimea becomes an Ottoman tributary 1475		Shaykh Ismail head of Safaviya order 1488
1500				Özbegs under Muhammad Shaybani take Samarqand 1500, Herat 1507 Safavid Shah Ismail kills Muhammad Shaybani 1510
		Russian conquest of Kazan 1552 Russian conquest of Astrakhan 1554		
1600				

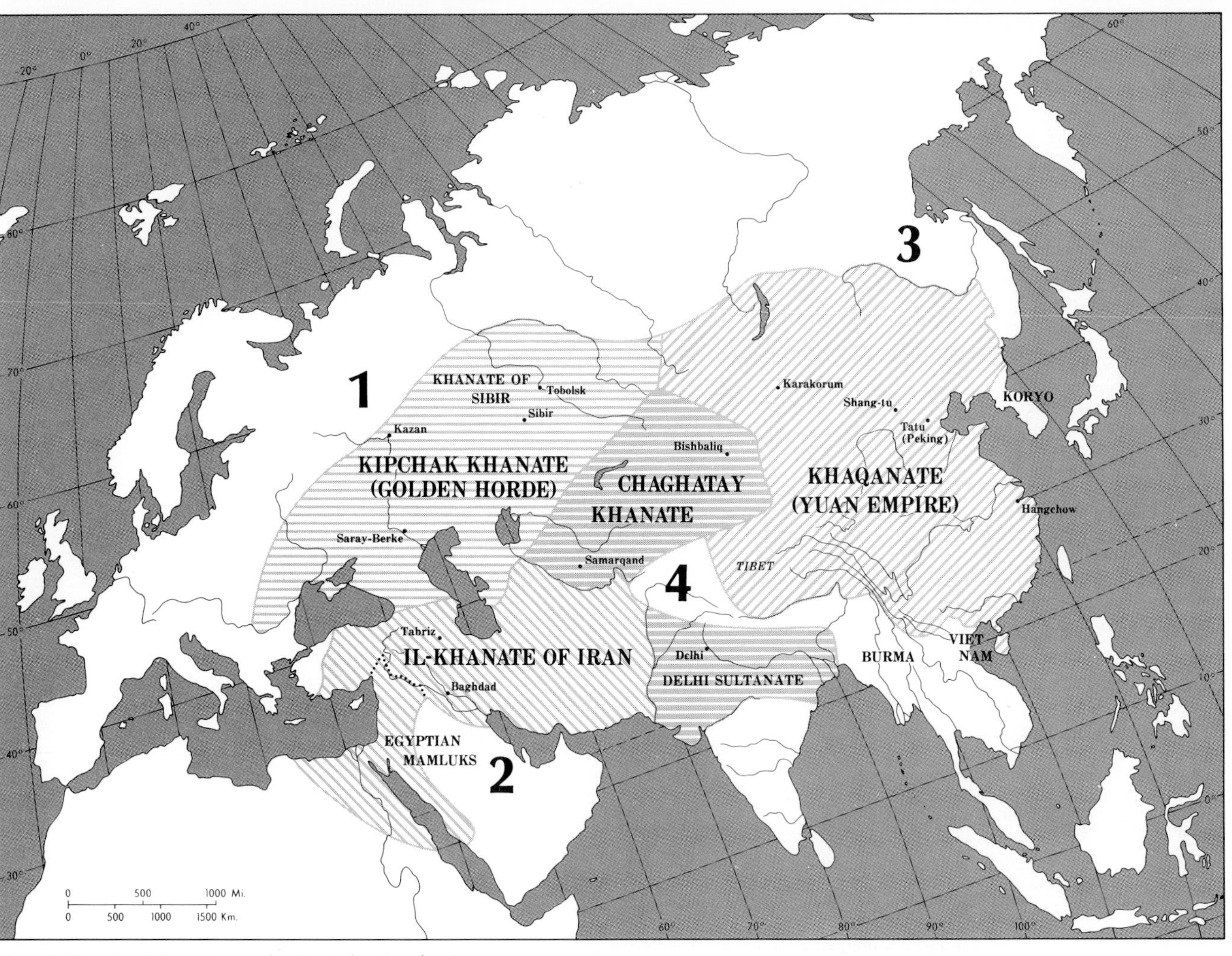

Map 33 Eurasian integration under Central Asian dominance

PROCESSES

In the thirteenth century most of the Eurasian continent was brought under the rule of the Mongol empire. All the civilized societies and their Inner Asian oasis outposts had been continously involved in interaction with pastoral-nomadic peoples of the steppes. Frontier states had been formed as a result of the conquest of agricultural and town-dwelling people by the nomads and, at times, the civilized societies, by war and diplomacy, had brought large areas of the steppe under their political control. Moreover, for about two millennia and perhaps longer than that, the peoples of the steppe, despite their differences in language and ethnic background, developed a fairly uniform culture from one end of the Eurasian steppe to the other. This resulted from a number of factors, including similar adaptations to analogous environmental conditions and relationships with the civilized societies; large-scale and long-term migrations usually leading westward from Mongolia; and the incorporation of different combinations of pastoral peoples in tribes and tribal federations, which resulted in close cooperation and mutual adaptation among the groups involved. The formation of the immense Mongol empire marked the culmination of the processes of steppe-sown interaction and the political integration of pastoral-nomadic peoples. For the first time, the steppe peoples under unified command simultaneously brought the sedentary societies of West Asia, Eastern Europe, and East Asia under their rule. The Mongol conquests resulted in the devastation of many cities, the ruin of vast areas of agricultural land, and enormous loss of life. On the other hand, under their unified rule communications across the continent were easier than ever before, trade flourished, and with the exchange of populations among all civilized societies from Western Europe to the Pacific and Southeast Asia, cultural diffusion among civilizations occurred at an unprecedented rate.

THE PERIOD

This chapter will focus on the formation of the Mongol empire under Chingiz Khan and its expansion to include the greater part of the Eurasian continent, from the Pacific coast to the Mediterranean, between ca. 1100 and ca. 1500. Consideration will also be given to the breakup of the Mongol empire and the formation of the spectacular, but short-lived, empire of Timur (Tamerlane), who tried to revive the universal empire of the Mongols.

The ephemeral political integration of Eurasia under the Mongols was preceded by several developments tending towards a community of civilizations. The spread of the universal religions had created a measure of cultural and religious community that survived regional fragmentation within and among the civilizations. Overland and maritime trade generated mobile, cosmopolitan, commercial classes able to forge economic and, later, political links among the civilizations. Our own era of global politics was prefigured by the early attempts at high-level political cooperation, as between crusading Europe and the imperialist Mongols. The Mongol era was followed by that of the early modern empires, the subject of the following chapter. The Ottoman and Safavid empires in West Asia, the Mughuls in South Asia, Ming China, and Tokugawa Japan all were in some degree products of the disintegration of the Mongol empire and institutionally and culturally influenced by it. One might add Czarist Russia to the list, if this study were not limited to non-European Eurasia.

The processes will be discussed in three main categories: first, the formation of a community of civilizations under the aspects of economy, culture, and politics; second, the formation of hybrid barbarian-civilized empires, in which we shall reexamine and enlarge upon processes of military and political interaction that have frequently been noted before; third, the processes associated with the breakup of the Mongol empire.

FORMATION OF A EURASIAN COMMUNITY OF CIVILIZATIONS

a. Trade

In the case of trade involving people of several different civilizations, all obtain goods that would otherwise be scarce or nonexistent in their own regions. They are to this extent enriched in their material culture. It should be borne in mind, however, that this gain was usually enjoyed in this period by relatively restricted classes of people; the high cost of land, and even sea, transport limited goods in trade to those having a high ratio of value to weight and these were of necessity what we might today call luxury goods. Cultural consequences of such trade might include the adoption by a participating civilization of new forms of production as a means of lowering the costs of goods once available only by trade. The adoption of silk cultivation in Syria in the sixth century A.D., for example, broke the East Asian monopoly. Moreover, trade in exotic goods did, however vaguely, communicate an awareness to the users of their place of origin, as reflected in the fact that at first Bactrian middlemen, and later the Chinese, were long known in the West as Seres, or "The Silk People." Of even greater importance is the fact that trade generated merchant classes, and these merchants, as dealers in luxury goods, were naturally in association with the wealthy and powerful in the several societies in question. By their wide-ranging contacts and by their skills—including organization, record keeping, economic calculation, knowledge of geography—they were well suited to the service of empire builders, who had a particular interest in being freed of the necessity of having to recruit administrators from the populations they had conquered.

b. Religious Community

The breakdown of the universal states involved a disintegration of the value systems associated with them. The resulting crisis of the civilizations was met, initially, by the adoption of popular religions of salvation that had often originated in regions foreign to those adopting them. The effect of this development was to bring enormous numbers of people into direct, or more often indirect or mediated, contact with the religious doctrines, institutions, ceremonials, iconography, and aesthetic traditions of other civilizations than their own. Thus, Mecca, an obscure Arabian town, became the object of religious awe for tens of millions of non-Arab Muslims. Benares, in India, likewise became a source and center of doctrinal authority for tens of millions of non-Indian Buddhists. Moreover, the spread of the universal religions, like the growth of Eurasian trade, contributed to the formation of a Eurasian community of civilizations as it gave rise to cosmopolitan classes of monks or religious scholars who were devoted to the study, translation, and interpretation of foreign religious literature. Despite the fragmentation of Asian civilizations prior to the Mongol conquest, shared religious beliefs and practices persisted across political boundaries.

FORMATION OF HYBRID BARBARIAN-CIVILIZED EMPIRES

c. Differential Adaptation: Steppe and Sown

During the first millennium B.C., peoples inhabiting the drier and more humid regions of Asia gradually diverged in their economic and social organization until in some regions of low rainfall they were fully committed to nomadic stock raising, while in the areas having enough rainfall or surface water to sustain a highly productive agriculture, the inhabitants became specialized as farmers. In each case the nomadic or farming people had arrived at their form of culture as an efficient adaptation to their geographic setting. Certain cultural and social consequences followed from this basic divergence in the form of food production. The herders of cattle, sheep, and horses were compelled to move about in order to exploit the natural range grass. Moreover, dependence on the natural grasses required a variable, but relatively low, limit on the size of herds. This, in turn, imposed a correspondingly low limit on the size of the human communities dependent on the herds. These two factors—enforced mobility and small scale of social organization—limited the possible degree of occupational and status differentiation in steppe society. In terms of material culture, therefore, steppe society was necessarily a "poor" society. The civilized societies based on agriculture were characterized, as we have seen, by extensive urbanization and by a proliferation of technological skills.

d. War and Trade: Barbarian-Civilized Frontiers and Symbiosis

The vast difference between civilized and steppe economies greatly affected the character of the relationship of civilized and steppe peoples. The herders were chronically short of certain necessary products as well as most luxury goods. They might obtain what they needed or wanted in either of two ways: by trade or by war. In the former case, they did have goods to barter for the grain, tea, textiles, and other goods of the civilized peoples: they had horses, which were usually prized as cavalry mounts, and they had cattle, hides, wool, felt, furs, and sometimes gold, which they mined or panned in the Inner Asian mountains. Thus, there was an economic basis for a symbiotic, mutually complementary relationship across the steppe-sown frontiers, and bartering went on continually to give effect to this relationship. However, peaceful trading relationships were often interrupted and replaced by armed raids. By and large, the civilized parties to the frontier trade had the advantage. Their populations were large, they usually were supported by powerful state organizations, they were served by professional traders and, in general, they had less need of steppe products than the steppe people had need of the farmers' grain. It often happened, therefore, that the herdsmen felt, and perhaps with reason, that they were being exploited economically. When this happened, or when soldiers of the civilized armies raided their camps to steal their horses and other livestock, the herdsmen would organize on a sufficient scale to raid the towns and villages, carrying off what they could otherwise obtain only at great cost by trade. Armed conflict, consequently, was a common alternative means of effecting the necessary exchanges between societies of the two basic types.

e. Adaptation of Political Institutions by Nomadic Societies

The differences between agrarian and nomadic societies was such as to limit the possible extent of mutual cultural influence (in contrast with the relations among civilized societies), but such influence as did occur was nevertheless of great importance. On the one hand, we will find that when steppe peoples did form large political systems, these usually arose in areas of cultural interpenetration with a civilized society. The very possibility of empire, to say nothing of the skills required for its implementation, was suggested by the examples provided by the universal states. Writing systems, law codes, standardized hierarchies of political authority all bore the imprint of civilization. Conversely, the civilized societies were profoundly influenced by the necessity of coping by a variety of means—economic, political, military, ceremonial, and ideological—with the fact of persisting and generally unstable or dangerous barbarian frontiers. Thus, a felt need for frontier defense was met by the construction of fortifications and the conscription or hiring of armies. Societies on both sides of the steppe-sown frontiers were to a degree militarized and politicized by their mutual economic and cultural anatagonisms.

From time to time, at least from the first millennium B.C., large segments of the steppe society were mobilized for war. War in the steppes was endemic on a small scale, with raiding parties (perhaps no larger than a family) seizing livestock, women, hostages, or other valuables. Family pride and ambition often led to long-continuing feuds among rival groups. For large-scale organization to occur, certain conditions had to be satisfied. One, clearly, was charismatic leadership—the emergence of a warrior of such skill and determination that other fighting men sought a place in his service. Another was the presence near at hand of opportunities for great material gain from large-scale military action. When the political and military organization of one or another of the civilized states began to disintegrate from internal causes, this condition was met. A third was the presence within the emerging steppe polity of men possessed of the needed knowledge and skill to assist in its organization and administration. The condition was most often met when the tribe or tribal federation was formed in a region near an agrarian society and when the leaders themselves were men of the frontier with some knowledge of both kinds of society. Legitimation of political authority in the steppes was often tied to recognition in some form on the part of the nearby civilized state. Intermarriage with a civilized ruling family or investiture with a title tended to bolster the prestige of leading clans and give them an inheritable aristocratic status vis-à-vis other steppe clans. Leadership of tribes or of federations of tribes usually came from such clans.

f. Steppe Imperialism

The transition from clan organization to a group of clans politically organized in a tribe under a common leader and, finally, a federation of tribes united under a steppe emperor (or *khan,* in Turkish and Mongolian) was always difficult and, once achieved, hard to sustain. Given good leadership and good fortune in battle against enemies well provided with treasure, a great organization of steppe peoples might last long enough to have an enormous impact on neighboring societies. One factor contributing to the formation of empires in the steppe was the fact that steppe society seems to have been remarkably uniform in its forms and values. Languages and physical appearances might be various, but the way of life, the social mores, and the personal and public ethics were relatively homogenous. At least among the Altaic peoples (Mongols, Turks, and Tungus), there was also a common religious foundation in the worship of a supreme sky god and in the widespread practices of shamans, persons who had the power of communication with the spirits. Shamans were typically an important element in the structure of steppe polities.

g. Mixed Feudal-Bureaucratic Polities

States of this type arose as the result of either domination of some part of steppe society by a civilized empire or the incorporation of some part of a civilized society within a conquering steppe empire. In either case this involved the incorporation of different economies, societies, value systems, and political structures within a single political system. In the former case, steppe leaders would be organized by law and ceremonial into a hierarchy or hierarchies of rank, lines of responsibility would be defined, and the whole structure would be placed under the control of an appropriate office or administrative agency in the distant imperial capital.

In the latter case, which is of greater interest in the present context, a state that originated among steppe peoples and came into possession of a population of conquered farmers and townsmen was faced with the choice of simply obliterating the subject society—destroying the towns and turning the farms into pastures for its cattle—or, as was often the case with more enduring conquests, minimizing the disruption of the conquered society and economy while maintaining political and military dominance over them in order to profit from this wealth through tax or tribute. The result again was a hybrid polity, with the conquerors retaining more or less of their own laws, customs, military values, etc., and with the subjugated people continuing to be governed by their laws, institutions, and procedures. Commonly, such mixed polities assumed a more or less feudal character. Usually before the achievement of major conquests, the steppe peoples would have passed over from a mere federation of tribes to an essentially feudal form of political organization, in which the tribal population would be broken up, organized into a hierarchy of military communities, with each of these, at least on the level of the higher units, being parcelled out to the command of noblemen who were personally loyal to the khan. Each of the communities, with its fighting men, its women, children, livestock, tents, and other goods, constituted a fief, and the rule of that fief was ordinarily hereditary in the family of the original officer, although it might be terminated for bad behavior. Thus it was that when the steppe regime imposed its rule on a population of farmers, it was itself often feudally organized. The defeated people, who might continue to be subject to the direct rule of their own officials and their bureaucratic institutions, would be for the most part indirectly subject to the domination of the conquering tribal elite, to whom they would be assigned as serfs or slaves.

REASSERTION OF INDIGENOUS POLITICAL CONTROL IN THE CIVILIZATIONS

h. Transformation of Transplanted Steppe Societies

Ordinarily, the empires of barbarian conquest left part of the participating steppe society in the steppes of the Inner Asian homeland, while settling part amongst their new sedentary subjects. Naturally, in the course of time, intense cultural interaction between the defeated people and the much less numerous conquerors led to the partial acculturation of the latter, who might become almost fully assimilated to the literary, agricultural, and commercial circles of their leading subjects. This had the effect of driving a wedge between the two segments of the conquering elite. The poor herdsmen in the steppe came to feel estranged from their citified cousins and their civilized ways. This had the effect of precipitating the formation of new tribal organizations in the steppes, which posed a threat to the conquest states despite their own steppe origins. Moreover, within the conquest states where the conquering military communities settled down among the farmers and townsmen, the aristocrats gradually assumed the life-style and habits of the indigenous landowners, treating their soldiers like serfs and losing their loyalty, a critical factor in the failure of alien elites to keep their conquered subjects under military control.

PATTERNS

1. FORMATION OF THE MONGOL EMPIRE IN CENTRAL ASIA

In 1206, Temuchin (later known as Chingiz) was elected khan of a federation of tribes in the eastern steppes by an assembly of tribal leaders known as a *kuriltai*. In 1279, his grandson, Kubilai, completed the conquest of south China, thereby adding the richest and most populous region to the Mongol empire. Kubilai's imperial authority ran from the Pacific coast of Korea westward across the continent into eastern Poland, and from south China westward across the Tibetan and Iranian plateaus into modern Iraq and Syria. The empire was bounded in the north by the forests of Siberia and in the south by the Persian Gulf and the Gulf of Oman, the Hindu Kush, the Himalayas, and the kingdoms of Burma and Vietnam. Roughly in the form of a great rectangle, the domains of the grand khan measured about eight thousand miles from east to west and nearly two thousand from north to south—or four or five times the land area of the United States. This empire was created and administered at a time when the fastest means of communication was by horse and rider. That it soon broke apart is less surprising than that it could have been created at all.

By the year of his death, 1227, Chingiz had unified Inner Asia, and the conquests of north China, Russia, and Iran were underway or imminent. Three of his four sons survived him. (The eldest, Jochi, had died shortly before his father.) In accordance with Chingiz' will, Batu, son of Jochi, ruled the Kipchak khanate, or Golden Horde, in the West. Chaghatay was khan of the central region including the oasis cities of Khwarazm, Mawarannahr, and

8.1 A Mongol soldier subduing a demon. Warfare, shamans dancing, giants and monsters featured in this style of painting, conveying the hard, lean quality of life on the steppes and the ceaseless struggle against a hostile environment. This scene, from an album in Istanbul, may have been painted in the Chaghatay or Kipchak Khanate, about 1350 to about 1450. Source: M. S. Ipsiroglu, *Painting and Culture of the Mongols* (London, 1967), Plate 3d. Reproduced by permission of Topkapi Saray Museum, Istanbul.

the Tarim basin, as well as the good pasture land of Dzungaria. Tolui, the youngest son, according to Mongol custom, was given the rule over the old homeland south of Lake Baikal. The third son, Ögedei, was khan in western Mongolia and the Altai. A new *kuriltai* in 1229 elevated Ögedei to be khaqan (literally "khan of khans," or "grand khan"). He and his successors in that office were to preside over the lesser khans of the empire. The heirs of Chingiz continued the conquests that he had begun: Batu in Russia, Ögedei in north China, and Hülegü, son of Tolui, in Iran and Mesopotamia. In the east, the momentun of conquest continued on through a third generation with Möngke and Kubilai conquering the rest of China, reducing the king of Korea to vassalage and invading Burma and Vietnam. Kubilai even attempted overseas conquests, fitting out naval expeditions against Japan and the Indonesian empire of Srivijaya.

This vast structure was tenuously held together by respect for Chingiz' will and by a less-than-compelling common interest in the preservation of peace. Succession disputes and rivalry among the several lineages descending from the sons of Chingiz soon began to undermine the empire at the highest level. A shift of the khaqanate from the line of Ögedei to the line of Tolui, Chinghiz' youngest son, in 1251, gave rise to a long and bitter struggle between the house of Tolui and the descendants of Ögedei and Chaghatay. At the same time, the il-khans, who were of the house of Tolui, fought with the Kipchak khans, descendants of Chingiz' eldest son, Jochi, over disputed territory in the Caucasus. To such rivalries were added the conflicts that arose within the several lineages and between the conquerors and their subjects. The il-khanate disintegrated into a number of rival states after 1335 and the khaqanate, internally divided by rival factions, fell victim to a vast Chinese rebellion that began in 1351 and ended with the expulsion of the khaqan, his court, and his armies and the founding of the Chinese Ming dynasty in 1368. The Mongol domination of European Russia was gradually terminated during the fifteenth century, as the Kipchak khanate was fragmented into several states that lacked the strength to stand before the rising power of Moscow. In the center of the Mongol realm, south of the Aral Sea, Timur (Tamerlane) attempted to revive the disintegrating empire by creating a new one on its ruins. Between 1370 and 1405, the year of his death, he unified by conquest the territories of the Chaghatay khanate and the il-khanate and added parts of northern India and the Kipchak khanate. After 1405, plans for the reconquest of the eastern regions of the empire were abandoned. Although leaders claiming descent from Chingiz long continued to appear in Russia, Central Asia, and northern India, the Mongol empire was at an end.

Civilized Societies in Inner Asia

Trade and the universal religions contributed to the development of civilized societies in Inner Asia. Both gave rise to contacts among different peoples and both created communities of interest and of shared values and life-styles among peoples of different cultures. Merchants engaged in trans-Eurasian trade needed conditions of order and security to pursue their vocation, and the Muslim, Buddhist, and Nestorian urban communities maintained ties of sentiment, scholarship, and organization across the great, sparsely inhabited distances that separated the cities of Inner Asia. Merchant caravans moved slowly across the continent from Iraq, Syria, or the Black Sea region eastward into China and on to the Pacific. Most of the journey was through arid regions of grassland or desert punctuated by oases and the cities that were built in them. The full journey in one direction took about one year, which gave the travelers time enough to become intimately acquainted with the customs, languages, religions, and politics—to say nothing of market conditions—in the places they visited. Other merchants, the greater number, remained in their cities and did business locally with those passing through.

At any given time, trade might be better or worse depending on political conditions. Most of the trade routes and the cities on which they were based were within easy striking distance of the Eurasian steppes and their nomadic peoples, who had a sharp eye for opportunities for successful raids and pillage. Some of the major concentrations of urban life, traveling from east to west, were along the Kansu panhandle leading from the upper Wei River valley in central Shensi northwestward to the dry Tarim basin, then strung out along the northern and southern margins of the basin westward and over the great mountain divide of the Pamirs to the headwaters of the Syr Darya and Amu Darya and the regions of Farghana and Mawarannahr. Other cities were associated with the trade routes across Iran and, northwestward, north of the Caspian into the Kipchak khanate.

The reason for spelling this out in some detail is to stress the fact that the cities of Inner Asia were distributed over a great distance through the heart of what was to become the Mongol empire and that in these cities were considerable concentrations of wealth and large numbers of men of cosmopolitan culture who had commercial and administrative skills. Thus, despite the fact that the vast majority of the population of the continent occupied the outer regions from Korea and China to mainland Southeast Asia and India, Inner Asia was provided with significant, albeit more limited, resources for the formation of states on a large scale.

The urban culture of Inner Asia was to a large extent derived from the surrounding civilizations and was strongly linked to the literature, teachings, and institutions of the universal religions—especially Islam and Buddhism. Long before the Mongol conquests, older Iranian populations had given way to successive waves of Turkish peoples, such as the Uigurs, who settled in the Tarim region, and the Seljuks, who dominated western Asia. The establishment of the ethnic and linguistic domination of the Turks was followed by their widespread adoption of Islam. The universal religions of Islam and Buddhism were in competition, with the latter rapidly yielding its hold. The presence of these religions in Inner Asia was reflected in the religious architecture and in the presence of a substantial class of literate, and even scholarly, teachers. Such cities of the interior as Samarqand, Bukhara, Khotan, and Kucha were therefore not only commercialized centers of international trade but part of great religious communities as well. In this ideological sense, too, they could make a contribution to Inner Asian imperialism.

In the preceding section we already considered rather abstractly the different cultural adaptations made by the pastoral peoples of the grasslands and the agricultural and urban peoples of regions provided with the necessary combinations of climate, soils, and surface water. Looked at in the context of Inner Asia in the twelfth and thirteenth centuries, we can see that the processes of adaptation, differentiation, and interaction were differently expressed in different regions. The most important single difference is that between the Chinese frontier in the east and the Iranian and Russian frontiers in the west. In the Chinese case, the frontier was relatively well defined, with the Great Wall somewhat arbitrarily sharpening the line dividing the two contrasting ways of life. Some interpenetration commonly occurred, with some nomadic peoples often occupying parts of north China within the wall for longer or shorter periods and even maintaining their pastoral way of life. This happened most often in the Ordos region of northern Shensi and in the strategic area of Kansu, where the eastern steppes approach the pastures of northeastern Tibet. With this reservation, however, one may say that the line between steppe and sown held relatively firm in the east. Moreover, the oasis cities of the Tarim region were fairly effectively divided from the steppe peoples by the natural barrier of the Tien Shan Mountains, although raids from the north did often occur. By contrast, farther west, nomadism and civilized culture were in much closer contact. Agriculture along the courses of the Syr Darya and Amu Darya and around the lower end of the Caspian Sea was confined to narrow irrigated regions merging into the nomadic habitat. The same was true of the steppes north of the Caspian and Black seas, where climatic conditions were suitable either for agriculture or grazing. This contrast between the hard frontier in the east and the more open or porous frontier in the west may hold the explanation of the "westward gradient" of Inner Asian history, the persistent phenomenon of long-term movement of peoples out of the eastern steppes, especially eastern or northern Mongolia, and across the continent toward, and sometimes into, Europe. The formation of the empire of the Mongols in the eastern steppes and its great expansion westward, where the Mongols had been recently preceded by the Uigurs and Seljuks, was one more instance of this process.

The differentiation of nomadic and agricultural-based societies in Inner Asia was largely an accomplished fact by about the third century B.C. on the frontiers of the eastern steppes and northern China and a few centuries earlier in the western steppes. The stability of the basic distinction is suggested by a reading of a careful description of the culture of the proto-Turkish *Hsiung-nu,* the main northern antagonists of the Han dynasty, written by the historian Ssu-ma Ch'ien about 100 B.C. There is little difference between this account and one written by the papal envoy of the Mongols, John of Plano Carpini, in the thirteenth century. Points stressed by these representatives of civilized societies were the mobility of the herdsmen, the absence of towns or cities, the people's great physical toughness and ability to sustain life in a harsh environment, the strong sense of honor among them in their mutual dealings, and their devastating military capacity, which was seen to be in part a consequence of their practice of hunting on horseback and with bow and arrow. Political organization also seems to have changed little. Ssu-ma Ch'ien notes that the great tribal federation of his day was headed by a *shan-yü*, equivalent to the khaqan of later times, and that his chief generals and counsellors were members of an hereditary aristocracy of leading clans. The *shan-yü* delegated authority over tracts of steppe lands to generals who were his vassals, and they, in turn, organized their subjects into armies on the "decimal principle," with units of ten thousand horse archers subdivided into units of one thousand, hundreds, and tens. All of this can also be said of Chingiz' empire some thirteen centuries later.

Formation of the Mongol Empire

But the Mongol conquests of the thirteenth century did not simply pit steppe nomads against the civilized populations; the path to empire had been prepared, as so often in the past, by the prior formation of conquest states. In the west, Turkish steppe peoples had already established their control over much of central and western Asia, and in the east, Mongolian Khitan and the closely related Tungusic people had successively conquered northern China. The conquests of Chingiz and his heirs in both east and west were made possible in part by the fact that the earlier conquerors retained enough of their original steppe culture and identity to be readily incorporated after their defeat into the ruling elite of the new and greater empire. Thus it was that the Mongol conquerors of the west soon merged almost completely with the dominant and numerically superior Muslim Turks, forming a new people, the Tatars of later Russian history, while in the east they brought surviving members of the Khitan and Jurchen rulers of the north China conquest dynasties of Liao and Chin into their regime in a privileged, although subordinate, capacity. Throughout the Mongol empire such men were invaluable to the new conquerors because of their long experience of administration and their intimate knowledge of the culture and society of the subject peoples.

The rise of Chingiz to a leading role in northern Mongolia, reasonably well described in Mongolian, Chinese, European, and Persian records, exemplifies the processes of steppe politics: the formation and maintenance of an aristocracy of leading clans or subclans, the political linking of clans into tribal states, intertribal war and diplomacy leading to a federation of tribes under a charismatic military leader, and finally, the reorganization of the tribal federation into an empire constructed on feudal principles. Chingiz was born into an aristocratic clan, the Borjigin, which had lately suffered disastrous military and political reverses. He claimed to be the great-grandson of a khan of the Mongol tribes who had created a state of such power that it was able to make raids on the territory of the Chin empire (1115-1234) in north China. The Chin, accordingly, befriended the rival Tatar tribes and incited them to attack and destroy the Mongols. The tactic was so successful that the Mongol federation was largely broken up around 1160. Only a few of the subordinate chiefs remained with Chingiz' father, who had to content himself with the more modest title of *bagatur* (meaning "hero").

When Chingiz was still a young boy, his father died from poison administered by a partisan of the Tatars, and most of the surviving dependents of the Mongol tribe now deserted him, his mother, and his brothers. Some circumstances were in his favor, however. Just before his father's death he was betrothed to Börte, daughter of a prosperous clan chieftain in northeastern Mongolia, and could eventually count on some support from that quarter. More important, however, was the fact that the Chin ruler, having used the Tatars to destroy the Mongols, soon looked for a new ally to use against the Tatars. He accordingly bestowed the Chinese title of *wang* ("prince") on the leader of the Kerait tribe with the understanding that he would attack the Tatars. This was a critical turn in Chingiz' fortunes because his father had been a sworn brother and an effective ally of the Kerait leader. Chingiz and his brothers presented themselves to the wang khan and were accepted in his service. When, shortly afterwards, Chingiz' wife was abducted by Merkit tribesmen, he was no longer defenseless. This time some groups of the old Mongol federation rallied to him, and together with Kerait allies he won a victory over the Merkits, recovering Börte and seizing a great amount of loot. The enhancement of his reputation as a leader, together with the political ineffectiveness of the wang khan, now made it possible for him to establish his control over a major proportion of the peoples of Mongolia.

From about 1201 Chingiz began to take the offensive against tribes or clans that refused to acknowledge his leadership (although he remained nominally the vassal of the wang khan). He attacked and defeated his cousin and rival, Jamuga, the Taijiuts, and the Tatars. The family of the wang khan, alarmed by the growing might of his vassal, Chingiz, turned on him but was defeated. The wang khan himself was killed and his son driven into exile. After each of these victories Chingiz distributed the ordinary subjects of the defeated leaders among his own vassals as serfs and, when it seemed expedient, allowed defeated nobles to become his vassals.

The only major obstacle in the way of Chingiz' total domination of the eastern steppes was the independence of the Naiman tribe, in western Mongolia. In preparation for war against them, Chingiz reorganized his following in the feudal pattern of steppe imperialism. The army, comprising most of the population of military age, was distributed among units of ten, a hundred, and a thousand, and he appointed officers from among the aristocracy to command the larger units. At the same time, he created an elite guard of young aristocrats under his personal command. In 1204 the Naimans were routed and reduced to servitude.

In the ten or more years since Chingiz had been acclaimed as their leader by his own followers, the number of clans and tribes under his authority had increased several times over. In 1206 he summoned the nobles of nearly all of the peoples of the eastern steppes to a great conference, or *kuriltai,* in order to reaffirm his leadership and to undertake the reorganization of his expanded domain. A powerful and respected shaman declared to the nobles that it was the will of Heaven that Chingiz and his descendants rule the entire world. The source of his authority was thus asserted to be divine, leaving it to the *kuriltai* merely to affirm the truth that had been revealed to them. The divine right of the Borjigin was so firmly accepted that it survived the collapse of the Mongol empire in the fourteenth century and continued down to the founding of the Mongolian People's Republic in 1924. In ideology, at least, the steppe regime had assumed the guise of a universal empire. The pattern of organization adopted before the campaign against the Naimans was now expanded until the entire subject population was brought into it. The army had grown so large that fourth and fifth layers were added to the hierarchy, with units of a thousand distributed among myriads (armies of ten thousand), and these among three "wings." Consistent with the aristocratic character of steppe society, only the nobles *(noyans)* and the principal officers were considered to be participants in the state. The ordinary herdsmen and all the captured commoners were treated as the property of the aristocrats. This facilitated the later incorporation of defeated peoples of many languages, religions, and cultures into the empire.

Also in 1206 Chingiz began to deal with the problems of civil administration. These would be of major importance only after large sedentary populations had been conquered, but already preparations were begun. The Naimans occupied the Altai Mountains and traded with the oases of the Tarim basin, which had been occupied for nearly four hundred years by the Uigur Turks. They had therefore been subject to more urban influence than had other steppe peoples. From them, Chingiz obtained a learned minister, Tatatunga, who introduced the Uigur script for administrative records and communications. At the same time, and perhaps under the same influence, Chingiz promulgated a written code of laws, the Yasa, which, as added to from time to time by his own decree, was to be the eternal code of the steppe lands. Only fragments of the Yasa have been transmitted, but it was evidently a standardization of customary law of the steppe peoples and in no sense derivative from the codes of the civilized societies. The tribal federation had now become an empire. In the subsequent sections we shall examine the integration of western and eastern Asia in the empire of Chingiz and his heirs.

2. THE MONGOL EMPIRE IN WEST ASIA

West Asia on the Eve of the Mongol Invasions

West Asia at the time of the Mongol invasions was not passing through an age of exceptional political or intellectual decadence. It was, however, experiencing a protracted crisis of fragmentation that had begun even before the death of the last of the Great Seljuks, Sanjar, in 1157 and, in the eastern Muslim lands, had been exacerbated by fresh invasions from out of the steppes. In the provinces that had once been subject to the Seljuk sultans, aspiring satraps everywhere asserted *de facto* independence while continuing, if it suited them, to recognize the nominal overlordship exercised by Sanjar's successors. Some of these were Turkish *amirs* supported by their own tribesmen, as the Seljuk royal house had been when it began its meteoric ascent to empire. Others were former *mamluks* of the Seljuks, among whom the most successful was a line of governors of Khwarazm who revived for themselves and their successors the ancient and sovereign title of Khwarazm-shah. It had been the custom for the Seljuk sultans to appoint cadets of the royal house as titular governors of provinces, placing them in the charge of *atabegs,* who were experienced soldiers and aministrators. In the late twelfth century across the entire Seljuk empire, except in Anatolia, these *atabegs* established hereditary principalities, some of which proved extraordinarily resilient and long lived. These rulers were sometimes enlightened patrons of scholars and writers but their military resources were necessarily modest in comparison with those of preceding regimes. The true successor state of the empire of the Great Seljuks was the long-lived Seljuk sultanate of Rum, with its capital at Konya, but Anatolia lay somewhat outside the main course of events on the Iranian plateau and in the Fertile Crescent, and the rulers of Konya tended to face westward towards Byzantium and the Mediterranean maritime states.

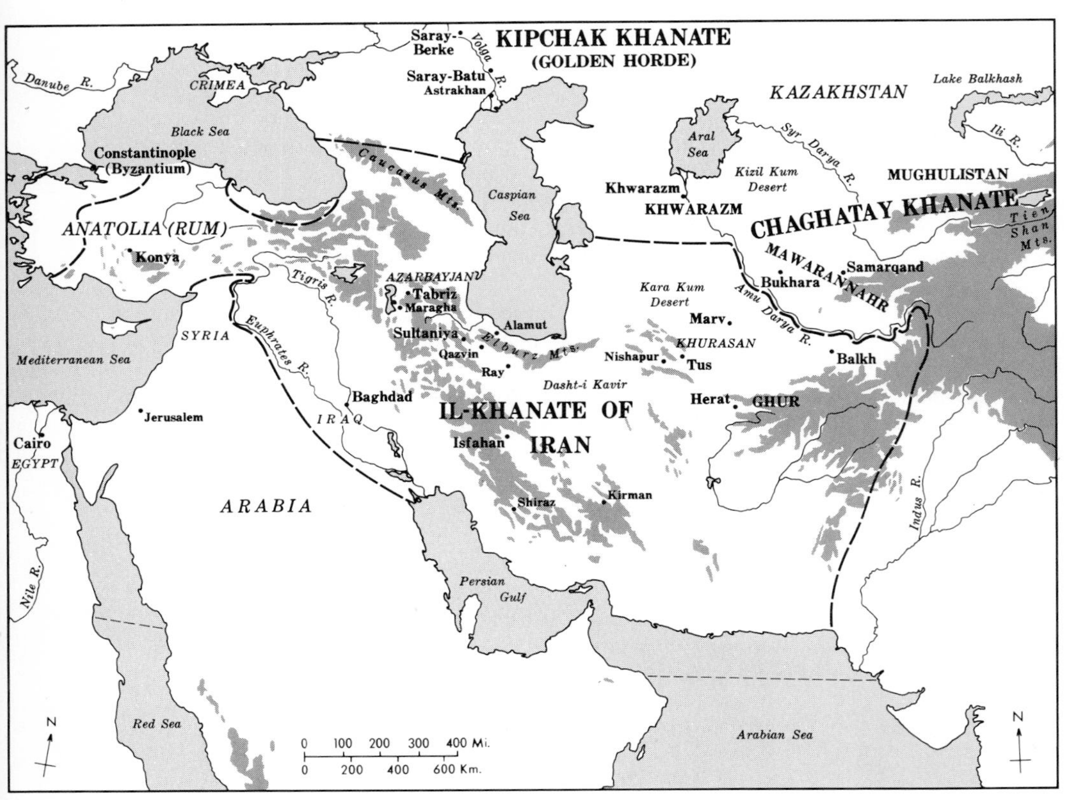

Map 34 The Il-khans of Iran, about 1300

In the eastern arc of the Fertile Crescent the close of the twelfth century saw a remarkable recovery in the authority of the Abbasid caliphate, which had sunk to its nadir during the tenth century but which now, thanks partly to the benevolent support of the Seljuk sultans, had recovered something of its former prestige, especially during the long reign of the caliph al-Nasir (1180-1225). However, Abbasid territorial ambitions were strictly circumscribed by the encircling ring of *atabeg* principalities to the north and by the continuing presence of a Shii "underground." The Ismaili theocracy established by Hasan-i Sabbah in the Elburz Mountains, with its headquarters at Alamut, was, however, past its peak, having become an essentially esoteric movement that had largely abandoned the political ambitions it had shown in the middle of the eleventh century.

In the western arc of the Fertile Crescent the rule of the Kurdish Ayyubids, based on Egypt and Syria, was also showing signs of decay, but here, almost coincidental with the second phase of the Mongol advance, there emerged in the middle of the thirteenth century a new regime that would provide the ultimate barrier to further Mongol penetration westward. Like other Muslim states, the Ayyubids possessed in addition to their own Kurdish followers a slave army of Turkish and Circassian *mamluks* recruited from the area north of the Black Sea and the Caspian, and from the Caucasus region, and who were, like the Mongols themselves, skilled horsemen and mounted archers. Between 1250 and 1259 these *mamluks* took over the Ayyubid sultanate and established a nonhereditary line of Mamluk sultans, which survived until 1517 and which in a succession of hard-fought campaigns in Syria gained the edge over the hitherto-invincible Mongol armies.

The Muslim world on the eve of the Mongol invasions was thus far from being moribund. In the southwest, Syria was soon to pass under the rule of the vigorous Mamluks. In the extreme west, Anatolia under the Seljuk sultans of Konya was enjoying a high level of material prosperity. In Baghdad, the authority of the caliphate was on the increase. In the area between the Amu Darya and the Syr Darya and in Khurasan the Khwarazmshah ruled an extensive empire in a region that had been the scene of earlier empire building by the Samanids, Ghaznavids, and Seljuks. Significantly, however, no great military power controlled the Iranian plateau or the mountainous country to the north of Iraq, while—as the Mongols were to prove so convincingly—the empire of the Khwarazm-shah, potentially so rich in manpower and resources, had yet to be consolidated, collapsing like a pack of cards at the first impact of the Mongol assault.

The Mongol Conquests in the West

There was no single invasion of the Muslim world by the Mongols but a series of incursions into Mawarannahr, Iran, and Iraq extending over a period of forty years in the first instance (ca. 1220-58) and followed by a series of deeper thrusts into Syria and Anatolia during the next half century. At first the Mongols raided, plundered, destroyed, and withdrew; only later did they become an occupying power, compelled to establish a formal administrative framework. Chingiz Khan's initial assault on the Khwarazmshah's kingdom began in 1220 with the crossing of the Syr Darya. Samarqand, Bukhara, and Khwarazm were sacked, and the Mongols advanced southwestward into Khurasan, destroying Balkh, Marv, Herat, Tus, and Nishapur, the principal centers of urban civilization and learning in the Muslim East. One Mongol army drew rein only on the west bank of the Indus; another, dispatched westward in pursuit of the fugitive Khwarazmshah, crossed northern Iran, penetrated the Caucasus, and returned to its base via the steppes north of the Caspian and Aral Sea. From that time onwards, Mawarannahr and Khurasan were occupied territory, subjected to unrestrained exactions on the part of the local representatives of the khaqan. The situation in the western part of Iran and in Iraq remained fluid. The upheavals in the east had sent a wave of refugees westward, including nomadic Turcoman tribes loyal to the son of the dead Khwarazmshah, who established themselves wherever they could, displacing former occupants of grazing grounds and perhaps causing little less destruction than the Mongols themselves. The fact remains, however, that few periods in the history of Islamic Iran and Iraq are more obscure than the thirty or forty years that separate the initial Mongol invasions from the final advance of Hülegü.

Acting in accordance with the instructions of his brother, the khaqan Möngke, Hülegü's invasion of Iran was no mere raid but an elaborate campaign of conquest and annexation: the troublesome Ismaili sectarians of Alamut were to be exterminated, the Abbasid caliphate was to be extinguished, and a great new fief was to be created for Hülegü and his heirs. Hülegü crossed the Amu Darya at the beginning of 1256, captured Alamut and most of the other Ismaili fortresses during 1257, and in February 1258 entered Baghdad. A general massacre followed, in which the last Abbasid caliph was put to death, but a relative of the dead caliph was spirited away to Egypt, where the Mamluk sultans, for their own convenience, thereafter maintained the fiction of an ongoing line of legitimate caliphs. Hülegü took the title of il-khan, meaning at that time a khan subordinate to the khaqan in Mongolia, and the fief that he and his descendants ruled between 1256 and 1353 is therefore known as the il-khanate of Iran.

Some twenty years earlier, however, the Mongols had also advanced westward into the rich grasslands that extend from what is now Kazakhstan across the Volga, the Don, and the Dnieper as far as Hungary. This movement was directed by Batu, a son of Chingiz Khan's eldest son, Jochi, who had predeceased his father. These lands were known collectively as the khanate of Kipchak, the name given by the Muslim world to the steppes north of the

Black and the Caspian Seas, but for some obscure reason they were known to the Slavs as the realm of the Golden Horde (Zolotaya Orda). Batu's conquests brought the frontiers of the Mongol empire within striking distance of Vienna; Hülegü's, of Jerusalem. Muslim Asia was now wholly in Mongol hands apart from the sultanate of Delhi in northern India, the Arabian peninsula, and the Seljuk sultanate in Anatolia, soon to become (after 1243) a Mongol client state.

The question naturally arises: Why did the relatively small armies of these nomadic steppe peoples meet with so little difficulty in conquering and annexing the vast expanses of western and southwestern Asia? Obviously, a major factor was the political fragmentation of the Muslim world of the time, the fragility of the Khwarazmshah's empire, and the modest resources of the various successor states of the former Seljuk empire. Then there was the superiority of Mongol military organization and tactics and the effectiveness of a policy of deliberate terrorism, although it should be remembered that the Mongols' chief opponents in West Asia were also mounted archers of Turkish origin, trained in a similar tradition of steppe warfare. Compared to the physical features of China, those of West Asia greatly assisted the Mongols. The steppe zone of Central Asia extends westward through the Ukraine as far as Hungary, and although in a southwestern direction it is broken by deserts such as the Kara Kum, the Kizil Kum, and the Dasht-i Kavir, as well as by extensive mountain ranges, there are tracts ideally suited for pastoral nomadism extending deep into Anatolia. Over this entire area the agricultural population was far smaller and more confined by the exigencies of the water supply than was the case in China, and the cities and towns were also far smaller. Furthermore, much of western Asia already sheltered nomadic tribes who could be co-opted without much difficulty into the Mongol system.

The Mongol invasions affected both the human and physical face of the lands they ravaged. Obviously, at the level of the ruling elite, the invasions destroyed the preexisting political structures—the caliphate, the Ismaili regime in Alamut, the Seljuk successor states—but it went far beyond that. Traditionally, in West Asia dynasties had come and gone without necessarily affecting the life of the ordinary man in the street, but the Mongol holocausts were something different. Although it is impossible to measure the extent of the destruction of human life, livestock, and property, there is no reason to suppose that contemporary historians exaggerated the extent of the devastation, especially with regard to the cities. Marv, Balkh, and many other cities never fully recovered; some, like Herat and Samarqand, recovered only very gradually; others again, like Tus and Ray, were replaced by new foundations located on nearby sites. Much of the surviving population was enslaved, especially women and craftsmen, and these latter were often transported far from their homelands to remote encampments in Central Asia. As always, under such circumstances, it was mainly the affluent and the well informed who were able to use their wealth and knowledge to escape, and a flow of illustrious and learned refugees made their way to Cairo, Konya, or Delhi. In terms of culture and education there was an absolute and catastrophic loss of what had been achieved over the preceding centuries: scholars and teachers slaughtered, books and manuscripts wantonly destroyed, and colleges left desolate. Most disastrous of all, the Mongols appear to have deliberately wrecked the elaborate irrigation systems that brought precious water to the fields as well as to centers of population, especially in lower Iraq, where hydraulic agriculture had a continuous history dating back to Babylonian times.

Although it is impossible to quantify the immediate consequences of the Mongol assault upon West Asia, it is probably safe to say that in the area extending southwest from the Syr Darya to the Mediterranean coastline of Syria there was a substantial fall in the total population, due not only to massacres but also to epidemics and famines following in the wake of the Mongol armies. There was also a reduction in the number of cities and towns, a contraction in the population of those that survived, and everywhere a decline in the quality of urban life, both material and cultural. There must also have been a contraction of the total area under cultivation and an accompanying contraction in the agricultural output. Finally, nomadism became more prevalent in certain areas, especially in Iran and eastern Anatolia.

Hybrid Barbarian-Civilized Empires: The Khanates in West Asia

After the initial conquests, the Mongols of the West were organized into three huge khanates. The first of these, the Chaghatay khanate (1227-1370), which took its name from Chingiz Khan's second son, Chaghatay, was created before Chingiz Khan's death in 1227. It consisted of the three distinct regions of Mawarannahr between the Amu Darya and the Syr Darya, the steppe region north of the Syr Darya and the Tien Shan Range, and Kashgaria south of the Tien Shan. Its population was thus partly nomadic and partly sedentary. The second, the Kipchak khanate, reached its greatest extent after 1241, when Batu's armies swept victoriously across southern Russia and into Poland, Silesia, and Hungary. The third, the il-khanate of Iran (1256-1353), extended southwest of the Amu Darya across the Iranian plateau, through Iraq and eastern Anatolia, to Syria and the Mediterranean.

All these three khanates, of which the il-khanate appears to have been the most powerful, were founded by outstanding leaders—Chaghatay (d. 1241), Batu (d. 1255) and his brother Berke (d. 1267), Hülegü (d. 1265) and his son Abaqa (d. 1282)—who ultimately derived their authority from the khaqan in Karakorum. The Mongol advances in the West were encouraged, supervised, and materially supported in men and mounts by the khaqans Ögedei and Möngke. The khanates were linked by the common interests of the imperial family, by dynastic marriages, by the movement back and forth across their frontiers of members of the ruling elite as well as of administrators and merchants, and by mutual concern to keep the caravans moving. Notwithstanding the immense distances involved, the exchange of men, merchandise, and ideas was a reality that gave meaning to the concept of a *Pax Mongolica*.

There were other reasons why the khanates of the West proved surprisingly stable in comparison with earlier nomadic incursions into the same areas: in particular, the Chingizkhanids were able to extend and maintain their control with the help of the predominantly Turkish nomadic tribes already settled in West Asia, who acted as intermediaries between them and the nonnomadic population (e.g., the Turkish tribes already occupying the Kipchak steppe), and because the various needs of the khanates were supplied by important collaborating groups whose readiness to work with the invaders offset the sullen hostility of the mass of the Muslim population. Some of these groups, such as those merchants who engaged in the transcontinental caravan trade, had a personal stake in the new order. Others had sectarian interests that they hoped the Mongols would advance. Shii Muslims like the astronomer-administrator Nasir al-Din Tusi (d. 1274), who allegedly incited Hülegü to attack Baghdad, welcomed the end of Sunni domination. Nestorian Christians and Jews also had great expectations of the Mongols and gravitated to their service. The Syriac Christian scholar Bar-Hebraeus (d. 1236) attached himself to Hülegü's court at Maragha in northwestern Iran, and Rashid al-Din (d. 1318), the first historian to attempt a genuine world history and an influential *vazir* of successive il-khans, was a converted Jew. The Christian rulers of Armenia and Georgia, and the Crusading states in Syria also attempted to come to terms with the Mongols. Everywhere, the ambitious and the opportunist endeavored to profit from friendship with or subservience to the new rulers once it became clear that Mongol rule was likely to prove long lasting. Among the Russian princes a number of prominent figures, including Alexander Nevsky (d. 1263), proved adept pupils of the Mongols, serving as their tax collectors vis-à-vis the subject Christian population. In the mountainous country of Ghur in central Afghanistan the Kart chieftain, Shams al-Din Muhammad (d. 1278), won the favor of successive Mongol rulers and thereby laid the foundations upon which his descendants would eventually establish an independent dynasty in Herat.

This process of collaboration was important because both the numerical inferiority of the Mongols and their personal inclinations led them to delegate authority to local rulers, over whom they exercised a loose suzerainty based on recognition of their own supremacy and the regular transmission of tribute. The Mongols of the West established themselves in areas where the climate and the grazing enabled them to maintain their traditional way of life with as little modification as possible. Thus, Chaghatay and his immediate successors located their principal encampments in the rich grasslands north of the Tien Shan Mountains beside the Ili River; Batu and his descendants favored the west bank of the lower Volga; and the il-khans identified with Azarbayjan in northwestern Iran. After their initial conquests they preferred to leave the Russian forest zone in the hands of indigenous rulers, and the same was true of much of the Caucasus region and Anatolia, where they tolerated the survival of the Seljuk sultans of Konya as obedient vassals. Their control over the mountainous regions of western Iran and of central Afghanistan was fairly nominal and they were content to leave the hot and arid regions of southern Iran under their former rulers, now Mongol tributaries. Thus neither Shiraz nor Kirman suffered the fate of the northeastern Iranian cities at the time of the initial conquests.

It follows from all this that the Mongols, once the first holocaust of death and destruction had subsided, interferred very little with their Muslim and Christian subjects so long as revenue was forthcoming. The Mongols governed themselves in accordance with their own law, the Yasa, and their Muslim, Christian, and Jewish subjects regulated their lives in accordance with the laws and customs of their own communities. Thus, so long as the Mongols retained their cultural identity intact the nonnomadic subject population maintained a quasi-autonomous status not unlike that of the Christian and Jewish *millets* (self-regulating religious communities) of the later Ottoman empire.

Acculturation of the Mongol Ruling Elites

Once the initial phase of invasion and rapine was over, the Mongols were forced to recognize that they would have to come to terms with the fact that in much of the il-khanate, and likewise in parts of the other two khanates, traditional patterns of government would have to be resuscitated if the nonnomadic population was to provide the necessary revenue, manpower, produce, and luxury commodities. The outcome, most highly developed in the case of the il-khanate, was the establishment of patterns of administration that conformed to a surprising extent to those of the traditional Muslim regimes so recently extinguished.

At the pinnacle of power stood the khan and his family, nominally subject to the khaqan in Karakorum, but with the passing of the years generating their own personal charisma and dynastic loyalty among their followers and military commanders, the *noyans, begs,* and *amirs*. These latter, although themselves often heads of powerful clans, were dependent on the khan for the allocation of pastures and for revenue assignments. In the il-khanate, of which far more is known than of the other two khanates, these assignments resembled the *iqtas* of Seljuk times and presented the same temptation for the assignee either to bleed the countryside dry or to try to establish inalienable possession. The *noyans, begs,* and *amirs* provided military leadership, but, as in the case of their Seljuk predecessors, they were unfit to undertake civil administration, lacking as they did the necessary bureaucratic skills to assess and collect the revenue. These skills were monopolized by urban-based and often hereditary officials, generally Iranians, who maintained important links with the *ulama* and the bazaar merchants. Recognition of the need for their services, demonstrated at a quite early stage of the conquests, constituted the beginning of a complex process of accommodation between rulers and ruled. Chaghatay, for example, although portrayed in the Muslim chronicles as a model of Mongol traditionalism, early on entrusted the administration of the settled areas of Mawarannahr to a Muslim merchant from Khwarazm and appointed another Muslim as his *vazir*.

It was these merchants and officials who serviced the elaborate courts that soon emerged in the Mongol encampments. The encampments had originally been the peripatetic headquarters of the khan and his administration, but it was not long before they became fixed in one place: Hülegü, for example, established his residence close to the old Seljuk town of Maragha; his successors favored the vicinity of the great commercial metropolis of Tabriz; finally, the il-khan Öljeitü (1304-17) laid out an imperial capital at Sultaniya midway between Tabriz and Qazvin. Batu's camp on the lower Volga, Saray-Batu, became the first capital of the Kipchak khanate, to be replaced in due course by a new site up river, Saray-Berke. The establishment of permanent capitals, which attracted a diverse population of traders, artisans, craftsmen, and entertainers, drew the khan and his entourage into a life-style resembling that of the former Muslim ruling elite and marked another important step in the process of Mongol acculturation.

The emergence of a court life and a court culture shaped by older indigenous traditions such as were to be found in il-khanid Tabriz or Sultaniya was one obvious indication of the way in which the new rulers were following in the footsteps of their Muslim predecessors, but the process did not stop there. Not only did the il-khans acquire a taste for urban pleasures. They also recognized the value of urban life as a source of profit to themselves, and some of the cities that had been rendered desolate at the time of the conquests were deliberately reestablished with such of their former inhabitants as could be found, as happened in the case of Herat, where the surviving weavers of that city, who had been transported to Bishbaliq north of the Tien Shan, were sent back to form the nucleus of the new foundation. Encouragement was given to both merchants and skilled craftsmen, the highways were made safe for travelers, tolls were standardized, caravanserais and milestones were erected at regular intervals along the roads, and each village was made responsible for the safety of travelers passing through its district.

Mongol Assimilation of Indigenous Religious Values

In their religious outlook the first generation of Mongol conquerors had shown themselves distinctly eclectic, since although they were shamanists, they were not averse to befriending Buddhist monks or Nestorian Christian priests and were perhaps also acquainted with vestiges of Central Asian Manichaeanism through their contacts with the Uigur Turks. In Iran the il-khans were no less eclectic than in Mongolia. Although Hülegü and Abaqa remained lifelong shamanists, Hülegü at first seemed to favor the Nestorians, some of his followers patronized Buddhism (although in a Kashmiri form and not the Tibetan form that entered Mongolia in the seventeenth century), and the third il-khan, Ahmad Tegüder (1282-84), became a Muslim, as his adopted name indicates. Similarly, in the Kipchak khanate, Batu remained a shamanist but one of his sons was supposedly a Christian and his brother Berke became a Muslim. These innovations were not welcome to the rank and file of the Mongol army and provoked sharp reactions among traditionalists. In fact, however, the issue was never in doubt, given the small number of the Mongol ruling elite. Conversion to Christianity might have gone some way to placating the Slav population in the Kipchak khanate and would have won the enthusiastic support of the Christians of the il-khanate, but the majority faith in western Asia was Islam and, perhaps of even greater significance, Islam was the faith of the Turkish nomadic population of the Kipchak steppe and of the pastoral zones in Iran, with whom the Mongols assimilated most easily. In the il-khanate the greatest of the line, Ghazan (1295-1304), converted to Islam in 1295, the Kipchak khanate became officially Muslim under Özbeg Khan (1312-41), and so did the Chaghatay khanate at about the same time. In Iran, Ghazan's brother and successor, Öljeitü, toyed with Shiism but

8.2 The mausoleum of the il-khan Öljeitü (1304-17); Sultaniya, northwestern Iran. On their conversion to Islam, the il-khans functioned as traditional Iranian rulers, maintaining a splendid court, patronizing men of letters, and endowing many colleges and mosques. Source: C. Texier, *Description de l'Armenie, la Perse et la Mesopotamia* (Paris, 1852), Vol. I, Plate 54.

finally gave his allegiance to Sunni Islam. These conversions were undoubtedly "political" in the way that Ashoka's conversion to Buddhism or Constantine's to Christianity had been. They did, however, assure the ultimate assimilation of the Mongols of the West into the cultural and ethnic "melting pot" of West Asia.

From the time of Ghazan, the il-khans in particular became lavish patrons of Islam, building enormous mosques and mausoleums, endowing shrines and colleges, and supporting Muslim men of letters. Significantly, when Öljeitü founded his new capital of Sultaniya, he planned to reinter there the bodies of the first and third Shii imams to make the new city a pilgrimage center, and, no less significantly, the foundation ceremonies were attended by several prominent *shaykhs* and dervishes. Hülegü and Abaqa were buried secretly in traditional Mongol style on an inaccessible rock on Lake Rezaiyeh, and Arghun (1284-91), Hülegü's grandson, was likewise buried in a forbidden sanctuary near Sujas, south of Sultaniya. His sons, Ghazan and Öljeitü, however, were buried in sumptuous Muslim tombs in Tabriz and Sultaniya, exemplifying the cultural distance the Mongol conquerors of Iran had traveled in half a century.

Disintegration of the Mongol Khanates of the West

By the second quarter of the fourteenth century all three khanates were in an advanced state of disintegration. Thereafter, however, the downward pace was uneven, with the khanate of Kipchak proving the most resilient. In no case was the Mongol ruling elite driven out, as happened in China, unless the Russian advance in the middle of the sixteenth century can be regarded as equivalent to the Ming expulsion. After 1335 the il-khanate, ruled by puppet khans, became fragmented among embattled kingmakers and would-be dynasts, as happened also in the Chaghatay khanate. By the end of the fourteenth century fragmentation also marked the fate of the Kipchak khanate, but there the successor states showed greater spirit. The khanates of Kazan and Astrakhan were not finally annexed by Russia until 1552 and 1554, the khanate of Sibir in the Tobolsk region survived down to the beginning of the seventeenth century, and the khanate of the Crimea, an Ottoman client state after 1475, withstood the Russian advance until 1783. Meanwhile there had emerged from among the diverse Turco-Mongol stock of the Kipchak khanate a new Muslim people, with their own language and distinctive culture, the Tatars, who were to maintain under Russian and later Soviet repression a robust awareness of their unique cultural identity.

Why were the descendants of the Mongols of the West assimilated rather than rejected by the societies over whom they had once ruled, as happened in the case of China? The answer appears to be, first, that the Mongol invaders, never very numerous, fraternized and intermarried with the preexisting Turkish nomadic population, forming a composite Turco-Mongol nomadic elite; second, that they were able to find a permanent place within the preexisting nomadic population because, unlike China proper, the khanates of the West included extensive and sparsely inhabited tracts ideally suited for preserving a nomadic way of life; and third, that the conversion of the Mongols to Islam integrated them into the dominant culture of the area. Unlike China, however, loss of military hegemony on the part of the Mongols was not followed by an immediate reassertion of political control on the part of the indigenous population. Even in Russia, the rulers of Muscovy, who would eventually become the heirs of the khanate of Kipchak, prudently retained the function of tax collectors for the khans and acted on their behalf vis-à-vis the other Russian rulers while slowly strengthening themselves for the inevitable trial of strength against their erstwhile overlords. In eastern Anatolia and the Caucasus the end of Mongol rule left a vacuum, to be filled by various Turcoman tribal confederacies. In Syria, the Mamluks ousted the garrisons of the il-khans, but they did so with troops and tactics drawn from the same steppe world of the Mongols themselves. In Iraq and northwestern Iran the rule of the il-khans gave way to that of another Mongol clan, the Jalayirids. Shiraz, Isfahan, and Kirman passed into the hands of a native dynasty, the Muzaffarids. Herat and the surrounding countryside was ruled by the Kart dynasty, which, like the Jalayirids and the Muzaffarids, had climbed to power in the service of the il-khans. All in the second half of the fourteenth century would collapse during Timur's short-lived attempt to repeat the Chingizkhanid achievement.

None of these dynasties, not even the Mamluks, had possessed the strength to dispossess the Mongols, and in retrospect it is clear that the Mongols destroyed themselves. First, despite the apparent harmony that had seemed to characterize the division of Chingiz Khan's empire into separate fiefs, the interests of these successor states were often diametrically opposed to each other. The Chaghatay khans exhausted themselves fighting the Mongol khaqans to the east and the il-khans to the west. The il-khans fought the Chaghatay khans, the Kipchak khans, and the Mamluks. External threats were compounded by internal upheavals as, with the passing of the years, the number of princes of the imperial house increased. Since Turco-Mongol sovereignty was held to be vested in the ruling family and not in an individual and since there was no clear recognition of the right of primogeniture, disputed successions and attempted usurpations were very frequent. This, in turn, encouraged the ambitions of the *noyans, begs,* and *amirs* who aspired to become kingmakers and exercise authority on behalf of puppet rulers.

It has often been remarked by historians who uncritically accept the idea that dynastic history involves a cyclical process of vigor, decay, revolution, and renewal, that the once-hardy il-khans and their contemporaries in the other khanates degenerated and that their successors, and the ruling elite as a whole, became effete. The process is more complicated and also more interesting than that. Nomadic military and therefore political power lost its effectiveness when, as can be clearly seen in the case of Mongol rule in Iran, it lost its tribal base, when the control of land, which had to be administered as a source of income and also defended, took the place of the leadership of people. Even more invidious than the administration and defense of land, however, was the administration and defense of cities, with all the concomitant temptations to modify a traditional life-style. Even in Azarbayjan, with its fine pastures, the il-khans were drawn into the complexities of urban and sedentary government. Preoccupied with essentially Islamic patterns of land control, revenue collection, political style, and elite culture, they lost the psychological as well as the physical superiority that they had formerly enjoyed as nomadic tribesmen ruling over a sedentary subject population.

3. MONGOL DOMINATION IN EAST ASIA

North China from 1234 and all of China from 1279 underwent the experience of being entirely incorporated as a mere province within a much larger empire of barbarian origin. This state of affairs presented problems of great difficulty for both conquerors and conquered. For the Chinese, some psychological comfort could be found in the fact that the Confucian state ideology affirmed the legitimacy of any dynasty that might assume undivided rule over the empire, even though this dynasty seemed otherwise disqualified by its barbarian origins and its exotic culture. But although the universal theory of the Chinese state could be stretched to accommodate even this turn of events, the conquerors' rapacious acquisition of wealth in every form eventually drove the Chinese to choose between active collaboration, at one extreme, and open resistance at the other. For the Mongols, on the other hand, the control of a population of more than sixty million (there were probably less than one million Mongols in all of East Asia) was an impossible task. This forced them into collaboration with Chinese who were willing to help them keep order and exploit the empire economically, in return for protection of their own interests. The problem of responsible administration at the critical local level, therefore, was never successfully solved. Moreover, Kubilai and his heirs drained much of the resources of China in further attempts at conquest by land and sea, thereby setting a new standard of imperial grandeur that would be imitated by succeeding dynasties in China.

The failure of the Mongols after over a century of rule in all or part of China resulted from their unwillingness to adjust completely to the Chinese social and cultural context, as the Manchus were to do four centuries later. Even after Kubilai committed himself to rule China in more or less Chinese fashion, the Mongols generally regarded the Chinese and their culture as alien and so had to rule them more by coercion and compromise than by leadership. At the same time, their own politics were bedeviled by feudal fragmentation and by bitter succession struggles, which rendered them incapable of offering resistance to the rebellion that resulted from misgovernment by themselves and their collaborators.

From the Chinese point of view, the Mongols were one more in a continuous succession of barbarian conquerors of the north beginning in the tenth century, so an outline of the Mongol conquest should begin with that century. During the period of the Five Dynasties, when China was divided among many independent states for about a half century, the Khitan, a Mongolian people from the steppe and mountain-forest margins of western Manchuria and eastern Mongolia, established a powerful frontier state. They expanded eastward, conquering the Manchurian tribal state of Pohai, then southward, occupying a narrow but strategically critical strip of territory within the Great Wall, including the site of Peking, and westward across the top of the loop of the Yellow River to the frontiers of Hsi Hsia, the Tibetan state based in Kansu and Shensi. The Khitan Liao state, which proclaimed its imperial status in 947, posed a constant threat to the northern Sung regime and had eventually to be bought off by a treaty in 1004, by the terms of which the Chinese were to pay an annual tribute. One of the Manchurian subject tribes of the Khitan, the Jurchen, revolted and, with Chinese encouragement, overthrew the Khitan, establishing an empire of their own, the Chin, in 1115. The Chin proved stronger and more aggressive than their Sung allies had expected and proceeded to expand southward, driving the Sung government from its capital at K'aifeng in 1126 to a new site at Hangchow. A new and stable frontier was established running eastward along the crest of the Ch'inling Mountains of southern Shensi to the upper Huai valley and along the Huai to the sea. Members of the defeated Liao regime fled westward with a considerable army, past Hsi Hsia, and established their control over the heart of Central Asia, including the Tarim basin, the Pamirs, and the region of Mawarannahr between the Amu Darya and Syr Darya. The boundaries of this new state, called Kara-Khitay, were almost identical with the later Chaghatay khanate.

Chingiz, in his own lifetime, destroyed both the Hsi Hsia and Kara-Khitay regimes, incorporating them into his empire. He also conducted successful invasions of the north China territory of the Chin, but the final conquest of Chin was accomplished only in 1234 by Chingiz' son Ögedei, the khaqan. In the reign of the third khaqan, Möngke, Mongol armies struck southward along the western frontier of Szechwan and into Yunnan, where the Thai state of Nanchao was destroyed and its capital, Tali, occupied. This southwestern region that had always escaped Chinese control was now added to the Chinese empire by the Mongol conquerors of China. The conquest of the rest of China was a long and costly undertaking, achieved under Kubilai. Stubborn Chinese resistance forced the invaders to accept years of siege warfare in order to capture the principal cities. The conquest of the Sung was formally concluded with the death of the last Sung emperor in a sea battle in 1279. The political relationship of China to the rest of the Mongol empire was determined during Kubilai's reign. He established himself as khaqan in the face of the bitter resistance of his younger brother, Arïq Böge, and his cousin, Kaydu, both of whom were more conservative than he in their adherence to the steppe culture of their ancestors. Kubilai moved from the rude capital at Karakorum, north of the Gobi on the banks of the Orkhon,

Map 35 Yuan China, about 1300

southward to the old Chin capital at Peking, well within the Great Wall and surrounded by a dense Chinese population of farmers and townspeople. He followed this move by the logical next step of reorganizing his government as a Chinese dynasty, which he called the Yuan, in 1271. At the same time, however, he retained his title of khaqan, with the intention of exercising control over the other khanates in the feudal pattern laid down under Chingiz.

The Mixed Feudal-Bureaucratic Polity of Mongol Rule in China

The establishment of foreign rule over China raised issues of the forms of government, political ideology, class and ethnic identity and relations, language, and religion. For north China this applies not only to the Mongols but to the Liao and Chin as well. Each conquering group made its own slightly different policies. All of them cast themselves in the role of primarily military elites and distributed authority feudally and hereditarily. All of them maintained more than one capital, so as to have at least one imperial seat in China proper and one in the steppes, thereby at least outwardly keeping faith with the herdsmen while attending to the tasks of administration in the conquered territory. All devised or borrowed writing systems in order to be able to use written communications in their own languages without becoming dependent on literary Chinese. All of them used the Confucian state ideology both to strengthen their internal authority and imperial succession and to facilitate administration of Chinese territory, and all followed their strong preference in generously patronizing Buddhism and religious Taoism which, unlike Confucianism, both made a bond with the Chinese common people and contrasted favorably with Confucian intolerance of non-Chinese cultural values and social customs. Moreover, each of the conquering peoples was able to recruit surviving members of the leading classes of the preceding regimes. Thus, the Chin employed former officials (Chinese as well as Khitan) of the Liao, and the Mongols employed Chinese, Khitan, and Jurchen who submitted to them. But there were differences as well. The Jurchen, perhaps because they were forest-dwelling people with a largely nonpastoral mixed economy of agriculture and hunting, and perhaps also because they were a very small minority in the vast population of north China, were more adaptable culturally and collaborated more readily with the north Chinese gentry. The advantages this brought them politically in the form of indigenous support were partially offset by the fact that like the other conquerors, they were quite uninhibited in the expropriation of lands for redistribution among leading clansmen. The Mongols, who were the most purely pastoral as well as the most powerful of all the conquerors, had the greatest difficulty adjusting to the demands of administration in China. They attempted under Kubilai to reverse the advanced feudalization of authority that followed quickly the conquest of the north, but the measures of centralization came too late to be of much use against the entrenched interests of the aristocracy and their Chinese collaborators. Ironically, the centralizing and despotic reforms of the late Mongol emperors were to prove more effective in the hands of the Chinese emperors of the succeeding Ming dynasty.

For the Mongols, the issue of the proper forms of administration in China was fully joined early in the reign of Ögedei (r. 1229-41). Territory wrested from the Chin was parcelled out to leading *noyans,* or "noblemen." Their authority was given formal status by the designation of their military headquarters as branch secretariats, but in practice there was no functional distinction between civil and military administration and the nobles behaved like the feudal lords they were, exercising independent jurisdiction over their lands and subjects. The Chinese were reduced to slavery by the Mongol officers, who simply continued the custom of the steppe in this regard. In the absence of any kind of regular or uniform taxation, the Mongol lords simply expropriated goods at will from their subjects. The most conservative faction at the court of Ögedei went so far as to argue that all the conquered territory should be converted into pasture for horses. The burden of the contrary argument was borne, fittingly, by a scholarly Khitan officer of the Chin government whose own ideological position was based on a combination of Confucian tradition for government and Buddhism for personal growth and guidance. Yeh-lü Ch'u-ts'ai fought shrewdly and successfully for a policy of compromise and accommodation that would at least avert the total destruction of Chinese society in the north while allowing the Mongols to enjoy the benefits of efficient and long-term exploitation of their conquests. He persuaded Ögedei to save the agricultural economy, establish civil administrative offices (*lu,* or "circuits"), institute regular taxation under central government control, and appoint Chinese officials with the required skills to manage the tasks of administration. When these measures proved their worth, Ögedei permitted Yeh-lü to reorganize the primitive chancellery of Chingiz into a Chinese-style central government administration. But the contradiction between bureaucratic and feudal principles was not so easily resolved. Full implementation of regular taxation and civil administration had to await the new population census after the final defeat of Chin in 1234. By this time, a vast number of the population, with their lands, had been appropriated by the nobles, and Ögedei liberally distributed lands and people to his supporters as hereditary fiefs. The early promise of administrative reform was thus not yet fulfilled except on a very limited scale. Similarly, when Yeh-lü succeeded in having thousands of Chinese scholars summoned to the capital to be examined for official service, the effects were limited and temporary. Many of the successful candidates, who had been slaves of Mongol officers, were freed and then given posts in the service of the nobles, but the examinations were not given again until long afterwards. During the last years of Ögedei's reign and the first years of regency of the dowager empress Töregene, Yeh-lü saw his work largely undone. The Mongols were unwilling to accept reasonable limits on the level of their exploitation of the Chinese, and imperial tax collection was taken out of the hands of the Chinese administrators and turned over to Muslim merchant companies. The chief tax farmer, Abd al Rahman, promised that he would squeeze far more revenues out of the taxpayers than had been done before.

In the reign of Kubilai (1260-94), the hybrid form of the Sino-Mongol state was finally worked out and extended to all of China. The main outlines of this arrangement may be summarized as follows. The whole population was divided among four ethnic or geographic census categories. The highest category was the Mongols, followed by the "miscellaneous categories," which consisted mainly of West Asian Muslim auxiliaries; third was "Han people," who were all the people of the Chin state and their descendants, supplemented by descendants of non-Mongol soldiers who helped conquer the Chin and including Chinese, Jurchen, Khitans, and Koreans; and finally was the "southern people," who had been subjects of the southern Sung state. The Mongols, for the most part, retained their original organization in myriads (armies of ten thousand, thousands, etc.) and were settled in Chinese territory, where they furnished troops for garrison duty and were supported by the Chinese lands and labor that were assigned to them or to their aristocratic officers. The emperor's own guard—the *kesig*—the elite army myriads, and most of the important offices of the government were filled exclusively with Mongols. North China was also garrisoned by non-Mongol auxiliaries under Mongol or West Asian officers. Much lower in legal status were the "Han people," who constituted the bulk of the subject population of north China. Some of them were recruited to serve in Han army myriads for active service or occupation duty in the south. Finally, the "southern people" stood lowest in the scale because of their long resistance to conquest and their reputation, no doubt deserved, of intransigent opposition. In the matter of military service they were used merely as a local constabulary and were very carefully controlled. In this fourfold division of the population, the Mongols and their West Asian collaborators constituted the official elite, while the Han and southern people provided the labor and the taxes and tribute for the conquerors.

The inevitable need for literate administrators and clerks was not met by the invention of new scripts for Mongolian, though two were used: the Uigur alphabet borrowed by Chingiz from the Naimans, and the new script devised by the Tibetan monk Phags-pa. Instead, for the most part, the Mongols recruited Chinese who were literate, but not necessarily educated in the Confucian sense. These recruits typically started in clinical jobs and constituted a pool of experienced candidates for promotion to civil administrative office. Although the literati were regarded with suspicion and their occupational status was lowered as a result, the ideology they represented was thought important enough to justify the reestablishment of an empirewide system of Confucian academies, and in 1315 there was a brief, if ineffectual, revival of the civil-service examination system. However, the school system, so impressive on paper, seems not to have been created on the scale planned, and the schools that were established were so badly administered that they served mainly as a refuge for people seeking the tax and service exemptions that were allowed the students. In a remarkable anticipation of the succeeding Ming and Ch'ing regimes, the Yuan in 1313 gave official orthodox status to the classical interpretations of the Sung philosopher Chu Hsi, but this had little practical effect at the time.

8.3 The Emperor Kubilai, robed in ermine, is shown here on a hunting trip. Kubilai moved his imperial capital from Karakorum in Mongolia to Peking in northern China. Like most of the Mongol rulers of China he retained some of the steppe culture of his forbears. Detail from painting attributed to Liu Kuan-tao. Collection of the National Palace Museum, Taipei, Taiwan, Republic of China.

This is necessarily a confused picture, full of contradictions: feudal versus bureaucratic structure; enthusiastic patronage of Buddhism and Taoism versus endorsement of Confucian official ideology for the Chinese part of the empire and the Yasa, as always, for the Mongols and their old allies; the will to dominate and exploit versus the necessary collaboration with certain Chinese interests. Under such circumstances of striking novelty and uncertainty, the effects on Chinese cultural and economic change were not altogether negative. The Mongols' enthusiasm for crafts and for trade created a climate favorable to economic enterprise, and both overland and maritime trade appear to have enjoyed a boom, at least when fighting was not in progress. In literature, Chinese drama may have enjoyed its highest development during the Yuan. The immensely wealthy and cosmopolitan capital at Peking saw a sudden flourishing of drama (building on earlier developments in Sung). No fewer than seven hundred plays are known to have been written in this brief period, and many more may have gone unrecorded. In religion, Buddhism and Taoism both enjoyed a vigorous revival. In the south, where the foreign presence was much less in evidence and the wealthy landlord families of Sung times were generally still in possession of their estates, there were patrons enough to sustain a great growth of the theatre there as well. As important as the drama was the emergence of the novel in Yuan times from the storyteller's books of Sung. Possibly the greatest of all Chinese novels, the *Romance of the Three Kingdoms,* was written at this time. What is most significant about these developments is that both the drama and the novel were composed in a style very close to the vernacular. The authors had broken the stylistic conventions of serious literature and written genuinely popular literature. It should be noted in this connection that since the Yuan made a practice of hiring Chinese administrators and clerks who were undereducated in the conventional sense, official documents also tended to be written in a style more nearly vernacular than classical. The most important cultural development of the period, however, was the fact that after the centuries of fragmentation, the empire was now a complex and interacting whole once again.

The Reassertion of Indigenous Political Control

The way in which the Mongol rule was ended in China presents a marked contrast with that in West Asia, but shows some resemblances to the Russian case. In contrast with West Asia, where the Mongols and their allies in the conquest were converted to the religion and, virtually, the civilization of the Islamic indigenous leadership, in China, as in Russia, ideology and culture continued to pose a great obstacle to assimilation. In Russia the Mongols generally adopted Islam, which placed them at a great cultural distance from their predominantly Orthodox Christian subjects. In China, the Confucian tradition, given its dense content of ethical and social prescriptions and its implied disapproval of other cultures, seems generally to have been regarded with intense hostility by the Mongols except insofar as it seemed necessary in the limited sphere of political organization. Since most of the leading Sung literati had turned away from Buddhism, that universal religion could not provide a common cultural ground with the gentry class either, although the Mongols in China strongly favored it. If one adds to this the fact that the Mongols isolated themselves from the Chinese, or tried to, by legal classification and by the maintenance of the old military communities, one can see why it was that when the end of their rule came, it was by expulsion rather than by absorption.

The expulsion of the Mongols from China resulted from the collapse of the military and political sanctions that had held the regime together in the face of widespread hostility among the conquered subjects. On one level, the government weakened at the center. Between 1308 and 1333 there were eight emperors, all of whom died young and at least two of whom died by assassination. The Mongols simply failed to adopt a strict and generally accepted rule of succession, and the death of an emperor became an occasion for violent conflict among different pretenders, all of whom might be able to make good claims to the throne. And when pretenders fell out, their military and family partisans joined in the struggle. These inner struggles became so intense that they were not even suspended during the last decades of Yuan rule when only a concerted effort could possibly have saved the regime from the Chinese rebellion. On a lower plane, the *noyans,* once the loyal and effective commanders of the myriads and thousands, rapidly were transformed into complacent landlords, using their soldiers as part of the labor force on their estates and exploiting them as thoroughly as they did their other dependents. Both among the Mongol and the Han units, therefore, low morale and general inefficiency were widespread, and when the troops were called upon to fight, they usually deserted at the first opportunity. The military sanction, at least in the south, was almost nonexistent by around 1350, and the burden of defense was passed to militiamen recruited by Chinese gentry, who were more interested in the security of their estates than in revolution. Finally, as Mongol exploitation intensified, collaboration became less attractive for many Chinese gentry and some of them were prepared to shift their allegiance to a rebel leader, although many did defend the regime to the end. By far the most important factor on the Chinese side, however, was the growth of peasant unrest. Caught between the Mongols and the landlords and with no authority of any real effectiveness to which to appeal for justice and protection, the peasants began to organize armed resistance. Given the tendency of the gentry to either collaborate or to retreat from politics, leadership of the anti-Yuan forces came from among the peasantry and from such marginal occupational groups as peddlers, fishermen, salt smugglers, and pirates. A revolutionary ideology was provided by the messianic White Lotus Society, which accounted for the major share of the rebellions. The devotees of the society believed in their imminent deliverance from their desperate circumstances by the coming of a divine savior, the Buddha Maitreya. Sporadic and local revolts gave way in the early 1350s to widespread rebellions. As these became successful in their destruction of Yuan and gentry authority, their leaders formed states that, they hoped, would triumph over their rivals and reunite the empire. Mongol intervention was so ineffectual that most of the fighting was among rebels rather than between them and the government. The ultimate victor was a peasant soldier, Chu Yuan-chang, whose armies first triumphed over all rivals in the south, then chased the Yuan regime from the capital and pursued the survivors into Mongolia. His new regime, the Ming (1368-1643), will be the subject of the next section on China as an early modern empire.

4. WEST ASIA UNDER TIMUR

West Asia on the Eve of Timur's Conquests

Despite the decline of the three Mongol khanates of the West during the first half of the fourteenth century, a further attempt was made to resurrect the form of these hybrid Eurasian steppe regimes in the second half of the century: first, by Tokhtamish (1376-95), a Chingizkhanid chieftain in the Kipchak khanate, and then by his more successful rival, Timur (1370-1405), known to Europeans as Tamerlane, a Turco-Mongol chieftain from the Chaghatay khanate. Timur's role as an empire builder was to be far less substantial than that of Chingiz Khan, but his conquests, which, for the Muslim world, probably exceeded in sheer destructiveness even those of the Chingizkhanids, had profound consequences for West Asia in the fifteenth century, even effecting the shape of the early modern empires that were to emerge in the first half of the sixteenth century.

Tokhtamish was a descendant of Batu's elder brother, Orda, whose clans, known as the White Horde, pastured their flocks between the Urals and the Aral Sea. With the decline of the ruling line of the khans of Kipchak, descendants of Batu, various usurpers attempted to exercise *de facto* authority in the khanate but none came so near success as Tokhtamish. The time was well chosen since, notwithstanding the unstable succession, the Kipchak khanate was still a formidable military power with a vigorous ruling elite eager for war and plunder, and there is no evidence that the processes of Islamicization and Tatarization had yet weakened the tribal social fabric. The reason for Tokhtamish's failure therefore seems, in the light of the scant evidence available, very clear: in Timur he was confronted by an opponent even more able and aggressive than himself.

The Chaghatay khanate in the middle years of the fourteenth century was seemingly less promising ground than the Kipchak khanate for the appearance of a potential empire builder. Excluding the remote and arid region of Kashgaria south of the Tien Shan, the Chaghatay khanate had from the outset consisted of two distinct regions: the grasslands northeast of the Syr Darya, which were ideally suited for pastoral nomadism and where the only agricultural or urban settlements were close to the river, and Mawarannahr, where there were extensive belts of cultivation bordering the Syr Darya, the Zarafshan, and the Amu Darya and where the oases sustained an intensive agricultural economy. Those Turco-Mongol chieftains and their followers who remained northeast of the Syr Darya endeavored to resist the lure of Islamic influences and to preserve the traditional life-style embodied in Chingiz Khan's Yasa. Those who had crossed the river into Mawarannahr, including the senior line of the descendants of Chaghatay, tended to become Muslims sooner or later. They also felt the lure of the Irano-Islamic life-style of such cities as Bukhara and Samarqand, which a century or more after the first Mongol onslaughts were now beginning to regain their importance as cultural centers. Little less significant for future cultural developments in the region, the language spoken by the Chaghatay ruling elite in Mawarannahr, deriving from older Turkish dialects spoken in the area, began to assume a flexible and expressive form, enriched by an extensive Persian and Arabic vocabulary. Known as Chaghatay Turkish, it was to become during the fifteenth and sixteenth centuries a vehicle for much fine literature, especially poetry, and the ancestor of modern Özbeg.

A literary language and culture exemplifying the regional synthesis of Turkish and Iranian traditions, conversion to Islam, and the availability of urban amenities—these were the elements that contributed to the taming of the Chaghatay khans in Mawarannahr, just as they had contributed to the taming of the il-khans in Iran. In consequence, the Chaghatay khans seem to have largely turned their backs on their ancestral pastures beyond the Syr Darya, where a cadet line of Chaghatay khans emerged around 1348. By the middle of the fourteenth century there were thus two khanates, both distracted by internal revolts, ambitious chieftains, and the curse of child or puppet rulers. In such a milieu Timur emerged as the most vigorous and successful of several would-be contenders for *de facto* control of the khanate, none of whom dared to supplant the line of Chaghatay since they themselves were not descendants of Chingiz Khan but exercised authority through a titular khan of the imperial house.

Elsewhere in West Asia the situation was no less inviting for a conqueror imbued with the traditions of Mongol imperialism. The Iranian plateau was divided among various local dynasties engaged in bitter rivalry with each other, of which the Jalayirids also controlled Iraq, while the Egyptian Mamluks held Syria, although not without some difficulty. Anatolia, following the demise of the Seljuk sultanate of Konya, was divided among warring Turcoman chieftains, who attracted to their service large numbers of *ghazis* ("warriors for the faith"). Among these emergent principalities, that of the Osmanli, or Ottoman Turks, was growing steadily in importance, although few at that time could have predicted its future greatness. The Ottomans' power base was located in western Anatolia, close to the Byzantine frontier, and at first their expansion had been mainly across the Bosporus and into the Balkans. They thus became a great territorial power in Europe long before they were a comparable power in Asia. Their history, too, would be temporarily deflected from its course by the career of Timur.

Timur's Bid to Revive the Mongol Empire in West Asia

Timur was born in 1336 in or near Shahrisabz, his father being chieftain of the Turco-Mongol Barlas clan. His early life, coinciding with a period of weak central government and recurring disorders throughout the Chaghatay khanate, was one of great vicissitude due to a decline in his family's position, and he was alternately freebooter, fugitive, and bandit. Gradually, however, his reputation as a daring and successful leader of a growing band of warriors drew men to his service and he eventually reached the point where, under the titular sovereignty of the Chaghatay khan, he was the most powerful figure in the khanate.

The story of his campaigns and conquests, although recorded in detail by contemporary historians, is a confusing one, but the broad outline is fairly clear. During the 1370s he consolidated his hold over Mawarannahr and campaigned to bring the steppe region northeast of the Syr Darya under his control, thereby reconstituting the Chaghatay khanate as it had been a hundred years before. He then turned toward Iran with the aim of reconstructing the il-khanate of Hülegü, a task that occupied the next seven years. He began with Khurasan and Sistan, taking Herat in 1380. He then proceeded westward across northern Iran, ravaging Azarbayjan, Georgia, and eastern Anatolia before turning south into Fars, where he sacked Shiraz in 1387. These campaigns witnessed not only massacres that probably exceeded even those perpetrated by the Chingizkhanids but also desperate resistance by some of Timur's victims, especially the resilient Jalayirids, Turco-Mongols who were to prove Timur's most obdurate opponents. Nevertheless, by the close of 1387 he was master of two of the original three Mongol khanates of the West. He therefore turned against his one-time patron, Tokhtamish, and for three years between 1388 and 1391 ravaged the Kipchak khanate, laying waste the caravan cities strung out across the steppes from the Black Sea port of Kaffa to the great entrepot of Khwarazm. Between 1392 and 1394 he was preoccupied with fighting the Jalayirids in western Iran and Iraq, capturing Baghdad in 1393. In 1395, exasperated by the recuperative powers of Tokhtamish, he once more ravaged the Kipchak khanate.

In 1398 Timur achieved what prudence or dread of the climate had prevented the Mongols from doing. He crossed the Indus and marched on Delhi. A general massacre followed his entry into the city, although craftsmen and the younger women were spared, to be sent to Samarqand, now the capital of the empire, along with the sultan's elephants. He then turned west again. During 1399-1401 he fought the Jalayirids, now allies of the Egyptian Mamluks, invaded Syria, and sacked Aleppo and Damascus, as well as Baghdad for the second time. In 1402 he marched against the Ottoman sultan, Bayezid I (1389-1403), defeated him in battle near Ankara, and took him prisoner. The Mamluks in Egypt were still undefeated, but Timur determined to undertake the invasion of China. He set off at the beginning of 1405 but got no farther than Otrar on the Syr Darya, where he died, at the age of seventy, worn out by the strain of a lifetime of almost ceaseless campaigning.

Timur's Empire as a Further Experiment in Hybrid Barbarian-Civilized Empire

Timur was probably the greatest military commander in the history of Asia; he may also have been the most cruel and the most destructive. If the chronicles are to be believed, the devastation he left behind him everywhere he went, the smoldering ruins of once-prosperous cities, the pyramids of skulls, were all on a scale exceeding even that of Chingiz Khan or Hülegü. If the thirteenth century Mongols had done irreparable harm to all aspects of civilized life in West Asia, Timur completed their handiwork. In the case of the khanate

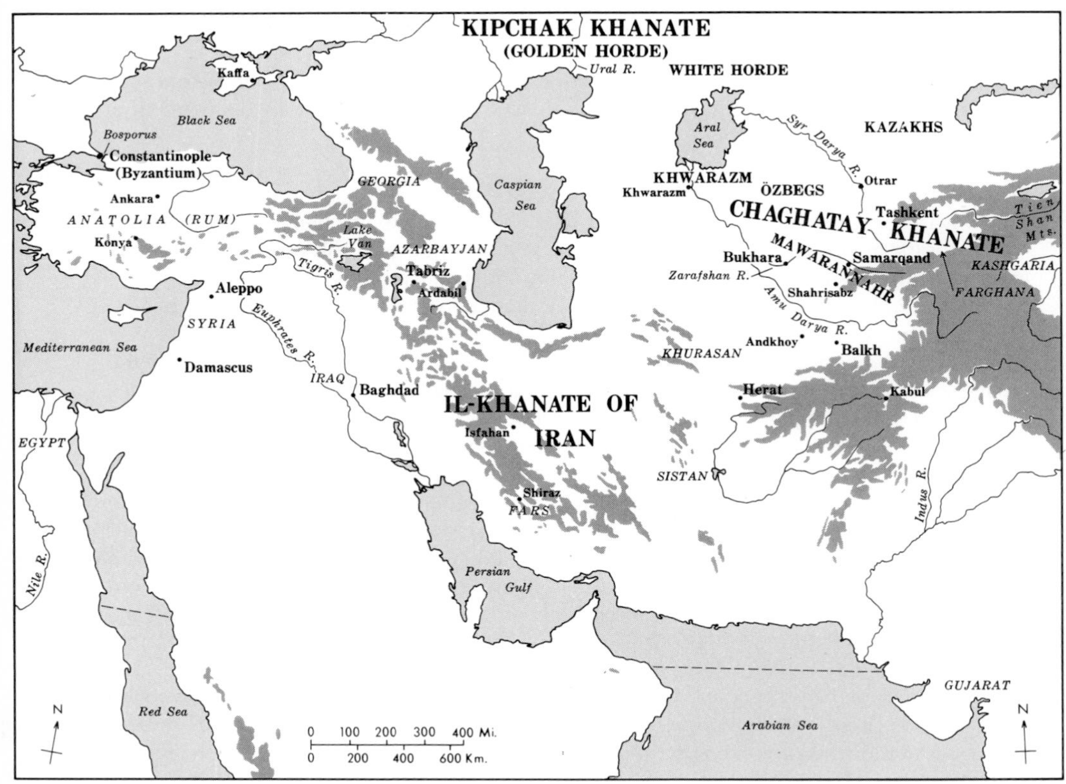

Map 36 West and Central Asia in the time of Timur, about 1400

of Kipchak, it is probable that he deliberately destroyed the settlements along the trade routes in order to divert the caravans south onto the older route crossing Anatolia to Tabriz in Azarbayjan and on through Khurasan to Samarqand. In the short term, he swept aside all those regimes in West Asia, except for that of the Egyptian Mamluks, which had emerged in the wake of the Mongols. In northwestern India he administered the *coup de grace* to Tughluq rule in Delhi, thus accelerating the process whereby the former Delhi sultanate would be replaced by regional sultanates such as those of Gujarat, Bengal, and Malwa. In the far west the defeat of Bayezid delayed further Ottoman expansion and, above all, the capture of Constantinople for another half century. In so doing Timur unwittingly contributed to the transmission of Greek learning to Renaissance Italy, since, but for his unexpected advance out of the East, it seems probable that sooner or later Bayezid would have taken the Byzantine capital.

Timur's career, however, was remarkable not only for the destruction that accompanied it, but also for its failure to improve upon or even to emulate effectively the model of a barbarian-civilized empire that had emerged under the il-khans. The fact is that, notwithstanding his superb talents as a military commander, Timur lacked the administrative skills and the imperial vision that characterized Chingiz Khan and several of his sons and grandsons. Timur's children were quarrelsome and ineffective and it seems that he himself did not draw to his service talented advisers and administrators such as had graced the Chingizkhanid courts. Certainly, he lacked one qualification the age demanded—the blood of Chingiz Khan flowing through his veins—and he was therefore compelled to maintain the fiction that he ruled on behalf of successive titular Chaghatay khans, who frequently accompanied him on his campaigns. He himself never assumed the title of khan but legitimized his position by marrying the daughter of the Chaghatay khan. This marriage enabled him to stress his connection with the Chingizkhanids by styling himself "son-in-law" on his coinage. Otherwise, he was apparently content with the title of *amir* or *beg*, although later panegyrists would refer to him as the Lord of the Fortunate Conjunction of the Planets. Those same panegyrists attempted to provide him with a spurious Mongol genealogy and also stressed the coincidence that he was born in the same (Muslim) year that the last effective il-khan died.

The ambiguity of Timur's position vis-à-vis successive Chaghatay khans was not the only aspect of his career that presents a certain paradox. Timur combined in himself and his regime two conflicting sets of values. On the one hand, to the Muslims of West Asia he seemed to be yet another "barbarian" conqueror, emerging out of the steppes to plunder and destroy, and such indeed was his function in relation to the settled population of Iran, Iraq, or Syria, who in the fourteenth century did not regard the Chaghatay khanate as being truly part of the Muslim world. But, conversely, Timur was not a product of a truly pastoral-nomadic society like that of Mongolia but of the hybrid society of Mawarannahr, where his function was that of a "lord of the marches" confronting the nomad "barbarians" of the steppes. In the final analysis he was a not untypical representative of that Turco-Iranian synthesis so characteristic of Islam in Central Asia. Ostensibly, he was an orthodox Sunni Muslim and apparently maintained good relations with the *ulama*. He established a lavish court in Samarqand, his capital, which he was determined to make more splendid than any other city in the world. In the day-to-day business of running an empire he relied on an army recruited from many different tribes and peoples and on that Iranian bureaucratic tradition without which not even the most successful conqueror could hope to maintain an uninterrupted supply of revenue.

Timur's attitude towards Islam is of great significance, although a great deal more has yet to be learned regarding Islam in general and Shiism in particular during the Timurid period (ca. 1370-ca. 1506). In many aspects of daily life Timur and his descendants strictly followed Chingizkhanid traditions, especially in matters of protocol. Timur's descendant Babur noted on a visit to Tashkent at the close of the fifteenth century how the Chaghatay khan ruling beyond the Syr Darya still retained the formal manners of his ancestors. For example, tribute or gifts, whether horses, slaves, or weapons, were given in units of nine—a sacred number. With regard to the succession to the throne and the division of the empire into great appanages for the members of the imperial family, Chingizkhanid traditions were also strictly observed. Yet, beyond the circle of the Timurid ruling elite, Islam was a standing challenge to Mongol values, an incalculable force that could be enlisted in the service of the ruler or, if he chose to disregard it, in his undoing. Islam meant, in terms of its influence, two distinct and sometimes rival groups. First there were the *ulama,* whether Sunni or Shii, who together with the bazaar merchants and minor officials formed a kind of urban patriciate and who, orthodox, conservative, and often worldly, exemplified the Muslim clerical establishment. Second, there were the dervishes, both Sunni and Shii, who were generally members of one of the Sufi orders. These dervishes were the embodiment of the "Little Traditions" of Islam, where folklore and pre-Islamic cults were somewhat casually absorbed into the religious life of the community. In the Eurasian steppe zone, these dervishes spearheaded the spread of Islam among the Turks and the steppe peoples generally, and their function and life-style therefore approximated to those of the shamans of pre-Islamic times.

Timur patronized the orthodox Sunni *ulama,* the *shaykhs,* and *sayyids* of Bukhara and Samarqand, but he also venerated, whether from superstition or political expediency, very much less orthodox figures. Thus, on the occasion of his march on Herat in 1380 he entered the town of Andkhoy and was received by a dervish of local fame who threw meat from the breast of an animal in front of the conqueror, which Timur interpreted as an omen of victory in the forthcoming campaign. When, on the same march, he passed through the village of Tayabad, another dervish refused to meet him. When the two men eventually met, Timur prostrated himself at the feet of the dervish, who pressed his hands heavily upon Timur's shoulders as a sign of his blessing in his war against the ruler of Herat. Such evidence of a close political relationship between the dervishes and the Timurid dynasty became even more apparent under Timur's successors, while under the Özbegs, who ruled in Bukhara and Khiva from the sixteenth to the nineteenth centuries, dervish influence became a major cause of the cultural backwardness of the region.

Disintegration of Timur's Empire and the Emergence of New Patterns in West Asia
Timur conquered everywhere but consolidated nowhere. His vast but loosely held possessions were divided among his sons and grandsons at his death, and while these fell to fighting among themselves, new forces emerged during the fifteenth century that provided the main catalysts for the evolution of West Asia down to the beginnings of European penetration in the eighteenth century. At first the fragility of the Timurid empire did not appear obvious. After a short struggle with his relatives, Timur's fourth son, Shah-Rukh (r. 1407-47), succeeded to the throne and although he was not particularly aggressive or warlike he had little difficulty in holding together the core of his father's conquests, the former Chaghatay khanate in Mawarannahr and the territories of the il-khanate. An outstanding patron of Islamic literature, learning, and the arts, he embodied all the traditional virtues of the exemplary Muslim ruler. Perhaps in order to draw closer to the Muslim heartlands and also to escape the complexities of politics on the steppe frontier, he transferred the seat of the empire from Samarqand to Herat, leaving the former city and the whole of Mawarannahr in the charge of his eldest son, Ulugh Beg, an amateur mathematician and astronomer who attracted to his observatory in Samarqand like-minded scholars with whom he compiled a celebrated set of astronomical tables. Shah-Rukh, like the Mongol rulers of a former age, made himself familiar to his contemporaries by rather pretentious diplomatic missions. In addition to exchanges with the Ming court he dispatched the historian Abd al-Razzaq Samarqandi on an embassy to south India, where he was welcomed by the rulers of Calicut and Vijayanagar. On his return he reported that the sultan of Bengal and the sultan of Jaunpur, engaged in a protracted quarrel, had agreed to accept the arbitration of his master. This may have been no more than skillful flattery on the envoy's part, but there seems no doubt that the feeble Sayyid dynasty in Delhi (1414-51) recognized Shah-Rukh's overlordship. Even before his death, however, his control over western Iran had come to an end, and after the brief reign of Ulugh Beg (1447-49) the Timurid empire disintegrated except in Khurasan and Mawarannahr. It is therefore appropriate to consider separately subsequent developments in each of the four main areas of the empire: (1) Khurasan and Mawarannahr; (2) the steppe zone north and northeast of Mawarannahr; (3) western Iran and eastern Anatolia; and (4) western Anatolia.

Khurasan and Mawarannahr
Timurid rule followed Turco-Mongol practice in dividing up the empire into appanages, which grew steadily smaller as each new generation of princes demanded and fought for a redistribution of fiefs. Following Ulugh Beg's death in 1449, a great-grandson of Timur, Abu Said, gained control of most of Khurasan and Mawarannahr, but after his death in 1469 the whole area split into mutually antagonistic principalities, the most important centering upon Herat, Balkh, Samarqand, Bukhara, and the Farghana valley (the upper reaches of the Syr Darya). These Timurid princelings proved themselves some of the most discriminating

patrons in the history of Islamic painting and architecture, and their courts, where both Persian and Chaghatay Turkish poets received generous encouragement, were distinguished by an attractive version of *fin de siècle* hedonism. Their individual resources, however, were extremely slender, they were temperamentally incapable of combining or regrouping into more stable units, and the old tribal supports of the dynasty had long since been eroded. They maintained some of the trappings of the hybrid barbarian-civilized empires of the past, but in reality were almost wholly assimilated into the prevailing Irano-Islamic cultural milieu. The process was a complex one and it is vividly illustrated in the *Tuzuk-i Baburi, The Memoirs of Babur,* a descendant of Timur who inherited the principality of Farghana, won and lost Samarqand, then seized control of Kabul and finally ended his days as the first of the Mughul conquerors of India (r. 1526-30).

The Timurids enjoy a well-deserved niche in the history of Persian and Chaghatay Turkish literature and also in the history of Islamic art and architecture, but their period of glory was brief and it was over by 1500. In that year Timur's former capital, Samarqand, fell to a new invading group, the Özbegs, and in 1507 the latter rounded off their conquests with the capture of Herat. With their occupation of Mawarannahr and much of Khurasan there began a new chapter in the history of West Asia, since the coming of the Özbegs and the rise of the Safavids in northwestern Iran together initiated a chain reaction that was to be felt from the Bosporus to the Bay of Bengal.

The Steppe Zone

Timur's wars against the Chaghatay khans beyond the Syr Darya and against the khanate of Kipchak appear to have brought about great changes in the tribal composition of these regions, although it is not now possible to see clearly what happened. Connected with these changes was the appearance of a new Turco-Mongol people on the north bank of the lower Syr Darya sometime during the first half of the fifteenth century. They had come from the region of the Tobol River in western Siberia, where they had been subjects of the khan of Kipchak, and their chieftains were descended from a younger brother of Batu. They had probably adopted Islam during the reign of the most powerful of the khans of Kipchak, Özbeg (1312-41), and had in consequence adopted the name of Özbegs. Their migration southeastward toward the Syr Darya had probably been part of a chain reaction resulting from Timur's campaigns in the steppes, but by the middle decades of the fifteenth century they were hovering on the northern frontier of the Timurid empire. From this vantage point their khan, Abul-Khayr (1429-68), proceeded to interfere in the internal affairs of the Timurid empire and might well have destroyed it altogether but for his death in 1468, fighting his own tribesmen. Abul-Khayr, like other tribal leaders, was plagued by the problem of how to coerce his own unruly kinsfolk and his *begs*. In this case, a number of mutinous clans broke away from his control and fled into the steppes northeast of the Syr Darya. This breakaway group, which acquired the name of Kazakhs, created in the sixteenth century a steppe empire extending eastward from the Ural River to the Dzungarian Gates, but by then the Özbegs had turned south across the Syr Darya to occupy Mawarannahr, Khwarazm, and much of northern Khurasan under the leadership of Abul-Khayr's grandson, Muhammad Shaybani (d. 1510).

Western Iran and Eastern Anatolia

By the middle of the fifteenth century the Timurids had lost control over western Iran and eastern Anatolia, where their place was taken successively by two powerful Turcoman confederacies: that of the Kara-Koyunlu (1380-1468), originating from the Lake Van region, and that of the Ak-Koyunlu (1378-1508), from near Diyarbakr. These confederacies dominated an area of rich pastures and inaccessible mountain retreats where tribal societies down to the twentieth century have managed to hold out against their neighbors, but while their strength was rooted in a nomadic tribal structure they too, like the Timurids, were notable patrons of Iranian urban culture. There is still much to be learned about both the Kara-Koyunlu and the Ak-Koyunlu, but one thing is clear: under their rule a great impetus was given to the spread of heterodox and especially Shii beliefs among the tribes of the area. The Kara-Koyunlu were Shii, the Ak-Koyunlu were Sunni, but under both dynasties Shiism spread rapidly, especially into central Anatolia, today almost exclusively Sunni. Of the various Sufi movements that flourished under the rule of the Ak-Koyunlu the most important was that of the Safaviya order, with its headquarters at Ardabil in eastern Azarbayjan. Founded by Shaykh Safi al-Din (d. 1334), who was almost certainly a Sunni, the movement seems to have acquired Shii tenets and politico-messianic aspirations under the leadership of one of his descendants, Shaykh Junayd (1447-60), who married a sister of the Ak-Koyunlu ruler Uzun Hasan, while his son and successor, Shaykh Haydar (r. 1460-88), married one of Uzun Hazan's daughters. Following the decline of the Ak-Koyunlu upon the death of Uzun Hazan in 1478, Shaykh Haydar's youngest son, Ismail, began to forge in the area a new tribal confederacy, the Qizilbash, with which to advance the cause of both Safaviya Shiism and his own Safavid dynasty, soon to seize control of the entire Iranian plateau. This rise of the Safavids was the second movement that, in conjunction with the coming of the Özbegs, began the chain reaction in West Asia that would lead inadvertently to the establishment of Mughul rule in India and of Ottoman rule throughout Anatolia, the Fertile Crescent and, eventually, Egypt.

The Ottomans in Western Anatolia

As has already been mentioned, Timur's sudden incursion into central and western Anatolia in 1402 diverted the immediate course of Ottoman expansionism, which had been about to deal a final blow at the moribund Byzantine empire. Bayezid's defeat and death and the subsequent struggle over the succession exposed the Ottomans to a ring of foes, and it is not therefore surprising that during the first half of the fifteenth century their history is one of internal consolidation, followed by renewed expansion in the Balkans. The Anatolian frontier was of less pressing concern than it was ever to be again. During the reign of Mehmed II (1451-81), who captured Constantinople in 1453, the new role of the Ottoman state as a Black Sea, Balkan, and eastern Mediterranean power overshadowed Anatolian problems, but certain developments need stressing at this stage to understand the course of events at the beginning of the sixteenth century. First, as has already been mentioned, there was the ever-increasing dissemination of Shiism among the Turcoman tribes of eastern and central Anatolia, which constituted a political threat to the Ottomans on account of the connections of those tribes with the powerful Turcoman confederacies of the Kara-Koyunlu, Ak-Koyunlu and the Safavids to their east. It also constituted an ideological challenge to the novel ecumenical claim of the Ottomans to be the champions not only of Islam but of orthodoxy. Second, during the 1470s the Ottoman advance into southeastern Anatolia threatened a direct confrontation with the still formidable Mamluk regime in Syria, protected to the north by a chain of Turcoman client principalities, a confrontation postponed until the second decade of the sixteenth century. Third, the growing strength of Uzun Hasan and his opposition to further Ottoman penetration into central and eastern Anatolia compelled Mehmed II to take the field against him in 1473, but without settling the issue of who was permanently to control that strategic area of West Asia. Thus it was clear by the end of the century that, sooner or later, the Ottoman sultans would have to deal with these three related problems: the spread of Shiism among the Turcoman tribes of Anatolia; the relationship of those tribes to whatever regime dominated Azarbayjan and western Iran; and the undefined frontier with the Mamluks.

8.4 A Turcoman prince and his mistress, illustrating Nizami's romance, *Khusru and Shirin*. Miniature of the Shiraz School, late fifteenth century. During the fifteenth century the Turco-Mongol and Turcoman ruling elites became increasingly assimilated to the culture and life-style of Iran. Courtesy: India Office Library, London.

CONCLUDING REMARKS

From the time of the first universal empires of Asia, the largest scale of political organization corresponded to the major mainland regions of civilized society in West, South, and East Asia. Frequently, in times of political fragmentation, the scale of organization was smaller. Only during the thirteenth and fourteenth centuries was the scale of political organization larger than that of the civilizations. The Mongols under Chingiz Khan and his heirs first created an Inner Asian empire by bringing the steppe and oasis peoples under their political control. They then sent their armies raiding and conquering in West and East Asia until they had brought China, Iran, and Mesopotamia into their empire. Northern India was spared conquest until the formation of the ephemeral empire of the Timurids, however. European Russia also was long subject to Mongol control. The Mongol conquest, therefore, was an experience shared by most of the agricultural and urban population of Eurasia and may be seen as the climactic episode in the long history of interaction and conflict between the peoples of steppe and sown.

Both in conquering and then in ruling the civilized populations, the Mongols enlisted the aid of other Inner Asian peoples who had preceded them. In Central and West Asia, the Mongols rapidly merged into the Turkish military aristocracies, and in China they found survivors of the Khitan and Jurchen conquests to be useful mediators between themselves and the Chinese. Moreover, at both ends of the empire, members of the landowning and urban elites, Iranians in the one case, Chinese in the other, were eventually recruited as administrators and tax gatherers.

There were contrasts as well as similarities, however. The cultural context in West Asia was relatively complex, with strong elements of Islamic and indigenous Iranian civilization both present. Moreover, many of the Mongols and their Turkish associates were better able to maintain their pastoral-nomadic values along with their adopted Islamic religion in the grassland settings of the Iranian plateau, Mawarannahr, Farghana, and Dzungaria, despite the tendency of their elite members to be captivated by the life-style of the cities. In East Asia, the cultural situation was simpler and more sharply drawn. The surviving representatives of the Liao and Chin rulers of north China were thoroughly assimilated to Chinese culture and so did not present as clear a contrast with the Chinese as the Turks did with respect to the Iranians and Russians. The Mongols in China, therefore, were faced with the dichotomous choice between resistance or accommodation to the Chinese pattern. Maintenance of their own cultural traditions was made more difficult, however, by the fact that the Chinese setting provided little support for pastoralism and its values. The split between traditionalists and assimilators among the Mongols in East Asia probably ran deeper and was more damaging socially than in the West. These differences help to explain why Mongol rule ended in the West in a process of gradual political disintegration of the il-khanate and the Chaghatay khanate into minor Turkish and Mongol states, whereas in China the Mongols were almost entirely driven out and were then supplanted by a new, unified regime of indigenous Chinese origin.

BIBLIOGRAPHY

8.P EURASIAN INTEGRATION UNDER CENTRAL ASIAN DOMINANCE: PROCESSES

Eberhard, W., *Conquerors and Rulers* (Leiden, 1965), 191 pp. A sociological study of Sino-barbarian interaction.

Krader, Lawrence. *Formation of the State* (New York, 1968), 118 pp. Chapter 5, 21 pp., offers an anthropological analysis of state building in the steppes.

Lattimore, Owen, *Inner Asian Frontiers of China* (New York, 1940), 585 pp. Part 4, 123 pp., of this classic study presents the author's analysis of Chinese frontier history.

Wittfogel, Karl A., *History of Chinese Society: Liao 907-1125* (New York, 1949), 752 pp. A detailed study of the frontier state by the controversial theorist of Chinese political organization.

8.1 FORMATION OF THE MONGOL EMPIRE IN CENTRAL ASIA

Bingham, Woodbridge, Hilary Conroy, and Frank W. Ikle, *A History of Asia,* 2 vols. (Boston, 1964), 582, 690 pp. Chapter 21, 19 pp., provides a survey of the formation of Chingiz' empire.

Dawson, Christopher, *Mission to Asia* (New York, 1955), 246 pp. This collection of contemporary travel accounts provides a vivid illumination of life in the Mongol empire.

Grousset, Rene, *Conqueror of the World: The Life of Chingis-Khan* (New York, 1966), 300 pp. A sound and readable account of Chingiz' career.

Hambly, Gavin, ed., *Central Asia* (London, 1969), 388 pp. A scholarly survey of the history of the region.

Prawdin, Michael, *The Mongol Empire* (New York, 1940), 581 pp. A popular but generally reliable book. Parts 1 and 2 (333 pp.) survey the history of the empire through the reign of Kubilai.

Saunders, J.J., *The History of the Mongol Conquests* (New York, 1971), 275 pp. This broad survey is particularly useful for the Central and West Asian phases of the conquests.

8.2 THE MONGOL EMPIRE IN WEST ASIA

Boyle, John A., ed., *The Cambridge History of Iran,* Vol. 5, *The Saljuq and Mongol Periods* (Cambridge, 1968), 679 pp. Essays by leading scholars, describing various aspects of life under the il-khans.

Cahen, Claude, *Pre-Ottoman Turkey* (New York, 1968), pp. 269-360. A description of the impact of il-khanid rule on the Seljuk sultanate of Rum. Illustrated.

Lambton, Ann K. S., *Landlord and Peasant in Persia* (Oxford, 1953), pp. 77-104. A definitive account of the effects of the Mongol invasions on preexisting agrarian relationships.

Saunders, John J., *The History of the Mongol Conquests* (London, 1971), pp. 119-54. A general introduction to the period.

Spuler, Bertold, *History of the Mongols Based On Eastern and Western Accounts of the Thirteenth and Fourteenth Centuries* (Berkeley, 1972), 207 pp. A useful anthology of readings.

Vernadsky, George, *The Mongols in Russia* (New Haven, 1953), 462 pp. The only detailed study in English.

8.3 MONGOL DOMINATION IN EAST ASIA

Bingham, Woodbridge, Hilary Conroy, and Frank W. Ikle, *A History of Asia* (Boston, 1964), 2 vols. Chapter 22 surveys the Mongol empire in East Asia.

Dardess, John W., *Conquerors and Confucians* (New York, 1973), 245 pp. A learned but readable examination of the disintegration of the Yuan state.

de Rachewiltz, Igor, "Yeh-lu Ch'u-ts'ai (1189-1243): Buddhist Idealist and Confucian Statesman," in Arthur F. Wright and Denis Twitchett, eds., *Confucian Personalities* (Stanford, 1962), 411 pp. Good account of policy issues relating to Mongol rule in north China.

Fairbank, John K., Edwin O. Reischauer, and Albert M.Craig, *East Asia: Tradition and Transformation* (Boston, 1973), 969 pp. Chapter 7 surveys the Mongol empire in East Asia.

Latham, Ronald, *Marco Polo: The Travels* (Baltimore, 1958), 380 pp. This is but one of many good translations of the medieval classic; much information on China from the point of view of a European in the service of the Yuan regime.

Schurmann, Herbert F., trans., *Economic Structure of the Yuan Dynasty* (Cambridge, 1956), 251 pp. This annotated translation of a major source for the economic history of the Yuan is somewhat technical, but useful for Mongol-Chinese interaction.

8.4 CENTRAL ASIA UNDER TIMUR

Bartold, Vasilii V., *Ulugh Beg,* trans. V. and T. Minorsky (Leiden, 1963), pp. 1-42. The best account of Timur's career available in English.

Hajianpur, Mahin, "The Timurid Empire and the Uzbek Conquest of Mawarannahr," in G. R. G. Hambly, ed., *Central Asia,* (New York, 1969), pp. 150-62. A concise introductory essay.

Hill, Derek, and Oleg Grabar, *Islamic Architecture and Its Decorations,* A.D. *800-1500* (Chicago, 1964), 88 pp. Describes, with illustrations, the remarkable architectural achievements of the Timurids.

Inalcik, Halil, "The Emergence of the Ottomans," *The Cambridge History of Islam,* 2 vols. (Cambridge, 1970), Vol. 1, pp. 263-91. The rise of the Ottomans described by one of the most distinguished of modern Turkish historians.

Markham, Sir Clements R., *Narrative of the Embassy of Ruy Gonzalez de Clavijo to the Court of Timour* (London, 1859, reprinted New York, 1963), 200 pp. A detailed description of Timur's court, by the envoy of Henry III of Castile.

Savory, R. M., "The Struggle for Supremacy in Persia After the Death of Timur," *Der Islam* 40.1:35-65 (1964). A lucid summary of events on the Iranian plateau during the fifteenth century.

GLOSSARY

Amir. Generally, a military commander or governor; occasionally a sovereign title, as in the case of the amir of Bukhara.

Beg (Turkish). Military commander.

Caliph (Arabic, **khalifa**). Originating with the title of the Prophet Muhammad's successor, Abu Bakr, Khalifat Rasul Allah, "Successor of the Messenger of God." The caliph was the head of the Islamic *umma,* "the community of believers," and was referred to as *amir al-muminin,* "commander of the faithful."

Chaghatay (d. 1241). Second son of Chingiz Khan and founder of the Chaghatay khanate in Central Asia; also, Chaghatay Turkish, the language spoken in that khanate and the precursor of present-day Özbeg.

Chaghatay Khanate. Extended over the central portions of the Mongol empire including parts of what are now Chinese and Russian Turkistan.

Chingiz Khan (ca. 1167-1227). The title of Temuchin of the Borjigin clan of Mongols, who organized the great federation of Mongolian and Turkish tribes of Inner Asia that later completed the conquest of most of the Eurasian continent.

Dervish. A Sufi; either a religious mendicant or a member of a Sufi brotherhood *(tariqa)* attached to a dervish convent *(khanqah).*

Ghazi. A warrior living in the frontier areas of the Muslim world and engaged in holy warfare (*jihad*) against non-Muslims.

Il-khan. The title assumed by the Chingizkhanid Mongol rulers of Iran (1256-1353), originally implying subordination to the supreme *khaqan* in Mongolia. In recent centuries some tribal chieftains in Iran, such as the chieftains of the Qashqai, have assumed the title.

Il-khanate. The Mongol khanate that extended over Iran, Iraq, and parts of Turkey and Afghanistan.

Iqta. The revenue assignment of a certain area, generally granted in exchange for military service.

Karakorum. The early capital city of the Mongol empire situated in northern Mongolia. The capital was shifted to Peking by the emperor Kubilai.

Kazakhs. A Turkish people who, since the middle decades of the fifteenth century, have practiced pastoral nomadism in the Central Asian steppe region north of the Aral Sea and the Syr Darya River.

Khan. A title widely used among the Turkish and Mongolian peoples of Central Asia, frequently, but not invariably, denoting a sovereign authority; also, a military commander, as in Muslim India.

Khaqan (also **khakhan, khaghan**). A title widely used among the Turkish and Mongolian peoples of Central Asia and usually, although not invariably, denoting suzerainty over an extended tribal confederacy.

Khurasan. Formerly a vast area extending northeastwards from the central Iranian desert to the Amu Darya River, with its metropolitan centers located at Nishapur, Marv, Herat, and Balkh. Today Khurasan consists of a province in northeastern Iran, bordering the U.S.S.R. and Afghanistan, and with its capital at Mashhad.

Khwarazm (ancient Chorasmia). The region south of the Aral Sea watered by the various channels of the Amu Darya delta, and known during the nineteenth century as Khiva.

Kipchak. The name given by the Arabs to the steppe region north of the Caspian and the Black Sea and inhabited by predominantly Turkish tribes. The Mongol khanate of Kipchak, known to the Russians as the Golden Horde, was the appanage of the descendants of Chingiz Khan's oldest son, Jochi. Acculturation between the Kipchak Turks and the Turco-Mongol armies of the Chingizkhanids produced the ethnic stock known in later Central Asian history as Tatars.

Kipchak Khanate. Also called the Golden Horde. The Mongol khanate that extended over the steppe regions north of the Caspian and the Black Seas, as well as over much of European Russia.

Kubilai Khan (r. 1260-94). Committed the khaqanate to a policy of permanent rule over China in an essentially Chinese manner. In doing so he became founder of the Yuan dynasty in 1271, while retaining his title as *khaqan*.

Kuriltai. The assembly of nobles that made major decisions on behalf of the steppe federations, such as the election of *khaqans* or the commencement of campaigns.

Mamluk. A slave-soldier, generally although not exclusively a Turk, a Georgian, or a Circassian.

Mawarannahr (literally, "that which lies beyond the river"). The Arabic name for the area lying between the Amu Darya and Syr Darya rivers, and including the cities of Samarqand and Bukhara. Known in ancient times as Sogdiana, the "land of the Sogdians," and to the Greeks as Transoxania, "the land beyond the Oxus" (i.e., the Amu Darya), it was generally referred to in the nineteenth century as Russian Turkistan.

Millet. A non-Muslim religious community living under the protection of a Muslim state (especially the Ottoman empire) and maintaining a considerable degree of internal autonomy under its own religious leaders.

Noyan (Mongolian). A noble or prince.

Ögedei Khan. The son and heir of Chingiz and the conqueror of north China and the state of Chin in 1234.

Özbegs (also, **Uzbeks**). A Turkish people who, since the second half of the fifteenth century, have occupied the area between the Syr Darya and Amu Darya Rivers (formerly Russian Turkistan and now divided between various Central Asian republics of the U.S.S.R).

Sayyid. A descendant of the Prophet Muhammad through his daughter, Fatima, and his son-in-law (and cousin), Ali.

Shaykh. A Sufi teacher, also known as a *murshid* or *pir*.

Shiis. Those who follow the *shia* (or party) of Ali, Muhammad's son-in-law and the fourth caliph of the Muslims. The Shiis, although subdivided into a number of sects, constitute the largest minority group (as opposed to the Sunni majority) within Islam and are today chiefly to be found in Iran and Iraq.

Sunnis. Those who follow the *sunna,* or practice of the Prophet Muhammad; the majority community in the Islamic world.

Turcoman. A term of unknown origin. One explanation of its derivation links it to the Persian *Turk manand,* meaning "Turk-like." Although appearing at different times in different areas, the Turcomans generally spoke a West Turkish language, retained memories of a pastoral-nomadic background, and displayed a life-style of a kind associated with Turkish peoples over an extensive area of West and Central Asia.

Uigurs. A Turkish people who in 744 founded an empire in Mongolia centered on the Orkhon River; in 762 their kaghan was converted to Manichaeanism. With the overthrow of the Uigur empire in 840, the Uigur tribes were dispersed, the majority fleeing into the Tarim basin in what is now Sinkiang, where they eventually displaced the indigenous Indo-European population and where they have remained ever since.

Ulama. The Arabic plural of *alim,* meaning a scholar trained in the Islamic "sciences." Collectively, the *ulama* enforced the Sharia and determined the social norms that governed the life of the Muslim community as a whole.

Vazir. The minister of a Muslim ruler. In fact, a ruler might appoint concurrently two or more *vazirs* to have charge over different areas of administration but the term is usually applied in the sense of a chief minister, as with the Ottoman "grand vizier."

Yasa. The public law of the Mongol empire of Chingiz Khan and his successors: a compilation, of which only random fragments have survived, combining the sayings and injunctions of Chingiz Khan and the customary law of the Mongol tribes during his lifetime.

9

Early Modern Empires in Asia

Early Modern Empires in Asia

1350 to 1850

Following a prolonged era of regional fragmentation and the brief experience of Central Asian domination, the principal culture zones of Asia were once again unified by great land-based empires. Included among these states of the period 1350 to 1850 were the Ottoman empire in West Asia, the Safavids in Iran, the Mughuls in India, the Ming and subsequent Ch'ing dynasties in China, and the Tokugawa regime in Japan. The Czarist Russian empire in northern Eurasia offers a counterexample with some Western cultural dimensions. The early modern empires resembled the universal empires of the ancient period in the sense that they were built upon a preindustrial agricultural base by hereditary military regimes employing foot soldiers and horsemen. They differed from their earliest predecessors, however, in that civilized society had grown in scale and complexity, considerable advances had been made in technology, and the passage of centuries had deepened the cultural traditions of each civilization. The universal religions, especially, tended to offer a measure by which Asians chose to define their civilizations. Early modern empires, in rationalizing their rule, gave special attention to this cultural dimension. The advent of printing and increased literacy made possible an intensive cultural policy on the part of the state. Early modern empires can be variously characterized as culturalistic or pluralistic, depending on their cultural policy and the foreign or indigenous origin of their rulers. In Anatolia a Turkish conquest group took up the Islamic banner in the long-standing hostilities with Christian Europe and others, and extended its holdings widely, bringing the Balkans as well as Egypt, Arabia, and Mesopotamia under its power. In Iran, a confederation of Qizilbash tribes consolidated a broad area into the Ṣafavid empire, a state that patronized Shii Islam. The Mughuls, a name derived from the word "Mongol," were an essentially Turkish conquest group that controlled northern India through a pluralistic state system based on Muslim rule but incorporating indigenous Hindu elements. In China the Ming expelled the Mongols in the fourteenth century and established a centralized bureaucratic polity that promoted Confucianism as a state ideology. The Ch'ing dynasty, which was founded by invading Manchus after 1644, continued the essential outlines of Ming institutions. The Tokugawa regime in Japan was based on a carefully maintained balance of feudal lords held in check by a military hegemon who ruled while the hereditary imperial line was preserved in impotent isolation. In the broadest terms the early modern empires may be regarded as agents of cultural conservatism, reviving and preserving traditional values after the Mongol conquests. Social and political stability were among the outstanding achievements of these states, a fact that has often prompted Westerners to view Asian societies as static.

9

PROCESSES

The Creation and Maintenance of Early Modern Empires

a. Military conquest
b. Reunification of the culture area: control of frontiers
c. Domination of the economy and society

The Cultural Legitimation of Early Modern Empires

d. Promotion of the cultural tradition: culturalism and pluralism
e. Manipulation and modification of cultural forms

Consequences of the Formation of Early Modern Empires

PATTERNS

1. **The Ottomans in West Asia**
2. **The Safavids in Iran**
3. **The Mughuls in South Asia**
4. **The Ming and Ch'ing Empires in China**
5. **Tokugawa Japan**

9. EARLY MODERN EMPIRES

	1	2	3	4	5
	OTTOMAN	SAFAVID	MUGHUL	MING-CH'ING	TOKUGAWA
1300	Sultan Bayezid I, r. 1389-1403			Rebellions and collapse of Mongol rule Ming dynasty founded at Nanking 1368 Elimination of post of prime minister 1380	
1400	Ottoman forces defeated by Timur at Ankara 1402 Sultan Mehmed II, The Conqueror, r. 1451-81 Conquest of Constantinople 1453 Khan of Crimea tributary to Ottoman sultan 1475			Usurpation by Yung-lo emperor, r. 1402-24 Conquest of Annam, Cheng Ho voyages to Africa, imperial campaigns to Mongolia, capital moved to Peking 1420	
1500	Selim I, The Grim, r. 1512-20 Ottomans defeat Safavid Shah Ismail at Caldiran 1514 Ottoman conquest of Egypt 1517 Sultan Süleyman I, The Magnificent, r. 1520-66 Ottomans capture Belgrade 1521 Siege of Vienna 1529	Shaykh Ismail of Safaviya order takes Tabriz, proclaims himself shah 1501 Safavids take Baghdad 1508 Safavids defeated by Ottomans at Caldiran1514 Death of Shah Ismail 1524	First Battle of Panipat 1526 Babur, r. 1526-30	Wang Yang-ming, neo-Confucian school of mind	

	Conquest of Baghdad 1534	Ottomans take Tabriz and Baghdad 1534 Shah Abbas I, r. 1588-1629	Humayun, r. 1530-40 and 1555-56 Second Battle of Panipat 1556 Akbar, r. 1556-1605	Development of syncretic trends challenging orthodox neo-Confucianism	Nobunaga deposes Ashikaga shogun 1573 Hideyoshi establishes hegemony 1590
1600		Portuguese expelled from Hormuz 1622 Safavids reconquer Baghdad 1623 Baghdad lost to Ottomans 1638 Shah Abbas II, r. 1642-66 Shah Sultan Husayn, r. 1694-1722	Jahangir, r. 1605-1627 Shah Jahan, r. 1627-58 Partial pacification of the Deccan 1636 Awrangzeb, r. 1658-1707 Awrangzeb leaves Delhi for Deccan 1681 Mughuls take sultanates of Bijapur and Golconda 1687	Factionalism at court intensified Wei Chung-hsien, eunuch dictator Peasant rebellions end Ming dynasty Manchus establish the Ch'ing dynasty 1644 K'ang-hsi, r. 1662-1772, Chinese resistance in the south suppressed	Tokugawa victory at Sekigahara 1600 Seclusion policy enforced 1620s and 1630s Neo-Confucian college established 1630
1700			Death of Awrangzeb 1707	Ch'ien-lung, r. 1736-95, patronage of Chinese scholarship Rapid population growth Increased corruption Spread of opium use	Yoshimune as shogun 1716
1800					

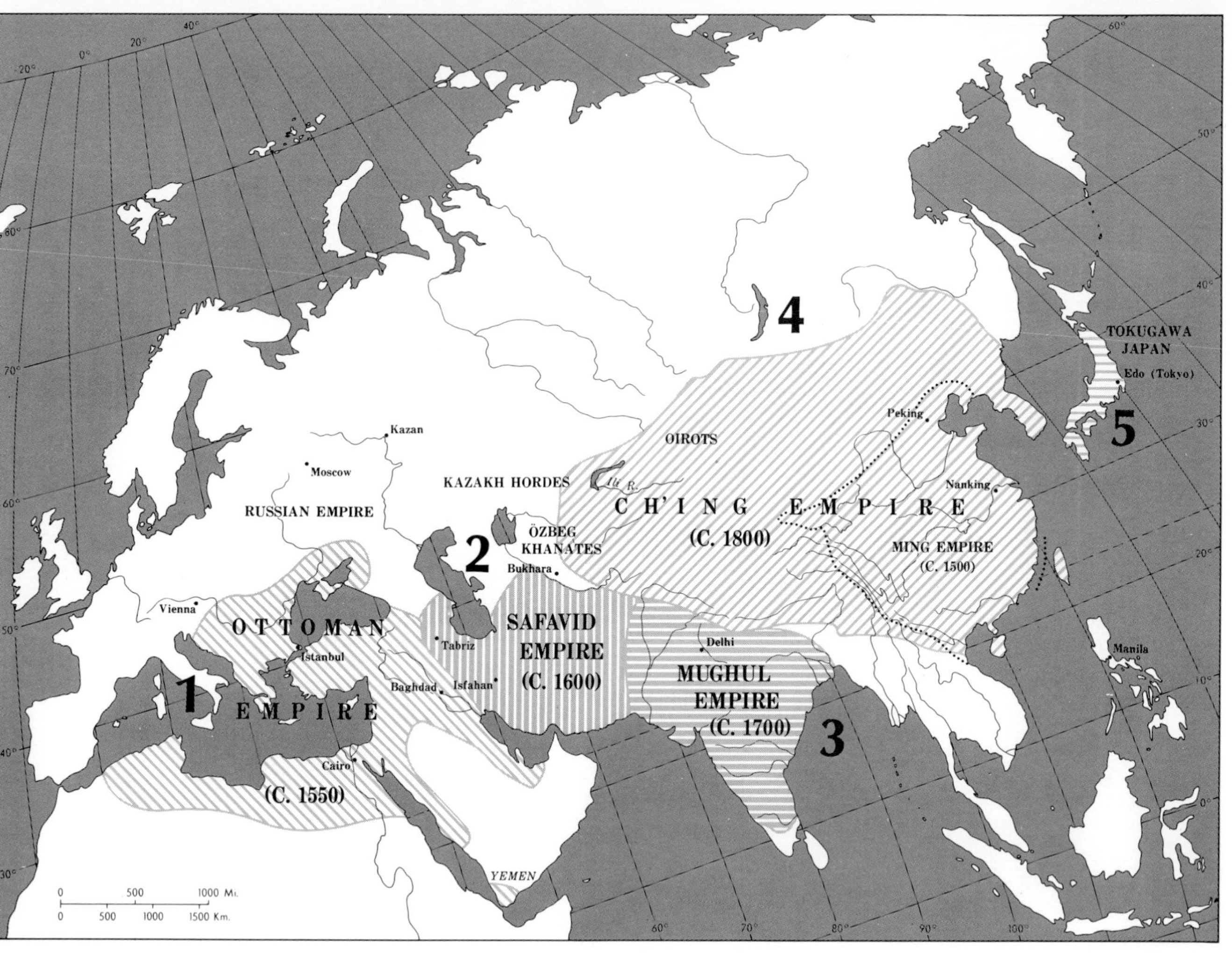

Map 37 Early modern empires in Asia

PROCESSES

Following the period of Central Asian domination, Asia came to be divided among a number of huge states that we call early modern empires. The era of these great empires lasted from around 1350 to 1850, and some of them persisted even into the twentieth century. Historically, these empires are significant both in terms of what preceded them and what came after them, for they provide a link between the earlier eras of regional cultural development and a more recent and familiar period of intensified global interaction. In their inception these empires constituted both an embodiment of the values of the cultural heritage derived from the historical experiences of universal empires and universal religions discussed in Chapters 4, 5, and 6, and a domestication of elements of Mongol rule considered in Chapter 8. In their demise, as will be seen in subsequent chapters, they constituted the forms of social organization that Western Europeans encountered in Asia in modern times and the institutional structures that conditioned the patterns of technological change and nationalism in Asia.

THE PERIOD

The early modern empires of Asia were roughly contemporaneous with the Portuguese, Spanish, Dutch, and English empires. Those empires were based on maritime expansion and differed in a number of fundamental respects from the Asian empires, which were formed by the control of contiguous land areas. For this reason the discussion of the European empires will be left to a later chapter in which they will be considered in terms of the interaction of civilizations under the title "Maritime Integration Under Western European Domination." The principal patterns to be considered here are: Safavid empire (1501-1722) in Iran; the Ottoman empire (1453-1918) formed by the Ottoman Turks in West Asia, eastern Europe, and northern Africa; the Mughul empire (1526-1739) in India; the indigenous Ming empire (1368-1644) and the foreign (Manchu) Ch'ing empire (1644-1911) in China. The Tokugawa state (1600-1868) in Japan was much more limited in size and cultural diversity than were any of the above but can fruitfully be treated under the same rubrics. The Russian empire (1480-1917) in northern Eurasia would be the most readily comparable "Western" example of an early modern empire.

In terms of the development of the various civilizations of Asia, the formation of early modern empires was in most cases a consequence of the experience of Mongol pressures in the preceding period. In some cases, notably China and Russia, the conquest and domination by Central Asians stimulated a reassertion of regional cultural values. To some extent, this response to external threats reflected a defensive or conservative psychology in which the peoples of a cultural area rallied to preserve the essential elements in their civilization from further intrusions. In other cases, especially the Safavids, Ottomans, Mughuls, and Manchus, Central Asian domination provided a model for the transformation of tribal organizations into empires through the conquest of civilized areas. Here, too, indigenous tradition played a significant role in defining the empire. The Safavid advocacy of an appeal to Shii loyalties helped to make Shiism the dominant faith in Iran. The Ottoman concept of the holy war against the unbelievers reinforced the historic sense of Islamic community in West Asia and northern Africa.

The early modern empires were vehicles of cultural resurgence in the sense that they reunified whole culture areas that had known unification before. In their scope the early modern empires were comparable to the universal empires of the ancient period. In a historical perspective, however, the two groups of empires differed markedly. In the first place, the universal states of the first millennium B.C. unified culture areas in a way that was without precedent, and by so doing shaped the subsequent development of the civilization in a unique way. All empires that followed, the early modern empires included, were constrained by established precedent and to varying degrees defined themselves retrospectively in terms of their predecessors. Secondly, the very fact that each culture area had experienced periods of relative political integration and division limited the claims that could be made for a new empire in the early modern period.

The significance of the early modern empires is perhaps best revealed by the degree to which they embodied developmental changes that were cumulative throughout history. Like the universal empires of the ancient period, the early modern empires were land empires based on a predominantly agricultural economy. The early modern "preindustrial" economy had evolved through incremental changes far beyond the stages reached in the pre-Christian era. Growth in population, increase in land area under cultivation, and improvements in techniques, tools, and seeds meant both that the total agricultural output was greater and that a greater portion of it was available to support nonagricultural activities. Likewise in industry, while the use of inanimate power sources and capital accumulation did not reach the stages of rationalization that characterized the industrial revolution, there were substantial advances in technologies, such as mining, smelting, weaving, pottery, silk production, paper making, boat building, architecture, chemicals, and weaponry. Applied to an activity like warfare, these incremental advances gave the early modern empire capabilities that surpassed previous eras in terms of equipment, techniques, and the scale of operations.

A most important technological advance in the early modern period was the development of printing, which significantly facilitated the collection, storage, and dissemination of information. The growth of a relatively large and sophisticated literate class, which staffed the elaborate bureaucracies of the early modern empires, made it possible for those regimes to pursue active managerial roles in their societies, particularly with regard to cultural and ideological affairs. While physical sciences, technology, and industrial practices did not undergo the open-ended, intentional, and cumulative rationalization that was characteristic of a later stage of modernization, advances in the social-control capabilities of the early modern empires were unprecedented. The fact that control was aimed primarily at social stability has often prompted Westerners, thinking in terms of economic development or an even vaguer notion of "progress," to regard Asian societies as static or stagnant. A better view would be to see the size and endurance of the great Asian empires as positive achievements in the management of the social environment. If one includes in the definition of modernization the enhancement of control over the human as well as the natural environment, then the political integration and bureaucratic organization of the early modern empires appear as significant developments.

THE CREATION AND MAINTENANCE OF EARLY MODERN EMPIRES

a. Military Conquest

Early modern empires were founded in all cases by military conquest. In some instances the conquest was the result of invasion by an outside or peripheral element (such as the Ottoman Turks in West Asia or the Manchus in China), and in other instances of unification by an indigenous group driving out foreign elements (the Ming founder in China) or success in internal warfare (Tokugawa Japan). In any case, the new ruling group faced the task of converting itself from a military machine into the core of a stable and reasonably efficient bureaucratic state. The goals of the ruler were paramount and the viability of the new regime depended on the ruler's ability to accomplish his goals within the conditions of the society he conquered. Such factors as the cultural and ethnic homogeneity of the society, the availability of resources, the strength of potential rivals, and geographical conditions influenced the character of the resulting regime.

b. Reunification of the Culture Area: Control of Frontiers

One of the primary objectives in the formation of an empire was the control of the frontier areas. Insofar as the empire was the instrument for the preservation of civilization, the defense of its perimeter may be considered to have been its paramount function. From this perspective, the empire was—in its most essential form—an instrument for delineating and enforcing the boundaries of a culture area. Stabilization of frontiers could take many forms, from defensive policies of exclusion aimed at keeping barbarians out to aggressive policies of inclusion by conquest, annexation, and assimilation. In addition to military activity, frontier arrangements involved the monitoring of travel, of trade, and of cultural contacts between the interior of the empire and the outside. As we shall see, the nature of frontier stabilization varied with the nature of the regime.

The ability to control territory and define frontiers—essential for any political system—was a function of power. It must be stressed that the early modern empires began as regimes of military conquest and always retained the configuration of military dictatorships. Once in power, the military apparatus was augmented by the creation of civil organs and programs to increase acceptance and support. Nevertheless, military power was always held in reserve. The degeneration of the military or rulers who neglected military affairs often imperiled the state. Usually there were special institutions that tied the military establishment to the ruler, such as a special royal guard composed of elite forces loyal to the ruler himself. Strict measures were designed to keep this group separate from powerful interests in the bureaucracy or the nobility. In extreme cases this royal guard might be composed of foreign elements, like the Swiss Guards who protected the Pope in the Vatican.

Military organization and technology in the early modern period showed clear signs of Mongol influence. The great innovations of the period of Central Asian domination were reflected in mixed forces, including infantry, mounted archers with increasingly effective armor, and siege-warfare specialists, organized in decimal units and coordinated through rapid signal and relay communications systems. Another feature that became characteristic of warfare during the thirteenth and fourteenth centuries was the increasing use of gunpowder and the development of artillery, which gave a relative advantage to imperial power at the expense of local autonomy.

c. Domination of the Economy and Society

Unification of the physical territory of an entire culture area under a single political authority—which was the continuing task of the ruler of an early modern empire—was possible only so long as the ruler could draw on the energies of the peoples under his rule. Reduced to the simplest terms, the politics of the early modern empire may be understood as a process by which the ruler attempted to exert his control over the society and extract from it the resources he needed. By resources we mean all the goods and services the ruler used to carry out the activities of the state: money, food, raw materials, manufactured products, manpower, and specialized talent. Social control includes measures that elevated the ruler above the rest of society and specified the forms of obligation and support that each sector in the polity owed to the state.

The total wealth at the disposal of any society and the way it was distributed within the society determined to a large extent what scale of a state could be supported. It was in the ruler's interest to have resources in as "free" a state as possible—that is, to have them available when needed and not become the preserve of some specialized group that might withhold support. This was a frequent source of conflict within the empire as the ruler tried

ز آواز صرنا و بانگ نفیر
گریزان شدی شیر و ببر دلیر
ز صیت کورگه فغان دهل
بجوش و تحرک فتاد آب پل

9.1

The military might of early modern empires owed much to Mongol experience with cavalry warfare.

9.1 The army of the Ottoman sultan, Süleyman the Magnificent (1520-66), crossing the river Drava in Hungary, 1566. Ottoman Turkish miniature, sixteenth century. The *sipahis* are crossing the river under the eyes of the sultan while the Janissaries wait on the left bank. Courtesy: Chester Beatty Library, Dublin.

9.2 A Qizilbash horseman of the seventeenth century. It was by means of the highly mobile cavalry provided by the nine Turcoman tribes known as Qizilbash ("Red Heads") that the Safavids acquired control of Iran and kept their Ottoman, Özbeg, and Mughul neighbors at bay. Source: J. Chardin, *Voyages du Chevalier Chardin, en Perse,* ed. Langles (Paris, 1811), Plate 29.

9.2

to consolidate his control over major resources. Normally the ruler of a bureaucratic empire would draw whatever goods and services he needed from his empire by means of a system of taxation and compulsory service. When the needed resources were the special preserve of some vested interest group, the ruler would be obliged to engage in a power struggle with competitors. For example, if monasteries held too much money in their treasuries or were keeping too much land off the tax roles or too many men out of military service, the ruler might find it necessary to enact laws restricting the operations of religious groups. Similarly, rich landlords and merchants could find themselves the victims of confiscatory policies. With specialized kinds of resources the bureaucratic regime usually organized its own source of supply in the form of state monopolies, mines, arsenals, horse farms, and the like.

One of the greatest powers the ruler of the bureaueratic empire possessed was control over the symbols of status. Rule was generally hereditary, and the royal house reserved special titles of kingship to its own line, which assigned it a unique role in the society and often characterized the ruler in terms of the welfare of the entire society as an agent of divine power or a link to the cosmic order. Close supporters of the ruling house might be given titles of nobility and social privileges. Being able to determine who would enjoy the most important ranks and privileges gave the ruler a powerful device for winning capable, ambitious, and powerful people over to his cause. Religious orders, feudal orders, tribal and other groups that still commanded great respect in the society represented limitations on the ruler's control over status and thus provided alternative modes of advancement for ambitious individuals which might not involve service to the regime and might even involve activities contrary to the imperial interests.

In the early modern society the bulk of the populace occupied mean or servile positions, variously characterized as peasants, serfs, slaves, retainers, or servants. Since the amount of wealth available was less than in a predominantly industrial society, the nonlaboring classes—especially the ruling elite, the military leadership, and religious authorities and scholars—represented a tiny segment of the total population. Consequently, the gap in standard of living between the elite and the mass of the commoners was correspondingly great. Strict enforcement of class distinctions was necessary to assure stability. Commoners and members of the lower classes were forbidden to take part in political activities. It was in the interests of the ruler and the state to discourage social change and to reinforce social distinctions that kept most of the populace in submissive roles. Special attention was given to recruiting and training talented individuals for service in the bureaucracy. Often the state organized its own training system to provide a supply of officials. An officialdom based on talent was a major asset to the centralized state because the individuals involved owed their allegiance to the state that recruited them and they lacked the security of a hereditary class.

THE CULTURAL LEGITIMATION OF EARLY MODERN EMPIRES

The rulers of early modern empires consciously and systematically sought to legitimize their rule by appeal to religious and ideological traditions. Thus, an emperor might claim to rule on behalf of a god or to be an authority in spiritual or ideological questions. Motivations for such claims could vary in individual instances, from the most cynical expediency to sincere conviction that a ruler was acting as an instrument of divine will. If we view this same matter from the perspective of the cultural tradition—from the point of view of religion, ideology, or other elite culture forms—the legitimation of the ruler takes on great importance. Where the ruler was successful in adapting cultural symbols to political ends, the whole corpus of cultural values could become politicized in the sense that they became so tied to the state that they no longer had an independent course of development. Political considerations and the interests of the state became prime determinants in the direction of cultural change. Where this tendency was most pronounced, the core values of the civilization were thought to be embodied in the institution of the early modern empire, and the demise of that empire was viewed as a blow to the civilized tradition itself. It is for this reason that we need to pay particular attention to the cultural orientation of the early modern empire.

d. Promotion of the Cultural Tradition: Culturism and Pluralism

In the creation of the early modern empire the rallying cry around which the society was to be united and a new polity formed was a sense of common culture either in the form of a religion or a state ideology. This culture provided the basis for a strong sense of identity and a distinction between the dominant group in the empire, which considered itself to be civilized, and outsiders, who were thought to be barbaric and a threat to civilization. The founding of the empire was infused with a sense of mission—the salvation and preservation of the cultural heritage.

Because the empire was inspired by a sense of mission, there was a strong tendency for the state to promote an orthodox religion or ideology. In practice, this orthodoxy might have extended only to certain classes of the population that were more politically potent and active. Where a church or religious leadership already existed, the state would forge links to those groups, often co-opting them into service to the throne. The state could either patronize existing institutions and organizations or form new ones. State schools and academic institutions elaborated and propagated orthodox values.

The form that cultural policy took was often determined by the relative cultural uniformity of the empire. Two types of orientation may be identified. Those empires that were based on culturally homogeneous societies we may call culturistic empires. Those that included diverse cultural elements we may characterize as pluralistic empires. The degree of cultural diversity influenced greatly the policies of the empires in a number of areas. In general, the more uniform, or culturistic, empires were those that were formed in response to external threats to a civilized area. These empires tended to place the greatest emphasis on tradition and the preservation of the heritage of the past. Internally there was a strong tendency for state policy to encourage cultural uniformity within the society and suppress deviance and change. Externally, the culturalistic state was defensively oriented and shunned extensive contact with outside influences. Examples of culturalistic states would be Safavid Iran, Ming China, and Tokugawa Japan.

The pluralistic empire by definition was one that incorporated diffuse cultural elements. Often these empires were the products of conquest. The ruling group was composed of outsiders who had to accommodate themselves to the culture of the people and the region they subdued. Cultural policy in these empires had to be flexible enough to accommodate to the differences of a mixed society and yet support the position of the rulers. In some cases, this could be accomplished by the rulers becoming cultural converts and then patrons of the indigenous culture. This placed the conqueror in the position of acting as the custodian of someone else's heritage. Inevitably, the result was a considerable reinterpretation of that heritage and particularly the suppression of those elements that were least congenial to the conquest group. Another development not uncommon to this situation was a tendency for these converts to take extreme and uncompromising views of their new faith. Internally, pluralistic empires were characterized by special administrative arrangements to accommodate the machinery of government to a mixed society. The imposition of an outside ruling group on top of a conquered society led to ethnic or racial stratification in which various classes could have distinct religious values, social customs, and even languages. Often the government found it necessary to utilize more than one language in official documents, staffing bureaucratic posts with multiple sets of officials, translators, and interpreters.

Externally, the pluralistic empires were more prone to expansion and wars of conquest. Ideologically, the rulers of pluralistic empires had to rationalize their rule in terms of universal sanctions that would justify their initial conquests. In the extreme case this could lead to the claim that the ruler was spreading a true faith and therefore had a right and duty to continue annexing new territories. Where the pluralistic empire could not easily convert subject peoples it could encapsulate them within its boundaries by allowing them varying degrees of self-rule. Examples of pluralistic empires are the Ottomans in West Asia, the Mughuls in India, and the Ch'ing in China. The Ottomans were a Turkish people who used Islam to justify widespread conquest of Islamic and non-Islamic peoples. The Manchus, who invaded China to form the Ch'ing empire, became ardent proponents of Chinese culture but also controlled vast areas of Manchuria, Mongolia, and Central Asia beyond China proper. The Mughuls are of particular interest because of the conflicting demands of the Hindu and Islamic cultural elements in their environment and because of the varied cultural policies of early Mughul rulers.

e. Manipulation and Modification of Cultural Forms

Where the early modern empire entered into the promotion of cultural values, it did so for political purposes. The patronage of culture by a bureaucratic state led inevitably to the modification of cultural forms. In the simplest cases, this modification of cultural values by political influences might have been nothing more than a reflection of the personal whims of a given monarch. A ruler who liked a particular style of architecture or painting might have chosen to patronize practitioners of that style at the expense of others. In other cases, the influence of state patronage took on a more systematic and penetrating character. Particularly in areas of religion and ideology, state patronage was selectively directed toward those thinkers and doctrines that were most supportive of the ruler's position. Patronage inevitably led the state to the practice of thought control. This could include such methods as the suppression of certain parts of the inherited tradition, the banning of heterodox interpretations of sacred texts, the persecution and elimination of heretical thinkers, the supervision of education, book burning, the patronage of orthodox scholarship, and various measures to discourage contact with other societies.

This intervention of the state into the realm of cultural values was by no means a new development with the early modern empires. What was new in the early modern period was the systematic, rational, and explicit character of state cultural policy. The state now saw itself as a legitimate custodian of tradition and took an active hand in modifying and manipulating tradition to state ends. The increase in literacy and the accumulation and circulation of printed material made it necessary for the state to be more active in these areas than had been the case in earlier ages.

CONSEQUENCES OF THE FORMATION OF EARLY MODERN EMPIRES

The processes of political control and cultural promotion discussed here were not essentially different from the core activities of other political systems. What was outstanding in the case of the early modern empires was the intensity and the persistence of the exercise of centralized political control. The result of this prolonged experience of political union was often to freeze the cultural forms of an area in such a manner that core values of the civilization became imbedded in the institutions of the empire. This very much influenced the direction in which the civilizations developed in the subsequent era of technological change, European intrusion, and nationalism. Those empires, like the Ch'ing, the Tokugawa, or the Russian, that showed the greatest stability lasted the longest but eventually faced the most extreme transformation of cultural forms. Confucianism died with the emperorship; samurai institutions with the shogunate. Those empires with the most pluralistic social bases, like the Mughuls and the Ottomans, displayed the lowest levels of national or group consciousness (as distinguished from religious affiliation). In other words, where the state was least influential, the cultural traditions were least threatened by its passing.

PATTERNS

1. THE OTTOMANS IN WEST ASIA

The Establishment of the Ottoman Empire

The early growth of the Ottoman sultanate has been briefly described in Chapter 8. One of several *ghazi* principalities that arose in western Anatolia upon the ruins of the former Seljuk sultanate of Rum, it had, by the second half of the fourteenth century, eliminated all would-be rivals and was already a formidable power in southeastern Europe. Sultan Bayezid I (r. 1389-1403) advanced the Ottoman frontier deep into the Balkans while maintaining a fairly effective blockade against Constantinople itself, which he would have surely conquered but for the intervention of Timur. In Asia he extended Ottoman rule into eastern Anatolia and seized the Mamluk frontier towns in the upper Euphrates valley, although by so doing he provoked the hostility of Timur, who brought the sultan's forces to bay at Ankara (1402), where Bayezid suffered the humiliation of defeat and capture. In the wake of Timur's destructive thrust into western Anatolia there occurred a temporary lull in the hitherto uninterrupted course of Ottoman expansion, and the next half century was characterized first by internal consolidation and then by renewed expansion in the Balkans.

It was Mehmed II (r. 1451-81), known as The Conqueror, who made the Ottoman Turks the dominant power in the eastern Mediterranean. In 1453 he besieged and captured Constantinople, which he renamed Istanbul and which now replaced Edirne in Thrace as capital of the empire. Master of both shores of the Bosporus, he vigorously pursued his goal of naval hegemony at sea as well as military hegemony on land, so that by 1477 Ottoman galleys were cruising in Venetian home waters while in 1480 an Ottoman expeditionary force actually seized the south Italian port of Otranto. In the Balkans the Ottoman grip over Greece and Serbia was tightened, while the northern frontier was extended, at least nominally, to the line of the Dniester. Symptomatic of the growing prestige of the empire, in 1475 the Tatar khan of the Crimea acknowledged the sultan as his overlord. In the east, Mehmed embarked upon the pacification of central and eastern Anatolia, but here he encountered fierce resistance from the Turcoman tribes of the region, which opposed both the establishment of the relatively centralized Ottoman administrative system and also a Sunni orthodoxy hostile to the syncretic folk-Islam of the nomads. They turned for assistance to Uzun Hasan (1453-78), ruler of the Ak-Koyunlu Turcoman confederacy, but Mehmed defeated him in 1473, thereby temporarily stabilizing a dangerously volatile frontier region.

After the exertions that characterized the reign of Mehmed the Conqueror, the reign of his successor, Bayezid II (r. 1481-1512), constituted a much-needed breathing space. The pace set by Mehmed had been too demanding and by the time of his death the treasury was depleted, the army mutinous, and the civilian population seething with discontent. Not that Bayezid's reign was a period of peace. The first decade of the sixteenth century saw the spectacular rise to power in Azarbayjan and eastern Iran of Shah Ismail, founder of the Safavid dynasty, and his vigorous dissemination of Shiism among the heterodox Turcoman tribes of eastern Anatolia, thus once again presenting the Ottoman empire with a serious threat to the security of its eastern marches. Bayezid failed to appreciate the nature of the danger but his son and successor, Selim I (r. 1512-20), did. Advancing eastward with a formidable army, he systematically massacred the Shii Turcoman tribes of central and eastern Anatolia and extirpated heterodoxy wherever he found it. In 1514 he forced Shah Ismail to give battle at Caldiran, in Azarbayjan, and there his artillery and the Janissaries, armed with handguns, routed the Qizilbash cavalry in an encounter as decisive as any in history. After plundering Tabriz, the Safavid capital, he withdrew southwestward to complete the pacification of eastern Anatolia. In so doing he trespassed on the northern marches of the Mamluk sultanate of Egypt, and a confrontation between these two great Turkish states became unavoidable. In 1516 Selim defeated the Mamluk army near Aleppo in northern Syria and then proceeded to march on Egypt, occupying Damascus and Jerusalem in the course of his advance. In Aleppo he had taken under his protection the descendant of a long line of titular Abbasid caliphs who had been pensioners of the Mamluk government since the fall of Baghdad to the Mongols in 1258. In Cairo, in 1517, he received the submission of the sharif of Mecca, who presented him with the keys of the Holy Cities of the Hijaz. He thus became the supreme ruler of the Muslim world in a way no ruler had been since the greatest days of the Abbasid caliphate of Baghdad.

Prior to the reign of Selim I the Ottoman Turks had possessed more territory in Europe than in Asia and much of their energies had been consumed by internal pacification and frontier warfare in the Balkans. Selim's Asian campaigns, however, changed the ethnic and communal composition of the empire, as a result of the acquisition of Syria, Palestine, and Egypt, areas inhabited mainly by Arabic-speaking Muslims. Thus, the Ottoman empire became in a geographical as well as in a spiritual sense the successor to the Umayyad and Abbasid caliphates and it only remained for Süleyman I (r. 1520-66), known to the Turks as the Lawgiver and to Europeans as The Magnificent, to complete his father's work with the conquest of Baghdad and the annexation of Iraq. The reign of Süleyman, although it did not mark the maximum extension of the imperial frontiers, is rightly regarded as constituting the apogee of Ottoman imperialism. In 1521 Belgrade was captured, followed in 1522 by the fall of Rhodes. In 1526 the greater part of the former kingdom of Hungary was incorporated into the empire as a vassal state, and in 1529 an Ottoman army was encamped beneath the walls of Vienna. This triumphal progress continued into the 1530s with the capture of Algiers and Tunis in the west and Baghdad in the east.

The last three decades of Süleyman's reign seem to have seen some perceptible loss of vigor, although successful campaigns continued to be mounted against the Safavids in the southern Caucasus region, the Habsburgs in Hungary, and the Venetians at sea. In the 1550s Tripoli in modern Libya and Bahrayn in the Persian Gulf were added to the empire, and due partly to the conquest of the Yemen earlier in the reign, the Ottoman Red Sea fleet penetrated into the Arabian Sea to measure itself against its Portuguese foes. These achievements, however, seemed to necessitate a greater degree of exertion than in the past, and in fact the empire was fast approaching a point where its resources were becoming visibly overstrained. Even before Süleyman's death there were ominous signs that the best days of the empire were over. In 1552 the Ottoman fleet in the Persian Gulf failed to dislodge the Portuguese from Ormuz. The Russian seizure of Kazan in 1552 and of Astrakhan in 1554 eliminated two weak but friendly Muslim regimes on the Volga, cut the Ottoman line of communication with the Özbeg khanates in Central Asia, and marked the beginning of the Russian advance into areas hitherto within the Ottoman sphere of influence. Most striking of all, the prodigious effort made by the Ottomans to conquer the island of Malta, the headquarters of the Knights of St. John, who earlier had been expelled from Rhodes, met with complete disaster.

The Reunification of Islamic West Asia and the Eastern Mediterranean Basin

Unlike the other empires of the early modern period described in this chapter, the Ottoman empire was not an exclusively Asian phenomenon since it was also felt as an imperial

Map 38 The Ottoman empire, about 1600

presence in Europe and Africa. The rise and fall of the Ottoman empire is therefore part of the history not only of West Asia, where the consequences of its demise are still apparent today, but also of North Africa and of southern and eastern Europe. It has long been a weakness of Europocentric historians that they have failed to take cognizance of the role of the Ottomans within the framework of the European experience, whether in a purely military and diplomatic context or, although more difficult to assess, in terms of social and cultural development. At this juncture it is perhaps not altogether inappropriate to compare, however superficially, the story of the emergence of the Ottomans as a world power between the second half of the fifteenth century and the first half of the seventeenth century with that of the Spaniards during much the same period. Both empires owed their beginnings to the military exploits of a frugal, hardy people occupying an arid and relatively infertile country, the high *mesta* of Castile and the western extension of the Anatolian plateau. Both peoples were habituated to the fervor and ferocity of crusading warfare in the marches that separated rival cultures, and both were capable of experiencing intense spiritual exaltation in the service of their faith. The Ottoman Turks and the Castilians were alike in the way they erupted from a poverty-stricken hinterland to dominate richer neighbors, to acquire control over the alien element of the sea and, finally, to become masters of vast and far-flung territories. Both, notwithstanding a genius for war and no small talent as proconsuls, lacked the manpower resources, the bureaucratic and fiscal expertise, and the commercial aptitudes to sustain the great adventure, and both were compelled to enlist the support of their subject peoples, the Turks utilizing the services of Serbs, Bosnians, Moldavians, Greeks, Armenians, and Jews just as the Castilians utilized the services of Catalans, Italians, Germans, and Flemings. If the armies and fleets of the king of Spain were a microcosm of the plural composition of the Habsburg empire, so too were the military forces of the sultan representative of the ethnic diversity of the Ottoman empire—the Janissaries recruited from Serbs, Albanians, Bosnians, and Bulgarians; the cavalry composed of Turks, Kurds, Wallachians, Moldavians, and Tatars; and the galleys manned by Greeks, Dalmatians, and Algerians. If Spain at the height of its power occasionally entrusted supreme military authority to foreigners, the Ottoman admirals too included more than one Christian renegade, while the Albanian ancestry of the Köprülü family of grand *vazirs* was typical of the higher echelons of the bureaucracy.

For the greater part of the sixteenth century and especially during the reign of Süleyman I, the Ottoman empire constituted the greatest concentration of military power from the Atlantic to the Pacific, a military power far more formidable than that of the contemporary Habsburg empire in Europe and America or of the Ming empire in East Asia. Outside China, the Ottoman sultan was the head of what was probably the most complex imperial administration to evolve between the fall of Rome and the emergence of the European colonial empires of the nineteenth century. The empire's maximum extent, measured in terms of the modern states that have arisen upon its ruins, was truly impressive. In Asia the sultan's rule extended over present-day Turkey, Iraq, Syria, Lebanon, Israel, Jordan, and much of the Arabian peninsula, including the Yemen. In Europe it extended over Greece, Cyprus, Albania, Yugoslavia, Bulgaria, Rumania, the greater part of Hungary and, in the Soviet Union, much of the Ukraine, the Crimea, and the western and southwestern flanks of the Caucasus region. In Africa it included Egypt and the coastal zones of Libya, Tunisia, and Algeria. The Mediterranean was virtually a Turkish lake, as were the Black Sea, the Persian Gulf, and the Red Sea. Ottoman galleys raided the Mediterranean shores of Italy, France, and Spain with impunity, but they also attempted to challenge Portuguese hegemony off the Horn of Africa and as far east as Gujarat. For sixteenth century Europeans the military might of the Ottomans, the secrecy and effectiveness with which they conducted their affairs, the mystery and awe that surrounded the sultan's government, and the knowledge that the principal *raison d'etre* of the empire was to wage war upon infidels and enslave them, all contributed towards a sense of psychological inferiority offset only by the counterbalancing spirit of Christian fanaticism.

The Organization of the Ottoman Empire

Deriving its institutional origins from the Turcoman *ghazi* principalities of central and western Anatolia but also from the earlier Seljuk sultanate of Rum, the Ottoman state system combined with this Turkish legacy older Islamic traditions derived from the Umayyad and Abbasid caliphates and also some aspects of the very different Byzantine heritage. Thus the Ottoman sultan personified the traditional leadership of a *ghazi* warlord, older and more remote traditions of Central Asian Turkish sovereignty, the Islamic ecumenicalism of the Abbasid caliphs, and the Caesaro-papalism of the Byzantine emperors. Originally the sultan's authority had been upheld by the bands of Turkish *ghazis* who had flocked to fight in the holy war against the Byzantines, but these had gradually been replaced by regular cavalry *(sipahis),* which, notwithstanding the fame of the Janissary infantry, probably remained the most important element in the Ottoman army down to the period of imperial decline in the early seventeenth century. These *sipahis* were of two kinds. The first constituted, with the Janissaries, the sultan's standing troops and were a part of the sultan's slave household. The second, often referred to by historians as the "feudal" *sipahis,* were stationed in the provinces but were available for active service during specified periods. In lieu of salary they received a grant of land known as a *timar,* which was exempt from revenue payment and by means of which they maintained themselves and provided their own weapons and mounts. When the *timar* exceeded a certain size they were also required to maintain a specified number of troops to accompany them when they went on campaign. Clearly, there was a great loss of potential revenue to the central exchequer from the *timars* granted to the "feudal" *sipahis* but, in compensation, the empire was able to maintain a very large body of cavalry without the necessity of making cash disbursements. In addition to the regular cavalry, the Ottoman army also included irregular cavalry units that served without pay, maintaining themselves by ravaging the enemy's countryside. Somewhat similar to these troops were the irregular cavalry forces provided by the voyevods of Wallachia and Moldavia and by the Tatar khan of the Crimea, useful auxiliaries who accompanied the Ottoman army on its European campaigns and also, in the case of the Tatars, on expeditions into the Caucasus.

The Ottoman cavalry vastly outnumbered the infantry but it was the celebrated Janissaries *(yenicheri,* "new troops") who were regarded as the crack troops of the empire and whose advance onto the battlefield usually filled their foes with the utmost consternation. While the "feudal" *sipahis* were freeborn Muslims, the Janissaries, who carried firearms and who, in the days of the warrior sultans, were subjected to an exacting training and discipline, were all recruited by means of the *devshirme.* The *devshirme* was the name given to the levy of male children from the Christian population of the Balkans, an operation that was undertaken every three to seven years, according to need. Recruitment was restricted solely to agricultural communities, with urban families and families with only one male child being exempted. The majority of boys recruited by the *devshirme* were trained as soldiers and entered the Janissary corps, although some of the more intelligent and those who showed little aptitude for bearing arms were separated from the rest and educated in the palace school as personal attendants upon the sultan and as elite administrators. Severed from their Christian surroundings at an early age and carefully instructed in the Muslim faith, in which they frequently became more zealous than freeborn Muslims, these *devshirme* children were meticulously trained to become members of the military and governing elite of a regime dedicated to war and the propagation of the faith.

Whether as soldiers or bureaucrats, the sultan's slaves *(kapikulus)* constituted the ruling elite of the empire, yet they remained his creatures from beginning to end and their power and position were entirely dependent on his goodwill. To this extent they were a "slave nobility" such as had been the governing elite of the early Delhi sultanate and Mamluk Egypt. Under the direction of the grand *vazir,* himself almost invariably of slave origin, the higher echelons of the administration were staffed exclusively by *kapikulus,* as were the more important administrative posts in the provinces. The largest provincial divisions were known as *beylerbeyiliks,* each of which was in the charge of a *beylerbeyi,* and these, in turn, were subdivided into *sanjaks,* administered by a *sanjak beyi.* Like other Muslim rulers, the Ottomans deliberately established institutional checks and balances to prevent the abuse of power by provincial officials. This was done by creating parallel hierarchies of authority in the provinces. From the sixteenth century onward, the *shaykh al-Islam,* as head of the *ulama* of the empire, acquired the right to recommend the appointment and dismissal of the provincial *qazis,* and the latter therefore showed little hesitation in complaining to Istanbul regarding the conduct of *beylerbeyis* and *sanjak beyis.* In addition, the central fiscal bureau in the capital appointed an official to administer the crown lands in each province, while yet another official superintended the lands granted as *timars* to the "feudal" *sipahis*. Most important of all, the *beylerbeyis* did not have direct control over the provincial garrisons.

In its greatest days Ottoman provincial administration appears to have been a highly efficient system, its severity mitigated by an elaborate set of checks and balances and by some sense of an imperial mission on the part of the highly trained and hand-picked *kapikulus*. The maintenance of administrative stability and continuity at the lower levels was dependent on a careful recording of rights and obligations, based on census and cadastral registers, which in their complexity and accuracy went far beyond those of earlier Islamic empires. The character of administration in the higher echelons depended very largely on the degree of the control exercised by the central government. Much, too, depended on the capacity and temperament of the individual sultans. Hardly less important was the influence of the grand *vazir* but he was not without rivals, of which the most obvious was the *shaykh al-Islam,* since, if the grand *vazir* was the deputy of the sultan in all executive matters, the *shaykh al-Islam* was his deputy in the spiritual sphere. Both, however, faced serious competition for the sultan's ear within the Topkapi Sarayi, the elaborate complex of buildings located on the promontory lying between the Golden Horn and the Bosporus, which housed both the imperial family and the government itself. The first of these would-be rivals for power was the *valide sultan,* or mother of the reigning sultan, and the second, who was also the principal agent of her authority, was the *kizlar aghasi,* or chief of the black eunuchs. Somewhat less influential, because his domain lay outside the forbidden precincts of the harem, was the *kapi aghasi,* or chief of the white eunuchs, who was directly responsible for the training and discipline of the slaves selected to become administrators or personal attendants upon the sultan. Finally, outside the Topkapi Sarayi itself, the *yenicheri aghasi,* or commander of the Janissaries, exercised great influence in the counsels of state by virtue of the physical force available at his disposal.

Ottoman Control over the Resources of the Empire

Among the great continental empires of the early modern period, that of the Ottomans was of quite exceptional ethnic, cultural, and sectarian diversity. In terms of manpower its population was enormous and was rapidly expanding throughout the sixteenth century, especially in the cities, which included what were then some of the largest metropolitan centers of the world—Istanbul, Cairo, and Baghdad. The Ottoman empire also contained large non-Muslim communities, especially in the Balkans, and these were organized into virtually autonomous *millets,* living according to their own traditional beliefs and laws, the latter administered by religious leaders who were also the official intermediaries between their coreligionists and the sultan's government. The majority of these non-Muslim subjects of the empire were agriculturists (Serbs, Bosnians, Bulgarians, Hungarians, etc.), but certain communities, especially the Greeks, the Armenians, and the Jews, occupied an important and in some areas a dominant position in the commercial life of the empire. When the Ottoman administration was functioning effectively, the non-Muslim minorities probably enjoyed a far greater degree of physical security than any minority could have hoped for in contemporary Europe. When the Jews were expelled from Spain in 1492, for example, many of the refugees sought sanctuary and later acquired great wealth and prosperity in the sultan's domains. In those parts of Hungary incorporated into the empire during the sixteenth century, Protestantism spread rapidly under Ottoman rule, where converts were secure from the persecution suffered by their coreligionists under Catholic Habsburg domination. Nor should it be forgotten that at the time of the initial Ottoman thrust into Serbia and Bosnia, the Orthodox Christian population, fearful of the Catholic zeal of the rulers of Hungary to the northeast, welcomed the coming of the Turks as the lesser of two evils. Unfortunately, European dread of Ottoman power during the sixteenth and seventeenth centuries, combined with nineteenth and twentieth century European sentiment in favor of the subject Christian nationalities of the empire, have created an almost ineradicable legend of Ottoman oppression, which, at least in the great days of the empire, is not borne out by modern research.

The great majority of the subjects of the sultan, whether Muslim or Christian, were agriculturists who supported the state by the payment of land revenue, unlike the tax-exempt *timar*-holding *sipahis,* the tribute-paying nomads, and the urban population, upon which various cesses were levied. The land itself was regarded as belonging to the state. The *timar*-holder was not a landowner in the European sense of the word and possessed only qualified occupancy rights, such as the right to collect the revenue instead of the government doing so. The cultivator, whether he worked on crown land or on a *timar,* enjoyed the status of a hereditary tenant who, although he could not dispose of the land at will except to his legal heirs, could not be dispossessed so long as he paid the revenue demand or its equivalent. It is impossible to generalize with regard to the actual conditions under which the cultivator lived without specific reference to period and area, but it is probably fair to say that the *timar* system brought *timar*-holder and cultivator into a more intimate relationship than would have been the case had the countryside been administered directly by officials of the central government or, as happened subsequently, by tax farmers. Many *timar*-holders maintained a paternal attitude towards their cultivators (*timars* varied greatly in extent and most *timar*-holders, when not on campaign, must have lived rather in the style of poorer knights in medieval Europe), and until the rapid expansion of population during the late sixteenth century there was a shortage of cultivators rather than pressure on land. Thus the *timar*-holders competed with each other to secure a sufficient labor force to work their estates or to extend the area already under cultivation. Moreover, since the *timar*-holder enjoyed a hereditary status, he was not tempted to bleed dry his *timar* in anticipation of a future transfer to another area, as happened in the case of Mughul India.

Ottoman Cultural Legitimation and the Islamic Tradition

The Ottoman sultan and his government were heirs to diverse, even rival, traditions—the *ghazi* principalities of Anatolia and the Byzantine empire, Central Asian nomadic sovereignty, and Abbasid sacerdotalism. In consequence, the Ottoman empire was perhaps especially receptive to outside influences, its cosmopolitan character being exemplified by the diverse social origins of the ruling elite and by the ethnic composition and life-style of the population of Istanbul, which by the beginning of the sixteenth century may well have numbered nearly 200,000 persons. With regard to their place in the Islamic world order, the Ottomans saw themselves as embodying the culmination of almost a thousand years of history, and they were for the most part condescending, if not overtly hostile, towards other Muslim states. Undoubtedly, the period of Ottoman greatness was also a period when Islamic intellectual life everywhere was becoming somewhat torpid, but several Ottoman rulers left a reputation as bibliophiles, as patrons of traditional scholarship, and as founders of lavishly endowed colleges, hospitals, and asylums. The Ottoman regime stimulated the growth of an impressive historiographical tradition and also encouraged the study of geography, mathematics, and astronomy. Mehmed II took into his service an astronomer, trained at Ulugh Beg's observatory in Samarqand, who established in Istanbul a tradition of scholarship in mathematics and astronomy which culminated in the construction of a short-lived observatory in Galata in 1577. Court poetry drew heavily, at least initially, from the classical Iranian masters so that even Selim I, although he was a relentless foe of the Safavids, wrote his verses in Persian (while, paradoxically, Shah Ismail wrote in Turkish, in order to spread his Shii doctrines among the Turkish-speaking tribes of Anatolia). Ottoman painting, on the other hand, owed much less to Iranian influences, and the robust and realistic vision of the Ottoman miniaturists is in striking contrast to the limpid elegance of their Safavid and Mughul contemporaries. No less distinctive than Ottoman painting was the Ottoman architectural achievement, which reached its stylistic apogee in the imperial mosques of Istanbul built by the great Sinan (d. 1588). It is an architectural tradition that is quite distinct from that of the Arab world, Iran or Muslim India, but in its monumentality and its spatial effect it seems to epitomize the formal grandeur of this greatest of all Islamic empires.

2. THE SAFAVIDS IN IRAN

The emergence during the first half of the sixteenth century of the three Islamic empires of the Ottomans, the Safavids, and the Mughuls was a interrelated development—as was also their decline during the first half of the eighteenth century. The central geographical position of the Iranian plateau ensured that the behaviour of the Safavid dynasty would serve as the principal catalyst for both these processes.

It has already been noted that among the consequences of the disintegration of the Timurid empire during the fifteenth century were: (1) the substitution of the Özbegs for the Timurids as the rulers of Mawarannahr (hereafter to be referred to as Turkistan) and part of Khurasan; (2) the gradual recovery of the Ottoman sultanate after Timur's victory at Ankara in 1402; and (3) the attempts made first by the Kara-Koyunlu Turcomans and then by the Ak-Koyunlu to fill the power vacuum left by Timur's ravages in western Iran, Iraq, and eastern Anatolia. Both attempts failed but they pointed the way for the Safavids, who, in part at least, built upon Timurid, Kara-Koyunlu, and Ak-Koyunlu foundations. Yet in one respect the Safavids were unique: they enlisted the military resources of a powerful tribal confederacy, the Qizilbash, to assist in the spread of their own particular form of "Twelver" Shiism.

The Establishment of the Safavid Empire

The Safavid regime was founded on three distinct, yet interconnected, elements. First, there was the charismatic leadership of the *murshid,* or spiritual director of the Safaviya order, the future Shah Ismail (d. 1524), who seems to have regarded himself as a living and hereditary incarnation of God. Second, there was the military support provided by the nine Turcoman tribes that formed the Shii confederacy known as the Qizilbash ("Red Heads"), a nickname deriving from the red headdress with its twelve points (symbolizing the Twelve Imams) which they wore as a sign of their allegiance to their *murshid,* Ismail, towards whom their chieftains assumed the role of disciples. Third, there was the support of the Shii urban population organized into solidarity groups (*futuwwa*). It seems unlikely that prior to the beginning of the sixteenth century Shiism was the faith of the majority of the population of Iran, but throughout the Il-Khanid and Timurid periods Shiism had been spreading unobstrusively, especially among the urban population. Even during the first half of the fourteenth century certain cities in central Iran—Ray, Qum, and Kashan, for example—were regarded as Shii strongholds.

Ismail attracted a following as much by his brilliant exploits as a warrior as by his spiritual charisma as a Sufi *murshid.* Starting from his base at Ardabil in eastern Azarbayjan he obtained possession of Tabriz in 1501, where he proclaimed himself shah, and thereafter brought the former Ak-Koyunlu territories in western Iran, Iraq, and eastern Anatolia under his control. The capture of Baghdad in 1508 marked the culmination of a process whereby yet another Turcoman dynasty had come to dominate the heartlands of West Asia. What made this new regime different from its predecessors and in a special sense "revolutionary" was its messianic Shiism, which demanded both the forceful propagation of Shii beliefs and the no less vigorous persecution of the recalcitrant Sunni population now living under Shii rule.

Map 39 The Safavid empire, about 1600

While Shah Ismail was pursuing his conquests in the west, the Özbeg chieftain, Muhammad Shaybani, was engaged in the annexation of the remaining Timurid principalities in Turkistan, where he seized Samarqand in 1500. Among the refugees who fled before the Özbeg advance was Babur, a descendant of Timur and a former ruler of Farghana and, very briefly, of Samarqand. In 1504 he established himself in Kabul in eastern Afghanistan. Here he remained until 1526, when he embarked upon the conquest of northern India, where he laid the foundations of the Mughul empire. Meanwhile, in 1507, Muhammad Shaybani gained possession of Herat in Khurasan, the last major center still controlled by the Timurids. A direct conflict between Muhammad Shaybani and Shah Ismail now became inevitable and their personal antagonism was reinforced by sectarian rivalry. While Shah Ismail harried the Sunnis, driving eminent *ulama* and scholars to seek refuge in Özbeg or Ottoman territory, Muhammad Shaybani reciprocated by persecuting the Shiis. Finally, in 1510, the Safavids and Özbegs met in battle near Marv and Muhammad Shaybani was defeated and killed.

Having had Muhammad Shaybani's skull made into a drinking cup, Shah Ismail sent the Özbeg's headless corpse, stuffed with straw, to the Ottoman sultan as a gratuitous insult. Selim I (r. 1512-20) accepted the challenge and in 1514 marched eastward, allegedly massacring 40,000 potential supporters of the Safavid cause among the Turcoman tribes of Anatolia and laying waste the Safavid ancestral homeland of Azarbayjan. At Caldiran the Ottoman artillery and the discipline of the Janissaries inflicted a crushing defeat on the

Qizilbash forces. Tabriz, Shah Ismail's capital, was occupied, but thereafter the Safavid "scorched earth" policy discouraged further Ottoman penetration into Iran. Shah Ismail continued to reign for another ten years until 1524, but both his personal self-confidence and his charisma among his followers had experienced an irrevocable setback.

Between 1524 and 1588 the Safavid empire was again and again hard pressed both by the Ottomans in the west and by the Özbegs in the east. Ottoman armies four times invaded Azarbayjan during the reign of Sultan Süleyman (1520-66) and in 1534 both Tabriz and Baghdad were occupied, and Iraq was incorporated into the Ottoman empire. Under the greatest of the Safavids, Shah Abbas I (r. 1588-1629), this trend was reversed, the northern frontier was secured against the Özbegs, and in 1623 Baghdad and much of Iraq passed back into Safavid hands. The shah's death, however, and the incapacity of his successor tilted the scales once more in favor of the Ottomans, and Baghdad was lost again in 1638. There followed a further revival under Shah Abbas II (r. 1642-66) but thereafter the Safavid empire sank into incurable lethargy during the long reigns of Shah Sulayman (1666-94), a drunken recluse, and Shah Sultan Husayn (1694-1722), a pious debauchee.

The Safavid Reunification of the Iranian Culture Zone

In retrospect, the Safavid period can be seen as the first phase in the emergence of modern Iran, the period when the present-day frontiers (allowing for some loss of territory during the nineteenth century) took shape and when Shiism was adopted as the religion of the majority of Iranians. The Safavids themselves, however, were not concerned with building a nation-state. Rather, Shah Ismail and his successors sought to create a traditional type of Islamic empire centering on the Iranian plateau but extending into the Fertile Crescent, the steppe zone of Anatolia, and even Turkistan. Had they been successful, the Safavid empire would have resembled in area and also to some extent in organization the earlier regimes of the Seljuks and the Il-Khans. Because they failed, and because twentieth-century Iranian historiography identifies the Safavid period with the resurgence of Iranian values after centuries of foreign domination by Arabs, Turks, and Mongols, the range of the Safavids' imperial aspirations has tended to be obscured by the more obvious success of their Ottoman and Mughul contemporaries. It is therefore worth stressing that whenever the Safavid shahs commanded sufficient resources, they invariably sought to extend their frontiers. At such times they probed deep into Anatolia and the Caucasus region, including Georgia. They held Baghdad and much of Iraq from 1508 to 1534 and again from 1623 to 1638. In 1511 and 1512 Shah Ismail dispatched troops into Turkistan and in 1602 Abbas I occupied Bahrayn. The Safavids always regarded the Kandahar province (claimed by the Indian Mughuls) as rightly theirs, and they were masters of the city for extended periods between 1556 and 1711. All this suggests that, far from containing their ambitions within the Persian-speaking lands of the Iranian plateau, the Safavids fitted the traditional pattern of empire builders in West Asia. It was their misfortune that there should have emerged so even a balance between their own forces and those of the Ottomans, Özbegs, and Mughuls in those vaguely defined frontier marches that constituted their mutual zones of expansion.

That the Safavids were able to hold their own against the Ottomans and the Mughuls, who possessed far greater resources than they did, was due partly to the rugged frontier terrain and partly to the fighting qualities of the Qizilbash tribes. Yet the military organization of the early Safavids was unsatisfactory on at least two counts: the irregular cavalry forces led by the Qizilbash chieftains did not perform particularly well in the face of artillery or regular troops and, far worse, their loyalty lay first and foremost with their own chieftains, who competed fiercely among themselves and sometimes against the throne itself in their quest for offices at court as well as provincial governorships. It was for this reason that Shah Abbas I endeavored to substitute for the Qizilbash tribal levies regular units upon which he could rely in a crisis without any fear of divided loyalties. He therefore established a corps of *ghulams* (the Persian equivalent of the Arabic *mamluk*) modeled on the Ottoman Janissaries and recruited from Georgian, Armenian, and Circassian slaves under the command of an officer who came from a non-Qizilbash background.

Following their exposure to Ottoman artillery fire in 1514, the Safavids gradually developed an artillery arm, although handguns had been known even during the Ak-Koyunlu period. Shah Abbas I, as part of his general policy of reforming and centralizing the military organization of the empire, greatly expanded the artillery and established a regiment of musketeers recruited from among the sedentary population. He also strengthened his exposed northeastern frontier while at the same time pursuing a policy of "divide and rule" among the tribal population by the enforced migration of turbulent elements to serve as a first line of resistance to Özbeg or Turcoman raiders from across the Amu Darya or the Kara Kum desert. In this way several Kurdish tribes were transferred to northern Khurasan, while two branches of the powerful Qizilbash tribe of Qajars were settled in Gurgan and Marv respectively. The Gurgan Qajars would provide the ruling dynasty in Iran between 1779 and 1925. Unlike the Ottomans, but like the Indian Mughuls, the Safavids appear to have been largely oblivious of the significance of sea power. When Shah Abbas I determined to expel the Portuguese from the island of Ormuz in 1622 he relied on ships of the British East India Company for offshore support.

The Organization of the Safavid Empire

As in the case of the other Islamic empires of the early modern period, the Safavids freely adopted the administrative structures of preceding regimes, although these had to be modified to take into account the peculiarly theocratic character of an empire founded by a militant Sufi order and also the dominant position of the Qizilbash *amirs,* who formed the higher echelons of the ruling elite. Otherwise, the Safavids were not particularly innovative in their administration, following precedents set by the Timurids, Kara-Koyunlu, and Ak-Koyunlu and clinging to well-established Irano-Islamic bureaucratic traditions. An exception to this, however, was the position of the *ulama,* which was bound to be highly ambiguous under a ruler such as Shah Ismail, who regarded himself, and was presumably regarded by many of his subjects also, as a divine emanation. It was the duty of the principal religious functionary, the *sadr,* and his provincial deputies to ensure the propagation of the official Shii faith, to supervise the conduct and teaching of the *ulama,* and to manage religious endowments. Much has yet to be learned regarding the social background, local connections, and economic position of the Safavid *ulama.* During the early years of the regime it appears that there did not exist in Iran a sufficient number of qualified persons to spread the new faith so that Shii divines had to be imported from the Arab world, especially from Bahrayn and Syria. But whether foreign- or native-born, the *ulama* of the early Safavid period were probably more closely supervised by the central government than had ever been the case before.

At the head of the civil administration stood the *vazir,* among whose functions the assessment, collection, and disbursement of the revenue took first place. Under him was an elaborate hierarchy of officeholders—secretaries, chancellery clerks, revenue assessors, and collectors—constituting that typical Iranian bureaucratic framework that both the Seljuks and the Il-Khans had recognized to be a prerequisite for ensuring a regular flow of revenue and an orderly administration. These Iranian officials were often objects of intense suspicion and hostility among the Qizilbash *amirs,* who claimed a virtual monopoly of the most important offices of state, including the provincial governorships. The *amirs* understood very well that the Iranian bureaucratic structure constituted a rival nucleus of power within the empire and that one of its functions was to maintain and extend the shah's authority at their expense and also to check their predatory activities, which were frequently exercised at the expense of the shah's own subjects rather than at that of his enemies. Prior to the accession of Shah Abbas I in 1588, the brute force that the Qizilbash *amirs* could bring to bear generally prevailed in their conflicts with the bureaucracy, due to their all-important role as military commanders and also to their grip on the great offices of state. For the Qizilbash *amirs* it was intolerable that Iranians should be appointed to the latter posts, and during the sixteenth century there were several instances of Iranians holding high office being abandoned in battle or even assassinated by the Qizilbash *amirs*. When, therefore, Shah Abbas I set about restructuring the Safavid state and its military establishment, he was striking not only at the ubiquitous turbulence of the Qizilbash chieftains among themselves but also at the destructive rivalry between the Turcoman and Iranian components of the ruling elite, a rivalry that also to some extent reflected cultural, ethnic, and even linguistic differences. Even down to the nineteenth century the Qajar dynasty, one of the original nine tribes of the Qizilbash, was Turkish speaking.

Under the Safavids Iran was divided into relatively small provinces ruled by Qizilbash governors, who provided for their military contingents and for the salaries of the local officials out of assignments on the land revenue. In each province the administrative hierarchy was modeled on that of the central government and was headed by a provincial *vazir* responsible for civil and fiscal administration. Khurasan, on account of its great size, its exposure to invasion by the Özbegs, and also because it was the traditional appanage of the heir apparent, had a somewhat more elaborate administrative structure, with a principal *vazir* stationed at Herat, where the heir apparent held court, and with subordinate *vazirs* in important local centers such as Mashhad and Sabzavar.

Safavid Control over the Economic and Human Resources of the Empire

The Safavids governed a society in which a substantial segment of the people were pastoralists and nomads or seminomads while the remainder were either sedentary agriculturists or town dwellers. Neither the relative size of the pastoral element nor the size of the population as a whole can now be known. The overwhelming majority of Iranians, however, lived in villages or tribal encampments and were engaged in cultivation of the land or animal husbandry, which provided the bulk of the revenue.

Safavid rule must have pressed fairly hard on the rural population, since the period was one in which the rigorous methods of land-revenue administration, initiated long before under the Seljuks and Il-Khans were further intensified by the centralizing trends of Safavid government. Like their predecessors and also their Mughul contemporaries in India, the Safavids endeavored to keep up their military establishment by making direct payments to the military commanders out of the central treasury. This proved impracticable and so they were forced to resort to the allotment of *iqtas,* or "revenue assignments." These went mainly to the members of the Qizilbash ruling families and, as had happened under previous regimes, such assignments showed an unfailing tendency to develop into personal and hereditary fiefs, which could be resumed by the crown only with very great difficulty. Unlike Mughul India, however, land in Safavid Iran was a marketable commodity and proprietary right was widely recognized, despite the theory that the shah was the sole owner of the soil. One peculiarity of the Safavid period was the transfer of large areas of land into clerical hands. Not only did the Shii shrines such as that of the Eighth Imam at Mashhad or that of the Safaviya order at Ardabil acquire extensive endowments, but the Shii clergy, owning land individually, became a major component of the landowning class.

The assessment of the land revenue varied from reign to reign and from province to province, but at its most favorable it may have been as little as one-quarter of the annual produce. Crop sharing was the normal method of payment in most areas, but cash payment probably prevailed on land in the vicinity of an urban center that could provide an accessible market for surplus produce. Over most of the Iranian plateau water for the soil could be obtained only by means of artificial irrigation, which had to be paid for. Sometimes the government granted advances or remitted revenue in order to extend the area under cultivation or to offset the consequences of drought, famine, or some other disaster. Apart from the hardships and misfortunes that were normal occurrences in the life cycle of the cultivator, he was also exposed to the fourfold miseries of forced labor, illegal exactions from his landlord, illegal exactions from government officials, and maltreatment at the hands of passing military or tribal contingents.

The Safavids were well aware of the advantages to be derived from actively encouraging commerce and indigenous manufacturing skills. Protection was extended to merchants and craftsmen, and it was partly in recognition of their commercial skills that Shah Abbas I transferred the Armenian population of Julfa in Armenia to a suburb of Isfahan, New Julfa, where they lived under the shah's special protection. The period as a whole saw the culmination of a long tradition of Iranian skill in the weaving, dyeing, and finishing of sumptuous cloths—brocades, velvets, damasks, cloth-of-gold, etc. In the Caspian provinces of Gilan and Mazandaran the silk-weaving industry flourished under royal patronage, and so did carpet weaving. Hostile relations with the Ottoman empire and the Özbeg khanates adversely affected Iranian participation in the traditional transcontinental caravan trade, which in any case was now in decline as a result of the opening of maritime trade routes between Europe and China. The Safavids therefore actively encouraged European merchants to trade in Iran, and Shah Abbas I founded the port of Bandar Abbas on the Persian Gulf, which serviced the important maritime trade with Gujarat and the Deccan sultanates, as well as with the Dutch and the British. Desire to stimulate trade resulted in the building of the many monumental caravanserais which are still to be seen along the old trade routes crossing the Iranian plateau and which are invariably ascribed by the local population to the beneficence of Abbas I, who also laid an impressive causeway across the low-lying countryside of Mazandaran.

Although the urban history of the Safavid period has yet to be written, it seems clear that some cities prospered exceedingly, especially manufacturing centers and those centers located far from the frontier regions, such as Isfahan, Kashan, Yazd, Qum, and Qazvin. So also did Mashhad, a major pilgrimage center, and some of the new foundations on the Caspian. On the other hand, the great commercial and cultural centers of Tabriz and Herat, repeatedly beseiged by Ottoman or Özbeg armies, probably declined in prosperity and population between 1500 and 1700, as did also the former Il-Khanid metropolis of Sultaniya. Tabriz had been the first capital of the dynasty, but its proximity to the Ottoman frontier led to its replacement by Qazvin. Later, Shah Abbas I transferred the capital to Isfahan, a more central and secure location, although both Qazvin and Tehran, already in existence in the Timurid period, were better placed as vantage points for watching the vulnerable northwestern and northeastern frontiers. Under the Safavids the cities enjoyed a certain measure of *de facto* self-government, as exercised by the more prominent *ulama,* the wealthier merchants, and long-established landowners in the neighborhood. The shah's authority was represented by a functionary known as the *kalantar,* who was a local man of consequence whose appointment was confirmed only after the heads of each quarter of the city had signified their approval. These latter were the real link between government and the urban population and it was they who provided the local knowledge necessary for assessing the allocation of taxes in each quarter. In return, they were the recognized channel for the expression of local grievances.

Safavid Promotion of the Iranian Cultural Tradition

The genesis of the Safavid empire lay in the unusual conjunction of a Turcoman tribal confederacy with a militant Shii Sufi order, although neither provided a particularly firm institutional base upon which to build. The Turcoman Qizilbash element in the empire tended to reduce all but the most vigorous rulers to the status of a mere *primus inter pares,* while once it became clear that the external danger to the empire came from the Ottomans and the Özbegs, Turks by race, culture, and language, there was a real need for the Safavids to disassociate themselves from their arch-foes by playing down their own Turkish origins. The Shii factor led to emphasis on the (probably spurious) descent of the Safavids from the Fifth Imam and ultimately from Ali and Fatima. To the clerical classes and to the pious in general this illustrious Arab genealogy was a source of deep satisfaction, but it did not in itself provide the kind of dynastic legitimation needed by a regime hard-pressed internally by turbulent and aspiring chieftains and by enemies beyond the frontiers with no less pretentious claims to world domination. Thus the Safavid rulers relied less and less on their position as leaders of the Qizilbash confederacy and on their charisma as *murshids* of the Safaviya order, identifying rather with those ancient traditions of Iranian absolutism that had managed to survive since Sasanid times throughout centuries of foreign domination. Those traditions, partly bureaucratic and institutional, partly literary and cultural, and always placing great stress on the charisma of monarchy, had reemerged briefly between the ninth and eleventh centuries under the patronage of Iranian dynasties such as the Saffarids, Samanids, and Buyids. Thereafter, the tradition had been taken over by the Turkish Ghaznavids and Seljuks and even by the Mongol Il-Khans and the Turco-Mongol Timurids. This was the tradition that the Safavids, at least from the time of Shah Abbas I, made their own. Consciously or unconsciously, the dynasty identified increasingly with its Iranian subjects, while the gorgeous trappings of kingship, designed to impress even those visitors who knew the courts of the Ottoman sultan or the Mughul padshah, provided the facade behind which lay an increasingly authoritarian and centralized regime.

Shah Abbas I beautified and enlarged his capital, Isfahan, in order to vie with and even outshine the splendor of Ottoman Istanbul. Certainly he planned on a truly imperial scale, and there can be little doubt that his example influenced the Mughul padshah, Shah Jahan, when the latter planned a new capital at Shahjahanabad (now Old Delhi) two decades later. Iranian architecture under the Safavids likewise evolved what may be called an imperial style. The architectural forms were less original than those of Seljuk or Il-Khanid times and the color and design of the tilework was less brilliant than Timurid decoration at its best, but the overall effect was one of sumptuous and dazzling opulence. Much the same may be said of the miniaturist's art, which, except during the early sixteenth century, never equalled that of the great masters of the Timurid period.

One important adjunct of the shah's authority was the support of the clerical classes. As Safavid rule stabilized itself and Shiism became the faith of the majority of the shah's subjects, the standing of the *ulama* in society rose accordingly, both in terms of their politico-religious influence with the masses and also in terms of their economic leverage. The regime recognized and supported this great growth in clerical power and pretensions. The authority of the *ulama* as a whole was upheld, individual teachers and theologians enjoyed royal favor, and Shii devotional literature was generously patronized. Unlike almost all previous regimes, whether indigenous Iranian, Turkish, or Turco-Mongol, the Safavids gave little or no encouragement to the composition of poetry, which over the centuries has been one of the crowning glories of Iranian civilization. The reason for this omission is clear. Poetry had long been closely associated with Sufism but now Sufism, apart from that manifested in the Safaviya and related orders, was positively discouraged and from time to time persecuted. Under the Safavids there emerged an alliance between the shah and the Shii clergy which served to counterbalance the less dependable alliance between the shah and the tribal ruling elite.

3. THE MUGHULS IN SOUTH ASIA

The Establishment of the Mughul Empire

In two decisive battles, against the Lodi Afghans at Panipat in 1526 and against a confederacy of Rajputs at Khanua in 1527, Babur laid the foundations of Mughul rule in India. At the time of his death in 1530 the frontiers of this new empire bounded an area that included the Panjab, the plains of the Jumna and the Ganges eastward into northern Bihar, and the country south of the Jumna and the Chambal as far as Gwalior. It also included the Kabul valley and much of what is now southeastern Afghanistan.

The term Mughul, as applied to Babur, his followers and descendants, is a misnomer now too firmly established to be dislodged, but a misnomer nonetheless. In Persian, *mughul* means "Mongol" (e.g., the race of Chingiz Khan and his descendants and especially the Il-Khanid dynasty), while *mughulistan* means "the land of the Mongols," the name traditionally given to the steppe region beyond the Syr Darya and, today, to the Mongolian People's Republic. Babur was not a Mongol but a Turk and his native tongue was the Turkish language known as Chaghatay, although he had Mongol ancestors on his mother's side, descended from Chingiz Khan's second son, Chaghatay. However, in this instance it was the paternal descent from Timur that mattered most. It was Timur's throne of Samarqand that Babur had aspired to seize in his adventurous youth, and it was as Timur's heir that he claimed the sultanate of Delhi on the strength of Timur's conquest of 1398. Strictly speaking, therefore, Babur and his descendants should be known as Timurids. In India they were frequently referred to as Chaghatays, but European travelers of the sixteenth and seventeenth centuries picked up the term Mughul, which was widely used to distinguish the foreign Muslim ruling elite from Indian-born Muslims, and the term is now sanctified by long usage. It is important to remember, however, that the Mughuls were Turks, like the majority of the earlier Muslim invaders of India, although they had undergone a much greater degree of Iranicization before entering the subcontinent than had any of their predecessors.

Under Babur's son, Humayun (r. 1530-40 and 1555-56), the empire, still unconsolidated, first expanded rapidly and then contracted. Having recklessly overextended his conquests, Humayun and his Mughuls were expelled from India in 1540 by the Afghans already settled in the Gangetic plain and were forced to seek temporary asylum in Safavid Iran. In 1555 Humayun made his way back to Delhi where he died in the following year, so that the work of reconquest and reconstruction had to begin all over again, under the nominal leadership of Humayun's thirteen-year-old son, Akbar (1556-1605). After a decisive victory, again at Panipat, over combined Afghan and Hindu elements, there was a short lull before the young ruler came into his own. Then, from 1561 until his death in 1605 the momentum of expansion continued unabated for four decades, advancing the Mughul frontier far beyond the Narbada, traditional southern boundary of north Indian empires. One by one, the sultanates of Malwa, Gujarat, and Bengal were annexed, as were areas such as Gondwana and Orissa in which the Muslims had hitherto taken little interest. To the north and west of the Panjab, the Kashmir valley was occupied, Mughul rule in the Kabul valley was strengthened to protect that strategic area from the formidable Özbeg ruler of Bukhara, Sind on the lower Indus was annexed, and Kandahar was acquired through the good offices of a defecting Safavid governor. At the same time, a nominal overlordship was asserted over the Pathan, Baluchi, and Brahui tribes of the northwestern frontier region.

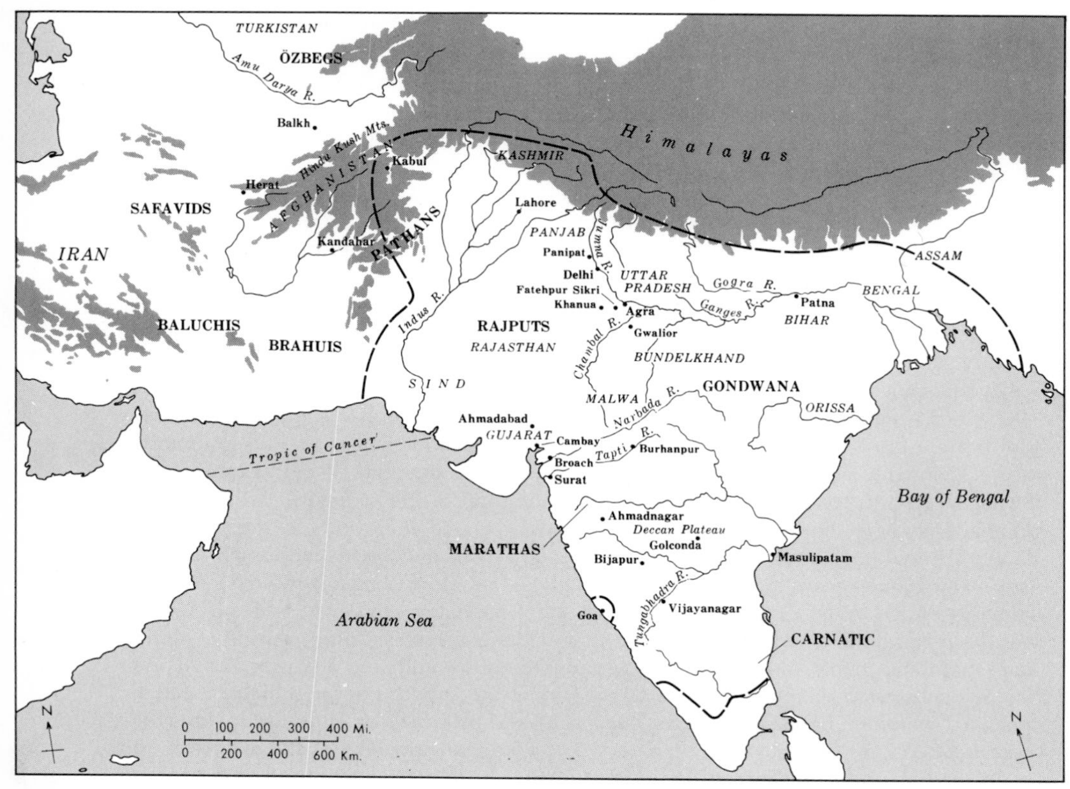

Map 40 Maximum extent of the Mughul empire under Awrangzeb, about 1700

These acquisitions can all be seen as part of a familiar pattern of expansionist dynamics. But while Akbar, like his predecessors, sought to enlarge the area under his rule, he was confronted within his own territory by the problem of the Rajputs, warlike and independent Hindu chieftains who occupied strategic fortresses or fortress cities not only in Rajasthan itself but also in Malwa and Bundelkhand. The retention of independence by these Rajput chieftains had always posed a threat to the Muslim rulers of northern India, first to the sultans of Delhi and later to the sultans of Malwa and Gujarat. Unless the Rajputs could be subjugated it was impossible for a Delhi-based regime to hold with complete security Gujarat, Malwa, and the highway to the Deccan. From apparently quite early in his reign, Akbar understood the significance of the Rajput problem and he dealt with it pragmatically, eliminating one Rajput stronghold after another with ferocious determination while shrewdly providing opportunities for the less recalcitrant Rajput chieftains to be co-opted into the imperial system by granting them positions of trust and honor.

During the last decade of his life Akbar felt his position in the north to be sufficiently strong for him to attempt to extend his empire into the Deccan, presumably with the ultimate intention of bringing the whole of peninsular India under Mughul rule. By the close of the sixteenth century the position in central and south India had changed radically from what it had been at the beginning of the century. The Bahmanid sultanate of the Deccan had disappeared and so had the Hindu kingdom of Vijayanagar south of the Tungabhadra River. No single state had arisen as successor to either, and compared to the Mughul empire, the sultanates of Ahmadnagar, Bijapur, and Golconda, the three principal regimes to emerge in the south, possessed only modest resources in terms of their military establishments. They did enjoy, however, substantial advantages in the difficult terrain and the tenuous line of communications which would face any invader whose base lay so far north as Delhi. Even the ablest of Mughul rulers seriously underestimated the difficulties involved in advancing southward.

From 1691 onward, Akbar sent envoys and armies to the south, but the rulers of the Deccan, divided though they were among themselves, resisted Mughul domination. Under Akbar's successor, Jahangir (r. 1605-27), a somewhat lethargic ruler, the pace of expansion slowed down while the empire enjoyed a breathing space in which to consolidate the gains of the previous half century. There followed a further burst of energy during the reign of Jahangir's successor, Shah Jahan (r. 1627-58), a vigorous expansionist. Shah Jahan set great store on regaining Kandahar, which had passed temporarily into Safavid hands in 1622. This he accomplished in 1638, but lost it again in 1648, and neither of the costly expeditions sent to recover it in 1649 and 1652 was successful. Shah Jahan also sent an expedition north of the Hindu Kush in 1646 to seize the Özbeg outpost of Balkh but without lasting success. Shah Jahan's attempts to recover the ancient possessions of his family in Central Asia were failures, but they were offset by his successes in the south, where the sultanates of Ahmadnagar, Bijapur, and Golconda were all brought to terms by 1636. Thereafter, the region stretching southward from the Narbada to the northern frontiers of Bijapur and Golconda was formed into a single viceroyalty (of which the core was the former sultanate of Ahmadnagar) over which Shah Jahan appointed as viceroy his third son, Awrangzeb, who served there from 1636 to 1644 and again from 1653 to 1657. Awrangzeb directed his considerable energies to pacifying and establishing effective control over the Mughul Deccan, but he never lost sight of his ultimate objective—the annexation of the two independent sultanates to the south. In 1656 his opportunity came when he intervened in a dispute between the sultan of Golconda and his Iranian general, Mir Jumla, who had recently conquered the Carnatic, the coastal area lying between the Eastern Ghats and the Bay of Bengal. Awrangzeb invaded the sultanate and was about to occupy Golconda itself when he received orders from Delhi to desist, sent by his father at the instigation of his jealous elder brother. A settlement was negotiated with the sultan, and Mir Jumla transferred his allegiance to Delhi, where he became imperial *vazir* and an influential partisan of Awrangzeb. In the following year, Shah Jahan's advancing senility provoked the long-expected contest for the throne among his four sons, from which Awrangzeb (r. 1658-1707) eventually emerged as sole ruler, having in the meantime rid himself of his brothers and several nephews.

Awrangzeb proclaimed himself padshah in 1658, but his father, Shah Jahan, survived as a prisoner until 1666. In consequence, notwithstanding his already considerable reputation as a general, the usurper felt the need to prove himself his father's equal and to conciliate the ruling elite by providing them with opportunities for patronage and personal enrichment such as they had enjoyed during previous reigns. For some years, therefore, the imperial court continued to be the setting for magnificance and extravagance on a scale comparable to Shah Jahan's time, while costly missions were dispatched to Mecca and to the courts of various Muslim rulers. Meanwhile, expansion into Assam on the northeast frontier, undertaken by Mir Jumla, provided substantial rewards in glory and plunder for the military classes. No doubt during these first decades of the reign Awrangzeb continued to think in terms of further aggression against Bijapur and Golconda, but affairs in the north engaged his attention until 1681. This was partly the result of his own high-handed dealings with the Pathan tribes across the Indus and with the Rajputs, hitherto an undoubted source of strength to the empire. Historians have traditionally attributed Awrangzeb's alienation of the Rajputs to his general aversion to Hindus but his motive may have been primarily fiscal, believing that the elimination of this particular component of the ruling elite was a price

worth paying for easing the overall pressure on patronage and revenue assignments. In any event, by 1681 patched-up settlements with the Rajputs and with the tribes of the northwestern frontier region enabled him to turn his attention once more to the Deccan and he abandoned Delhi for the south, never to return. For the remaining twenty-six years of the reign he remained in the Deccan, where he achieved his life-long ambition of conquering the sultanates of Bijapur and Golconda but where he failed to solve a greater problem, the intransigence of the warlike Marathas who occupied the rugged terrain of the northwestern Deccan, where they had been subjects of the former sultans of Ahmadnagar. It was a failure that contributed substantially to the ultimate disintegration of the empire.

The Mughul Unification of the Indian Subcontinent

The history of the Mughul empire from the first battle of Panipat (1526) to the annexation of the sultanate of Golconda (1687) covered a span of 160 years, and although expansion was to bring almost the entire subcontinent under Mughul rule—at least nominally—it would be unwise to postulate that the Mughuls envisaged themselves as fulfilling some kind of "manifest destiny" to which, as rulers of India, they were bound to aspire. The Mughuls were aliens in India and the traditions of the dynasty were characteristically Turco-Mongol and Central Asian. In attacking the Delhi sultanate, Babur saw himself reclaiming a lost appanage of the Timurids, but he probably also viewed it as being of less worth than Samarqand and the ancestral homelands of his dynasty north of the Hindu Kush and of the Amu Darya, now in the hands of the Özbegs. It took the Mughuls a long time to accustom themselves to a purely Indian role. Babur, Humayun, and Akbar were all compelled to keep a watchful eye on what was happening north of the Hindu Kush. There was an ongoing awareness of the exposed frontier with the Özbegs and the Safavids and also of the strategic importance of the country lying between the Indus and Kabul. In his costly wars against Balkh and Kandahar, Shah Jahan was reaffirming (although for the last time) the dynasty's historic preoccupation with Central Asia.

In India itself, by way of contrast, the Mughuls encountered no rivals for hegemony: only refractory centers of local power (such as the Rajput principalities) or decaying sultanates such as those of Bengal and the Deccan whose inherent weakness made them tempting objects for aggression and whose inability to control their own frontier regions provided opportune pretexts for intervention. The Mughuls occupied these power vacuums one after another not because they possessed a compulsive urge to bring the entire subcontinent under a single rule but because the Mughul dynasty, like all such dynasties, was naturally predatory (Akbar declared on one occasion: "A monarch should be ever intent on conquest; otherwise, his enemies rise in arms against him. The army should be exercised in warfare, lest from want of training they become self-indulgent.") and because it could maintain itself only by the continuous acquisition of new sources of revenue and land with which to reward its followers.

The Mughul war machine included such disparate elements as the highly mobile mounted archers who had been the shock troops of former Turkish invaders of India, the massed infantry and elephants of traditional Hindu warfare, and also artillery. Notwithstanding assertions to the contrary, firearms in India were not a Mughul innovation, for they were already known in the sultanates of Gujarat and the Deccan. In general, the Mughuls made rather ineffective use of both artillery and handguns, being content to employ mostly foreigners—deserters from the Ottoman provinces or European renegades—as artillerymen and gunsmiths. Artillery was valued mainly for siege operations

---

9.3 Mughul siege guns being dragged into position at the siege of the Rajput fortress of Ranthambhor, Rajasthan, in 1568. Mughul miniature, late sixteenth century. Courtesy: Victoria and Albert Museum, London.

and so, as in the case of the Ottoman empire, there was a tendency for cannon to get larger and larger, but also more clumsy and difficult to handle. At the beginning of the eighteenth century, for example, some cannon were removed from the Lahore fort which were so heavy that it took 250 oxen and five or six elephants ten days to move them a distance of three or four miles.

The Mughul empire in its great days did not, except perhaps in the first decade of its existence, depend on the support of a single group in the way that the early Safavid empire depended on the Qizilbash. Rather, the strength of the Mughul empire lay in the diversity of its ruling elite, the loyalty of which was assured so long as it had access to a continuous flow of titles and honorifics, appointments and revenue assignments. The initial conquests had been the work of a fairly homogeneous Iranicized Turco-Mongol military elite, confronting two preexisting power groups that had dominated northern India for the preceding century or more—the Afghans and the Rajputs. During the sixteenth century both these groups were gradually co-opted into the new Mughul system, although not without some show of resistance from the resentful Afghans, who regarded the Mughuls as having supplanted them, and also from those Rajput clans that saw their traditional Rajput rivals already well entrenched within the new order. At the same time, the opportunities for enrichment provided by service in the Mughul army or bureaucracy tempted many enterprising soldiers of fortune, *ulama,* and scholars to immigrate into India from the Muslim lands to the northwest, especially from Bukhara and the surrounding regions. Immigrants from Bukhara were mainly Turks and therefore Sunni, in contrast to the immigrants from Iran, who were Shii. Numerically, the Iranian immigrants were in a minority but they included some of the ablest among the newcomers. Sometimes the immigrants were political or religious refugees, but irrespective of the reasons that brought them into India (then regarded as a land of opportunity), their departure from their homeland constituted a veritable drain of talent, which in the case of Safavid Iran in particular must have contributed to the prevailing decline of the late seventeenth century. These Turkish and Iranian immigrants were the backbone of the Mughul system, but during the seventeenth century the Mughul advance into the Deccan led to the recruitment of new groups into the ruling elite—Deccani Muslims who had formerly served the sultans of Ahmadnagar, Bijapur, and Golconda, and also Hindu Marathas.

The Organization of the Mughul Empire

While the size and complexity of Mughul administration far exceeded that of the Muslim regimes that had established themselves in India between the thirteenth and sixteenth centuries, it is important to stress that the Mughuls built upon preexisting foundations. Akbar was not the first Muslim to rule an extensive area of the subcontinent and devise an elaborate bureaucracy to collect the land revenue and maintain order. The organization of the Mughul empire as it emerged in the second half of the sixteenth century was rooted in the traditions of the Delhi sultanate, but it also—like all the later Islamic empires—derived much of its institutional structure and its dynastic life-style from a common Turco-Mongol heritage. The decimal chain of command in the army, for example, was based on Chingizkhanid practice, and when Shah Jahan styled himself Lord of the Fortunate Conjunction of the Planets he was deliberately reviving the title used by his famous ancestor, Timur. But it is not enough to emphasize the Mughuls' Central Asian antecedents and the heritage of the Delhi sultanate. A number of features of Mughul government—the functions of the *vazir,* for example, and the separation of the revenue administration in the provinces from the executive arm—derived from long-established practices going back to the great days of the Abbasid caliphs in Baghdad. It is less easy to detect truly indigenous elements in the Mughul system of government in the higher echelons, although the fact that the land revenue was assessed and collected mainly by subordinate Hindu officials ensured that the modes of control and coercion at subdistrict and village level followed traditional patterns.

As in the case of the Ottomans and the Safavids, it is convenient to divide the power structure of the Mughul empire into two distinct hierarchies, one religious and the other bureaucratic. The plural composition of Indian society and the diversity of the Mughul ruling elite (Indian and non-Indian, Muslim and Hindu, Sunni and Shii) necessarily involved some relaxation of the application of the *Sharia*. Partly in consequence of this, the *ulama* under the Mughuls enjoyed less prestige than they did in other Islamic empires. This was due not only to the peculiar situation of Islam in India as a minority religion but also to the place of the *ulama* in Indo-Muslim society. The power of the *ulama* in traditional Muslim society was based on the influence they exercised over the entire "community of believers," which in turn gave them political leverage to put pressure on the state or its representatives. In India, however, where the Muslims had always been a minority, the *ulama* were far more dependent on the goodwill and the patronage of the state than were the clerical classes in the Muslim lands farther west, and this necessarily bound them to the reigning sultan, who alone could assure them of such practical necessities as official posts, pensions, and revenue assignments. At the same time, leadership of the Muslim community as a whole had long been preempted by the Sufis, a tradition going back to the great Chishtiya *murshids* of the thirteenth and fourteenth centuries. Under the Mughuls the *ulama,* therefore, continued to be an "establishment" clergy, widely regarded as being venal and time serving.

The head of the *ulama* in Mughul India was the *sadr* or *shaykh al-Islam,* who had charge of religious endowments and institutions of religious learning. Muslim law was administered by a chief *qazi,* sometimes the same person as the chief *sadr,* to whom all provincial *qazis* were subordinate. The relationship of these officials to the padshah was necessarily an ambiguous one and demanded discretion on both sides. In 1578-79, for example, the behavior of the *ulama* at court so irritated Akbar that he assumed certain functions—the reading of the *khutba* and the handing down of judicial decisions based on his own interpretation of religious law—which in turn deeply offended orthodox opinion. Under more conventional rulers such as Shah Jahan and Awrangzeb the *ulama* enjoyed a somewhat higher prestige than under Akbar. Nevertheless, even then, the distribution of power among the ruling elite of the empire and the great personal prestige enjoyed by the Sufis in Indo-Muslim society gave the *ulama* less importance than might have been expected. Significantly, the disintegration of the empire did not result in an increase in the influence or authority of the *ulama* such as the Shii *ulama* in Iran gained from the decline of the Safavids.

Mughul India was governed by a service nobility in which every nobleman held a military rank called a *mansab* and was consequently known as a *mansabdar*. This rank was determined by the number of troops the nobleman was required to maintain on a war footing. The most junior *mansabdars* maintained a mere ten men while in Awrangzeb's reign there were *mansabdars* who maintained as many as seven thousand. A *mansabdar* might have exclusively administrative duties—as a revenue official, for example—but he remained part of a military hierarchy in which promotion was measured by the number of troops attached to each *mansab*. Only the *ulama* were outside the system, and even Hindu tributaries such as the Rajput Maharajas held *mansab* ranks. It was a highly effective system since it provided a steel framework within which the entire military and civil administration (apart from the judiciary) operated.

Mansabdars were recruited from various social and ethnic backgrounds ranging from immigrants and local supporters to erstwhile foes, and included both princes of the imperial house and also self-made men such as Mir Jumla, who had started life as an oil-merchant's son in a village outside Isfahan. One category was, however, almost wholly unrepresented—persons of slave origin. Unlike their Ottoman and Safavid contemporaries or the former sultans of Delhi, the Mughuls apparently had no use for *mamluks*.

It had been Akbar's intention that every *mansabdar* should receive his salary in cash, the logical consequence of his intention that the land revenue should be paid in cash. This, however, proved impossible. Instead, *mansabdars* were granted territorial revenue assignments known as *jagirs* on which they were required to collect the land revenue for the government, deducting an agreed amount to cover their salary, including the maintenance of their troops and the cost of collection. A *mansabdar* might be granted *jagirs* in several different provinces, sometimes in localities remote from where he was serving. Necessarily, therefore, he was compelled to employ agents to administer these *jagirs* on his behalf. Even so, the government was determined to prevent *jagirs* from being converted into private fiefs and so they were systematically transferred from one officeholder to another every three or four years.

The higher echelons of the administrative system were closely supervised by the rulers in person, and the ablest padshahs—Akbar, Shah Jahan, and Awrangzeb—were very much in control. Under their watchful direction the *vazir* (sometimes known also as the *diwan*) supervised the entire bureaucracy and especially the revenue-collecting arm of the government, while other great officeholders were in charge of the military commissariat, the administration of the imperial household, and various secretariats.

In the middle years of Akbar's reign the empire was divided into twelve provinces, known as *subahs,* but these increased in number with the later conquests until by 1687 they numbered twenty-one. Differing from each other in extent of area, size of population, and revenue yield, their boundaries were for the most part predetermined by the historical growth of the empire. There were also, however, extensive tracts of country which were excluded from the provincial structure and left in the hands of local rulers on condition that they paid tribute regularly. Such areas usually consisted of jungle or hill country considered difficult to control and unlikely to be very remunerative in terms of their revenue yield.

In charge of each province was a governor, known as a *subahdar,* who headed the administrative hierarchy of district officers responsible for upholding the padshah's authority. The *subahdar* did not, however, appoint the district officers to their posts. They, like the police officials in charge of the larger towns and the commandants of important fortresses in the provinces, were all appointed from Delhi itself. The prime function of all these officials and also of their subordinates at subdistrict level was the maintenance of law and order of a rough-and-ready kind. They played no part whatever in the most important function of government—the assessment and collection of the land revenue. This was separately administered by a provincial *diwan,* who was appointed by and was solely answerable to the imperial *vazir,* or *diwan,* in Delhi. Under the provincial *diwan,* throughout the districts and subdistricts, there was a skilled staff, composed mainly of Hindus, which determined the amount of the land revenue to be paid and supervised its collection. The majority of subdistrict officials were local men and in many cases the office became hereditary.

Mughul Control over the Economic and Human Resources of the Empire

The overwhelming majority of the subjects of the Mughul padshah were engaged in agriculture, living in relatively stable village communities where land was not a marketable commodity and where contacts with the outside world were few. The state impinged on the village communities to obtain revenue but for hardly anything else. Throughout the empire it was the custom for the government to demand a proportion of the crop or its equivalent in cash, but while this proportion had fluctuated under former dynasties it had rarely reached the level exacted by the Mughuls, which was one-third of the crop during the second half of the sixteenth century and one-half a century later. Under Mughul rule areas directly administered from Delhi were divided for revenue assessment purposes into two distinct categories: crown lands administered by state officials, and revenue assignments *(jagirs)* administered by the *jagirdars* or their agents.

Unlike the townsfolk, of whom a substantial minority were Muslims and therefore subject to the *Sharia* administered by the *qazi,* most cultivators were Hindus who conducted their lives in accordance with Hindu religious traditions upheld by the local brahman or embodied in the consensus judgments of the village council of elders. For the bulk of the population, therefore, the sole link between the imperial government and themselves—at least under normal circumstances—was the payment of the land revenue, while at subdistrict level the revenue officials were generally Hindus and local men. Thus the average villager was no more likely to come into contact with Mughul officialdom than he was later to come into contact with British officialdom. But if the cultivator saw little of the pomp and splendor of Mughul rule he nevertheless felt its weight upon his shoulders, and all the evidence points to the conclusion that Mughul rule pressed upon him very heavily indeed. The available statistics are exceptionally difficult to interpret for purposes of comparison with earlier or subsequent regimes, but what does seem certain is that the revenue demand, heavy enough during the sixteenth century, had increased substantially by the second half of the seventeenth century and that, concurrently, serious abuses had crept into its administration, especially in the form of illegal exactions by the revenue officials themselves.

Inspired by the vigorous administrative reforms undertaken by Sher Shah Sur (r. 1540-45), an Afghan predecessor who reigned in Delhi all too briefly, Akbar and his advisers devised an improved system of revenue assessment and collection, which was probably superior to anything hitherto known in the subcontinent. The principles upon which this system was based were (1) the accurate measurement and classification of all land under cultivation, (2) fixed rates of assessment made, wherever possible, with the actual cultivator of the soil, and (3) payment in cash rather than kind, wherever market conditions allowed. Admirable as these principles were, they had to be modified to a very considerable extent in the interests of administrative expediency. The accurate assessment of the revenue demand envisaged by this system necessitated the creation of an extensive subordinate bureaucracy that required constant supervision from above. Revenue settlements made with the cultivators were extremely laborious to administer in comparison with settlements made with intermediaries, whether village headmen, local notables, or revenue farmers. Cash payments were possible only where a cash economy was already well established at village level. Above all, it was not possible to find the ready cash to cover the day-to-day cost of running the court and government and in particular to pay the salaries of the *mansabdars.* Hence, even during Akbar's lifetime the regime was forced to fall back on the time-honored device of making revenue assignments—the *jagirdari* system.

Surviving instructions to Mughul revenue officials invariably include passages to the effect that the cultivator should be treated with justice and consideration, and it was certainly in the long-term interests of the empire to encourage expansion of the area under cultivation, with a view to a future increase of revenue. But the *mansabdar* who had received a temporary revenue assignment that he knew was to be transferred to a fellow *mansabdar* within three or four years felt no incentive to invest in the future prosperity of his *jagir.* On the contrary, it was in his interest to squeeze the maximum profit out of it in the shortest possible time. For this reason the *jagirdari* system, excellent as it was as a political device for preventing the growth of local bases of power among the *mansabdars,* was ruinous for agriculture.

It is curious to note how many European visitors to India during the seventeenth century, coming as they did from countries where the lot of the peasant was far from idyllic, nevertheless commented on the brutal treatment of the Indian villager by the agents of the government. It seems clear that, notwithstanding the professed concern of the Mughul government for the welfare of the cultivator, the fiscal needs of the regime were virtually insatiable and those who could not or would not meet the revenue demand were savagely punished. Apart from being beaten and tortured, cultivators who defaulted on their revenue payments, or the members of their families, were frequently sold into slavery. Sometimes widespread and persistent oppression by revenue officials provoked an uprising over an extended area and when this occurred the revolt would be put down with exemplary ferocity, a ferocity that generally far exceeded that shown in the case of outbursts of insubordination and fractiousness on the part of dissident nobles.

It should be stressed, however, that exemplary punishment for rebels was a response to the rather limited means of coercion that were, under normal circumstances, available to the authorities. The Mughul regime in its prime possessed a highly effective military machine, which was certainly more powerful than anything known in India before the sixteenth century, but it lacked the means to undertake the constant regulation of its subjects in the form of law-enforcement agents and basic statistical information such as enables even democratic governments in the twentieth century to exercise an all-pervasive authority over the lives of their subjects. Inadequate communications, a relatively small administrative cadre, the dispersal of regular troops over a vast area, shortage of ready cash, and the need for tacit support from the population as a whole resulted in the exercise of some degree of restraint in all aspects of government in which the acquisition of revenue was not directly involved.

One severe burden traditionally endured by the cultivator in premechanized societies—forced labor—seems to have been rather limited in Mughul India. The regime undertook few hydraulic or irrigation schemes except in the immediate vicinity of Delhi and Lahore, and the lavish building of palaces, mosques, and mausoleums appears to have been done by hired laborers. Another traditional abuse, the conscription of peasants to assist in the transport of military supplies and grain for the army, seems to have been rather rare, being undertaken normally by occupational groups such as the nomadic Banjaras, who supplied grain for Indian armies on the move well into the nineteenth century. It should, however, be stressed that the Mughul period was as accustomed to the prevalence of chattel slavery as were the preceding two millennia of Indian history, although the presence of a large slave population was less obvious than in some other societies because the overwhelming majority of slaves were employed in domestic service.

Mughul rule pressed much more lightly upon the urban population, which apart from the payment of miscellaneous taxes and customs dues, contributed much less in the way of state revenue than did the agricultural population. Under the Mughuls, urban life continued to flourish, as it had done throughout the three preceding centuries of Muslim rule. Great manufacturing centers such as Patna and Ahmadabad, ports such as Broach, Cambay, and Surat, and towns located on important trade routes such as Burhanpur on the Tapti prospered and expanded along with the imperial capitals of Agra, Delhi, and Lahore. Many small towns mushroomed into important local centers, especially in the area between the Jumna and the Gogra in what is now Uttar Pradesh. It has also been suggested that Akbar's endeavor to enforce the payment of the land revenue in cash stimulated the emergence of nuclear townships, where grain dealers, money lenders, money changers, *jagirdari* agents, and local officials gathered for convenience and perhaps security.

Mughul urban prosperity was based largely on a growth in the demand for manufactured commodities of all kinds. This demand was partly a natural consequence of the creation of the Mughul empire itself, which had brought into being a vast free-trade area in which merchants and their goods could pass with relative ease and safety over vast distances from Kabul to the Deccan and from Gujarat to Bengal. It was also a response to the insatiable demand for luxury commodities on the part of the exceedingly affluent ruling elite. In addition, there was a growing foreign demand for Indian manufactured goods, especially textiles, which were sought after not only in the traditional marts of West Asia and of the lands bordering the Indian Ocean, but also in increasing quantities by the European traders who now began to frequent the ports of the subcontinent and even some of the manufacturing centers up country, rubbing shoulders with their Arab, Iranian, Armenian, and Indian competitors.

The Mughul regime well understood the value of merchants and bankers. It therefore encouraged them, protected them, and even went into partnership with them, having perhaps more need of these useful subjects than they had need of any such imperial superstructure. In any event, the creation of an empire that in course of time came to include the greater part of the subcontinent, together with the establishment of an orderly administrative system, served to boost trading activities of all kinds, as did government initiative in repairing and making safe the main commercial arteries of the country, in the construction of bridges, caravanserais and milestones, and in the attempted standardization of currency, weights, and measures. All these activities favored the commercial classes. In addition, the Mughuls involved themselves directly in the affairs of those same commercial classes in three specific spheres of activity. First, they maintained workshops, often located within the fortress-palaces of their capital cities, where luxury commodities and, in particular, textiles were manufactured under the direction of state officials, a practice emulated by many of the wealthier *mansabdars.* Second, they invested directly in a wide range of capitalist activities, including maritime ventures across the Arabian Sea and the Bay of Bengal. That a *mansabdar* with a commercial background such as Mir Jumla should have gone into partnership with local merchants and also established monopolies in certain commodities was only to be expected, but similar enterprises were also undertaken by members of the ruling house, including some of the women in the imperial harem. Third, the regime was frequently compelled to turn to the capitalist classes for loans in times of emergency, such as at the outset of a campaign. It also sought from them bills of exchange for the transfer of large sums of money over great distances, as when tribute was to be sent from Golconda to Delhi or when the land revenue collected in the province of Bengal was needed to pay troops operating in the southern Deccan.

Under such circumstances, the commercial and banking classes seem to have flourished under Mughul rule. The same can hardly be said of the urban proletariat, steadily growing in number in consequence of an unregulated drift to the towns, where the squalor of the slums might be regarded as preferable to the exactions of the government's revenue officials in the villages. Artisans were paid virtually subsistence wages, and the more skillful were subjected to periodical seizure by nobles who sought their services, often *gratis,* in their own factories. Vast numbers of persons, both in towns and villages, were engaged in the manufacture of textiles, of which cotton weaving undoubtedly employed the most.

Mughul bureaucracy, whatever its achievement in the coercion and manipulation of a vast and diverse population, provided little or nothing in the way of assistance or security for these people, beyond maintaining order of a rather heavy-handed kind. The government's revenue demands and the additional exactions of its servants left the cultivator little or no margin to protect himself against the onset of bad times, and much the same may be said of the pitiful wages of the weaver or unskilled laborer. Both cultivator and artisan alike were exposed to the violence and rapacity of those above them, and both were the first victims of those periodical natural disasters such as drought or famine against which the age knew no protection.

Mughul Cultural Legitimation and the Indian Cultural Tradition

The Safavids, as was shown in the preceding section, acquired cultural legitimation first by linking the fortunes of the Safaviya Sufi order with a tribal Turcoman confederacy, the Qizilbash, and then by gradually identifying their interests with those of their Iranian subjects. The result was to link the dynasty with messianic Shiism, with ancient traditions of Iranian absolutism, and with the Iranian sense of cultural identity and its corollary, the Iranian sense of antagonism towards Ottoman and Arab neighbors. In the case of the Ottomans, the sultan, engaged in *jihad* ("religious warfare") against the infidel in Anatolia and the Balkans, was able to stand forth as the supreme *ghazi,* or "fighter for the faith." In course of time this role was enlarged, first by taking over the imperial Byzantine heritage and then that of the long-defunct Abbasid caliphate of Baghdad. By way of contrast, the Mughuls were confronted by peculiar difficulties in acquiring cultural legitimation as the *de facto* rulers of the subcontinent. Nowhere in their past could they claim a spiritual charisma such as the Safavids claimed through their descent from the *shaykhs* of Ardabil. The role of *ghazi* was inappropriate in a land where, notwithstanding the fact that the majority of the population was non-Muslim, Muslim states had been in existence for three centuries and which, except at its peripheries, was regarded as an extension of the Muslim world of West Asia. Yet the heritage of the sultans of Delhi did not offer an attractive source of legitimation either. The sultans, it is true, had sometimes assumed the role of *ghazis,* but the chronicles of their reigns seem to be mostly tales of unrighteous tyrants and bloody usurpations. Moreover, with one exception, the sultans of Delhi had never claimed to be more than lieutenants of the Abbasid caliphs. They had humbly styled themselves "Helper of the Commander of the Faithful," and Indo-Muslim coins had continued to be struck in the name of the last caliph long after the Mongol sack of Baghdad in 1258. This was hardly an appealing tradition to conquerors with such pretensions as the Mughuls, and indeed they had at hand a far more persuasive tradition of cultural legitimation—that of their Turco-Mongol ancestors, the Chingizkhanids and the Timurids, with their lofty claims to universal empire. This was a tradition of empire in the true sense of the word, a tradition of mastery over men, without regard to geography, race, or creed, and it was reinforced by the folk memory and life-style of the dynasty and its followers and also by that Iranian historiographical tradition, going back to the thirteenth century, which had been brought into existence largely to serve first the Chingizkhanid Il-Khans and then the Timurids.

Significantly, Babur adopted the title of padshah not when he conquered the Delhi sultanate in 1526 but some twenty years earlier, at the time of the death of the senior ruler of his house, Sultan Husayn Baykara of Herat. It was an unusual title since the Timurids (apart from Timur himself, who was content with the title of *amir*) were traditionally styled mirza and occasionally sultan. It seems that in assuming the title of padshah, Babur was proclaiming himself head of all those ruling lineages and clans throughout Central Asia to whom he was related, whether Timurid or Chaghatay. It was with just such a claim, supported by a pedigree to match it, that he and his descendants built up their empire in India, operating within the traditional framework of the steppe empires of their Turco-Mongol ancestors.

For many years the Mughuls and their Central Asian followers continued to regard the Indian subcontinent as an alien environment, due partly to the strength of the cultural heritage they had brought with them from the lands beyond the Indus and partly to their instinctive rejection of the climate, living conditions, and patterns of behavior which they met with in India and which Babur denounced in his memoirs in no uncertain terms. Above all, there was that antipathy between the Islamic and the Hindu world view which has been a continuous factor in shaping the attitudes of Indian Muslims from the time of Sultan Mahmud of Ghazni and al-Biruni down to the twentieth century.

In dress, diet, and in many other respects the Mughuls only slowly and very partially adapted themselves to an Indian life-style. Persian remained the language of the imperial court, of higher administration, and of polite learning, while as late as the reign of Awrangzeb the imperial princes and princesses were still taught Chaghatay Turkish. The Persian poetry written in India continued to mirror the tastes of Shiraz or Herat, and virtually everyone in the long list of poets attached to Akbar's court was a foreigner. Akbar's favorite authors were the classical masters of Iran—Firdawsi, Rumi, Sadi, and Hafiz—and it is arguable that his intellectual predilections, like his eclecticism in religious matters, his lavish patronage of the arts, his magnificent life-style, and his openhanded generosity to suppliants and supporters were a legacy of his Turco-Mongol ancestors rather than a response to a specifically Indian situation.

In general, the imperial family and the foreign nobility did not marry Hindus (Akbar's marriage alliances with Rajput princesses were exceptions which proved the rule) or even Indian Muslims, carefully choosing their sons' brides from other foreign families. Babur, Humayun, and Akbar were of partly Turco-Mongol and partly Iranian descent. Jahangir, however, had a Rajput mother, and so had Shah Jahan. Shah Jahan, in turn, married an Iranian, in whose memory he built the Taj Mahal at Agra, and so Awrangzeb was Iranian on his mother's side. Two centuries later, European visitors at the court of the last Mughul padshahs commented upon their pale complexions and Central Asian features.

Against all this, however, must be weighed the consequence of the rulers having harems inhabited by Indian concubines and slave girls, being surrounded by Hindu servants and retainers, and being exposed to the novelties—sexual, dietary, and recreational—of an Indian milieu. In music and dancing, painting and architecture, indigenous influence proved especially pervasive. By the reign of Jahangir, for example, miniature painting had emancipated itself from the constricting traditions of the Safavid court and had evolved a distinctly Mughul style, as much Indian as Iranian. Pre-Mughul Muslim architecture in India had long shown a tendency to draw inspiration from Hindu forms and decorative motifs, a process that reached its culmination in the sixteenth century in Akbar's new foundation of Fatehpur Sikri.

It was in the sphere of religious life that the polarization of attitudes—indigenous versus foreign—found most complete expression. This was expressed not so much in terms of Hinduism versus Islam as in terms of Sufi heterodoxy versus Sunni orthodoxy. Tracing its origins back to the days of the great Chishtiya *murshids* of the early Delhi sultanate, Sufism in India had assumed during the fifteenth and sixteenth centuries increasingly syncretic and esoteric forms, of which the religious eclecticism of Akbar's court was only one manifestation. Whether these developments should be regarded as the direct consequence of Hindu influence or of a fluidity peculiarly characteristic of Islam in a frontier setting (e.g., in the marches of Byzantine Anatolia or in Southeast Asia), they posed an undoubted threat to Sunni orthodoxy and, by implication, to Muslim political domination. A predictable reaction, therefore, occurred at the close of the sixteenth century, spearheaded by a Sufi order new to India, the Naqshbandiya, which in Bukhara, its home territory, had long been celebrated for its close association with the ruling elite (in contrast to orders like the Chishtiya) and for a spiritual discipline somewhat at variance with the liberal Sufi traditions of the subcontinent. The most effective spokesman of the Naqshbandiya position was Shaykh Ahmad Sirhindi (1564-1624), who cast himself in the role of a millennial renovator of Islam (a thousand years having passed since the *hijra,* the Prophet's flight from Mecca to Medina), much to the apprehension of the self-indulgent Jahangir. The success of his movement, however, probably owed as much to the conventional piety of Jahangir's successors, Shah Jahan and Awrangzeb, as to the work of the *shaykh* himself. Neither during the seventeenth century nor later were these polarizing tensions and conflicts within the Indo-Islamic tradition resolved, and they have come to be seen in retrospect as aspects of another conflict, between those who were willing to adapt and to acculturate themselves to the Indian situation and those who were not. It seems unlikely, however, that contemporaries would have seen the problem in such terms. Rather, they would have seen it in the light of the age-old problem of integrating the personal vision of the Sufis into the rigid framework of the Sunni great tradition.

4. THE MING AND CH'ING EMPIRES IN CHINA

In China the period that followed the era of Central Asian domination is conventionally designated by the names of the two dynasties that succeeded the Mongol Yuan. These dynasties, the Ming (1368-1644) and the Ch'ing (1644-1911), are thus the Chinese counterparts of the early modern empires that existed in the other subdivisions of Asia. In viewing the Ming and Ch'ing dynasties as early modern empires two questions at once arise: (1) How are these regimes different from other dynasties in earlier periods of Chinese history? (2) What is the difference between the Ming and the Ch'ing—should we think of them as distinct or as a single block?

The answer to both of these questions flows from the processes defined at the outset of this chapter. First, in designating an early modern period we are specifically referring to the post-Mongol period and asserting that the regimes that supplanted the Central Asian conquest empires were different from those that went before. There were three types of differences: those resulting from the continuation or adaptation of institutions or practices from the period of Central Asian dominance, those that were part of a reaction to Central Asian dominance, and those that stemmed from ongoing changes within the societies. In the Chinese case it will be seen that the post-Mongol dynasties were different from the pre-Mongol dynasties in a number of significant ways. In general, the elements to be stressed relate to the influence of the political structure upon the society and the tendency for essential cultural values to be shaped by political forces. Second, the Ming and Ch'ing empires both fall into the period designated and both illustrate the trends associated with the early modern empire. However, since these two states were of fundamentally different origins—the Ming was the last indigenous Chinese dynasty while the Ch'ing was a Manchu conquest empire—it will be necessary to discuss them separately in order to understand their separate contributions to the evolution of political institutions and cultural forms. The Chinese state will be viewed as a culturalistic empire and the Manchu state as a pluralistic empire.

The Chinese Ming Empire

Mongol rule in China lasted less than a century after the establishment of the Yuan dynasty in 1279. By the 1340s the empire was torn by dissension and civil disorder at every level: factionalism among the ruling group itself led to fighting over the throne, regional commanders defied central authority, local gentry organized their own security forces, and Chinese peasants rose in armed rebellion. It was peasant rebellion that ultimately dismembered the Yuan. In revolt equally against the harsh exploitation of a ruthless landlord class and the oppressions of a foreign Mongol regime, the common people were inspired by the millennarian doctrines of secret societies which promised them deliverance from the suffering of the traditional order. These organizations, of which the White Lotus Society was the best known, existed deep within the body of peasant society and there harbored values and beliefs strikingly at odds with the high culture of the Chinese elite classes—the ideology of the Confucian state. By the mid-fourteenth century there was widespread belief in a Prince of Brightness (Ming Wang) who would appear and save the world. This doctrine, which combined elements of Maitreya, the popular Buddha of the Future, with traces of Manichaeanism (the West Asian religious dualism, in Chinese *ming chiao*), was combined by the rebels with the demand for the restoration of the Sung dynasty.

Chu Yuan-chang (1328-98), the founder of the Ming empire, started his career as a member of one of the rebel bands. Like the Han founder some fifteen centuries before, he began life as a peasant and was only the second such person in history to rule China. Orphaned and destitute, Chu Yuan-chang spent some of his early years as a wandering monk, begging for his food. Shrewd and ruthless, he rose rapidly once he joined the rebels. A cautious but adequate military strategist and a better judge of men, he soon attracted a large following. Establishing his seat at Nanking on the southern bank of Yangtze, he set about the business of destroying his rivals and annexing territory. Motivated in part by a strong hatred of the landlord class and ever mindful of his own experience of poverty, Chu Yuan-chang took stern measures to prevent his soldiers from harming the common people. Partly because of this solicitude for the peasantry but also because of good generalship and the centrality of his location, Chu Yuan-chang was able to eliminate competing Chinese leaders with regimes similar to his own. Initially, he maintained his allegiance to the secret society elements and to the fledgling state of Sung, which they had created. At the same time he set about building an administrative apparatus of scholars, gentry members, and former Yuan civil servants. By 1367, when he sent his armies north to sweep the Mongol remnants from China, he was ready to disavow his connections with the secret societies and their heterodox doctrines and put himself forward as a champion of orthodoxy qualified to take the Chinese throne. In 1368 he became the first emperor of the Ming dynasty. The name Ming was an ingenious touch, because its meaning—"brightness"—could be variously interpreted as referring to the popular notion of a savior—the Prince of Brightness, Ming Wang—or to a Confucian value (perfect understanding). A gesture in the direction of Sung restoration was made in the same year when the new ruler proposed to make Kaifeng, the first Sung capital, an imperial city (the plan was never realized).

Once in power Chu Yuan-chang devoted his energies to the task of reuniting the Chinese peoples into a single state. Faced with the problem of holding power and building an administration, the Ming founder soon forgot the radical ideals of the peasant movement in favor of an orthodox Confucianism. Thus did potential social revolution turn to cultural conservatism once power was attained. Chu Yuan-chang spent thirty years on the throne, designing and redesigning the institutions that would make his house and government endure. In this enterprise he borrowed freely from the Mongol example as well as from precedents in the Chinese historical record.

Domination over Society and Economy

Imperial domination over Chinese society was guaranteed by an elaborate prescription of the status of all strata of Chinese society. Rule was the monopoly of the imperial family. All offspring of the founder were granted hereditary titles as princes or princesses and were supported by government stipends. Succeeding generations were granted lesser titles. All were barred from government service or any useful occupation. By the end of the Ming, the ranks of the royal family had swollen to more than 100,000 members. The generals who participated in the founding, originally peasants, were converted into a hereditary nobility that intermarried with the imperial clan. Forced to reside in the capital, this group of loyal supporters became a pool from which military commanders were drawn. Actual military forces were scattered about the empire in small guard units organized on a decimal system of Mongol origin. When campaigns were ordered, generals were sent out from the capital to command the troops of the guard units. In this manner a commander was prevented from developing more than temporary ties to his troops. Moreover, the retention of his family in the capital as virtual hostages encouraged the general's loyalty in the field. Beneath this hereditary stratum of the Ming ruling elite lay the two traditional divisions of Chinese society—the gentry and the commoners. The status of the gentry—the wealthy and influential class of literati that had been growing in number ever since the Sung period—was formally fixed by the government through the device of the examination system. Success in passing a government examination conferred a degree, and with the degree went a special social status that extended to the members of the degree-holder's family. Elaborate sumptuary laws specified in detail the clothing and life-style appropriate to each level of society. Nobles and gentry members might wear silk gowns and ride in sedan chairs, while peasants were obliged to wear cotton and to walk. Tax and labor-service regulations and criminal laws were likewise specifically favorable to the upper classes.

The vast bureaucratic apparatus that the Ming founder assembled to run his empire was probably the most sophisticated administrative organization created anywhere up to that time. Organized into the traditional tripartite divisions of civil, military, and censorial elements, it was staffed throughout by salaried officials recruited into imperial service on the basis of merit and dependent on the emperor's trust for continuance in office. Military administration was divided among five regions and numerous military commissions. Civil administration adhered to the traditional units of provinces, prefectures, and counties, while the small body of censors circulated throughout the government and the empire monitoring the efficiency of administration, investigating, criticizing, and exposing all sorts of abuses.

Manpower for the administration was recruited through the traditional examination system, which was now elaborated and regularized on a scale that surpassed the practice of earlier dynasties. Examinations were held in three-year cycles starting at the county level, then moving to more stringent elimination rounds at the provincial level and then at the capital, where the final runoff was held under imperial supervision within the Forbidden City. Degrees were awarded at all three levels, and placing first in the palace examination was a guarantee of fame and fortune for life. Such was the prestige associated with success in the examination system that families of any wealth and ambition whatsoever tutored their sons for the competition. Passing even at the lowest level brought the reward of gentry status. Winners of the higher two degrees might reasonably expect to be appointed to government service. So desirable were the rewards of the degree system and so totally did the degree holders dominate Chinese society that it was not uncommon for ambitious men to spend decades in preparation and attempt repeatedly to pass the examinations. Far more rigorous and restrictive than even the most advanced graduate training in our own degree-conscious society, the examinations drove many to nervous collapse, madness, or suicide. Administration of the examinations was scrupulously fair and every effort was made to avoid cheating or bias of any kind. Examinees were sealed up in cubicles while they wrote their examinations and their papers were coded to preclude favoritism on the part of the judges. Quotas at the provincial level restricted the number of successful graduates, the largest number being assigned to the capital and the richest and most culturally developed areas in the lower Yangtze. The average number of doctorates (the highest degree) awarded in the ninety triennial metropolitan examinations was about 275. In all, the civil service consisted of some ten to fifteen thousand degree holders in eighteen grades, whose careers were carefully regulated. Laws of avoidance kept them from serving in their home districts, thereby reducing the chance of conflict of interest. Efficiency reports evaluated their performance and transfers took place at regular intervals. The effect of recruitment through the examination system was to guarantee the emperor a continuous supply of talented and willing administrators and to preclude the development of entrenched opposition. All officials served at the emperor's pleasure and none held hereditary claim to high office. To continue in office, a family had to educate sons who could pass the examinations—a feat that few could sustain over very many generations. So stable and well regulated was the Ming administration that it operated without major change for more than 250 years.

Mobilization of resources in Ming society was related to the social policy of the Ming government. Just as the nobility monopolized command over military forces, so the gentry supplied administrative talent for the bureaucracy. Lower classes, precluded from participating in government affairs or the political process, were also expected to support the state. The populace was divided into military households, artisans, and commoners. Military families were obliged to supply sons for service in the armed forces. Artisans served terms of rotation as skilled craftsmen on government construction projects. The great bulk of the population, the commoners, were obligated to pay grain taxes and perform labor service. At the founder's behest a comprehensive survey of all the agricultural land in the empire was carried out, along with a census of the population. Compiled for tax purposes, the land survey consisted of annotated diagrams depicting each parcel of land. The "yellow registers" of the census, first completed in the 1390s, described a population of about 60 million persons—a population that was to climb as high as 150 million by the year 1600. Taxation was assigned by quotas at the county level according to the wealth of the area. The basic grain tax, which the peasants paid in two annual portions, was collected by "tax captains," who were chosen from the wealthiest families in each area. This policy, which in effect placed control of landed wealth in the hands of the local elite, was one of the foundations of Chu Yuan-chang's accommodation to the landlord gentry class. It prompted the charge from one modern Chinese historian that Chu had "sold out" the peasantry. At the most local level the peasants were organized in the traditional *li-chia* system—groups of 10 and 110 households that rotated the duties of tax collection and labor service among their members, relieving the government of the need to extend its own agencies down as far as the village level.

One feature of the Ming government which differed decisively from earlier Chinese dynasties was the centralization of power at the top, particularly in the person of the emperor. Organizationally, the most important innovation was the elimination of the office of prime minister. Traditionally, the power of the Chinese emperor was partially balanced by that of the prime minister, who headed the bureaucracy and provided continuity of executive control over government operations. Acting on a report that his highest official was planning a coup d'etat, the first Ming ruler executed his prime minister in 1380 and eliminated for all time the office that the offender had occupied. This event initiated a thorough reorganization of the government in which all of the highest official posts were eliminated. The result of these changes was that the emperor made himself the sole central source of coordination for both the civil and military sides of the government. Reporting directly to him were the five military commissions and the six civil ministries of personnel, revenue, rites, war, justice, and works. All executive coordination had now to come from within the palace. Eventually the emperor appointed civil officials to the various administrative halls within the palace to handle the enormous flow of documents. These officers, called grand secretaries, gradually evolved enormous power and prestige, at times exercising control over the government like that of a prime minister. Unlike prime ministers, however, they were not a check on the ruler but agents of imperial power. Reorganization of the government was accompanied by a prolonged series of purges that eventually put to death twenty or thirty thousand persons suspected of plotting against the emperor. In large part this bloodletting was an outgrowth of the founder's paranoia, but it may also reflect to some extent the brutalization of Chinese life under Mongol rule. The first Ming ruler was, after all, a peasant who had risen to the throne through armed struggle. It was not uncommon for high officials to be fatally beaten right in the court. The emperor is even quoted as having threatened to put a few individuals to death with his own hands. Doubtless some of his fury came from his hatred of the literati and the fact that he had to deal with them in order to rule. On one occasion he had the skin of an official caught pilfering funds stuffed with straw and hung up outside the office as a warning to others. These changes in imperial rule, both institutional and behavioral, are often referred to as Ming despotism. They represented a marked departure from the more temperate and decorous style of the Sung court.

Promotion of the Cultural Tradition

The Ming empire was a culturalistic empire in the sense that its territory encompassed little more than China proper. Its ruling group came to power by expelling the foreign Yuan house so that Chinese self-rule could be reestablished. Reviving a sense of Chinese identity and unity required considerable effort. North China, after all, had been under non-Chinese rule for more than two centuries, parts of it for four centuries. It is little wonder that the new government found it necessary to decree that all Chinese should return to the dress style of the T'ang dynasty and that the practice of Mongol customs and the use of Mongol surnames be discontinued. The Ming regime was based in south China, at this time the Yangtze region (an area Marco Polo had referred to as Manzi, in effect a separate country from the north). In a sense the founding of the Ming was a reassertion of the rich and culturally developed south. It was the first regime ever to rule north China from a capital south of the Yangtze.

Military policy is revealing of the cultural claims of the Ming empire. With the exception of the Liao River valley in the northeast (Manchuria), the northern frontier followed the general contours of the Great Wall, with only purely military installations "beyond the passes." The Ming made no attempt to rule Mongolia as the Mongols had ruled China. The empire was defined essentially in terms of the location of the Chinese population. Peripheral states and tribes were dealt with through a combination of diplomatic and military means but were not incorporated in the territory of the empire. A huge military establishment was maintained across north China with the sole aim of preventing a return of the Mongols. Chu Yuan-chang was obsessed with the danger of a Mongol comeback. He sent his best generals to the north and later stationed his sons in princedoms along the frontier so they could patrol the border.

The Ming state was a Confucian state. So thoroughly had Confucian values colored Chinese history, literature, and statecraft that anyone who governed in China by Ming times was obliged to explain his actions in terms of Confucian prescriptions. In the Ming case the vigorous effort to unify China and to rationalize its administration had the effect of pushing Confucian norms deeper into society than had previously been the case. The examination system was more extensively used than it had been in earlier dynasties. It was under the Mongols that the neo-Confucian *li-hsueh* of Chu Hsi became the core curriculum for the examinations, in effect making ideological purity a prerequisite for government service. Perhaps because he harbored such hostility to the upper classes, the first Ming emperor greatly opened access to the examination system by establishing schools at the local level throughout China. Various imperial codes aimed at bringing Chinese society into conformity with imperial ideals and there stabilizing it. The classification of the population, already alluded to, was part of this effort. An imperial will was issued by the founder governing the affairs of the royal family. Designed to protect the throne, it stipulated the order of succession, regulated the movements of the princes, and specified distinctions between their ranks. For the populace at large there was a comprehensive Ming Code, which covered both criminal law and sumptuary social regulations. The emperor also issued a number of Grand Pronouncements, which covered a wide range of criminal and economic issues. These were in the form of imperial warnings against certain kinds of abuses. Mere possession of these documents entitled the bearer to reduction of criminal sentences by one degree.

The founder's death in 1398 was followed by a period of civil war in which the prince who was stationed at the old Mongol capital at Peking turned his army south and seized the throne from the rightful heir. The usurper, Yung-lo (r. 1402-24), made a number of important changes in Ming government. First, his efforts to rationalize his usurpation of the throne led to drastic alteration of the historical record. The whole reign period from 1399 to 1402 was simply erased. Many historical documents were forged and many more destroyed. Imperial influence in literature reached a new stage with the compilation of the *Yung-lo Encyclopedia* in some twenty-two thousand chapters. Selecting words for inclusion provided an opportunity to search out and destroy undesirable literature. Many officials found their loyalties to the preceding ruler hard to overcome, and the usurper had to make extensive use of less scrupulous agents like the palace eunuchs. This practice led later to the most serious abuses of Ming government.

Second, Yung-lo carried out an extraordinarily aggressive foreign policy that extended Ming influence in all directions at the same time. The emperor's attention to foreign affairs may well have been part of an effort to bolster his prestige by increasing the number of states that paid him tribute. Toward the south he sent his armies into Annam and annexed it as a province. By sea a series of great maritime expeditions was sent out under the direction of the Muslim eunuch Cheng Ho. Using huge, oceangoing junks that carried thousands of soldiers, the expeditions, seven in all, sailed to Southeast Asia, India, Persia, Arabia, and the east coast of Africa. States visited were encouraged to send tributary missions to the Chinese court and some rulers who resisted were attacked. Coming a century before the first European ships reached China, the expeditions reveal Ming technological sophistication in the early fifteenth century. The Yung-lo emperor also undertook a series of five military expeditions into Mongolia. These he led himself. The largest armies numbered more than half a million men and drove as far into the steppe as Karakorum. None of these aggressive efforts expanded Chinese territory. Annam proved ungovernable and had to be given up in the 1430s. The voyages were discontinued at about the same time. Imperial expeditions in the north harassed the Mongols but could not control them. A subsequent emperor, campaigning north of the Wall, was even taken prisoner by the Mongols in 1449.

The third accomplishment of the Yung-lo period was to move the capital to Peking in the north, thus enabling the emperor to keep a closer control over his frontier defenses. Considerable costs were involved, however, for the Grand Canal had to be reopened to bring grain from south China to support the capital at Peking. A more subtle cost was the removal of the government apparatus from the Chinese heartland to the site of what had previously been an alien political center.

Late Ming Developments

The first Westerners to report extensively on China in the sixteenth century were astounded at the orderliness and stability of Chinese society. No doubt this was due in large part to the conscious effort of the Ming government to control change and impose its pattern on Chinese society. Its mere survival as an institution for nearly three centuries testifies to its success. Nevertheless, changes did come with the passage of time. If one compares early Ming China with China of the late Ming, one sees that both the government and the social order were drastically altered. Since the focus of our attention is the impact of the early modern empire on Chinese civilization, and not the fate of the Ming empire as such, it will suffice here simply to note the sort of forces at work in late Ming times as a background to the Manchu invasion and the founding of the Ch'ing dynasty in 1644.

Already in the fifteenth century, drift was apparent in the higher reaches of Ming government. Weak emperors were controlled by ambitious eunuchs who elaborated the imperial bodyguard into a vast secret police apparatus that could terrorize the entire civil service. The number of eunuchs mounted to the tens of thousands. They busied themselves

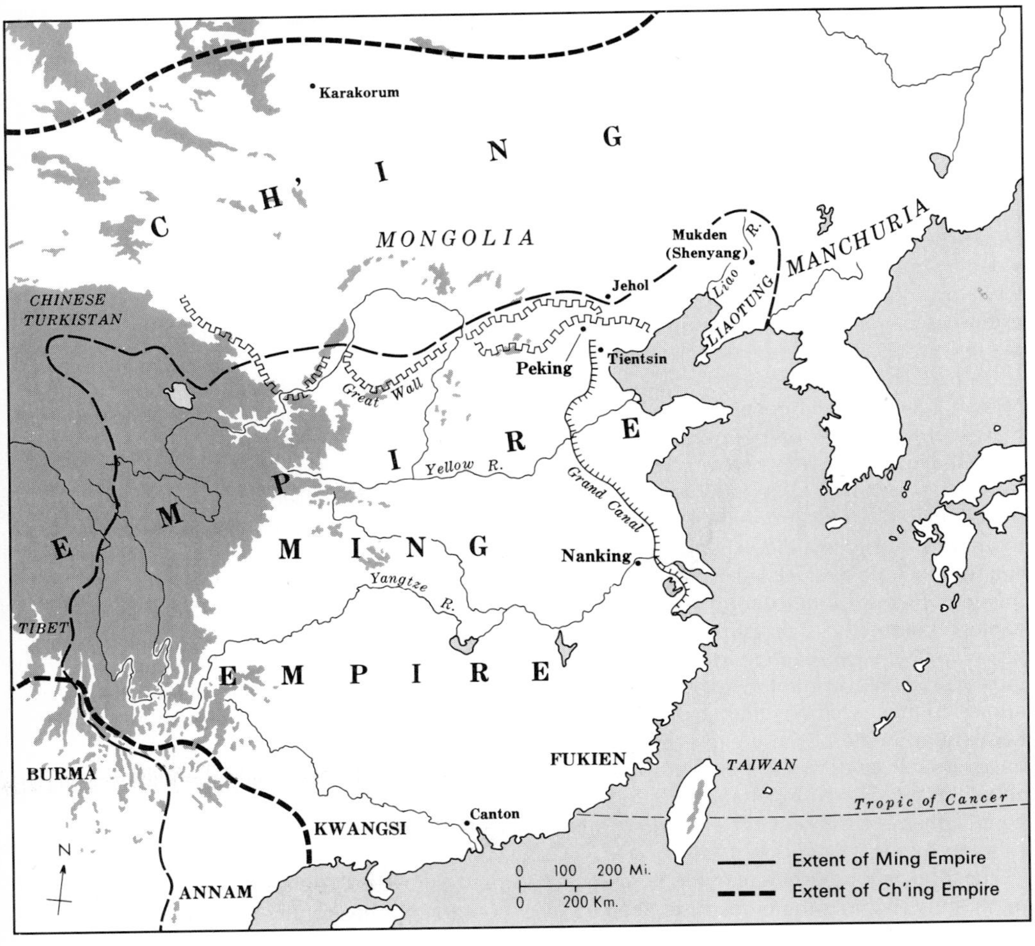

Map 41 Ming and Ch'ing China, 1400-1700

throughout the empire appropriating land that was converted into eunuch-run "imperial estates," making the palace establishment a state within a state. As the central government lost its vigor, it also lost touch with changes in Chinese society. Powerful forces were at work in south China—the wealthy and populous area along the lower Yangtze. The volume of trade increased, urban populations grew, and the whole economy became monetized. What had been a grain economy now became a money economy as labor service and tax payments in kind were converted to payment in silver. Silver flowed into China from the great mines of Mexico as the growth of external trade provided the first preview of the European and American maritime commerce to come.

Remote in the north, dependent on the grain shipments up the Grand Canal for its sustenance, the Ming court was ill-suited to convert its fiscal machinery to the demands of a new economic reality. In the sixteenth century, when new Mongol threats materialized in the north, the government discovered that its old hereditary military system was no longer adequate. It became necessary to raise revenues and hire a whole new army. Piecemeal reforms were instituted and the government muddled through, but not without placing strains on its own cohesion as well as the tolerance of the peasantry, who were asked to bear additional burdens in a tax structure now grossly inequitable.

Changes in the economy and the society were mirrored in art and literature. An acquisitive wealthy class demanded the symbols of cultured existence even when the substance was lacking. The volume of porcelain production, for example, rose to satisfy an expanded market, but the quality fell. Austere and refined motifs of the early wares gave way increasingly to the vulgar symbols of long life, wealth, and happiness. Paintings, too, were turned out in greater number but increasingly by mere copyists to grace the walls of uncultured consumers. Printing reached great heights in the Ming, especially techniques of illustration and color printing. Here also quantity was at odds with quality. Many of the Ming editions were poorly edited and full of mistakes—printed more for display than for reading. One of the liveliest areas of literature was popular colloquial fiction. The growth of literacy is no way better evidenced than in the conversion of storytellers' tales into vernacular novels. Stories like *All Men Are Brothers* and *Monkey,* which had long been part of an oral tradition, appeared as books in the late Ming. Short stories were also extremely popular. The facts that these novels were written in a style that approached the spoken language and that some of them, like *Chin P'ing Mei (Golden Lotus)* and *Jou Pu Tuan (Prayer Mat of Flesh),* were overtly pornographic is indicative of the breakdown of Confucian standards.

So unsure did people become about the norms of behavior that handbooks for everyday conduct were written to tell people how to manage their affairs. Morality books were written as guides to ethical action, and "ledgers of merit and demerit" allowed the reader to score his behavior by totaling up points for good deeds and bad. Another aspect of the confusion about values was the continuing tendency for elements of Confucianism, Buddhism, and Taoism to be fused together as the distinctions between the "three teachings" became blurred. The popular traditions, Buddhism and Taoism, interacted with the elite tradition, Confucianism, with influences running both ways. Elite patterns were emulated by lower classes but the literati were also receptive to new values. These developments can best be seen in the realm of philosophy.

The greatest philosophical thinker of the Ming period was Wang Yang-ming (1472-1529), who is credited with bringing to fruition the second major branch of neo-Confucianism, the School of Mind *(hsin hsueh).* By the end of the fifteenth century the orthodox interpretations of Chu Hsi's *li-hsueh* school had lost their vitality and intellectual appeal, although students continued to memorize the orthodox commentaries so that they could pass the examinations and become degree holders. Orthodox learning was a badge of ideological conformity to the state but it could not answer the pressing intellectual and morai questions of the day. Confucian scholars were tormented by the demands of loyalty to a state that had grown corrupt and was at times the antithesis of the Confucian ideal. The effect of Wang Yang-ming's innovation was to move the locus of moral and epistomological authority from an externally discovered principle *(li)* to an internal source: the mind *(hsin).* For Wang, the universal principles of which Chu Hsi had spoken were the same as the true substance of the mind and therefore could be discovered by looking inward. This innovation had two major implications: (1) much formal book learning and scholarship could be dispensed with since the truth could be attained through introspection, and (2) since it was no longer necessary to be a learned scholar to gain enlightenment, the way was open to sagehood for the common man.

Wang Yang-ming led an active career as a high official, distinguishing himself in military pacification work by putting down rebels and insurgent tribal groups in South China. For him there was no conflict between the dictates of his mind and the social demands of his role as an official in the service of the emperor. He did not question that the norms that were enshrined within the mind were the same as those that orthodox thought approached through the "investigation of things" or through conventional scholarship. Inevitably, however, Wang's thought, with its emphasis on the mind and on quiet sitting, meditation akin to that practiced by Taoists and Chan (Zen) Buddhists, led later thinkers further and further from orthodoxy and official careers. The changes in Chinese philosophy after Wang Yang-ming were so great in the sixteenth century that they have been characterized as a near revolution in thought. Doctrines of the School of Mind were transmitted, studied, and discussed in academies, centers of Confucian learning that sprang up throughout China in the Ming. By the latter half of the sixteenth century something approaching a counterculture had emerged. Popularization of revitalized Confucianism was manifested in mass meetings, complete with group singing and uplifting speeches by itinerant evangelists. Eventually, radical thinkers emerged who broke out of the Confucian mold entirely. Where Wang Yang-ming's thought had sought a kind of psychic adjustment to the conflicting demands of conscience and duty in a corrupt society, these thinkers attacked the society and its institutions. The most outspoken of them were hunted down, jailed, and put to death or driven to suicide.

The philosophy of Wang Yang-ming represented a major innovation within Confucianism but it failed to overturn the orthodox *li-hsueh* school. Wang's most lasting influence was felt not in China but in Japan (where he is known as Ōyōmei). In China Wang's thought was attacked by orthodox thinkers as Buddhism in disguise. By the beginning of the seventeenth century an intellectual reaction had set in and conservative Confucians tried to restore strict moral standards to the decadent government. Organized around academies like the Tung-lin, they soon became enmeshed in the factional struggles of the court involving rival groups of officials and eunuchs in unstable alliances.

Ming politics reached bottom in the 1620s with the emergence of the eunuch dictator Wei Chung-hsien (1568-1627). Utterly unscrupulous, Wei rose to power in the palace establishment through manipulation of a child emperor and quickly established control over both the police apparatus and the fiscal machinery of the state. All who resisted him were subjected to persecution. A blacklist was drawn up of those, such as the Tung-lin faction, who dared to criticize his actions. Government was perverted utterly. At the height of his power officials throughout the empire competed to build temples to his honor while students in the imperial academy compared him to Confucius. As the Ming government degenerated, the Chinese people rose in armed rebellion. Massive peasant uprisings swept the northern and western provinces in the 1630s and early 1640s. Rebel leaders like Li Tzu-ch'eng (d. 1645) and Chang Hsien-chung (1605-47), after years of bloody campaigning, assumed imperial titles in direct challenge to the Ming house.

Manchu Conquest and Establishment of the Ch'ing Dynasty

With the Manchu seizure of Peking in 1644 China entered upon another era of foreign rule, which was to last until the twentieth century (1911). In subsequent chapters we shall have cause to notice various ways in which the fact of foreign rule influenced China's response to forces of change and inhibited the development of Chinese nationalism.

Unlike the Central Asian Mongols, the Manchus were descended from tribes of hunter-fisher peoples in the forested slopes of the Liaotung area northeast of China. Of Jurched stock, they were related to the founders of the Chin dynasty (1115-1234), which had ruled north China in pre-Mongol times. Under the Ming the Manchus were nominally organized into a commandery on the Chinese frontier. As Ming power declined this tribal group transformed itself from the status of a tributary loosely affiliated with the court to an independent and aggressive state. Much of the later Manchu success is traceable to the fact they were able to devote several decades to state building in the relative security of Manchuria before they invaded China. In this incubation period they enjoyed an advantage over the Chinese rebels who were obliged to build their regimes within China proper in territory contested by the Ming.

The most remarkable aspect of the Manchu conquest of China was the almost total social and institutional transformation that the Manchus underwent. In but half a century they developed from a loose group of tribes into a highly mobilized war machine with an administrative arm capable of managing the largest empire on earth. Many of the processes of the formation of hybrid barbarian-civilized empires discussed in the preceding chapter were repeated in this transition. The Manchus survived their transition and erected a state that long outlived any the Mongols attempted. Essential to the effort was a judicious and pragmatic blending of traditional tribal elements, Chinese bureaucratic institutions, and outright innovations.

The first steps were taken around 1600 by Nurhaci (1559-1626), who unified the Jurched tribes and created a flexible military organization. Called the banner system, this involved the division of his fighting forces into units designated by colored flags. The four initial units were expanded to eight by adding borders to the banners, and later eight Mongol and eight Chinese banners were added. The size of the banner units grew to encompass the whole Manchu and allied population and the function was generalized to include a variety of administrative matters. In this way tribal organization was gradually displaced by more rational and bureaucratic forms and the entire society was mobilized for service under a central leadership. Nurhaci extended his territory and fought enough battles with the Ming to control the area east of the Liao River. He established his capital at Mukden (Shenyang).

The Manchus were keenly aware of the superiority of Chinese governmental organization. They therefore set out in a very systematic way to learn as much as they could from the Chinese. As they came into control of towns and cities in the Liaotung area and as Ming forces surrendered to them in battle, Chinese officials and officers were induced to teach them the arts of government. A new written script was created for the Manchu language and numerous Chinese texts were translated. Nurhaci's successor, Abahai (1592-1643), set up a civil administration in the Chinese style with six boards, slightly modified to accommodate Manchu princes in the top positions.

It is often true in politics that the essence of political authority resides more in the imagery of power than in its substance. Nowhere was this better appreciated than China, where Confucian political culture explicitly stressed the importance of the "rectification of names." This matter is worthy of our attention for it has to do with the relationship between the Manchus and the Chinese cultural tradition. If the Manchus were to conquer China and rule it they had to create an image of legitimacy. Nurhaci had originally called his state Chin in reference to the earlier conquest dynasty. This title Abahai changed in 1636 to Ch'ing ("pure"), suggesting a reform much needed in China. The term Jurched and the name of the old commandery were suppressed and the new term Manchu was coined to obscure the fact that the Ch'ing had once been tributaries of the Ming. The greatest boon to the Manchus came in 1644, when the rebel Li Tzu-ch'eng entered Peking and the Ming emperor committed suicide. This spared the would-be invaders the onus of extinguishing a legitimate Chinese rule. The Manchus by this time had conquered most of the territory north of the Great Wall and were poised to invade China. The Ming Chinese general who was guarding the passes against the Manchus, Wu San-kuei (1612-78), now invited the Manchus to enter China and attack Li Tzu-ch'eng. This allowed the Manchus to pose as the agents of order and orthodoxy even as they occupied the Ming capital.

Domination over Chinese Society

Control over the empire and acceptance by the Chinese was not quick in coming to the new Ch'ing dynasty. Before entering China the Manchus built alliances with the peoples on their flanks, the Koreans and the Mongols. Initially this multiethnic military alliance controlled only north China as a civil administration was gradually elaborated. In the southern provinces a number of regional satrapies were tolerated for several decades under such Chinese collaborators as Wu San-kuei. A series of Ming princes offered token resistance along the seacoast and southern frontier. Wu San-kuei pursued the last of these pretenders into Burma and brought him back for strangulation. The most colorful of the Ming loyalists was a half-Japanese pirate named Cheng Ch'eng-kung (1624-62), better known to Europeans as Koxinga. He fought for the Ming cause along the coast south of the Yangtze and then was forced across the strait to Taiwan, where he defeated the Dutch and took over the island. The Manchu conquest of China was not completed until 1683, by which time the regional satraps and Ming pretenders had been eliminated and Taiwan taken. Nearly forty years had elapsed since the fall of Peking.

Initially the Manchus were obliged to utilize such persons as were willing to collaborate with them. One of their first Chinese grand secretaries, for example, was an official who had done some of the dirty work for the eunuch Wei Chung-hsien. Wu San-kuei was a temporary ally. Another example is Koxinga's father, Cheng Chih-lung (1604-61). A political opportunist, he touched all the bases in a western Pacific community where Portuguese, Spanish, and Dutch intermingled freely with Chinese and Japanese and commerce shaded indistinguishably into piracy. A native of Fukien, he was baptized Nicholas Gaspard in Macao before going on to Manila, Taiwan, and Japan, where he married. Becoming a pirate he operated out of Taiwan against both the Chinese and the Dutch. Later he went over to the Ming and worked for them against the pirates. After the fall of the Ming he served a Ming pretender briefly and then defected to the Manchus. Residing in Peking, he came under suspicion when his son continued to lead the fight against the Ch'ing. Eventually he was imprisoned and executed.

Reliance on allies such as these could not guarantee the Ch'ing rulers continued control over China. Since the Manchus were outnumbered by their subjects on the order of a hundred to one, the durability of their government depended on their ability to recruit capable Chinese administrators into their service. The system that resulted was a Manchu-Chinese dyarchy, or dual form of government. Basically, the Ch'ing continued the Ming organization of civil administration with Manchu control elements added at the top. The highest positions were divided among Manchus, some Mongols, and reliable Chinese, many of whom descended from earlier collaborators in Manchuria. Governors of provinces were typically Chinese officials, but imposed upon them, usually with responsibility for two provinces, were governors general (normally Manchus), whose concurrent reports provided the emperor with a reliable check on the Chinese. Another safeguard in the provinces was the presence of banner forces under Manchu command. In the central government the heads of the six boards, or ministries, were staffed by two officials, one Manchu and one Chinese. The Chinese provided bureaucratic expertise while the Manchus guaranteed political reliability. The highest organ continued to be the grand secretariat, which the early Ming emperors had developed as an agency of the throne. In the early eighteenth century a new body was superimposed at the top. Called the Grand Council (literally "military plans office"), it consisted of a select group of grand secretaries who met informally with the emperor to decide the most sensitive issues. This marked the culmination of a number of steps by which the emperors tightened their hold over the administration by channeling the flow of the most sensitive secret reports directly into the palace.

Patronage of Chinese Culture

Because it was a conquest dynasty, the Ch'ing can be classified as a pluralistic empire. Although the Ch'ing continued Ming institutions in a wholesale manner, it nevertheless differed from its predecessor in a number of fundamental respects. For one thing, its territory included vast tracts of Mongolia and Central Asia. Peking, at the northern edges of the Ming, was in the southern half of the great eighteenth century map of the Ch'ing empire. The Ch'ing ruler, like other conquerors before, extended his rule both north and south of the Great Wall. Court business was conducted in two languages—Chinese and Manchu—and court documents were prepared in bilingual form. The Manchu homeland was maintained as a preserve for the tribal peoples and Chinese settlement there was restricted for the first two centuries of the dynasty. Mukden continued to rank as a subsidiary capital, while Jehol, just beyond the Wall, was the site of a summer palace. Relations with areas such as Mongolia, Tibet, and Chinese Turkistan were handled through a Superintendency of Dependencies, which paralleled the civil organs for China proper. In military terms the Ch'ing were not content as the Ming had been to rule just China. Frontiers were expanded vigorously—especially in the north and west, where aggressive campaigning continued into the middle of the eighteenth century.

In matters of cultural policy the Ch'ing rulers carefully nurtured different traditions to meet the needs of their pluralistic empire. To keep alive their own customs they encouraged the use of the Manchu language and even established an examination system in Manchu similar to that in Chinese. An important part of Ch'ing policy toward Central Asian subjects was imperial patronage of Lamaism, a faith that was important to Mongols as well as Tibetans. Toward the Chinese, of course, the Manchus presented themselves as champions of Confucian values. Much of their success in building a permanent empire on Chinese soil was due to the fact that early emperors, K'ang-hsi (r. 1662-1722) and Ch'ien-lung (r. 1736-95) in particular, were able to demonstrate great proficiency in Chinese learning. Tireless administrators who personally handled heroic quantities of documents, these men approached the ideal of Confucian kingship. They were equally familiar with civil and military administration; they wrote poetry and patronized the arts. K'ang-hsi was the first Manchu ruler to travel south to the Yangtze region to inspect the conditions of the Chinese heartland and enhance his prestige among the Chinese literati.

The Ch'ing revived the civil-service examination system of the Ming which continued the patronage of Sung neo-Confucianism. The works of Chu Hsi were reprinted under imperial sponsorship during the K'ang-hsi reign. Resistance to Manchu rule by Ming scholars was widespread. It was several decades before special imperial examinations were held as a device for recruiting Chinese scholars to take part in the compiling of the official history of the Ming dynasty *(Ming-shih).* Some refused to take part, others did so under duress, while many who participated were tormented by the conflict between a desire to accurately record the history of their dynasty and a revulsion at collaboration with a foreign conqueror. The resulting *Ming-shih* was not completed until the 1720s. It is regarded as one of the most accurate of the twenty-four official histories. Still, the *Ming-shih* is purposely obscure on a number of points dealing with the Mongols and the Manchus.

Imperial patronage of scholarly activity not only bound scholars to the state, it also gave the state an opportunity to shape the content of learning itself. So boldly did the Manchu rulers act in this regard that the whole picture of modern Chinese history was distorted by their efforts. The K'ang-hsi emperor undertook projects of the same scale as had the early Ming rulers. The great illustrated encyclopedia, *Ku-chin t'u-shu chi-ch'eng,* ten thousand chapters, completed in 1725, ranks with the *Yung-lo Encyclopedia* as an effort to summarize all knowledge. The *K'ang-hsi Dictionary* (1716) contains definitions for forty-seven thousand individual Chinese characters arranged according to a list of 214 radicals (parts of characters) and then ranked by the number of brush strokes used in writing the characters. This system of classification, which functions as alphabetical ordering does in our language, has remained a standard feature of Chinese ever since. In the Ch'ien-lung era an even grander project was undertaken. This was the compilation called *Ssu-k'u ch'uan-shu,* or *Complete Books of the Four Treasuries.* Occupying an editorial board of 361 scholars from 1773 to 1782, the final manuscript consisted of more than seventy-eight thousand chapters arranged under the four traditional categories of classics, history, philosophers, and belles lettres. As important as the collection itself was the selection process involved in its creation, for it provided the opportunity for a massive purge of Chinese literature. Rare works were actively solicited from throughout the empire, brought to Peking and examined. Only 3,461 books were eventually copied into the manuscript, but all of the works were described and evaluated in a catalogue that contained more than ten thousand entries. Hand in hand with this scholarly survey of Chinese literature there proceeded an equally thorough effort to identify, collect, and destroy all works offensive to the Manchu house. In the 1780s a Bureau of Book Censorship was set up and an *Index* of banned books issued which contained more than two thousand titles. Proclamations were issued, homes and libraries searched, and books seized for burning in every province.

The fact that systematic purges of Chinese literature came after more than a century of Manchu rule reflects the change in political conditions. The policies of the K'ang-hsi emperor in the late seventeenth century were patronizing toward the Chinese scholars and aimed at drawing them into government service. Considerable tolerance was involved. The great Ming scholar and loyalist Huang Tsung-hsi (1610-95), for example, refused to join in the compilation of the *Ming-shih,* but the emperor ordered that his works be made available to the editorial board. In this way, Huang's resistance was overlooked and his learning acknowledged by the Manchu ruler. By the 1770s Ch'ien-lung realized that the scholarship of the preceding century contained many elements dangerous to Manchu supremacy. Works that dealt with Ming history, border affairs, defense, conquest dynasties or that contained even the most subtle criticisms of Manchu rule were ruthlessly suppressed. One result of the suppression was to obscure or distort the portrayal of early modern Chinese history. Only in the last few decades have copies of banned works been discovered and reprinted and scholars set about the task of reconstructing the story of Ming history.

Another effect of Ch'ien-lung's book burning was to deflect Chinese scholarship away from sensitive issues. Already by the end of the Ming, scholars were in reaction against the idealism of the Wang Yang-ming school, which stressed the mind. Late Ming and early Ch'ing scholarship turned increasingly to concrete subjects like geography, history, and bibliography. The result was Ch'ing empiricism—a rigorous and systematic scholarship that was protoscientific in its rules for collection of data, use of evidence, and citation of sources. It did not include experimentation, however, and there was little interest in the realm of nature. The favored subject matter was the literary tradition itself, and some of the greatest achievements were in areas like philology, phonology, lexicography, and textual analysis of the classics. Thus by the twin sanctions of sponsorship and suppression, the Manchu state was able to channel the energies of the Chinese literati into harmless endeavors. As scholarship became less relevant to the issues of the day it also declined in vigor and creativity.

In China the era of the early modern empires saw a continued development of the centralized power of the imperial state. The Ming, which arose in response to Mongol rule, was self-conscious in its culturism. The state took an active role in the promotion of Chinese high culture and in stabilizing the social and administrative institutions of the empire. The jurisdiction of the Ming was essentially China proper, an area the state governed and defended as a self-contained island of cultural superiority. The Manchu conquest in the seventeenth century reduced the Chinese to the status of a subordinate, though large, majority within a pluralistic Ch'ing empire. The Manchu rulers assiduously adopted and promoted the Ming forms but transformed them to the needs of a foreign rule. The result in the first century and a half was a prosperous empire under stable and capable administration. Under the Ch'ing government, China attained in the eighteenth century its greatest prosperity—perhaps the greatest wealth known to any society in history up to that time.

Internal peace and moderate levels of taxation contributed to a doubling of the population from 150 million to more than 300 million by the end of the century. In subsequent chapters we will have cause to note that the very successes of the Ming and Ch'ing governments created problems for China in the nineteenth century. Ming institutions worked so well that innovation was hard to justify or even to conceive, Manchu cultural policy was so effective that the Chinese were tardy in developing a sense of nationalism, and the growth of population undermined the prosperity of the whole society.

5. TOKUGAWA JAPAN

During the era of Mongol dominance in China and other parts of Asia, Japanese society remained largely outside the historical developments on the Eurasian continent. Although the abortive attempts at invasion by Mongol naval forces at the end of the thirteenth century perhaps played a role in further weakening the Kamakura government, there was no foreign conquest and the major currents in Japanese history down to the sixteenth century were primarily indigenous in origin. Nevertheless, the creation of the Tokugawa early modern empire at the turn of the seventeenth century does in numerous ways resemble the rallying of other Asian societies to restore cultural stability after an extended period of turmoil.

From the middle of the fifteenth century the tempo of change within Japanese society had increased dramatically. Foreign trade had stimulated the growth of the domestic economy, and cities and towns had sprung up outside the framework of the older social structure. Social and geographical mobility had increased to produce a much more fluid society. Contact with the outside world reached new proportions in Japanese history and in the late sixteenth century Europeans for the first time appeared on the scene, albeit in small numbers and with limited impact. These developments were accompanied in the fifteenth and sixteenth centuries by a breakdown in the political system and near anarchy, as the warrior elite became locked in protracted struggles for power. Thus the Tokugawa regime can be viewed as the result of a concerted effort at cultural conservatism, an attempt to stem the tide of change by reasserting the older ideal of a government capable of dominanting social and cultural life. As such it was an effort that did slow the tempo of change in certain sectors and largely reverse the process by which Japan had become increasingly involved in the outside world. It is this aspect of early modern Japanese history that will be emphasized here, leaving to later chapters the more dynamic story of how the changes in the Tokugawa period paved the way for the modern transformation of Japan of the nineteenth and twentieth centuries.

Creation and Maintenance of the Tokugawa State

The Tokugawa regime in Japan, like other early modern empires in Asia, was first established through military might. From the fifteenth century on the Japanese military elite, described in Chapter 7, had engaged in almost incessant conflict in the attempt to create a stable configuration of political power. In the early stages, from about 1330 to about 1460, it was primarily the regional overlords, the heirs of the military governors of the Kamakura period, who struggled among themselves for the position formerly held by the Minamoto, a position that continued to elude the Ashikaga despite their claims to the title of shogun. After the middle of the fifteenth century central authority became a myth to which few bothered to pay even lip service, and for a century effective control over regions as large as the old provincial units proved beyond the capacities of most competing warlords.

Political power had become fragmented to the point where stability and peace were at best temporary phenomena, achieved only in local areas constantly defended by force of arms. Political authority was thus largely equated with military force. The synthesis of familial and bureaucratic norms that had aided in holding together the political system of the previous era gave way to something resembling very closely the feudalism of medieval Europe, the significant political groupings being local networks of fighting men tied together by the institutions of vassalage and fiefs. These shifting alliances based on feudal vassalage were too unstable and the ghost of a single national hegemony too strong an ideal to permit a lasting equilibrium, and in the late sixteenth century the struggles for power entered a new stage. Although firearms introduced via the Portuguese played a small role in these struggles, the key factors here were new types of regional leaders who utilized new institutional arrangements to more fully mobilize the economic, social, and military resources of their domains to piece together larger and more stable territorial bases. The three most successful of these leaders were Oda Nobunaga (1534-82), Toyotomi Hideyoshi (1537-98), and finally Tokugawa Ieyasu (1542-1616).

Oda Nobunaga had been a relatively obscure warrior leader with a small local base near the present-day city of Nagoya and the vassal of a warlord with an expanding territory in eastern Japan. In the fashion that had become increasingly prevalent in the late Ashikaga period, Nobunaga turned on his liege lord and usurped control over his network of vassals. He then marched on the imperial city of Kyoto, established dominance over central Japan, and eventually deposed the last Ashikaga shogun in 1573. Although Nobunaga died in the struggle to expand his authority at the expense of other regional hegemons, his power base passed intact to Toyotomi Hideyoshi. Hideyoshi, whose rise from the peasantry to become Nobunaga's chief lieutenant illustrates the openness and fluidity of the social structure at this time, was an extraordinarily gifted military leader, and by the early 1590s the rival leagues of warlords in the eastern and southwestern regions of Japan were forced to acknowledge Hideyoshi's supremacy. His hold over the country was extremely tenuous, however, and his death in 1598 threatened to pitch Japan into a new round of bloody conflict. It was only after another of Nobunaga's former vassals, Tokugawa Ieyasu, combined crucial victories in the battle of Sekigahara in 1600 and the siege of the castle of Hideyoshi's heir in 1615 with skillful political compromises that the great regional leaders of the country were convinced that little was to be gained by further recourse to arms.

It is important to note that Ieyasu's military victories did not eliminate his opposition. The settlement that created the Tokugawa regime was a series of compromises, a fact that is a key to understanding the political life of Japan over the next two and a half centuries. Whatever Ieyasu's own ambitions and views of the ideal political system may have been—and it is quite possible that he did not envisage a highly centralized bureaucratic state since his own experience and that of his contemporaries was limited to the feudal milieu of his times—his forces simply did not have the strength to destroy the other warlords within the country. The advantage he did possess over his rivals rested on a larger network of alliances, family ties, and feudal vassalage linking the Tokugawa house with other military lords. This network was strong only so long as Ieyasu's own vassals were assured of their rightful status as feudal lords and hence of a measure of autonomy within their own domains or fiefs. The military supremacy of this network over the rival leaders of the northeast and southwest was sufficient to persuade them to pay homage to the Tokugawa, but, again, only so long as these lords were not forced to choose between losing control over their own domains, on the one hand, and a new round of battles on the other. In short, the Tokugawa in the early seventeenth century did not have the capacity nor perhaps the will to create a truly centralized state; rather, Ieyasu sought a grand compromise in which the more powerful of his own vassal lords and those outside his network were confirmed as rulers within their own territories in return for accepting Tokugawa overlordship and authority in matters of overall national policy.

As a consequence of this compromise, the political map of Japan between 1600 and

1868 remained a patchwork quilt. The largest single area, comprising approximately a fifth of the country and a third of the population, consisted of Tokugawa houselands administered directly by Tokugawa officials and liege vassals. The bulk of the land and its peoples, however, was divided into over 200 semiautonomous domains administered by lords over whom the Tokugawa shogun's influence varied greatly. The majority of the very largest domains were held by the descendants of the warlords classified as *tozama,* or "outside lords," who had originally resisted Tokugawa hegemony. Their size, the tradition of independence, and their strategic geographical position (the more important were located in the southwest, outside of the central regions around Kyoto and Tokyo) gave them considerable autonomy, although they were largely excluded from any role in the formulation of Tokugawa policy. The second category of domains were governed by *fudai,* or "inside lords," the heirs of men who had early sworn personal allegiance to Ieyasu. The more important of these "inside" lords sat in the higher councils of the Tokugawa shogun and provided the administrative leadership for the regime. The remainder of the *fudai* lords participated at lower levels in the Tokugawa government and were also subject to closer supervision over the internal affairs of their domains.

Despite the basically decentralized character of the political system that took shape in Japan during the early seventeenth century, there were critical restrictions placed on the lords in their semiautonomous domains, and certain key powers were reserved to the Tokugawa central government in Edo (modern-day Tokyo). Given the Tokugawa's direct control over a large share of the nation's resources and people, these powers and restrictions constituted a significant degree of centralized power, and a complex system of interlocking checks on the activities of the lords, whether "outside" or "inside," served to create a political equilibrium in which Tokugawa hegemony could be maintained for over two and a half centuries. These restrictions included prohibitions against expanding military fortifications or forming political alliances through marital ties. Perhaps the most significant of these, however, was the system of alternate attendance, under which all lords were required to be present in Edo for specified periods of time to pay homage to the Tokugawa shogun. This served both to siphon off some of the economic means of challenging Tokugawa supremacy—the heavy expenses incurred in the long journeys to and from and the maintenance of large mansions in Edo were a continual drain on the finances of the lords—and as a thinly veiled hostage system. When the lord himself was not present in Edo, other members of his family were to reside there both as symbolic acknowledgement of submission to Tokugawa overlordship and as a concrete guarantee of good conduct.

Reunification of the Cultural Area

One of the most important of the powers reserved to the central government was that of making foreign policy, a power the Tokugawa utilized to further ensure stability and shield against disrupting influences. By the middle of the seventeenth century the Tokugawa had all but cut Japan off from intercourse with the outside world. Vessels were limited to sizes suitable only to coastal shipping, and Japanese who traveled abroad were subject to permanent exile or severe punishment. Foreigners, with the exception of some Chinese merchants and employees of the Dutch East Indies Trading Company, which was permitted a specified number of voyages per year, were forbidden to land on Japanese territory. Even the Dutch were allowed outside their trading factory in Nagasaki only to report to Edo upon shogunate demand. This policy of isolation was a radical reversal of trends in the late sixteenth century toward greater involvement in the wider world. Japanese pirates then had flaunted Ming authority on the China coast, while merchants had sought profits as far abroad as Southeast Asia, and adventurers had sold their military skills in the service of both sides in the conflicts that accompanied European probes in that part of Asia. This outward

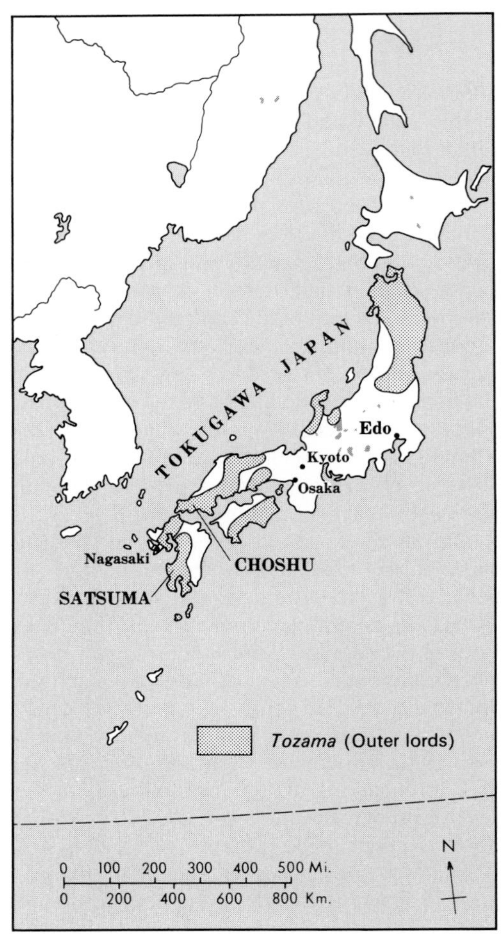

Map 42 Tokugawa Japan, about 1700

thrust had culminated in the 1590s when Hideyoshi, combining an ambition for conquest with a shrewd plan for diverting his rivals' attention from domestic politics, had launched two ill-fated expeditions up the Korean peninsula.

During this period, Hideyoshi and others welcomed the European traders and their missionary companions, exhibiting great interest in the goods, technology, and even ideas carried with them. The details of this early interaction with the West will be discussed in a later chapter; here our concern is with the reasons the Tokugawa insisted on decision-making power in foreign affairs and why they utilized it to enforce an almost total ban on interaction with the world. Stated in simplest terms, foreign contacts posed an internal and an external threat. The external threat was vividly described for them by the accounts of European military victories elsewhere in Asia—accounts supplied in part by competing Europeans who sought to advance their own nation's interests in Japan by warning the Japanese of their rivals' greed. The internal threat was posed in part by the fact, dictated by simple geography, that foreign contact had taken place first in the southwest domains of the *tozama,* or "outside," lords. Profits from trade and military advantages from European weapons were seen by the Tokugawa as potentially undermining its own supremacy. Even the conversion of members of the elite to the Christian faith appeared a political threat insofar as it served to forge new ties between anti-Tokugawa forces. Although the Tokugawa did keep the door slightly ajar for a small volume of trade via the Dutch, its own views of the role of commerce in the economy precluded any serious interest in the long-range possibilities of foreign trade. Hence, on the balance there was little to be gained and much, in the form of disruption of the newly established balance of power within Japan, to be lost by foreign contacts.

Domination of Economy and Society

Having eliminated foreign trade as a major factor, the Tokugawa also consolidated its control over other aspects of the economy. Its general view of economics was derived from the experience gained in successfully mobilizing resources for the military campaigns of the late sixteenth century. What adaptations were needed for peacetime were made ad hoc or suggested by Chinese neo-Confucian precepts. Agriculture was seen as the all-important foundation for strong government and an affluent society, and following the lead of Hideyoshi the new regime took steps to ascertain precisely what the land would produce and to routinize tax collections. Direct Tokugawa control, however, applied only to its own houselands. Although the various lords were required from time to time to contribute to such special projects as the rebuilding of the imperial city of Kyoto or the repair of fire damage in Edo, there was no systematic taxation of their domains by the shogunate. On the other hand, the estimated yield of the Tokugawa lands in the early period amounted to as much as 25 percent of the whole country's agrarian production. Revenue from this for the most part flowed directly into the Tokugawa treasury, since by the end of the seventeenth century few of the Tokugawa liege vassals had any direct economic power over their fiefs. Tax policy was set by the shogunate councils, collected by agents of the shogunate, and stored in shogunate granaries. Levies on the peasantry in the form of labor services were also controlled from the castle town. Most vassals who held title to specified villages as fiefs merely collected their income from the granary officials. The campaigns of Nobunaga and Hideyoshi had earlier broken the economic power of the central Buddhist temples and Shinto shrines, and these too were now supported by payments from revenue collected by shogunal officials. Although in large part autonomous, the various lords within their own domains followed a similar pattern, imposing a more centralized control over agrarian production by removing their vassals from the land and substituting stipends for fiefs of the type common in earlier periods.

Commerce as such was not viewed as a source of regular revenue by the Tokugawa government. It was seen rather as potentially disruptive to a smoothly functioning, agrarian-based economy and subjected to a wide variety of restrictions, particularly with regard to merchant activities in the rural areas. The prohibition on merchants acquiring land was indicative of the Tokugawa attempt to separate urban commerce from rural agriculture and keep important resources in its own hands. The Tokugawa was therefore careful to bring the major urban centers of consumption and trade under its own direct supervision, for political as well as economic reasons. Thus Kyoto (the seat of the imperial court and an important consumption center), Osaka (which had replaced its neighbor Sakai as chief port along the inland sea), Nagasaki (the only outlet for foreign trade), as well as the Tokugawa castle town of Edo were administered by Tokugawa officials. None was allowed opportunity to develop the type of independence found in Western European cities. Whereas large merchant houses did achieve a position of influence over the economy, they were forced to operate in a political atmosphere basically hostile to commercial interests. Even the fact that the Tokugawa did not regularly tax trade was partially offset by the practice of forced "loans," licensing fees, and even outright confiscation in some instances. These practices were imposed on an irregular basis and were at times compensated for by grants of monopolies, but they are evidence that the Tokugawa was far more concerned with keeping the activities of the merchant class within limited channels than with promoting its growth. The ultimate failure of this attempt is an important part of the story of the decline of the Tokugawa system.

The Tokugawa, moreover, recognized the strategic importance of some economic goods and placed them under tight control. The chief sources of precious metals for coinage—which was one of the important economic powers reserved to the central government—were monopolized by the shogunate, whose officials supervised the production and minting of gold, silver, and copper. The resulting opportunities for manipulation of currency, although in the long run detrimental to Tokugawa economic stability, were frequently made use of for short-run goals.

Despite the severe limitations on political freedom and the many harsh features of government in the Tokugawa period, there were very real restraints on shogunal power both in principle and in practice. The nature of the relationship to the imperial throne gave political authority a dualistic character; even though the emperor in Kyoto was a puppet, his mere existence prevented the shogun from acquiring the full status of national monarch. While Japanese feudalism had never developed the concepts of contractual rights that came to be present in European vassalage, the status of samurai was an honorable one, and no lord could ignore entirely the claims upon his benevolence if his authority was to remain legitimate (hence, for example, when the Tokugawa and other lords in economic difficulties resorted to reductions in the stipends of their samurai retainers, they also resorted to such euphemisms as "loans" to soften the impact). In practice, there were more tangible restraints on Tokugawa despotism. As noted above, the continued existence of domains economically and militarily independent of the shogunate meant that political power remained somewhat fragmented in Japan. While able to dictate policy on foreign affairs and require lords to pay homage at the castle in Edo, even Ieyasu at the height of his military victories had been cautious about direct interference into the internal affairs of the larger outer domains.

If we shift the focus from the Tokugawa as a national government and consider the shogunate and the domain governments as parts of a single political system, we do see a number of features that combined to give the elite in power greater control over Japanese society than any previous regime had achieved.

One development, or set of developments, that made this social control possible was the rapid growth of bureaucratic institutions and techniques. Both the shogunate and the individual domain governments built upon the advances inherited from the late sixteenth century in their efforts to mobilize human and material resources. The responsibility for such administrative functions as finances, religious affairs, urban government, mining and other monopolies, as well as military matters, was divided among hierarchically structured offices operating according to routinized procedures. Hereditary rank within the samurai class was still the essential qualification for official positions; but since the pool of samurai at any given level was larger than the number of offices to be filled, it was usually possible to pass over the obviously incompetent and select officials from among those with the proper rank who exhibited particular merit. On the other hand, promotion across hereditary rank lines remained uncommon, although here again consideration of competency or political favoritism sometimes prevailed over the strict adherence to hereditary status. By the late Tokugawa period there was also greater concern for training appropriate to the specialized functions to be assumed by these samurai civil servants. On the whole, although the Tokugawa bureaucracy was far less developed in terms of specialization of function, codification of regulations, or recruitment according to impersonal standards than either the contemporary Chinese or twentieth century Western standards, there had been a marked departure from the style of administration of medieval Japan.

The country was also now far more effectively knit together by means of communication than it had ever been in Japanese history. The mountainous terrain and the dictates of military defense hindered road building (rivers were often left unbridged in order to prevent the easy movement of troops and checkpoints were established to control illegal travel), but overland transportation did improve greatly with such major arteries as the Tokkaido road linking Edo and Osaka. In addition to providing for administrative needs, the major roads were well traveled by merchants, pilgrims, and tourists, giving rise to thriving post towns where innkeepers, prostitutes, bearers, and money changers competed to make the journey more comfortable, if also more expensive. The shipping of foodstuffs and other commercial goods was cheaper by sea, and by the beginning of the eighteenth century a well-developed system of coastal routes encircled the islands. The annual arrival in Edo of the first barrels of premium *sake* wine from the Osaka region became a festive occasion with public acclamation for the captain who won the race. One of the chief stimuli for this vastly increased movement of people and goods through the country was the alternate attendance system created as a political device for controlling the feudal lords. Facilities for both land and sea transportation were necessary to accommodate the large entourages of the lords' processions to Edo, and the heavy costs were offset by shipping tax grain and other domain products to Osaka or Edo for the urban markets.

The flow of elite and their samurai retainers in and out of Edo also stimulated a national exchange of information, ideas, and fashions, serving to reduce regionalism and parochialism. The most significant development in this process of knitting Japanese society more closely together, however, was the dramatic increase in literacy. Bureaucratic requirements for record keeping and the neo-Confucian faith in moral education transformed the unlettered, unpolished swordsman of the medieval battlefield into a literate official capable of producing formal reports and, when the occasion demanded, quoting the appropriate Confucian precept. Literacy became increasingly common among the general populace as well; it has been estimated that by the end of the Tokugawa period the majority of all males routinely experienced some formal schooling. Journalism as such did not develop until after Western influence, but by the end of the seventeenth century there was a thriving publishing industry meeting the demand for theatre announcements, advertising handbills, travel guides, and earthy novels, as well as the more solemn works on moral inspiration and success through crop selection. Thus, despite the self-contained character of the separate domains and the many legal restrictions on travel by the lower classes, information moved relatively freely throughout Japan and promoted a higher degree of cultural homogeneity.

From the point of view of those in political power in Japan, however, communications were most often conceived of as another means of furthering social control. The effort at controlling status in particular gave the Tokugawa regime some of its most marked characteristics. Ieyasu and his successors, as well as the lords of the various domains, were acutely sensitive to the political importance of rank, titles, and honors, including those associated with the imperial court and the Buddhist and Shinto establishment, even though these structures had lost the substance of economic or political power. In general, the good society was equated with stability, and stability was thought best achieved by strict maintenance of hereditary status. This was sought not only within the ranks of the samurai class but within the functional divisions of the larger society. Hence, the samurai class took on the character of a closed caste with very little movement across the line between it and the general populace. The late sixteenth century practice of removing warriors from the land and stationing them permanently in castle towns became the almost universal rule in the

9.4

Symbolic of the social stratification of early modern societies are the fortifications which protected the governmental elites of China anc Japan.

9.4 Corner of the Peking city wall. In the Ming period the earthern walls of the former Mongol capital were strengthened and faced with brick. Numerous city walls were built in the Ming and portions of the Great Wall were refurbished and garrisoned. Source: Sir Charles Eliot, *Letters from the Far East* (London, 1907).

9.5 The "White Heron" castle at Himeji is one of the most impressive extant examples of the headquarters of Japanese daimyo lords. Built at the turn of the seventeenth century as a military fortress, it was even more an expression of the vast wealth and power held by the samurai leaders of the early modern period. Courtesy: Japan Information Service, Consulate General, San Francisco.

9.5

seventeenth century, although the domain of Satsuma was a notable exception. The peasantry, which had included large numbers of part-time participants in medieval warfare, were stripped of their weapons and legally bound to agrarian pursuits within their native villages. A system of official registration and passport requirements for domestic travel was devised to impede both occupational and geographical mobility. Prohibitions against selling or dividing land and establishing new families without parental consent, and sumptuary laws to curtail conspicuous consumption, were also aimed at creating social stability. In the same fashion the merchant and artisan classes within urban areas were subjected to measures intended to enforce the status quo. In the long run, as economic changes provided incentive for migration to the cities and expanded commercial opportunities in the rural hinterland, these legal checks were less and less effective, and it proved impossible to maintain in actuality the official hierarchy of social prestige. Nevertheless, considerable attention and energy were given to this elaborate attempt at social engineering, which contributed greatly to the longevity of the Tokugawa system.

Cultural Legitimation

No regime rules long by military might alone, and an essential pillar in the Tokugawa political structure was its claim to legitimacy. Although this came to be most frequently articulated in terms of the Chinese neo-Confucianism that the Tokugawa adopted as official orthodoxy, the three most important sanctions invoked in this appeal for respect stressed continuity with basic elements in Japan's own political history. The title of shogun and the style of the shogunate as a government derived from the Kamakura period and had clear historical precedents. The Tokugawa also emphasized the ideal, if not the reality, of the shogun's role as agent of the imperial throne; they took great pains to restore the material symbols of court life in Kyoto, thereby reversing the long trend toward obscurity that had marked the medieval period and reviving a substantial measure of prestige, if not power, for the throne. This outward show of respect for the throne as the fountainhead of authority in Japanese political culture bolstered the Tokugawa's own position as interpreter of the imperial will and permitted the shogunate to claim a national hegemony without violating the sanctity of the imperial dynasty. Third, the Tokugawa made full use of the values of *bushido*, the code of the heroic warrior of the late Ashikaga period, in invoking the principles of feudal vassalage. The shogun stood at the apex of the vertical chains of lord-vassal relationships. The swearing of homage by the various lords in theory was an acknowledgement of Tokugawa overlordship over all samurai. This combination of appeals to historical precedent, the sacrosanct character of the throne, and central values of the military class, once systematized in neo-Confucian terms, formed a potent ideological justification for Tokugawa rule which was not seriously challenged until the mid-nineteenth century.

The Tokugawa preoccupation with political and social control was matched by its concern for cultural activities. As already noted, its own legitimacy rested in part on the prestige of the imperial court, which had suffered a decline during the long period of political turmoil. Tokugawa patronage of the court served to prevent further decline and to an extent stimulated a revival of classic court culture. In addition to restoring physically much of the old capital at Kyoto, the Tokugawa shoguns and the local lords lavished wealth and energy on building new urban centers dominated by monumental castle architecture. Furnished with richly decorated screens and other art work, these castles of the late sixteenth and early seventeenth centuries were intended as much to symbolize political authority as to protect against military attack. This symbolic function is even more apparent in the mausoleum built for Ieyasu at Nikko—a shrine complex of almost incredible ornateness dedicated to the glorification of the Tokugawa founder. In a similar fashion, official patronage of the Shinto and Buddhist religious establishments was intended to preserve and control traditional cultural values and to give substance to the Tokugawa claim to have restored peace and order. The greater patronage, however, went to neo-Confucianism.

Ieyasu employed, as did other warlords, a number of learned men to aid in the bureaucratic tasks of civil administration and to advise in the formulation of new policy. Buddhist priests had played this role in earlier periods but the bitter struggle with Buddhism as a secular power and the absence of political doctrine appropriate to the new Tokugawa structure turned the feudal elite in the direction of neo-Confucian scholars. Although always subordinate to the regular samurai officialdom and never achieving the direct influence of the Confucian literati in China, these scholar-advisers played an important part in establishing the world view that was to remain the orthodox social and political view until the mid-nineteenth century. They provided philosophical underpinnings to the feudal code of *bushido,* systematizing the amalgam of traditional values in Confucian terms, and supplied historical precedents for justifying Tokugawa policy. Their greatest influence came in the educational institutions where the process of civilizing and preparing the warrior class for its role as a political and cultural elite took place. The Confucian academy established in Edo with Tokugawa subsidies in the seventeenth century became the seat of orthodox interpretations of social doctrine.

Although the means available to the Tokugawa shogunate to enforce, whether through coercion or co-option, cultural uniformity were somewhat limited by the decentralized pattern of local political power, the Tokugawa state can nevertheless be characterized as culturalistic. Japanese society, effectively sealed off from the larger world by geography and foreign policy, was racially, ethnically, and linguistically quite homogeneous. The local lords, moreover, shared a common interest in measures conducive to maintaining their collective hegemony. Thus there was a marked tendency toward common cultural policies in the various domains.

This orientation toward culturalism, however, did not mean the total absence of intellectual diversity. Despite strict bans on Christianity and occasional attempts to eliminate domestic heresies, heterodoxy continued to flourish throughout the Tokugawa period. Here again the autonomy of the various powerful domains was conducive to an intellectual diversity, which was tolerated by the political elite so long as it was not seen as posing a direct challenge to the status quo. The problems of synthesizing Chinese and Japanese cultural values—for example, the contradiction between the Confucian stress on merit and the Japanese system of hereditary status—kept alive a certain tension that resisted the imposition of intellectual uniformity. This was further fed by the ferment that accompanied the growth of a new urban culture semiindependent of the feudal elite.

The diverse aspects of Japanese intellectual life in the Tokugawa no doubt made the society somewhat open to novel ideas. Certainly, despite the restrictions on contact with the Europeans, curiosity about "Dutch learning" continued among Japanese, and this in turn is indicative of a considerable degree of ambivalence inTokugawa views of the outside world. The official policy of self-containment was itself contradicted by the acceptance of a neo-Confucian orthodoxy that was foreign in origin. It may be argued as a generalization that, because of this diversity and the nature of the cultural relationship with China, Tokugawa intellectuals never achieved the degree of self-assuredness or confidence in cultural identity that characterized their Chinese counterparts. In any case, as we shall see in a later chapter, intellectual heterodoxy increased toward the end of the Tokugawa period and was directly related to the flexibility with which Japanese society responded to the Western challenge in the nineteenth century.

Consequences of the Formation of the Tokugawa State

Assessments of the Tokugawa period in the overall unfolding of Japanese history have varied considerably. Some historians, often working from an evolutionary model of socioeconomic development drawn largely from the European experience, have seen the formation of the Tokugawa regime as a major setback. In their view it represented a "refeudalization" of Japanese society that curtailed social development by reimposing samurai control over "free" cities and an independent peasantry, thus freezing the society at a "medieval" stage of history and delaying its entry into modernity by several centuries. This view has been sharply criticized by others who would challenge both the Europocentric conceptual premises and the accuracy of the claim that sixteenth century Japanese society was as highly developed as this interpretation would imply. There is somewhat more agreement among historians regarding the consequences of the Tokugawa policy of seclusion. Certainly the Japanese did cut off themselves from the stimulus of cross-fertilization that played such a large role in the early modern technological and economic advances of Western Europe. Moreover, to the extent that such traditional values as respect for hierarchical authority and vertically organized groups were embedded in the institutions of Tokugawa state, this period can be viewed as one in which older cultural patterns were hardened in a manner that precluded some alternative directions for cultural growth even after the onset of industrialization ushered in by late nineteenth century contact with the Western world.

As we shall see in later chapters, however, Tokugawa society did not stagnate to the extent that such interpretations might imply. On the contrary, despite the intentions of the Tokugawa elite, many of the trends within Tokugawa history were to pave the way for the modern transformation of Japan. To the extent that this was true, the Tokugawa heritage must be seen in a different light.

CONCLUDING REMARKS

The early modern empires that followed the period of Central Asian domination were notable for their stability and longevity. They differed, however, in the extent to which they continued the pattern of the Mongol achievement. In West Asia, Turkish tribal federations formed three Muslim conquest empires. The Ottomans, championing the cause of Sunni orthodoxy, captured control of the old Muslim heartland and waged a vigorous holy war on the periphery of a vast and diverse empire. In Iran, the Qizilbash tribes built the Safavid state on the foundation of a preexisting Iranian society. Farther east the Mughuls, following Timurid precedents, failed in Central Asia but succeeded in India in creating an empire of unprecedented wealth and power. In East Asia the Ming empire represented the reverse of the tribal conquest model, since it was the result of the Chinese expelling the Mongols from south of the Great Wall. The following Ch'ing regime, however, was again an instance of a tribal federation conquering a sedentary population. In Japan, the Tokugawa state was the product of internal civil war and cannot be attributed to Central Asian influences.

These empires may be compared by asking what was the basis of their power and how they were integrated politically. The Ottomans built a central core of military forces and administrators by the training and enslavement of youths levied from the subject population, which was allowed to remain divided in terms of custom, religion, and language. Safavid power was based on an uneasy combination of Qizilbash tribal forces and an Iranian administrative apparatus. How did the Ottoman administration compare with that of the Mughuls, where an effort was made to prevent the entrenchment of supporters in specific locations? Or how would these cases contrast with Japan and Iran, where tribal chieftains and "inner" and "outer lords" held lands and loyalties at the local level which were a check on the power of the central government? How does one account for the fact that Ming China avoided the formation of such a regional military elite? How would the Ming case compare with that of the Ch'ing in regard to the control of the military establishment?

How did the structures of the early modern empires affect their cultural policies? Could one argue that the success with which the Safavids and the Ming vigorously promoted Shiism and neo-Confucianism, respectively, can be explained by the fact that they controlled areas of relative cultural uniformity? To what may one attribute the failure of the Mughuls to develop a strong state ideology? How were intellectual and religious elites integrated into the regime? What factors account for the relatively defensive postures of the Safavids, Ming, and Tokugawa and the more expansionist tendancies of the Ottomans, Mughuls, and Ch'ing?

A further set of questions can be asked regarding the social and economic life of these societies. Each case varied in the degree to which the regime systematically attempted to control mobility within the social hierarchy and regulate relations between various classes and status groups. Moreover, although the Tokugawa in Japan was an extreme example of an effort to circumscribe some types of commercial activity, other regimes also attempted to channel economic behavior into acceptable patterns. What factors account, for example, for the different policies toward foreign trade, a topic of particular importance in Chapter 11? To what extent was mercentile wealth convertible into social status and political influence?

BIBLIOGRAPHY

9.P EARLY MODERN EMPIRES: PROCESSES

Eisenstadt, Shmuel N., *The Political System of Empires* (Free Press paperback, 1969), 524 pp. A monumental analysis of the forces at work within "historical bureaucratic societies," with material drawn from a wide spectrum of examples. The same author has produced many articles or related subjects, all challenging reading.

Parsons, Talcott, *Societies: Evolutionary and Comparative Perspectives* (Prentice-Hall paperback, 1966), 120 pp. A theoretical analysis of political organization; it assigns the empires of China, India, and Islam to the same category as Rome, that of historic intermediate empires.

Toynbee, Arnold J., *A Study of History,* Vol. 7A, *Universal States* (Oxford University Press paperback, 1963), 379 pp. Full of insights from the perspective of a great overview of human history.

Weber, Max, *The Religion of China: Confucianism and Taoism* (Free Press paperback, 1964), 308 pp. English translation of a great German social theorist considering the role of ideological values in the organization of premodern Chinese society.

Wittfogel, Karl A., *Oriental Despotism* (Yale Press paperback, 1963), 556 pp. A controversial but often stimulating theory of totalitarian states; much of the data drawn from Chinese history.

9.1 THE OTTOMANS IN WEST ASIA

Gibb, Hamilton A. R., and H. Bowen, *Islamic Society and the West,* 2 vols. (London, 1950), Vol. 1, pp. 19-173. An in-depth analysis of the governing institutions of the Ottoman empire.

Holt, Peter M., *Egypt and the Fertile Crescent, 1516-1922. A Political History* (Cornell University Press paperback, 1966), pp. 1-57. A straightforward account of the Ottoman conquests in Asia.

Inalcik, Halil, "The Rise of the Ottoman Empire," *Cambridge History of Islam* (Cambridge, 1970), Vol. 1, pp. 295-323. A reliable narrative, by one of the leading authorities.

———, *The Ottoman Empire: The Classical Age, 1300-1600* (New York, 1973), 202 pp. A detailed analysis of institutions, to be read in conjunction with the same author's narrative account, listed above.

Lewis, Bernard, *Istanbul and the Civilization of the Ottoman Empire* (Norman, Oklahoma, 1963), 176 pp. A brilliant evocation of Istanbul in its age of splendor.

Lewis, Raphaela, *Everyday Life in Ottoman Turkey* (New York, 1971), 197 pp. A vivid reconstruction of social life, with illustrations.

9.2 THE SAFAVIDS IN IRAN

Blunt, Wilfred, *Isfahan, Pearl of Persia* (New York, 1966), 208 pp. A popular account of the history, monuments, and social life of the Safavid capital, lavishly illustrated.

Lambton, Ann K.S., "Islamic Society in Persia," in L. E. Sweet, ed., *Peoples and Cultures of the Middle East,* 2 vols. (New York, 1970), Vol. 1, pp. 74-101. A succinct overview by a leading scholar, stressing urban patterns, especially during the Safavid and Qajar periods.

———, *Landlord and Peasant in Persia* (Oxford, 1953), pp. 105-128. Discusses the impact of the Safavids upon preexisting agrarian relationships.

Mazzaoui, Michel M., *The Origins of the Safavids* (Wiesbaden, 1972), 109 pp. A monograph of seminal importance, recommended only for the advanced student.

Nasr, Seyyed Hossein, ' Ithnā 'Asharī Shī'ism and Iranian Islam," *Religion in the Middle East,* ed. A. J. Arberry, 2 vols. (Cambridge, 1969), Vol. 2, pp. 96-118. A brief introduction to Shiism in Iran.

Savory, R. M., "Safavid Persia," *The Cambridge History of Islam,* 2 vols. (Cambridge, 1970), Vol. 1, pp. 394-429. The best account of the dynasty available in English.

9.3 THE MUGHULS IN SOUTH ASIA

Ahmad, Aziz, *Studies in Islamic Culture in the Indian Environment* (Oxford, 1964), pp. 22-54 and 167-200. Scholarly essays on Indo-Islamic civilization in the Mughul period. Strongly recommended.

Ali, M. Athar, *The Mughal Nobility under Aurangzeb* (New York, 1970), 174 pp. The best account available of the governing institutions of the Mughul empire.

Ikram, Sheikh Mohamad, *Muslim Civilization in India* (New York, 1964), pp. 134-253. The best general account.

Mujeeb, Mohammed, *The Indian Muslims* (London, 1967), pp. 236-388. A leisurely narrative by a scholar of great learning and perception.

Sharma, Sri Ram, *The Religious Policy of the Mughul Emperors* (New York, 1962), 185 pp. Attempts to assess the significance of the various measures initiated by the first six Mughul rulers with regard to matters of religion.

Spear, Percival, "The Mughul *Mansabdari* System," in Edmund Leach and S. N. Mukherjee, eds., *Elites in South Asia* (Cambridge, 1970), pp. 1-15. A lucid introduction to a complicated institution.

9.4 THE MING AND CH'ING EMPIRES IN CHINA

de Bary, William Theodore, ed., *Self and Society in Ming Thought* (Columbia University Press paperback, 1970), 550 pp. Monumental work on late Ming intellectual history with articles describing the revolutionary trends in Chinese thought in the sixteenth and seventeenth centuries.

Fairbank, John K., Edwin O. Reischauer, and Albert M. Craig, *East Asia: Tradition and Transformation* (Boston, 1973), 969 pp. Chapters 8 and 9 give the best textbook account of Ming and Ch'ing China.

Hsu, Immaneul C. Y., *The Rise of Modern China* (New York, 1970), pp. 1-121. The best textbook account of the early Ch'ing empire with bibliographies at the end of each chapter.

Hucker, Charles O., *The Traditional Chinese in Ming Times (1368-1644)* (University of Arizona Press, 1961), 85 pp. Brief but informative description of the Ming empire, stressing the political organization.

Michael, Franz, *The Origin of Manchu Rule in China* (Baltimore, 1942), 127 pp. Describes the transformation of the Manchu tribal society for the purpose of conquest of the Chinese empire.

Wu Ching-tzu, *The Scholars* (Grosset and Dunlap paperback, 1972), 721 pp. English translation of the satirical novel aimed at the actions of Chinese literati and officials of the Ming.

9.5 TOKUGAWA JAPAN

Dore, Ronald P., *Education in Tokugawa Japan* (Berkeley, 1965), 346 pp. A brilliantly written analysis of the central values and the relationships between hereditary status, education, and the social order.

Hall, John W., *Government and Local Power in Japan, 500-1700* (Princeton, 1966), 446 pp. A careful analysis of the institutional innovations and the underlying political dynamics that produced and supported the Tokugawa regime is contained in Chapters 12 and 13.

Hall, John W., and Marius B. Jansen, eds., *Studies in the Institutional History of Early Modern Japan* (Princeton University Press paperback, 1970), 396 pp. Parts 1-3 include seminal articles on various political and social aspects of the seventeenth and eighteenth centuries.

Sansom, George B., *A History of Japan, 1334-1615* (Stanford University Press paperback, 1960), 462 pp. Chapters 17-26 of this standard survey describe the centralization of power achieved by the military coalition eventually headed by Tokugawa Ieyasu.

———, *A History of Japan, 1615-1867* (Stanford University Press paperback, 1963), 270 pp. Although not of the quality of the first two volumes in this series, Chapters 1-9 give a concise description of the Tokugawa political and social systems as they took shape in the seventeenth century.

Tsunoda, Ryusaku, *et. al.*, comps., *Sources of Japanese Tradition,* Vol. 1 (Columbia University Press paperback, 1964), 506 pp. Chapters 15-21 are well annotated translations from early Tokugawa materials.

GLOSSARY

Amir. Generally, a military commander or governor; occasionally a sovereign title, as in the case of the amir of Bukhara.

Ashikaga. A family of military aristocrats who held an increasingly tenuous hegemony over Japan between 1333 and 1573, giving their name to that historical period.

Banners. Military-political units of Manchu society formed in mobilizing for the conquest of China; later hereditary garrisons, some containing Chinese and Mongols.

Caliph (Arabic, **khalifa**). Originating with the title of the Prophet Muhammad's successor, Abu Bakr, Khalifat Rasul Allah, "Successor of the Messenger of God." The caliph was the head of the Islamic *umma,* "the community of believers," and was referred to as *amir al-muminin,* "commander of the faithful."

Chaghatay (d. 1241). Second son of Chingiz Khan and founder of the Chaghatay khanate in Central Asia; also, Chaghatay Turkish, the language spoken in that Khanate and the precursor of the present-day Ozbeg.

Cheng Ho. A Muslim eunuch who led Chinese imperial maritime expeditions to South Asia, Arabia, and the eastern coast of Africa in the early fifteenth century.

Chu Yuan-chang (1328-98). Founder of the Ming dynasty, which expelled the Mongols from China and increased the power of the emperor; the second peasant to rule China.

Confucianism. A social and political philosophy based upon the doctrines of Confucius (sixth century B.C.), this became the ideology of an elite bureaucratic-scholar class and the official learning promoted by the imperial Chinese state.

Deccan. The great tableland of central India. The Narbada River was traditionally regarded as constituting the dividing line between the northern India and the Deccan plateau.

Devshirme. The system whereby the Ottoman empire recruited slaves for the administration and the army by levying a child tribute upon the Christian provinces in the Balkans (Rumelia.)

Edo (Tokyo). The castle city that was built as headquarters for the Tokugawa at the end of the sixteenth century and grew into the largest city in the world. Renamed Tokyo ("Eastern Capital") in 1868 when the imperial court took possession of the Tokugawa castle.

Eunuch. A castrated male used in China, India, and West Asia as imperial servants and harem guards; during the Ming period they often exercised great political influence.

Fudai daimyo. Regional leaders who held fiefs from the Tokugawa and, in addition to being lords over their own domains, served as councillors and administrators within the Tokugawa central government; hence referred to here as "inner lords."

Futuwwa. Associations or solidarity groups, generally composed of young Muslim males drawn mainly although not invariably from the poorer elements of the urban population.

Ghazi. A warrior living in the frontier areas of the Muslim world and engaged in holy warfare *(jihad)* against non-Muslims.

Hijra. The flight of the Prophet Muhammad from Mecca to Medina in 622, an event that marked the beginning of the Islamic calendar.

Iqta. The revenue assignment of a certain area, generally granted in exchange for military service.

Jagirdar. The holder of a *jagir,* or revenue assignment, in Mughul India.

Janissaries (from Turkish, *yenicheri*, "new troops"). Technically slaves, recrutied by means of the *devshirme,* or child tribute, levied upon the Christian population of the Balkans. The Janissaries were the best disciplined and most feared troops of the Ottoman sultans, especially during the centuries of imperial expansion.

Jihad. The holy warfare that Muslims were enjoined to wage against non-Muslims.

Kamakura. The historical period from 1185 to 1333, so named because the Minamoto shoguns who held power had their headquarters in this city in eastern Japan.

Kapikulus. The personal slaves of the Ottoman sultans.

Khurasan. Formerly a vast area extending northeastward from the central Iranian desert to the Amu Darya River, with its metropolitan centers located at Nishapur, Marv, Herat, and Balkh. Today Khurasan consists of a province in northeastern Iran, bordering the U.S.S.R. and Afghanistan, and with its capital at Mashhad.

Khutba. The sermon given in the congregational mosque on a Friday, in which are included prayers for the well-being of the ruler. The usual proof of sovereignty in Islam is to have one's name read in the *khutba* and impressed upon the coinage.

Mamluk. A slave-soldier, generally although not exclusively a Turk, a Georgian, or a Circassian.

Manchus. A tribal hunter-fisher people from the region north of the Korean peninsula who adopted Chinese techniques of statecraft and conquered China in the seventeenth century.

Mansabdar. The holder of a *mansab,* a salaried rank in the administrative hierarchy of the Mughul empire.

Mawarannahr (literally, "that which lies beyond the river"). The Arabic name for the area lying between the Amu Darya and Syr Darya rivers, and including the cities of Samarqand and Bukhara. Known in ancient times as Sogdiana, the "land of the Sogdians," and to the Greeks as Transoxania, "the land beyong the Oxus" (i.e., the Amu Darya), it was generally referred to in the nineteenth century as Russian Turkistan.

Millet. A non-Muslim religious community living under the protection of a Muslim state (especially the Ottoman empire) and maintaining a considerable degree of internal autonomy under its own religious leaders.

Murshid. A Sufi teacher, also known as a *shaykh* or *pir.*

Nurhaci (1559-1626). The Manchu leader who unified the tribes and built the military organization that later conquered China.

Özbegs (also, **Uzbeks**). A Turkish people who, since the second half of the fifteenth century, have occupied the area between the Syr Darya and Amu Darya rivers (formerly Russian Turkistan and now divided between various Central Asian republics of the U.S.S.R.

Qazi. The Islamic judge who administers the Sharia.

Qizilbash (Turkish, "red head"). A confederacy of nine Turcoman tribes assembled by Shah Ismail Safavi and thereafter forming the dominant military class of the Safavid empire. Among the Qizilbash tribes were the Afshars and the Qajars, who provided the dynasties that succeeded the Safavids. The nickname Qizilbash refers to the peculiar red headdress (with twelve points in honor of the twelve Shii imams) worn by the followers of Shah Ismail.

Sharia. The Law of Islam, derived from the Quran, the *Hadith,* or *Sayings of the Prophet,* and the analogical interpretations of the jurists.

Shaykh al-Islam. The title held by the chief religious dignitary of the Ottoman and Mughul empires.

Shiis. Those who follow the *shia* (or "party") of Ali, Muhammad's son-in-law and the fourth caliph of the Muslims. The Shiis, although subdivided into a number of sects, constitute the largest minority group (as opposed to the Sunni majority) within Islam, and are today chiefly to be found in Iran and Iraq.

Shogun. An old court title given to imperial commanders in chief but adopted by the leading military family in the Kamakura period (1185-1333) and subsequently by the Ashikaga and then Tokugawa Ieyasu to signify their national hegemony.

Sipahi (Persian "soldier," hence the Anglo-Indian term, sepoy). In the Ottoman empire the *sipahi* was a cavalryman who maintained himself, his horse, and arms, and in some cases mounted retainers out of a revenue assignment known as a *timar.*

Subahdar (also **nawab**). A Mughul provincial governor; the officer in charge of a *subah*, the largest unit of administration in the Mughul empire.

Sufi. A dervish or mystic. Hence, Sufism, Islamic mysticism.

Sultan. A ruler, "one who exercises power"; the title adopted by territorial rulers in the Muslim world from the eleventh century onwards.

Sunnis. Those who follow the *sunna,* or "practice," of the Prophet Muhammad; the majority community in the Islamic world.

Timar. A revenue assignment in the Ottoman empire for the maintenance of a *sipahi,* or cavalryman.

Tokugawa Ieyasu (1542-1616). The leader of a large military coalition who triumphed over rival lords to found the Tokugawa regime; he assumed the title shogun in 1603.

Tozama daimyo. Regional leaders who were confirmed as lords of their semiautonomous domains after agreeing to accept the Tokugawa as their leige lord and national hegemon. They were largely excluded from the inner council of the Tokugawa central government, hence the term "outer lords."

Turcoman. A term of unknown origin. One explanation of its derivation links it to the Persian *Turk manand,* meaning "Turk-like." Although appearing at different times in different areas, the Turcomans generally spoke a West Turkish language, retained memories of a pastoral-nomadic background, and displayed a life-style of a kind associated with Turkish peoples over an extensive area of West and Central Asia.

Turkistan (literally, "the land of the Turks"). A term sometimes used to describe all those areas of Central Asia inhabited by Turkish peoples. During the nineteenth century, the term Russian Turkistan was applied to the area between the Amu Darya and Syr Darya rivers, together with the steppe region beyond the Syr Darya. The term Chinese Turkistan was used to describe the Tarim basin, modern Sinkiang.

Ulama. The Arabic plural of *alim,* meaning a scholar trained in the Islamic "sciences." Collectively, the *ulama* enforced the Sharia and determined the social norms that governed the life of the Muslim community as a whole.

Vazir. The minister of a Muslim ruler. In fact, a ruler might appoint concurrently two or more *vazirs* to have charge over different areas of administration, but the term is usually applied in the sense of a chief minister, as with the Ottoman "grand vizier."

Wang Yang-ming (1472-1529). Chinese bureaucrat and thinker who developed the School of Mind, an introspective and individualistic trend in Confucianism symptomatic of social changes in south China.

Yuan (1279-1368). Dynastic title for the period of Mongol rule in China; the first period that all of China came under foreign rule.

Index

Note: Volume 1 includes pages 1–474, while Volume 2 contains pages 404–797. (Pages 404–474 are included in both volumes.) Bold numerals in the index indicate a glossary entry, and italic numerals indicate a map or an illustration.

CHRONOLOGICAL CHART OF CHAPTERS (approximate span on sliding tim

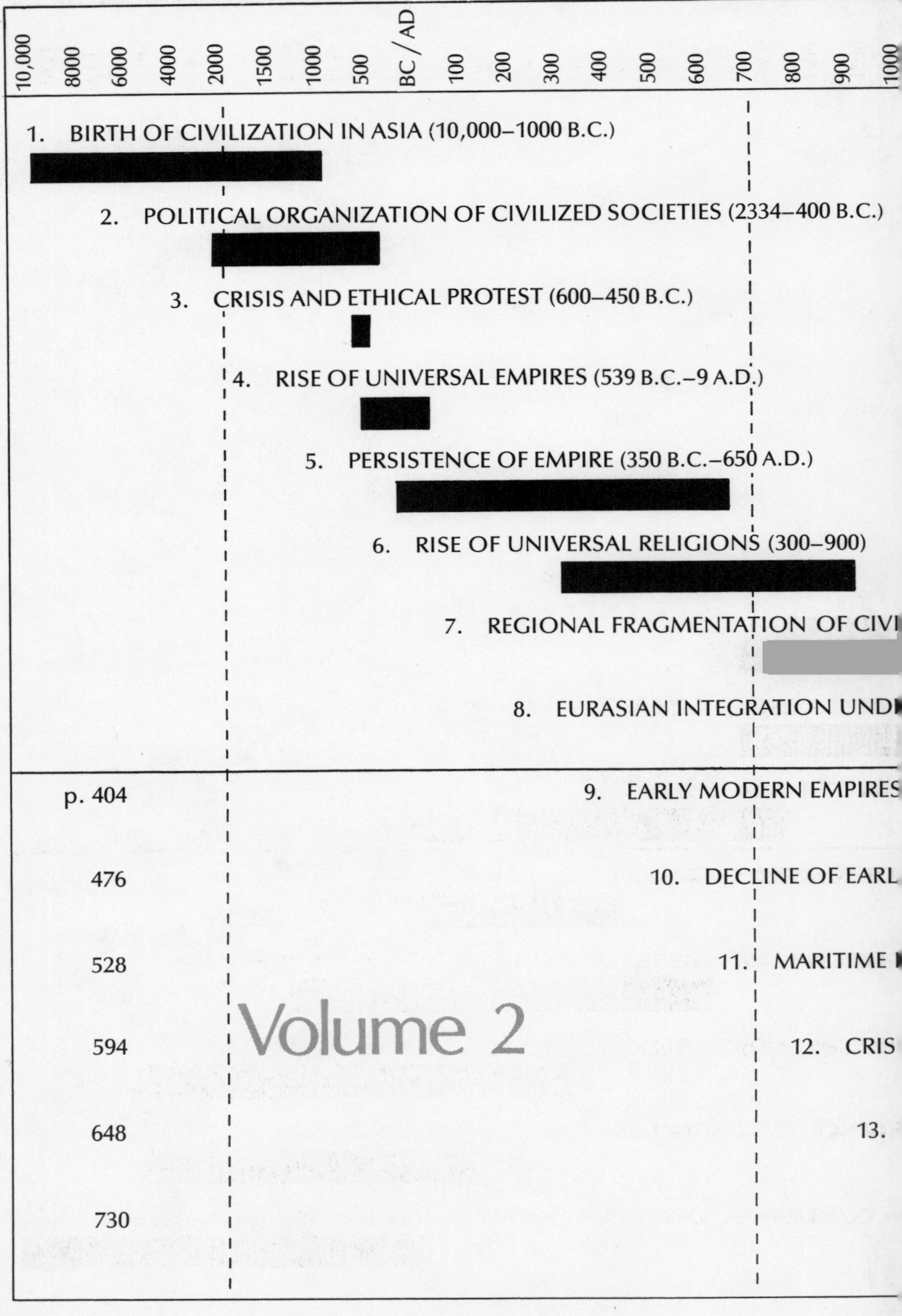

10,000 | 8000 | 6000 | 4000 | 2000 | 1500 | 1000 | 500 | BC / AD | 100 | 200 | 300 | 400 | 500 | 600 | 700 | 800 | 900 | 1000

1. BIRTH OF CIVILIZATION IN ASIA (10,000–1000 B.C.)

2. POLITICAL ORGANIZATION OF CIVILIZED SOCIETIES (2334–400 B.C.)

3. CRISIS AND ETHICAL PROTEST (600–450 B.C.)

4. RISE OF UNIVERSAL EMPIRES (539 B.C.–9 A.D.)

5. PERSISTENCE OF EMPIRE (350 B.C.–650 A.D.)

6. RISE OF UNIVERSAL RELIGIONS (300–900)

7. REGIONAL FRAGMENTATION OF CIVI

8. EURASIAN INTEGRATION UND

Volume 2

p. 404 9. EARLY MODERN EMPIRES

476 10. DECLINE OF EARL

528 11. MARITIME

594 12. CRIS

648 13.

730